# Atlas contents

Scale 1:160,000 or 2.52 miles to 1 inch

| | |
|---|---|
| **Map pages** | inside front cover |
| ***Route planning*** | ***2–16*** |
| *Route planner* | *2–5* |
| *London district* | *6–7* |
| *Road safety cameras* | *8* |
| *Tourist sites with satnav friendly postcodes* | *9* |
| *Caravan and camping sites in Britain* | *10–11* |
| *Traffic signs and road markings* | *12–13* |
| *Channel hopping* | *14–15* |
| *Ferries to Ireland and the Isle of Man* | *16* |
| **Atlas symbols** | **1** |
| **Road maps 1:160,000 scale** | **2–152** |
| Channel Islands 1:113,000 scale | 12–13 |
| Isle of Man 1:200,000 scale | 102 |
| Western Isles 1:696,000 scale | 152 |
| Orkney and Shetland Islands 1:725,000 scale | 152 |

**Ferry ports**

| | | | | | |
|---|---|---|---|---|---|
| Aberdeen Harbour | 133 | Holyhead Harbour | *16* | Port of Tyne | 101 |
| Channel Tunnel | 17 | Liverpool Docks | *16* | Portsmouth Harbour | *15* |
| Dover, Port of | *15* | Newhaven Harbour | *15* | Southampton, Port of | 13 |
| Fishguard Harbour | *16* | Pembroke Dock | *16* | Weymouth Harbour | *14* |
| Harwich Int. Port | 47 | Plymouth, Port of | *14* | | |
| Heysham Harbour | *16* | Poole, Port of | *14* | | |

**Town plans**

| | | | | | |
|---|---|---|---|---|---|
| Aberdeen | 133 | Harrogate | 155 | Peterborough | 157 |
| Aberystwyth | 48 | Inverness | 155 | Plymouth | 4 |
| Bath | 153 | Ipswich | 47 | Portsmouth | 157 |
| Birmingham | 153 | Kingston upon Hull | 155 | Ramsgate | 35 |
| Blackpool | 82 | Leeds | 155 | St Andrews | 125 |
| Bradford | 153 | Leicester | 155 | Salisbury | 157 |
| Bristol | 153 | Lincoln | 156 | Scarborough | 93 |
| Cambridge | 153 | Liverpool | 74 | Sheffield | 157 |
| Canterbury | 153 | Llandudno | 73 | Shrewsbury | 157 |
| Cardiff | 154 | LONDON | 156 | Southampton | 158 |
| Chester | 154 | Manchester | 156 | Southend-on-Sea | 35 |
| Coventry | 154 | Middlesbrough | 93 | Stratford-upon-Avon | 158 |
| Derby | 154 | Milton Keynes | 156 | Sunderland | 101 |
| Dundee | 125 | Newcastle upon Tyne | 101 | Swansea | 26 |
| Durham | 154 | Newquay | 3 | Swindon | 158 |
| Edinburgh | 154 | Norwich | 156 | Wolverhampton | 158 |
| Exeter | 9 | Nottingham | 156 | Worcester | 158 |
| Glasgow | 155 | Oxford | 157 | York | 158 |
| Great Yarmouth | 71 | | | | |

| | |
|---|---|
| **Motorways** | **159–161** |
| M25 London orbital | 159 |
| M6 Toll motorway | 160 |
| Restricted junctions | 161 |
| **Index to place names** | **162–192** |
| County, administrative area map | 162 |
| **Distances and journey times** | inside back cover |

8th edition June 2012

Revised version of atlas formerly known as Maxi Scale Atlas Britain

Original edition printed 1990.

**Cartography:**
All cartography in this atlas edited, designed and produced by the Mapping Services Department of AA Publishing (A04861).

**Publisher's notes:**
Published by AA Publishing (a trading name of AA Media Limited, whose registered office is Fanum House, Basing View, Basingstoke, Hampshire RG21 4EA, UK. Registered number 06112600).

ISBN: 978 0 7495 7345 4 (spiral bound)
ISBN: 978 0 7495 7344 7 (paperback)

A CIP catalogue record for this book is available from The British Library.

The publishers would welcome information to correct any errors or omissions and to keep this atlas up to date. Please write to the Atlas Editor, AA Publishing, The Automobile Association, Fanum House, Basing View, Basingstoke, Hampshire RG21 4EA, UK.
E-mail: *roadatlasfeedback@theaa.com*

**Acknowledgements:**
**RoadPilot**® AA Publishing would like to thank the following for their assistance in producing this atlas:
Information on fixed speed camera locations provided by and © 2012 RoadPilot® Driving Technology. Crematoria data provided by the Cremation Society of Great Britain. Cadw, English Heritage, Forestry Commission, Historic Scotland, Johnsons, National Trust and National Trust for Scotland, RSPB, The Wildlife Trust, Scottish Natural Heritage, Natural England, The Countryside Council for Wales (road maps).

**Printer:**
Printed in Italy by Rotolito Lombarda.
Paper: 80gsm W/F matt coated FSC.

102
Isle of Man
Ramsey
Peel
Douglas
Castletown
Isle of Man (Ronaldsway)
(Apr-Sept)
To help you navigate safely and easily, see the AA's Ireland atlases... theAA.com/shop
IRISH SEA
(Nov-Mar)
(Mar-Oct)
(Apr-Sept)
DUBLIN
Dún Laoghaire
REPUBLIC OF IRELAND
Rosslare Harbour
(July-Sept)
Egremont
LAKE DISTRICT
Ambleside
Windermere
Ravenglass
Kendal
Sedbergh
Kirkby Lonsdale
YORKSHIRE DALES
Millom
Brough
Barrow-in-Furness
Morecambe
Heysham
Lancaster
82
84
Settle
Skipton
Fleetwood
Clitheroe
Keighley
Blackpool
Burnley
Preston
Blackburn
Southport
Rochdale
Ormskirk
Skelmersdale
Bolton
Bury
Formby
Wigan
Oldham
Crosby
St Helens
MANCHESTER
LIVERPOOL
Warrington
Stockport
Birkenhead
Widnes
Manchester
72
74
Holyhead
Anglesey
Llandudno
Colwyn Bay
Rhyl
Holywell
Ellesmere Port
Runcorn
Knutsford
Bangor
Conwy
Abergele
Northwich
Macclesfield
Bethesda
Denbigh
Queensferry
Mold
Chester
Caernarfon
Congleton
Crewe
Kidsgrove
Ruthin
Nantwich
STOKE-ON-TRENT
60
SNOWDONIA
Betws-y-coed
62
Wrexham
Newcastle-under-Lyme
64
Pwllheli
Porthmadog
Llangollen
Whitchurch
Stone
Abersoch
Bala
Oswestry
Market Drayton
Stafford
Barmouth
Dolgellau
Newport
Shrewsbury
Cannock
Welshpool
Telford
Machynlleth
48
Cardigan Bay
50
WALES
Newtown
Church Stretton
WOLVERHAMPTON
Bridgnorth
52
Dudley
Aberystwyth
Llangurig
Stourbridge
Halesowen
Kidderminster
Ludlow
Knighton
Bromsgrove
Rhayader
Redditch
Aberaeron
Tregaron
Llandrindod Wells
Leominster
Worcester
Kington
Lampeter
Builth Wells
Great Malvern
Cardigan
36
Newcastle Emlyn
38
40
Hay-on-Wye
Hereford
Ledbury
Fishguard
Llandovery
Brecon
Tewkesbury
St David's
Ross-on-Wye
Carmarthen
Llandeilo
BRECON BEACONS
Gloucester
Cheltenham
PEMBROKESHIRE COAST
Haverfordwest
St Clears
Abergavenny
Milford Haven
Monmouth
Stroud
Pembroke Dock
Pembroke
Tenby
Llanelli
Merthyr Tydfil
26
Swansea
Neath
Cwmbran
28
Chepstow
Port Talbot
Pontypridd
Newport
Bridgend
CARDIFF
Avonmouth
Chippenham
Cardiff
Clevedon
BRISTOL
Bristol Channel
Weston-super-Mare
Bristol
Bath
Trowbridge
18
Lundy
Ilfracombe
Lynton
20
Minehead
Cheddar
Wells
22
Frome
Warminster
EXMOOR
Glastonbury
Shepton Mallet
Barnstaple
Bridgwater
Bideford
Great Torrington
South Molton
Taunton
Wincanton
Yeovil
Shaftesbury
6
Tiverton
Ilminster
Sherborne
Bude
Hatherleigh
8
Crediton
Chard
10
Crewkerne
Blandford Forum
Wimborne Minster
Holsworthy
Okehampton
Exeter
Honiton
Axminster
Bridport
Exeter
Lyme Regis
Dorchester
Poole
Launceston
Exmouth
DARTMOOR
Dawlish
Weymouth
Wadebridge
Tavistock
Teignmouth
Fortuneswell
Newquay
Bodmin
Newton Abbot
Buckfastleigh
Plymouth
Torquay
2
Isles of Scilly inset
4
Liskeard
Lostwithiel
Saltash
PLYMOUTH
Totnes
Paignton
Torpoint
St Austell
Redruth
Truro
Kingsbridge
Dartmouth
Camborne
Penzance
Land's End
Helston
Falmouth
Lizard
Santander (Mar-Oct)
Roscoff
Guernsey Jersey St-Malo
Cherbourg (Apr-Oct) Guernsey (Apr-Oct) Jersey (Apr-Oct) St-Malo (May-Sept)
ENGLISH
2
Isles of Scilly

# Route planner

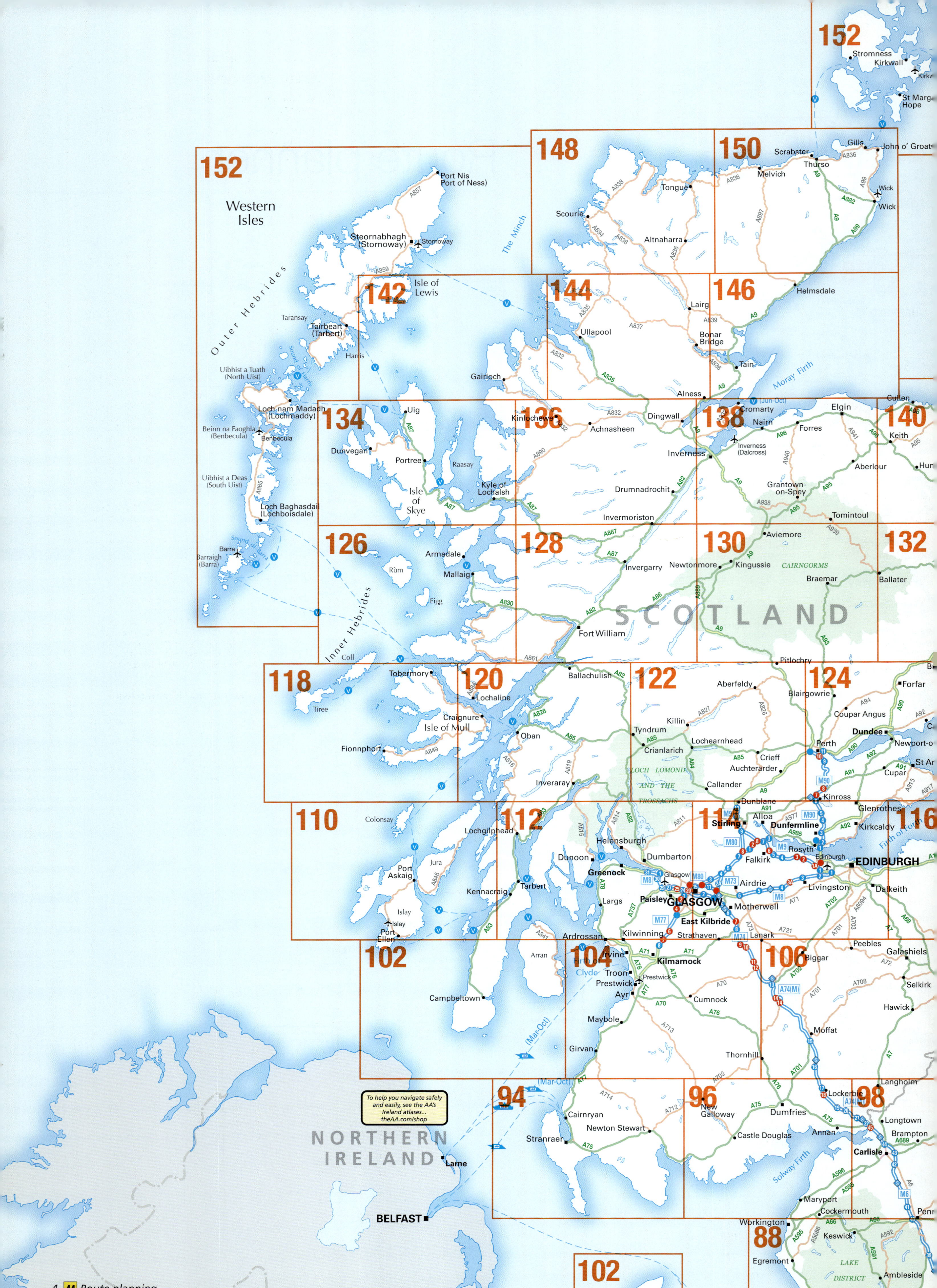

152
Stromness
Kirkwall
St Margaret's Hope
152
Western Isles
Outer Hebrides
Port Nis (Port of Ness)
Steornabhagh (Stornoway)
Stornoway
Isle of Lewis
Taransay
Tairbeart (Tarbert)
Harris
Sound of Harris
Uibhist a Tuath (North Uist)
Loch nam Madadh (Lochmaddy)
Beinn na Faoghla (Benbecula)
Benbecula
Uibhist a Deas (South Uist)
Loch Baghasdail (Lochboisdale)
Barra
Barraigh (Barra)
Sound of Barra
The Minch
148
Scourie
Tongue
Altnaharra
150
Scrabster
Thurso
Gills
John o' Groats
Melvich
Wick
142
144
Ullapool
Lairg
Bonar Bridge
Tain
146
Helmsdale
Moray Firth
Gairloch
Alness
134
Uig
Dunvegan
Portree
Raasay
Isle of Skye
Kyle of Lochalsh
136
Kinlochewe
Achnasheen
Dingwall
138
Cromarty
Nairn
Inverness
Inverness (Dalcross)
Drumnadrochit
Invermoriston
Forres
Elgin
Cullen
140
Keith
Aberlour
Grantown-on-Spey
Tomintoul
126
Armadale
Mallaig
Rùm
Eigg
Inner Hebrides
Coll
128
Invergarry
Fort William
130
Aviemore
Newtonmore
Kingussie
CAIRNGORMS
Braemar
132
Ballater
SCOTLAND
Pitlochry
118
Tiree
Tobermory
120
Lochaline
Craignure
Isle of Mull
Fionnphort
Oban
Ballachulish
122
Aberfeldy
Killin
Tyndrum
Crianlarich
Lochearnhead
Crieff
Auchterarder
Callander
LOCH LOMOND AND THE TROSSACHS
Inveraray
124
Blairgowrie
Forfar
Coupar Angus
Dundee
Perth
Newport-on-Tay
St Andrews
Cupar
Kinross
110
Colonsay
Lochgilphead
Jura
Port Askaig
Islay
Port Ellen
Kennacraig
Tarbert
112
114
Helensburgh
Dumbarton
Dunoon
Greenock
Largs
Paisley
GLASGOW
Glasgow
East Kilbride
Motherwell
Airdrie
Kilwinning
Ardrossan
Strathaven
Lanark
Dunblane
Stirling
Alloa
Dunfermline
Falkirk
Rosyth
Edinburgh
EDINBURGH
Livingston
Dalkeith
Glenrothes
Kirkcaldy
Firth of Forth
116
102
Arran
Campbeltown
104
Irvine
Firth of Clyde
Troon
Kilmarnock
Prestwick
Ayr
Cumnock
Maybole
Girvan
106
Biggar
Peebles
Galashiels
Selkirk
Hawick
Moffat
Thornhill
(Mar-Oct)
To help you navigate safely and easily, see the AA's Ireland atlases... theAA.com/shop
NORTHERN IRELAND
Larne
BELFAST
94
Cairnryan
Newton Stewart
Stranraer
96
New Galloway
Dumfries
Castle Douglas
Lockerbie
Langholm
98
Longtown
Annan
Brampton
Carlisle
Solway Firth
Maryport
Cockermouth
Workington
88
Keswick
Egremont
LAKE DISTRICT
Ambleside
Windermere
Ravenglass
Kendal
Penrith
102
Isle of Man
Ramsey

## FERRY INFORMATION

| | |
|---|---|
| **Hebrides and west coast Scotland** | |
| *calmac.co.uk* | 0800 066 5000 |
| *skyeferry.co.uk* | 01599 522 756 |
| *western-ferries.co.uk* | 01369 704 452 |
| **Orkney and Shetland** | |
| *northlinkferries.co.uk* | 0845 6000 449 |
| *pentlandferries.co.uk* | 01856 831 226 |
| *orkneyferries.co.uk* | 01856 872 044 |
| *shetland.gov.uk/ferries* | 01595 693 535 |
| **Isle of Man** | |
| *steam-packet.com* | 08722 992 992 |
| **Ireland** | |
| *irishferries.com* | 08717 300 400 |
| *poferries.com* | 08716 642 020 |
| *stenaline.co.uk* | 08447 70 70 70 |
| **North Sea (Scandinavia and Benelux)** | |
| *dfdsseaways.co.uk* | 08715 229 955 |
| *poferries.com* | 08716 642 020 |
| *stenaline.co.uk* | 08447 70 70 70 |
| **Isle of Wight** | |
| *wightlink.co.uk* | 0871 376 1000 |
| *redfunnel.co.uk* | 0844 844 9988 |
| **Channel Islands** | |
| *condorferries.co.uk* | 0845 609 1024 |
| **Channel hopping (France and Belgium)** | |
| *brittany-ferries.co.uk* | 0871 244 0744 |
| *condorferries.co.uk* | 0845 609 1024 |
| *eurotunnel.com* | 08443 35 35 35 |
| *ldlines.co.uk* | 0844 576 8836 |
| *dfdsseaways.co.uk* | 08715 229 955 |
| *poferries.com* | 08716 642 020 |
| *transeuropaferries.com* | 01843 595 522 |
| *transmancheferries.co.uk* | 0844 576 8836 |
| **Northern Spain** | |
| *brittany-ferries.co.uk* | 0871 244 0744 |
| *poferries.com* | 08716 642 020 |

## EMERGENCY DIVERSION ROUTES

In an emergency it may be necessary to close a section of motorway or other main road to traffic, so a temporary sign may advise drivers to follow a diversion route. To help drivers navigate the route, black symbols on yellow patches may be permanently displayed on existing direction signs, including motorway signs. Symbols may also be used on separate signs with yellow backgrounds.

For further information see www.highways.gov.uk

Motorway
Toll motorway
Primary route dual carriageway
Primary route single carriageway
Other A road
Vehicle ferry
Fast vehicle ferry or catamaran
National Park
96 Atlas page number

0 10 20 30 miles
0 10 20 30 40 kilometres

Central London Congestion Charging Zone
2 miles
3 kilometres
NORTHWOOD
EDGWARE
STANMORE
Harefield
PINNER
HARROW
KENTON
RUISLIP
Eastcote
Ickenham
WEMBLEY
BRENT
WILLESDEN
NORTHOLT
GREENFORD
HILLINGDON
UXBRIDGE
Yeading
HAYES
SOUTHALL
EALING
ACTON
Hanwell
West Drayton
Harmondsworth
HEATHROW AIRPORT
Cranford
Heston
HOUNSLOW
Isleworth
Brentford
Osterley
RICHMOND UPON THAMES
TWICKENHAM
FELTHAM
Ashford
Stanwell
Sunbury-on-Thames
Teddington
KINGSTON UPON THAMES
Hampton
Barnes
Mortlake
Richmond Park
Bushy Park
Queen Mary Reservoir
Hounslow Heath
Kingsbury
Queensbury
Greenhill
Sudbury
Perivale
Northolt Aerodrome
Harlesden
Chiswick
Kew
Whitton
Hanworth
Petersham
Ham
Kingston Vale
Coombe

FINCHLEY
HENDON
HARINGEY
TOTTENHAM
WALTHAM FOREST
WALTHAMSTOW
HAMPSTEAD
CAMDEN
HACKNEY
ISLINGTON
KENSINGTON
WESTMINSTER
CITY
LAMBETH
TOWER HAMLETS
CHELSEA
FULHAM
GREENWICH
SOUTHWARK
CLAPHAM
LEWISHAM
PUTNEY
WANDSWORTH
CATFORD
WIMBLEDON
STREATHAM
BECKENHAM
MERTON
MITCHAM
Hampstead Heath
Regent's Park
Hyde Park
Battersea Park
Clapham Common
River Thames

# Road safety cameras

First, the advice you would expect from the AA – we advise drivers to always follow the signed speed limits - breaking the speed limit is illegal and can cost lives.

Both the AA and the Government believe that safety cameras ('speed cameras') should be operated within a transparent system. By providing information relating to road safety and speed hotspots, the AA believes that the driver is better placed to be aware of speed limits and can ensure adherence to them, thus making the roads safer for all users.

Most fixed cameras are installed at accident 'black spots' where four or more fatal or serious road collisions have occurred over the previous three years. It is the policy of both the police and the Department for Transport to make the location of cameras as well known as possible. By showing speed camera locations in this atlas the AA is identifying the places where extra care should be taken while driving. Speeding is illegal and dangerous and you MUST keep within the speed limit at all times.
There are currently more than 4,000 fixed cameras in Britain and the road mapping in this atlas identifies their on-the-road locations.

**Gatso™**

**Truvelo™**

**SPECS™**

**Traffipax™**

Mobile cameras are also deployed at other sites where speed is perceived to be a problem and mobile enforcement often takes place at the fixed camera sites shown on the maps in this atlas. Additionally, regular police enforcement can take place on any road.

60 This symbol is used on the mapping to identify **individual** camera locations - with speed limits (mph)

40 This symbol is used on the mapping to identify **multiple** cameras on the same stretch of road - with speed limits (mph)

20 This symbol is used on the mapping to highlight SPECS™ camera systems which calculate your **average speed** along a stretch of road between two or more sets of cameras - with speed limits (mph)

## Camera locations – read this before you use the atlas

1 The camera locations were correct at the time of finalising the information to go to press.
2 Camera locations are approximate due to limitations in the scale of road mapping used in this atlas.
3 In towns and urban areas camera locations are shown only on roads that appear on the road maps in this atlas.
4 Where two or more cameras occur close together, a special symbol is used to indicate multiple cameras on the same stretch of road.
5 Our symbols do not indicate the direction in which cameras point.
6 On the mapping we symbolise more than 4,000 fixed camera locations. Mobile laser device locations, roadworks cameras and 'fixed red light' cameras cannot be shown.

**Speed Limits**

| Types of vehicle | Built up areas* MPH (km/h) | Single carriageways MPH (km/h) | Dual carriageways MPH (km/h) | Motorways MPH (km/h) |
|---|---|---|---|---|
| **Cars & motorcycles** (including car derived vans up to 2 tonnes maximum laden weight) | 30 (48) | 60 (96) | 70 (112) | 70 (112) |
| **Cars towing caravans or trailers** (including car derived vans and motorcycles) | 30 (48) | 50 (80) | 60 (96) | 60 (96) |
| **Buses, coaches and minibuses** (not exceeding 12 metres (39 feet) in overall length) | 30 (48) | 50 (80) | 60 (96) | 70 (112) |
| **Goods vehicles** (not exceeding 7.5 tonnes maximum laden weight) | 30 (48) | 50 (80) | 60 (96) | 70† (112) |
| **Goods vehicles** (exceeding 7.5 tonnes maximum laden weight) | 30 (48) | 40 (64) | 50 (80) | 60 (96) |

* The 30mph (48km/h) limit usually applies to all traffic on all roads with street lighting unless signs show otherwise.
† 60mph (96km/h) if articulated or towing a trailer.

The fixed camera symbols on the mapping show the maximum speed in mph that applies to that particular stretch of road and above which the camera is set to activate. The actual road speed limit however will vary for different vehicle types and you must ensure that you drive within the speed limit for your particular class of vehicle at all times. The chart above details the speed limits applying to the different classes. Don't forget that mobile enforcement can take account of vehicle class at any designated site.

Be alert to accident black spots
even before seeing the cameras
65
60


## The AA brings you a Smart Phone app that provides 'real-time' updates of safety camera locations

The AA Safety Camera app brings the latest safety camera location system to your Smart Phone. It improves road safety by alerting you to the location of fixed and mobile camera sites and accident black spots.

The AA Safety Camera app ensures that you will always have the very latest data of fixed and mobile sites on your Smart Phone without having to connect it to your computer. Updates are made available automatically.

Powered by RoadPilot®

Available on the App Store

Available in Android Market

**Visual Countdown**
To camera location

**Your Speed**
The speed you are travelling when approaching a camera. Dial turns red as an additional visual alert

**Camera Types Located**
Includes fixed cameras (Gatso, Specs etc.) and mobile cameras

**Speed Limit at Camera**

**Smart Phone Apps**

AA

# Tourist sites with satnav friendly postcodes

## ENGLAND

- **Acorn Bank Garden** CA10 1SP Cumb 89 Q1
- **Aldborough Roman Site** YO51 9ES N York 85 N2
- **Alfriston Clergy House** BN26 5TL E Susx 15 P10
- **Alton Towers** ST10 4DB Staffs 65 K3
- **Anglesey Abbey** CB25 9EJ Cambs 57 K8
- **Anne Hathaway's Cottage** CV37 9HH Warwks 53 M9
- **Antony House** PL11 2QA Cnwll 4 F5
- **Appuldurcombe House** PO38 3EW IoW 13 J8
- **Apsley House** W1J 7NT Gt Lon 33 K6
- **Arlington Court** EX31 4LP Devon 19 M5
- **Ascott** LU7 0PS Bucks 44 C7
- **Ashby-de-la-Zouch Castle** LE65 1BR Leics 66 B9
- **Athelhampton House & Gardens** DT2 7LG Dorset 11 J6
- **Attingham Park** SY4 4TP Shrops 63 P10
- **Audley End House & Gardens** CB11 4JF Essex 45 P4
- **Avebury Manor & Garden** SN8 1RF Wilts 30 C8
- **Baconsthorpe Castle** NR25 6LN Norfk 70 H5
- **Baddesley Clinton Hall** B93 0DQ Warwks 53 M6
- **Bamburgh Castle** NE69 7DF Nthumb 109 K3
- **Barnard Castle** DL12 8PR Dur 90 H3
- **Barrington Court** TA19 0NQ Somset 21 N9
- **Basildon Park** RG8 9NR W Berk 31 M7
- **Bateman's** TN19 7DS E Susx 16 B6
- **Battle of Britain Memorial Flight** LN4 4SY Lincs 80 D12
- **Beamish Open Air Museum** DH9 0RG Dur 100 G7
- **Beatrix Potter Gallery** LA22 0NS Cumb 89 K7
- **Beaulieu House** SO42 7ZN Hants 12 F4
- **Belton House** NG32 2LS Lincs 67 M4
- **Belvoir Castle** NG32 1PD Leics 67 K5
- **Bembridge Windmill** PO35 5SQ IoW 13 L7
- **Beningbrough Hall & Gardens** YO30 1DD N York 85 Q3
- **Benthall Hall** TF12 5RX Shrops 64 C11
- **Berkeley Castle** GL13 9BQ Gloucs 29 K3
- **Berrington Hall** HR6 0DW Herefs 51 N8
- **Berry Pomeroy Castle** TQ9 6NJ Devon 5 P4
- **Beth Chatto Gardens** CO7 7DB Essex 47 J7
- **Biddulph Grange Garden** ST8 7SD Staffs 76 G11
- **Bishop's Waltham Palace** SO32 1DH Hants 25 J10
- **Blackpool Zoo** FY3 8PP Bpool 82 H8
- **Blenheim Palace** OX20 1PX Oxon 43 J8
- **Blickling Hall** NR11 6NF Norfk 70 H6
- **Blue John Cavern & Mine** S33 8WP Derbys 77 L7
- **Bodiam Castle** TN32 5UA E Susx 16 D6
- **Bolsover Castle** S44 6PR Derbys 78 D9
- **Boscobel House** ST19 9AR Staffs 64 F10
- **Bovington Tank Museum** BH20 6JG Dorset 11 K7
- **Bowes Castle** DL12 9LD Dur 90 G4
- **Bradford Industrial Museum** BD2 3HP W York 85 J8
- **Bradley Manor** TQ12 6BN Devon 8 F10
- **Bramber Castle** BN44 3WW W Susx 14 H8
- **Brinkburn Priory** NE65 8AP Nthumb 109 J10
- **Bristol Zoo** BS8 3HA Bristl 28 H7
- **British Library** NW1 2DB Gt Lon 33 K6
- **British Museum** WC1B 3DG Gt Lon 33 K6
- **Brockhampton Estate** WR6 5TB Herefs 52 C9
- **Brough Castle** CA17 4EJ Cumb 90 C4
- **Buckfast Abbey** TQ11 0EE Devon 5 M3
- **Buckingham Palace** SW1A 1AA Gt Lon 33 K6
- **Buckland Abbey** PL20 6EY Devon 4 G3
- **Buscot Park** SN7 8BU Oxon 30 F3
- **Byland Abbey** YO61 4BD N York 92 B11
- **Caldicot Castle & Country Park** NP26 4HU Mons 28 G5
- **Calke Abbey** DE73 7LE Derbys 66 B7
- **Canons Ashby House** NN11 3SD Nhants 54 F10
- **Canterbury Cathedral** CT1 2EH Kent 35 L10
- **Carisbrooke Castle** PO30 1XY IoW 12 H7
- **Carlyle's House** SW3 5HL Gt Lon 33 K7
- **Castle Drogo** EX6 6PB Devon 8 D7
- **Castle Howard** YO60 7DA N York 86 D1
- **Castle Rising Castle** PE31 6AH Norfk 69 M7
- **Charlecote Park** CV35 9ER Warwks 53 P9
- **Chartwell** TN16 1PS Kent 33 N12
- **Chastleton House** GL56 0SU Oxon 42 F6
- **Chatsworth** DE45 1PP Derbys 77 N9
- **Chedworth Roman Villa** GL54 3LJ Gloucs 42 C9
- **Chessington World of Adventures** KT9 2NE Gt Lon 32 H10
- **Chester Cathedral** CH1 2HU Ches 75 L10
- **Chester Zoo** CH2 1LH Ches 75 L9
- **Chesters Roman Fort** NE46 4EP Nthumb 99 P4
- **Chiswick House** W4 2RP Gt Lon 33 J7
- **Chysauster Ancient Village** TR20 8XA Cnwll 2 D7
- **Clandon Park** GU4 7RQ Surrey 32 E12
- **Claremont Landscape Garden** KT10 9JG Surrey 32 G9
- **Claydon House** MK18 2EY Bucks 43 P6
- **Cleeve Abbey** TA23 0PS Somset 20 G5
- **Clevedon Court** BS21 6QU N Som 28 F8
- **Cliveden** SL6 0JA Bucks 32 C5
- **Clouds Hill** BH20 7NQ Dorset 11 K6
- **Clumber Park** S80 3AZ Notts 78 G8
- **Colchester Zoo** CO3 0SL Essex 46 G7
- **Coleridge Cottage** TA5 1NQ Somset 21 K5
- **Coleton Fishacre** TQ6 0EQ Devon 5 Q6
- **Compton Castle** TQ3 1TA Devon 5 P4
- **Conisbrough Castle** DN12 3HH Donc 78 E4
- **Corbridge Roman Site** NE45 5NT Nthumb 100 C5
- **Corfe Castle** BH20 5EZ Dorset 11 M8
- **Corsham Court** SN13 0BZ Wilts 29 P8
- **Cotehele** PL12 6TA Cnwll 4 F3
- **Coughton Court** B49 5JA Warwks 53 K8
- **Courts Garden** BA14 6RR Wilts 29 P10
- **Cragside** NE65 7PX Nthumb 108 H9
- **Crealy Adventure Park** EX5 1DR Devon 9 J6
- **Crich Tramway Village** DE4 5DP Derbys 65 Q1
- **Croft Castle** HR6 9PW Herefs 51 M7
- **Croome Park** WR8 9DW Worcs 41 P3
- **Deddington Castle** OX15 0TE Oxon 43 K5
- **Didcot Railway Centre** OX11 7NJ Oxon 31 L4
- **Dover Castle** CT16 1HU Kent 17 P2
- **Drayton Manor Theme Park** B78 3TW Staffs 65 M11
- **Dudmaston** WV15 6QN Shrops 52 D3
- **Dunham Massey** WA14 4SJ Traffd 76 D6
- **Dunstanburgh Castle** NE66 3TT Nthumb 109 L6
- **Dunster Castle** TA24 6SL Somset 20 F5
- **Durham Cathedral** DH1 3EH Dur 100 H10
- **Dyrham Park** SN14 8ER S Glos 29 L7
- **East Riddlesden Hall** BD20 5EL Brad 84 G7
- **Eden Project** PL24 2SG Cnwll 3 P4
- **Eltham Palace** SE9 5QE Gt Lon 33 M7
- **Emmetts Garden** TN14 6AY Kent 33 N11
- **Exmoor Zoological Park** EX31 4SG Devon 19 M5
- **Farleigh Hungerford Castle** BA2 7RS Somset 29 N10
- **Farnborough Hall** OX17 1DU Warwks 54 C10
- **Felbrigg Hall** NR11 8PR Norfk 71 J4
- **Fenton House** NW3 6RT Gt Lon 33 J5
- **Finch Foundry** EX20 2NW Devon 8 C6
- **Finchale Priory** DH1 5SH Dur 100 H9
- **Fishbourne Roman Palace** PO19 3QR W Susx 13 P4
- **Flag Fen Bronze Age Centre & Archaeology Park** PE6 7QJ Cambs 56 D1
- **Flamingo Land** YO17 6UX N York 92 F10
- **Forde Abbey** TA20 4LU Somset 9 Q4
- **Fountains Abbey & Studley Royal** HG4 3DY N York 85 K1
- **Gawthorpe Hall** BB12 8UA Lancs 84 B8
- **Gisborough Priory** TS14 6HG R & Cl 92 C3
- **Glendurgan Garden** TR11 5JZ Cnwll 3 J9
- **Goodrich Castle** HR9 6HY Herefs 41 J7
- **Great Chalfield Manor** SN12 8NH Wilts 29 P9
- **Great Coxwell Barn** SN7 7LZ Oxon 30 F3
- **Greenway** TQ5 0ES Devon 5 P6
- **Haddon Hall** DE45 1LA Derbys 77 N10
- **Hailes Abbey** GL54 5PB Gloucs 42 B6
- **Ham House** TW10 7RS Gt Lon 32 H8
- **Hampton Court Palace** KT8 9AU Gt Lon 32 H8
- **Hanbury Hall** WR9 7EA Worcs 52 H8
- **Hardwick Hall** S44 5QJ Derbys 78 D11
- **Hardy's Cottage** DT2 8QJ Dorset 10 H6
- **Hare Hill** SK10 4QB Ches 76 G8
- **Hatchlands Park** GU4 7RT Surrey 32 F12
- **Heale Gardens** SP4 6NT Wilts 23 P6
- **Helmsley Castle** YO62 5AB N York 92 C10
- **Hereford Cathedral** HR1 2NG Herefs 40 G4
- **Hergest Croft Gardens** HR5 3EG Herefs 51 J9
- **Hever Castle & Gardens** TN8 7NG Kent 15 N2
- **Hidcote Manor Garden** GL55 6LR Gloucs 42 E3
- **Hill Top** LA22 0LF Cumb 89 K7
- **Hinton Ampner** SO24 0LA Hants 25 K8
- **Holkham Hall** NR23 1AB Norfk 70 C4
- **Housesteads Roman Fort** NE47 6NN Nthumb 99 M4
- **Howletts Wild Animal Park** CT4 5EL Kent 35 M11
- **Hughenden Manor** HP14 4LA Bucks 32 B3
- **Hurst Castle** SO41 0TR Hants 12 E7
- **Ickworth House & Gardens** IP29 5QE Suffk 58 38
- **Ightham Mote** TN15 0NT Kent 33 Q11
- **Ironbridge Gorge Museums** TF8 7DQ Wrekin 64 C11
- **Kedleston Hall** DE22 5JH Derbys 65 P4
- **Kenilworth Castle** CV8 1NE Warwks 53 P6
- **Kenwood House** NW3 7JR Gt Lon 33 K5
- **Kew Gardens** TW9 3AB Gt Lon 32 H7
- **Killerton House & Garden** EX5 3LE Devon 9 J5
- **King John's Hunting Lodge** BS26 2AP Somset 21 P2
- **Kingston Lacy** BH21 4EA Dorset 11 N4
- **Kirby Hall** NN17 3EN Nhants 55 M2
- **Knightshayes Court** EX16 7RQ Devon 20 E10
- **Knole House** TN15 0RP Kent 33 P11
- **Knowsley Safari Park** L34 4AN Knows 75 M5
- **Lacock Abbey** SN15 2LG Wilts 29 Q8
- **Lamb House** TN31 7ES E Susx 16 G7
- **Lanhydrock House** PL30 5AD Cnwll 3 Q2
- **Launceston Castle** PL15 7DR Cnwll 7 L8
- **Leeds Castle** ME17 1PL Kent 34 E11
- **Lindisfarne Castle** TD15 2SH Nthumb 109 J1
- **Lindisfarne Priory** TD15 2RX Nthumb 109 J1
- **Little Moreton Hall** CW12 4SD Ches 76 F12
- **Liverpool Cathedral** L1 7AZ Lpool 75 K6
- **Longleat** BA12 7NW Wilts 22 H5
- **Losely Park** GU3 1HS Surrey 14 D1
- **Lost Gardens of Heligan** PL26 6EN Cnwll 3 N5
- **Ludgershall Castle** SP11 9QR Wilts 24 D3
- **Lydford Castle** EX20 4BH Devon 7 P8
- **Lyme Park** SK12 2NX Ches 76 H7
- **Lytes Cary Manor** TA11 7HU Somset 22 C8
- **Lyveden New Bield** PE8 5AT Nhants 55 N4
- **Maiden Castle** DT2 9PP Dorset 10 G7
- **Mapledurham House** RG4 7TR Oxon 31 N7
- **Marble Hill House** TW1 2NL Gt Lon 32 H7
- **Marwell Zoological Park** SO21 1JH Hants 24 H9
- **Melford Hall** CO10 9AA Suffk 46 F2
- **Merseyside Maritime Museum** L3 4AQ Lpool 75 K6
- **Minster Lovell Hall** OX29 0RR Oxon 42 G9
- **Mompesson House** SP1 2EL Wilts 23 P7
- **Monk Bretton Priory** S71 5QD Barns 78 B2
- **Montacute House** TA15 6XP Somset 22 C10
- **Morwellham Quay** PL19 8JL Devon 4 G3
- **Moseley Old Hall** WV10 7HY Staffs 64 H11
- **Mottisfont Abbey & Garden** SO51 0LP Hants 24 E8
- **Mottistone Manor Garden** PO30 4ED IoW 12 G8
- **Mount Grace Priory** DL6 3JG N York 91 Q7
- **National Gallery** WC2N 5DN Gt Lon 33 K6
- **National Maritime Museum** SE10 9NF Gt Lon 33 M7
- **National Motorcycle Museum** B92 0EJ Solhll 53 M4
- **National Portrait Gallery** WC2H 0HE Gt Lon 33 K6
- **National Railway Museum** YO26 4XJ York 86 B5
- **National Space Centre** LE4 5NS C Leic 66 F11
- **Natural History Museum** SW7 5BD Gt Lon 33 K6
- **Needles Old Battery** PO39 0JH IoW 12 E8
- **Nene Valley Railway** PE8 6LR Cambs 56 C1
- **Netley Abbey** SO31 5FB Hants 12 G3
- **Newark Air Museum** NG24 2NY Notts 79 L12
- **Newtown Old Town Hall** PO30 4PA IoW 12 G6
- **North Leigh Roman Villa** OX29 6QB Oxon 43 J8
- **Norwich Cathedral** NR1 4DH Norfk 71 J10
- **Nostell Priory** WF4 1QE Wakefd 85 N11
- **Nunnington Hall** YO62 5UY N York 92 D11
- **Nymans** RH17 6EB W Susx 15 J5
- **Old Royal Naval College** SE10 9LW Gt Lon 33 M7
- **Old Sarum** SP1 3SD Wilts 23 P7
- **Old Wardour Castle** SP3 6RR Wilts 23 L8
- **Oliver Cromwell's House** CB7 4HF Cambs 57 K4
- **Orford Castle** IP12 2ND Suffk 59 N10
- **Ormesby Hall** TS7 9AS R & Cl 92 B3
- **Osborne House** PO32 6JY IoW 13 J6
- **Osterley Park & House** TW7 4RB Gt Lon 32 G7
- **Overbeck's** TQ8 8LW Devon 5 M9
- **Oxburgh Hall** PE33 9PS Norfk 69 P12
- **Packwood House** B94 6AT Warwks 53 M6
- **Paignton Zoo** TQ4 7EU Torbay 5 P5
- **Paycocke's** CO6 1NS Essex 46 E7
- **Peckover House & Garden** PE13 1JR Cambs 69 J10
- **Pendennis Castle** TR11 4LP Cnwll 3 K8
- **Petworth House & Park** GU28 0AE W Susx 14 D6
- **Pevensey Castle** BN24 5LE E Susx 16 B10
- **Peveril Castle** S33 8WQ Derbys 77 L7
- **Polesden Lacey** RH5 6BD Surrey 32 G12
- **Portland Castle** DT5 1AZ Dorset 10 G10
- **Portsmouth Historic Dockyard** PO1 3LJ C Port 13 L5
- **Powderham Castle** EX6 8JQ Devon 8 H8
- **Prior Park Landscape Garden** BA2 5AH BaNES 29 M9
- **Prudhoe Castle** NE42 6NA Nthumb 100 E5
- **Quarry Bank Mill** SK9 4LA Ches 76 F7
- **Quebec House** TN16 1TD Kent 33 N11
- **Ramsey Abbey Gatehouse** PE17 1DH Cambs 56 F4
- **Reculver Towers** CT6 6SU Kent 35 M8
- **Red House** DA6 8JF Gt Lon 33 N7
- **Restormel Castle** PL22 0EE Cnwll 3 Q2
- **Richborough Roman Fort** CT13 9JW Kent 35 P10
- **Richmond Castle** DL10 4QW N York 91 K6
- **Roche Abbey** S66 8NW Rothm 78 E6
- **Rochester Castle** ME1 1SX Medway 34 C8
- **Rockbourne Roman Villa** SP6 3PG Hants 23 P10
- **Roman Baths & Pump Room** BA1 1LZ BaNES 29 M9
- **Royal Observatory Greenwich** SE10 8XJ Gt Lon 33 M7
- **Rufford Old Hall** L40 1SG Lancs 83 L12
- **Runnymede** SL4 2JJ W & M 32 E7
- **Rushton Triangular Lodge** NN14 1RP Nhants 55 K4
- **Rycote Chapel** OX9 2PA Oxon 43 N11
- **Salisbury Cathedral** SP1 2EJ Wilts 23 P7
- **Saltram** PL7 1UH C Plym 4 H5
- **Sandham Memorial Chapel** RG20 9JT Hants 31 K10
- **Sandringham House & Grounds** PE35 6EN Norfk 69 N6
- **Saxtead Green Post Mill** IP13 9QQ Suffk 59 K8
- **Scarborough Castle** YO11 1HY N York 93 L9
- **Science Museum** SW7 2DD Gt Lon 33 K6
- **Scotney Castle** TN3 8JN Kent 16 B4
- **Shaw's Corner** AL6 9BX Herts 44 H8
- **Sheffield Park Garden** TN22 3QX E Susx 15 M6
- **Sherborne Old Castle** DT9 3SA Dorset 22 E10
- **Sissinghurst Castle Garden** TN17 2AB Kent 16 E3
- **Sizergh Castle & Garden** LA8 8AE Cumb 89 M9
- **Smallhythe Place** TN30 7NG Kent 16 F5
- **Snowshill Manor** WR12 7JU Gloucs 42 C5
- **Souter Lighthouse** SR6 7NH S Tyne 101 K5
- **Speke Hall** L24 1XD Lpool 75 M7
- **Spinnaker Tower** PO1 3TT C Port 13 L5
- **St Leonard's Tower** ME19 6PE Kent 34 B11
- **St Michael's Mount** TR17 0HT Cnwll 2 E8
- **St Paul's Cathedral** EC4M 8AD Gt Lon 33 L6
- **Stokesay Castle** SY7 9AH Shrops 51 M4
- **Stonehenge** SP4 7DE Wilts 23 P5
- **Stourhead** BA12 6QD Wilts 22 H6
- **Stowe Landscape Gardens** MK18 5EH Bucks 43 P4
- **Sudbury Hall** DE6 5HT Derbys 65 M6
- **Sulgrave Manor** OX17 2SD Nhants 43 M3
- **Sunnycroft** TF1 2DR Wrekin 64 C10
- **Sutton Hoo** IP12 3DJ Suffk 59 K10
- **Sutton House** E9 6QJ Gt Lon 33 L5
- **Tate Britain** SW1P 4RG Gt Lon 33 K6
- **Tate Liverpool** L3 4BB Lpool 75 K6
- **Tate Modern** SE1 9TG Gt Lon 33 K6
- **Tattershall Castle** LN4 4LR Lincs 80 D12
- **Tatton Park** WA16 6QN Ches 76 D7
- **The Lowry** M50 3AZ Salfd 76 E4
- **The Vyne** RG24 9HL Hants 31 N11
- **The Weir** HR4 7QF Herefs 40 F3
- **Thornton Abbey** DN39 6TU N Linc 87 L11
- **Thorpe Park** KT16 8PN Surrey 32 E8
- **Tilbury Fort** RM18 7NR Thurr 34 B7
- **Tintagel Castle** PL34 0HE Cnwll 6 F7
- **Tintinhull Garden** BA22 8PZ Somset 22 C9
- **Totnes Castle** TQ9 5NU Devon 5 N5
- **Tower of London** EC3N 4AB Gt Lon 33 L6
- **Townend** LA23 1LB Cumb 89 L6
- **Treasurer's House** YO1 7JL York 86 B5
- **Trelissick Garden** TR3 6QL Cnwll 3 K6
- **Trengwainton Garden** TR20 8RZ Cnwll 2 C8
- **Trerice** TR8 4PG Cnwll 3 K3
- **Twycross Zoo** CV9 3PX Leics 65 P11
- **Upnor Castle** ME2 4XG Medway 34 D8
- **Uppark House & Garden** GU31 5QR W Susx 25 N10
- **Upton House & Garden** OX15 6HT Warwks 42 H3
- **Victoria & Albert Museum** SW7 2RL Gt Lon 33 K6
- **Waddesdon Manor** HP18 0JH Bucks 43 Q8
- **Wakehurst Place** RH17 6TN W Susx 15 L4
- **Wall Roman Site** WS14 0AW Staffs 65 L11
- **Wallington House** NE61 4AR Nthumb 100 D1
- **Walmer Castle & Gardens** CT14 7LJ Kent 35 Q12
- **Warkworth Castle** NE65 0UJ Nthumb 109 L8
- **Warwick Castle** CV34 4QU Warwks 53 P7
- **Washington Old Hall** NE38 7LE Sundld 101 J7
- **Waterperry Gardens** OX33 1JZ Oxon 43 N10
- **Weeting Castle** IP27 0RQ Norfk 57 P3
- **Wenlock Priory** TF13 6HS Shrops 64 B12
- **West Midland Safari Park** DY12 1LF Worcs 52 E5
- **West Wycombe Park** HP14 3AJ Bucks 32 B3
- **Westbury Court Garden** GL14 1PD Gloucs 41 L9
- **Westminster Abbey** SW1P 3PA Gt Lon 33 K6
- **Westonbirt Arboretum** GL8 8QS Gloucs 29 N4
- **Westwood Manor** BA15 2AF Wilts 29 N10
- **Whitby Abbey** YO22 4JT N York 92 H4
- **Wightwick Manor** WV6 8EE Wolves 52 F1
- **Wimpole Hall & Home Farm** SG8 0BW Cambs 56 F10
- **Winchester Cathedral** SO23 9LS Hants 24 H7
- **Winchester City Mill** SO23 0EJ Hants 24 H7
- **Windsor Castle** SL4 1NJ W & M 32 D7
- **Winkworth Arboretum** GU8 4AD Surrey 14 E3
- **Wisley RHS Garden** GU23 6QB Surrey 32 F10
- **Woburn Safari Park** MK17 9QN Beds 44 D5
- **Wookey Hole Caves** BA5 1BB Somset 22 C4
- **Woolsthorpe Manor** NG33 5NR Lincs 67 M7
- **Wordsworth House** CA13 9RX Cumb 97 M12
- **Wrest Park** MK45 4HS Beds 44 F4
- **Wroxeter Roman City** SY5 6PR Shrops 63 P11
- **WWT Arundel Wetland Centre** BN18 9PB W Susx 14 E9
- **Yarmouth Castle** PO41 0PB IoW 12 F7
- **York Minster** YO1 7JF York 86 B5
- **ZSL London Zoo** NW1 4RY Gt Lon 33 K6
- **ZSL Whipsnade Zoo** LU6 2LF Beds 44 E8

## SCOTLAND

- **Aberdour Castle** KY3 0SL Fife 115 M4
- **Alloa Tower** FK10 1PP Clacks 114 F3
- **Angus Folk Museum** DD8 1RT Angus 124 H3
- **Arbroath Abbey** DD11 1EG Angus 125 M4
- **Arduaine Garden** PA34 4XQ Ag & B 120 E10
- **Bachelors' Club** KA5 5RB S Ayrs 104 H4
- **Balmoral Castle Grounds** AB35 5TB Abers 131 N5
- **Balvenie Castle** AB55 4DH Moray 139 P7
- **Bannockburn Heritage Centre** FK7 0LJ Stirlg 114 E3
- **Blackness Castle** EH49 7NH Falk 115 J5
- **Blair Castle** PH18 5TL P & K 130 F11
- **Bothwell Castle** G71 8BL S Lans 114 C9
- **Branklyn Garden** PH2 7BB P & K 124 C8
- **Brodick Castle** KA27 8HY N Ayrs 103 Q2
- **Brodie Castle** IV36 2TE Moray 138 H4
- **Broughton House & Garden** DG6 4JX D & G 96 D8
- **Burleigh Castle** KY13 9GG P & K 124 C12
- **Burrell Collection** G43 1AT C Glas 113 Q9
- **Caerlaverock Castle** DG1 4RU D & G 97 L5
- **Cardoness Castle** DG7 2EH D & G 96 C7
- **Carnasserie Castle** PA31 8RQ Ag & B 112 B1
- **Castle Campbell** FK14 7PP Clacks 114 H1
- **Castle Fraser** AB51 7LD Abers 132 H2
- **Castle Kennedy & Gardens** DG9 8BX D & G 94 G6
- **Castle Menzies** PH15 2JD P & K 123 L3
- **Corgarff Castle** AB36 8YL Abers 131 P3
- **Craigievar Castle** AB33 8JF Abers 132 E2
- **Craigmillar Castle** EH16 4SY C Edin 115 P7
- **Crarae Garden** PA32 8YA Ag & B 112 E2
- **Crathes Castle & Garden** AB31 5QJ Abers 132 H5
- **Crichton Castle** EH37 5QH Mdloth 115 Q8
- **Crossraguel Abbey** KA19 5HQ S Ayrs 104 E8
- **Culloden Battlefield** IV2 5EU Highld 138 D7
- **Culross Palace** KY12 8JH Fife 114 H4
- **Culzean Castle & Country Park** KA19 8LE S Ayrs 104 D8
- **Dallas Dhu Distillery** IV36 2RR Moray 139 J4
- **David Livingstone Centre** G72 9BT S Lans 114 C9
- **Dirleton Castle** EH39 5ER E Loth 116 C4
- **Doune Castle** FK16 6EA Stirlg 114 D1
- **Drum Castle** AB31 5EY Abers 133 J4
- **Dryburgh Abbey** TD6 0RQ Border 107 P3
- **Duff House** AB45 3SX Abers 140 H3
- **Dumbarton Castle** G82 1JJ W Duns 113 M6
- **Dundrennan Abbey** DG6 4QH D & G 96 F8
- **Dunnottar Castle** AB39 2TL Abers 133 L7
- **Dunstaffnage Castle** PA37 1PZ Ag & B 120 G6
- **Edinburgh Castle** EH1 2NG C Edin 115 N6
- **Edinburgh Zoo** EH12 6TS C Edin 115 M7
- **Edzell Castle** DD9 7UE Angus 132 F10
- **Elgin Cathedral** IV30 1HU Moray 139 N3
- **Falkland Palace & Garden** KY15 7BU Fife 124 E11
- **Fort George** IV2 7TE Highld 138 D4
- **Fyvie Castle** AB53 8JS Abers 141 J8
- **Georgian House** EH2 4DR C Edin 115 N6
- **Gladstone's Land** EH1 2NT C Edin 115 N6
- **Glamis Castle** DD8 1RJ Angus 124 H3
- **Glasgow Botanic Gardens** G12 0UE C Glas 113 Q8
- **Glasgow Cathedral** G4 0QZ C Glas 114 A8
- **Glasgow Science Centre** G51 1EA C Glas 113 Q8
- **Glen Grant Distillery** AB38 7BS Moray 139 N6
- **Glenluce Abbey** DG8 0AF D & G 94 H6
- **Greenbank Garden** G76 8RB E Rens 113 Q10
- **Haddo House** AB41 7EQ Abers 141 L9
- **Harmony Garden** TD6 9LJ Border 107 N3
- **Hermitage Castle** TD9 0LU Border 107 M10
- **Highland Wildlife Park** PH21 1NL Highld 130 E4
- **Hill House** G84 9AJ Ag & B 113 L4
- **Hill of Tarvit Mansionhouse & Garden** KY15 5PB Fife 124 H10
- **Holmwood** G44 3YG C Glas 113 R9
- **House of Dun** DD10 9LQ Angus 125 N1
- **House of the Binns** EH49 7NA W Loth 115 J6
- **Hunterian Museum** G12 8QQ C Glas 113 Q8
- **Huntingtower Castle** PH1 3JL P & K 124 B8
- **Huntly Castle** AB54 4SH Abers 140 E7
- **Hutchesons' Hall** G1 1EJ C Glas 114 A8
- **Inchmahome Priory** FK8 3RA Stirlg 113 R1
- **Inveresk Lodge Garden** EH21 7TE E Loth 115 Q7
- **Inverewe Garden** IV22 2LG Highld 143 M9
- **Inverlochy Castle** PH33 6SN Highld 128 F9
- **Kellie Castle & Garden** KY10 2RF Fife 125 K11
- **Kildrummy Castle** AB33 8RA Abers 132 C1
- **Killiecrankie Visitor Centre** PH16 5LG P & K 130 G11
- **Leith Hall Garden** AB54 4NQ Abers 140 E10
- **Linlithgow Palace** EH49 7AL W Loth 115 J6
- **Lochleven Castle** KY13 8AS P & K 124 C12
- **Logan Botanic Garden** DG9 9ND D & G 94 G9
- **Malleny Garden** EH14 7AF C Edin 115 L8
- **Melrose Abbey** TD6 9LG Border 107 N3
- **National Museum of Scotland** EH1 1JF C Edin 115 N6
- **Newark Castle** PA14 5NH Inver 113 L6
- **Palace of Holyroodhouse** EH8 8DX C Edin 115 N6
- **Pitmedden Garden** AB41 7PD Abers 141 L10
- **Preston Mill** EH40 3DS E Loth 116 E6
- **Priorwood Garden** TD6 9PX Border 107 N3
- **Robert Smail's Printing Works** EH44 6HA Border 107 J2
- **Rothesay Castle** PA20 0DA Ag & B 112 G8
- **Royal Botanic Garden Edinburgh** EH3 5LR C Edin 115 N6
- **Royal Yacht Britannia** EH6 6JJ C Edin 115 N6
- **Scone Palace** PH2 6BD P & K 124 C7
- **Smailholm Tower** TD5 7PG Border 107 Q3
- **Souter Johnnie's Cottage** KA19 8HY S Ayrs 104 D8
- **St Andrews Aquarium** KY16 9AS Fife 125 K9
- **Stirling Castle** FK8 1EJ Stirlg 114 E2
- **Sweetheart Abbey** DG2 8BU D & G 97 J5
- **Tantallon Castle** EH39 5PN E Loth 116 D4
- **Tenement House** G3 6QN C Glas 113 R8
- **The Lighthouse** G1 3NU C Glas 113 R8
- **Threave Castle** DG7 1TJ D & G 96 E6
- **Threave Garden** DG7 1RX D & G 96 F6
- **Tolquhon Castle** AB41 7LP Abers 141 L10
- **Traquair House** EH44 6PW Border 107 J3
- **Urquhart Castle** IV63 6XJ Highld 137 P10
- **Weaver's Cottage** PA10 2JG Rens 113 M8
- **Whithorn Priory** DG8 8PY D & G 95 N10

## WALES

- **Aberconwy House** LL32 8AY Conwy 73 N8
- **Aberdulais Falls** SA10 8EU Neath 27 J2
- **Beaumaris Castle** LL58 8AP IoA 73 K8
- **Big Pit: National Coal Museum** NP4 9XP Torfn 40 B10
- **Bodnant Garden** LL28 5RE Conwy 73 P9
- **Caerleon Roman Amphitheatre** NP18 1AE Newpt 28 D4
- **Caernarfon Castle** LL55 2AY Gwynd 72 H11
- **Cardiff Castle** CF10 3RB Cardif 28 A7
- **Castell Coch** CF15 7JS Cardif 27 Q6
- **Chirk Castle** LL14 5AF Wrexhm 63 J4
- **Colby Woodland Garden** SA67 8PP Pembks 37 M9
- **Conwy Castle** LL32 8AY Conwy 73 N8
- **Criccieth Castle** LL52 0DP Gwynd 60 H5
- **Dan-yr-Ogof Showcaves** SA9 1GJ Powys 39 K8
- **Dinefwr Park** SA19 6RT Carmth 38 F7
- **Dolaucothi Gold Mines** SA19 8US Carmth 38 G4
- **Erddig** LL13 0YT Wrexhm 63 K3
- **Ffestiniog Railway** LL49 9NF Gwynd 61 J4
- **Harlech Castle** LL46 2YH Gwynd 61 K6
- **Llanerchaeron** SA48 8DG Cerdgn 48 H8
- **Penrhyn Castle** LL57 4HN Gwynd 73 K9
- **Plas Newydd** LL61 6DQ IoA 72 H9
- **Plas yn Rhiw** LL53 8AB Gwynd 60 C6
- **Portmeirion** LL48 6ET Gwynd 61 K5
- **Powis Castle & Garden** SY21 8RF Powys 62 H11
- **Raglan Castle** NP15 2BT Mons 40 F10
- **Sygun Copper Mine** LL55 4NE Gwynd 61 K2
- **Tintern Abbey** NP16 6SE Mons 28 H2
- **Tudor Merchant's House** SA70 7BX Pembks 37 M10
- **Tŷ Mawr Wybrnant** LL25 0HJ Conwy 61 N2
- **Valle Crucis Abbey** LL20 8DD Denbgs 62 H3

# Caravan and camping sites in Britain

These pages list the top 300 AA-inspected Caravan and Camping (C & C) sites in the Pennant rating scheme. Five Pennant Premier sites are shown in **green**, Four Pennant sites are shown in **blue**.

Listings include addresses, telephone numbers and websites together with page and grid references to locate the sites in the atlas. The total number of touring pitches is also included for each site, together with the type of pitch available. The following abbreviations are used: C = Caravan CV = Campervan T = Tent

To find out more about the AA's Pennant rating scheme and other rated caravan and camping sites not included on these pages please visit *theAA.com*

## ENGLAND

**Abbey Farm Caravan Park**
Dark Lane, Ormskirk
L40 5TX
Tel: 01695 572686 75 M2
*abbeyfarmcaravanpark.co.uk*
Total Pitches: 56 (C, CV & T)

**Alders Caravan Park**
Home Farm, Alne, York
YO61 1RY
Tel: 01347 838722 85 P2
*alderscaravanpark.co.uk*
Total Pitches: 87 (C, CV & T)

**Alpine Grove Touring Park**
Forton, Chard
TA20 4HD
Tel: 01460 63479 9 Q3
*alpinegrovetouringpark.com*
Total Pitches: 40 (C, CV & T)

**Andrewshayes Caravan Park**
Dalwood, Axminster
EX13 7DY
Tel: 01404 831225 9 N5
*andrewshayes.co.uk*
Total Pitches: 150 (C, CV & T)

**Appuldurcombe Gardens Holiday Park**
Appuldurcombe Road, Wroxall, Isle of Wight
PO38 3EP
Tel: 01983 852597 13 J8
*appuldurcombegardens.co.uk*
Total Pitches: 100 (C, CV & T)

**Ayr Holiday Park**
St Ives, Cornwall
TR26 1EJ
Tel: 01736 795855 2 E6
*ayrholidaypark.co.uk*
Total Pitches: 40 (C, CV & T)

**Back of Beyond Touring Park**
234 Ringwood Rd, St Leonards, Dorset
BH24 2SB
Tel: 01202 876968 11 Q4
*backofbeyondtouringpark.co.uk*
Total Pitches: 80 (C, CV & T)

**Bagwell Farm Touring Park**
Knights in the Bottom, Chickerell, Weymouth
DT3 4EA
Tel: 01305 782575 10 G8
*bagwellfarm.co.uk*
Total Pitches: 320 (C, CV & T)

**Bardsea Leisure Park**
Priory Road, Ulverston
LA12 9QE
Tel: 01229 584712 89 J11
*bardsealeisure.co.uk*
Total Pitches: 83 (C & CV)

**Barn Farm Campsite**
Barn Farm, Birchover, Matlock
DE4 2BL
Tel: 01629 650245 77 N11
*barnfarmcamping.com*
Total Pitches: 25 (C, CV & T)

**Barnstones C & C Site**
Great Bourton, Banbury
OX17 1QU
Tel: 01295 750289 43 K3
Total Pitches: 49 (C, CV & T)

**Beaconsfield Farm Caravan Park**
Battlefield, Shrewsbury
SY4 4AA
Tel: 01939 210370 63 N8
*beaconsfield-farm.co.uk*
Total Pitches: 60 (C & CV)

**Bellingham C & C Club Site**
Brown Rigg, Bellingham
NE48 2JY
Tel: 01434 220175 99 M2
*campingandcaravanningclub.co.uk/bellingham*
Total Pitches: 64 (C, CV & T)

**Bingham Grange Touring & Camping Park**
Melplash, Bridport
DT6 3TT
Tel: 01308 488234 10 D5
*binghamgrange.co.uk*
Total Pitches: 150 (C, CV & T)

**Bo Peep Farm Caravan Park**
Bo Peep Farm, Aynho Road, Adderbury, Banbury
OX17 3NP
Tel: 01295 810605 43 K5
*bo-peep.co.uk*
Total Pitches: 104 (C, CV & T)

**Briarfields Motel & Touring Park**
Gloucester Road, Cheltenham
GL51 0SX
Tel: 01242 235324 41 P7
*briarfields.net*
Total Pitches: 72 (C, CV & T)

**Broadhembury C & C Park**
Steeds Lane, Kingsnorth, Ashford
TN26 1NQ
Tel: 01233 620859 16 H3
*broadhembury.co.uk*
Total Pitches: 110 (C, CV & T)

**Brokerswood Country Park**
Brokerswood, Westbury
BA13 4EH
Tel: 01373 822238 23 J3
*brokerswoodcountrypark.co.uk*
Total Pitches: 69 (C, CV & T)

**Budemeadows Touring Park**
Widemouth Bay, Bude
EX23 0NA
Tel: 01288 361646 7 J4
*budemeadows.com*
Total Pitches: 145 (C, CV & T)

**Burrowhayes Farm C & C Site**
West Luccombe, Porlock, Minehead
TA24 8HT
Tel: 01643 862463 20 D4
*burrowhayes.co.uk*
Total Pitches: 120 (C, CV & T)

**Burton Constable Holiday Park & Arboretum**
Old Lodges, Sproatley, Hull
HU11 4LN
Tel: 01964 562508 87 M8
*burtonconstable.co.uk*
Total Pitches: 140 (C, CV & T)

**Calloose C & C Park**
Leedstown, Hayle
TR27 5ET
Tel: 01736 850431 2 F7
*calloose.co.uk*
Total Pitches: 109 (C, CV & T)

**Camping Caradon Touring Park**
Trelawne, Looe
PL13 2NA
Tel: 01503 272388 4 C6
*campingcaradon.co.uk*
Total Pitches: 85 (C, CV & T)

**Carlton Meres Country Park**
Rendham Road, Carlton, Saxmundham
IP17 2QP
Tel: 01728 603344 59 M7
*carlton-meres.co.uk*
Total Pitches: 96 (C & CV)

**Carlyon Bay C & C Park**
Bethesda, Cypress Avenue, Carlyon Bay
PL25 3RE
Tel: 01726 812735 3 P4
*carlyonbay.net*
Total Pitches: 180 (C, CV & T)

**Carnevas Holiday Park & Farm Cottages**
Carnevas Farm, St Merryn
PL28 8PN
Tel: 01841 520230 6 B10
*carnevasholidaypark.co.uk*
Total Pitches: 195 (C, CV & T)

**Carnon Downs C & C Park**
Carnon Downs, Truro
TR3 6JJ
Tel: 01872 862283 3 K6
*carnon-downs-caravanpark.co.uk*
Total Pitches: 150 (C, CV & T)

**Carvynick Country Club**
Summercourt, Newquay
TR8 5AF
Tel: 01872 510716 3 L3
*carvynick.co.uk*
Total Pitches: 47 (CV)

**Castlerigg Hall C & C Park**
Castlerigg Hall, Keswick
CA12 4TE
Tel: 017687 74499 89 J2
*castlerigg.co.uk*
Total Pitches: 48 (C, CV & T)

**Cheddar Bridge Touring Park**
Draycott Rd, Cheddar
BS27 3RJ
Tel: 01934 743048 21 P3
*cheddarbridge.co.uk*
Total Pitches: 45 (C, CV & T)

**Cheddar C & C Club Site**
Townsend, Priddy, Wells
BA5 3BP
Tel: 01749 870241 22 C3
*campingandcaravanningclub.co.uk/cheddar*
Total Pitches: 90 (C, CV & T)

**Chiverton Park**
East Hill, Blackwater
TR4 8HS
Tel: 01872 560667 3 J5
*chivertonpark.co.uk*
Total Pitches: 12 (C, CV & T)

**Church Farm C & C Park**
The Bungalow, Church Farm, High Street, Sixpenny Handley, Salisbury
SP5 5ND
Tel: 01725 552563 23 M10
*churchfarmcandcpark.co.uk*
Total Pitches: 35 (C, CV & T)

**Claylands Caravan Park**
Cabus, Garstang
PR3 1AJ
Tel: 01524 791242 83 L5
*claylands.com*
Total Pitches: 30 (C, CV & T)

**Clippesby Hall**
Hall Lane, Clippesby, Great Yarmouth
NR29 3BL
Tel: 01493 367800 71 N9
*clippesby.com*
Total Pitches: 120 (C, CV & T)

**Cofton Country Holidays**
Starcross, Dawlish
EX6 8RP
Tel: 01626 890111 8 H8
*coftonholidays.co.uk*
Total Pitches: 450 (C, CV & T)

**Colchester Holiday Park**
Cymbeline Way, Lexden, Colchester
CO3 4AG
Tel: 01206 545551 46 H6
*colchestercamping.co.uk*
Total Pitches: 168 (C, CV & T)

**Constable Burton Hall Caravan Park**
Constable Burton, Leyburn
DL8 5LJ
Tel: 01677 450428 91 K8
*cbcaravanpark.co.uk*
Total Pitches: 120 (C & CV)

**Coombe Touring Park**
Race Plain, Netherhampton, Salisbury
SP2 8PN
Tel: 01722 328451 23 N7
*coombecaravanpark.co.uk*
Total Pitches: 50 (C, CV & T)

**Corfe Castle C & C Club Site**
Bucknowle, Wareham
BH20 5PQ
Tel: 01929 480280 11 M8
*campingandcaravanningclub.co.uk/corfecastle*
Total Pitches: 80 (C, CV & T)

**Cornish Farm Touring Park**
Shoreditch, Taunton
TA3 7BS
Tel: 01823 327746 21 K9
*cornishfarm.com*
Total Pitches: 50 (C, CV & T)

**Cosawes Park**
Perranarworthal, Truro
TR3 7QS
Tel: 01872 863724 3 J7
*cosawestouringandcamping.co.uk*
Total Pitches: 40 (C, CV & T)

**Cote Ghyll C & C Park**
Osmotherley, Northallerton
DL6 3AH
Tel: 01609 883425 91 Q7
*coteghyll.com*
Total Pitches: 77 (C, CV & T)

**Cotswold View Touring Park**
Enstone Road, Charlbury
OX7 3JH
Tel: 01608 810314 42 H7
*cotswoldview.co.uk*
Total Pitches: 125 (C, CV & T)

**Dell Touring Park**
Beyton Road, Thurston, Bury St Edmunds
IP31 3RB
Tel: 01359 270121 58 D8
*thedellcaravanpark.co.uk*
Total Pitches: 60 (C, CV & T)

**Diamond Farm C & C Park**
Islip Road, Bletchingdon
OX5 3DR
Tel: 01869 350909 43 L8
*diamondpark.co.uk*
Total Pitches: 37 (C, CV & T)

**Dibles Park**
Dibles Road, Warsash, Southampton
SO31 9SA
Tel: 01489 575232 12 H3
*diblespark.co.uk*
Total Pitches: 14 (C, CV & T)

**Dolbeare Park C & C**
St Ive Road, Landrake, Saltash
PL12 5AF
Tel: 01752 851332 4 E4
*dolbeare.co.uk*
Total Pitches: 60 (C, CV & T)

**Dornafield**
Dornafield Farm, Two Mile Oak, Newton Abbot
TQ12 6DD
Tel: 01803 812732 5 P3
*dornafield.com*
Total Pitches: 135 (C, CV & T)

**East Fleet Farm Touring Park**
Chickerell, Weymouth
DT3 4DW
Tel: 01305 785768 10 G9
*eastfleet.co.uk*
Total Pitches: 400 (C, CV & T)

**Eden Valley Holiday Park**
Lanlivery, Nr Lostwithiel
PL30 5BU
Tel: 01208 872277 3 Q3
*edenvalleyholidaypark.co.uk*
Total Pitches: 56 (C, CV & T)

**Eskdale C & C Club Site**
Boot, Holmrook
CA19 1TH
Tel: 019467 23253 88 G6
*campingandcaravanningclub.co.uk/eskdale*
Total Pitches: 80 (CV & T)

**Exe Valley Caravan Site**
Mill House, Bridgetown, Dulverton
TA22 9JR
Tel: 01643 851432 20 E7
*exevalleycamping.co.uk*
Total Pitches: 50 (C, CV & T)

**Fallbarrow Park**
Rayrigg Road, Windermere
LA23 3DL
Tel: 015394 44422 89 L7
*slholidays.co.uk*
Total Pitches: 32 (C & CV)

**Fernwood Caravan Park**
Lyneal, Ellesmere
SY12 0QF
Tel: 01948 710221 63 M5
*fernwoodpark.co.uk*
Total Pitches: 60 (C & CV)

**Fields End Water Caravan Park & Fishery**
Benwick Road, Doddington, March
PE15 0TY
Tel: 01354 740199 56 G2
*fieldsendcaravans.co.uk*
Total Pitches: 52 (C, CV & T)

**Fishpool Farm Caravan Park**
Fishpool Road, Delamere, Northwich
CW8 2HP
Tel: 01606 883970 75 P10
*fishpoolfarmcaravanpark.co.uk*
Total Pitches: 50 (C, CV & T)

**Flusco Wood**
Flusco, Penrith
CA11 0JB
Tel: 017684 80020 98 F12
*fluscowood.co.uk*
Total Pitches: 53 (C & CV)

**Forest Glade Holiday Park**
Kentisbeare, Cullompton
EX15 2DT
Tel: 01404 841381 9 L3
*forest-glade.co.uk*
Total Pitches: 80 (C, CV & T)

**Globe Vale Holiday Park**
Radnor, Redruth
TR16 4BH
Tel: 01209 891183 2 H5
*globevale.co.uk*
Total Pitches: 138 (C, CV & T)

**Golden Cap Holiday Park**
Seatown, Chideock, Bridport
DT6 6JX
Tel: 01308 422139 10 C6
*wdlh.co.uk*
Total Pitches: 108 (C, CV & T)

**Golden Square Touring Caravan Park**
Oswaldkirk, Helmsley
YO62 5YQ
Tel: 01439 788269 92 C10
*goldensquarecaravanpark.com*
Total Pitches: 129 (C, CV & T)

**Golden Valley C & C Park**
Coach Road, Ripley
DE55 4ES
Tel: 01773 513881 66 C2
*goldenvalleycaravanpark.co.uk*
Total Pitches: 45 (C, CV & T)

**Goosewood Caravan Park**
Sutton-on-the-Forest, York
YO61 1ET
Tel: 01347 810829 86 B3
*flowerofmay.com*
Total Pitches: 100 (C & CV)

**Greenacres Touring Park**
Haywards Lane, Chelston, Wellington
TA21 9PH
Tel: 01823 652844 21 J9
*greenacres-wellington.co.uk*
Total Pitches: 40 (C & CV)

**Greenhill Leisure Park**
Greenhill Farm, Station Road, Bletchingdon, Oxford
OX5 3BQ
Tel: 01869 351600 43 K8
*greenhill-leisure-park.co.uk*
Total Pitches: 92 (C, CV & T)

**Grouse Hill Caravan Park**
Flask Bungalow Farm, Fylingdales, Robin Hood's Bay
YO22 4QH
Tel: 01947 880543 93 J7
*grousehill.co.uk*
Total Pitches: 175 (C, CV & T)

**Gunvenna Caravan Park**
St Minver, Wadebridge
PL27 6QN
Tel: 01208 862405 6 D9
*gunvenna.co.uk*
Total Pitches: 75 (C, CV & T)

**Gwithian Farm Campsite**
Gwithian Farm, Gwithian, Hayle
TR27 5BX
Tel: 01736 753127 2 F6
*gwithianfarm.co.uk*
Total Pitches: 87 (C, CV & T)

**Harbury Fields**
Harbury Fields Farm, Harbury, Nr Leamington Spa
CV33 9JN
Tel: 01926 612457 54 B8
*harburyfields.co.uk*
Total Pitches: 32 (C & CV)

**Hawthorn Farm Caravan Park**
Station Road, Martin Mill, Dover
CT15 5LA
Tel: 01304 852658 17 P2
*keatfarm.co.uk*
Total Pitches: 147 (C, CV & T)

**Heathfield Farm Camping**
Heathfield Road, Freshwater, Isle of Wight
PO40 9SH
Tel: 01983 407822 12 E7
*heathfieldcamping.co.uk*
Total Pitches: 60 (C, CV & T)

**Heathland Beach Caravan Park**
London Road, Kessingland
NR33 7PJ
Tel: 01502 740337 59 Q3
*heathlandbeach.co.uk*
Total Pitches: 63 (C, CV & T)

**Hele Valley Holiday Park**
Hele Bay, Ilfracombe, North Devon
EX34 9RD
Tel: 01271 862460 19 K4
*helevalley.co.uk*
Total Pitches: 50 (C, CV & T)

**Heron's Mead Fishing Lake & Touring Park**
Marsh Lane, Orby, Skegness
PE24 5JA
Tel: 01754 811340 81 K10
*heronsmeadtouringpark.co.uk*
Total Pitches: 21 (C, CV & T)

**Hidden Valley Park**
West Down, Braunton, Ilfracombe
EX34 8NU
Tel: 01271 813837 19 K5
*hiddenvalleypark.com*
Total Pitches: 115 (C, CV & T)

**Highfield Farm Touring Park**
Long Road, Comberton, Cambridge
CB23 7DG
Tel: 01223 262308 56 H9
*highfieldfarmtouringpark.co.uk*
Total Pitches: 120 (C, CV & T)

**Highlands End Holiday Park**
Eype, Bridport, Dorset
DT6 6AR
Tel: 01308 422139 10 C6
*wdlh.co.uk*
Total Pitches: 195 (C, CV & T)

**Hill Cottage Farm C & C Park**
Sandleheath Road, Alderholt, Fordingbridge
SP6 3EG
Tel: 01425 650513 23 P10
*hillcottagefarmcampingandcaravanpark.co.uk*
Total Pitches: 35 (C, CV & T)

**Hill Farm Caravan Park**
Branches Lane, Sherfield English, Romsey
SO51 6FH
Tel: 01794 340402 24 E8
*hillfarmpark.com*
Total Pitches: 70 (C, CV & T)

**Hill of Oaks & Blakeholme**
Windermere
LA12 8NR
Tel: 015395 31578 89 L9
*hillofoaks.co.uk*
Total Pitches: 43 (C & CV)

**Hillside Caravan Park**
Canvas Farm, Moor Road, Thirsk
YO7 4BR
Tel: 01845 537349 91 Q9
*hillsidecaravanpark.co.uk*
Total Pitches: 35 (C & CV)

**Hollins Farm C & C**
Far Arnside, Carnforth
LA5 0SL
Tel: 01524 701508 89 M11
*holgates.co.uk*
Total Pitches: 12 (C, CV & T)

**Homing Park**
Church Lane, Seasalter, Whitstable
CT5 4BU
Tel: 01227 771777 35 K9
*homingpark.co.uk*
Total Pitches: 43 (C, CV & T)

**Honeybridge Park**
Honeybridge Lane, Dial Post, Horsham
RH13 8NX
Tel: 01403 710923 14 H7
*honeybridgepark.co.uk*
Total Pitches: 130 (C, CV & T)

**Hurley Riverside Park**
Park Office, Hurley, Nr Maidenhead
SL6 5NE
Tel: 01628 824493 32 B5
*hurleyriversidepark.co.uk*
Total Pitches: 200 (C, CV & T)

**Hutton-le-Hole Caravan Park**
Westfield Lodge, Hutton-le-Hole
YO62 6UG
Tel: 01751 417261 92 E9
*westfieldlodge.co.uk*
Total Pitches: 42 (C, CV & T)

**Hylton Caravan Park**
Eden Street, Silloth
CA7 4AY
Tel: 016973 31707 97 M7
*stanwix.com*
Total Pitches: 90 (C, CV & T)

**Isle of Avalon Touring Caravan Park**
Godney Road, Glastonbury
BA6 9AF
Tel: 01458 833618 22 C5
Total Pitches: 120 (C, CV & T)

**Jacobs Mount Caravan Park**
Jacobs Mount, Stepney Road, Scarborough
YO12 5NL
Tel: 01723 361178 93 L9
*jacobsmount.com*
Total Pitches: 156 (C, CV & T)

**Jasmine Caravan Park**
Cross Lane, Snainton, Scarborough
YO13 9BE
Tel: 01723 859240 93 J10
*jasminepark.co.uk*
Total Pitches: 94 (C, CV & T)

**Juliot's Well Holiday Park**
Camelford, North Cornwall
PL32 9RF
Tel: 01840 213302 6 F8
*juliotswell.com*
Total Pitches: 39 (C, CV & T)

**Kenneggy Cove Holiday Park**
Higher Kenneggy, Rosudgeon, Penzance
TR20 9AU
Tel: 01736 763453 2 E9
*kenneggycove.co.uk*
Total Pitches: 45 (C, CV & T)

**Kennford International Caravan Park**
Kennford, Exeter
EX6 7YN
Tel: 01392 833046 8 G7
*kennfordinternational.co.uk*
Total Pitches: 96 (C, CV & T)

**King's Lynn Caravan & Camping Park**
New Road, North Runcton, King's Lynn
PE33 0RA
Tel: 01553 840004 69 M9
*kl-cc.co.uk*
Total Pitches: 150 (C, CV & T)

**Kloofs Caravan Park**
Sandhurst Lane, Bexhill
TN39 4RG
Tel: 01424 842839 16 C9
*kloofs.com*
Total Pitches: 50 (C, CV & T)

**Kneps Farm Holiday Park**
River Road, Stanah, Thornton-Cleveleys, Blackpool
FY5 5LR
Tel: 01253 823632 83 J6
*knepsfarm.co.uk*
Total Pitches: 60 (C & CV)

**Knight Stainforth Hall Caravan & Campsite**
Stainforth, Settle
BD24 0DP
Tel: 01729 822200 84 B2
*knightstainforth.co.uk*
Total Pitches: 100 (C, CV & T)

**Ladycross Plantation Caravan Park**
Egton, Whitby
YO21 1UA
Tel: 01947 895502 92 G5
*ladycrossplantation.co.uk*
Total Pitches: 130 (C, CV & T)

**Lamb Cottage Caravan Park**
Dalefords Lane, Whitegate, Northwich
CW8 2BN
Tel: 01606 882302 75 Q10
*lambcottage.co.uk*
Total Pitches: 45 (C & CV)

**Langstone Manor C & C Park**
Moortown, Tavistock
PL19 9JZ
Tel: 01822 613371 7 P10
*langstone-manor.co.uk*
Total Pitches: 40 (C, CV & T)

**Larches Caravan Park**
Mealsgate, Wigton
CA7 1LQ
Tel: 016973 71379 97 P10
Total Pitches: 73 (C, CV & T)

**Lebberston Touring Park**
Filey Road, Lebberston, Scarborough
YO11 3PE
Tel: 01723 585723 93 M10
*lebberstontouring.co.uk*
Total Pitches: 125 (C & CV)

**Lee Valley Campsite**
Sewardstone Road, Chingford, London
E4 7RA
Tel: 020 8529 5689 33 M3
*leevalleypark.org.uk*
Total Pitches: 100 (C, CV & T)

**Lemonford Caravan Park**
Bickington (near Ashburton), Newton Abbot
TQ12 6JR
Tel: 01626 821242 8 E10
*lemonford.co.uk*
Total Pitches: 82 (C, CV & T)

**Lickpenny Caravan Site**
Lickpenny Lane, Tansley, Matlock
DE4 5GF
Tel: 01629 583040 77 Q11
*lickpennycaravanpark.co.uk*
Total Pitches: 80 (C & CV)

**Lime Tree Park**
Dukes Drive, Buxton
SK17 9RP
Tel: 01298 22988 77 K9
*limetreeparkbuxton.co.uk*
Total Pitches: 106 (C, CV & T)

**Lincoln Farm Park Oxfordshire**
High Street, Standlake
OX29 7RH
Tel: 01865 300239 43 J11
*lincolnfarmpark.co.uk*
Total Pitches: 90 (C, CV & T)

**Little Cotton Caravan Park**
Little Cotton, Dartmouth
TQ6 0LB
Tel: 01803 832558 5 P6
*littlecotton.co.uk*
Total Pitches: 95 (C, CV & T)

**Little Lakeland Caravan Park**
Wortwell, Harleston
IP20 0EL
Tel: 01986 788646 59 K4
*littlelakeland.co.uk*
Total Pitches: 38 (C, CV & T)

**Little Trevarrack Holiday Park**
Laity Lane, Carbis Bay, St Ives
TR26 3HW
Tel: 01736 797580 2 E7
*littletrevarrack.co.uk*
Total Pitches: 200 (C, CV & T)

**Long Acre Caravan Park**
Station Road, Old Leake, Boston
PE22 9RF
Tel: 01205 871555 68 G2
*longacres-caravanpark.co.uk*
Total Pitches: 40 (C, CV & T)

**Lowther Holiday Park**
Eamont Bridge, Penrith
CA10 2JB
Tel: 01768 863631 89 N1
*lowther-holidaypark.co.uk*
Total Pitches: 180 (C, CV & T)

**Lytton Lawn Touring Park**
Lymore Lane, Milford on Sea
SO41 0TX
Tel: 01590 648331 12 E6
*shorefield.co.uk*
Total Pitches: 136 (C, CV & T)

**Manor Wood Country Caravan Park**
Manor Wood, Coddington, Chester
CH3 9EN
Tel: 01829 782990 63 M1
*cheshire-caravan-sites.co.uk*
Total Pitches: 45 (C, CV & T)

**Maustin Caravan Park**
Kearby with Netherby, Netherby
LS22 4DA
Tel: 0113 288 6234 85 L6
*maustin.co.uk*
Total Pitches: 25 (C, CV & T)

**Mayfield Touring Park**
Cheltenham Road, Cirencester
GL7 7BH
Tel: 01285 831301 42 B10
*mayfieldpark.co.uk*
Total Pitches: 72 (C, CV & T)

**Meadowbank Holidays**
Stour Way, Christchurch
BH23 2PQ
Tel: 01202 483597 12 B6
*meadowbank-holidays.co.uk*
Total Pitches: 41 (C & CV)

**Merley Court**
Merley, Wimborne Minster
BH21 3AA
Tel: 01590 648331 11 N5
*shorefield.co.uk*
Total Pitches: 160 (C, CV & T)

**Middlewood Farm Holiday Park**
Middlewood Lane, Fylingthorpe, Robin Hood's Bay, Whitby
YO22 4UF
Tel: 01947 880414 93 J6
*middlewoodfarm.com*
Total Pitches: 100 (C, CV & T)

**Minnows Touring Park**
Holbrook Lane, Sampford Peverell
EX16 7EN
Tel: 01884 821770 20 G10
*ukparks.co.uk/minnows*
Total Pitches: 59 (C, CV & T)

**Moon & Sixpence**
Newbourn Road, Waldringfield, Woodbridge
IP12 4PP
Tel: 01473 736650 47 N3
*moonandsixpence.eu*
Total Pitches: 65 (C, CV & T)

**Moss Wood Caravan Park**
Crimbles Lane, Cockerham
LA2 0ES
Tel: 01524 791041 83 L5
*mosswood.co.uk*
Total Pitches: 25 (C, CV & T)

**Naburn Lock Caravan Park**
Naburn
YO19 4RU
Tel: 01904 728697 86 B6
*naburnlock.co.uk*
Total Pitches: 100 (C, CV & T)

**Newberry Valley Park**
Woodlands, Combe Martin
EX34 0AT
Tel: 01271 882334 19 L4
*newberryvalleypark.co.uk*
Total Pitches: 120 (C, CV & T)

**New House Caravan Park**
Kirkby Lonsdale
LA6 2HR
Tel: 015242 71590 89 Q11
Total Pitches: 50 (C & CV)

**Newlands C & C Park**
Charmouth, Bridport
DT6 6RB
Tel: 01297 560259 10 B6
*newlandsholidays.co.uk*
Total Pitches: 240 (C, CV & T)

**Newperran Holiday Park**
Rejerrah, Newquay
TR8 5QJ
Tel: 01872 572407 3 K4
*newperran.co.uk*
Total Pitches: 357 (C, CV & T)

**Newton Mill Holiday Park**
Newton Road, Bath
BA2 9JF
Tel: 0844 272 9503 29 L9
*newtonmillpark.co.uk*
Total Pitches: 106 (C, CV & T)

**Northam Farm Caravan & Touring Park**
Brean, Burnham-on-Sea
TA8 2SE
Tel: 01278 751244 21 M2
*northamfarm.co.uk*
Total Pitches: 350 (C, CV & T)

**North Morte Farm C & C Park**
North Morte Road, Mortehoe, Woolacombe, N Devon
EX34 7EG
Tel: 01271 870381 19 J4
*northmortefarm.co.uk*
Total Pitches: 180 (C, CV & T)

**Oakdown Country Holiday Park**
Gatedown Lane, Sidmouth
EX10 0PT
Tel: 01297 680387 9 M7
*oakdown.co.uk*
Total Pitches: 150 (C, CV & T)

**Oathill Farm Touring & Camping Site**
Oathill, Crewkerne
TA18 8PZ
Tel: 01460 30234 10 B4
*oathillfarmleisure.co.uk*
Total Pitches: 13 (C, CV & T)

**Old Barn Touring Park**
Cheverton Farm, Newport Road, Sandown
PO36 9PJ
Tel: 01983 866414 13 J8
*oldbarntouring.co.uk*
Total Pitches: 60 (C, CV & T)

**Old Hall Caravan Park**
Capernwray, Carnforth
LA6 1AD
Tel: 01524 733276 83 M1
*oldhallcaravanpark.co.uk*
Total Pitches: 38 (C & CV)

**Orchard Farm Holiday Village**
Stonegate, Hunmanby
YO14 0PU
Tel: 01723 891582 93 M11
*orchardfarmholidayvillage.co.uk*
Total Pitches: 91 (C, CV & T)

**Orchard Park**
Frampton Lane, Hubbert's Bridge, Boston
PE20 3QU
Tel: 01205 290328 68 E4
*orchardpark.co.uk*
Total Pitches: 87 (C, CV & T)

**Ord House Country Park**
East Ord, Berwick-upon-Tweed
TD15 2NS
Tel: 01289 305288 117 L11
*ordhouse.co.uk*
Total Pitches: 79 (C, CV & T)

**Otterington Park**
Station Farm, South Otterington, Northallerton
DL7 9JB
Tel: 01609 780656 91 P9
*otteringtonpark.com*
Total Pitches: 62 (C & CV)

**Oxon Hall Touring Park**
Welshpool Road, Shrewsbury
SY3 5FB
Tel: 01743 340868 63 M9
*morris-leisure.co.uk*
Total Pitches: 105 (C, CV & T)

**Padstow Touring Park**
Padstow
PL28 8LE
Tel: 01841 532061 6 C10
*padstowtouringpark.co.uk*
Total Pitches: 150 (C, CV & T)

**Park Cliffe Camping & Caravan Estate**
Birks Road, Tower Wood, Windermere
LA23 3PG
Tel: 01539 531344 89 L8
*parkcliffe.co.uk*
Total Pitches: 60 (C, CV & T)

**Parkers Farm Holiday Park**
Higher Mead Farm, Ashburton, Devon
TQ13 7LJ
Tel: 01364 654869 8 E10
*parkersfarmholidays.co.uk*
Total Pitches: 100 (C, CV & T)

**Pear Tree Holiday Park**
Organford Road, Holton Heath, Organford, Poole
BH16 6LA
Tel: 0844 272 9504 11 M6
*peartreepark.co.uk*
Total Pitches: 154 (C, CV & T)

**Penrose Holiday Park**
Goonhavern, Truro
TR4 9QF
Tel: 01872 573185 3 K4
penroseholidaypark.com
Total Pitches: 110 (C, CV & T)

**Polmanter Touring Park**
Halsetown, St Ives
TR26 3LX
Tel: 01736 795640 2 E7
polmanter.com
Total Pitches: 270 (C, CV & T)

**Porlock Caravan Park**
Porlock, Minehead
TA24 8ND
Tel: 01643 862269 20 D4
porlockcaravanpark.co.uk
Total Pitches: 40 (C, CV & T)

**Portesham Dairy Farm Campsite**
Portesham, Weymouth
DT3 4HG
Tel: 01305 871297 10 F7
porteshamdairyfarm.co.uk
Total Pitches: 90 (C, CV & T)

**Porth Beach Tourist Park**
Porth, Newquay
TR7 3NH
Tel: 01637 876531 3 K2
porthbeach.co.uk
Total Pitches: 200 (C, CV & T)

**Porthtowan Tourist Park**
Mile Hill, Porthtowan, Truro
TR4 8TY
Tel: 01209 890256 2 H5
porthtowantouristpark.co.uk
Total Pitches: 80 (C, CV & T)

**Quantock Orchard Caravan Park**
Flaxpool, Crowcombe, Taunton
TA4 4AW
Tel: 01984 618618 21 J6
quantock-orchard.co.uk
Total Pitches: 69 (C, CV & T)

**Ranch Caravan Park**
Station Road, Honeybourne, Evesham
WR11 7PR
Tel: 01386 830744 42 C3
ranch.co.uk
Total Pitches: 120 (C & CV)

**Ripley Caravan Park**
Knaresborough Road, Ripley, Harrogate
HG3 3AU
Tel: 01423 770050 85 L3
ripleycaravanpark.com
Total Pitches: 100 (C, CV & T)

**River Dart Country Park**
Holne Park, Ashburton
TQ13 7NP
Tel: 01364 652511 5 M3
riverdart.co.uk
Total Pitches: 170 (C, CV & T)

**Riverside C & C Park**
Marsh Lane, North Molton Road, South Molton
EX36 3HQ
Tel: 01769 579269 19 P8
exmoorriverside.co.uk
Total Pitches: 42 (C, CV & T)

**Riverside Caravan Park**
High Bentham, Lancaster
LA2 7FJ
Tel: 015242 61272 83 P1
riversidecaravanpark.co.uk
Total Pitches: 61 (C & CV)

**Riverside Caravan Park**
Leigham Manor Drive, Marsh Mills, Plymouth
PL6 8LL
Tel: 01752 344122 4 H5
riversidecaravanpark.com
Total Pitches: 259 (C, CV & T)

**Riverside Holidays**
21 Compass Point, Ensign Way, Hamble
SO31 4RA
Tel: 023 8045 3220 12 H3
riversideholidays.co.uk
Total Pitches: 77 (C, CV & T)

**Riverside Meadows Country Caravan Park**
Ure Bank Top, Ripon
HG4 1JD
Tel: 01765 602964 91 N12
flowerofmay.com
Total Pitches: 80 (C, CV & T)

**River Valley Holiday Park**
London Apprentice, St Austell
PL26 7AP
Tel: 01726 73533 3 N4
rivervalleyholidaypark.co.uk
Total Pitches: 45 (C, CV & T)

**Rosedale C & C Park**
Rosedale Abbey, Pickering
YO18 8SA
Tel: 01751 417272 92 E7
flowerofmay.com
Total Pitches: 100 (C, CV & T)

**Rose Farm Touring & Camping Park**
Stepshort, Belton, Nr Great Yarmouth
NR31 9JS
Tel: 01493 780896 71 P11
rosefarmtouringpark.co.uk
Total Pitches: 145 (C, CV & T)

**Ross Park**
Park Hill Farm, Ipplepen, Newton Abbot
TQ12 5TT
Tel: 01803 812983 5 P3
rossparkcaravanpark.co.uk
Total Pitches: 110 (C, CV & T)

**Rudding Holiday Park**
Follifoot, Harrogate
HG3 1JH
Tel: 01423 871350 85 L4
ruddingpark.co.uk/caravans-camping
Total Pitches: 109 (C, CV & T)

**Rutland C & C**
Park Lane, Greetham, Oakham
LE15 7FN
Tel: 01572 813520 67 M9
rutlandcaravanandcamping.co.uk
Total Pitches: 130 (C, CV & T)

**Seaview International Holiday Park**
Boswinger, Mevagissey
PL26 6LL
Tel: 01726 843425 3 N6
seaviewinternational.com
Total Pitches: 201 (C, CV & T)

**Severn Gorge Park**
Bridgnorth Road, Tweedale, Telford
TF7 4JB
Tel: 01952 684789 64 D11
severngorgepark.co.uk
Total Pitches: 10 (C & CV)

**Shamba Holidays**
230 Ringwood Road, St Leonards, Ringwood
BH24 2SB
Tel: 01202 873302 11 Q4
shambaholidays.co.uk
Total Pitches: 150 (C, CV & T)

**Shrubbery Touring Park**
Rousdon, Lyme Regis
DT7 3XW
Tel: 01297 442227 9 P6
shrubberypark.co.uk
Total Pitches: 120 (C, CV & T)

**Silverbow Park**
Perranwell, Goonhavern
TR4 9NX
Tel: 01872 572347 3 J4
chycor.co.uk/parks/silverbow
Total Pitches: 100 (C, CV & T)

**Silverdale Caravan Park**
Middlebarrow Plain, Cove Road, Silverdale, Nr Carnforth
LA5 0SH
Tel: 01524 701508 89 M11
holgates.co.uk
Total Pitches: 80 (C, CV & T)

**Skelwith Fold Caravan Park**
Ambleside, Cumbria
LA22 0HX
Tel: 015394 32277 89 K6
skelwith.com
Total Pitches: 150 (C & CV)

**Somers Wood Caravan Park**
Somers Road, Meriden
CV7 7PL
Tel: 01676 522978 53 N4
somerswood.co.uk
Total Pitches: 48 (C & CV)

**Southfork Caravan Park**
Parrett Works, Martock
TA12 6AE
Tel: 01935 825661 21 P9
southforkcaravans.co.uk
Total Pitches: 27 (C, CV & T)

**South Lytchett Manor C & C Park**
Dorchester Road, Lytchett Minster, Poole
BH16 6JB
Tel: 01202 622577 11 M6
southlytchettmanor.co.uk
Total Pitches: 150 (C, CV & T)

**Springfield Holiday Park**
Tedburn St Mary, Exeter
EX6 6EW
Tel: 01647 24242 8 F6
springfieldholidaypark.co.uk
Total Pitches: 48 (C, CV & T)

**Stanmore Hall Touring Park**
Stourbridge Road, Bridgnorth
WV15 6DT
Tel: 01746 761761 52 D2
morris-leisure.co.uk
Total Pitches: 131 (C, CV & T)

**St Helens Caravan Park**
Wykeham, Scarborough
YO13 9QD
Tel: 01723 862771 93 K10
sthelenscaravanpark.co.uk
Total Pitches: 250 (C, CV & T)

**Stowford Farm Meadows**
Berry Down, Combe Martin
EX34 0PW
Tel: 01271 882476 19 L5
stowford.co.uk
Total Pitches: 700 (C, CV & T)

**Stroud Hill Park**
Fen Road, Pidley
PE28 3DE
Tel: 01487 741333 56 G5
stroudhillpark.co.uk
Total Pitches: 60 (C, CV & T)

**Sumners Ponds Fishery & Campsite**
Chapel Road, Barns Green, Horsham
RH13 0PR
Tel: 01403 732539 14 G5
sumnersponds.co.uk
Total Pitches: 85 (C, CV & T)

**Sun Haven Valley Holiday Park**
Mawgan Porth, Newquay
TR8 4BQ
Tel: 01637 860373 6 B11
sunhavenvalley.com
Total Pitches: 109 (C, CV & T)

**Sun Valley Holiday Park**
Pentewan Road, St Austell
PL26 6DJ
Tel: 01726 843266 3 N5
sunvalleyholidays.co.uk
Total Pitches: 29 (C, CV & T)

**Swiss Farm Touring & Camping**
Marlow Road, Henley-on-Thames
RG9 2HY
Tel: 01491 573419 31 Q6
swissfarmcamping.co.uk
Total Pitches: 140 (C, CV & T)

**Tanner Farm Touring Caravan & Camping Park**
Tanner Farm, Goudhurst Road, Marden
TN12 9ND
Tel: 01622 832399 16 C3
tannerfarmpark.co.uk
Total Pitches: 100 (C, CV & T)

**Tattershall Lakes Country Park**
Sleaford Road, Tattershall
LN4 4RL
Tel: 01526 348800 80 D12
tattershall-lakes.com
Total Pitches: 186 (C, CV & T)

**Teversal C & C Club Site**
Silverhill Lane, Teversal
NG17 3JJ
Tel: 01623 551838 78 D11
campingandcaravanningclub.co.uk/teversal
Total Pitches: 126 (C, CV & T)

**The Inside Park**
Down House Estate, Blandford Forum
DT11 9AD
Tel: 01258 453719 11 L4
theinsidepark.co.uk
Total Pitches: 125 (C, CV & T)

**The Old Brick Kilns**
Little Barney Lane, Barney, Fakenham
NR21 0NL
Tel: 01328 878305 70 E5
old-brick-kilns.co.uk
Total Pitches: 65 (C, CV & T)

**The Old Oaks Touring Park**
Wick Farm, Wick, Glastonbury
BA6 8JS
Tel: 01458 831437 22 C5
theoldoaks.co.uk
Total Pitches: 100 (C, CV & T)

**The Orchards Holiday Caravan Park**
Main Road, Newbridge, Yarmouth, Isle of Wight
PO41 0TS
Tel: 01983 531331 12 G7
orchards-holiday-park.co.uk
Total Pitches: 171 (C, CV & T)

**The Quiet Site**
Ullswater, Watermillock
CA11 0LS
Tel: 07768 727016 89 L2
thequietsite.co.uk
Total Pitches: 100 (C, CV & T)

**Tollgate Farm C & C Park**
Budnick Hill, Perranporth
TR6 0AD
Tel: 01872 572130 3 J3
tollgatefarm.co.uk
Total Pitches: 102 (C, CV & T)

**Townsend Touring Park**
Townsend Farm, Pembridge, Leominster
HR6 9HB
Tel: 01544 388527 51 L9
townsendfarm.co.uk
Total Pitches: 60 (C, CV & T)

**Treloy Touring Park**
Newquay
TR8 4JN
Tel: 01637 872063 3 L2
treloy.co.uk
Total Pitches: 223 (C, CV & T)

**Trencreek Holiday Park**
Hillcrest, Higher Trencreek, Newquay
TR8 4NS
Tel: 01637 874210 3 K2
trencreekholidaypark.co.uk
Total Pitches: 194 (C, CV & T)

**Trethem Mill Touring Park**
St Just-in-Roseland, Nr St Mawes, Truro
TR2 5JF
Tel: 01872 580504 3 L7
trethem.com
Total Pitches: 84 (C, CV & T)

**Trevalgan Touring Park**
Trevalgan, St Ives
TR26 3BJ
Tel: 01736 792048 2 D6
trevalgantouringpark.co.uk
Total Pitches: 120 (C, CV & T)

**Trevarth Holiday Park**
Blackwater, Truro
TR4 8HR
Tel: 01872 560266 3 J5
trevarth.co.uk
Total Pitches: 30 (C, CV & T)

**Trevella Tourist Park**
Crantock, Newquay
TR8 5EW
Tel: 01637 830308 3 K3
trevella.co.uk
Total Pitches: 313 (C, CV & T)

**Troutbeck C & C Club Site**
Hutton Moor End, Troutbeck, Penrith
CA11 0SX
Tel: 017687 79149 89 K1
campingandcaravanningclub.co.uk/troutbeck
Total Pitches: 54 (C, CV & T)

**Truro C & C Park**
Truro
TR4 8QN
Tel: 01872 560274 3 J5
trurocaravanandcampingpark.co.uk
Total Pitches: 51 (C, CV & T)

**Tudor C & C**
Shepherds Patch, Slimbridge, Gloucester
GL2 7BP
Tel: 01453 890483 41 L11
tudorcaravanpark.com
Total Pitches: 75 (C, CV & T)

**Two Mills Touring Park**
Yarmouth Road, North Walsham
NR28 9NA
Tel: 01692 405829 71 K6
twomills.co.uk
Total Pitches: 81 (C, CV & T)

**Ulwell Cottage Caravan Park**
Ulwell Cottage, Ulwell, Swanage
BH19 3DG
Tel: 01929 422823 11 N8
ulwellcottagepark.co.uk
Total Pitches: 77 (C, CV & T)

**Vale of Pickering Caravan Park**
Carr House Farm, Allerston, Pickering
YO18 7PQ
Tel: 01723 859280 92 H10
valeofpickering.co.uk
Total Pitches: 120 (C, CV & T)

**Warcombe Farm C & C Park**
Station Road, Mortehoe
EX34 7EJ
Tel: 01271 870690 19 J4
warcombefarm.co.uk
Total Pitches: 250 (C, CV & T)

**Wareham Forest Tourist Park**
North Trigon, Wareham
BH20 7NZ
Tel: 01929 551393 11 L6
warehamforest.co.uk
Total Pitches: 200 (C, CV & T)

**Waren Caravan Park**
Waren Mill, Bamburgh
NE70 7EE
Tel: 01668 214366 109 J3
meadowhead.co.uk
Total Pitches: 150 (C, CV & T)

**Watergate Bay Touring Park**
Watergate Bay, Tregurrian
TR8 4AD
Tel: 01637 860387 6 B11
watergatebaytouringpark.co.uk
Total Pitches: 171 (C, CV & T)

**Waterrow Touring Park**
Wiveliscombe, Taunton
TA4 2AZ
Tel: 01984 623464 20 G8
waterrowpark.co.uk
Total Pitches: 45 (C, CV & T)

**Wayfarers C & C Park**
Relubbus Lane, St Hilary, Penzance
TR20 9EF
Tel: 01736 763326 2 E8
wayfarerspark.co.uk
Total Pitches: 39 (C, CV & T)

**Wells Holiday Park**
Haybridge, Wells
BA5 1AJ
Tel: 01749 676869 22 C4
wellsholidaypark.co.uk
Total Pitches: 72 (C, CV & T)

**Westwood Caravan Park**
Old Felixstowe Road, Bucklesham, Ipswich
IP10 0BN
Tel: 01473 659637 47 N3
westwoodcaravanpark.co.uk
Total Pitches: 100 (C, CV & T)

**Whitefield Forest Touring Park**
Brading Road, Ryde, Isle of Wight
PO33 1QL
Tel: 01983 617069 13 K7
whitefieldforest.co.uk
Total Pitches: 80 (C, CV & T)

**Whitemead Caravan Park**
East Burton Road, Wool
BH20 6HG
Tel: 01929 462241 11 K7
whitemeadcaravanpark.co.uk
Total Pitches: 95 (C, CV & T)

**Whitsand Bay Lodge & Touring Park**
Millbrook, Torpoint
PL10 1JZ
Tel: 01752 822597 4 F6
whitsandbayholidays.co.uk
Total Pitches: 49 (C, CV & T)

**Widdicombe Farm Touring Park**
Marldon, Paignton
TQ3 1ST
Tel: 01803 558325 5 P4
widdicombefarm.co.uk
Total Pitches: 180 (C, CV & T)

**Widemouth Fields C & C Park**
Park Farm, Poundstock, Bude
EX23 0NA
Tel: 01288 361351 7 J4
widemouthbaytouring.co.uk
Total Pitches: 156 (C, CV & T)

**Widend Touring Park**
Berry Pomeroy Road, Marldon, Paignton
TQ3 1RT
Tel: 01803 550116 5 P4
widend.co.uk
Total Pitches: 207 (C, CV & T)

**Wild Rose Park**
Ormside, Appleby-in-Westmorland
CA16 6EJ
Tel: 017683 51077 90 A3
wildrose.co.uk
Total Pitches: 226 (C, CV & T)

**Wilksworth Farm Caravan Park**
Cranborne Road, Wimborne Minster
BH21 4HW
Tel: 01202 885467 11 N4
wilksworthfarmcaravanpark.co.uk
Total Pitches: 85 (C, CV & T)

**Wolds Way Caravan & Camping**
West Farm, West Knapton, Malton
YO17 8JE
Tel: 01944 728463 92 H12
rydalesbest.co.uk
Total Pitches: 70 (C, CV & T)

**Wooda Farm Holiday Park**
Poughill, Bude
EX23 9HJ
Tel: 01288 352069 7 J3
wooda.co.uk
Total Pitches: 200 (C, CV & T)

**Woodclose Caravan Park**
High Casterton, Kirkby Lonsdale
LA6 2SE
Tel: 01524 271597 89 Q11
woodclosepark.com
Total Pitches: 29 (C, CV & T)

**Wood Farm C & C Park**
Axminster Road, Charmouth
DT6 6BT
Tel: 01297 560697 9 Q6
woodfarm.co.uk
Total Pitches: 216 (C, CV & T)

**Woodhall Country Park**
Stixwold Road, Woodhall Spa
LN10 6UJ
Tel: 01526 353710 80 D10
woodhallcountrypark.co.uk
Total Pitches: 80 (C, CV & T)

**Woodlands Grove C & C Park**
Blackawton, Dartmouth
TQ9 7DQ
Tel: 01803 712598 5 N6
woodlands-caravanpark.com
Total Pitches: 350 (C, CV & T)

**Woodland Springs Adult Touring Park**
Venton, Drewsteignton
EX6 6PG
Tel: 01647 231695 8 D6
woodlandsprings.co.uk
Total Pitches: 81 (C, CV & T)

**Woodovis Park**
Gulworthy, Tavistock
PL19 8NY
Tel: 01822 832968 7 N10
woodovis.com
Total Pitches: 50 (C, CV & T)

**Woolsbridge Manor Farm Caravan Park**
Three Legged Cross, Wimborne
BH21 6RA
Tel: 01202 826369 11 Q4
woolsbridgemanorcaravanpark.co.uk
Total Pitches: 60 (C, CV & T)

**Yeatheridge Farm Caravan Park**
East Worlington, Crediton
EX17 4TN
Tel: 01884 860330 8 E3
yeatheridge.co.uk
Total Pitches: 85 (C, CV & T)

**Zeacombe House Caravan Park**
Blackerton Cross, East Anstey, Tiverton
EX16 9JU
Tel: 01398 341279 20 D8
zeacombeadultretreat.co.uk
Total Pitches: 50 (C, CV & T)

## SCOTLAND

**Aird Donald Caravan Park**
London Road, Stranraer
DG9 8RN
Tel: 01776 702025 94 F6
aird-donald.co.uk
Total Pitches: 100 (C, CV & T)

**Anwoth Caravan Site**
Gatehouse of Fleet, Castle Douglas
DG7 2JU
Tel: 01557 814333 96 C7
auchenlarie.co.uk
Total Pitches: 28 (C, CV & T)

**Beecraigs C & C Site**
Beecraigs Country Park, The Park Centre, Linlithgow
EH49 6PL
Tel: 01506 844516 115 J6
beecraigs.com
Total Pitches: 36 (C, CV & T)

**Blair Castle Caravan Park**
Blair Atholl, Pitlochry
PH18 5SR
Tel: 01796 481263 130 F11
blaircastlecaravanpark.co.uk
Total Pitches: 241 (C, CV & T)

**Brighouse Bay Holiday Park**
Brighouse Bay, Borgue
DG6 4TS
Tel: 01557 870267 96 D9
gillespie-leisure.co.uk
Total Pitches: 190 (C, CV & T)

**Cairnsmill Holiday Park**
Largo Road, St Andrews
KY16 8NN
Tel: 01334 473604 125 K10
Total Pitches: 62 (C, CV & T)

**Castle Cary Holiday Park**
Creetown, Newton Stewart
DG8 7DQ
Tel: 01671 820264 95 N7
castlecary-caravans.com
Total Pitches: 50 (C, CV & T)

**Craigtoun Meadows Holiday Park**
Mount Melville, St Andrews
KY16 8PQ
Tel: 01334 475959 125 J10
craigtounmeadows.co.uk
Total Pitches: 57 (C, CV & T)

**Crossburn Caravan Park**
Edinburgh Road, Peebles
EH45 8ED
Tel: 01721 720501 106 H1
crossburncaravans.co.uk
Total Pitches: 45 (C, CV & T)

**Drum Mohr Caravan Park**
Levenhall, Musselburgh
EH21 8JS
Tel: 0131 665 6867 115 Q7
drummohr.org
Total Pitches: 120 (C, CV & T)

**East Bowstrips Caravan Park**
St Cyrus, Nr Montrose
DD10 0DE
Tel: 01674 850328 132 H11
caravancampingsites.co.uk/aberdeenshire/eastbowstrips.htm
Total Pitches: 32 (C, CV & T)

**Gart Caravan Park**
The Gart, Callander
FK17 8LE
Tel: 01877 330002 122 G11
theholidaypark.co.uk
Total Pitches: 128 (C & CV)

**Glenearly Caravan Park**
Dalbeattie
DG5 4NE
Tel: 01556 611393 96 G6
glenearlycaravanpark.co.uk
Total Pitches: 39 (C, CV & T)

**Glen Nevis C & C Park**
Glen Nevis, Fort William
PH33 6SX
Tel: 01397 702191 128 F10
glen-nevis.co.uk
Total Pitches: 380 (C, CV & T)

**Hoddom Castle Caravan Park**
Hoddom, Lockerbie
DG11 1AS
Tel: 01576 300251 97 N4
hoddomcastle.co.uk
Total Pitches: 200 (C, CV & T)

**Huntly Castle Caravan Park**
The Meadow, Huntly
AB54 4UJ
Tel: 01466 794999 140 E8
huntlycastle.co.uk
Total Pitches: 90 (C, CV & T)

**Invercoe C & C Park**
Glencoe, Ballachulish
PH49 4HP
Tel: 01855 811210 121 L1
invercoe.co.uk
Total Pitches: 60 (C, CV & T)

**Linnhe Lochside Holidays**
Corpach, Fort William
PH33 7NL
Tel: 01397 772376 128 F9
linnhe-lochside-holidays.co.uk
Total Pitches: 85 (C, CV & T)

**Lomond Woods Holiday Park**
Old Luss Road, Balloch, Loch Lomond
G83 8QP
Tel: 01389 755000 113 M5
holiday-parks.co.uk
Total Pitches: 100 (C & CV)

**Machrihanish Caravan Park**
East Trodigal, Machrihanish, Mull of Kintyre
PA28 6PT
Tel: 01586 810366 102 H6
campkintyre.co.uk
Total Pitches: 90 (C, CV & T)

**Milton of Fonab Caravan Site**
Bridge Road, Pitlochry
PH16 5NA
Tel: 01796 472882 123 N1
fonab.co.uk
Total Pitches: 154 (C, CV & T)

**River Tilt Caravan Park**
Blair Atholl, Pitlochry
PH18 5TE
Tel: 01796 481467 130 G11
rivertilt.co.uk
Total Pitches: 30 (C, CV & T)

**Riverview Caravan Park**
Marine Drive, Monifieth
DD5 4NN
Tel: 01382 535471 125 K6
riverview.co.uk
Total Pitches: 49 (C & CV)

**Sands of Luce Holiday Park**
Sands of Luce, Sandhead, Stranraer
DG9 9JN
Tel: 01776 830456 94 G8
sandsofluceholidaypark.co.uk
Total Pitches: 120 (C, CV & T)

**Seaward Caravan Park**
Dhoon Bay, Kirkudbright
DG6 4TJ
Tel: 01557 870267 96 D8
gillespie-leisure.co.uk
Total Pitches: 26 (C, CV & T)

**Shieling Holidays**
Craignure, Isle of Mull
PA65 6AY
Tel: 01680 812496 120 D5
shielingholidays.co.uk
Total Pitches: 90 (C, CV & T)

**Silver Sands Leisure Park**
Covesea, West Beach, Lossiemouth
IV31 6SP
Tel: 01343 813262 147 M11
silver-sands.co.uk
Total Pitches: 140 (C, CV & T)

**Skye C & C Club Site**
Loch Greshornish, Borve, Arnisort, Edinbane, Isle of Skye
IV51 9PS
Tel: 01470 582230 134 F5
campingandcaravanningclub.co.uk/skye
Total Pitches: 105 (C, CV & T)

**Springwood Caravan Park**
Kelso
TD5 8LS
Tel: 01573 224596 108 B3
springwood.biz
Total Pitches: 20 (C & CV)

**Thurston Manor Leisure Park**
Innerwick, Dunbar
EH42 1SA
Tel: 01368 840643 116 G6
thurstonmanor.co.uk
Total Pitches: 120 (C, CV & T)

**Trossachs Holiday Park**
Aberfoyle
FK8 3SA
Tel: 01877 382614 113 Q2
trossachsholidays.co.uk
Total Pitches: 66 (C, CV & T)

**Witches Craig C & C Park**
Blairlogie, Stirling
FK9 5PX
Tel: 01786 474947 114 E2
witchescraig.co.uk
Total Pitches: 60 (C, CV & T)

## WALES

**Anchorage Caravan Park**
Bronllys, Brecon
LD3 0LD
Tel: 01874 711246 39 Q5
anchoragecp.co.uk
Total Pitches: 110 (C, CV & T)

**Barcdy Touring C & C Park**
Talsarnau
LL47 6YG
Tel: 01766 770736 61 K5
barcdy.co.uk
Total Pitches: 80 (C, CV & T)

**Beach View Caravan Park**
Bwlchtocyn, Abersoch
LL53 7BT
Tel: 01758 712956 60 E7
Total Pitches: 47 (C, CV & T)

**Bodnant Caravan Park**
Nebo Road, Llanrwst, Conwy Valley
LL26 0SD
Tel: 01492 640248 73 P11
bodnant-caravan-park.co.uk
Total Pitches: 54 (C, CV & T)

**Bron Derw Touring Caravan Park**
Llanrwst
LL26 0YT
Tel: 01492 640494 73 N11
bronderw-wales.co.uk
Total Pitches: 43 (C & CV)

**Bron-Y-Wendon Caravan Park**
Wern Road, Llanddulas, Colwyn Bay
LL22 8HG
Tel: 01492 512903 74 B8
northwales-holidays.co.uk
Total Pitches: 130 (C & CV)

**Bryn Gloch C & C Park**
Betws Garmon, Caernarfon
LL54 7YY
Tel: 01286 650216 73 J12
campwales.co.uk
Total Pitches: 160 (C, CV & T)

**Caerfai Bay Caravan & Tent Park**
Caerfai Bay, St David's, Haverfordwest
SA62 6QT
Tel: 01437 720274 36 E5
caerfaibay.co.uk
Total Pitches: 106 (C, CV & T)

**Cenarth Falls Holiday Park**
Cenarth, Newcastle Emlyn
SA38 9JS
Tel: 01239 710345 37 P2
cenarth-holipark.co.uk
Total Pitches: 30 (C, CV & T)

**Deucoch Touring & Camping Park**
Sarn Bach, Abersoch
LL53 7LD
Tel: 01758 713293 60 E7
deucoch.com
Total Pitches: 70 (C, CV & T)

**Dinlle Caravan Park**
Dinas Dinlle, Caernarfon
LL54 5TW
Tel: 01286 830324 72 G12
thornleyleisure.co.uk
Total Pitches: 175 (C, CV & T)

**Eisteddfa**
Eisteddfa Lodge, Pentrefelin, Criccieth
LL52 0PT
Tel: 01766 522696 61 J4
eisteddfapark.co.uk
Total Pitches: 100 (C, CV & T)

**Erwlon C & C Park**
Brecon Road, Llandovery
SA20 0RD
Tel: 01550 721021 39 J5
erwlon.co.uk
Total Pitches: 75 (C, CV & T)

**Hendre Mynach Touring C & C Park**
Llanaber Road, Barmouth
LL42 1YR
Tel: 01341 280262 61 K8
hendremynach.co.uk
Total Pitches: 240 (C, CV & T)

**Home Farm Caravan Park**
Marian-Glas, Isle of Anglesey
LL73 8PH
Tel: 01248 410614 72 H7
homefarm-anglesey.co.uk
Total Pitches: 98 (C, CV & T)

**Hunters Hamlet Caravan Park**
Sirior Goch Farm, Betws-yn-Rhos, Abergele
LL22 8PL
Tel: 01745 832237 74 C9
huntershamlet.co.uk
Total Pitches: 23 (C & CV)

**Islawrffordd Caravan Park**
Tal-y-bont, Barmouth
LL43 2AQ
Tel: 01341 247269 61 K8
islawrffordd.co.uk
Total Pitches: 105 (C, CV & T)

**Llys Derwen C & C Site**
Ffordd Bryngwyn, Llanrug, Caernarfon
LL55 4RD
Tel: 01286 673322 73 J11
llysderwen.co.uk
Total Pitches: 20 (C, CV & T)

**Pencelli Castle C & C Park**
Pencelli, Brecon
LD3 7LX
Tel: 01874 665451 39 P7
pencelli-castle.com
Total Pitches: 80 (C, CV & T)

**Penisar Mynydd Caravan Park**
Caerwys Road, Rhuallt, St Asaph
LL17 0TY
Tel: 01745 582227 74 F8
penisarmynydd.co.uk
Total Pitches: 75 (C, CV & T)

**Pen-y-Bont Touring Park**
Llangynog Road, Bala
LL23 7PH
Tel: 01678 520549 62 C5
penybont-bala.co.uk
Total Pitches: 95 (C, CV & T)

**Plas Farm Caravan Park**
Betws-yn-Rhos, Abergele
LL22 8AU
Tel: 01492 680254 74 B9
plasfarmcaravanpark.co.uk
Total Pitches: 40 (C, CV & T)

**Pont Kemys C & C Park**
Chainbridge, Abergavenny
NP7 9DS
Tel: 01873 880688 40 D10
pontkemys.com
Total Pitches: 65 (C, CV & T)

**Riverside Camping**
Seiont Nurseries, Pont Rug, Caernarfon
LL55 2BB
Tel: 01286 678781 72 H11
riversidecamping.co.uk
Total Pitches: 60 (C, CV & T)

**River View Touring Park**
The Dingle, Llanedi, Pontarddulais
SA4 0FH
Tel: 01269 844876 38 E10
riverviewtouringpark.com
Total Pitches: 60 (C, CV & T)

**The Plassey Leisure Park**
The Plassey, Eyton, Wrexham
LL13 0SP
Tel: 01978 780277 63 K3
plassey.com
Total Pitches: 90 (C, CV & T)

**Trawsdir Touring C & C Park**
Llanaber, Barmouth
LL42 1RR
Tel: 01341 280999 61 K8
barmouthholidays.co.uk
Total Pitches: 70 (C, CV & T)

**Trefalun Park**
Devonshire Drive, St Florence, Tenby
SA70 8RD
Tel: 01646 651514 37 L10
trefalunpark.co.uk
Total Pitches: 90 (C, CV & T)

**Tyddyn Isaf Caravan Park**
Lligwy Bay, Dulas, Isle of Anglesey
LL70 9PQ
Tel: 01248 410203 72 H6
tyddynisaf.co.uk
Total Pitches: 30 (C, CV & T)

**Tyn Cornel C & C Park**
Frongoch, Bala
LL23 7NU
Tel: 01678 520759 62 B4
tyncornel.co.uk
Total Pitches: 67 (C, CV & T)

**Well Park C & C Site**
Tenby
SA70 8TL
Tel: 01834 842179 37 M10
wellparkcaravans.co.uk
Total Pitches: 100 (C, CV & T)

**Ynysymaengwyn Caravan Park**
Tywyn
LL36 9RY
Tel: 01654 710684 61 K11
ynysy.co.uk
Total Pitches: 80 (C, CV & T)

## CHANNEL ISLANDS

**Beuvelande Camp Site**
Beuvelande, St Martin, Jersey
JE3 6EZ
Tel: 01534 853575 13 d2
campingjersey.com
Total Pitches: 150 (T)

**Fauxquets Valley Campsite**
Castel, Guernsey
GY5 7QL
Tel: 01481 236951 12 c2
fauxquets.co.uk
Total Pitches: 120 (T)

**Rozel Camping Park**
Summerville Farm, St Martin, Jersey
JE3 6AX
Tel: 01534 855200 13 d1
rozelcamping.co.uk
Total Pitches: 100 (C, CV & T)

# Traffic signs and road markings

## Traffic signs

### Signs giving orders

**Signs with red circles are mostly prohibitive. Plates below signs qualify their message.**

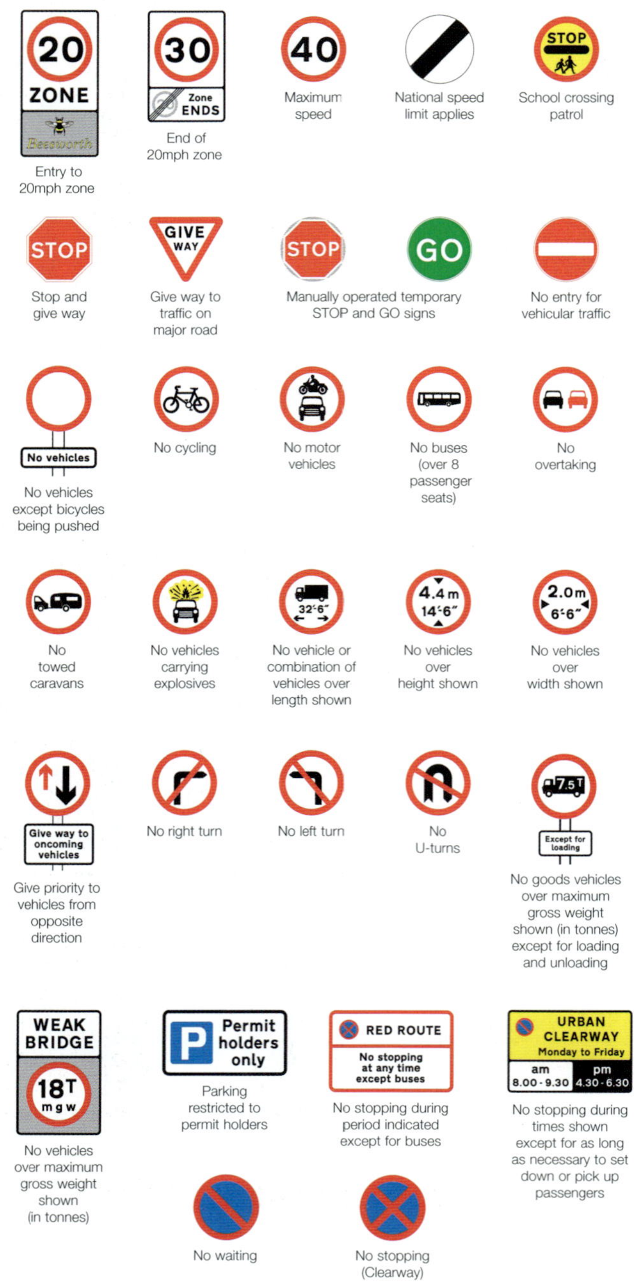


Entry to 20mph zone

End of 20mph zone

Maximum speed

National speed limit applies

School crossing patrol

Stop and give way

Give way to traffic on major road

Manually operated temporary STOP and GO signs

No entry for vehicular traffic

No vehicles except bicycles being pushed

No cycling

No motor vehicles

No buses (over 8 passenger seats)

No overtaking

No towed caravans

No vehicles carrying explosives

No vehicle or combination of vehicles over length shown

No vehicles over height shown

No vehicles over width shown

Give priority to vehicles from opposite direction

No right turn

No left turn

No U-turns

No goods vehicles over maximum gross weight shown (in tonnes) except for loading and unloading

No vehicles over maximum gross weight shown (in tonnes)

Parking restricted to permit holders

No stopping during period indicated except for buses

No stopping during times shown except for as long as necessary to set down or pick up passengers

No waiting

No stopping (Clearway)

**Signs with blue circles but no red border mostly give positive instruction.**

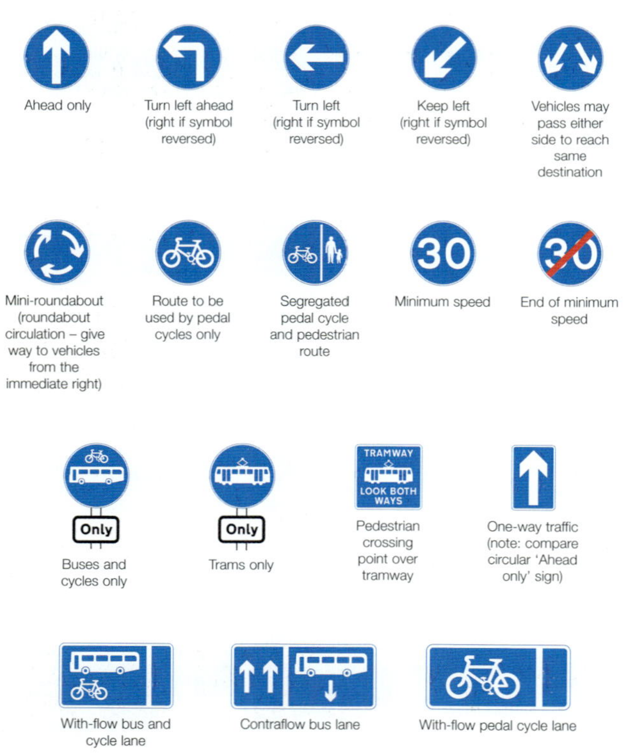


Ahead only

Turn left ahead (right if symbol reversed)

Turn left (right if symbol reversed)

Keep left (right if symbol reversed)

Vehicles may pass either side to reach same destination

Mini-roundabout (roundabout circulation – give way to vehicles from the immediate right)

Route to be used by pedal cycles only

Segregated pedal cycle and pedestrian route

Minimum speed

End of minimum speed

Buses and cycles only

Trams only

Pedestrian crossing point over tramway

One-way traffic (note: compare circular 'Ahead only' sign)

With-flow bus and cycle lane

Contraflow bus lane

With-flow pedal cycle lane

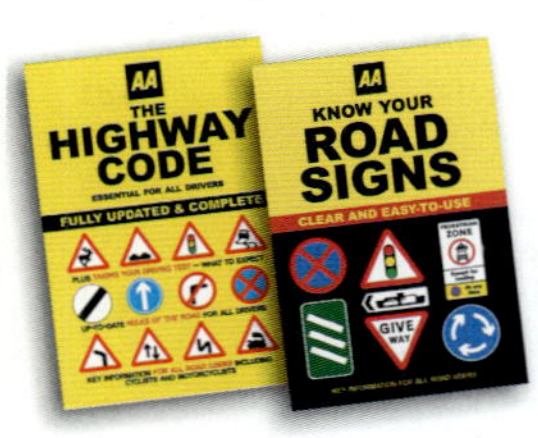


Note: Although this road atlas shows many of the signs commonly in use, a comprehensive explanation of the signing system is given in the AA's handbook *Know Your Road Signs*, which is on sale at theaa.com/shop and booksellers. The booklet also illustrates and explains the vast majority of signs the road user is likely to encounter. The signs illustrated in this road atlas are not all drawn to the same scale. In Wales, bilingual versions of some signs are used including Welsh and English versions of place names. Some older designs of signs may still be seen on the roads.

### Warning signs

**Mostly triangular**

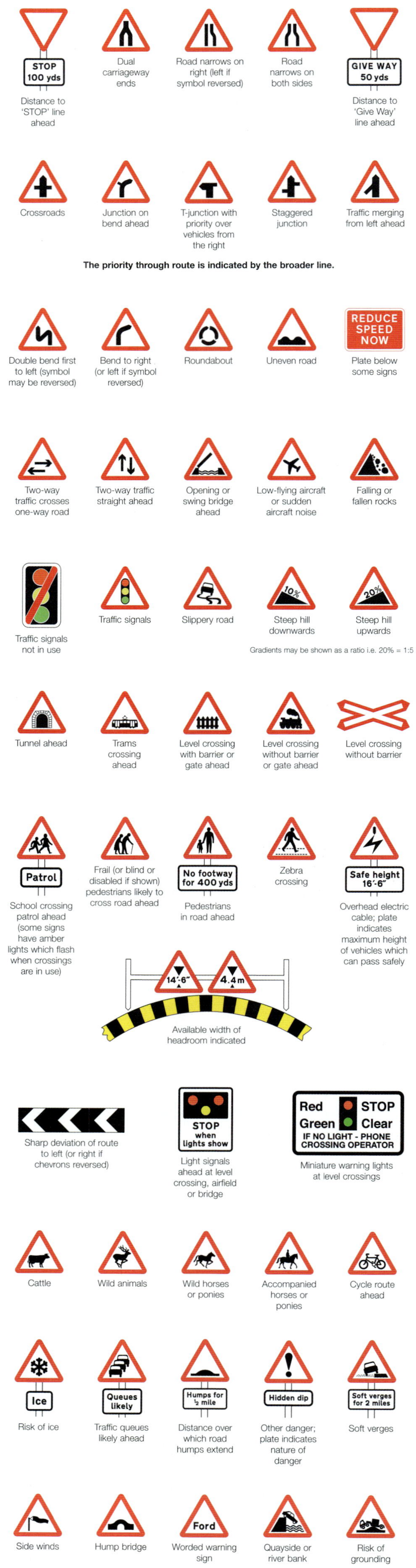


Distance to 'STOP' line ahead

Dual carriageway ends

Road narrows on right (left if symbol reversed)

Road narrows on both sides

Distance to 'Give Way' line ahead

Crossroads

Junction on bend ahead

T-junction with priority over vehicles from the right

Staggered junction

Traffic merging from left ahead

**The priority through route is indicated by the broader line.**

Double bend first to left (symbol may be reversed)

Bend to right (or left if symbol reversed)

Roundabout

Uneven road

Plate below some signs

Two-way traffic crosses one-way road

Two-way traffic straight ahead

Opening or swing bridge ahead

Low-flying aircraft or sudden aircraft noise

Falling or fallen rocks

Traffic signals not in use

Traffic signals

Slippery road

Steep hill downwards

Steep hill upwards

Gradients may be shown as a ratio i.e. 20% = 1:5

Tunnel ahead

Trams crossing ahead

Level crossing with barrier or gate ahead

Level crossing without barrier or gate ahead

Level crossing without barrier

School crossing patrol ahead (some signs have amber lights which flash when crossings are in use)

Frail (or blind or disabled if shown) pedestrians likely to cross road ahead

Pedestrians in road ahead

Zebra crossing

Overhead electric cable; plate indicates maximum height of vehicles which can pass safely

Available width of headroom indicated

Sharp deviation of route to left (or right if chevrons reversed)

Light signals ahead at level crossing, airfield or bridge

Miniature warning lights at level crossings

Cattle

Wild animals

Wild horses or ponies

Accompanied horses or ponies

Cycle route ahead

Risk of ice

Traffic queues likely ahead

Distance over which road humps extend

Other danger; plate indicates nature of danger

Soft verges

Side winds

Hump bridge

Worded warning sign

Quayside or river bank

Risk of grounding

### Direction signs

**Mostly rectangular**

**Signs on motorways – blue backgrounds**

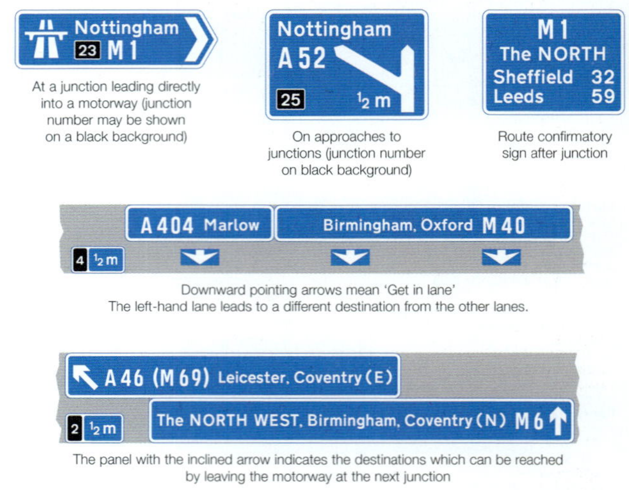


At a junction leading directly into a motorway (junction number may be shown on a black background)

On approaches to junctions (junction number on black background)

Route confirmatory sign after junction

Downward pointing arrows mean 'Get in lane'
The left-hand lane leads to a different destination from the other lanes.

The panel with the inclined arrow indicates the destinations which can be reached by leaving the motorway at the next junction

**Signs on primary routes - green backgrounds**

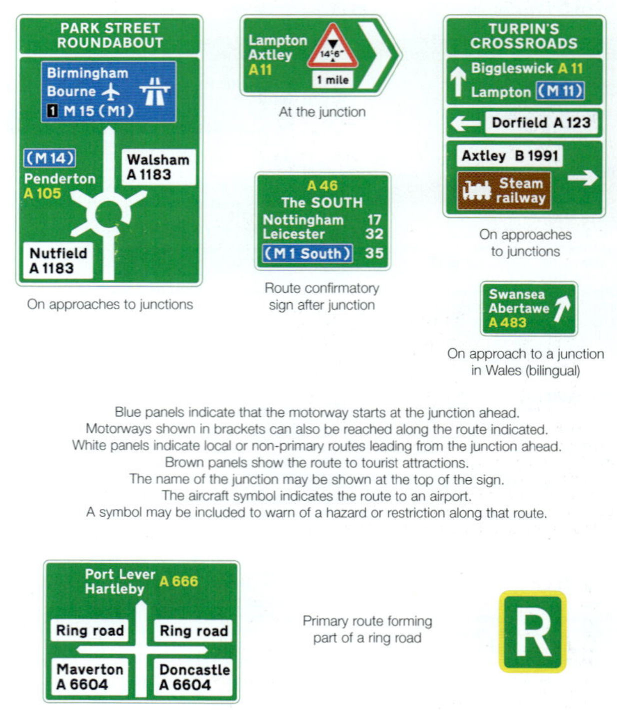


On approaches to junctions

At the junction

Route confirmatory sign after junction

On approaches to junctions

On approach to a junction in Wales (bilingual)

Blue panels indicate that the motorway starts at the junction ahead.
Motorways shown in brackets can also be reached along the route indicated.
White panels indicate local or non-primary routes leading from the junction ahead.
Brown panels show the route to tourist attractions.
The name of the junction may be shown at the top of the sign.
The aircraft symbol indicates the route to an airport.
A symbol may be included to warn of a hazard or restriction along that route.

Primary route forming part of a ring road

**Signs on non-primary and local routes - black borders**

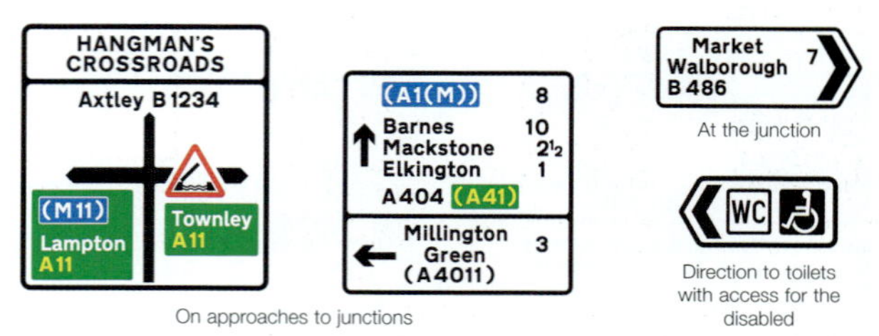


On approaches to junctions

At the junction

Direction to toilets with access for the disabled

Green panels indicate that the primary route starts at the junction ahead.
Route numbers on a blue background show the direction to a motorway.
Route numbers on a green background show the direction to a primary route.

**Other direction signs**

Picnic site

Ancient monument in the care of English Heritage

Direction to a car park

Tourist attraction

Direction to camping and caravan site

Advisory route for lorries

Route for pedal cycles forming part of a network

Recommended route for pedal cycles to place shown

Route for pedestrians

**Emergency diversion routes**

Symbols showing emergency diversion route for motorway and other main road traffic

Diversion route

In an emergency it may be necessary to close a section of motorway or other main road to traffic, so a temporary sign may advise drivers to follow a diversion route. To help drivers navigate the route, black symbols on yellow patches may be permanently displayed on existing direction signs, including motorway signs. Symbols may also be used on separate signs with yellow backgrounds.

For further information see www.highways.gov.uk

# Information signs

**All rectangular**

Entrance to controlled parking zone

Entrance to congestion charging zone

Greater London Low Emission Zone (LEZ)

Advance warning of restriction or prohibition ahead

Parking place for solo motorcycles

With-flow bus lane ahead which pedal cycles and taxis may also use

Lane designated for use by high occupancy vehicles (HOV) - see rule 142

Vehicles permitted to use an HOV lane ahead

End of motorway

Start of motorway and point from which motorway regulations apply

Appropriate traffic lanes at junction ahead

Traffic on the main carriageway coming from right has priority over joining traffic

Additional traffic joining from left ahead. Traffic on main carriageway has priority over joining traffic from right hand lane of slip road

Traffic in right hand lane of slip road joining the main carriageway has prority over left hand lane

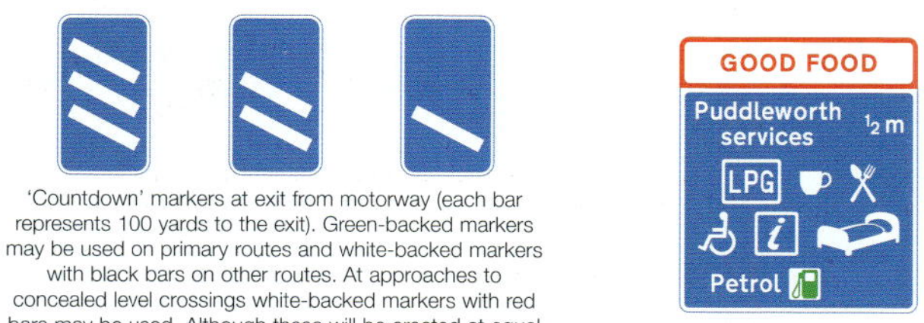


'Countdown' markers at exit from motorway (each bar represents 100 yards to the exit). Green-backed markers may be used on primary routes and white-backed markers with black bars on other routes. At approaches to concealed level crossings white-backed markers with red bars may be used. Although these will be erected at equal distances the bars do not represent 100 yard intervals.

Motorway service area sign showing the operator's name

Traffic has priority over oncoming vehicles

Hospital ahead with Accident and Emergency facilities

Tourist information point

No through road for vehicles

Recommended route for pedal cycles

Home Zone Entry

Area in which cameras are used to enforce traffic regulations

Bus lane on road at junction ahead

*Home Zone Entry – You are entering an area where people could be using the whole street for a range of activities. You should drive slowly and carefully and be prepared to stop to allow people time to move out of the way.

# Roadworks signs

Road works

Loose chippings

Temporary hazard at roadworks

Temporary lane closure (the number and position of arrows and red bars may be varied according to lanes open and closed)

Slow-moving or stationary works vehicle blocking a traffic lane. Pass in the direction shown by the arrow.

Mandatory speed limit ahead

Roadworks 1 mile ahead

End of roadworks and any temporary restrictions including speed limits

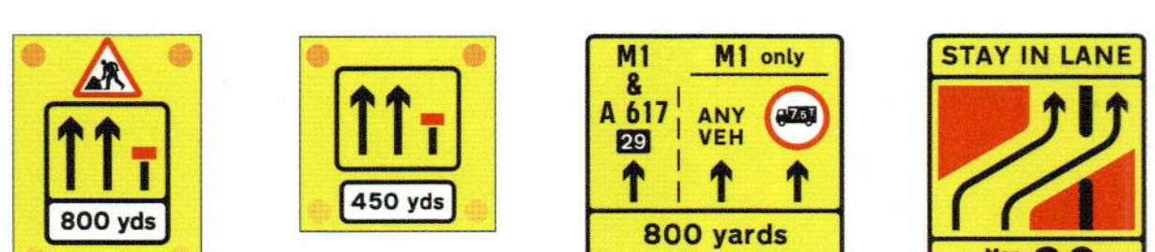


Signs used on the back of slow-moving or stationary vehicles warning of a lane closed ahead by a works vehicle. There are no cones on the road.

Lane restrictions at roadworks ahead

One lane crossover at contraflow roadworks

# Road markings

## Across the carriageway

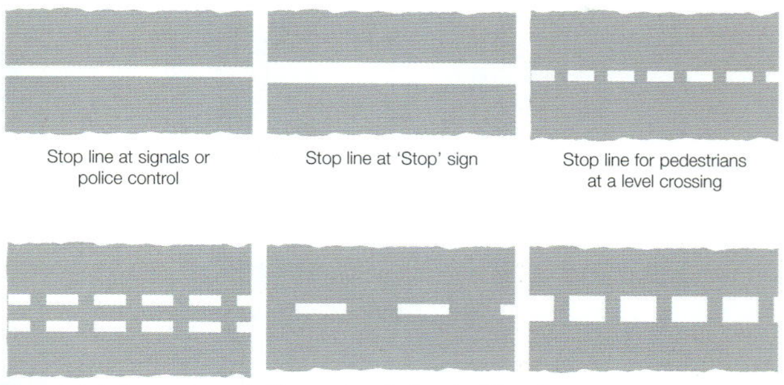

Stop line at signals or police control

Stop line at 'Stop' sign

Stop line for pedestrians at a level crossing

Give way to traffic on major road (can also be used at mini roundabouts)

Give way to traffic from the right at a roundabout

Give way to traffic from the right at a mini-roundabout

## Along the carriageway

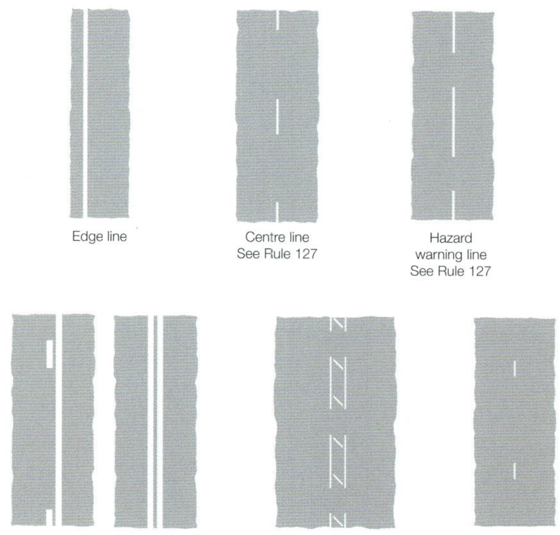

Edge line

Centre line See Rule 127

Hazard warning line See Rule 127

Double white lines See Rules 128 and 129

See Rule 130

Lane line See Rule 131

## Along the edge of the carriageway

**Waiting restrictions**

Waiting restrictions indicated by yellow lines apply to the carriageway, pavement and verge. You may stop to load or unload (unless there are also loading restrictions as described below) or while passengers board or alight. Double yellow lines mean no waiting at any time, unless there are signs that specifically indicate seasonal restrictions. The times at which the restrictions apply for other road markings are shown on nearby plates or on entry signs to controlled parking zones. If no days are shown on the signs, the restrictions are in force every day including Sundays and Bank Holidays. White bay markings and upright signs (see below) indicate where parking is allowed.

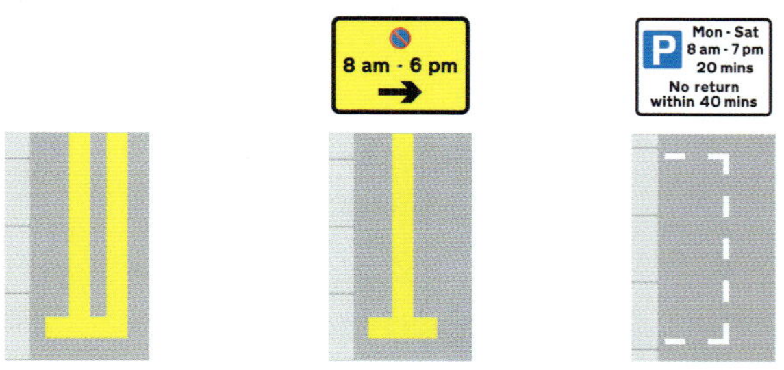


No waiting at any time

No waiting during times shown on sign

Waiting is limited to the duration specified during the days and times shown

**Red Route stopping controls**

Red lines are used on some roads instead of yellow lines. In London the double and single red lines used on Red Routes indicate that stopping to park, load/unload or to board and alight from a vehicle (except for a licensed taxi or if you hold a Blue Badge) is prohibited. The red lines apply to the carriageway, pavement and verge. The times that the red line prohibitions apply are shown on nearby signs, but the double red line ALWAYS means no stopping at any time. On Red Routes you may stop to park, load/unload in specially marked boxes and adjacent signs specify the times and purposes and duration allowed. A box MARKED IN RED indicates that it may only be available for the purpose specified for part of the day (e.g. between busy peak periods). A box MARKED IN WHITE means that it is available throughout the day.

RED AND SINGLE YELLOW LINES CAN ONLY GIVE A GUIDE TO THE RESTRICTIONS AND CONTROLS IN FORCE AND SIGNS, NEARBY OR AT A ZONE ENTRY, MUST BE CONSULTED.

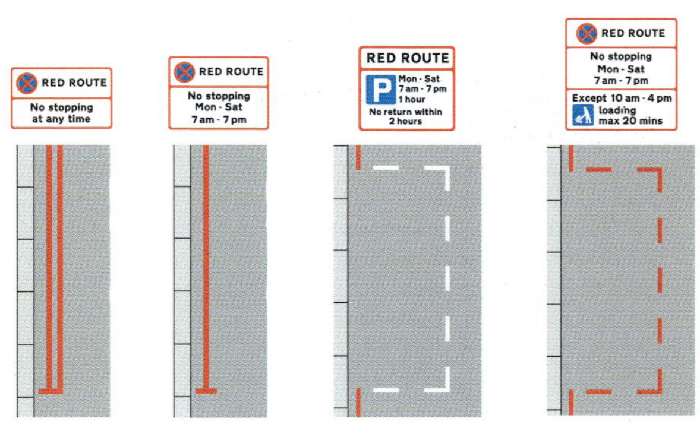


No stopping at any time

No stopping during times shown on sign

Parking is limited to the duration specified during the days and times shown

Only loading may take place at the times shown for up to a maximum duration of 20 mins

## On the kerb or at the edge of the carriageway

**Loading restrictions on roads other than Red Routes**

Yellow marks on the kerb or at the edge of the carriageway indicate that loading or unloading is prohibited at the times shown on the nearby black and white plates. You may stop while passengers board or alight. If no days are indicated on the signs the restrictions are in force every day including Sundays and Bank Holidays.

ALWAYS CHECK THE TIMES SHOWN ON THE PLATES.

Lengths of road reserved for vehicles loading and unloading are indicated by a white 'bay' marking with the words 'Loading Only' and a sign with the white on blue 'trolley' symbol. This sign also shows whether loading and unloading is restricted to goods vehicles and the times at which the bay can be used. If no times or days are shown it may be used at any time. Vehicles may not park here if they are not loading or unloading.

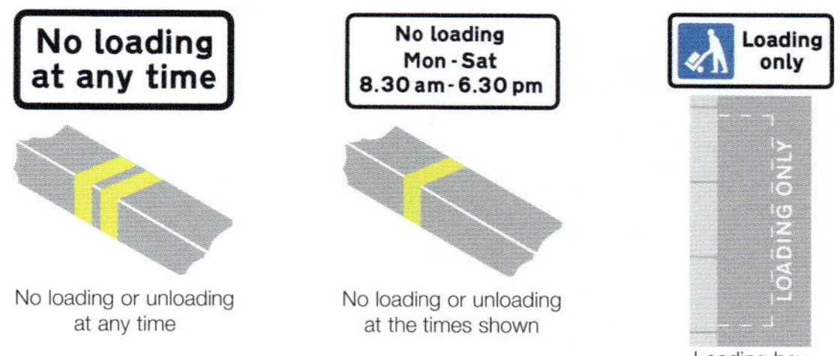


No loading or unloading at any time

No loading or unloading at the times shown

Loading bay

## Other road markings

Keep entrance clear of stationary vehicles, even if picking up or setting down children

Warning of 'Give Way' just ahead

Parking space reserved for vehicles named

See Rule 243

See Rule 141

Box junction - See Rule 174

Do not block that part of the carriageway indicated

Indication of traffic lanes

# Light signals controlling traffic

## Traffic Light Signals

RED means 'Stop'. Wait behind the stop line on the carriageway

RED AND AMBER also means 'Stop'. Do not pass through or start until GREEN shows

GREEN means you may go on if the way is clear. Take special care if you intend to turn left or right and give way to pedestrians who are crossing

AMBER means 'Stop' at the stop line. You may go on only if the AMBER appears after you have crossed the stop line or are so close to it that to pull up might cause an accident

A GREEN ARROW may be provided in addition to the full green signal if movement in a certain direction is allowed before or after the full green phase. If the way is clear you may go but only in the direction shown by the arrow. You may do this whatever other lights may be showing. White light signals may be provided for trams

## Flashing red lights

**Alternately flashing red lights mean YOU MUST STOP**

At level crossings, lifting bridges, airfields, fire stations, etc.

## Motorway signals

You **MUST NOT** proceed further in this lane

Change lane

Reduced visibility ahead

Lane ahead closed

Temporary maximum speed advised and information message

Leave motorway at next exit

Temporary maximum speed advised

End of restriction

## Lane control signals



Green arrow – lane available to traffic facing the sign

Red crosses – lane closed to traffic facing the sign

White diagonal arrow – change lanes in direction shown

# Channel Hopping

For business or pleasure, hopping on a ferry across to France, Belgium or the Channel Islands has never been easier.

The vehicle ferry routes shown on this map give you all the options, together with detailed port plans to help you navigate to and from the ferry terminals. Simply choose your preferred route, not forgetting the fast sailings; then check the colour-coded table for ferry operators, crossing times and contact details.

Bon voyage!

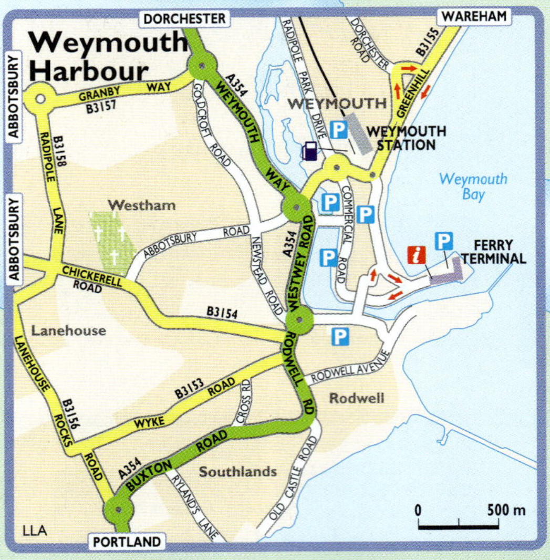

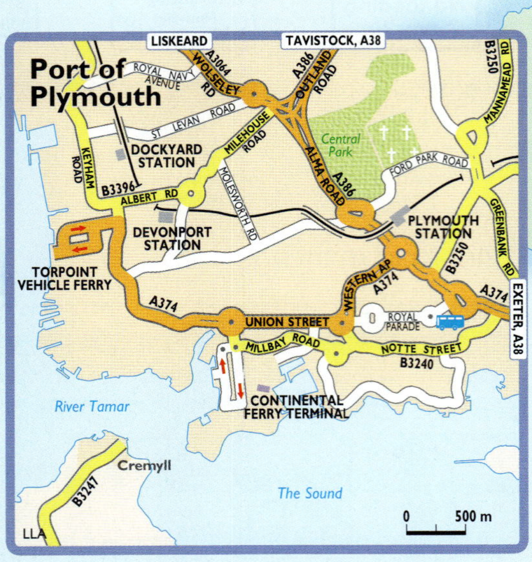

## ENGLISH CHANNEL FERRY CROSSINGS AND OPERATORS

| To | From | Journey Time | Operator | Telephone | Website |
|---|---|---|---|---|---|
| Caen (Ouistreham) | Portsmouth | 6 - 7 hrs | Brittany Ferries | 0871 244 0744 | *brittany-ferries.co.uk* |
| Caen (Ouistreham) | Portsmouth | 3 hrs 45 mins (Mar-Oct) | Brittany Ferries | 0871 244 0744 | *brittany-ferries.co.uk* |
| Calais | Dover | 1 hr 30 mins | P&O Ferries | 0871 664 2020 | *poferries.com* |
| Calais (Coquelles) | Folkestone | 35 mins | Eurotunnel | 08443 35 35 35 | *eurotunnel.com* |
| Cherbourg | Poole | 2 hrs 30 mins (April-Oct) | Brittany Ferries | 0871 244 0744 | *brittany-ferries.co.uk* |
| Cherbourg | Portsmouth | 3 hrs (Mar-Oct) | Brittany Ferries | 0871 244 0744 | *brittany-ferries.co.uk* |
| Cherbourg | Portsmouth | 4 hrs 30 mins(day) 8 hrs(o/night) | Brittany Ferries | 0871 244 0744 | *brittany-ferries.co.uk* |
| Cherbourg | Portsmouth | 5 hrs 30 mins (May-Sept) | Condor | 0845 609 1024 | *condorferries.co.uk* |
| Dieppe | Newhaven | 4 hrs | Transmanche Ferries | 0844 576 8836 | *transmancheferries.co.uk* |
| Dunkerque | Dover | 2 hrs | DFDS Seaways | 0871 522 9955 | *dfdsseaways.co.uk* |
| Guernsey | Poole | 2 hrs 30 mins (April-Oct) | Condor | 0845 609 1024 | *condorferries.co.uk* |
| Guernsey | Portsmouth | 7 hrs | Condor | 0845 609 1024 | *condorferries.co.uk* |
| Guernsey | Weymouth | 2 hrs 10 mins | Condor | 0845 609 1024 | *condorferries.co.uk* |
| Jersey | Poole | 3 hrs (April-Oct) | Condor | 0845 609 1024 | *condorferries.co.uk* |
| Jersey | Portsmouth | 10 hrs 30 mins | Condor | 0845 609 1024 | *condorferries.co.uk* |
| Jersey | Weymouth | 3 hrs 25 mins | Condor | 0845 609 1024 | *condorferries.co.uk* |
| Le Havre | Portsmouth | 5 hrs 30 mins - 8 hrs | LD Lines | 0844 576 8836 | *ldlines.co.uk* |
| Le Havre | Portsmouth | 3 hrs 15 mins (Mar-Sept) | LD Lines | 0844 576 8836 | *ldlines.co.uk* |
| Oostende | Ramsgate | 4 hrs - 4hrs 30 mins | Transeuropa | 01843 595 522 | *transeuropaferries.com* |
| Roscoff | Plymouth | 6 - 8 hrs | Brittany Ferries | 0871 244 0744 | *brittany-ferries.co.uk* |
| St-Malo | Poole | 4 hrs 35 mins (May-Sept) | Condor | 0845 609 1024 | *condorferries.co.uk* |
| St-Malo | Portsmouth | 9 - 10 hrs 45 mins | Brittany Ferries | 0871 244 0744 | *brittany-ferries.co.uk* |
| St-Malo | Weymouth | 5 hrs 15 mins | Condor | 0845 609 1024 | *condorferries.co.uk* |

Portsmouth Harbour
500 m
M27, SOUTHAMPTON, CHICHESTER
CONTINENTAL FERRY TERMINAL
Buckland
Landport
HM Naval Base
Portsea
PORTSMOUTH & SOUTHSEA STA
Fratton
FRATTON STA
PORTSMOUTH HARBOUR STA
Spinnaker Tower
ISLE OF WIGHT FERRY TERMINAL
Somers Town
Old Portsmouth
Newhaven Harbour
LEWES
EASTBOURNE
BRIGHTON
NEWHAVEN TOWN STATION
FERRY TERMINAL
NEWHAVEN
NEWHAVEN HARBOUR STATION
Lifeboat Station
Newhaven Harbour
Newhaven Marina
EAST QUAY COMMERCIAL TERMINAL
Rec Ground
500 m
Port of Dover
CANTERBURY, RAMSGATE
DOVER
Dover Castle
Police Station
FERRY TERMINAL
Tower Hamlets
DOVER PRIORY STATION
Clarendon
Western Heights
Western Docks
Outer Harbour
Eastern Docks
CRUISE TERMINAL
Inner Harbour
LONDON, FOLKESTONE, CHANNEL TUNNEL
500 m
Ramsgate
Portsmouth
Folkestone
Dover
Newhaven
Oostende
Calais
Dunkerque
Calais (Coquelles)
CHANNEL
Dieppe
le Havre
Caen (Ouistreham)
Calais
1 km
CAR FERRY TERMINAL
Stadium
Notre Dame
Citadelle
GARE CENTRALE
Hypermarket
Hospital
Fort Nieulay
Hypermarket
SANGATTE
BOULOGNE
Cité de l'Europe
CALAIS CHANNEL TUNNEL TERMINAL ENTRANCE
EXIT FROM CHANNEL TUNNEL
GUÎNES
ST OMER
PARIS
DUNKERQUE

# Ferries to Ireland and the Isle of Man

With so many sea crossings to Ireland and the Isle of Man this map will help you make the right choice.

The vehicle ferry routes shown on this map give you all the options, together with detailed port plans to help you navigate to and from the ferry terminals. Simply choose your preferred route, not forgetting the fast sailings; then check the colour-coded table for ferry operators, crossing times and contact details.

Fast ferry   Conventional ferry

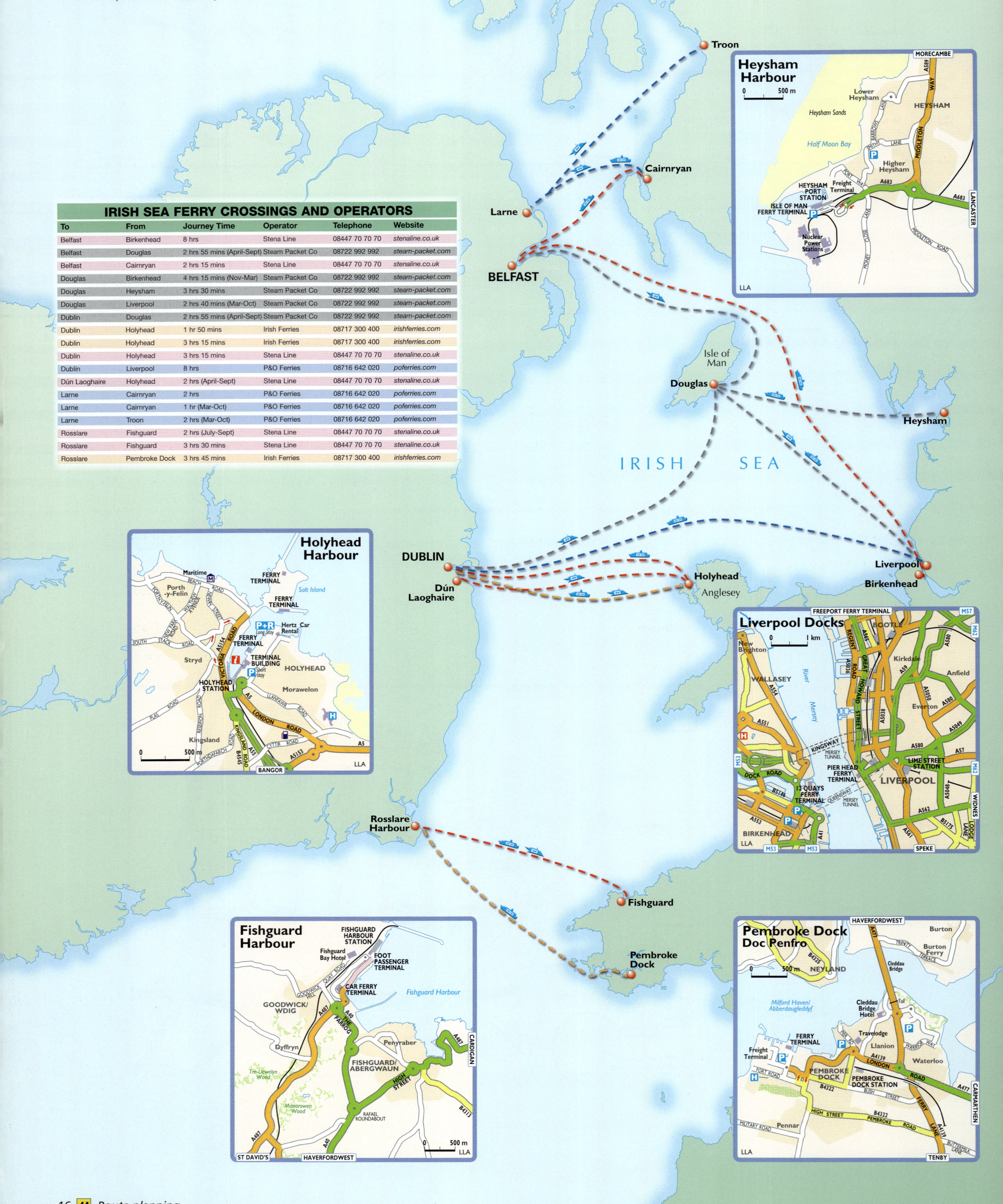


**IRISH SEA FERRY CROSSINGS AND OPERATORS**

| To | From | Journey Time | Operator | Telephone | Website |
|---|---|---|---|---|---|
| Belfast | Birkenhead | 8 hrs | Stena Line | 08447 70 70 70 | *stenaline.co.uk* |
| Belfast | Douglas | 2 hrs 55 mins (April-Sept) | Steam Packet Co | 08722 992 992 | *steam-packet.com* |
| Belfast | Cairnryan | 2 hrs 15 mins | Stena Line | 08447 70 70 70 | *stenaline.co.uk* |
| Douglas | Birkenhead | 4 hrs 15 mins (Nov-Mar) | Steam Packet Co | 08722 992 992 | *steam-packet.com* |
| Douglas | Heysham | 3 hrs 30 mins | Steam Packet Co | 08722 992 992 | *steam-packet.com* |
| Douglas | Liverpool | 2 hrs 40 mins (Mar-Oct) | Steam Packet Co | 08722 992 992 | *steam-packet.com* |
| Dublin | Douglas | 2 hrs 55 mins (April-Sept) | Steam Packet Co | 08722 992 992 | *steam-packet.com* |
| Dublin | Holyhead | 1 hr 50 mins | Irish Ferries | 08717 300 400 | *irishferries.com* |
| Dublin | Holyhead | 3 hrs 15 mins | Irish Ferries | 08717 300 400 | *irishferries.com* |
| Dublin | Holyhead | 3 hrs 15 mins | Stena Line | 08447 70 70 70 | *stenaline.co.uk* |
| Dublin | Liverpool | 8 hrs | P&O Ferries | 08716 642 020 | *poferries.com* |
| Dún Laoghaire | Holyhead | 2 hrs (April-Sept) | Stena Line | 08447 70 70 70 | *stenaline.co.uk* |
| Larne | Cairnryan | 2 hrs | P&O Ferries | 08716 642 020 | *poferries.com* |
| Larne | Cairnryan | 1 hr (Mar-Oct) | P&O Ferries | 08716 642 020 | *poferries.com* |
| Larne | Troon | 2 hrs (Mar-Oct) | P&O Ferries | 08716 642 020 | *poferries.com* |
| Rosslare | Fishguard | 2 hrs (July-Sept) | Stena Line | 08447 70 70 70 | *stenaline.co.uk* |
| Rosslare | Fishguard | 3 hrs 30 mins | Stena Line | 08447 70 70 70 | *stenaline.co.uk* |
| Rosslare | Pembroke Dock | 3 hrs 45 mins | Irish Ferries | 08717 300 400 | *irishferries.com* |

# Atlas symbols

## Motoring information

- M4 Motorway with number
- T4 Toll Toll motorway with toll station
- 11 Motorway junction with and without number
- 3 Restricted motorway junctions
- S Fleet Motorway service area
- Motorway and junction under construction
- A3 Primary route single/dual carriageway
- 11 Primary route junction with and without number
- 3 Restricted primary route junctions
- S Primary route service area
- BATH Primary route destination
- A1123 Other A road single/dual carriageway
- B2070 B road single/dual carriageway
- Minor road more than 4 metres wide, less than 4 metres wide
- Roundabout
- Interchange/junction
- Narrow primary/other A/B road with passing places (Scotland)
- Road under construction/ approved
- Road tunnel
- Toll Road toll, steep gradient (arrows point downhill)
- 5 Distance in miles between symbols
- or V Vehicle ferry
- Fast vehicle ferry or catamaran
- F International freight terminal
- Railway line, in tunnel
- Railway station and level crossing
- Tourist railway
- City, town, village or other built-up area
- Airport, heliport
- H H 24-hour Accident & Emergency hospital, other hospital
- C Crematorium
- Sandy beach
- 30 Speed camera site (fixed location) with speed limit in mph
- 50 Section of road with two or more fixed speed cameras, with speed limit in mph
- 40 40 Average speed (SPECS™) camera system with speed limit in mph
- V Fixed speed camera with variable speed limit
- P+R Park and Ride (at least 6 days per week)
- 628 637 Lecht Summit Height in metres, mountain pass
- National boundary
- County, administrative boundary

## Touring information

To avoid disappointment, check opening times before visiting

- Scenic Route
- Tourist Information Centre
- Tourist Information Centre (seasonal)
- Visitor or heritage centre
- Picnic site
- Caravan site (AA inspected)
- Camping site (AA inspected)
- Caravan & camping site (AA inspected)
- Abbey, cathedral or priory
- Ruined abbey, cathedral or priory
- Castle
- Historic house or building
- Museum or art gallery
- Industrial interest
- Aqueduct or viaduct
- Garden
- Arboretum
- Vineyard
- Country park
- Agricultural showground
- Theme park
- Farm or animal centre
- Zoological or wildlife collection
- Bird collection
- Aquarium
- RSPB site
- National Nature Reserve (England, Scotland, Wales)
- Wildlife Trust reserve
- Local nature reserve
- Forest drive
- National trail
- Viewpoint
- Hill-fort
- Roman antiquity
- Prehistoric monument
- 1066 Battle site with year
- Steam railway centre
- Cave
- Windmill, monument
- Golf course
- County cricket ground
- Rugby Union national stadium
- International athletics stadium
- Horse racing, show jumping
- Motor-racing circuit
- Air show venue
- Ski slope (natural, artificial)
- National Trust property
- National Trust for Scotland property
- English Heritage site
- Historic Scotland site
- Cadw (Welsh heritage) site
- Other place of interest
- Boxed symbols indicate attractions within urban areas
- World Heritage Site (UNESCO)
- National Park
- National Scenic Area (Scotland)
- Forest Park
- Heritage coast
- Major shopping centre

## Town plans (pages 153–158)

- 2 Motorway and junction
- Primary road single/ dual carriageway
- A road single/ dual carriageway
- B road single/ dual carriageway
- Local road single/ dual carriageway
- Other road single/ dual carriageway, minor road
- One-way, gated/ closed road
- Restricted access
- Pedestrian area
- Footpath
- Road under construction
- Road tunnel
- Level crossing
- Railway station
- Tramway
- London Underground station
- London Overground station
- Rail interchange
- Docklands Light Railway (DLR) station
- Light rapid transit system station
- Airport, heliport
- R Railair terminal
- P+ Park and Ride (at least 6 days per week)
- P Car park
- Bus/coach station
- H H 24-hour Accident & Emergency hospital, other hosptial
- Toilet, with facilities for the less able
- Building of interest
- Ruined building
- City wall
- Cliff lift
- Cliff escarpment
- River/canal, lake
- Lock, weir
- Park/sports ground/ open space
- Cemetery
- Woodland
- Built-up area
- Beach
- Tourist Information Centre
- Visitor or heritage centre
- Post Office
- Public library
- Shopping centre
- Shopmobility
- Theatre or performing arts centre
- Cinema
- Museum
- Castle
- Castle mound
- Monument, statue
- Viewpoint
- Abbey, chapel, church
- Synagogue
- Mosque
- Golf Course
- Racecourse
- Nature reserve
- Aquarium
- World Heritage Site (UNESCO)
- English Heritage site
- Historic Scotland site
- Cadw (Welsh heritage) site
- National Trust site
- National Trust Scotland site

Isles of Scilly
White Island
ST. MARTIN'S
St Martin's Head
BRYHER
Old Grimsby
Higher Town
New Grimsby
Lizard Point
Isles of Scilly Heritage Coast
Pool
Tresco Abbey
Great Ganilly
Samson
TRESCO
Great Arthur
ST MARY'S
Crow Sound
Longstone
Deep Point
North West Channel
Hugh Town
Porth Hellick Downs Tombs
Isles of Scilly (St Mary's)
Old Town
Garrison Walls
Peninnis Head
Annet
St Mary's Sound
Broad Sound
Middle Town
Gugh
ST AGNES
Horse Point
Smith Sound
Western Rocks
St Ives
St Ives Bay
Carbis Bay
Hayle
Camborne
Redruth
Penzance
Newlyn
Mousehole
MOUNT'S BAY
St Michael's Mount
Marazion
Helston
Porthleven
St Just
Cape Cornwall
LAND'S END
Land's End
Sennen
Sennen Cove
Whitesand Bay
Porthcurno
Lamorna
Zennor
Pendeen
St Buryan
Mullion Cove
Mullion
Lizard
LIZARD POINT
Kynance Cove
Portreath
Porthtowan
Godrevy Point
Gwithian
Coverack Bridges
Penwith Heritage Coast
South West Coast Path
The Lizard Heritage Coast
Godrevy-Portreath Heritage Coast
St Agnes Heritage Coast
ST AGNES HEAD
Gunwalloe
Poldhu Point
Predannack Head
Vellan Head
Lizard Head

Bedruthan Steps
Carnewas
Trenance
Downhill
St Eval
Ervan
Trelow
St Jidgey
St Breock Downs Monolith
Crealy Great Adventure Park
Nine Maidens
Polbrock
Brocton
Washaway
Lane End
Dunmere
Bodmin
Cardinham
Cooksland
Fletchersbridge
Bodmin & Wenford Railway
Berrys Point
Griffins Point
Mawgan Porth
Trevarrian
St Mawgan
Carloggas
Talskiddy
Rosenannon
St Wenn
Withiel
Withielgoose
Tremore
Ruthernbridge
Tregawne
Nanstallon
Boscarne
St Lawrence
Lanivet
Tregullon
Lamorick
Retire
Demelza
Watergate Bay
Tregurrian
Newquay
Gluvian
Reterth
Tregonetha
Town Head
Newquay Bay
Porth
St Columb Minor
Tregaswith
Trevithick
St Columb Major
Belowda
Victoria
Higher Town
Criggan
Trebyan
Bokiddick
Cutmadoc
Sweetshouse
Lockengate
Helman Tor
Restormel Castle
West Taphouse
Middle Taphouse
Braddock
Boconnoc
Lostwithiel
Couch's Mill
Castle
Milltown
Lerryn
Lanreath
Bocaddon
Porfell Animal Land
Fistral Bay
Kelsey Head
West Pentire
Pentire
Crantock
Trenowah
Holywell Bay
Holywell
Penhale Point
Ligger Point
Perran Beach
Colan
Trebudannon
Mountjoy
Bosoughan
Black Cross
Ruthvoes
Tregoss
Goss Moor
Roche
Carbis
Bodwen
Tredinnick
Penhale
Lanlivery
Treninnick
Lane
Trevemper
Quintrell Downs
Rosecliston
St Columb Road
Trevarren
Toldish
Enniscaven
Fraddon
Indian Queens
Carne
Bugle
Carnsmerry
Rosevean
Luxulyan
Luxulyan Valley
Tresean
Treveal
Trevoll
Kestle Mill
Dairyland
Retyn
Trerice
Gummow's Shop
Lappa Valley
Trevilson
Troan
St Enoder
Penhale
Blue Anchor
St Dennis
Whitemoor
Stenalees
Treverbyn
Penwithick
Trethurgy
Tywardreath Highway
Penpillick
Cubert
Newlyn East
Rejerrah
Mount
Summercourt
Chapel Town
Burthy
Treviscoe
Melbur
Nanpean
Carthew
Wheal Martyn Heritage Centre
Foxhole
Eden Project
St Blazey
Tywardreath
Treesmill
Torfrey
Golant
St Veep
Penpoll
Rose
Fiddlers Green
Mitchell
Scarcewater
Carpalla
Ruddlemoor
Carclaze
Tregrehan Mills
Boscoppa
St Blazey Gate
Par
Polmear
Lanteglos Highway
Perranporth
Goonhavern
World in Miniature
Carland Cross
Brighton
Trethosa
High Street
St Austell
Trewoon
Holmbush
Biscovey
Bolingey
Cocks
Carnkief
Perranwell
Perranzabuloe
Trelassick
Trendeal
St Stephen
Gwindra
Lanjeth
Trelion
Carlyon Bay
Polkerris
Fowey
Bodinnick
Lansallos
Penhallow
Zelah
St Allen
Ladock
New Mills
Coombe
St Mewan
Hay
Polgooth
Charlestown
Menabilly
Mithian
Callestick
Marazanvose
Trispen
Grampound Road
Tregorrick
Porthpean
St Austell Bay
St Catherine's Castle
Polruan
Pencarrow Head
Lantivet Bay
Lantic Bay
Barkla Shop
Treworgan
St Erme
Treverbyn
Hewas Water
Sticker
Levalsa Meor
London Apprentice
Gribbin Head
Allet Common
Idless
Probus
Grampound
Rescorla
Trenarren
Black Head
Shortlanesend
Creed
Town
Lost Gardens of Heligan
Pentewan
Three Burrows
Tresillian
Tresawle
St Ewe
Mevagissey Bay
Chacewater
Threemilestone
Kenwyn
Truro
River Fal
Tucoyse
Polmassick
Kestle
Tregiskey
Penare Point
Mevagissey
Saveock
Higher Town
Merther
Trevithick
Portmellon
Newbridge
Baldhu
Calenick
Malpas
St Clement
Tregony
Trevarrick
Chapel Point
Gwennap Mining District
Kea
Tregenna
Gorran High Lanes
Rescassa
Gorran Churchtown
Cross Lanes
Killiow
St Michael Penkevil
Ruan Lanihorne
St Michael Caerhays
Treveor
Gorran Haven
Twelveheads
Chyewoling
Porthkea
Playing Place
Lamorran
Portholland
Boswinger
Maenease Point
Frogpool
Bissoe
Carnon Downs
Coombe
Old Kea
Ruan High Lanes
Veryan Green
Treviskey
Penare
Gwennap
Perranwell
Penelewey
Trelissick Garden
Trelissick
Philleigh
Treworga
Treworthal
Veryan
Portloe
Veryan Bay
Dodman Point
Perranarworthal
Devoran
Penpol
Trevilla
Treworlas
Carne
Kennall Vale
Perran Wharf
Devoran & Perran
Feock
Treluggan
The Roseland Heritage Coast
Ponsanooth
Angarrick
Mylor Bridge
Restronguet
Trewithian
Cargurrel
Gerrans Bay
Nare Head
Burnthouse
Lower Treluswell
St Just-in-Roseland
Rosevine
Portscatho
Trelew
St Gluvia's
Mylor
Carrick Roads
Gerrans
Mabe Burnthouse
Penryn
Tregew
Flushing
Greeb Point
Trenoweth
Budock Water
Castle
St Mawes
Pendennis Castle
Treverva
Falmouth
Bohortha
Lamanva
Pendennis Point
South West Coast Path
Penjerrick
Zone Point
High Cross
Bareppa
Carlidnack
Maenporth
Falmouth Bay
Mawnan Smith
Trebah
Carwinion
Rosemullion Head
Glendurgan Garden
Durgan
Mawnan
Helford River
Helford
St Anthony
Manaccan
Gillan
Nare Point
Carne
Lestowder
St Martin
Roskorwell
Tregidden
Porthallow
Tregarne
Trenance
Porthoustock
Treleague
Manacle Point
Traboe
Rosenithon
St Keverne
Zoar
Lowland Point
Trelan
Ponsongath
North Corner
Coverack
Trewillis
Treleaver
Black Head
A39
A30
A392
A3059
A3058
A3076
A3075
A390
A391
A389
A38
A3082
A3078
B3274
B3276
B3279
B3266
B3268
B3269
B3285
B3284
B3275
B3287
B3273
B3289
B3293
B3294
Newquay
Newquay Bay
Fistral Beach
Atlantic Hotel
Memorial
Fly Cove
Tolcarne Beach
Best Western Hotel Bristol
First Aid
Towan Beach
Great Western Beach
Great Western Hotel
Lifeboat Station
The Island
Lifeguard Stn
Newquay Golf Club
Superstore
Blue Reef
Travelodge
Newquay Station
Police Sta.
The Royal British Legion
Hotel Victoria
Register Office
Jobcentre Plus
Christian Ctr
Newquay School
Salvation Army
Ambulance Sta
Superstore
Quarry Park Rd Industrial Estate
St John's Ambulance
Buccaneer Bay
St Michael's
Trenance School
Surgery
Heron Tennis Centre
Newquay Zoo
Trenance Leisure Park
Skate Park
Waterworld
Newquay AFC
Fire Station
Trenance Holiday Park
The Bishops School
Trevemper Caravan Park
Gannel Road
Gannel
Trevemper Road
Edgcumbe Ave
Hilgrove Road
St Columb Minor
Redruth, Bodmin

BODMIN MOOR
Tresinney
Wesley's Cottage
Trewint
Fivelanes
Lewannick
Tregonoe
Hexworthy
Bradstone
Milton Abbot
North Brentor
Blackdown
Horndon
Mary Tavy
Cudlipton
Peter Tavy
COXTOR
BROWN WILLY
Palmersbridge
Jamaica Inn
Bolventor
Plusha
Trevadlock
Congdon's Shop
Illand
Trebullett
Newtown
Lower Trebullett
Lanoy
Lezant
Penrest
Trekenner
Landue
Rezare
Bealsmill
Dunterton
Chaddlehanger
Lamerton
Rushford
Portontown
Tutwell
Kingston
Treburley
Sydenham Damerel
Coad's Green
Trebartha
North Hill
Middlewood
Bathpool
Bray Shop
Venterdon
Horsebridge
Townlake
Tavistock
Moortown
Middlemore
Whitchurch
Grenofen
Churchtown
St Breward
De Lank River
Bradford
River Fowey
SMALLACOMBE DOWNS
Colliford Lake
Henwood
Rillaton
Stoke Climsland
Oldmill
Luckett
Latchley
Waterloo
Temple
Colliford Lake Park
Siblyback
Sharptor
Cheesewring
The Hurlers Stone Circle
Minions
BROWNGELLY DOWNS
Upton
Upton Cross
Rilla Mill
Plushabridge
Linkinhorne
South Hill
Downgate
Coxpark
Chilsworthy
Gulworthy
Gunnislake
Drakewalls
St Ann's Chapel
Kit Hill
Kelly Bray
Mornick
Caradon Town
Sterts Open-Air Theatre
Trewoodloe
Golberdon
Haye
Harrowbarrow
A30
Millpool
Caradon Mining District
Common Moor
Darite
Crow's Nest
Pensilva
Trevigro
Dupath Well
Norris Green
Albaston
Morwellham Quay
Horrabridge
Warleggan
Trethevy Quoit
Middlehill
Charaton
Gang
Callington
Metherell
Cotehele
Calstock
Calstock Viaduct
The Garden House
Buckland Monachorum
Crapstone
Yelverton
Mount
St Neot
Golitha
King Doniert's Stone
Tremar
St Cleer
Frogwell
St Dominick
Pantersbridge
Lampen
Tredinnick
Ley
Carnglaze Caverns
Merrymeet
St Ive
St Ive Cross
Cadson Bury
Bealbury
Burraton
Bohetherick
Tamar Valley Mining District
St Mellion
Buckland Abbey
Bere Alston
Milton Combe
Sowton
Clearbrook
Fletchersbridge
Bodmin & Wenford Railway
Doublebois
Dobwalls
Trembraze
Liskeard
Pengover Green
Newton Ferrers
Quethiock
Pillaton
Halton Quay
Cotts
Weir Quay
Maristow
West Taphouse
Middle Taphouse
Moorswater
Trevelmond
Lamellion
Trehunist
Trewint
Pillatonmill
Bere Ferrers
Cargreen
Hatt
Landulph
Tamerton Foliot
Roborough
Bickleigh
East Taphouse
St Pinnock
Menheniot
Blunts
Cuttivett
Botusfleming
Restormel Castle
Braddock
Boconnoc
Herodsfoot
St Keyne
Paul Corin Music
Doddy Cross
Cutmere
Tideford Cross
Tideford
Horningtops
Carkeel
Notter
Saltash
Landrake
Trematon
Lostwithiel
Couch's Mill
Porfell Animal Land
Trewidland
Widegates
Budge's Shop
St Erney
Crownhill
PLYMOUTH
Bocaddon
Duloe
Lanreath
Shorta Cross
Trerulefoot
Markwell
Trehan
St Stephens
Eggbuckland
Lerryn
Muchlarnick
Tredinnick
Sandplace
Morval
No Man's Land
Hessenford
Trelowia
Polbathic
Narkurs
St Germans
Churchtown Farm Community
Antony House
Devonport
St Veep
Penpoll
Pelynt
St Martin
Monkey Sanctuary
Sheviock
Antony
Torpoint
St John
St John's Lake
Stonehouse
Cremyll
Saltram
Golant
Torrfey
Lanteglos Highway
Trenewan
Trelawne
Looe
Looe Bay
Bodigga Cliff
Seaton
Downderry
Portwrinkle
Craftholе
Penhale
Insworke
Plymouth Dome
Plymstock
Turnchapel
Hooe
Fowey
Bodinnick
Crumplehorn
Model Village
Portlooe
Porthallow
Looe or St George's Island
Higher Tregantle
Freathy
Millbrook
Mount Edgcumbe
Anderton
Spriddlestone
Staddiscombe
St Catherine's Castle
Polruan
Lansallos
Polperro
Talland Bay
Lantivet Bay
Lantic Bay
Pencarrow Head
South West Coast Path
Gribbin Head - Polperro Heritage Coast
Whitsand Bay
South West Coast Path
Cawsand
Kingsand
Cawsand Bay
The Sound
Down Thomas
Rame
West Wembury
Wembury
Heybrook Bay
Penlee Point
Wembury Bay
The Old Mill
Gara Point
RAME HEAD
Rame Head Heritage Coast
Santander (Mar-Oct)
Roscoff
Plymouth
TORPOINT
KINGSBRIDGE
A38, LISKEARD
Armada
City Market
Drake Circus
Charles Church
Plymouth College of Art
University of Plymouth
Police Station
St Peter's School
Casino
Plymouth Pavilions
Plymouth Athenaeum
Royal Clock Tower
Civic Centre
Guildhall
Crown & County Courts
Magistrates' Court
St Andrew's
Arts Centre
Merchant's House
Holiday Inn
YMCA
Register Office
Black Friar's Distillery
Custom House
Sutton Harbour
Sue Wills Art Gallery
Mayflower Visitor & Exhibition Centre
Barbican
Duke of Cornwall Hotel
St Andrew's School
Millbay Recreation Ground
TA Centre
Quality Hotel
War Memorial
Royal Navy Memorial
Hoe Park
Drake Statue
Memorials
Royal Citadel (MOD)
West Hoe Park
The Hoe
Smeaton's Tower
St Katherine upon the Hoe
Millbay Marina Village
Lifeboat Station
Yacht Club
200 m
miles
kilometres

DARTMOOR
FOREST
NATIONAL PARK
Postbridge
Two Bridges
Princetown
Hexworthy
Dunstone
Widecombe in the Moor
Haytor Vale
Ilsington
Bovey Tracey
Chudleigh Knighton
Kingsteignton
Newton Abbot
Teignmouth
Dawlish
Shaldon
Ashburton
Buckfastleigh
Buckfast
Kingskerswell
TORQUAY
Babbacombe Bay
Paignton
Tor Bay
Brixham
BERRY HEAD
Totnes
Dartington
Dartmouth
Kingswear
Plympton
Ivybridge
Modbury
Kingsbridge
Salcombe
Bigbury Bay
Bigbury-on-Sea
Burgh Island
Start Bay
Start Point
Prawle Point
Bolt Head
Bolt Tail
Slapton
Torcross
Stokenham
South Devon Heritage Coast
South West Coast Path
Hopes Nose
Sharkham Point
Scabbacombe Head
A38
A380
A381
A385
A384
A379
A3122
A3121
A383
Burrator Reservoir
Venford Reservoir
Sheepstor
Yealmpton
Noss Mayo
Holbeton
Aveton Gifford
Loddiswell
Harbertonford
Halwell
Blackawton
Stoke Fleming
Strete
Chillington
Frogmore
Malborough
Hope
Thurlestone
Marldon
Compton
Cockington
Ipplepen
Denbury
Staverton
Dean Prior
South Brent
Wrangaton
Bittaford
Ermington
Ugborough
Harford
Cornwood
Lee Mill
Sparkwell
Hemerdon
Galmpton
Churston Ferrers
Stoke Gabriel
Ashprington
Cornworthy
Dittisham
Berry Pomeroy
Littlehempston
Broadhempston
Woodland
Bickington
East Ogwell
Abbotskerswell
Coffinswell
Stokeinteignhead
Combeinteignhead
Bishopsteignton
Ideford
Luton
Holcombe
Chivelstone
East Prawle
South Pool
Beesands
Hallsands
Beeson
Kellaton
East Portlemouth
Soar
Rickham
Collaton
Bolberry
Galmpton
South Huish
South Milton
Bantham
West Alvington
Churchstow
Goveton
East Allington
Woodleigh
Moreleigh
Diptford
North Huish
Avonwick
Kingston
Ringmore
Mothecombe
Challaborough
Ashford
East Charleton
West Charleton
Sherford
Harleston
Blackpool
Warfleet
Bugford
Capton
Allaleigh
Washbourne
Tuckenhay
Harberton
Belsford
Tigley
Rattery
Lutton
Aish
Hillside
Harbourneford
Deancombe
Holne
Scorriton
Michelcombe
Poundsgate
Ponsworthy
Buckland in the Moor
Lower Town
Rew
Dartmeet
Huccaby
Babeny
Bellever
Cator Court
Southcott
Water
Hennock
Lower Gabwell
Higher Gabwell
Maidencombe
Watcombe
St Marychurch
Ellacombe
Babbacombe
Goodrington
Yalberton
Collaton St Mary
Longcombe
Blagdon
Westerland
Preston
Hollicombe
Waddeton
Woodhuish
Hillhead
Higher Brixham
Plymouth
Greenway
Paignton & Dartmouth Railway
South Devon Railway
Dartmouth Castle
Bayard's Cove Fort
Coleton Fishacre House
Overbeck's Museum & Garden
Kingsbridge Estuary
River Erme
River Avon
R Dart
R Teign
Hound Tor Medieval Village
Becky Falls
Ugbrooke Park
Stover
Bradley Manor
Hedgehog Hospital
Model Village
Berry Pomeroy Castle
Sharpham
Butterfly Farm
Hembury Castle
River Dart
Wistman's Wood
Merrivale
Clapper Bridge
Church House
Dartmoor Wildlife Park
Upper Plym Valley
Erme Mouth
Beacon Point
Stoke Point
Netton
Lighthouse
J K L M N P Q R
1 2 3 4 5 6 7 8 9 10 11 12

Morwenstow
Higher Sharpnose Point
South West Coast Path
Lower Sharpnose Point
Steeple Point
Sandy Mouth
Northcott Mouth
Bude Bay
Lynstone
Widemouth Bay
Millook
Dizzard Point
Dizzard
Poundstock
Penlean
Tregole
St Gennys
Crackington Haven
Cambeak
Coxford
Sweets
Rosecare
Wainhouse Corner
B3263
A39
Beeny
Marshgate
Witchcraft
Pentire Point - Widemouth Heritage Coast
Boscastle
Tresparrett
Treworld
Lesnewth
Trevalga
Otterham
Otterham Station
TINTAGEL HEAD
Castle
Tintagel
Trethevey
Bossiney
B3266
B3262
Old Post Office
Tregatta
Davidstow
Penhallic Point
Trewarmett
Treknow
Trewassa
Tremail
R Inny
British Cycling
B3314
Trebarwith
Penpethy
Rockhead
Treligga
Trefrew
Tregoodwell
Delabole
St Clether
South West Coast Path
Westdowns
Pengelly
Valley Truckle
Camelford
Crowdy Reservoir
Port Isaac Bay
Trewalder
Lanteglos
Pencarrow
Bowithick
Rumps Point
Port Quin Bay
Kelland Head
Varley Head
Helstone
Watergate
Port Gaverne
St Teath
Tresinney
Wesley's
Pentire Point
Port Quin
Port Isaac
Trewetha
Knightsmill
Padstow Bay
New Polzeath
Bee Centre
Long Cross
B3267
Treburgett
Treveighan
BROWN WILLY
Hayle Bay
Plain Street
Trelights
Pendoggett
Stepper Point
Polzeath
Treharrock
Michaelstow
BODMIN
Trebetherick
B3314
St Endellion
Trelill
Trenewth
Palmersbridge
Trevose Head Heritage Coast
Gunver Head
Trevanger
St Minver
Tregellist
Churchtown
TREVOSE HEAD
Mother Ivey's Bay
Pityme
St Tudy
Jamaica Inn
Crugmeer
Tredrizzick
Trequite
St Breward
Dinas Head
Trevose
Harlyn Bay
Prideaux Place
Rock
Splatt
Trewethern
St Kew
St Kew Highway
De Lank River
Trevone
Stoptide
Hendra
Lank
Row
Constantine Bay
Treator
Bradford
Harlyn
Padstow
Chapel Amble
Wenfordbridge
Windmill
Dinas
Constantine Bay
Towan
Treyarnon
St Merryn
Tregonce
Tregunna
Bodieve
St Mabyn
Penpont
Colliford Lake
Trehemborne
Shop
Edmonton
Trevanson
Blisland
Porthcothan
Trevorrick
St Issey
Wadebridge
Egloshayle
Waterloo
Temple
B3276
A389
Whitecross
Tredethy
Colliford Lake Park
Little Petherick
St Breock
Croanford
Hellandbridge
Park Head
Treburrick
Penrose
Trenance
Royal Cornwall
Treneague
Sladesbridge
Pencarrow
A30
Millpool
St Ervan
Rumford
Tredinnick
Burlawn
Colquite
Helland
Engollan
Hay
Washaway
Bedruthan Steps
Downhill
Trelow
St Jidgey
St Breock Downs Monolith
Polbrock
Lane End
Warleggan
Carnewas
St Eval
Crealy Great Adventure Park
Brocton
Camel Valley
Trenance
Nine Maidens
Dunmere
Cardinham
Mount
St Neot
Berryls Point
Mawgan Porth
B3274
Rutherbridge
Boscarne
Cooksland
Pantersbridge
Griffins Point
A39
Tregawne
Nanstallon
Fletchersbridge
Trevarrian
St Mawgan
Rosenannon
Withielgoose
St Lawrence
Bodmin
Tredinnick
Ley
Carglaze Caverns
Watergate Bay
Carloggas
Talskiddy
Tremore
Bodmin & Wenford Railway
A38
Doublebois
St Wenn
Withiel
Retire
Tregullon
Tregurrian
Newquay
Gluvian
Reterth
Demelza
Lamorick
Lanivet
West Taphouse
Middle Taphouse
Towan Head
Newquay Bay
St Columb Minor
A3059
St Columb Major
Tregonetha
Cutmadoc
Newquay
Porth
Tregaswith
Trevithick
Lanhydrock
Trebyan
A390
East Taphouse
Trebudannon
Belowda
Victoria
Higher Town
A391
Bokiddick
Sweetshouse
Braddock
West Pentire
Colan
Black Cross
Lockengate
Restormel Castle
Crantock
Trenowah
Bosoughan
Ruthvoes
Tregoss
Criggan
Bodwen
Boconnoc
Herod
Goss Moor
Roche
Carbis
Tredinnick
Penhale
Lostwithiel
Porfell Animal Land
miles
kilometres

Woolfardisworthy
Parkham
Monkleigh
Great Torrington
St Giles in the Wood
Bickington
Kingscott
Roborough
Burrington
Beaford
Little Torrington
Taddiport
Rosemoor
Frithelstock Stone
Buckland Brewer
Ashmansworthy
East Putford
West Putford
Welcombe
Darracott
Meddon
Woolley
East Youlstone
West Youlstone
Dinworthy
Gnome Reserve
Colscott
Haytown
Thornehillhead
Langtree
Southcott
Langtree Week
Great Potheridge
Little Potheridge
Berry Cross
Stibb Cross
Peters Marland
Winswell
Little Marland
Halsdon
Riddlecombe
Ashreigney
Dolton
Hollocombe
Merton
Huish
Bradworthy
Bulkworthy
Abbots Bickington
Kimworthy
Tamar Lakes
Alfardisworthy
Sutcombe
Sutcombemill
Kilkhampton
Stibb
Brocklands
Dinscott
Newton St Petrock
Venngreen
Milton Damerel
Thurdon
Soldon
Soldon Cross
North Town
Petrockstow
Dowland
Iddesleigh
Ingleigh Green
Barwick
Meeth
Ash
Shebbear
Thornbury
Buckland Filleigh
Woodacott
Bradford
Priestacott
Holsworthy Beacon
Dunsdon
Poughill
Flexbury
Bush
Hersham
Grimscott
Lana
Stratton
Launcells
Launcells Cross
Kingford
Pancrasweek
Chilsworthy
Brendon
Lashbrook
Dippermill
Sheepwash
R Torridge
Fishleigh
Cookbury
Cookbury Wick
Anvil Corner
Holemoor
Black Torrington
Monkokehampton
Broadwood Kelly
Splatt
Red Post
Buttsbear Cross
Derril
Derriton
Holsworthy
Hollacombe
Brandis Corner
Highampton
Hatherleigh
Marhamchurch
Whimble
Bridgerule
Pyworthy
Chasty
Headon
Odham
Chilla
Winsford Walled Garden
Jacobstowe
Honeychurch
Exbourne
Sampford Courtenay
Titson
Leworthy
R Claw
Buckhorn
Halwill
Halwill Junction
Whiddon
Crowden
Eastcott
Inwardleigh
Northlew
Oak Cross
Bangors
Kitleigh
Treskinnick Cross
Whitstone
Penhallam
Week St Mary
East Balsdon
North Tamerton
Clawton
Tetcott
Langaford
Stowford
Beaworthy
Patchacott
East Kimber
Ashbury
Folly Gate
Brightley
Chichacott
Cruft
Quoditch
Higher Prestacott
Ashmill
Nethercott
Ashwater
Brockscombe
Broadbury
Southcott
Maddaford
Okehampton
South Tawton
Sticklepath
Belstone
Finch Foundry
Castle
Dartmoor Railway
Trecott
Corscombe
Taw Green
Greena Moor
Luffincott
West Peeke
Henford
Bradaford
Eworthy
Germansweek
Boasley Cross
Thorndon Cross
Meldon
Meldon Reservoir
West Curry
Maxworthy
Clubworthy
Chapmans Well
Virginstow
Grinacombe Moor
Roadford Reservoir
Bratton Clovelly
South Wheatley
Bennacott
Troswell
Copthorne
Boyton
Northcott
East Panson
Frankaborough
Sitcott
Forda
Sourton
Lake
Black-a-Tor
Yes Tor
High Willhays
Cawsand Beacon
West Okement River
Billacott
Brazacott
Tamar Otter & Wildlife Centre
South Beer
West Panson
Langdon
Bridgetown
Warbstow
Trillacott
North Petherwin
Tremaine
Splatt
Petherwin Gate
Hellescott
Ladycross
Yeolmbridge
Crossgate
Downicarey
St Giles-on-the-Heath
Kellacott
Rexon
Broadwoodwidger
Ebsworthy
Bridestowe
Thrushelton
Stowford
Foxcombe
Lobhillcross
Lewdown
Lewtrenchard
Lydford
Lydford Gorge
Cross Green
River Ottery
Three Hammers
Tresmeer
Trebeath
Tregeare
Egloskerry
Werrington
Langore
Badgall
Badharlick
Truscott
St Stephens
Launceston
Newport
Dutson
Liftondown
Tinhay
Lifton
Portgate
Dippertown
Great Kneeset
Whitehorse Hill
Dartmoor Forest
Hidden Valley
Laneast
Pipers Pool
Tregadillett
Trethorne Leisure Farm
Trewen
Trebullett
Tregunnon
Kennards House
Daw's House
South Petherwin
Lawhitton
Marystow
Coryton
Beardon
Liddaton Green
Polyphant
Tredaule
Trelinnoe
Trecogo
Hexworthy
Meadwell
Kelly
Chillaton
Sittaford Tor
Willsworthy
Fivelanes
Lewannick
Bradstone
Milton Abbot
North Brentor
Blackdown
Mary Tavy
Horndon
Lynch Tor
Postbridge
Plusha
Trevadlock
Landue
Dunterton
Chaddlehanger
Lamerton
Cudliptown
Cocks Hill
Congdon's Shop
Illand
Newtown
Lower Trebullett
Lezant
Trekenner
Penrest
Rezare
Godsworthy
Peter Tavy
Great Mis Tor
Wistman's Wood
Trebartha
Coad's Green
Lanoy
Treburley
Bealsmill
Portontown
Rushford
Cox Tor
Merrivale
Two Bridges
North Hill
Middlewood
Kingston
Tutwell
Sydenham Damerel
Bathpool
Bray Shop
Venterdon
Horsebridge
Townlake
Tavistock
Moortown
Princetown
Smallacombe Downs
Rillaton
Stoke Climsland
Oldmill
Middlemoore
Sampford Spiney
Henwood
Sharptor
Cheesewring
Upton
Rilla Mill
Plushabridge
Linkinhorne
Luckett
Downgate
Latchley
Chilsworthy
Gulworthy
Whitchurch
Grenofen
Royal Hill
Whiteworks
Siblyback
The Hurlers Stone Circle
Upton Cross
Caradon Town
Sterts Open-Air Theatre
Minions
South Hill
Trewoodloe
Mornick
Kelly Bray
Kit Hill
Coxpark
St Ann's Chapel
Gunnislake
Drakewalls
Morwellham Quay
Caradon Mining District
Downgate
Pensilva
Golberdon
Haye
Harrowbarrow
Norris Green
Albaston
Horrabridge
Walkhampton
Common Moor
Darite
Crow's Nest
Trevigro
Callington
Dupath Well
Metherell
Calstock
The Garden House
Burrator Reservoir
Dousland
Yelverton
Sheepstor
Golitha
King Doniert's Stone
Trethevy Quoit
Middlehill
Tremar
Charaton
Gang
Frogwell
St Dominick
Cotehele
Calstock Viaduct
Buckland Monachorum
Buckland Abbey
Crapstone
Meavy
St Cleer
Merrymeet
St Ive
St Ive Cross
Cadson Bury
Burraton
Bohetherick
Tamar Valley Mining District
Bere Alston
Milton Combe
Hoo Meavy
Upper Plym Valley
Clearbrook
Briseworthy
Trembraze
Dobwalls
Newton Ferrers
Bealbury
St Mellion
Halton Quay
Cotts
Sowton
Goodameavy
Liskeard
Pengover Green
Quethiock
Pillaton
Weir Quay
Maristow
Dewerstone
Shell Top
Moorswater
Trevelmond
Lamellion
Trehunist
Trewint
Pillatonmill
Cargreen
Bere Ferrers
Shaugh Prior
Bickleigh
Pinnock
Moorswater
Menheniot
Blunts
Cuttivett
Hatt
Landulph
Tamerton Foliot
Roborough
Wotter
Lee Moor
Paul Corin Music
Doddy Cross
Tideford Cross
Botusfleming
Plymouth
St Keyne
Horningtops
Cutmere
Tideford
Notter
Carkeel
Saltash
Landrake
Budge's
Boringdon
Dartmoor
Lutton
A386
A388
A3072
A3124
B3227
B3217
B3216
A3079
A30
B3260
B3215
A395
B3254
B3257
B3362
A390
B3357
B3212
B3257
A38
B3252
B3251
B3373
B3432

Chittlehamholt
High Bickington
Kings Nympton
Romansleigh
Rose Ash
Oakford
Dolton
St Giles in the Wood
Kingscott
Roborough
Burrington
Beaford
Riddlecombe
Ashreigney
Chulmleigh
Cheldon
Chawleigh
Worlington
Witheridge
Nomansland
Washford Pyne
Edgeworthy
Templeton
Calverleigh
Withleigh
Tiverton
Stoodleigh
Loxbeare
Washfield
Creacombe
Rackenford
Merton
Huish
Hollocombe
Ashley
Eggesford
Dowland
Wembworthy
Nymet Rowland
Lapford
Eastington
Morchard Bishop
Black Dog
Woolfardisworthy
Pennymoor
Puddington
Way Village
Poughill
Upham
Butterleigh
Cadeleigh
Bickleigh
Iddesleigh
Ingleigh Green
Winkleigh
Brushford
Coldridge
Kennerleigh
Stockleigh English
East Village
Cheriton Fitzpaine
Meeth
Monkokehampton
Hatherleigh
Broadwood Kelly
Bondleigh
Zeal Monachorum
Down St Mary
Copplestone
Newbuildings
Sandford
Upton Hellions
Stockleigh Pomeroy
Cadbury
Thorverton
Splatt
Honeychurch
Exbourne
Jacobstowe
Sampford Courtenay
North Tawton
Bow
Coleford
Knowle
Colebrooke
Nymet Tracey
Crediton
Shobrooke
Yeoford
Sweetham
Brampford Speke
Rewe
Stoke Canon
Upton Pyne
Inwardleigh
Oak Cross
Folly Gate
Brightley
Taw Green
Spreyton
Hittisleigh
Cheriton Bishop
Tedburn St Mary
Whitestone
Newton St Cyres
Cowley
Okehampton
South Tawton
Sticklepath
South Zeal
Belstone
Whiddon Down
Crockernwell
Drewsteignton
Longdown
EXETER
Meldon
Meldon Reservoir
Sourton
Gooseford
Throwleigh
Sandy Park
Murchington
Chagford
Easton
Dunsford
Shillingford Abbot
Shillingford St George
Dunchideock
Exminster
Topsham
Kennford
Doddiscombsleigh
Moretonhampstead
Doccombe
Bridford
Christow
North Bovey
Lustleigh
Manaton
Trusham
Harcombe
Hennock
Bovey Tracey
Chudleigh
Chudleigh Knighton
DARTMOOR
DARTMOOR NATIONAL PARK
FOREST
Postbridge
Widecombe in the Moor
Haytor Vale
Ilsington
Liverton
Kingsteignton
Teignmouth
Newton Abbot
Kingskerswell
Princetown
Two Bridges
Hexworthy
Poundsgate
Buckland in the Moor
Ashburton
Buckfastleigh
Staverton
Dartington
Totnes
Berry Pomeroy
Marldon
Compton
Paignton
TORQUAY
Babbacombe Bay
Walkhampton
Yelverton
Sheepstor
Dousland
Harbourneford
Dean Prior
Rattery
Blagdon
Shaldon
Combeinteignhead
Stokeinteignhead
Maidencombe
Ideford
Luton
Bishopsteignton
Powderham
Kenton
Cofton
Ashcombe

Wellington
Cullompton
Honiton
Ilminster
Chard
Axminster
Ottery St Mary
Sidmouth
Seaton
Lyme Regis
Exmouth
Budleigh Salterton
BLACKDOWN HILLS
Lyme Bay
Jurassic Coast World Heritage Site
East Devon Heritage Coast
South West Coast Path
Ladram Bay
Dawlish Warren
Exeter
Uplyme
Charmouth
Beer
Branscombe
Colyton
Axmouth
Sidbury
Feniton
Whimple
Broadclyst
Woodbury
East Budleigh
Otterton
Lympstone
Dunkeswell
Hemyock
Culmstock
Uffculme
Sampford Peverell
Willand
Bradninch
Kentisbeare
Payhembury
Stockland
Kilmington
Musbury
Membury
Chardstock
Tatworth
Winsham
Thorncombe
Broadhembury
Upottery
Yarcombe
Exeter Central Station
Rougemont Castle
Exeter Cathedral
Guildhall
Bonhay Road
Western Way
New North Road
A30
A303
A35
A3052
A375
A358
A373
M5

Lyme Regis
Bridport
Chard
Ilminster
Crewkerne
Martock
Yeovil
Sherborne
Dorchester
Weymouth
Fortuneswell
Beaminster
Charmouth
Uplyme
Axminster
Abbotsbury
Portesham
Chickerell
Puncknowle
Burton Bradstock
West Bay
Seatown
Eype
Chideock
Symondsbury
Netherbury
Broadwindsor
Misterton
Maiden Newton
Cerne Abbas
Frampton
Charminster
Poundbury
Martinstown
Winterbourne Abbas
Winterborne Came
Preston
Osmington
Poxwell
Wyke Regis
Portland Harbour
Easton
Southwell
PORTLAND
PORTLAND BILL
Portland Bill Lighthouse
Portland Museum & Shipwreck Centre
Portland Castle
Chesil Beach
LYME BAY
Weymouth Bay
Jurassic Coast World Heritage Site
South West Coast Path
Swannery
Abbey Remains
Chapel
Maiden Castle
Hardy Monument
Valley of Stones
Nine Stones
Kingston Russell
Hog Cliff
The Giant
Mapperton
Forde Abbey
Pilsdon Pen
Barrington Court
Montacute House
Tintinhull Garden
Treasurer's House
Hurst Priory
Old Castle
Castle
White Horse
Jordan Hill
Deep Sea Adventure
Nothe Fort
Water Gardens
Chesil Bank & The Fleet
Kingston Maurward
Yetminster
Evershot
Stoford
Bradford Abbas
Barwick
Montacute
Stoke sub Hamdon
Norton sub Hamdon
South Petherton
Shepton Beauchamp
Whitelackington
Dowlish Wake
Hinton St George
Merriott
Haselbury Plucknett
North Perrott
South Perrott
Mosterton
Drimpton
Thorncombe
Hawkchurch
Marshwood
Whitchurch Canonicorum
Morcombelake
Catherston Leweston
Wootton Fitzpaine
Monkton Wyld
Loders
Uploders
Askerswell
Powerstock
Litton Cheney
Long Bredy
Littlebredy
Langton Herring
Fleet
Charlestown
Upwey
Broadwey
Sutton Poyntz
Bincombe
Broadmayne
Whitcombe
Stinsford
Puddletown
Godmanstone
Sydling St Nicholas
Frome St Quintin
Chetnole
Leigh
Holnest
Longburton
Folke
Thornford
Beer Hackett
Holwell
A35
A37
A30
A303
A354
A352
A356
A3066
A358
A3088
A3052
A353
B3157
B3159
B3162
B3163
B3164
B3165
B3143
B3146
B3148
B3150
B3155
B3156
B3167
B3168
B3030
21
22
0 1 2 3 4 5 miles
0 1 2 3 4 5 6 7 8 kilometres
A
B
C
D
E
F
G
H

Fifehead Magdalen
Stour Provost
Todber
Guy's Marsh
Cann
West Melbury
Melbury Abbas
St John
Cobley
Martin Drove End
East Martin
Whitsbury
Woodfalls
Marnhull
Moorside
Margaret Marsh
Hartgrove
Compton Abbas
Fontmell & Melbury Downs
Tollard Royal
New Town
Dean End
Deanland
Woodyates
Martin
Tidpit
Rockbourne
Upper Street
North Street
Breamore
Walton Elm
East Orchard
Woodbridge
Ashmore
Fontmell Down
Bedchester
West Orchard
Fontmell Magna
Cranborne Chase
Woodcutts
Tollard Farnham
Sixpenny Handley
Pentridge
North End
Outwick
Hinton St Mary
Manston
Sutton Waldron
Dean
Farnham
Boveridge
Damerham
Lower Burgate
Upper Burgate
Sturminster Newton
Bagber
Hammoon
Fontmell Parva
Iwerne Minster
Stubhampton
New Town
Minchington
Chettle
Gussage St Andrew
Cashmoor
Monkton Up Wimborne
Cranborne
Bellows Cross
South End
Sandleheath
Fordingbridge
Manor
Gold Hill
Tarrant Gunville
Stuckton
Bisslford
Frogham
Rivers Corner
Fiddleford
Child Okeford
Hambledon Hill
Iwerne Courtney or Shroton
Gussage St Michael
Wimborne St Giles
Alderholt
Bickton
Hyde
Hungerford
Fifehead Neville
Sturminster Common
Okeford Fitzpaine
Little Hanford
Hanford
Tarrant Hinton
Cripplestyle
Church & Earthworks
Edmondsham
Dorset Heavy Horse Centre
Harbridge Green
North Gorley
South Gorley
Fifehead St Quintin
Belchalwell
Shillingstone
Hod Hill
Ash
Stourpaine
Pimperne
Tarrant Launceston
Long Crichel
Gussage All Saints
Knowlton
Romford
Verwood
Harbridge
Ibsley
Ibsley Common
Belchalwell Street
Durweston
Tarrant Monkton
Moor Crichel
Woodlands
Whitmore
Mockbeggar
Rockford
Droop
Ibberton
Turnworth
Royal Signals
Manswood
Horton
Ellingham
Rock
Woolland
Bryanston
Blandford Camp
Tarrant Rawston
New Town
Chalbury
Chalbury Common
Crab Orchard
Blashford
North Poulner
Linford
Stoke Wake
Bulbarrow Hill
Blandford Forum
Witchampton
Uppington
Mannington
Three Legged Cross
Ringwood
Poulner
Shobley
Winterborne Houghton
Blandford St Mary
Langton Long Blandford
Tarrant Rushton
Hinton Martell
Gaunt's Common
Holt Heath
Lower Mannington
Moors Valley
Ashley Heath
Hightown
Liberty's Raptor & Reptile Centre
Ansty
Ansty Cross
Winterborne Stickland
Charlton on the Hill
Charlton Marshall
Tarrant Keyneston
Stanbridge
St Leonards
St Ives
Ashley
Crow
Hilton
Winterborne Clenston
Tarrant Crawford
Badbury Rings
Holt
Pig Oak
West Moors
Moortown
North Kingston
Milton
Thornicombe
Honeybrook
Clapgate
Broom Hill
Avon Heath
Kingston
Sandford
Bingham's Melcombe
Milton Abbas
Higher Whatcombe
Spetisbury
Kingston Lacy
Abbott Street
Hillbutts
Furzehill
Merry Field Hill
Pilford
Colehill
Ferndown
Foxbury Hill
Bisterne
Lower Whatcombe
Shapwick
Sturminster Marshall
Pamphill
Canford Bottom
Stapehill
Trickett's Cross
North Ripley
Bingham
Winterborne Whitechurch
Almer
Wimborne Minster
Leigh Park
Hampreston
Knoll
Dewlish
Lower Street
Winterborne Kingston
Winterborne Tomson
Winterborne Zelston
Ashington
Oakley
Longham
Dudsbury
East Parley
Bournemouth
Avon
Ripley
Milborne St Andrew
Sleight
Combe Almer
Merley
Canford Magna
Knighton
West Parley
Parley Green
Hurn
Sopley
Bockhampton
Anderson
Corfe Mullen
Bearwood
West Howe
Kinson
Red Hill
Adventure Wonderland
Mid Bockhampton
Winkton
Athelhampton
Tolpuddle
Bere Regis
Newport
West Morden
Morden
Lychett Matravers
Broadstone
Upton Heath
Cudnell
Ensbury
East Howe
Throop
South Bockhampton
Burton
Burleston
Affpuddle
Turners Puddle
Bloxworth
East Morden
East Bloxworth
Post Green
Waterloo
Canford Heath
Moordown
Winton
Iford
Somerford
Christchurch
Briantspuddle
Throop
Sherford
Slepe
Upton
Newtown
Wallisdown
Talbot Village
Castle
Tincleton
Pallington
Morden Bog
Organford
Lytchett Minster
Branksome
Pokesdown
Tuckton
Wick
Boscombe
Southbourne
Clouds Hill
Hurst
River Piddle or River Trent
River Frome
Hamworthy
Lake
Parkstone
Westbourne
Branksome Park
Lilliput
Bournemouth
Bovington Camp
Holton Heath
Lower Hamworthy
Poole
Canford Cliffs
Moreton
Crossways
Tank
Monkey World
Bovington
Sandford
Northport
Arne
Poole Harbour
RSPB
Brownsea Island
Sandbanks
East Burton
Stokeford
Binnegar
Worgret
Wareham
Poole Bay
Owermoigne
Giddy Green
Wool
Bindon
East Stoke
Stoborough
Ridge
Toll
East Knighton
West Holme
East Holme
Stoborough Green
Stoborough Heath
Purbeck Heritage Coast
(Apr-Oct)
Winfrith Newburgh
Coombe Keynes
Creech
Hartland Moor
Studland Bay
Blue Pool
East Creech
P+R
Isle of Purbeck
The Foreland
West Chaldon
East Chaldon (Chaldon Herring)
East Lulworth
Studland
Cherbourg Guernsey Jersey St-Malo (May-Sept)
Chaldon Down
Lulworth Camp
Lulworth Castle
Corfe Castle
Swanage Railway
Church Knowle
Harman's Cross
Ulwell
Ballard Point
West Lulworth
Bindon Hill
Purbeck Hills
Tyneham Village
Steeple
Swanage Bay
Lulworth Cove
Durdle Door
Worbarrow Bay
Kingston
Swanage
Kimmeridge
Herston
Kimmeridge Bay
South West Coast Path
Acton
Langton Matravers
Durlston
Jurassic Coast World Heritage Site
Chapman's Pool
Worth Matravers
Anvil Point
Durlston Head
St Aldhelm's or St Alban's Head
Guernsey Jersey St-Malo
A350
A354
A357
A31
A35
A338
A348
A341
A347
A3049
A3060
A351
A352
B3081
B3078
B3072
B3073
B3074
B3075
B3082
B3068
B3369
B3065
B3061
B3070
B3071
B3351
B3069
B3390
B3347
B3091
B3092
23
12
J K L M N P Q R
1 2 3 4 5 6 7 8 9 10 11 12

WHITSBURY DOWN
BREAMORE DOWN
East Martin
Whitsbury
Upper Street
Rockbourne
North End
Damerham
South End
Outwick
Lower Burgate
Upper Burgate
Fordingbridge
Sandleheath
Alderholt
Stuckton
Bickton
Godshill
Blissford
Frogham
Hungerford
Fritham
Woodfalls
Morgan's Vale
Redlynch
Langley Wood
Lover
Hale
North Charford
Hamptworth
Landford
Nomansland
Woodgreen
Breamore
Wick
North Street
Ditford
West Wellow
East Wellow
Canada
Furzley
Wigley
Bramshaw
Newbridge
Brook Hill
Brook
Upper Canterton
Cadnam
Stoney Cross
Ower
Stonyford
Copythorne
Winsor
Woodlands
Minstead
Newtown
Netley Marsh
Totton
Eling
Ashurst
Foxhills
Lyndhurst
Emery Down
Bank
Clayhill
NEW FOREST
NATIONAL PARK
Beaulieu River
Beaulieu Road Station
North Baddesley
Chandler's Ford
Chilworth
Toothill
Lee
Upton
Rownhams
Nursling
Hillstreet
Calmore
Testwood
Millbrook
Shirley
Portswood
Bassett
Swaythling
EASTLEIGH
West End
Bitterne
Thornhill
Hedge End
SOUTHAMPTON
Marchwood
Woolston
Sholing
Bursledon
Lower Swanwick
Netley
Dibden
Dibden Purlieu
Langdown
Hythe
Southampton Water
Hamble-le-Rice
Sarisbury
Park Gate
Locks Heath
Warsash
Royal Victoria
Buttsash
Hardley
Fawley
Holbury
Ashlett
Calshot Castle
Calshot
Blackfield
Otterwood
Langley
Stanswood Bay
Hill Top
Beaulieu
National Motor Museum
Hatchet Gate
Bucklers Hard
North Solent
Exbury
Lower Exbury
East Boldre
Lepe
Needs Ore Point
Romford
Verwood
Harbridge
Harbridge Green
Ibsley
North Gorley
South Gorley
Mockbeggar
Linwood
Rockford
Rockford Common
Ellingham
Blashford
North Poulner
Linford
Poulner
Shobley
Picket Post
Three Legged Cross
Ringwood
Ashley Heath
St Leonards
St Ives
Ashley
Hightown
Burley Street
Crow
Moortown
Kingston
North Kingston
Burley Lawn
Burley
MARKWAY HILL
Rhinefield Ornamental Drive
Brockenhurst
Balmerlawn
Setley
Sandford
Bisterne
North Ripley
Ripley
Thorney Hill
FOXBURY HILL
Tricketts Cross
Avon Heath
Avon
Bransgore
North Bockhampton
Neacroft
Godwinscroft
Hurn
Sopley
Mid Bockhampton
Winkton
South Bockhampton
Burton
Hinton Admiral
Hinton
Bashley
Beckley
Wootton
Tiptoe
Sway
Battramsley Cross
Boldre
Pilley Bailey
Pilley
Portmore
Buckland
Norleywood
South Baddesley
East End
Walhampton
Lymington
Woodside
Upper Pennington
Pennington
Everton
Lower Pennington
Keyhaven
New Milton
Ashley
Hordle
Downton
Barton-on-Sea
Milford on Sea
Hurst Castle
Highcliffe
Walkford
Somerford
Christchurch
Mudeford
Christchurch Bay
HENGISTBURY HEAD
Tuckton
Wick
Southbourne
Boscombe
Pokesdown
Iford
BOURNEMOUTH
West Parley
Parley Green
East Parley
Throop
Moordown
Winton
Ensbury
Red Hill
Dudsbury
POOLE BAY
THE SOLENT
Cowes
Gurnard Bay
Gurnard
Rew Street
Thorness Bay
Hillis Corner
Northwood
Hamstead Heritage Coast
Newtown Bay
Porchfield
Newtown
Mark's Corner
Hamstead
Cranmore
Old Town Hall
Locksgreen
Forest Side
Sconce Point
Yarmouth
Bouldnor
Thorley
Ningwood
Shalfleet
Carisbrooke
Colwell Bay
Norton
Totland
Totland Bay
Norton Green
Thorley Street
Wellow
Newbridge
Freshwater
Afton
Watermill
Chessell Pottery
Calbourne
Bowcombe
Blackwater
BRIGHSTONE DOWN
Rowborough
Alum Bay
Dimbola Lodge
Freshwater Bay
Afton, Compton & Brook Downs
Shalcombe
Hulverstone
Gatcombe
Chillerton
THE NEEDLES
Needles Old Battery
West Wight
Compton Bay
Brook
Hanover Point
Manor Garden
Mottistone
Mortown
Limerstone
Cheverton
Shorwell
Rookley Green
Tennyson Heritage Coast
Brighstone
Yafford
Kingston
Chilton Chine
Thorncross
Brighstone Bay
Little Atherfield
Chale Green
Atherfield Green
Atherfield Point
St Catherine's Down
St Catherine's Oratory
Whale Chine
Chale
Bierley
Niton
Blackgang Chine
Blackgang
Rocken End
ST CATHERINE'S POINT
St Catherine's Lighthouse
ISLE OF WIGHT
Channel Islands
ALDERNEY
St Anne
St Peter Port
HERM
SARK
GUERNSEY
JERSEY
St Helier
FRANCE
Guernsey
L'Ancresse Bay
Fort le Marchant
Grande Havre
L'Ancresse
La Fontenelle
Déhus Dolmen
Rousse Tower
La Passee
Vale
La Greve
Clos du Valle
Bordeaux
Islet Village
Grandes Rocques
Saline Bay
Pleinheaume
St Sampson
Cobo Bay
Fort Hommet
Saumarez Park Folk
Capelles
Les Quartiers
Belle Greve Bay
Vazon Bay
Cobo
La Rousaillerie
Le Villocq
St Peter Port
Poole
Weymouth
Richmond Fort
Perelle Bay
Perelle
Vazon Bay
Castel
Lihou Island
L'Erée
Mont Saint
King's Mills
Castle Cornet
Havelet Bay
Jersey Portsmouth
Rocquaine Bay
La Houguette
St Saviour Reservoir
St Saviour
Les Lohiers
Four Cabots
St Andrew
Guernsey Aquarium
Fort Grey Shipwreck Museum
Les Arquêts
Le Gron
German Underground Hospital
Les Hubits
Les Terres Point
St Martin
Les Sages
St Peter's
Villiaze
Moulpied
Sausmarez Manor
Village de Putron
Fermain Bay
Pleinmont Point
Le Bourg
Bellieuse
Jersey St-Malo
Torteval
Les Murchez
Forest
Les Nicolles
La Villette
La Fosse
Le Bigard
German Occupation Museum
Les Villets
Petit Bot Bay
Moulin Huet Bay
Jerbourg
St Martins Point
Point de la Moye
Icart Point
2 miles
2 kilometres
5 miles
8 kilometres

Upham
Exton
Corhampton
Coombe
Meonstoke
Bishop's Waltham
Droxford
Brockbridge
Chidden
Clanfield
Buriton
South Harting
East Harting
Didling
Treyford
Bepton
Cocking
Midhurst
Heyshott
Graffham
East Lavington
Duncton
Upwaltham
Hambledon
Catherington
Horndean
Blendworth
Chalton
Compton
West Marden
North Marden
East Marden
Up Marden
Chilgrove
Singleton
West Dean
Charlton
East Dean
Swanmore
Soberton
Shirrell Heath
Waltham Chase
Curdridge
Shedfield
Wickham
Newtown
Hoe Gate
Denmead
Anmore
Worlds End
Soake
Cowplain
Lovedean
Rowland's Castle
Forestside
Deanlane End
Lordington
Stoughton
Bow Hill
Walterton
Woodend
West Stoke
Funtington
Aldsworth
Waterlooville
Southwick
North Boarhunt
Purbrook
Stakes
Widley
Havant
Westbourne
Woodmancote
West Ashling
East Ashling
Lavant
Mid Lavant
East Lavant
Waterbeach
Strettington
Westerton
Halnaker
Boxgrove
Tangmere
Aldingbourne
Eartham
Fontwell
M27
Fareham
Portchester
Wallington
Boarhunt
Funtley
Knowle Village
Titchfield
Titchfield Common
Catisfield
Cosham
Drayton
Bedhampton
Farlington
Hermitage
Brockhampton
Langstone
Emsworth
Southbourne
Hambrook
Prinsted
Nutbourne
Chidham
Bosham
Bosham Hoe
Broadbridge
Walton
Fishbourne
Dell Quay
Chichester
Shopwyke
Westhampnett
Oving
Westergate
Woodgate
Merston
Colworth
Runcton
North Mundham
South Mundham
Apuldram
Donnington
Hunston
Portsmouth Harbour
Port Solent
Hilsea
Whale Island
Stubbington
Hill Head
Peel Common
Bridgemary
Elson
Rowner
Hardway
Gosport
Lee-on-the-Solent
Alverstoke
Stokes Bay
Southsea
Portsea
Fratton
Eastney
North End
Langstone Harbour
North Hayling
Stoke
Northney
Tye
Hayling Island
West Town
South Hayling
Hayling Bay
Thorney Island
West Thorney
Chichester Harbour
West Itchenor
Birdham
Shipton Green
Somerley
Sidlesham
Sidlesham Common
Street End
Fisher
West Wittering
East Wittering
Bracklesham
Earnley
Almodington
Highleigh
Pagham Harbour
Pagham
Church Norton
Selsey
Selsey Bill
Bracklesham Bay
Portsmouth
Gilkicker Point
Cowes
Osborne Bay
Spithead
Wootton Bridge
Fishbourne
Ryde
Puckpool Point
Nettlestone Point
Seaview
Nettlestone
St Helens
Binstead
Quarr Hill
Havenstreet
Little Whitefield
East Ashey
Bembridge
Foreland
Brading
Yarbridge
Alverstone
Morton
Queen's Bower
Yaverland
Culver Cliff
Whitecliff Bay
Newchurch
Branstone
Winford
Sandown
Sandown Bay
Apse Heath
Sandford
Whiteley Bank
Shanklin
Wroxall
Luccombe Village
Luccombe Chine
Dunnose
Bonchurch
Ventnor
Steephill
St Lawrence
The Undercliff
Cherbourg
Guernsey
Jersey
St-Malo
Caen (Ouistreham)
Bilbao (Mar-Nov)
Le Havre
Santander
Caen (Ouistreham)
Le Havre (Mar-Sept)
(Mar-Oct)
Port of Southampton
Southampton Central Station
Western Esp
City Cruise Terminal
Dock Gate 8
Dock Gate 10
Red Funnel Terminal
Terminal 2
Ocean Cruise Terminal
Ocean Village
National Oceanography Centre (Southampton)
Itchen Bridge
River Itchen
500 m
Jersey
Grosnez Point
Plemont Point
Plemont
Sorel Point
Ronez Point
St John's Bay
Fremont Point
Belle Hougue Point
La Colombière
Vicard Point
Bouley Bay
Nez du Guet
Rozel Bay
Rozel
La Coupe Point
Fliquet Bay
Verclut Point
St Catherine's Bay
Archirondel
Faldouet
Mont Orgueil
Gorey
Royal Bay of Grouville
Grouville
La Rocque
La Rocque Point
Plat Rocque Point
St Clement's Bay
Le Bourg
Pontac
Le Hocq
Le Haguais
Le Croc
St Clement
Samarès Manor
Longueville
St Saviour
St Helier
St Aubin's Bay
St Aubin
Beaumont
Millbrook
Belcroute Bay
Noirmont Point
Portelet Bay
Point La Fret
St Brelade's Bay
St Brelade
Corbière
Corbière Point
La Pulente
Point La Moye
Les Quennevais
St Ouen's Bay
St Peter
St Ouen
L'Etacq
Millais
Ville la Bas
Portinfer
La Grève de Lecq
Rouge Nez
St Mary
Six Rues
Carrefour
St Lawrence
Trois Bois
St John
Hautes Croix
Trinity
Bellozanne Valley
Vallée des Vaux
Bécquet Vincent
Grand Chemins
Maufant
La Hougue Bie
Queen's Valley Reservoir
Five Oaks
St Martin
Swiss Valley
St Peter's Valley
Mourier Valley
Grève de Lecq Valley
Handois Reservoir
Poole
Weymouth via Guernsey
St-Malo
2 miles
2 kilometres

32
25
13
Aldershot
Farnham
GUILDFORD
Dorking
Shalford
Godalming
Haslemere
Liphook
Whitehill & Bordon
Cranleigh
Billingshurst
Southwater
Midhurst
Petworth
Pulborough
West Chiltington
Storrington
Steyning
Arundel
Chichester
Southbourne
Littlehampton
Rustington
Angmering
East Preston
Ferring
Lancing
WORTHING
Sompting
Middleton-on-Sea
BOGNOR REGIS
Selsey
SELSEY BILL
SOUTH DOWNS NATIONAL PARK
A
B
C
D
E
F
G
H
0 1 2 3 4 5 miles
0 1 2 3 4 5 6 7 8 kilometres

Redhill
Reigate
Salfords
Horley
Gatwick
Lowfield Heath
Copthorne
Crawley Down
CRAWLEY
Three Bridges
Maidenbower
Tilgate
Pease Pottage
St Leonards Forest
Handcross
Staplefield
Slaugham
Widening in progress
Warninglid
Bolney
Cuckfield
Haywards Heath
Lindfield
Ardingly
Ardingly Reservoir
Horsted Keynes
Danehill
West Hoathly
Sharpthorne
Highbrook
Birchgrove
Balcombe
Wivelsfield
Burgess Hill
Hurstpierpoint
Keymer
Ditchling
Hassocks
Clayton
Pyecombe
Poynings
Pangdean
Saddlescombe
Fulking
Devil's Dyke
Patcham
Withdean
Hollingbury
Hangleton
Portslade
Southwick
Portslade-by-Sea
HOVE
BRIGHTON
Rottingdean
Ovingdean
Woodingdean
Kemp Town
Moulsecoomb
Bevendean
Falmer
Stanmer
Lewes
Kingston near Lewes
Iford
Rodmell
Southease
Telscombe
Telscombe Cliffs
Peacehaven
Piddinghoe
Newhaven
South Heighton
Tarring Neville
Denton
Bishopstone
Norton
East Blatchington
Seaford
Seaford Bay
Seaford Head
Dieppe
Beddingham
Glynde
Glyndebourne
Ringmer
Firle
Firle Beacon
Charleston Farmhouse
Selmeston
Alciston
Berwick
Alfriston
Litlington
Lullington
Wilmington
Long Man of Wilmington
Folkington
Jevington
Westdean
Friston
Exceat
Seven Sisters
East Dean
Birling Gap
Beachy Head
Sussex Heritage Coast
Beachy Head Countryside Centre
EASTBOURNE
Polegate
Willingdon
Hampden Park
Langney
Westham
Pevensey Levels
Hailsham
Hellingly
Horsebridge
Herstmonceux Castle & Observatory
Magham Down
Heathfield
Horam
Cross in Hand
Waldron
Blackboys
Framfield
Uckfield
Buxted
Maresfield
Nutley
Fairwarp
Crowborough
Ashdown Forest
Forest Row
East Grinstead
Felbridge
Lingfield
Dormansland
Edenbridge
Hever
Chiddingstone
Penshurst
Tonbridge
Southborough
TUNBRIDGE WELLS
Groombridge
Frant
Mayfield
Rotherfield
Wadhurst
Hildenborough
Newhaven
SOUTH DOWNS NATIONAL PARK
South Downs Way
Offham
Hamsey
Barcombe
Chailey
North Chailey
Newick
Fletching
Piltdown
Sheffield Park
Isfield
Laughton
Chiddingly
East Hoathly
Halland
Bentley Wildfowl & Motor Museum
Plumpton
Westmeston
Lavender Line
Bluebell Railway
Spa Valley Railway
Weir Wood Reservoir
M23
A23
A22
A26
A27
A264
A272
A259
A275
A267
A21

34
15
Tonbridge
Tunbridge Wells
Pembury
Paddock Wood
Hadlow
East Peckham
Coxheath
Marden
Staplehurst
Headcorn
Ashford
Cranbrook
Tenterden
Hawkhurst
Wadhurst
Goudhurst
Lamberhurst
Rolvenden
Newenden
Sandhurst
Benenden
Biddenden
Sissinghurst
Frittenden
Smarden
Bethersden
Woodchurch
Kenardington
Appledore
Warehorne
Hamstreet
Snargate
Brookland
Rye
Rye Harbour
Camber
East Guldeford
Playden
Iden
Peasmarsh
Beckley
Northiam
Bodiam
Ewhurst Green
Salehurst
Robertsbridge
Etchingham
Hurst Green
Ticehurst
Stonegate
Burwash
Burwash Common
Burwash Weald
Mayfield
Heathfield
Punnett's Town
Dallington
Netherfield
Mountfield
Battle
Sedlescombe
Westfield
Three Oaks
Guestling Green
Pett
Fairlight
Cliff End
Winchelsea
Winchelsea Beach
Icklesham
Udimore
Brede
Broad Oak
Ore
St Helens
Hastings
St Leonards
Bulverhythe
Bexhill
Sidley
Little Common
Cooden
Ninfield
Catsfield
Crowhurst
Hooe
Herstmonceux
Windmill Hill
Boreham Street
Wartling
Hailsham
Pevensey Levels
Pevensey
Westham
Pevensey Bay
Norman's Bay
Stone Cross
Langney
Langney Point
Eastbourne
Beachy Head
Beachy Head Countryside Centre
Rye Bay
Walland Marsh
Isle of Oxney
Wittersham
Stone in Oxney
Royal Military Canal
Rother Levels
River Rother
River Brede
River Tillingham
Kent Ditch
River Limden
River Dudwell
River Teise
River Beult
River Medway
Bewl Water
Darwell Reservoir
Bedgebury Pinetum
National Pinetum & Garden
Scotney Castle
Bayham Old Abbey
Owl House
Marle Place
Sissinghurst Castle Garden
Bodiam Castle
Great Dixter
Bateman's
Pashley Manor
Merriments
Kent & East Sussex Railway
Historic Vehicles Collection
Tenterden Vineyard Park
Smallhythe Place
Camber Castle
Castle Water
Rye Harbour
Herstmonceux Castle & Observatory
The Truggery
Pevensey Castle
Union Mill
Iden Croft Herbs
Godinton House
South of England Rare Breeds Centre
Sutton Valence Castle
Hop Farm
Finchcocks
North Downs Way
Sandway
Lenham
Charing
Chilmington Green
Kingsnorth
Great Chart
Shadoxhurst
Orlestone
Ulcombe
Sutton Valence
Chart Sutton
Boughton Monchelsea
Linton
Laddingford
Yalding
Mockbeggar
Matfield
Brenchley
Horsmonden
Kilndown
Flimwell
Frant
Bells Yew Green
A21
A26
A229
A262
A268
A28
A274
A2070
A20
A252
A264
A267
A265
A271
A269
A259
A27
A22
A2100
A2036
M20
1066

Molash
Godmersham
Bilting
Sole Street
Petham
Waltham
Crundale
Wye
Wye Crown
Pet Street
Whiteacre
Kempe's Corner
Hassell Street
Hastingleigh
Bodsham
Brook
Naccolt
Elmsted
Whatsole Street
West Brabourne
Stowting Common
Stowting
Hinxhill
Willesborough Lees
Willesborough
Brabourne
Brabourne Lees
Sevington
Mersham
Smeeth
Monks Horton
Broad Street
Sellindge
Moorstock
Stanford
The Forstal
South Stour
Clap Hill
Stonestreet Green
Westenhanger
Aldington
Aldington Corner
Court-at-Street
Newingreen
Lympne
Port Lympne
Bonnington
Bilsington
Ruckinge
Botolph's Bridge
Donkey Street
Burmarsh
Newchurch
ROMNEY MARSH
Norwood
Romney, Hythe & Dymchurch Railway
Dymchurch
Martello Tower
St Mary in the Marsh
Ivychurch
St Mary's Bay
Romney Marsh
Old Romney
New Romney
Littlestone-on-Sea
Greatstone-on-Sea
Lydd
RSPB
Pilot Inn
Old Lighthouse
DUNGENESS
Upper Hardres Court
Bossingham
Stelling Minnis
North Leigh
Maxted Street
Wheelbarrow Town
Sixmile Cottages
Exted
Lymbridge Green
Rhodes Minnis
Woodland
Elham
Ottinge
Lyminge
Newbarn
Postling
Paddlesworth
Etchinghill
Channel Tunnel Terminal
Peene
Newington
Battle of Britain
Horn Street
Brockhill
Saltwood
Pedlinge
Seabrook
Hythe
West Hythe
Sandgate
Cheriton
Morehall
FOLKESTONE
Bottom
Kingston
Elmstead
Elham Valley
Marley
Derringstone
Barham
Bladbean
Breach
Denton
Wingmore
North Elham
Swingfield Minnis
Ridge Row
Hawkinge
Butterfly Centre
Womenswold
Frogham
Woolage Village
Woolage Green
Barfrestone
East Kent Railway
Shepherdswell
Lydden
Coldred
Wootton
Selsted
Swingfield Street
Densole
Upper Standen
Lower Standen
Capel-le-Ferne
Ewell Minnis
Kearsney
Chilton
Alkham
South Alkham
Drellingore
Wolverton
St Radigund's
West Hougham
Satmar
Samphire Hoe
Dover - Folkestone Heritage Coast
East Wear Bay
Holt St
Tilmanstone
Elvington
Lower Eythorne
Eythorne
North Downs Way
Ashley
Sutton Downs
West Langdon
Whitfield
Temple Ewell
River
Buckland
Maxton
Farthingloe
Great Mongeham
Little Mongeham
East Studdal
Sutton
Ringwould
Martin
East Langdon
Guston
Kingsdown
St Margaret's at Cliffe
St Margaret's Bay
West Cliffe
Pines
SOUTH FORELAND
Lighthouse
South Foreland Heritage Coast
Castle
Gateway to the White Cliffs
DOVER
Dunkerque
Calais
Channel Tunnel (Rail)
STRAIT OF DOVER
A28
A20
A2070
A261
A259
B2067
B2071
B2075
M20
A260
B2011
A2
A256
A258
Stop 24

Folkestone Terminal
400 yards
500 metres
Ashley Wood
Peene
Newington
Beachborough Crossroads
Terminal Building
CHANNEL TUNNEL TERMINAL
Check-in
Police Station
ASHFORD ROAD
Cheriton Interchange
Superstore
Cheriton
ASHFORD, MAIDSTONE, M25 & LONDON
DOVER, FOLKESTONE, CANTERBURY
Departures to France follow
Arrivals from France follow

Calais / Coquelles Terminal
400 yards
500 metres
Coquelles
D243E
Ibis Hotel
Etap Hotel
Novotel
Cité de l'Europe
PASSENGER TERMINAL
Petrol Station
Check-in
Frontier Controls
BOULEVARD DE LA CÔTE D'OPALE
A16 (E402)
ROCADE LITTORALE
HGV Fuel Station
Freight Terminal
Eurotunnel Administration Headquarters
Parc d'activites les Terrasses
BOULOGNE
CALAIS
DUNKERQUE, A26 (PARIS)
D304
Departures to England follow
Arrivals from England follow

North West Point
Lundy Heritage Coast
LUNDY
142
Marisco
Surf Point
Shutter Point
Baggy Point
Putsborough
Croyde Bay
Croyde Bay
North Devon Heritage Coast
BARNSTAPLE
OR
BIDEFORD BAY
Westward Ho!
HARTLAND POINT
Shipload Bay
Damehole Point
Titchberry
Hartland Abbey & Garden
Brownsham
Hartland Heritage Coast
Abbotsham
Hartland Quay
Stoke
Hartland
B3248
Velly
Clovelly
Higher Clovelly
Buck's Mills
Fairy Cross
Ford
Horns Cross
Woodtown
Yeo Vale
Spekes Mill Mouth
Milford
Docton Mill Gardens
Philham
Milky Way
Buck's Cross
A39
Goldworthy
Elmscott
Edistone
Woolfardisworthy
Cranford
Parkham
Cabbacott
Hardisworthy
Tosberry
Parkham Ash
Buckland Brewer
South Hole
Melbury
Welcombe
Ashmansworthy
Frithelstock
Mead
Darracott
Meddon
East Putford
Gooseham Mill
Woolley
Thornehillhead
Gooseham
Eastcott
East Youlstone
Dinworthy
Gnome Reserve
West Putford
Morwenstow
Colscott
Haytown
Higher Sharpnose Point
West Youlstone
Shop
Bradworthy
Bulkworthy
South West Coast Path
Woodford
Tamar Lakes
Kimworthy
Abbots Bickington
Lower Sharpnose Point
A388
Kilkhampton
Sutcombe
Newton St Petrock
Steeple Point
Stibb
Brocklands
Alfardisworthy
Sutcombemill
Venngreen
Dinscott
Thurdon
River
Soldon
Milton Damerel
Sandy Mouth
B3254
Soldon Cross
Waldon
Thornbury
Shebbear
Northcott Mouth
Maer
Poughill
Dunsdon
Holsworthy Beacon
Woodacott
Bradford
Bush
Hersham
Brendon
Flexbury
Grimscott
Lana
Chilsworthy
Lashbrook
Bude Bay
Bude
Stratton
Launcells
Launcells Cross
Kingford
Cookbury
Pancrasweek
Lynstone
A3072
Red Post
Anvil Corner
Cookbury Wick
Holemoor
Upton
Buttsbear Cross
Derril
Derriton
Holsworthy
A3072
Brandis Corner
Helebridge
Marhamchurch
Whimble
Hollacombe
0 1 2 3 4 5 miles
0 1 2 3 4 5 6 7 8 kilometres

J
K
L
M
N
P
Q
R
Foreland Point
Lynmouth Bay
Countisbury Cove
Countisbury
Lynton
Lynmouth
Wilsham
Brendon
Malmsmead
Culbone
Porlock Bay
Porlock Weir
West Porlock
Oare
Rockford
Tippacott
Watersmeet House
Brass Rubbing
Woody Bay
Elwill Bay
Martinhoe
Trentishoe
Hunter's Inn
Heale
Kemacott
Killington
Lynbridge
West Lyn
Barbrook
Dean
East Ilkerton
West Ilkerton
Cheriton
Furzehill
Lynton & Barnstaple Railway
Parracombe
Churchtown
Ilfracombe
Hele Bay
Hele
Water Mouth
Watermouth Castle
Combe Martin Bay
Combe Martin
Haggington Hill
Berrynarbor
Chambercombe Manor
The Old Corn Mill
Lee Bay
Lee
Slade
Bull Point
Damage Cliffs
Mortehoe
Lincombe
Two Pots
Mullacott Cross
Wildlife & Dinosaur Park
Kentisbury
Kentisbury Ford
Patchole
Berry Down Cross
East Down
Bittadon
Trimstone
Bradwell
West Down
Wistlandpound Reservoir
Arlington Beccott
Arlington
Arlington Court
Stowford
Exmoor Zoological Park
Swincombe
Challacombe
Barton Town
EXMOOR FOREST
HOARoak HILL 474
DRY HILL 444
EXMOOR NATIONAL PARK
River Exe
River Barle
Simonsbath
Newland
Edgcott
Exford
Dunkery & Horner Woods
Kinsford Water
SPAN HEAD 493
Withypool
North Radworthy
South Radworthy
Tarr Steps
Tarr
Hawkridge
Twitchen
North Buckland
Netherocott
Darracott
Croyde
Winsham
Halsinger
Knowle
Higher Muddiford
Milltown
Muddiford
Clifton
Churchill
Loxhore
Loxhore Cott
Lower Loxhore
Knightacott
Lobb
Boode
Marwood
Pippacott
Marwood Hill
Guineaford
Kingsheanton
Heanton Punchardon
Prixford
Shirwell
Bratton Fleming
Benton
Leworthy
Fullaford
R Bray
Lydcott
Whitefield
Braunton
Braunton Burrows
Wrafton
Chivenor
Ashford
Bradiford
Burridge
Northleigh
Goodleigh
Stoke Rivers
Brayford
High Bray
Bentwichen
Charles
North Heasley
Heasley Mill
River Taw
Pilton
Derby
Willesleigh
Gunn
Barnstaple
Fremington
Bickington
Bradninch
Stoodleigh
Elwell
Crow Point
Yelland
Horsacott
Landkey
Swimbridge Newland
West Buckland
East Buckland
North Molton
Instow
Bickleton
Tawstock
Lake
Yarnacott
Northam
Tapeley Park
Westleigh
St John's Chapel
Bishop's Tawton
Hannaford
Swimbridge
Kerscott
Castle Hill
Bremridge
Upcott
Molland
West Anstey
Horwood
Eastleigh
Lower Lovacott
Newton Tracey
Harracott
Herner
East Stowford
Filleigh
South Molton
Slade
Yeo Mill
East Anstey
Pillhead
East-the-Water
Hiscott
Ensis
Week
Chapelton
Cobbaton
Quince Honey Farm
Aller
Bish Mill
Newtown
Bishop's Nympton
Alverdiscott
Delley
Chittlehampton
Clapworthy
George Nympton
Radley
Crooked Oak
Knowstone
East Knowstone
Roachill
Landcross
Yarnscombe
Umberleigh
Atherington
Warkleigh
Satterleigh
Alswear
Mariansleigh
Ash Mill
Rose Ash
Huntshaw
Huntshaw Cross
Langridgeford
River Mole
Yard
Weare Giffard
High Bullen
Chittlehamholt
Kings Nympton
Romansleigh
Meshaw
Great Torrington
Taddiport
Dodscott
St Giles in the Wood
High Bickington
Creacombe
Rackenford
Little Torrington
Rosemoor
Kingscott
Cadbury Barton
Queen Dart
Little Dart River
Roborough
Week
Langtree Week
Great Potheridge
Beaford
Burrington
Colleton Mills
Elstone
Berry Cross
Little Potheridge
Chulmleigh
Witheridge
Drayford
Edgeworthy
Peters Marland
Winswell
Little Marland
Riddlecombe
Ashreigney
Bridge Reeve
Cheldon
Chawleigh
Worlington
Nomansland
Halsdon
Leigh
Thelbridge Cross
Washford Pyne
Merton
Huish
Dolton
Hollocombe
Ashley
Eggesford
Filleigh
Hele Lane
Littleborough
Pennymoor
Cruwys Morchard
North Town
Puddington
Way Village
Petrockstow
Dowland
Wembworthy
Moor End
Nymet Rowland
Eastington
Lapford
Black Dog
Morchard Bishop
Woolfardisworthy
Poughill
Upham
Buckland Filleigh
Ash
Meeth
Iddesleigh
Ingleigh Green
Brushford
Coldridge
Kennerleigh
Stockleigh English
Cheriton Fitzpaine
Sheepwash
R Torridge
Fishleigh
Barwick
Winkleigh
Broadwood Kelly
West Leigh
Weeke
East Village
Black Torrington
Monkokehampton
Splatt
Bondleigh
Loosebeare
Highampton
Hatherleigh
Lowton
East Leigh
Zeal Monachorum
Down St Mary
Copplestone
New Buildings
Upton Hellions
Chilton
Honeychurch
Sandford
Odham
Sutton
Woolsgrove
A39
A399
A3123
A361
A3125
A377
A386
A3124
A3072
B3343
B3230
B3229
B3226
B3227
B3232
B3217
B3220
B3096
B3042
B3137
B3358
B3223
B3224
B3225
B3233
B3216
20
7
8

Foreland Point
Lynmouth Bay
Countisbury Cove
Lynton
Brass Rubbing
Countisbury
Lynbridge
Lynmouth
Wilsham
Brendon
West Lyn
Toll
Dean
Barbrook
Rockford
Malmsmead
Culbone
Porlock Weir
Porlock Bay
Hurlstone Point
SELWORTHY BEACON 308
South West Coast Path
Exmoor Heritage Coast
West Porlock
Bossington
Allerford
East Ilkerton
Tippacott
Oare
A39
B3225
Woodcombe
Minehead
Ilkerton
Cheriton
Watersmeet House
Porlock
Holnicote
Selworthy
Bratton
Periton
Furzehill
Horner
Tivington
Alcombe
Marsh Street
Dunster Water Mill
Blue Anchor Bay
Blue Anchor
West Somerset Railway
Watchet
St Audries Bay
HOAROAK HILL 474
B3223
Luccombe
Dunkery & Horner Woods
Huntscott
Wootton Courtenay
Butter Cross
Dunster
Gallox Bridge
Dunster Castle
B3191
St Decumans
Doniford
EXMOOR FOREST
EXMOOR NATIONAL PARK
19
Ranscombe
Knowle
Carhampton
Old Cleeve
Five Bells
Swincombe
Challacombe
444 DRY HILL
519 Dunkery Beacon DUNKERY HILL
Burrow
Timberscombe
Tropiquaria
Washford
Williton
River Exe
B3358
Withycombe
Bilbrook
Hungerford
Cleeve Abbey
Torre
Stream
Sampford Brett
Woolston
Capton
River Barle
Simonsbath
B3223
Edgcott
B3224
Wheddon Cross
A396
Cutcombe
Rodhuish
Luxborough
Golsoncott
Lower Roadwater
Roadwater
Vellow
Escott
Kingswood
410
Newland
Exford
Luckwell Bridge
424
Kingsbridge
Treborough
Monksilver
Stogumber
493 SPAN HEAD
Kinsford Water
BRENDON HILLS
Leighland Chapel
Sticklepath
Combe Sydenham
Preston
Whitefield
Withypool
B3224
B3190
Elworthy
North Radworthy
Winsford
West Howetown
Gupworthy
WINSFORD HILL
B3188
Willett
High Bray
Bentwichen
Brendon Hill
Clatworthy Reservoir
Brompton Ralph
Rooks Nest
North Heasley
South Radworthy
Tarr Steps
Liscombe
Exton
Bridgetown
Withiel Florey
Tolland
Heasley Mill
Tarr
Woolcotts
Clatworthy
Wimbleball Lake
Gaulden Manor
Hawkridge
Brompton Regis
Twitchen
North Molton
Highercombe
Whitefield
316
Hartford
Huish Champflower
Langley Marsh
Hoccombe
Chapel Leigh
Bremridge
Upcott
Molland
HADDON HILL
355
Maundown
Langley
Ford
Fitzhead
B3223
West Anstey
Dulverton
Upton
Wiveliscombe
Slade
Bury
Battleton
B3222
Chipstable
B3227
Hartswell
Quince Honey Farm
South Molton
Yeo Mill
East Anstey
Skilgate
Raddington
Milverton
Aller
Timewell
Waterrow
B3226
Bish Mill
Newtown
B3227
Oldways End
Brushford
Morebath
Petton
Bathealton
B3187
Bishop's Nympton
Sowerhill
Exbridge
Shillingford
B3227
George Nympton
Crooked Oak
Clayhanger
North Hele
Langford Budville
Radley
Knowstone
Stawley
Langford Heathfield
B3137
East Knowstone
Roachill
Ash Mill
Oakfordbridge
Bampton
Kyrle
Kittisford
Thorne St Margaret
Alswear
Mariansleigh
Ashbrittle
Appley
Mole
Rose Ash
A361
Tracebridge
Westford
Yard
Oakford
Huntsham
Staple Cross
Greenham
Holywell Lake
Romansleigh
19
Meshaw
Cove
Hockworthy
White Ball
A38
R Lowman
Exe Valley
Creacombe
Holcombe Rogus
Sampford Arundel
Stoodleigh
Sampford Moor
Rackenford
Westleigh
Red Ball
Wrangway
Queen Dart
Little Dart River
Knightshayes Court
East Mere
Pitt
Burlescombe
Week
Loxbeare
Washfield
Hayne
Uplowman
Ayshford
Nicholashayne
Culm Davy
Chevithorne
Craze Lowman
Whitnage
Appledore
Woodgate
Chulmleigh
Witheridge
Lurley
Bolham
Chettiscombe
A361
Sampford Peverell
Prescott
Culmstock
Cheldon
Drayford
B3137
Edgeworthy
Templeton
Calverleigh
Waterloo Cross
Uffculme
B3096
Worlington
Nomansland
B3137
Northcott
Chawleigh
Thelbridge Cross
Withleigh
Tiverton
Halberton
Coldharbour
Craddock
Leigh
B3042
Washford Pyne
Cruwys Morchard
R Dart
Canal
Smithincott
Coldharbour Mill
B3042
Pennymoor
8
9
Willand
Ashill
Filleigh
Hele Lane
Littleborough
Puddington
Way Village
Well Town
River Exe
Little Silver
Diggerland
Blackborough
R Dalch
Black Dog
Devon Railway Centre
Butterleigh
Bradfield
Nymet Rowland
Eastington
Poughill
Upham
River Culm
Kentisbeare
Lapford
Morchard Bishop
Woolfardisworthy
Cullompton
Coldridge
Kennerleigh
Stockleigh English
Cheriton Fitzpaine
Cadeleigh
Bickleigh Mill
Bickleigh
Cullompton
Saint Hill
A377
Weeke
East Village
Knowle
Colebrook
Dulford
Kerswell
R Yeo
Uppincott
Bickleigh
Fursdon
East Leigh
Loosebeare
Down St Mary
Chilton
A3072
Cadbury
Westcott
Mutterton
Broadhembury
Zeal Monachorum
Newbuildings
Upton Hellions
Stockleigh Pomeroy
Up Exe
Bradninch
Norman's Green
Colliton
A373
Hembury
Sutton
Woolsgrove
Lower
West Raddon
Silverton
Hele
Langford
Plymtree
Luton
Upton
0 1 2 3 4 5 miles
0 1 2 3 4 5 6 7 8 kilometres

WESTON-SUPER-MARE
Steep Holm
Kewstoke
Worle
St Georges
Locking
Hutton
Uphill
Oldmixon
Bleadon
Brean
Lympsham
Berrow
Brent Knoll
East Brent
Burnham-on-Sea
Highbridge
BRIDGWATER
BAY
Stolford
Steart
Huntspill
Pawlett
Puriton
Woolavington
Cossington
POLDEN HILLS
Bawdrip
Chedzoy
Bridgwater
Wembdon
North Petherton
Durleigh
Cannington
Nether Stowey
Over Stowey
QUANTOCK HILLS
Kilve
Stogursey
Holford
Crowcombe
Bishops Lydeard
Taunton
Wellington
Ruishton
Creech St Michael
North Curry
Athelney
Stoke St Gregory
Langport
Somerton
Street
Glastonbury
Wells
Cheddar
MENDIP HILLS
Winscombe
Banwell
Sandford
Churchill
Blagdon
Axbridge
Wedmore
Mark
Westhay
Meare
Shapwick
Ashcott
Walton
Butleigh
Compton Dundon
Kingsweston
Charlton Mackrell
Keinton Mandeville
Ilchester
Yeovilton
Martock
Stoke sub Hamdon
Montacute
Yeovil
South Petherton
Ilminster
Hatch Beauchamp
Curry Rivel
Huish Episcopi
Long Sutton
Crewkerne
Chard
Cricket St Thomas
Misterton
Merriott
Whitelackington
Broadway
Buckland St Mary
Churchinford
Hemyock
Blagdon Hill
Corfe
Pitminster
BLACKDOWN HILLS
Yarcombe
Wambrook
Tatworth
Chardstock
Membury
Stockland
Axminster
Thorncombe
Drimpton
Broadwindsor
Haselbury Plucknett
North Perrott
South Perrott
Corscombe
Halstock
A38
A39
A361
A372
A378
A358
A303
A30
A37
A371
A368
A370
M5
1
2
3
4
5
6
7
8
9
10
11
12
J
K
L
M
N
P
Q
R

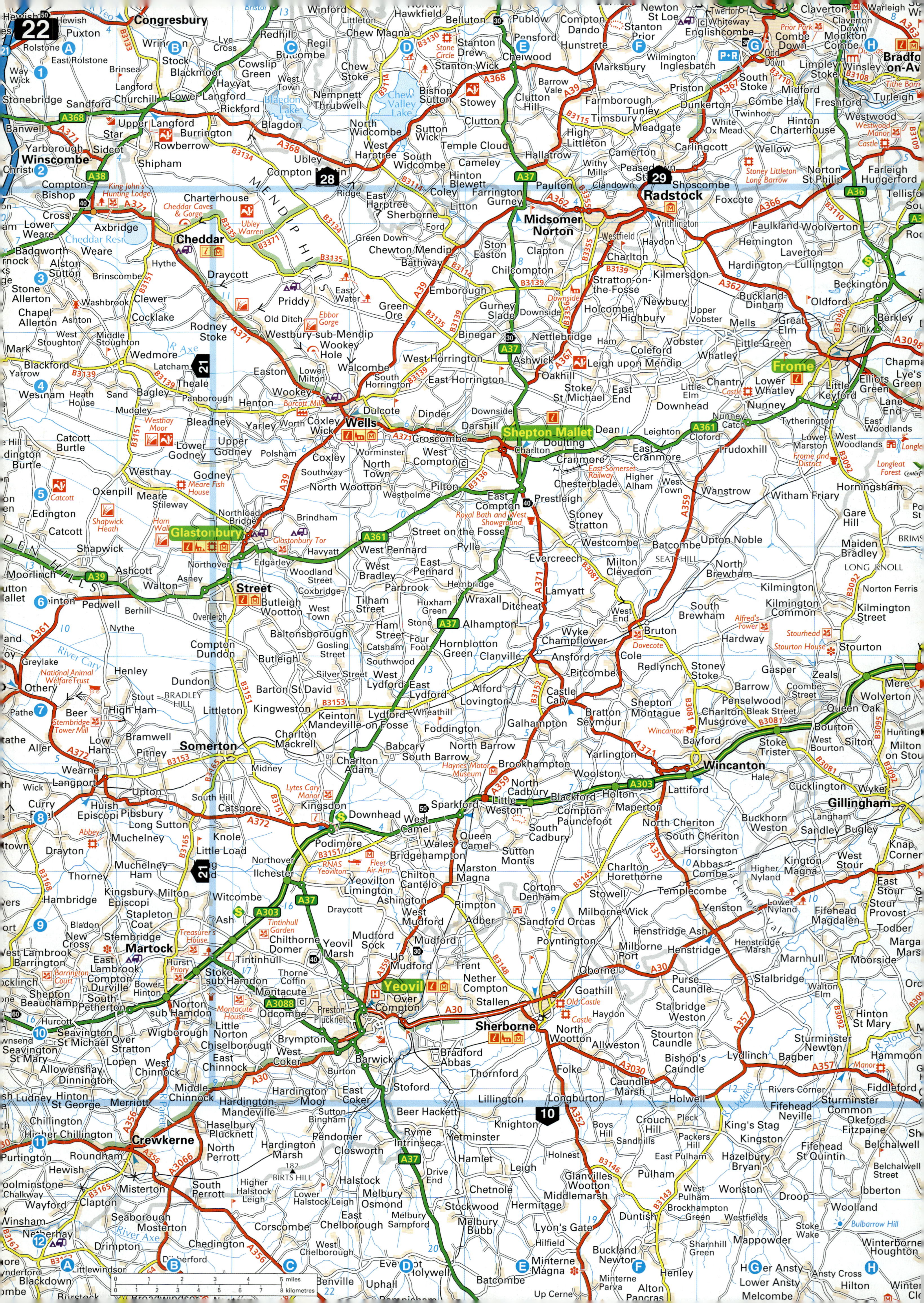

Congresbury
Winscombe
Cheddar
MENDIP HILLS
Wells
Shepton Mallet
Midsomer Norton
Radstock
Frome
Glastonbury
Street
Somerton
Langport
Wincanton
Gillingham
Yeovil
Sherborne
Martock
Crewkerne
Ilchester
Castle Cary
Bruton
Chew Valley Lake
Blagdon Lake
Cheddar Caves & Gorge
Ebbor Gorge
Longleat Forest
Stourhead
Haynes Motor Museum
Fleet Air Arm
RNAS Yeovilton
Royal Bath and West Showground
Montacute House
Barrington Court
Treasurer's House
Tintinhull Garden
Glastonbury Tor
Stoney Littleton Long Barrow
Farleigh Hungerford
Alfred's Tower
Stourton House
Wincanton
King John's Hunting Lodge
Ubley Warren
Westhay Moor
Meare Fish House
Shapwick Heath
Catcott
Ham Wall
Stembridge Tower Mill
National Animal Welfare Trust
Lytes Cary Manor
Old Castle
Castle
Dovecote
Downside
Barcott Mill
Wookey Hole
Westbury-sub-Mendip
Cleeve
A37
A39
A303
A30
A361
A371
A368
A362
A366
A356
A357
A3088
A3030
A372
A36
A350
28
29
21
10

Melksham
Devizes
Trowbridge
Westbury
Warminster
Tidworth
Durrington
Bulford
Amesbury
Wilton
Salisbury
Shaftesbury
Fordingbridge
Ringwood
Verwood
Blandford Forum
Great Chalfield
Broughton Gifford
Bradford Leigh
Holt
Whaddon
Staverton
Hilperton
Semington
Seend
Seend Cleeve
Bowerhill
Redstocks
St Edith's Marsh
Sells Green
Rowde
Roundway
Dunkirk
Little Horton
Horton
Allington
Stanton St Bernard
Alton Barnes
Alton Priors
Honeystreet
West Stowell
Oare
Wootton Rivers
Pewsey
Fyfield
Milton Lilbourne
Easton Royal
Burbage
Eastcourt
West Grafton
East Grafton
Wexcombe
Coate
All Cannings
Nursteed
Etchilhampton
Vale of Pewsey
Woodborough
Wilcot
Beechingstoke
Broad Street
Gores
Manningford Bruce
Manningford Bohune
North Newnton
Pewsey Down
Easton Hill
Inmarsh
Poulshot
Bulkington
The Strand
Great Hinton
Keevil
Bleet
Ashton Common
Ashton Hill
Worton
Potterne
Potterne Wick
Stert
Wedhampton
Urchfont
Patney
Marden
Hilcott
Chirton
Wilsford
Charlton St Peter
Rushall
Wilsford Down
Aughton
Collingbourne Kingston
Steeple Ashton
Rood Ashton
Marston
West Ashton
Woodmarsh
Yarnbrook
North Bradley
Heywood
Dunge
Coulston
Edington
Erlestoke
Great Cheverell
Littleton Pannell
Eastcott
Easterton
Market Lavington
Little Cheverell
West Lavington
Charlton Down
Upavon
Lower Everleigh
Everleigh
East Everleigh
Sunton
Cadley
Collingbourne Ducis
West Chisenbury
East Chisenbury
Littlecott
Compton
Enford
Longstreet
Coombe
Fifield
Fittleton
Sidbury Hill
Haxton Down
Enford Down
Hawkeridge
Brokerswood
Bratton
Bratton Camp
Stradbrook
Penleigh
Chalford
Westbury Leigh
White Horse
Tenantry Down
Littleton Down
Tilshead
Westdown Camp
Netheravon
Haxton
Figheldean
Ablington
Alton
Milston
Perham Down
Dilton
Upton Scudamore
Warminster Down
Corsley
Corsley Heath
Cold Harbour
Battlesbury Hill
Boreham
Scratchbury Hill
Salisbury Plain
Orcheston
Elston
Knighton Down
Larkhill
Shipton Bellinger
Beacon Hill
Bulford Camp
Crockerton
Bishopstrow
Norton Bavant
Heytesbury
Chitterne
Shrewton
Maddington
Stonehenge
Countess
Ratfyn
Quarley
Quarley Hill
Cholderton
Shear Cross
Longbridge Deverill
Sutton Veny
Knook
Upton Lovell
Codford St Peter
Codford St Mary
Tytherington
Tytherington Hill
Corton
Boyton
Sherrington
Winterbourne Stoke
West Amesbury
Normanton
Rare Breeds Farm
Newton Tony
Palestine
Hill Deverill
Brixton Deverill
Fisherton de la Mere
Stockton
Deptford
Steeple Langford
Berwick St James
Wilsford
Lake
Allington
Boscombe
Over Wallop
Monkton Deverill
Bapton
Wylye
Hanging Langford
Little Langford
Overstreet
Stapleford
Upper Woodford
Middle Woodford
Great Durnford
Netton
Idmiston
Porton
Jack's Bush
Kingston Deverill
Pertwood
Salterton
High Post
Heale
Winterbourne Dauntsey
Gomeldon
Winterbourne Gunner
Lopcombe Corner
Keysley Down
Chicklade
Great Wishford
Stoford
Lower Woodford
Little Durnford
Winterbourne Earls
Hurdcott
Figsbury Ring
Middle Winterslow
East Winterslow
Firsdown
Winterslow
West Winterslow
The Common
West Knoyle
Berwick St Leonard
Fonthill Bishop
Teffont Magna
Baverstock
Barford St Martin
Ditchampton
South Newton
Old Sarum
Stratford sub Castle
Ford
Paul's Dene
Laverstock
Pitton
Upton
Hindon
Fonthill Gifford
Ridge
Chilmark
Dinton
Dinton Park
Teffont Evias
Farmer Giles Farmstead
Quidhampton
Bemerton
The Medieval Hall
The Green
Barrow Street
East Knoyle
Holloway
Tisbury
Lower Chicksgrove
Upper Chicksgrove
Burcombe
Compton Chamberlayne
Fovant
Bulbridge
Netherhampton
West Harnham
East Harnham
Farley
Tuckingmill
Newtown
East Hatch
West Hatch
Sutton Mandeville
Regimental Badges
Britford
Alderbury
East Grimstead
Sedgehill
West End
Semley
Ansty
Swallowcliffe
Old Wardour Castle
Fyfield Bavant
Broad Chalke
Bishopstone
Stratford Tony
Coombe Bissett
Odstock
Bodenham
Nunton
Whaddon
West Dean
West Grimstead
Motcombe
Donhead St Mary
Donhead St Andrew
Ebbesborne Wake
Stoke Farthing
Croucheston
Homington
Pepperbox Hill
Whiteparish
Enmore Green
Ivy Cross
West End
Alvediston
Mount Sorrel
Bowerchalke
Charlton-All-Saints
Ludwell
Charlton
Berwick St John
Woodminton
Downton
Newton
Redlynch
Guy's Marsh
Cann
West Melbury
Melbury Abbas
Cobley
Martin Drove End
Whitsbury Down
Breamore Down
Wick
Morgan's Vale
Woodfalls
Langley Wood
Hartgrove
Compton Abbas
Ashmore
Fontmell & Melbury Downs
Tollard Royal
New Town
Dean End
Woodyates
Deanland
Martin
East Martin
Tidpit
Whitsbury
Upper Street
North Street
Breamore
Hale
Lover
Hamptworth
Landford
Bedchester
Fontmell Down
West Orchard
Fontmell Magna
Cranborne Chase
Tollard Farnham
Woodcutts
Sixpenny Handley
Pentridge
Rockbourne
North End
Outwick
Woodgreen
Hale Purlieu
Nomansland
Sutton Waldron
Dean
Farnham
Boveridge
Damerham
Lower Burgate
Upper Burgate
Godshill
Bramshaw
Fontmell Parva
Iwerne Minster
New Town
Stubhampton
Minchington
Chettle
Gussage St Andrew
Cashmoor
Monkton Up Wimborne
Cranborne
Bellows Cross
South End
Sandleheath
Blissford
Frogham
Fritham
Iwerne Courtney or Shroton
Tarrant Gunville
Gussage St Michael
Wimborne St Giles
Alderholt
Stuckton
Bickton
Hyde
Hungerford
Stoney Cross
Hambledon Hill
Little Hanford
Hanford
Hod Hill
Tarrant Hinton
Long Crichel
Church & Earthworks
Edmondsham
Cripplestyle
Dorset Heavy Horse Centre
Harbridge Green
Harbridge
Ibsley
North Gorley
South Gorley
Ibsley Common
Linwood
Rockford Common
Mockbeggar
Rockford
Emery Down
Ash
Stourpaine
Pimperne
Tarrant Launceston
Tarrant Monkton
Gussage All Saints
Moor Crichel
Knowlton
Woodlands
Whitmore
Romford
Ellingham
Durweston
Royal Signals
Manswood
Horton
North Poulner
Linford
Bryanston
Blandford Camp
Tarrant Rawston
New Town
Witchampton
Chalbury
Chalbury Common
Crab Orchard
Blashford
Poulner
Shobley
Picket Post
Hightown
Burley Street
Blandford St Mary
Langton Long Blandford
Tarrant Rushton
Uppington
Hinton Martell
Gaunt's Common
Mannington
Holt Heath
Three Legged Cross
Moors Valley
Ashley Heath
Lower Mannington
St Leonards
St Ives
Ashley
Moortown
Liberty's Raptor & Reptile Centre
Crow
Kingston Great Common
Burley Lawn
Markway
Winterborne Stickland
Charlton on the Hill
Charlton Marshall
Littleton
Tarrant Keyneston
Stanbridge
Holt
West Moors
North Kingston
Thornicombe
Tarrant Crawford
Badbury Rings
Honeybrook
Pig Oak
Broom Hill
Avon Heath
Crawford
Clay Hill
Cley Hill
Great Chalfield Manor
The Courts Garden
A350
A365
A361
A342
A360
A3098
A338
A345
A346
A3026
A36
A303
A344
A3028
A30
A3094
A354
A31
A357
A366
A363
B3098
B3107
B3105
B3087
B3086
B3083
B3089
B3081
B3078
B3080
B3072
B3414
B3095
B3099
B390
29
30
24
11
12

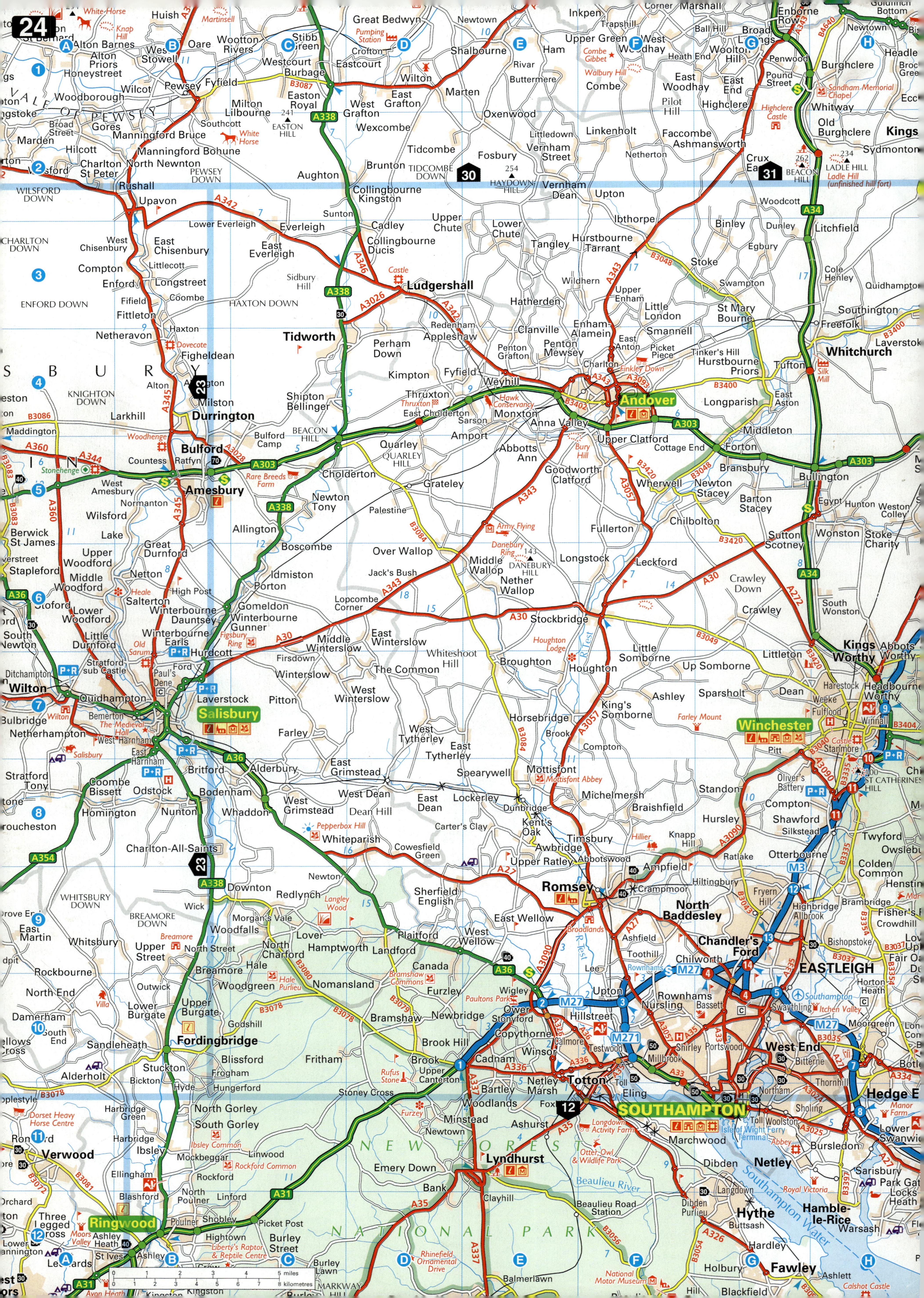
Great Bedwyn
Newtown
Inkpen
Marshall
Enborne Row
Goldfinch Bottom
Pumping Station
Crofton
Shalbourne
Ham
Upper Green
West Woodhay
Ball Hill
Broad Layings
Newtown
Headley
Alton Barnes
Alton Priors
Honeystreet
Oare
Wootton Rivers
Stibb Green
Westcourt
Burbage
Eastcourt
Wilton
Rivar
Buttermere
Combe Gibbet
Walbury Hill
Combe
Heath End
Woolton Hill
East End
Penwood
Pound Street
Burghclere
Sandham Memorial Chapel
Woodborough
Wilcot
Pewsey
Fyfield
Milton Lilbourne
Easton Royal
West Grafton
East Grafton
Marten
East Woodhay
Pilot Hill
Highclere
Highclere Castle
Whitway
Old Burghclere
Kings
VALE OF PEWSEY
Broad Street
Gores
Manningford Bruce
Southcott
White Horse
EASTON HILL
Wexcombe
Oxenwood
Littledown
Vernham Street
Linkenholt
Faccombe
Ashmansworth
Netherton
Crux Easton
Sydmonton
Marden
Hilcott
Manningford Bohune
Charlton St Peter
North Newnton
Wilsford
PEWSEY DOWN
Aughton
Tidcombe
TIDCOMBE DOWN
Fosbury
HAYDOWN HILL
Vernham Dean
Upton
BEACON HILL
LADLE HILL
Ladle Hill (unfinished hill fort)
WILSFORD DOWN
Rushall
Upavon
Collingbourne Kingston
Sunton
Woodcott
Lower Everleigh
Everleigh
East Everleigh
Cadley
Collingbourne Ducis
Upper Chute
Lower Chute
Tangley
Hurstbourne Tarrant
Ibthorpe
Binley
Dunley
Litchfield
CHARLTON DOWN
West Chisenbury
East Chisenbury
Littlecott
Compton
Enford
Longstreet
Fifield
Coombe
Fittleton
Sidbury Hill
HAXTON DOWN
Castle
Ludgershall
Egbury
Stoke
Wildhern
Upper Enham
Swampton
Cole Henley
Quidhampton
ENFORD DOWN
Hatherden
Little London
St Mary Bourne
Southington
Freefolk
Netheravon
Haxton
Tidworth
Redenham
Appleshaw
Clanville
Enham Alamein
Smannell
East Anton
Picket Piece
Tinker's Hill
Hurstbourne Priors
Whitchurch
Laverstoke
Dovecote
Figheldean
Perham Down
Penton Grafton
Penton Mewsey
Charlton
Finkley Down
Tufton
Silk Mill
Alton
Ablington
Milston
Durrington
Kimpton
Fyfield
Weyhill
Andover
Longparish
East Aston
KNIGHTON DOWN
Larkhill
Shipton Bellinger
Thruxton
Hawk Conservancy
East Cholderton
Sarson
Monxton
Anna Valley
Middleton
Maddington
Woodhenge
BEACON HILL
Bulford
Bulford Camp
Quarley
QUARLEY HILL
Amport
Abbotts Ann
Upper Clatford
Bury Hill
Cottage End
Forton
Stonehenge
Countess
Ratfyn
Cholderton
Rare Breeds Farm
Grateley
Goodworth Clatford
Wherwell
Newton Stacey
Bransbury
Bullington
West Amesbury
Amesbury
Normanton
Newton Tony
Palestine
Barton Stacey
Egypt
Hunton
Weston Colley
Wilsford
Allington
Army Flying
Chilbolton
Fullerton
Sutton Scotney
Wonston
Stoke Charity
Berwick St James
Lake
Great Durnford
Boscombe
Over Wallop
Danebury Ring
DANEBURY HILL
Longstock
Leckford
Upper Woodford
Middle Wallop
Nether Wallop
Crawley Down
Stapleford
Middle Woodford
Netton
Idmiston
Jack's Bush
Porton
Heale
High Post
Salterton
Lopcombe Corner
Crawley
South Wonston
Stoford
Lower Woodford
Winterbourne Dauntsey
Gomeldon
Winterbourne Gunner
Stockbridge
Winterbourne Earls
Figsbury Ring
Little Durnford
Old Sarum
Hurdcott
Middle Winterslow
East Winterslow
Houghton Lodge
Little Somborne
Kings Worthy
Abbots Worthy
South Newton
Stratford sub Castle
Firsdown
Whiteshoot Hill
Broughton
Houghton
Up Somborne
Littleton
Headbourne Worthy
Ditchampton
Paul's Dene
Ford
Winterslow
The Common
Harestock
Wilton
Quidhampton
Laverstock
West Winterslow
Pitton
King's Somborne
Ashley
Sparsholt
Dean
Weeke
Fulflood
Bemerton
The Medieval Hall
Salisbury
Farley Mount
Winchester
Bulbridge
Netherhampton
West Harnham
Farley
West Tytherley
Horsebridge
Brook
Compton
Winnall
Castle
Stanmore
Pitt
East Tytherley
Mottisfont
Mottisfont Abbey
East Harnham
Britford
Alderbury
East Grimstead
Spearywell
Oliver's Battery
ST CATHERINE'S HILL
Stratford Tony
Coombe Bissett
Odstock
Bodenham
West Dean
Lockerley
Michelmersh
Standon
Compton
West Grimstead
Dean Hill
East Dean
Braishfield
Shawford
Homington
Nunton
Whaddon
Dunbridge
Kent's Oak
Carter's Clay
Hursley
Silkstead
Twyford
Broughton
Pepperbox Hill
Whiteparish
Awbridge
Timsbury
Hillier
Knapp Hill
Otterbourne
Owslebury
Charlton-All-Saints
Cowesfield Green
Upper Ratley
Abbotswood
Ratlake
Colden Common
Ampfield
Crampmoor
Newton
Romsey
Hiltingbury
Fryern Hill
Highbridge
Allbrook
Brambridge
WHITSBURY DOWN
Downton
Redlynch
Langley Wood
Sherfield English
North Baddesley
Fisher's Pond
Crowdhill
Wick
Morgan's Vale
East Wellow
Broadlands
Ashfield
Chandler's Ford
Bishopstoke
East Martin
BREAMORE DOWN
Woodfalls
Lover
Plaitford
West Wellow
Toothill
Chilworth
EASTLEIGH
Fair Oak
Whitsbury
Breamore
Upper Street
North Street
North Charford
Hamptworth
Landford
Lee
Rownhams
Horton Heath
Rockbourne
Hale
Canada
Rownhams Nursling
Southampton
Itchen Valley
Breamore
Hale Purlieu
Bramshaw Commons
Furzley
Wigley
Upton
North End
Woodgreen
Nomansland
Paultons Park
Ower
Hillstreet
Bassett
Swaythling
Damerham
Villa
Lower Burgate
Upper Burgate
Bramshaw
Newbridge
Stonyford
Moorgreen
South End
Godshill
Copythorne
Calmore
Testwood
Shirley
Portswood
West End
Sandleheath
Fordingbridge
Brook Hill
Cadnam
Winsor
Millbrook
Bitterne
Hedge End
Alderholt
Stuckton
Blissford
Fritham
Brook
Upper Canterton
Netley Marsh
Totton
Eling
Thornhill
Frogham
Rufus Stone
Bartley
Northam
Bickton
Hyde
Hungerford
Stoney Cross
Woodlands
Fox
SOUTHAMPTON
Sholing
Manor Farm
Dorset Heavy Horse Centre
Harbridge Green
North Gorley
Furzey
Minstead
Ashurst
Longdown Activity Farm
Woolston
Isle of Wight Ferry Terminal
Lower Swanwick
Harbridge
South Gorley
Newtown
Marchwood
Bursledon
Ibsley
Ibsley Common
NEW FOREST
Netley Abbey
Verwood
Mockbeggar
Linwood
Rockford Common
Emery Down
Lyndhurst
Otter Owl & Wildlife Park
Dibden
Netley
Sarisbury
Ellingham
Rockford
Bank
Beaulieu River
Langdown
Southampton Water
Royal Victoria
Park Gate
Locks Heath
Blashford
North Poulner
Linford
Clayhill
Beaulieu Road Station
Dibden Purlieu
Hythe
Hamble-le-Rice
Three Legged Cross
Ringwood
Poulner
Shobley
Picket Post
NATIONAL PARK
Buttsash
Warsash
Moors Valley
Ashley Heath
Hightown
Liberty's Raptor & Reptile Centre
Burley Street
Hardley
St Leonards
St Ives
Ashley
Burley Lawn
Rhinefield Ornamental Drive
Holbury
Fawley
Ashlett
MARKWAY
Kingston
Avon Heath
Balmerlawn
National Motor Museum
Hill
Blackfield
Calshot Castle
5 miles
8 kilometres

A 31 towards New Arlesford
Alton -> Farnham
Rt 272 towards Petersfield

Kidwelly (Cydweli)
Llansaint
Mynydd-y-garreg
Pontyates
Ponthenry
Llannon
Trimsaran
Pembrey
Burry Port
Pwll
Llanelli
Millennium Coastal Park
Llangennech
Hendy
Pontarddulais
Fforest
Felindre
Clydach
Pontardawe
Birchgrove
Gorseinon
Pontlliw
Penllergaer
Loughor
Gowerton
Dunvant
Killay
Sketty
Upper Killay
Bishopston
Mayals
Black Pill
West Cross
Norton
Oystermouth
The Mumbles
Mumbles Head
Langland
Caswell Bay
Pwlldu Head
Southgate
Pennard
Parkmill
Penmaen
Nicholaston
Oxwich
Oxwich Bay
Oxwich Point
Oxwich Green
Horton
Port Eynon
Port Einon Point
Port Einon Bay
Overton
Pilton Green
Scurlage
Knelston
Reynoldston
Llanddewi
Rhossili
Rhossili Bay
Rhossili Downs
Middleton
Worms Head
Hillend
Llangennith
Burry Holms
Broughton Bay
Llanmadoc
Cheriton
Landimore
Burry Green
Oldwalls
Llanrhidian
Wernffrwd
Crofty
Penclawdd
Salthouse Point
Burry Inlet
Llanmorlais
Poundffald
Three Crosses
Ilston
G O W E R
Cefn-y-Bryn
Arthur's Stone
Weobley Castle
Parc le Breos
Culver Hole
Paviland
Gower Heritage Coast
SWANSEA (ABERTAWE)
Swansea Bay
Morriston
Llansamlet
Landore
Cwmdu
Port Tennant
National Waterfront
Jersey Marine
Skewen
Baglan
Aberavon
Port Talbot
M4
38
19
Swansea
CARMARTHEN, M4 WEST
CARDIFF, M4 EAST
THE MUMBLES, GOWER
Swansea Metropolitan University
Swansea Castle
Parc Tawe Leisure & Retail Park
Civil Justice Centre
The Dylan Thomas Centre
Leisure Centre
National Waterfront
South Dock Marina
HM Prison
Observatory
Ilfracombe
Combe Martin Bay
Watermouth Castle
Woody Bay
Martinhoe
Trentishoe
Lynton
Lynmouth Bay
Lynmouth
0 1 2 3 4 5 miles
0 1 2 3 4 5 6 7 8 kilometres

Glynneath
Seven Sisters
Hirwaun
Penywaun
Aberdare
(Aberdâr)
Merthyr Tydfil
(Merthyr Tudful)
Tredegar
Ebbw Vale
Rhymney
New Tredegar
Bargoed
(Bargod)
Treharris
Gelligaer
Oakdale
Blackwood
Pengam
Treherbert
Treorchy
Maerdy
Mountain Ash
Ferndale
Ystrad
Tonypandy
Trealaw
Porth
Penygraig
Ynysybwl
Abercynon
Pontypridd
Tonyrefail
Caerphilly
(Caerffili)
Llanbradach
Bedwas
Glyncorrwg
Cymmer
Maesteg
Cwmafan
Ogmore Vale
Gilfach Goch
Pontycymer
Betws
Bryncethin
Pencoed
Llanharan
Llantrisant
Beddau
Church Village
Radyr
Tongwynlais
Pyle
Kenfig
Bridgend
(Pen-y-Bont-ar-Ogwr)
Coity
Laleston
Porthcawl
Cowbridge
Llantwit Major
Barry
(Y Barri)
Penarth
Dinas Powys
Sully
Lavernock
Rhoose
Aberthaw
Nash Point
Glamorgan Heritage Coast
Afan Forest Park
Vale of Neath
Neath
Aberdulais
Tonna
Mynydd Maendy
BRIDGWATER BAY
Porlock
Porlock Bay
Hurlstone Point
Bossington
Countisbury Cove
Brendon
Malmsmead
Culbone
Exmoor Heritage Coast
South West Coast Path
M4
A465
A470
A4119
A48
A4232
20
28
39

28
Ebbw Vale (Glynebwy)
Blaenavon
Abertillery (Abertyleri)
Abersychan
Pontypool (Pont-y-Pŵl)
Usk
Raglan
Llanhilleth
Crumlin
Oakdale
Blackwood
Newbridge
Cwmbran (Cwmbrân)
Caerleon
Risca
Crosskeys
Caerphilly (Caerffili)
Bedwas
Llanbradach
Rogerstone
NEWPORT (CASNEWYDD-AR-WYSG)
Caldicot (Cil-y-coed)
Chepstow (Cas-Gwent)
Tintern Parva
Magor
Undy
Redwick
Portskewett
Sudbrook
Severn Beach
Second Severn Crossing
CARDIFF (CAERDYDD)
Penarth
Lavernock Point
Flat Holm
Steep Holm
Sully Island
SEVERN ESTUARY
Portishead
Avonmouth
Clevedon
Nailsea
Long Ashton
Easton-in-Gordano
Yatton
Congresbury
WESTON-SUPER-MARE
Winscombe
Cheddar
Burnham-on-Sea
Brean
Berrow
Lympsham
Axbridge
MENDIP HILLS
Wye Valley
Forest Park
M4
M5
M48
M49
A48(M)
A4042
A449
A370
A38
A368
A371
A403
40
27
21
22
0 1 2 3 4 5 miles
0 1 2 3 4 5 6 7 8 kilometres

Lydney
Stroud
Stonehouse
Nailsworth
Minchinhampton
Cirencester
Dursley
Wotton-under-Edge
Tetbury
Malmesbury
Thornbury
Yate
Chipping Sodbury
Pucklechurch
Chippenham
Corsham
Keynsham
BATH
Melksham
Bradford-on-Avon
Trowbridge
Westbury
Radstock
Midsomer Norton
Frampton on Severn
Berkeley
Slimbridge
Chalford
Cam
Uley
Kingswood
Hawkesbury Upton
Marshfield
Box
Calne
Sherston
Luckington
Badminton
Acton Turville
Castle Combe
Tormarton
Dyrham
Wick
Saltford
Peasedown St John
Paulton
Freshford
Hilperton
Steeple Ashton
Rode
Beckington
Berkley
Dilton Marsh
River Severn
Severn
Sharpness
Oldbury-on-Severn
Tytherington
Alveston
Rudgeway
Winterbourne
Frenchay
Hambrook
Mangotsfield
Fishponds
Kingswood
Hanham
Bitton
Whitchurch
Pensford
Chew Magna
Farmborough
Timsbury
Hinton Charterhouse
Norton St Philip
Wingfield
Southwick
North Bradley
Semington
Seend
Bowerhill
Lacock
Derry Hill
Kington Langley
Sutton Benger
Christian Malford
Seagry
Hullavington
Grittleton
Leigh Delamere
Kemble
Culkerton
Ashley
Long Newnton
Crudwell
Hankerton
Oaksey
Brokenborough
Charlton
Lea
Garsdon
Cleverton
Great Somerford
Little Somerford
Dauntsey
Bradenstoke
Lyneham
Chelwood
Stanton Drew
Temple Cloud
Farrington Gurney
Clutton
Hallatrow
Camerton
Dunkerton
Writhlington
Kilmersdon
Mells
Frome
Chapmanslade
Upton Scudamore
Warminster Down
Tenantry Down
Littleton Down

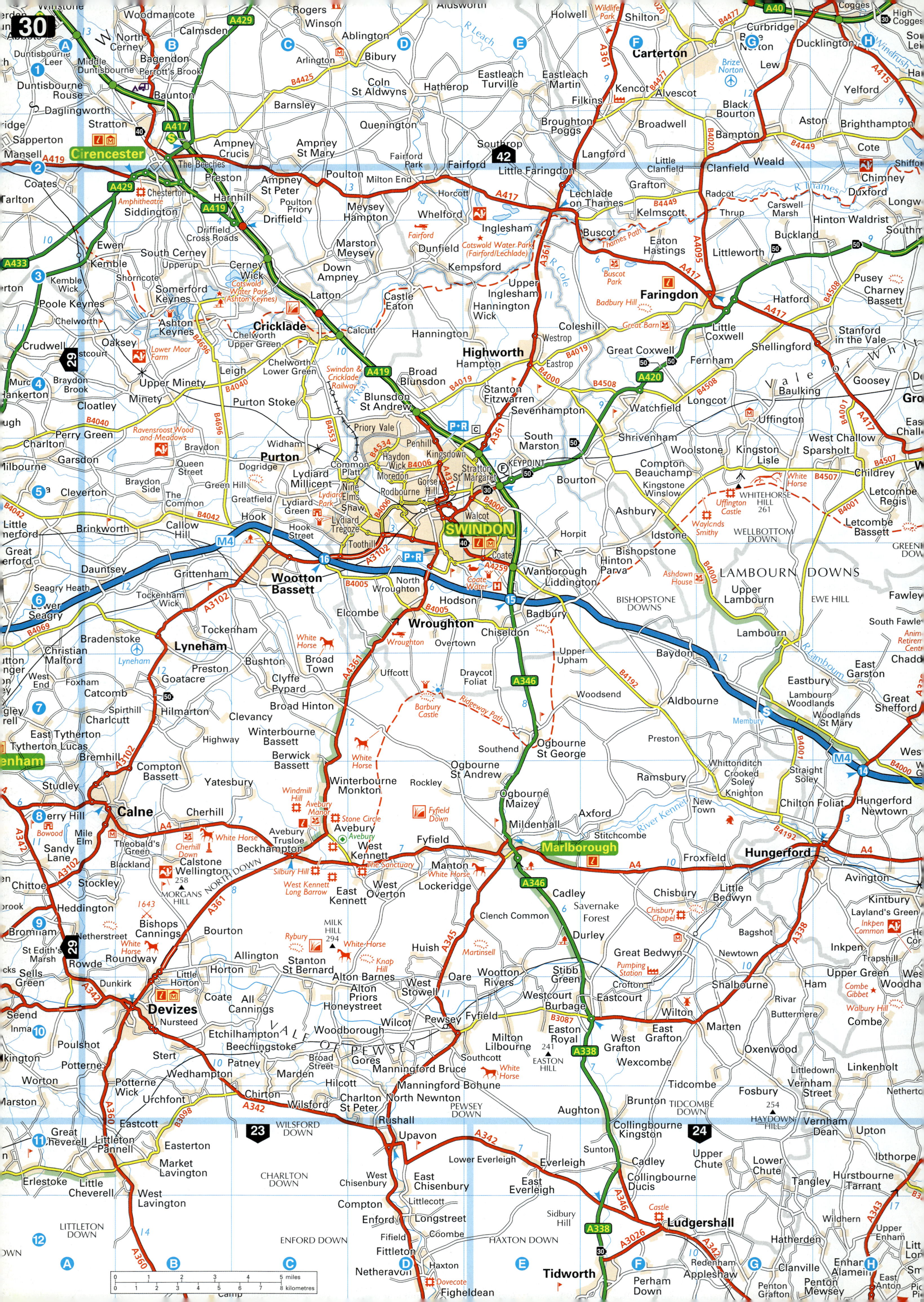
Woodmancote
North Cerney
Calmsden
Bagendon
Perrott's Brook
Baunton
Duntisbourne Leer
Middle Duntisbourne
Duntisbourne Rouse
Daglingworth
Stratton
Sapperton
Cirencester
The Beeches
Chesterton
Amphitheatre
Siddington
Preston
Harnhill
Driffield
Driffield Cross Roads
Ampney Crucis
Ampney St Mary
Ampney St Peter
Poulton
Poulton Priory
Barnsley
Rogers
Winson
Ablington
Arlington
Bibury
Coln St Aldwyns
Quenington
Hatherop
Aldsworth
Eastleach Turville
Eastleach Martin
Holwell
Filkins
Broughton Poggs
Wildlife Park
Shilton
Carterton
Kencot
Alvescot
Curbridge
Brize Norton
Ducklington
Lew
Black Bourton
Yelford
Bampton
Aston
Brighthampton
Cote
Broadwell
Langford
Southrop
Fairford Park
Fairford
Little Faringdon
Milton End
Horcott
Whelford
Inglesham
Cotswold Water Park (Fairford/Lechlade)
Dunfield
Kempsford
Meysey Hampton
Marston Meysey
Down Ampney
Lechlade on Thames
Buscot
Buscot Park
Thames Path
Eaton Hastings
Kelmscott
Grafton
Little Clanfield
Clanfield
Weald
Chimney
Radcot
Thrup
Carswell Marsh
Duxford
Hinton Waldrist
Buckland
Littleworth
Longworth
Pusey
Charney Bassett
Hatford
Faringdon
Badbury Hill
Great Barn
Little Coxwell
Shellingford
Stanford in the Vale
Fernham
Great Coxwell
Coleshill
Upper Inglesham
Hannington Wick
Castle Eaton
Hannington
Highworth
Westrop
Eastrop
Hampton
Latton
Cerney Wick
Cotswold Water Park (Ashton Keynes)
Somerford Keynes
South Cerney
Upperup
Ewen
Kemble
Kemble Wick
Shorncote
Poole Keynes
Ashton Keynes
Chelworth
Cricklade
Chelworth Upper Green
Chelworth Lower Green
Calcutt
Crudwell
Oaksey
Lower Moor Farm
Upper Minety
Minety
Leigh
Braydon Brook
Hankerton
Cloatley
Perry Green
Charlton
Garsdon
Ravensroost Wood and Meadows
Braydon
Purton Stoke
Purton
Widham
Queen Street
Braydon Side
The Common
Green Hill
Dogridge
Lydiard Millicent
Greatfield
Lydiard Green
Lydiard Park
Lydiard Tregoze
Hook
Hook Street
Callow Hill
Brinkworth
Little Somerford
Cleverton
Swindon & Cricklade Railway
Broad Blunsdon
Blunsdon St Andrew
Priory Vale
Penhill
Kingsdown
Haydon Wick
Moredon
Rodbourne
Gorse Hill
Stratton St Margaret
Common Platt
Nine Elms
Shaw
Toothill
SWINDON
Walcot
Coate
Coate Water
KEYPOINT
Stanton Fitzwarren
Sevenhampton
South Marston
Bourton
Watchfield
Shrivenham
Longcot
Uffington
Woolstone
Kingston Lisle
Compton Beauchamp
Kingstone Winslow
Ashbury
Uffington Castle
WHITEHORSE HILL 261
White Horse
Waylands Smithy
WELLBOTTOM DOWN
Idstone
Bishopstone
Hinton Parva
Ashdown House
LAMBOURN DOWNS
Upper Lambourn
Lambourn
West Challow
Sparsholt
Childrey
Letcombe Regis
Letcombe Bassett
Baulking
Goosey
Vale of White Horse
Horpit
Wanborough
Liddington
BISHOPSTONE DOWNS
EWE HILL
Fawley
South Fawley
Dauntsey
Seagry Heath
Lower Seagry
Grittenham
Tockenham Wick
Wootton Bassett
North Wroughton
Hodson
Elcombe
Wroughton
Chiseldon
Badbury
Overtown
Tockenham
Bradenstoke
Lyneham
Christian Malford
West End
Foxham
Catcomb
White Horse
Broad Town
Bushton
Preston
Goatacre
Clyffe Pypard
Uffcott
Draycot Foliat
Upper Upham
Baydon
Aldbourne
Woodsend
Barbury Castle
Ridgeway Path
Broad Hinton
Hilmarton
Clevancy
Spirthill
Charlcutt
East Tytherton
Tytherton Lucas
Bremhill
Highway
Winterbourne Bassett
Berwick Bassett
Compton Bassett
Yatesbury
Studley
Calne
Cherhill
Winterbourne Monkton
Rockley
Southend
Ogbourne St George
Ogbourne St Andrew
Ogbourne Maizey
Mildenhall
Axford
Ramsbury
Preston
Whittonditch
Crooked Soley
Knighton
Straight Soley
Chilton Foliat
New Town
River Kennet
Hungerford Newtown
Eastbury
Lambourn Woodlands
Woodlands St Mary
East Garston
Great Shefford
Membury
Windmill Hill
Avebury Manor
Stone Circle
Avebury
Avebury Trusloe
Fyfield Down
Fyfield
West Kennett
The Sanctuary
Beckhampton
Silbury Hill
West Kennett Long Barrow
East Kennett
West Overton
Manton
Lockeridge
Marlborough
Stitchcombe
Froxfield
Hungerford
Avington
Kintbury
Layland's Green
Inkpen Common
Inkpen
Bagshot
Little Bedwyn
Chisbury
Chisbury Chapel
Cadley
Savernake Forest
Durley
Great Bedwyn
Pumping Station
Crofton
Newtown
Shalbourne
Ham
Trapshill
Upper Green
Combe Gibbet
Walbury Hill
Combe
Rivar
Buttermere
Eastcourt
Wilton
Marten
East Grafton
West Grafton
Wexcombe
Oxenwood
Littledown
Vernham Street
Linkenholt
Fosbury
Tidcombe
TIDCOMBE DOWN
HAYDOWN HILL 254
Vernham Dean
Upton
Clench Common
Martinsell
Huish
Oare
Wootton Rivers
Stibb Green
Westcourt
Burbage
Easton Royal
EASTON HILL 241
Milton Lilbourne
Southcott
White Horse
Pewsey
Fyfield
West Stowell
Alton Barnes
Alton Priors
Honeystreet
Wilcot
Woodborough
VALE OF PEWSEY
Manningford Bruce
Manningford Bohune
North Newnton
PEWSEY DOWN
Gores
Broad Street
Hilcott
Charlton St Peter
Rushall
Upavon
Aughton
Brunton
Collingbourne Kingston
Sunton
Cadley
Collingbourne Ducis
Everleigh
East Everleigh
Lower Everleigh
Sidbury Hill
HAXTON DOWN
Ludgershall
Castle
Tidworth
Perham Down
Redenham
Appleshaw
Clanville
Penton Grafton
Penton Mewsey
East Anton
Enham Alamein
Hatherden
Wildhern
Upper Enham
Tangley
Hurstbourne Tarrant
Ibthorpe
Lower Chute
Upper Chute
Theobald's Green
Cherhill Down
White Horse
Calstone Wellington
Blackland
MORGANS HILL 258
NORTH DOWN
Bourton
Bishops Cannings
1643
Netherstreet
White Horse
Roundway
Rybury
MILK HILL 294
White Horse
Knap Hill
Stanton St Bernard
Allington
Horton
Little Horton
All Cannings
Coate
Devizes
Nursteed
Etchilhampton
Beechingstoke
Patney
Marden
Stert
Wedhampton
Chirton
Wilsford
WILSFORD DOWN
Urchfont
Potterne Wick
Potterne
Worton
Poulshot
Eastcott
Easterton
Market Lavington
West Lavington
Littleton Pannell
Little Cheverell
Great Cheverell
Erlestoke
LITTLETON DOWN
CHARLTON DOWN
West Chisenbury
East Chisenbury
Littlecott
Compton
Longstreet
Enford
Coombe
Fifield
Fittleton
Haxton
Netheravon
Dovecote
Figheldean
ENFORD DOWN
Camp
Derry Hill
Bowood
Mile Elm
Sandy Lane
Chittoe
Stockley
Heddington
Bromham
St Edith's Marsh
Rowde
Dunkirk
Sells Green
Seend
Inmarsh
Sandy Lane
Great Somerford
Lyneham
Spirthill
0 1 2 3 4 5 miles
0 1 2 3 4 5 6 7 8 kilometres

OXFORD
Eynsham
Wytham
Farmoor
Sutton
Stanton Harcourt
Cumnor
Wheatley
Horspath
Cuddesdon
Garsington
Great Milton
Tiddington
Thame
Haddenham
Long Crendon
Shabbington
Chinnor
Princes Risborough
Kennington
Sandford-on-Thames
Radley
Abingdon-on-Thames
Culham
Clifton Hampden
Dorchester
Berinsfield
Drayton
Sutton Courtenay
Milton
Steventon
Didcot
Harwell
Chilton
Wallingford
Crowmarsh Gifford
Benson
Ewelme
Watlington
Stokenchurch
Lewknor
Cholsey
Moulsford
Goring
Streatley
Pangbourne
Henley-on-Thames
Twyford
READING
Caversham
Earley
Woodley
Theale
Tilehurst
Wokingham
Shinfield
Newbury
Thatcham
Hermitage
Compton
East Ilsley
Kingsclere
Tadley
Basingstoke
BASINGSTOKE
Hook
Odiham
Fleet
Hartley Wintney
Yateley
Whitchurch
Overton
Oakley
Farnham

ST ALBANS
HEMEL HEMPSTEAD
Berkhamsted
Wendover
Princes Risborough
Great Missenden
Chesham
Amersham
Bovingdon
Kings Langley
Radlett
Shenley
WATFORD
Borehamwood
Bushey
Chorleywood
Rickmansworth
HIGH WYCOMBE
Beaconsfield
Chalfont St Giles
Chalfont St Peter
Gerrards Cross
Harefield
Harrow
Wembley
Marlow
Cookham
Maidenhead
SLOUGH
Uxbridge
Ealing
Henley-on-Thames
Wargrave
Twyford
Eton
Windsor
Datchet
Old Windsor
Hounslow
Richmond
Wokingham
Binfield
BRACKNELL
Ascot
Egham
STAINES-UPON-THAMES
Sunbury
Walton-on-Thames
Chertsey
Addlestone
Weybridge
Esher
Sandhurst
Crowthorne
Bagshot
Windlesham
Lightwater
Chobham
CAMBERLEY
Yateley
Byfleet
Cobham
Epsom
WOKING
Leatherhead
Hartley Wintney
Fleet
Farnborough
Aldershot
Send
East Horsley
GUILDFORD
Dorking
Heathrow
M25
M40
M4
M3
A40
A404
A4
A30
A31
A3
A322
A329(M)
A404(M)
5 miles
8 kilometres

Hatfield
Hoddesdon
Brookmans Park
Cuffley
Cheshunt
Potters Bar
Waltham Abbey
Epping
North Weald Bassett
Chipping Ongar
Enfield
Barnet
Theydon Bois
Chigwell
BRENTWOOD
Romford
Barking
Camden Town
Islington
Hackney
LONDON
Woolwich
Greenwich
Rainham
South Ockendon
Aveley
Grays
Lewisham
Dartford
Bromley
Swanley
Orpington
Croydon
Sutton
New Addington
Biggin Hill
Eynsford
West Kingsdown
Meopham
Otford
Kemsing
Borough Green
Banstead
Westerham
Sevenoaks
Caterham
Limpsfield
Oxted
Redhill
Reigate
Hildenborough
Hadlow
Hammersmith

CHELMSFORD
Maldon
Danbury
Little Baddow
Woodham Walter
Woodham Mortimer
Heybridge
Goldhanger
River Blackwater
Bradwell Waterside
Osea Is
Northey Is
St Lawrence
Tillingham
Dengie
Steeple
Mayland
Maylandsea
Asheldham
Southminster
Latchingdon
Althorne
Burnham-on-Crouch
River Crouch
Ostend
Creeksea
Margaretting
Ingatestone
Mountnessing
Stock
Hanningfield Reservoir
West Hanningfield
South Hanningfield
East Hanningfield
Rettendon
South Woodham Ferrers
North Fambridge
South Fambridge
Hullbridge
Runwell
Battlesbridge
Rawreth
Hockley
Hawkwell
Ashingdon
Rochford
Canewdon
Paglesham
Wallasea Island
FOULNESS ISLAND
Potton Is
Barling
Little Wakering
Great Wakering
North Shoebury
Shoeburyness
Shoebury Ness
SOUTHEND-ON-SEA
Southchurch
Prittlewell
Eastwood
Leigh-on-Sea
Westcliff-on-Sea
Hadleigh
Rayleigh
Thundersley
BRENTWOOD
Billericay
Wickford
Shotgate
Nevendon
Crays Hill
Ingrave
Herongate
BASILDON
Laindon
Pitsea
Vange
Bowers Gifford
South Benfleet
Canvey Island
Canvey Point
Leigh Beck
Fobbing
Corringham
Stanford le Hope
Coryton
Mucking
Orsett
Bulphan
West Horndon
Horndon on the Hill
South Ockendon
North Stifford
Chadwell St Mary
West Tilbury
East Tilbury
Tilbury
Grays
THAMES ESTUARY
Allhallows-on-Sea
Allhallows
Isle of Grain
Grain
Cliffe
Cooling
St Mary's Hoo
High Halstow
Lower Stoke
Middle Stoke
Hoo St Werburgh
Cliffe Woods
Higham
GRAVESEND
Northfleet
Sheerness
Minster
Queenborough
Eastchurch
ISLE OF SHEPPEY
Rushenden
River Medway
The Swale
Strood
ROCHESTER
CHATHAM
GILLINGHAM
Rainham
Upchurch
Newington
Sittingbourne
Teynham
Faversham
Kemsley
Milton Regis
Bapchild
Tunstall
Borden
Bredgar
Snodland
Aylesford
Ditton
Larkfield
West Malling
Kings Hill
MAIDSTONE
Bearsted
Hollingbourne
Harrietsham
Lenham
Leeds
Boxley
Detling
Meopham
Cobham
Wrotham
Coxheath
Hadlow
East Peckham
Headcorn
Charing
Doddington
Eastling
33
46
16
5 miles
8 kilometres

Southend-on-Sea
LONDON, BASILDON
SOUTHEND VICTORIA STATION
QUEENSWAY
SOUTHCHURCH ROAD
SOUTHEND CENTRAL STATION
The Victoria
The Royals
Porters Grange School
Kursaal Entertainment Centre
SeaLife Adventure
Adventure Island
Pier
SHOEBURYNESS
SHOEBURY
Ramsgate
BROADSTAIRS
LONDON, (M2), CANTERBURY
MARGATE RD
CHATHAM ST
Royal Victoria Pavilion
Maritime
Royal Harbour
Lifeboat Station
LD Lines & Transeuropa Ferries
St Augustine's Abbey
Granville
Bandstand
Sales Point
Holliwell Point
Foulness Point
Courtsend
Warden Point
Warden
Leysdown-on-Sea
Shell Ness
Whitstable
Whitstable Bay
Herne Bay
Reculver
Reculver Towers
Minnis Bay
MARGATE
Westgate on Sea
Birchington
Foreness Point
Cliftonville
Northdown
Kingsgate
NORTH FORELAND
Broadstairs
ISLE OF THANET
RAF Manston
Kent International
Manston
Minster
Pegwell Bay
Ramsgate
Oostende
Sandwich
Sandwich Bay
Royal St George's
Richborough Roman Fort
Canterbury
Sturry
Blean
Faversham
Chartham
Bridge
Wingham
Ash
Eastry
Deal
Walmer
Kingsdown
The Downs
Barham
Aylesham
Shepherdswell
East Kent Railway
North Downs Way
Goodnestone
Dargate
Yorkletts
Seasalter
Graveney
Boughton St
Selling
Molash
Godmersham
Crundale
Waltham
Petham
Bossingham
Derringstone
Elham Valley
Higham Park
Howletts
Wildwood Forest Park
Druidstone
Old Town Hall
Fordwich
Littlebourne
Wickhambreaux
Stodmarsh
Preston
Elmstone
Westbere
Hersden
Upstreet
Chislet
Sarre
St Nicholas at Wade
Monkton
Acol
Sholden
Northbourne
Great Mongeham
Ripple
Sutton
Eythorne
Nonington
Adisham
Bekesbourne
Patrixbourne
Kingston

Rosslare Harbour
(July-Sept)
Rosslare Harbour
STRUMBLE HEAD
Pen Brush
Pwll Deri
Pembrokeshire Coast Path
Trefasser
Manorowen
St Nicholas
Panteg
Ynys Daullyn
Granston
Carreg Sampson
Abercastle
Llangloffan
Jordanston
Porthgain
Trefin
Mathry
Castle Morris
B4331
Abereiddy
Llanrhian
A487
Square & Compass
Llangloffan Fen
Berea
Croes-goch
Tretio
Treffynnon
Letterston
ST DAVID'S HEAD
Treleddyd-fawr
Carnhedryn
Treglemais
Cerbyd
B4330
Whitesand Bay
Rhodiad-y-brenin
Caer Farchell
River Solva
Llandeloy
Tancredston
Pont-yr-hafod
B4583
Bishop's Palace
Whitchurch
Middle Mill
Treffgarne Owen
Hayscastle
Hayscastle Cross
St David's
RAMSEY ISLAND
Ramsey Sound
RSPB
Nine Wells
Solva
Pen-y-cwn
178
DUDWELL MT
St David's Peninsula Heritage Coast
Newgale
Leweston
Roch
Wolfsdale
PEMBROKESHIRE COAST NATIONAL PARK
Roch Gate
Simpson Cross
Rickets Head
Keeston
Nolton Haven
Nolton
Pelcomb Cross
St Brides Bay
St Brides Bay Heritage Coast
Lambston
Pelcomb Bridge
Druidston
Sutton
Haroldston West
Portfield Gate
B4341
Broad Haven
Broadway
B4327
Dreen Hill
Pembrokeshire Coast Path
Little Haven
Walton West
Solbury
Talbenny
Tiers Cross
St Brides
Walwyn's Castle
SKOMER ISLAND
Wooltack Point
Marloes
Hasguard
Sandy Haven
Thornton
St Ishmael's
Herbrandston
Steynton
Broad Sound
Hubberston
Hakin
Waterston
Marloes and Dale Heritage Coast
Dale
Great Castle Head
Llanstadwell
SKOKHOLM ISLAND
Westdale Bay
Dale Point
Milford Haven
Milford Haven (Aberdaugleddau)
Angle
Angle Bay
Pwllcrochan
St Anns Head
Rhoscrowther
B4320
Rosslare Harbour
Castlemartin Brook
Freshwater West
B4319
Castlemartin
Warren
Linney Head
Pembrokeshire Coast Path
0 1 2 3 4 5 miles
0 1 2 3 4 5 6 7 8 kilometres

Gwbert on Sea
Y Ferwig
Tremain
Blaenannerch
Poppit Sands
Pembrokeshire Coast Path
St Dogmaels Moylgrove Heritage Coast
Penparc
Blaenporth
Glynarthen
Rhydlewis
Cardigan
(Aberteifi)
St Dogmaels
Abbey
Bridgend
Llangoedmor
Beulah
Bettws Evan
Hawen
Troedyraur
Penrhiw-pal
Moylegrove
Gelbwr Bay
Monington
Teifi Marshes
Llechryd
Ponthirwaun
Brongest
Coed-y-Bryn
Maesllyn
Llandygwydd
Llangynllo
Trwyn-y-bwa
Pen-y-bryn
Castle
Cilgerran
TIVY SIDE
Cwm-cou
Dinas Head Heritage Coast
DINAS HEAD
Glanrhyd
Tredrissi
A487
Bridell
Abercych
Cenarth
Adpar
Llandyfriog
Aber-banc
Teifi Valley Railway
Horeb
Penrhiw
Newport Bay
Strumble Head
Pwllgwaelod
Fishguard Bay
Berry Hill
Nevern
B4582
Pontgarreg
Pengelli Forest
Rhoshill
Pen-rhiw
Newcastle Emlyn
(Castell Newydd Emlyn)
Henllan
Llangeler
Bryn-Henllan
Parrog
Newport
Felindre Farchog
Castell Henllys
Newchapel
Aber-arad
Pentre-cagel
Drefach
Felindre
National Wool
Glynteg
Ocean Lab
Dinas
A487
Carreg Coetan
Eglwyswrw
B4332
Boncath
Penrherber
Cwmhiraeth
Lower Town
Mynydd Melyn
Pontygynon
Blaenffos
Drefelin
Saron
Fishguard
(Abergwaun)
311
MYNYDD CAREGOG
Pentre Ifan
Crosswell
Llanfair-Nant-Gwyn
Whitechurch
Capel Iwan
Llanychaer Bridge
Pontyglasier
Bwlch-y-groes
Clydey
335
Cwmpengraig
Rhos
Penlan-Uchaf
Brynberian
Star
Cilrhedyn
Scleddau
PEMBROKESHIRE COAST
Crymmych
Cwm Morgan
362
Pontfaen
Tafarn-y-bwlch
Llwyn-drain
B4313
MYNYDD PRESELI
NATIONAL PARK
Tegryn
Trecwn
Hermon
Foel Eryr
536
FOEL CWMCERWYN
Mynachlog ddu
Pentregalar
265
Hermon
Little Newcastle
Puncheston
Rosebush
368
FOEL DRYCH
Llanfyrnach
Dinas
Trelech
Gors-Fawr
Glandwr
Esgair
Castlebythe
Tufton
Llandre Isaf
St Dogwells
Henry's Moat
(Castell Hendre)
Maenclochog
Hebron
Blaenwaun
Blaen-y-Coed
Cynwyl
Llangolman
Llanglydwen
Cefn-y-pant
The Welsh Chocolate Farm
Cwmbach
Llanwinio
Trelech a'r Betws
Rinaston
Wallis
Woodstock
Pantymenyn
Cwmfelin Mynach
Talog
Ambleston
Llys-y-fran Resr
New Moat
Efailwen
Bwlchnewydd
Triffleton
Llys-y-fran
Llanycefn
Login
Maesgwynne
Llanboidy
Gellywen
Abernant
Spittal
Walton East
Pen-ffordd
Crosshands
Scolton
Clarbeston
Llandissilio
Meidrim
Merthyr
Great Rudbaxton
Clarbeston Road
Bletherston
Llanfallteg
Henllan Amgoed
Carmarthen
(Caerfyrddin)
A40
Clunderwen
Gelly
Poyston Cross
Cwmfelin Boeth
Llangynin
B4298
Sarnau
Castle
Crundale
Wiston
Llanfallteg West
Whitland Abbey
United Counties
Fenton Brook
Castle
Bethesda
Bancyfelin
Llanllwch
Llawhaden
Haverfordwest
(Hwlffordd)
Robeston Wathen
Redstone Cross
A40
Whitland
Pwll Trap
St Clears
Croesyceiliog
Slebech
Pentlewin
Llanddewi Velfrey
Trevaughan
Backe
Canaston Bridge
Uzmaston
Blackpool Mill
B4314
Narberth
Crinow
Lampeter Velfrey
Llwyn-y-brain
Llangynog
Merlin's Bridge
Millin Cross
Picton Castle
Cold Blow
Melinau
Llanddowror
Boulston
Oakwood Theme Park
Bluestone
B4315
B4314
Tavernspite
A477
Llanybri
Minwear
Cross Hands
Princes Gate
A4066
Landshipping
Templeton
Red Roses
Laugharne
Llansteffan
Hook
Ludchurch
Lanteg
Crunwear
Llandawke
Martletwy
Thomas Chapel
Longstone
Llansadurnen
Laugharne
Ferryside
Broadway
Llangwm
Black Tar
Cwm Deri
Yerbeston
Marros
Brook
Wharley Point
Rosemarket
NATIONAL PARK
Folly Farm
Colby Woodland Garden
Pendine
Llanmiloe
Ginst Point
Llansaint
Newton Mountain
Loveston
Reynalton
Begelly
Stepaside
Amroth
Museum of Speed
Houghton
Lawrenny
Cresswell
Jeffreyston
Kilgetty
Summerhill
Burton
Cresselly
Broadmoor
West Williamston
Cross Inn
Pentlepoir
Wiseman's Bridge
Neyland
Upton
Carew Newton
Redberth
Wooden
Saundersfoot
Toll
Tide Mill
Carew Cross
Carew
East Williamston
A478
Waterloo
Milton
Broadfield
Cosheston
Monkstone Point
East Pennar
Golden Hill
A477
Sageston
New Hedges
B4322
Carew Cheriton
B4318
Manor House
Gumfreston
Tenby
(Dinbych-y-Pysgod)
Pembroke
(Penfro)
A4075
Bishop's Palace
St Florence
Lamphey
Manorbier Newton
CARMARTHEN BAY
Grove
Maiden Wells
B4584
Hodgeston
A4139
Penally
Jameston
Giltar Point
Freshwater East
Lydstep
Trewent
Manorbier
B4585
Lydstep Point
St Petrox
Cheriton or Stackpole Elidor
Trewent Point
Monastery
CALDEY ISLAND
Stackpole
Barafundle Bay
South Pembrokeshire Heritage Coast
Stackpole Head
St Govan's Chapel
St Govan's Head
J
K
L
M
N
P
Q
R

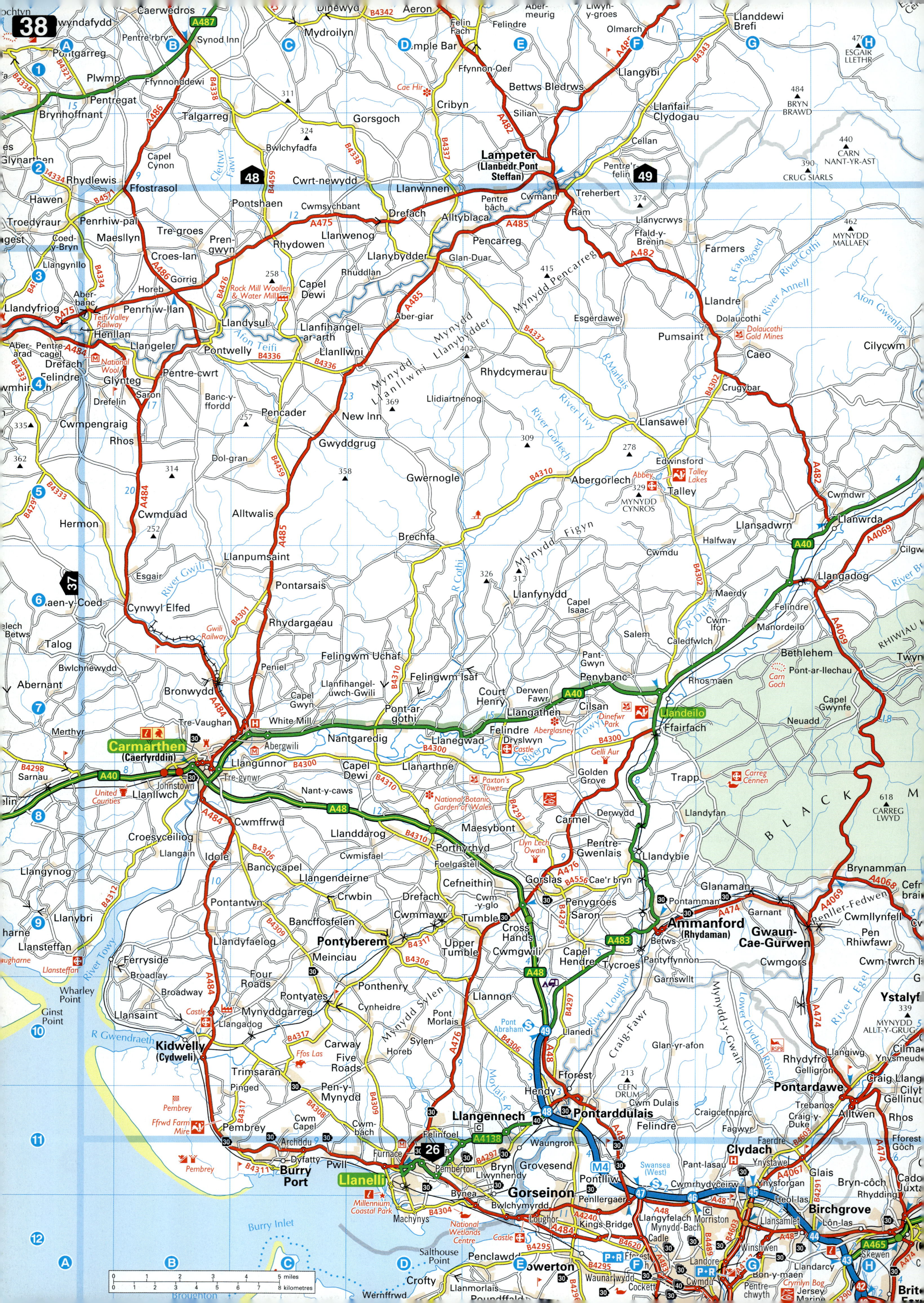

Caerwedros
Synod Inn
A487
Mydroilyn
Aeron
Dihewyd
B4342
Felin Fach
Felindre
Aber-meurig
Llwyn-y-groes
Olmarch
Llanddewi Brefi
Pontgarreg
Plwmp
Pentregat
Brynhoffnant
Fynnonddewi
Talgarreg
Gorsgoch
Cribyn
Temple Bar
Ffynnon-Oer
Bettws Bledrws
Llangybi
Silian
Llanfair Clydogau
ESGAIR LLETHR
BRYN BRAWD
CARN NANT-YR-AST
CRUG SIARLS
Cellan
Capel Cynon
Bwlchyfadfa
Lampeter (Llanbedr Pont Steffan)
Pentre'r-felin
Glynarthen
Rhydlewis
Ffostrasol
Cwrt-newydd
Llanwnnen
Cwmann
Treherbert
Hawen
Pontshaen
Cwmsychbant
Drefach
Alltyblaca
Pentre bach
Ram
Llanycrwys
Ffald-y-Brenin
Troedyraur
Penrhiw-pal
Tre-groes
Pren-gwyn
Rhydowen
Llanwenog
Llanybydder
Pencarreg
Farmers
MYNYDD MALLAEN
Coed-y-Bryn
Maesllyn
Croes-lan
Gorrig
Horeb
Capel Dewi
Rhuddlan
Glan-Duar
Mynydd Pencarreg
Rock Mill Woollen & Water Mill
Llangynllo
Aber-banc
Penrhiw-llan
Llandysul
Llanfihangel-ar-arth
Aber-giar
Mynydd Llanybydder
Esgerdawe
Llandre
Dolaucothi
Dolaucothi Gold Mines
River Cothi
River Annell
Afon Gwenlais
Llandyfriog
Teifi Valley Railway
Henllan
Llangeler
Pontwelly
Afon Teifi
Llanllwni
Pumsaint
Caeo
Cilycwm
Aber-arad
Pentre-cagel
Drefach
Felindre
National Wool Museum
Glynteg
Saron
Drefelin
Pentre-cwrt
Rhydcymerau
Crugybar
Cwmpengraig
Banc-y-ffordd
Pencader
New Inn
Mynydd Llanllwni
Llidiartnenog
River Gorlech
River Liwy
Llansawel
Rhos
Dol-gran
Gwyddgrug
Edwinsford
Talley Lakes
Talley
Abbey
Abergorlech
MYNYDD CYNROS
Gwernogle
Cwmdwr
Llanwrda
Cwmduad
Hermon
Alltwalis
Brechfa
Llansadwrn
Halfway
Cwmdu
Llanpumsaint
Esgair
River Gwili
Pontarsais
Mynydd Figyn
Llanfynydd
Capel Isaac
Llangadog
Maerdy
Felindre
Manordeilo
Cwm-Ifor
Caledfwlch
Salem
Laen-y-Coed
Cynwyl Elfed
Rhydargaeau
Gwili Railway
Talog
Bwlchnewydd
Felingwm Uchaf
Felingwm Isaf
Pant-Gwyn
Penybanc
Bethlehem
Pont-ar-llechau
Carn Goch
RHIWIAU
Twyn
Abernant
Bronwydd
Peniel
Llanfihangel-uwch-Gwili
Capel Gwyn
Court Henry
Derwen Fawr
Cilsan
Rhosmaen
Capel Gwynfe
Pont-ar-gothi
Llangathen
Dinefwr Park
Llandeilo
Ffairfach
Neuadd
Tre-Vaughan
White Mill
Nantgaredig
Llanegwad
Felindre
Dryslwyn Castle
Aberglasney
Merthyr
Carmarthen (Caerfyrddin)
Abergwili
Llangunnor
Capel Dewi
Llanarthne
Gelli Aur
Golden Grove
Trapp
Carreg Cennen
B4298
Sarnau
A40
Tre-gynwr
Johnstown
Llanllwch
United Counties
Nant-y-caws
Paxton's Tower
National Botanic Garden of Wales
A48
Carmel
Derwydd
Llandyfan
CARREG LWYD
Cwmffrwd
Llanddarog
Maesybont
Croesyceiliog
Llangain
Idole
Porthyrhyd
Llyn Llech Owain
Pentre-Gwenlais
Llandybie
Cwmisfael
Bancycapel
Foelgastell
Llangynog
Llangendeirne
Cefneithin
Gorslas
Cae'r bryn
Brynamman
Glanaman
Crwbin
Drefach
Cwm-y-glo
Penygroes
Pontamman
Garnant
Cwmllynfell
Pontantwn
Saron
Ammanford (Rhydaman)
Gwaun-Cae-Gurwen
Llanybri
Bancffosfelen
Cwmmawr
Tumble
Cross Hands
Betws
Pen Rhiwfawr
Llansteffan
Llandyfaelog
Pontyberem
Upper Tumble
Cwmgwili
Capel Hendre
Tycroes
Cwmgors
Cwm-twrch
Ferryside
Meinciau
Pantyffynnon
Broadlay
Four Roads
Garnswllt
Wharley Point
Broadway
Pontyates
Ponthenry
Llannon
Ystalyfera
Ginst Point
Llansaint
Castle
Mynyddgarreg
Cynheidre
Mynydd Sylen
Pont Morlais
Pont Abraham
Llanedi
Craig-Fawr
Mynydd-y-Gwair
MYNYDD ALLT-Y-GRUG
R Gwendraeth
Kidwelly (Cydweli)
Llangadog
Carway
Ffos Las
Five Roads
Horeb
Sylen
Glan-yr-afon
Rhydyfro
Gelligron
Ynysmeudw
Trimsaran
Pinged
Pen-y-Mynydd
Fforest
CEFN DRUM
Cwm Dulais
Pontardawe
Craig Llangiwg
Pembrey
Ffrwd Farm Mire
Pembrey
Cwm Capel
Cwm-bach
Llangennech
Hendy
Pontarddulais
Felindre
Craigcefnparc
Fagwyr
Trebanos
Craig-y-Duke
Alltwen
Rhos
Gellinudd
Archddu
Dyfatty
Pwll
Burry Port
Felinfoel
Furnace
Pemberton
Waungron
Bryn
Grovesend
Llwynhendy
Swansea (West)
Clydach
Ynystawe
Pant-lasau
Glais
Ffforest Goch
Llanelli
Millennium Coastal Park
Bynea
Gorseinon
Pontlliw
Penllergaer
Cwmrhydyceirw
Ynysforgan
Heol-las
Bryn-côch
Rhydding
Birchgrove
Lôn-las
Llansamlet
Machynys
Bwlchymyrdd
Loughor
Kingsbridge
Llangyfelach
Morriston
Mynydd-Bach
Cadle
Landore
Winsh-wen
Skewen
Llandarcy
Burry Inlet
National Wetlands Centre
Castle
Salthouse Point
Penclawdd
Gowerton
Waunarlwydd
Fforestfach
Cockett
Cwmdu
Bon-y-maen
Crymlyn Bog
Jersey Marine
Pentre-chwyth
Crofty
Wernffrwd
Llanmorlais
Poundffald
Broughton
5 miles
8 kilometres

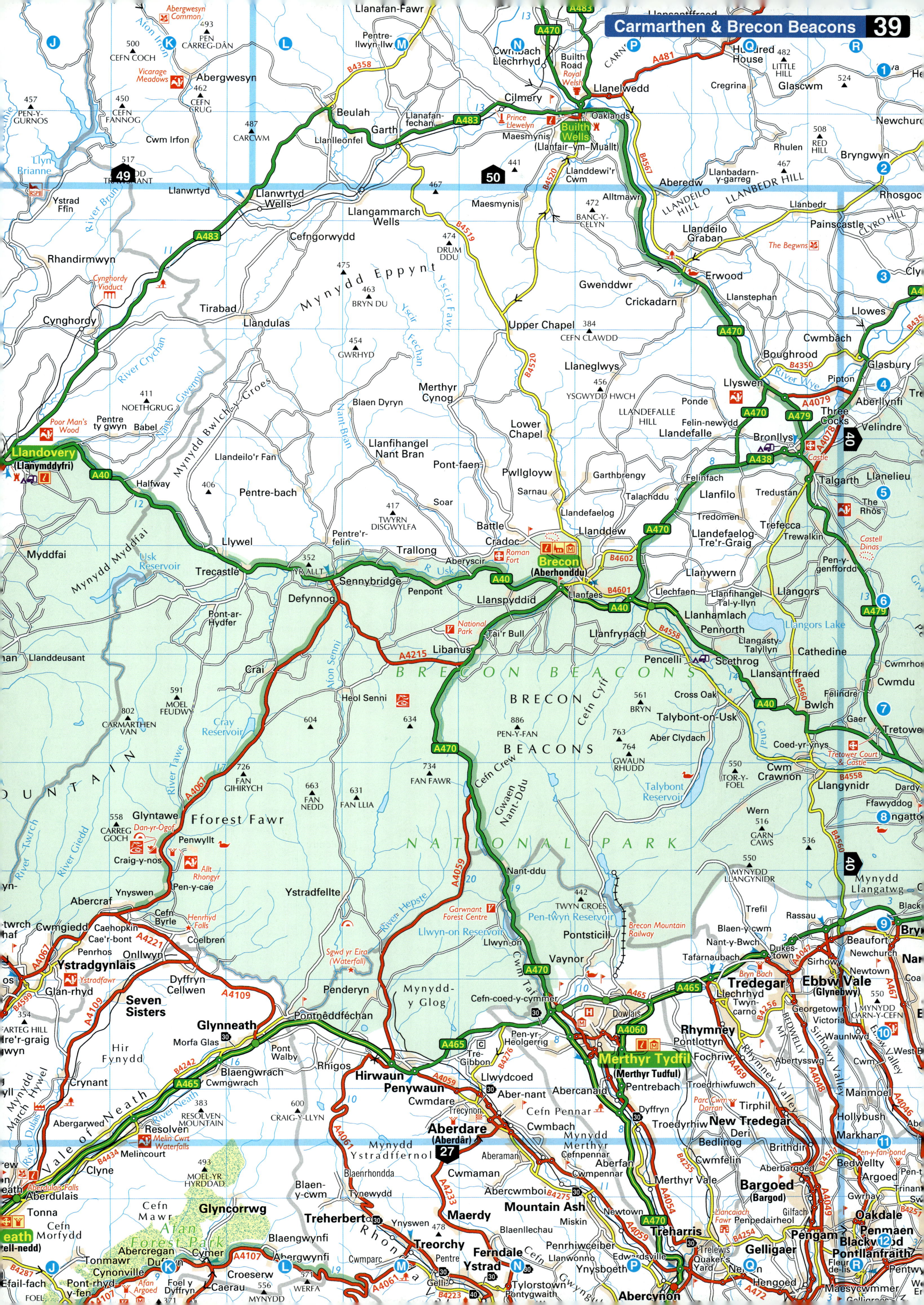
Llanafan-Fawr
Abergwesyn Common
Pentre-llwyn-llwyd
Cwmbach Llechrhyd
Builth Road
Royal Welsh
Llanelwedd
Hundred House
Little Hill
Cregrina
Glascwm
Newchurch
Abergwesyn
Vicarage Meadows
Cefn Coch
Pen Carreg-dân
Cefn Crug
Cefn Fannog
Pen-y-Gurnos
Carcwm
Cwm Irfon
Beulah
Garth
Llanafan-fechan
Cilmery
Prince Llewelyn
Oaklands
Builth Wells
(Llanfair-ym-Muallt)
Maesmynis
Llanlleonfel
Rhulen
Red Hill
Bryngwyn
Llyn Brianne
Llanwrtyd
Llanwrtyd Wells
Llanddewi'r Cwm
Llanbadarn-y-garreg
Aberedw
Llanbedr Hill
Llandeilo Hill
Rhosgoch
Ystrad Ffin
River Bran
Llangammarch Wells
Banc-y-Celyn
Alltmawr
Llanbedr
Painscastle
Clyro Hill
Cefngorwydd
Drum Ddu
Llandeilo Graban
The Begwns
Rhandirmwyn
Cynghordy Viaduct
Mynydd Eppynt
Bryn Du
Erwood
Gwenddwr
Crickadarn
Llanstephan
Tirabad
Llandulas
Cynghordy
Gwrhyd
Upper Chapel
Cefn Clawdd
Llowes
Cwmbach
Boughrood
River Crychan
Llaneglwys
Ysgwydd Hwch
Llyswen
River Wye
Glasbury
Pipton
Noethgrug
Pentre ty gwyn
Babel
Poor Man's Wood
Blaen Dyrryn
Merthyr Cynog
Llandefalle Hill
Ponde
Felin-newydd
Llandefalle
Three Cocks
Aberllynfi
Velindre
Mynydd Bwlch-y-Groes
Nant Bran
Lower Chapel
Bronllys
Llandovery
(Llanymddyfri)
Llanfihangel Nant Bran
Llandeilo'r Fan
Pont-faen
Pwllgloyw
Garthbrengy
Felinfach
Talgarth
Llanelieu
Halfway
Pentre-bach
Sarnau
Talachddu
Llanfilo
Tredustan
The Rhos
Soar
Twyrn Disgwylfa
Battle
Llandefaelog
Tredomen
Trefecca
Trewalkin
Llywel
Myddfai
Mynydd Myddfai
Usk Reservoir
Pentre'r-felin
Trallong
Cradoc
Roman Fort
Llanddew
Llandefaelog-Tre'r-Graig
Castell Dinas
Trecastle
Yr Allt
Sennybridge
Aberyscir
Brecon
(Aberhonddu)
Pen-y-genffordd
Llanywern
Defynnog
Penpont
Llanspyddid
Llanfaes
Llechfaen
Llanfihangel Tal-y-llyn
Llangors
Pont-ar-Hydfer
National Park
Tai'r Bull
Llanhamlach
Llanfrynach
Pennorth
Llangors Lake
Llanddeusant
Libanus
Llangasty-Talyllyn
Cathedine
Crai
Brecon Beacons
Pencelli
Scethrog
Llansantffraed
Cwmrhos
Cwmdu
Heol Senni
Afon Senni
Moel Feudwy
Cefn Cyff
Bryn
Cross Oak
Felindre
Bwlch
Carmarthen Van
Cray Reservoir
Pen-y-Fan
Talybont-on-Usk
Gaer
Aber Clydach
Coed-yr-ynys
Tretower
Tretower Court & Castle
Gwaun Rhudd
Fan Gihirych
Fan Fawr
Cefn Crew
Tor-y-Foel
Cwm Crawnon
Llangynidr
Canal
Talybont Reservoir
Fan Nedd
Fan Llia
Gwaen Nant-Ddu
Dardy
Ffawyddog
Wern
Garn Caws
Carreg Goch
Glyntawe
Dan-yr-Ogof
Fforest Fawr
Penwyllt
River Tawe
National Park
Craig-y-nos
Allt Rhongyr
Nant-ddu
Mynydd Llanynidr
Mynydd Llangatwg
Ynyswen
Pen-y-cae
Ystradfellte
Twyn Croes
Abercraf
River Hepste
Garwnant Forest Centre
Pen-twyn Reservoir
Trefil
Rassau
Cefn Byrle
Henrhyd Falls
Llwyn-on Reservoir
Pontsticill
Brecon Mountain Railway
Blaen-y-cwm
Cwmgiedd
Caehopkin
Coelbren
Cae'r-bont
Llwyn-on
Nant-y-Bwch
Dukes-town
Beaufort
Penrhos
Onllwyn
Sgwd yr Eira (Waterfall)
Vaynor
Tafarnaubach
Sirhowy
Newchurch
Ystradgynlais
Ystradfawr
Glan-rhyd
Dyffryn Cellwen
Penderyn
Mynydd-y Glog
Cwm Taf
Cefn-coed-y-cymmer
Bryn Bach
Tredegar
Ebbw Vale
(Glynebwy)
Newtown
Seven Sisters
Llechrhyd
Twyn-carno
Georgetown
Mynydd Carn-y-Cefn
Victoria
Glynneath
Pontneddfechan
Dowlais
Rhymney
Pontlottyn
Waunlwyd
Morfa Glas
Hir Fynydd
Pont Walby
Rhigos
Pen-yr-Heolgerrig
Merthyr Tydfil
(Merthyr Tudful)
Fochriw
Abertysswg
Cwm
Blaengwrach
Cwmgwrach
Tre-Gibbon
Hirwaun
Penywaun
Llwydcoed
Pentrebach
Troedrhiwfuwch
Rhymney Valley
Sirhowy Valley
Ebbw Valley
Crynant
Abercanaid
Manmoel
Resolven Mountain
Craig-y-Llyn
Aber-nant
Cwmdare
Trecynon
Cefn Pennar
Parc Cwm Darran
Tirphil
Dyffryn
Troedyrhiw
New Tredegar
Hollybush
Mynydd March Hywel
Abergarwed
Vale of Neath
River Neath
Resolven
Melin Cwrt Waterfalls
Aberdare
(Aberdâr)
Cwmbach
Mynydd Merthyr
Cefnpennar
Deri
Markham
Bedlinog
Brithdir
River Dulais
Melincourt
Mynydd Ystradffernol
Abercwmboi
Aberaman
Aberfan
Cwmpennar
Cwmfelin
Aberbargoed
Pen-y-fan-pond
Bedwellty
Clyne
Moel-yr Hyrddad
Blaenrhondda
Cwmaman
Merthyr Vale
Bargoed
(Bargod)
Argoed
Aberdulais Falls
Aberdulais
Blaen-y-cwm
Tynewydd
Mountain Ash
Gilfach
Gwrhay
Oakdale
Tonna
Cefn Mawr
Glyncorrwg
Afan Forest Park
Treherbert
Ynyswen
Maerdy
Miskin
Newtown
Llancaiach Fawr
Penpedairheol
Treharris
Neath
(Castell-nedd)
Cefn Morfydd
Abercregan
Blaengwynfi
Treorchy
Blaenllechau
Ferndale
Penrhiwceiber
Pengam
Penmaen
Blackwood
Gelligaer
Pontllanfraith
Tonmawr
Cynonville
Duffryn
Cymer
Abergwynfi
Cwmparc
Pentre
Rhondda
Ystrad
Llanwonno
Ynysboeth
Edwardsville
Trelewis
Quaker's Yard
Nelson
Fleur-de-lis
Pentwyn
Efail-fach
Pont-rhyd-y-fen
Afan Argoed
Foel y Dyffryn
Croeserw
Caerau
Gelli
Tylorstown
Pontygwaith
Abercynon
Hengoed
Maesycwmmer
Foel
Werfa
Mynydd
Llanfair-ym-Muallt

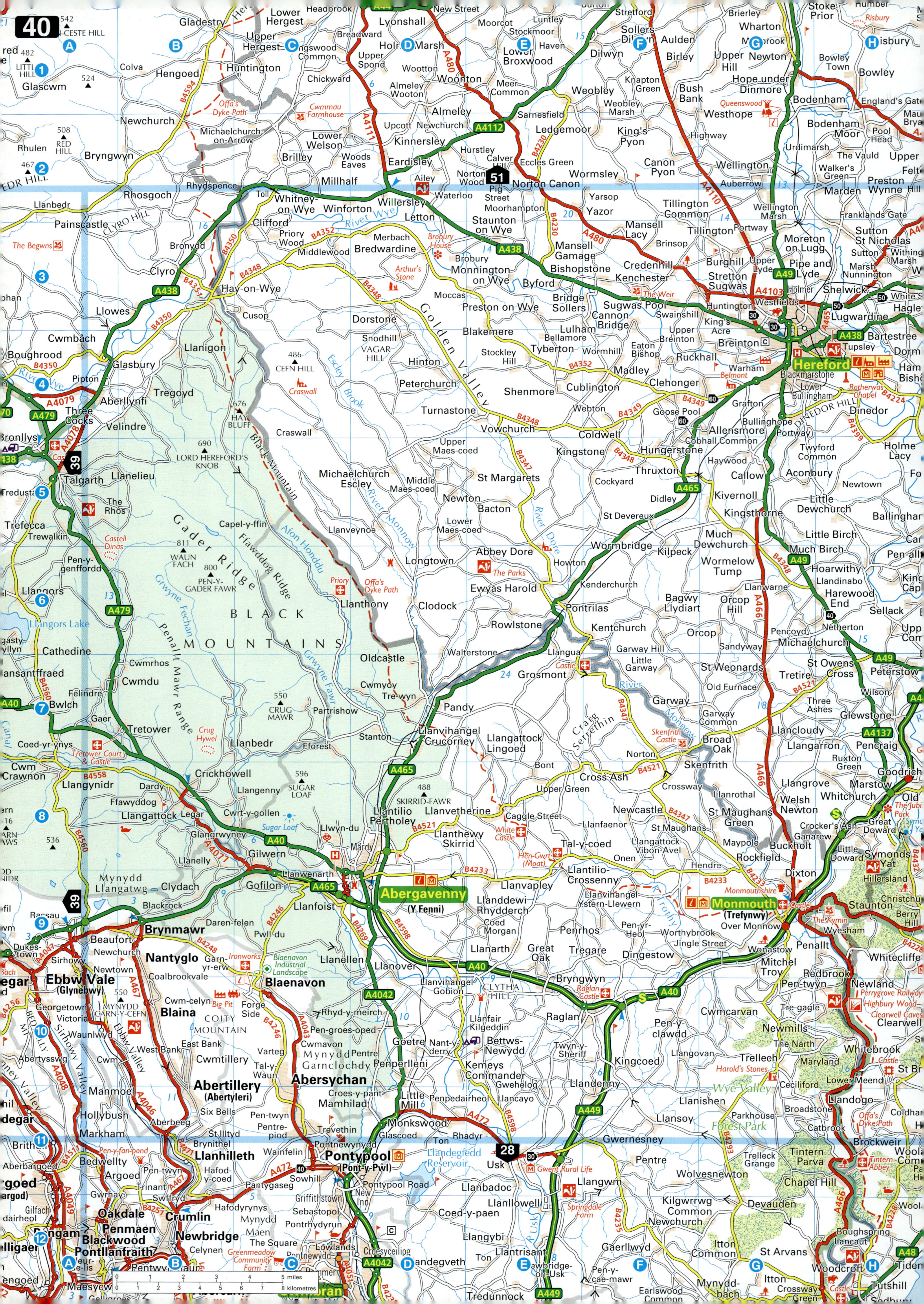
Gladestry
Lower Hergest
Upper Hergest
Kingswood Common
Huntington
Hengoed
Colva
Glascwm
Newchurch
Michaelchurch-on-Arrow
Rhulen
Bryngwyn
Brilley
Lower Welson
Woods Eaves
Rhydspence
Rhosgoch
Lyonshall
Holme Marsh
Upper Spond
Almeley
Almeley Wooton
Woonton
Kinnersley
Eardisley
Millhalf
Whitney-on-Wye
Winforton
Willersley
Letton
Clifford
Priory Wood
Middlewood
Bredwardine
Merbach
Brobury House
Arthur's Stone
Dorstone
Snodhill
Vagar Hill
Hinton
Peterchurch
Turnastone
Vowchurch
Golden Valley
Painscastle
Clyro
Clyro Hill
The Begwns
Hay-on-Wye
Cusop
Llowes
Cwmbach
Boughrood
Glasbury
Llanigon
Tregoyd
Aberllynfi
Three Cocks
Velindre
Bronllys
Talgarth
Llanelieu
The Rhos
Trefecca
Trewalkin
Pen-y-genffordd
Llangors
Llangors Lake
Cathedine
Bwlch
Llansantffraed
Felindre
Gaer
Tretower
Coed-yr-ynys
Cwm Crawnon
Llangynidr
Crickhowell
Llangattock
Llangenny
Cwrt-y-gollen
Sugar Loaf
Gilwern
Glangrwyney
Llanelly
Clydach
Gofilon
Llanfoist
Abergavenny
(Y Fenni)
Llanwenarth
Mardy
Llantilio Pertholey
Llanvetherine
Lower Hergest
Gader Ridge
Black Mountains
Black Mountain
Hay Bluff
Lord Hereford's Knob
Waun Fach
Pen-y-Gader Fawr
Crug Mawr
Crug Hywel
Penallt Mawr Range
Grwyne Fechan
Grwyne Fawr
Ffawddog Ridge
Afon Honddu
Capel-y-ffin
Llanthony
Llanbedr
Partrishow
Eforest
Cwmyoy
Tre-wyn
Pandy
Oldcastle
Stanton
Llanvihangel Crucorney
Craswall
Cefn Hill
Escley Brook
Michaelchurch Escley
Llanveynoe
Longtown
Clodock
Walterstone
Middle Maes-coed
Upper Maes-coed
Lower Maes-coed
Newton
Bacton
St Margarets
Abbey Dore
Ewyas Harold
Rowlstone
Pontrilas
Kentchurch
Llangua
Grosmont
Garway
Garway Hill
Little Garway
Craig Serrethin
Skenfrith
Broad Oak
Llangattock Lingoed
Bont
Cross Ash
Upper Green
Newcastle
Llanfaenor
Caggle Street
Skirrid-Fawr
Llanthewy Skirrid
White Castle
Tal-y-coed
Llantilio-Crossenny
Llanvapley
Llanddewi Rhydderch
Coed Morgan
Llanarth
Great Oak
Tregare
Penrhos
Dingestow
Llanvihangel-Ystern-Llewern
Pen-yr-Heol
Jingle Street
Worthybrook
Monmouth
(Trefynwy)
Over Monnow
Wonastow
Mitchel Troy
Rockfield
Hendre
Onen
Llangattock-Vibon-Avel
St Maughans
St Maughans Green
Maypole
Buckholt
Dixton
Llanrothal
Welsh Newton
Whitchurch
Llangrove
Marstow
Goodrich
Ganarew
Crocker's Ash
Great Doward
Little Doward
Symonds Yat
Hillersland
Staunton
Christchurch
Berry Hill
Wyesham
Penallt
Redbrook
Newland
Whitecliff
Clearwell
Whitebrook
Trellech
Maryland
Lower Meend
St Briavels
Llandogo
Newmills
The North
Tre-gagle
Pen-twyn
Cwmcarvan
Raglan
Raglan Castle
Bryngwyn
Llanover
Llanvihangel Gobion
Clytha Hill
Llanfair Kilgeddin
Bettws-Newydd
Kemeys Commander
Twyn-y-Sheriff
Pen-y-clawdd
Llangovan
Kingcoed
Llandenny
Llanishen
Llansoy
Gwernesney
Pentre
Wolvesnewton
Kilgwrrwg Common
Newchurch
Devauden
Itton Common
Itton
St Arvans
Mynydd-bach
Earlswood Common
Tintern Parva
Tintern Abbey
Chapel Hill
Trelleck Grange
Parkhouse
Catbrook
Brockweir
Wye Valley
Forest Park
Usk
Llanbadoc
Llanllowell
Llantrisant
Gwernesney
Gwent Rural Life
Springdale Farm
Llangwm
Gaerllwyd
Pen-y-cae-mawr
Newbridge-on-Usk
Tredunnock
Llangybi
Coed-y-paen
Rhadyr
Glascoed
Monkswood
Little Mill
Penpedairheol
Llancayo
Gwehelog
Goetre
Nant-y-derry
Penperlleni
Mamhilad
Croes-y-pant
Llanellen
Pwll-du
Blaenavon
Blaenavon Industrial Landscape
Garn-yr-erw
Forge Side
Varteg
Cwmavon
Pen-groes-oped
Rhyd-y-meirch
Abersychan
Mynydd Garnclochdy
Pontypool
(Pont-y-Pŵl)
Pontnewynydd
Trevethin
Wainfelin
Sowhill
Griffithstown
Sebastopol
Pontrhydyrun
New Inn
Croesyceiliog
Llanfrechfa
Pontnewydd
Llandegfedd Reservoir
Daren-felen
Brynmawr
Beaufort
Nantyglo
Coalbrookvale
Ebbw Vale
(Glynebwy)
Blaina
Cwm-celyn
Coity Mountain
Cwmtillery
Abertillery
(Abertyleri)
Six Bells
Tal-y-Waun
Pen-twyn
Pentre-piod
Llanhilleth
Brynithel
Hafod-y-coed
Aberbeeg
Cwm
Waunlwyd
Victoria
Georgetown
Manmoel
Hollybush
Markham
Aberbargoed
Bedwellty
Argoed
Oakdale
Penmaen
Blackwood
Pontllanfraith
Crumlin
Newbridge
Celynen
Treowen
Hafodyrynys
Mynydd Maen
The Square
Greenmeadow Community Farm
Abersychan
Cwmbran
Ebbw Valley
Sirhowy Valley
Mynydd Llangatwg
Dukestown
Rassau
Sirhowy
Newtown
Tredegar
Hereford
Holmer
Shelwick
Lugwardine
Bartestree
Tupsley
Hampton Bishop
Dinedor
Dinedor Hill
Rotherwas Chapel
Grafton
Bullinghope
Lower Bullingham
Belmont
Warham
Breinton
Ruckhall
Eaton Bishop
Clehonger
Madley
Cublington
Tyberton
Blakemere
Preston on Wye
Moccas
Monnington on Wye
Byford
Bridge Sollers
Canon Bridge
Lulham
Swainshill
Upper Breinton
Kenchester
Credenhill
The Weir
Sugwas Pool
Stretton Sugwas
Burghill
Tillington
Tillington Common
Mansel Lacy
Mansell Gamage
Bishopstone
Yazor
Yarsop
Brinsop
Norton Canon
Staunton on Wye
Moorhampton
Pig Street
Waterloo
Norton Wood
Ailey
Calver Hill
Hurstley
Eccles Green
Ledgemoor
Sarnesfield
Meer Common
Lower Broxwood
Moorcot
Stockmoor
Luntley
Haven
Dilwyn
Sollers Dilwyn
Weobley
Weobley Marsh
Knapton Green
King's Pyon
Canon Pyon
Wormsley
Mansell Lacy
Birley
Aulden
Bush Bank
Upper Hill
Westhope
Queenswood
Hope under Dinmore
Bodenham
Bodenham Moor
Wellington
Wellington Marsh
Moreton on Lugg
Marden
Sutton St Nicholas
Pipe and Lyde
Upper Lyde
Portway
Auberrow
Huntington
King's Acre
Wormhill
Webton
Goose Pool
Kingstone
Allensmore
Cobhall Common
Hungerstone
Thruxton
Cockyard
Haywood
Callow
Kivernoll
Didley
St Devereux
Wormbridge
Kilpeck
Much Dewchurch
Kingsthorne
Little Dewchurch
Wormelow Tump
Howton
Kenderchurch
Bagwy Llydiart
Orcop
Orcop Hill
Llanwarne
Much Birch
Little Birch
Hoarwithy
Harewood End
Sellack
Pencoyd
Michaelchurch
Sandyway
St Weonards
Old Furnace
Tretire
St Owens Cross
Peterstow
Glewstone
Three Ashes
Llancloudy
Llangarron
Pencraig
Ruxton Green
Welsh Newton
Aconbury
Twyford Common
Portway
Holme Lacy
Ballingham
Brierley
Wharton
Newton
Stoke Prior
Humber
Risbury
Hisbury
Bowley Town
Bowley
Pool Head
The Vauld
Walker's Green
Preston Wynne
Urdimarsh
Frankland Gate
Withington Marsh
Nunnington
Marsh
Hagley
Dormington
Hampton Bishop
Croft
Headbrook
Broadward
New Street
Burton
Stretford
Upcott
Newchurch
Chickward
Cwmmau Farmhouse
Offa's Dyke Path
Brynmawr
Castell Dinas
The Parks
Priory
Skenfrith Castle
Hen-Gwrt (Moat)
Perrygrove Railway
Highbury Wood
Clearwell Caves
Harold's Stones
Ceciliford
Broadstone
Offa's Dyke Path
River Wye
River Dore
River Monnow
River Usk
Usk
Tretower Court & Castle
Ironworks
Big Pit
0 1 2 3 4 5 miles
0 1 2 3 4 5 6 7 8 kilometres

Bromyard
Great Malvern
Malvern Wells
Upton upon Severn
Pershore
Ledbury
Tewkesbury
Newent
Ross-on-Wye
Bishop's Cleeve
CHELTENHAM
Charlton Kings
GLOUCESTER
Brockworth
Cinderford
Coleford
Lydney
Stonehouse
Stroud
Chalford
Cirencester
Minchinhampton
Nailsworth
Dursley
Newnham
Leigh Sinton
Colwall
Eastnor
Bromsberrow Heath
Dymock
Kempley
Staunton
Hartpury
Longford
Churchdown
Quedgeley
Whaddon
Painswick
Birdlip
Winchcombe
Eckington
Kemerton
Ashchurch
Deerhurst
Tredington
Woodmancote
Southam
Cam
Uley
Frampton on Severn
Slimbridge
Berkeley
Sharpness
Blakeney
Awre
Westbury on Severn
Flaxley
Mitcheldean
Ruardean
Drybrook
Parkend
Yorkley
Bream
Alvington
Woolaston
A44
A4103
A449
A438
A417
A4172
A4136
A48
A40
A46
A4019
A435
A436
A419
A38
A4135
A433
A429
M5
M50
B4211
B4208
B4215
B4216
B4221
B4063
B4070
B4066
B4058
B4008
B4080
B4084
B4104
River Severn
Forest of Dean
Wildfowl & Wetlands Trust
Cotswold Way
Dean Forest Railway
Three Counties
Three Choirs
Croome Park
Hellen's House
Birds of Prey Centre
Westbury Court Garden
Woodchester Park
Chavenage
Odda's Chapel
Tithe Barn
Elgar Birthplace
52
29
42

Kington
Abbots Morton
Weethley
Exhall
Red Hill
Temple Grafton
Lighthorne Heath
Flyford Flavell
Goom's Hill
Bevington
Wood Bevington
Ragley Hall
Wixford
Ardens Grafton
Shottery
Tiddington
Stratford upon-Avon
Wellesbourne
Wellesbourne Mountford
Morrell
Moreton Paddox
Heritage Motor Centre
Gaydon
M40
Piddle
Abberton
Rous Lench
Dunnington
Broom
Bidford-on-Avon
Cranhill
Binton
Anne Hathaway's Cottage
Luddington
Butterfly Farm
Walton
Compton Verney
Naunton Beauchamp
Church Lench
Cock Bevington
Iron Cross
Welford-on-Avon
Weston-on-Avon
Clifford Chambers
Loxley
Chadshunt
Bishampton
Ab Lench
Salford Priors
Atherstone on Stour
Combrook
Kineton
Atch Lench
Abbot's Salford
Marlcliff
Barton
Preston on Stour
Little Kineton
Throckmorton
Dorsington
Willicote
Alderminster
Butlers Marston
Edgehill 1642
Pinvin
Harvington
Cleeve Prior
Long Marston
Wimpstone
Ettington
Pillerton Hersey
Radway
Upper Moor
Norton
Lenchwick
North Littleton
Lower Quinton
Pebworth
Crimscote
Pillerton Priors
Edgehill
Wyre Piddle
Lower Moor
Offenham
Middle Littleton
Tithe Barn
South Littleton
Broad Marston
Upper Quinton
Newbold on Stour
Fladbury
Chadbury
Charlton
Cropthorne
Wick
Evesham
Aldington
Bretforton
Honeybourne
Admington
Halford
Fullready
Oxhill
Whatcote
Lower Tysoe
Middle Tysoe
Upper Tysoe
Upton House
Armscote
Idlicote
Little Comberton
Bengeworth
Hampton
Badsey
The Fleece Inn
Mickleton
Kiftsgate Court
Hidcote Bartrim
Hidcote Manor Garden
Blackwell
Ilmington
Tredington
Honington
Alderton
Shenington
Great Comberton
Bricklehampton
Netherton
Vale of Evesham
Aston-sub-Edge
Weston-sub-Edge
Hidcote Boyce
Darlingscott
Shipston on Stour
Balscote
Elmley Castle
Wickhamford
Hinton Green
Ebrington
Charingworth
Winderton
Shutford
Upper Brailes
Epwell
Bredon Hill
Kersoe
Hinton on the Green
Murcot
Willersey
Saintbury
Chipping Campden
Barcheston
Willington
Stretton on Fosse
Lower Brailes
Tidmington
Burmington
Swalcliffe
Ashton under Hill
Childswickham
Aston Somerville
Cotswold Way
Sutton-under-Brailes
Grafton
Sedgeberrow
Broad Campden
Paxford
Sibford Gower
Sibford Ferris
Conderton
Beckford
Wormington
Broadway
Todenham
Cherington
Stourton
Kemerton
Buckland
Draycott
Broadway Tower
Blockley
Aston Magna
Little Wolford
Ascott
Silk Mill
Great Washbourne
Little Washbourne
Dumbleton
Laverton
Stanton
Snowshill
Snowshill Manor
Lavender
Batsford
Dorn
Lower Lemington
Great Wolford
Whichford
Waterfowl Sanctuary & Children's Farm
Aston Cross
Hook Norton
Toddington
Alderton
Cotswold Falconry Centre
Long Compton
Wigginton
Teddington
Four Shire Stone
Barton-on-the-Heath
Stanway
Bourton-on-the-Hill
Bourton Downs
Moreton-in-Marsh
Alstone
Oxenton
Stanley Pontlarge
Gloucestershire Warwickshire Railway
Taddington
Sezincote
Kitebrook
Swerford
Dixton
Didbrook
Hailes Abbey
Great Rollright
Little Rollright
Rollright Stones
Gretton
Greet
Cutsdean
Longborough
Chastleton
Little Compton
Hailes
Ford
Langley Hill
Nottingham Hill
Farmcote
Condicote
Evenlode
Chastleton House
Salford
Over Norton
Dunthrop
Heythrop
Woodmancote
Langley
Winchcombe
Sudeley
Temple Guiting
Donnington
Broadwell
Adlestrop
Cornwell
The Common
Chipping Norton
Church Enstone
Cleeve Hill
Cotswold
Upper Swell
Lower Swell
Stow-on-the-Wold
Daylesford
Southam
Kineton
Barton
Oddington
Maugersbury
Kingham
Churchill
Enstone
Belas Knap
Prestbury
Guiting Power
Upper Slaughter
Naunton
Charlton Abbots
Hawling
Icomb
Wyck Rissington
Bledington
Sarsden
Dean
Cheltenham
Brockhampton
Lower Slaughter
Bourton-on-the-Water
Miniatures
Model Village
Foscot
Chadlington
Spelsbury
Taston
Fulwell
Battledown
Ham
Sevenhampton
Whittington
Salperton
Aylworth
Westcote
Nether Westcote
Foxholes
Lyneham
Greenend
Charlbury
Charlton Kings
Syreford
Andoversford
Shipton
Notgrove
Motor & Toy
Little Rissington
Upper Rissington
Idbury
Fifield
Bruern Abbey
Chilson
Dowdeswell
Leckhampton Hill
Hazleton
Cold Aston
Clapton-on-the-Hill
Milton-under-Wychwood
Ascott Earl
Ascott-under-Wychwood
Shipton-under-Wychwood
Wychwood
Fawler
Foxcote
Turkdean
Seven Springs
Compton Abdale
Withington
Great Rissington
Habber Gallows Hill
Langley
Finstock
Coberley
Upper Coberley
Hampnett
Farmington
Fullbrook Hill
Leafield
Ramsden
Cowley
Yanworth
Northleach
Sherborne
Great Barrington
Taynton
Fordwells
Whiteoak Green
Delly End
Colesbourne
Chedworth Roman Villa
World of Mechanical Music
Eastington
Windrush
Little Barrington
Upton
Fulbrook
Asthall Leigh
Crawley
Hailey
North Leigh
New Yatt
Elkstone
Chedworth
Swinbrook
Minster Lovell Hall
Minster Lovell
Burford
Witney
Asthall
Coln St Dennis
Fossebridge
Calcot
Coln Rogers
Rendcomb
Winson
Westwell
Signet
Cotswold Wildlife Park
Shilton
Brize Norton
Charterville Allotments
Woodgreen
Newland
Cogges
High Cogges
Caudle Green
Winstone
Woodmancote
Aldsworth
Holwell
Calmsden
North Cerney
Ablington
Carterton
Curbridge
Ducklington
Duntisbourne Abbots
Duntisbourne Leer
Middle Duntisbourne
Bagendon
Perrott's Brook
Arlington
Bibury
Brize Norton
Lew
Duntisbourne Rouse
Baunton
Coln St Aldwyns
Hatherop
Eastleach Turville
Eastleach Martin
Kencot
Alvescot
Yelford
Daglingworth
Barnsley
Filkins
Black Bourton
Stratton
Quenington
Broughton Poggs
Broadwell
Aston
Brighthampton
Sapperton
Ampney Crucis
Ampney St Mary
Southrop
Bampton
Mansell
Cirencester
The Beeches
Fairford Park
Fairford
Langford
Little Clanfield
Clanfield
Weald
Cote
Shifford
Coates
Preston
Ampney St Peter
Poulton
Milton End
Little Faringdon
Grafton
Chimney
Tarlton
Chesterton
Amphitheatre
Harnhill
Poulton Priory
Horcott
Lechlade on Thames
Radcot
Duxford
Siddington
Driffield
Meysey Hampton
Whelford
Kelmscott
Thrup
Carswell Marsh
Hinton Waldrist
Longworth
Driffield Cross Roads
Inglesham
Buscot
Thames Path
Eaton Hastings
Buckland
Ewen
Kemble
South Cerney
Upperup
Marston Meysey
Fairford
Dunfield
Cotswold Water Park (Fairford/Lechlade)
Littleworth
Cerney Wick
Cotswold Water Park
Down Ampney
Kempsford
Buscot Park
Pusey
Kemble
Shorncote
Somerford Keynes
Latton
Castle Eaton
Upper Inglesham
Hannington Wick
Badbury Hill
Faringdon
Hatford
Charney Bassett
Poole Keynes
Chelworth
Ashton Keynes
Cricklade
miles
kilometres
A44
A46
A429
A422
A3400
A435
A436
A40
A417
A419
A433
A361
A424
A4095
A415
A38
B4035
B4632
B4077
B4068
B4425
B4449
B4020
B4477
B4437
B4026
B4022
B4450
B4450
53
41
30

Banbury
Brackley
Towcester
Buckingham
Bicester
Kidlington
OXFORD
Wheatley
Thame
Haddenham
Aylesbury
Winslow
MILTON KEYNES
Abingdon-on-Thames
Kennington
Eynsham
Chinnor
Stokenchurch
Woodstock
Charwelton
Preston Capes
Farthingstone
Litchborough
Pattishall
Eastcote
Astcote
Blisworth
Courteenhall
Roade
Hartwell
Piddington
Quinton
Byfield
Woodford Halse
Adstone
Canons Ashby
Moreton Pinkney
Maidford
Grimscote
Cold Higham
Blakesley
Greens Norton
Tiffield
Caldecote
Shutlanger
Stoke Bruerne
Ashton
Stoke Goldington
Wormleighton
Upper Boddington
Lower Boddington
Aston le Walls
Chipping Warden
Culworth
Weston
Plumpton
Weedon Lois
Slapton
Bradden
Woodend
Alderton
Grafton Regis
Hanslope
Paulerspury
Yardley Gobion
Potterspury
Cosgrove
Old Stratford
Deanshanger
Wicken
Passenham
Calverton
Leckhampstead
Akeley
Maids Moreton
Thornton
Nash
Whaddon
Thornborough
Singleborough
Great Horwood
Little Horwood
Adstock
Padbury
Gawcott
Radclive
Tingewick
Finmere
Mixbury
Water Stratford
Westbury
Evenley
Turweston
Whitfield
Biddlesden
Dadford
Shalstone
Chackmore
Stowe Gardens
Syresham
Silverstone
Whittlebury
Lillingstone Dayrell
Lillingstone Lovell
Wappenham
Abthorpe
Helmdon
Sulgrave
Thorpe Mandeville
Wardington
Cropredy
Mollington
Farnborough
Avon Dassett
Fenny Compton
Great Bourton
Little Bourton
Hanwell
Drayton
Middleton Cheney
Thenford
Greatworth
Marston St Lawrence
Farthinghoe
Halse
Radstone
Warkworth
Bodicote
Adderbury
Bloxham
Milton
King's Sutton
Newbottle
Charlton
Hinton-in-the-Hedges
Croughton
Aynho
Walton Grounds
Barford St John
Barford St Michael
South Newington
Deddington
Clifton
Hempton
North Aston
Souldern
Fritwell
Somerton
Ardley
Upper Heyford
Lower Heyford
Steeple Aston
Middle Aston
Duns Tew
Great Tew
Over Worton
Middle Barton
Westcote Barton
Steeple Barton
Kiddington
Rousham
Glympton
Wootton
Tackley
Kirtlington
Weston-on-the-Green
Bletchingdon
Shipton-on-Cherwell
Hampton Poyle
Thrupp
Bladon
Begbroke
Yarnton
Church Hanborough
Cassington
Combe
Stonesfield
Long Hanborough
Freeland
Eynsham
Swinford
Wytham
Farmoor
Sutton
Stanton Harcourt
Cumnor
Eaton
Appleton
Northmoor
Bessels Leigh
Wootton
Sandleigh
Sunningwell
Cothill
Shippon
Frilford
Marcham
Kingston Bagpuize
Fyfield
Tubney
Drayton
Sutton Wick
Culham
Clifton Hampden
Long Wittenham
Dorchester
Berinsfield
Drayton St Leonard
Berrick Prior
Newington
Chalgrove
Britwell Salome
Cuxham
Pyrton
Watlington
Brightwell Baldwin
Easington
Stadhampton
Chiselhampton
Marsh Baldon
Toot Baldon
Nuneham Courtenay
Sandford-on-Thames
Radley
Garsington
Cuddesdon
Great Milton
Little Milton
Great Haseley
Little Haseley
Stoke Talmage
Tetsworth
Latchford
Adwell
Wheatfield
South Weston
Lewknor
Aston Rowant
Kingston Blount
Crowell
Postcombe
Sydenham
Emmington
Chalford
Kingston Stert
Towersey
Kingsey
Ilmer
Longwick
Owlswick
Meadle
Askett
Monks Risborough
Princes Risborough
Saunderton
Bledlow
Bledlow Ridge
Radnage
Bennett End
The City
Horsley's Green
Piddington
Tiddington
Rycote
Moreton
Milton Common
Waterstock
Waterperry
Albury
Holton
Forest Hill
Stanton St John
Horspath
Headington
Marston
Binsey
Wolvercote
Botley
North Hinksey Village
South Hinksey
Cowley
Littlemore
Iffley
Elsfield
Water Eaton
Noke
Woodeaton
Beckley
Horton-cum-Studley
Boarstall
Oddington
Islip
Murcott
Fencott
Charlton-on-Otmoor
Merton
Heathfield Village
Oakley
Brill
Little London
Worminghall
Ickford
Shabbington
Long Crendon
Chearsley
Easington
Chilton
Dorton
Ashendon
Upper Pollicott
Lower Pollicott
Nether Winchendon
Upper Winchendon
Cuddington
Dinton
Upton
Westlington
Stone
Sedrup
Bishopstone
Ford
Aston Sandford
Church End
Kimble Wick
Little Kimble
Stoke Mandeville
Lower Hartwell
Southcourt
Waddesdon
Westcott
Wotton Underwood
Ludgershall
Kingswood
Woodham
Quainton
Hardwick
Weedon
Bierton
Pitchcott
Oving
Whitchurch
North Marston
Granborough
Hoggeston
Swanbourne
Mursley
Drayton Parslow
East Claydon
Middle Claydon
Steeple Claydon
Botolph Claydon
Calvert
Grendon Underwood
Edgcott
Marsh Gibbon
Launton
Twyford
Poundon
Charndon
Godington
Hillesden
Preston Bissett
Addington
Chetwode
Barton Hartshorn
Newton Purcell
Hethe
Fringford
Cottisford
Hardwick
Stoke Lyne
Fewcott
Bucknell
Bainton
Stratton Audley
Caversfield
Middleton Stoney
Caulcott
Northbrook
Chesterton
Ambrosden
Wendlebury
Blackthorn
Lower Arncott
Upper Arncott
Piddington
Muswell Hill
Ledwell
Sandford St Martin
Hopcrofts Holt
Broughton
Horley
Hornton
Shotteswell
Claydon
Mollington
Williamscot
Chacombe
Overthorpe
Great Purston
Upper Astrop
Astrop
Evenley
Fosse
Sandleigh
Boars Hill
Bayworth
Henwood
Dry Sandford
Appleton
Netherton
Newbridge
A5
A43
A422
A421
A413
A418
A4129
A40
A34
A44
A41
A4260
A4095
A361
A423
A415
A420
A4142
A4010
A508
A329
A4074
A4183
A338
A4009
M1
M40
Shenley Brook End
Shenley Church End
Beachampton
Upper Weald
Stony Stratford
Wolverton
Tathall End
Castlethorpe
Haversham
Little Linford

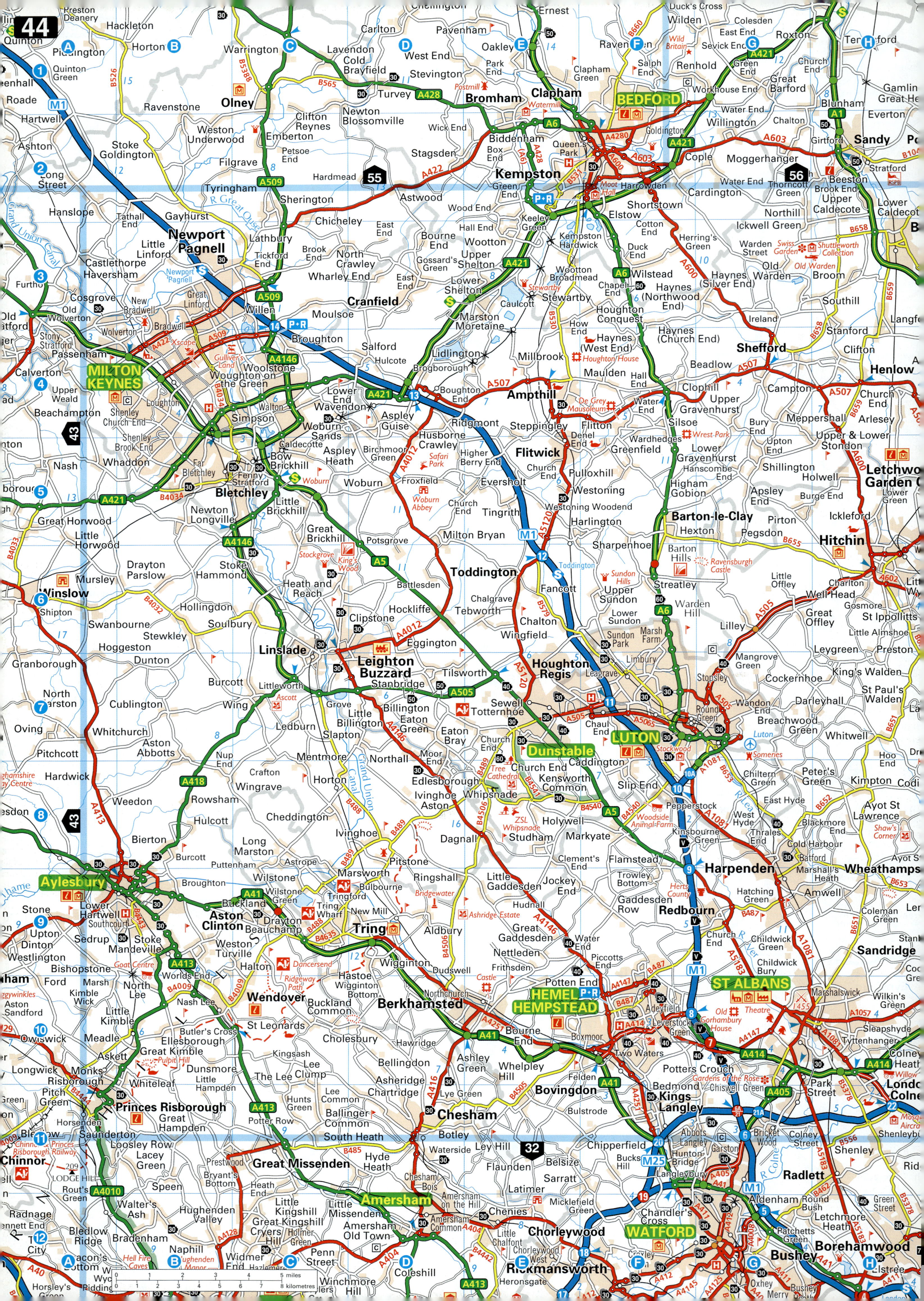

Olney
Bedford
Clapham
Bromham
Kempston
Sandy
Newport Pagnell
Milton Keynes
Cranfield
Ampthill
Flitwick
Shefford
Henlow
Letchworth Garden City
Hitchin
Barton-le-Clay
Toddington
Bletchley
Woburn
Leighton Buzzard
Linslade
Winslow
Houghton Regis
Dunstable
Luton
Harpenden
Aylesbury
Tring
Wendover
Berkhamsted
Hemel Hempstead
St Albans
Princes Risborough
Chesham
Great Missenden
Amersham
Chorleywood
Rickmansworth
Watford
Bushey
Borehamwood
Radlett
Kings Langley
Redbourn
Wheathampstead
Sandridge
Chinnor

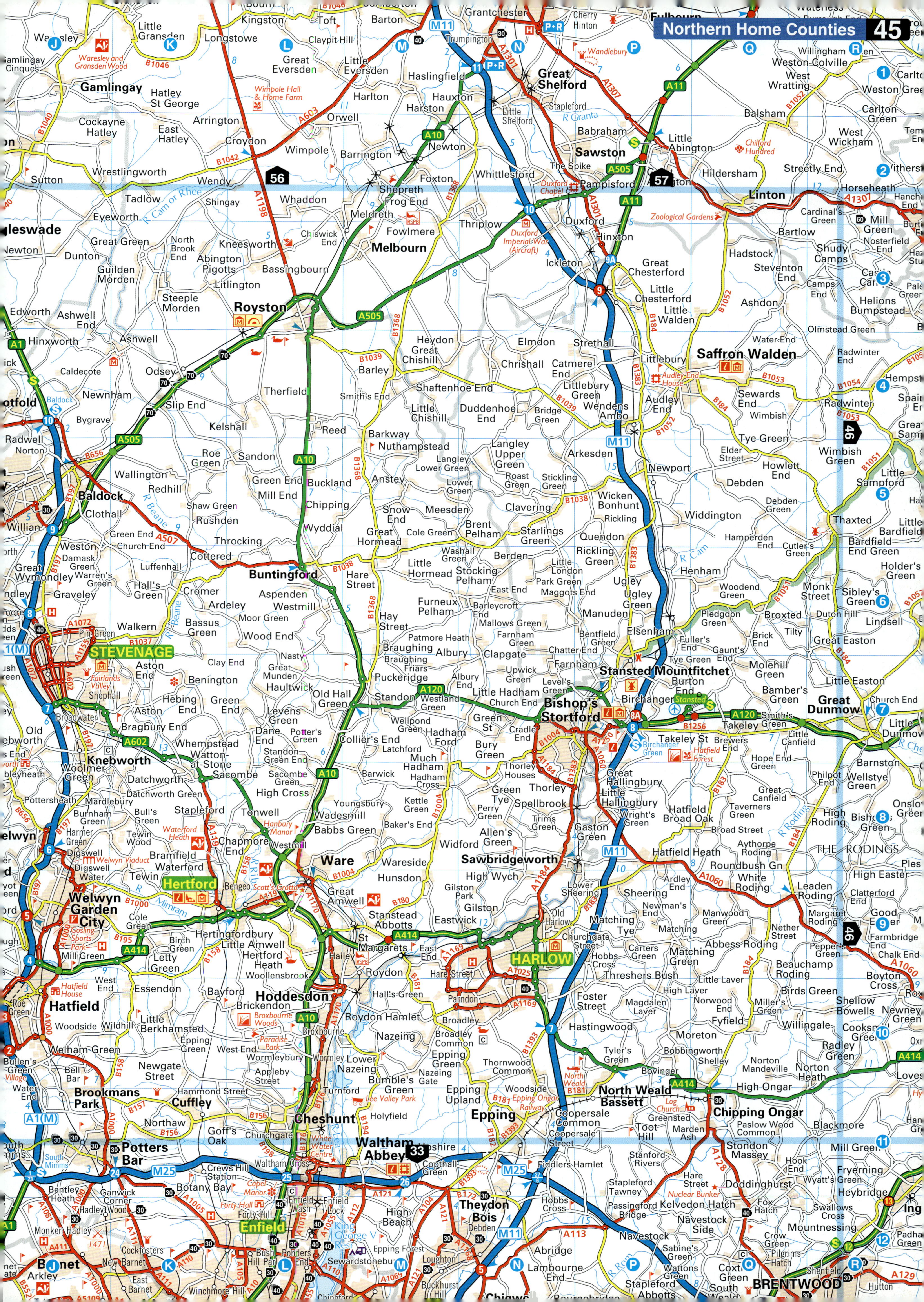

Gamlingay
Royston
Melbourn
Great Shelford
Sawston
Linton
Saffron Walden
Baldock
Stevenage
Knebworth
Buntingford
Bishop's Stortford
Stansted Mountfitchet
Great Dunmow
Ware
Hertford
Welwyn Garden City
Hatfield
Hoddesdon
Harlow
Sawbridgeworth
Cheshunt
Waltham Abbey
Epping
Chipping Ongar
North Weald Bassett
Potters Bar
Enfield
Barnet
Theydon Bois
Brentwood
Thaxted
Duxford
Hinxton
Great Chesterford
Newport
Wendens Ambo
Ickleton
Barrington
Shepreth
Meldreth
Kneesworth
Bassingbourn
Therfield
Barkway
Puckeridge
Standon
Much Hadham
Wadesmill
Tonwell
Watton-at-Stone
Datchworth
Welwyn
Brookmans Park
Cuffley
Nazeing
Roydon
Sheering
Matching
Hastingwood
Moreton
High Ongar
Stapleford Abbotts
Loughton
THE RODINGS
Duxford Imperial War Museum (Aircraft)
Audley End House
Zoological Gardens
Wimpole Hall & Home Farm
Chilford Hundred
Waresley and Gransden Wood
Wandlebury
Fairlands Valley
Scott's Grotto
Hatfield House
Gosling Sports Park
Paradise Park
Broxbourne Woods
Lee Valley Park
Epping Ongar Railway
Capel Manor
Forty Hall
Nuclear Bunker
Hatfield Forest
Stansted
Hanbury Manor
Waterford Heath
Welwyn Viaduct
Log Church
M11
M25
A1(M)
A1
A10
A505
A120
A414
A11
A602
56
57
33
46

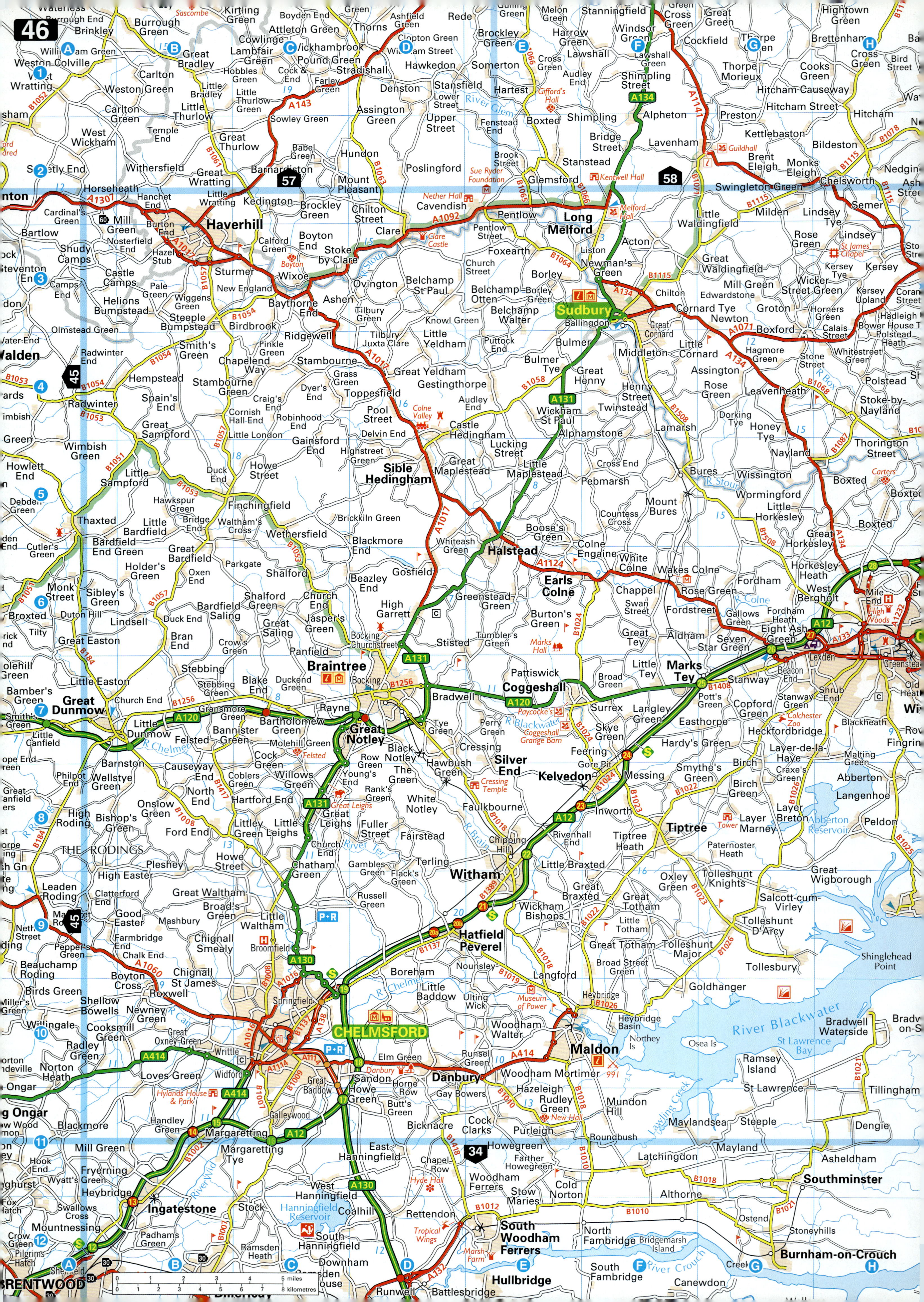

Haverhill
Long Melford
Sudbury
Sible Hedingham
Halstead
Earls Colne
Coggeshall
Braintree
Great Dunmow
Great Notley
Witham
Kelvedon
Marks Tey
Tiptree
Hatfield Peverel
CHELMSFORD
Maldon
Danbury
Ingatestone
South Woodham Ferrers
Burnham-on-Crouch
Southminster
Hullbridge
BRENTWOOD
Walden
Thaxted
Great Bardfield
Finchingfield
Wethersfield
Castle Hedingham
Great Yeldham
Glemsford
Cavendish
Clare
Stoke by Clare
Kedington
Steeple Bumpstead
Helions Bumpstead
Radwinter
Great Sampford
Little Sampford
Wimbish
Hempstead
Ashen
Ridgewell
Stambourne
Toppesfield
Gestingthorpe
Bulmer
Pebmarsh
Colne Engaine
White Colne
Wakes Colne
Chappel
Aldham
Fordham
West Bergholt
Copford
Stanway
Lexden
Layer-de-la-Haye
Abberton
Langenhoe
Peldon
Great Wigborough
Salcott-cum-Virley
Tolleshunt D'Arcy
Tolleshunt Knights
Tolleshunt Major
Tollesbury
Goldhanger
Heybridge
Langford
Great Totham
Little Totham
Wickham Bishops
Great Braxted
Little Braxted
Rivenhall End
Silver End
Cressing
Black Notley
White Notley
Faulkbourne
Terling
Fairstead
Great Leighs
Little Leighs
Felsted
Rayne
Stebbing
High Easter
Pleshey
Great Waltham
Little Waltham
Broomfield
Springfield
Boreham
Little Baddow
Great Baddow
Writtle
Sandon
Howe Green
Woodham Walter
Woodham Mortimer
Hazeleigh
Purleigh
Cold Norton
Stow Maries
Woodham Ferrers
Rettendon
Battlesbridge
Runwell
Downham
East Hanningfield
West Hanningfield
South Hanningfield
Hanningfield Reservoir
Margaretting
Margaretting Tye
Stock
Mountnessing
Fryerning
Blackmore
Mill Green
Highwood
Roxwell
Chignall St James
Chignall Smealy
Good Easter
Leaden Roding
Margaret Roding
Beauchamp Roding
Willingale
Norton Heath
Chipping Ongar
THE RODINGS
Mundon
Latchingdon
Steeple
Maylandsea
Mayland
St Lawrence
Tillingham
Dengie
Asheldham
Althorne
North Fambridge
South Fambridge
Canewdon
Bradwell Waterside
Bradwell-on-Sea
River Blackwater
Osea Is
Northey Is
Ramsey Island
Shinglehead Point
Bridgemarsh Island
River Crouch
Abberton Reservoir
Nayland
Stoke-by-Nayland
Boxted
Great Horkesley
Little Horkesley
Wormingford
Bures
Lamarsh
Twinstead
Alphamstone
Henny Street
Middleton
Great Cornard
Little Cornard
Boxford
Groton
Assington
Leavenheath
Polstead
Chilton
Acton
Borley
Foxearth
Pentlow
Belchamp Otten
Belchamp St Paul
Belchamp Walter
Ovington
Birdbrook
Sturmer
Withersfield
Great Thurlow
Little Thurlow
Great Bradley
Stradishall
Hawkedon
Somerton
Hartest
Boxted
Shimpling
Alpheton
Lavenham
Brent Eleigh
Monks Eleigh
Chelsworth
Bildeston
Kettlebaston
Hitcham
Preston
Milden
Lindsey
Kersey
Semer
Little Waldingfield
Great Waldingfield
Stanstead
Stansfield
Denston
Wickhambrook
Cowlinge
Great Wratting
Little Wratting
Barnardiston
Hundon
Poslingford
Chilton Street
Mount Pleasant
Horseheath
Bartlow
Shudy Camps
Castle Camps
Great Easton
Little Easton
Lindsell
Broxted
Tilty
Barnston
High Roding
Shalford
Panfield
Gosfield
Stisted
Bradwell
Feering
Inworth
Messing
Birch
Layer Marney
Great Tey
Little Tey
Pattiswick
Greenstead Green
Wickham St Paul
Great Henny
Great Maplestead
Little Maplestead
A120
A131
A12
A130
A134
A1017
A1092
A414
A1060
A1307
A143
A1124
Nether Hall
Kentwell Hall
Melford Hall
Colne Valley
Paycocke's
Coggeshall Grange Barn
Cressing Temple
Hylands House & Park
Museum of Power
Hyde Hall
Tropical Wings
Marsh Farm
Colchester Zoo
Gifford's Hall
Sue Ryder Foundation
57
58
45
34
0 1 2 3 4 5 miles
0 1 2 3 4 5 6 7 8 kilometres

Needham Market
Ipswich
Woodbridge
Felixstowe
Harwich
Manningtree
Hadleigh
Colchester
Brightlingsea
Clacton-on-Sea
Walton on the Naze
Frinton-on-Sea
Jaywick
St Osyth
Martlesham Heath
Orford
Holbrook Bay
River Stour
River Orwell
River Deben
Hollesley Bay
Pennyhole Bay
Hoek van Holland
Esbjerg
Suffolk Heritage Coast
Harwich International Port
Ipswich

Aberystwyth
200 m
Cardigan Bay
Parc Natur Penglais
MACHYNLLETH, LLANGURIG
PENGLAIS ROAD
LLANBADARN ROAD
A44
A487
B4346
Town Hall
St Paul Methodist
St David's URC
The Morlan Centre
Capel y Morfa
Ceredigion Museum & Gallery
Surgery
Royal Pier
Conference Centre
Coastguard Station
University (Old College)
Bethel
CAB
STRYD FAWR
Salvation Army
Clock Tower
Market Hall
St Michael's
Monument
North Tower
Castle
Eglwys y Santes Fair
ABERYSTWYTH STATION
ALEXANDRA ROAD
Holy Trinity
University
School
Government Offices
Rheidol
Ystwyth Retail Park
Vale of Rheidol Steam Railway Station
Recreation Ground
BRIDGE STREET
MILL ST
PARK AVENUE
Pont Aberystwyth
Slipway
Government Offices
Afon Rheidol
Aberystwyth Town FC
Marina
Police Station
Ysgol
Fire Station
TA Centre
Lifeboat Station
PENPARCAU ROAD
CARDIGAN
Aqua Terra
LLA
CARDIGAN
BAY
Aberarth
Aberaeron
Llansantffraid
Llanon
Pennant
Llyswen
Llanerchaeron
A482
New Quay
Foss-y-ffin
Llanina
Ceredigion Heritage Coast
Maen-y-groes
Gilfachrheda
Llwyncelyn
Llanarth
Cross Inn
Oakford
Cwmtydu
Nanternis
A486
B4342
B4339
Ynys-Lochtyn
Caerwedros
Dihewyd
Llwyndafydd
A487
Synod Inn
Mydroilyn
Pentre'rbryn
Llangranog
Pontgarreg
B4321
B4334
Morfa
Plwmp
Ffynnonddewi
Penbryn
Pentregat
B4338
311
Ceredigion Heritage Coast
Parcllyn
Aberporth
Cardigan Island
Mwnt
Tresaith
Sarnau
Brynhoffnant
Talgarreg
Gorsgoch
Cardigan Island Coastal Farm Park
Felinwynt Rainforest & Butterfly Centre
B4333
324
Gwbert on Sea
Y Ferwig
Tremain
Blaenannerch
Tan-y-groes
Bwlchyfadfa
Poppit Sands
Glynarthen
Capel Cynon
Blaenporth
Penparc
Pembrokeshire Coast Path
B4546
B4548
Rhydlewis
Ffostrasol
Cwrt-newydd
Cardigan
(Aberteifi)
Beulah
Bettws Evan
Hawen
38
Pontshaen
Cwmsychbant
Ceibwr Bay
St Dogmaels
Abbey
Bridgend
Llangoedmor
B4570
Troedyraur
Penrhiw-pal
Tre-groes
A475
Moylegrove
Monington
Teifi Marshes
A484
37
Ponthirwaun
Brongest
Coed-y-Bryn
Maesllyn
Pren-gwyn
Rhydowen
Llanwenog
Llandygwydd
Llangynllo
Croes-lan
Llanybydder
Pen-y-bryn
Castle
B4333
B4571
B4334
Gorrig
Rhuddlan
258
Glanrhyd
Cilgerran
Afon Teifi
TIVY SIDE
Cwm-cou
Aber-banc
Horeb
Rock Mill Woollen & Water Mill
Capel Dewi
A487
Bridell
Abercych
Cenarth
Adpar
Llandyfriog
Penrhiw-llan
B4476
B4582
Pontgarreg
A478
Teifi Valley Railway
Llandysul
Nevern
Felindre Farchog
Pengelli Forest
Rhosl
Pen-rhiw
B4332
Newcastle Emlyn
(Castell Newydd Emlyn)
Aber-arad
Pentre-cagel
Henllan
Llangeler
Pontwelly
B4336
Llanfihangel-ar-arth
Llanllwni
Drefach
National
0 1 2 3 4 5 miles
0 1 2 3 4 5 6 7 8 kilometres

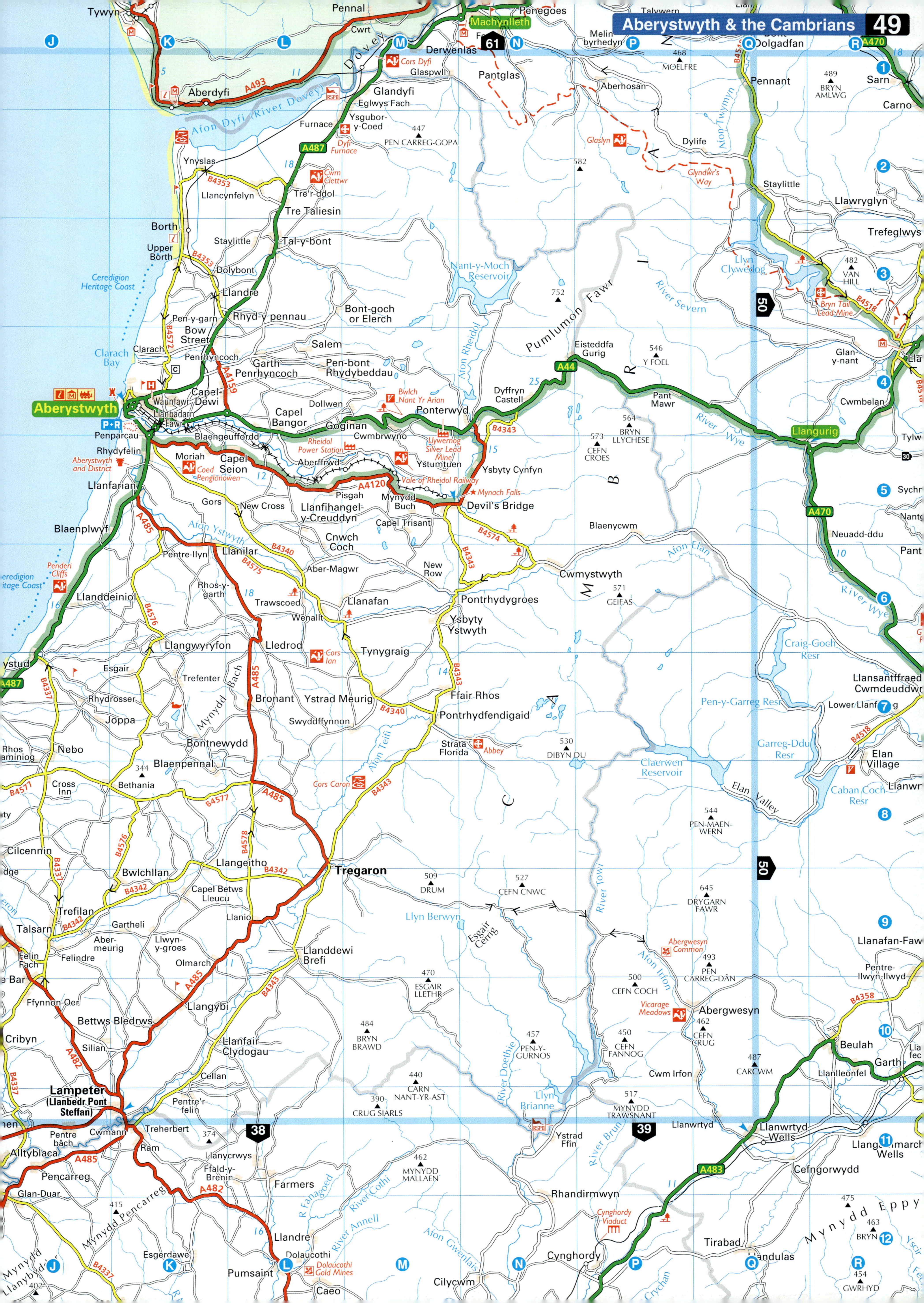
Tywyn
Pennal
Cwrt
Machynlleth
Penegoes
Derwenlas
61
Pantglas
Glaspwll
Cors Dyfi
Aberdyfi
A493
Glandyfi
Eglwys Fach
Afon Dyfi (River Dovey)
RSPB
Furnace
Ysgubor-y-Coed
Dyfi Furnace
447
PEN CARREG-GOPA
A487
Ynyslas
B4353
Llancynfelyn
Cwm Clettwr
Tre'r-ddol
Tre Taliesin
Borth
Upper Borth
Staylittle
Tal-y-bont
Ceredigion Heritage Coast
Dolybont
Llandre
Pen-y-garn
Rhyd-y pennau
Bow Street
B4572
Bont-goch or Elerch
Salem
Clarach
Clarach Bay
Penrhyncoch
Garth Penrhyncoch
Pen-bont Rhydybeddau
A4159
Capel-Dewi
Waunfawr
Llanbadarn Fawr
Aberystwyth
Dollwen
Capel Bangor
Bwlch Nant Yr Arian
Ponterwyd
Goginan
Cwmbrwyno
Penparcau
Blaengeuffordd
Rhydyfelin
Aberystwyth and District
Moriah
Capel Seion
Coed Penglanowen
Rheidol Power Station
Aberffrwd
Llywernog Silver Lead Mine
Ystumtuen
Vale of Rheidol Railway
Pisgah
A4120
Mynydd Buch
Mynach Falls
Devil's Bridge
Ysbyty Cynfyn
Llanfarian
Gors
New Cross
Llanfihangel-y-Creuddyn
Capel Trisant
Blaenplwyf
A485
Afon Ystwyth
Cnwch Coch
B4574
Pentre-llyn
Llanilar
B4340
B4575
Aber-Magwr
New Row
B4343
Cwmystwyth
Penderi Cliffs
Ceredigion Heritage Coast
Rhos-y-garth
Llanddeiniol
Trawscoed
Wenallt
Llanafan
Pontrhydygroes
Ysbyty Ystwyth
B4576
Llangwyryfon
Lledrod
Cors Ian
Tynygraig
Esgair
Trefenter
Mynydd Bach
B4337
Rhydrosser
Bronant
Ystrad Meurig
Ffair Rhos
Pontrhydfendigaid
Joppa
Swyddffynnon
Strata Florida
Abbey
Nebo
Bontnewydd
Blaenpennal
344
Bethania
Cross Inn
B4577
B4578
Afon Teifi
Cors Caron
B4577
Cilcennin
Bwlchllan
Llangeitho
B4342
Tregaron
Capel Betws Lleucu
Trefilan
Gartheli
Llanio
Talsarn
Felin Fach
Aber-meurig
Felindre
Llwyn-y-groes
Olmarch
Ffynnon-Oer
Bettws Bledrws
Llangybi
Llanddewi Brefi
Cribyn
Silian
Llanfair Clydogau
A482
Cellan
Lampeter (Llanbedr Pont Steffan)
Pentre'r-felin
Pentre bâch
Cwmann
Treherbert
374
Alltyblaca
A485
Ram
Llanycrwys
Pencarreg
Ffald-y-Brenin
Glan-Duar
415
Mynydd Pencarreg
Farmers
Esgerdawe
Pumsaint
Llandre
Dolaucothi
Dolaucothi Gold Mines
Caeo
402
Mynydd Llanybydder
Melin byrhedyn
468
MOELFRE
Aberhosan
Glaslyn
582
Dylife
Glyndŵr's Way
Afon Twymyn
Pennant
489
BRYN AMLWG
Sarn
Carno
Staylittle
Llawryglyn
Trefeglwys
Llyn Clywedog
482
VAN HILL
Bryn Tail Lead Mine
B4518
Nant-y-Moch Reservoir
752
Pumlumon Fawr
River Severn
Afon Rheidol
Eisteddfa Gurig
546
Y FOEL
A44
Dyffryn Castell
Pant Mawr
Glan-y-nant
Cwmbelan
564
BRYN LLYCHESE
573
CEFN CROES
River Wye
Llangurig
A470
Blaenycwm
Neuadd-ddu
Afon Elan
571
GEIFAS
River Wye
Craig-Goch Resr
Llansantffraed Cwmdeuddwr
Pen-y-Garreg Resr
Lower Llanfadog
530
DIBYN DU
Garreg-Ddu Resr
Elan Village
Claerwen Reservoir
Caban Coch Resr
Elan Valley
544
PEN-MAEN-WERN
509
DRUM
527
CEFN CNWC
645
DRYGARN FAWR
Llyn Berwyn
Esgair Cerrig
River Tywi
Abergwesyn Common
493
PEN CARREG-DÂN
Llanafan-Fawr
Pentre-llwyn-llwyd
470
ESGAIR LLETHR
500
CEFN COCH
Afon Irfon
Vicarage Meadows
Abergwesyn
462
CEFN CRUG
B4358
484
BRYN BRAWD
457
PEN-Y-GURNOS
450
CEFN FANNOG
Beulah
Garth
487
CARCWM
Llanlleonfel
Cwm Irfon
440
CARN NANT-YR-AST
390
CRUG SIARLS
River Doethie
Llyn Brianne
517
MYNYDD TRAWSNANT
38
39
Llanwrtyd
Llanwrtyd Wells
Ystrad Ffin
River Bran
Llangammarch Wells
A483
Cefngorwydd
462
MYNYDD MALLAEN
Rhandirmwyn
R Fanagoed
River Cothi
River Annell
Afon Gwenlais
Cynghordy Viaduct
Cynghordy
Cilycwm
Tirabad
Llandulas
475
Mynydd Eppynt
463
BRYN
454
GWRHYD
50

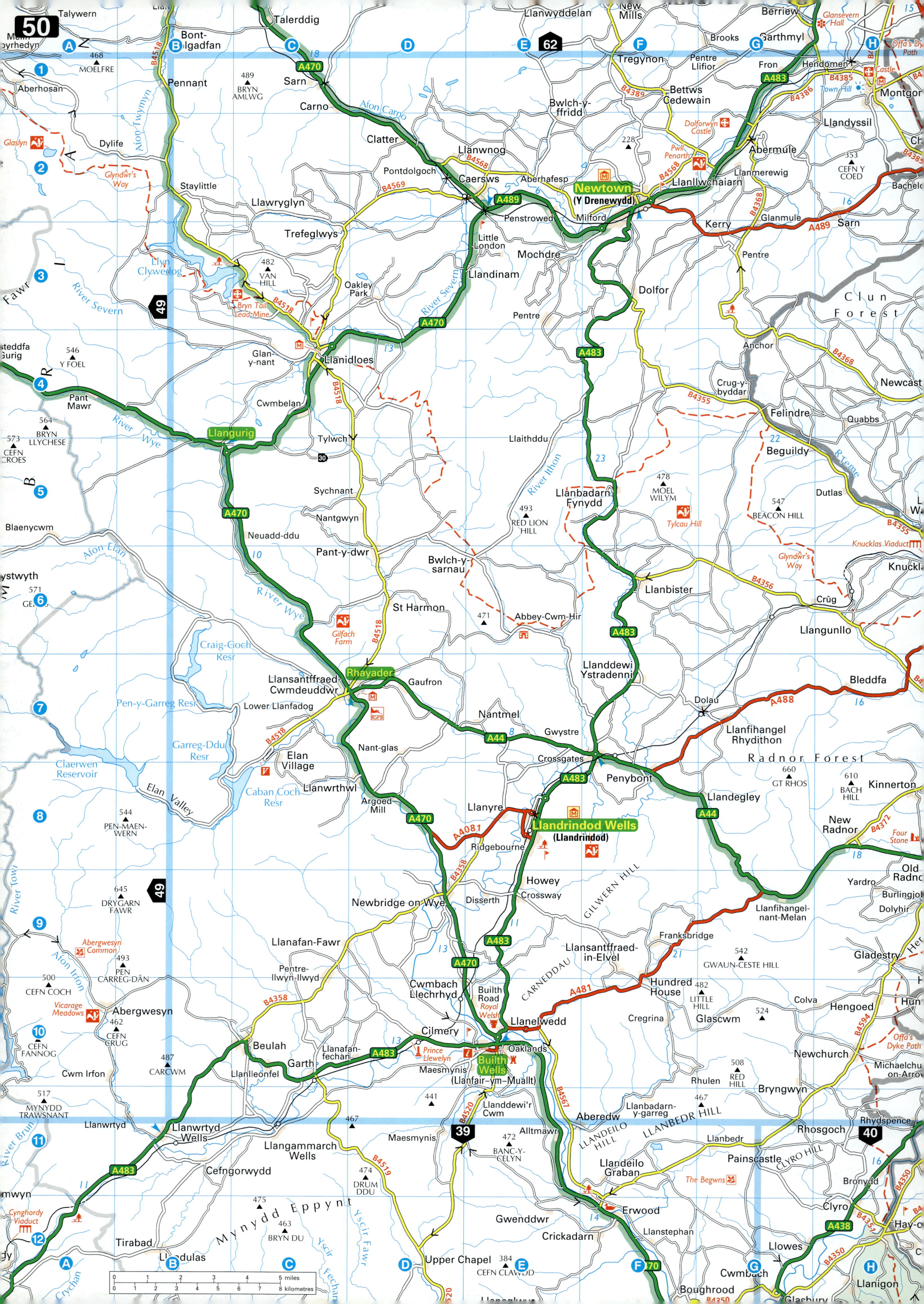

Talywern
Talerddig
Llanwyddelan
New Mills
Berriew
Glansevern Hall
Bont-dolgadfan
Pennant
Sarn
Carno
Afon Carno
Tregynon
Pentre Llifior
Brooks
Garthmyl
Fron
Hendomen
Castle
Town Hill
Montgomery
Moelfre
Aberhosan
Bryn Amlwg
Bwlch-y-ffridd
Bettws Cedewain
Dolforwyn Castle
Llandyssil
Glaslyn
Dylife
Afon Twymyn
Clatter
Llanwnog
Pwll Penarth
Abermule
Glyndŵr's Way
Staylittle
Pontdolgoch
Caersws
Aberhafesp
Newtown
(Y Drenewydd)
Llanllwchaiarn
Llanmerewig
Cefn y Coed
Bacheldre
Llawryglyn
Penstrowed
Milford
Kerry
Glanmule
Sarn
Trefeglwys
Little London
Mochdre
Pentre
Llyn Clywedog
Van Hill
Llandinam
Dolfor
Clun Forest
River Severn
Oakley Park
Bryn Tail Lead Mine
Pentre
Steddfa Gurig
Y Foel
Glan-y-nant
Llanidloes
Anchor
Crug-y-byddar
Newcastle
Pant Mawr
Cwmbelan
Felindre
Quabbs
Bryn Llychese
Cefn Croes
River Wye
Llangurig
Tylwch
Llaithddu
Beguildy
R. Teme
Sychnant
Llanbadarn Fynydd
Moel Wilym
Dutlas
Tylcau Hill
Beacon Hill
Red Lion Hill
Blaenycwm
Nantgwyn
Neuadd-ddu
Afon Elan
Pant-y-dwr
Bwlch-y-sarnau
Knucklas Viaduct
Knucklas
Aberystwyth
Llanbister
Crûg
St Harmon
Abbey-Cwm-Hir
Gilfach Farm
Llangunllo
Craig-Goch Resr
Llanddewi Ystradenni
Rhayader
Llansantffraed-Cwmdeuddwr
Gaufron
Bleddfa
Pen-y-Garreg Resr
Lower Llanfadog
Dolau
Nantmel
RSPB
Gwystre
Llanfihangel Rhydithon
Garreg-Ddu Resr
Nant-glas
Elan Village
Crossgates
Radnor Forest
Claerwen Reservoir
Penybont
Rhos
Gt Rhos
Bach Hill
Kinnerton
Elan Valley
Caban Coch Resr
Llanwrthwl
Argoed Mill
Llandegley
Llanyre
Pen-maen-wern
Llandrindod Wells
(Llandrindod)
New Radnor
Four Stones
Ridgebourne
Old Radnor
Howey
Gilwern Hill
Yardro
Burlingjobb
Drygarn Fawr
Newbridge on Wye
Disserth
Crossway
Dolyhir
River Towi
Llanfihangel-nant-Melan
Abergwesyn Common
Llanafan-Fawr
Franksbridge
Afon Irfon
Pen Carreg-Dân
Pentre-llwyn-llwyd
Llansantffraed-in-Elvel
Gwaun-Ceste Hill
Gladestry
Cefn Coch
Cwmbach Llechrhyd
Builth Road
Royal Welsh
Carneddau
Hundred House
Little Hill
Colva
Hengoed
Vicarage Meadows
Abergwesyn
Cefn Crug
Llanelwedd
Cregrina
Glascwm
Cefn Fannog
Beulah
Cilmery
Prince Llewelyn
Oaklands
Offa's Dyke Path
Llanafan-fechan
Builth Wells
(Llanfair-ym-Muallt)
Newchurch
Cwm Irfon
Carcwm
Garth
Llanlleonfel
Maesmynis
Rhulen
Red Hill
Michaelchurch-on-Arrow
Mynydd Trawsnant
Llanddewi'r Cwm
Bryngwyn
Aberedw
Llanbadarn-y-garreg
Llanbedr Hill
Rhydspence
Llanwrtyd
Llanwrtyd Wells
Maesmynis
Alltmawr
Banc-y-celyn
Llandeilo Hill
Llanbedr
Rhosgoch
Llangammarch Wells
Painscastle
Clyro Hill
Cefngorwydd
Drum Ddu
Llandeilo Graban
The Begwns
Bronydd
River Bran
Mynydd Eppynt
Erwood
Clyro
Cynghordy Viaduct
Gwenddwr
Ysgir Fawr
Llanstephan
Hay-on-Wye
Bryn Ddu
Crickadarn
Tirabad
Llandulas
Ysgir Fechan
Upper Chapel
Cefn Clawdd
Llowes
Cwmbach
Llanigon
Crychan
Boughrood
Glasbury
0 1 2 3 4 5 miles
0 1 2 3 4 5 6 7 8 kilometres

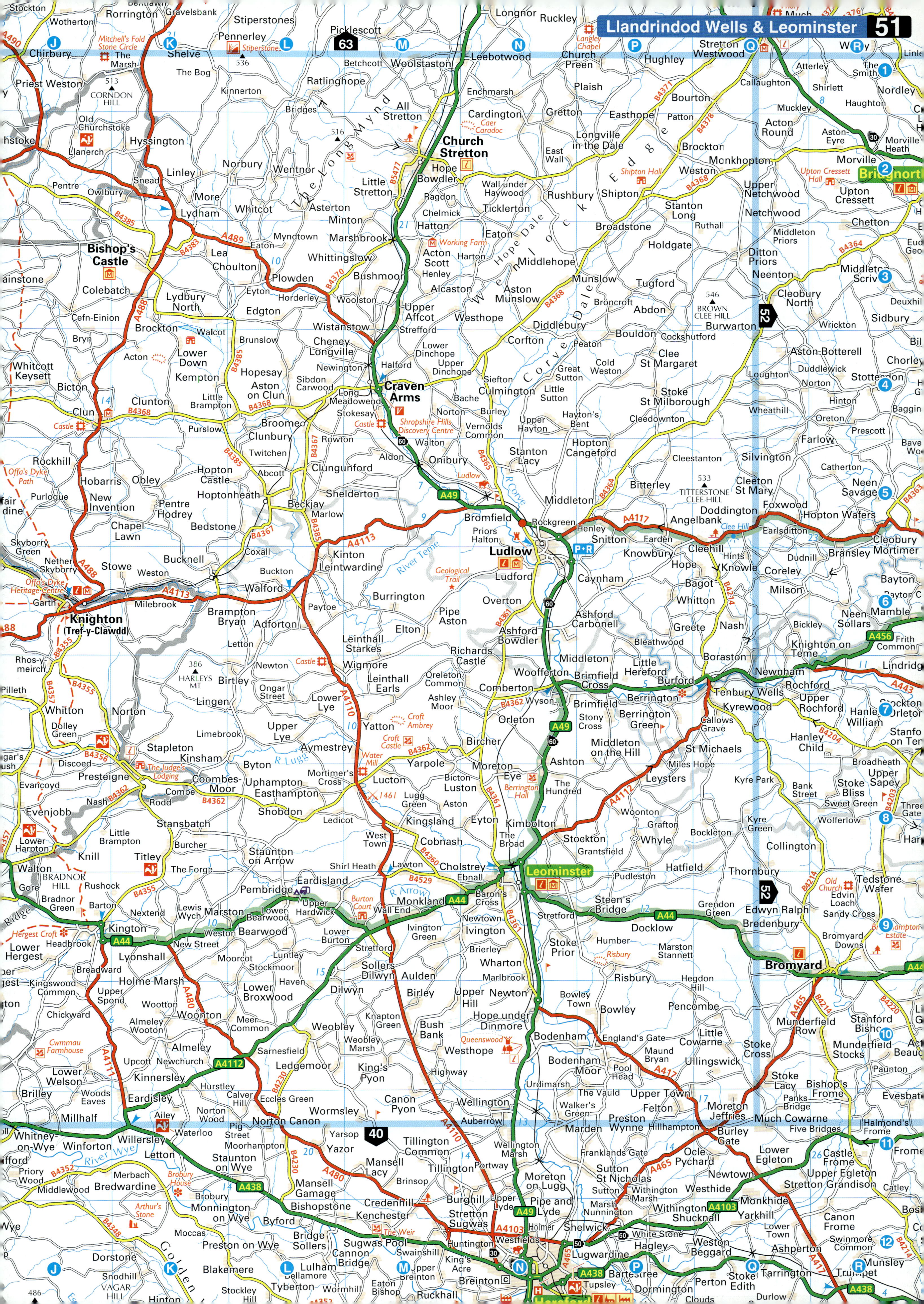
Church Stretton
Bishop's Castle
Craven Arms
Ludlow
Knighton (Tref-y-Clawdd)
Leominster
Bromyard
Tenbury Wells
Kington
Cleobury Mortimer
Bridgnorth
The Long Mynd
Wenlock Edge
Corve Dale
Hope Dale
River Teme
River Arrow
River Wye
River Lugg
Clun
Lydham
Eardisland
Pembridge
Weobley
Wigmore
Bromfield
Onibury
Woofferton
Orleton
Yarpole
Lucton
Kingsland
Hereford
Brown Clee Hill
Titterstone Clee Hill
Offa's Dyke Path
A49
A44
A4117
A4113
A4110
A4112
A438
A4103
A465
A489
A488
A456

52
Church Preen
Hughley
The Bank
Stretton Westwood
Much Wenlock
Barrow
Willey
Linleygreen
Norton
Stockton
Stableford
Badger
Pattingham
64
Kingslow
Nurton
Perton
Tettenhall
WOLVERHAMPTON
Atterley
The Smithies
Colemore Green
Ackleton
Chesterton
Callaughton
Shirlett
Nordley
Astley Abbots
Catstree
Allscott
Worfield
Trescott
Wightwick Manor
Merryhill
Bourton
Easthope
Patton
Muckley
Haughton
Cross Lane Head
Rindleford
Wyken
Hilton
Shipley
Upper Ludstone
Lower Penn
Penn
Acton Round
Aston Eyre
Morville Heath
Tasley
Bromley
Swancote
Burcote
Hopstone
Orton
Seisdon
Gospel End
Sedgley
Brockton
Monkhopton
Morville
Roughton
Woundale
Aston
Trysull
The Bratch
Weston
Upton Cressett Hall
Bridgnorth
Claverley
Draycott
Ounsdale
Wombourne
Shipton
Upper Netchwood
Upton Cressett
Danesford
Upper Farmcote
Heathton
Smestow
Halfpenny Green
Stanton Long
Netchwood
Cross Houses
Oldbury
Quatford
Farmcote
Lower Beobridge
Swindon
Himley
Lower Gornal
DUDLEY
Broadstone
Ruthall
Chetton
Eardington
Bobbington
Wolverhampton Business
Hinksford
Holdgate
Middleton Priors
Ditton Priors
Eudon George
Mose
Six Ashes
Wall Heath
Kingswinford
Brockmoor
Brierley Hill
Neenton
Middleton Scriven
Chelmarsh
Quatt
Highgate Common
Four Ashes
Ashwood
Tugford
Abdon
Brown Clee Hill
Cleobury North
Glazeley
Dudmaston
Tuckhill
Enville
Prestwood
Audnam
Amblecote
Cradley Heath
Burwarton
Deuxhill
Sutton
Hampton Loade
Coxgreen
Boulton
Cockshutford
Wrickton
Sidbury
Hampton
Turleygreen
Birdsgreen
Compton
Stourton
Clee St Margaret
Aston Botterell
Billingsley
Alveley
Potter's Cross
Dunsley
Wollaston
HALESOWEN
Cold Weston
Loughton
Duddlewick
Chorley
Woodhill
Severn Valley
Romsley
Kinver
STOURBRIDGE
Norton
Stottesdon
High Green
Highley
Stanley
Fenn Green
Whittington
Stoke St Milborough
Hinton
Netherton
Nash End
Bodenham Arboretum
Kingsford
Pedmore
Hayley Green
Hasbury
Cleedownton
Wheathill
Bagginswood
Blakeshall
Caunsall
Cookley
Hagley
Hagley Hall
Oreton
Kinlet
Upper Arley
Shatterford
Drakelow
Islandpool
Clent Hills
Prescott
Baveney Wood
Coppicegate
Severn Valley Railway
Wolverley
Churchill
Lower Clent
Clent
Romsley
Cleestanton
Silvington
Farlow
Catherton
Buttonbridge
Pound Green
Trimpley
Low Habberley
Axborough
Broome
Holy Cross
Dayhouse Bank
Bitterley
Titterstone Clee Hill
Cleeton St Mary
Neen Savage
Buttonoak
Wyre Forest
Habberley
Franche
Broadwaters
Blakedown
Hackman's Gate
Yieldingtree
Newtown
Bell End
Angelbank
Doddington
Foxwood
Hopton Wafers
Lem Hill
Bewdley
Wribbenhall
Blakebrook
KIDDERMINSTER
Belbroughton
Drayton
Stoneybridge
Snitton
Farden
Earlsditton
Cleobury Mortimer
Far Forest
Long Bank
West Midland
Stone
Broom Hill
Wildmoor
Knowbury
Cleehill
Hints
Bransley
Wyre Forest
Pound Bank
Callow Hill
Stanklin
Harvington
Bluntington
Fairfield
Hope
Knowle
Dudnill
Coreley
Ribbesford
Hoobrook
Summerfield
Mustow Green
Brockencote
Bournheath
Catshill
Bagot
Bayton
Lye Head
Bliss Gate
Upper Milton
Wilden
Shenstone
Chaddesley Corbett
Dodford
Whitton
Milson
Bayton Common
Gorst Hill
Cakebole
Woodcote Green
Park Gate
Greete
Neen Sollars
Mamble
Clows Top
Rock
Heightington
Stourport-on-Severn
Charlton
Torton
Rushock
Purshull Green
Sidemoor
Nash
Bickley
Areley Kings
Hartlebury
Bromsgrove
Bleathwood
Knighton on Teme
Frith Common
Greenway
Astley Cross
Waresley
Titton
Cooksey Green
Rock Hill
Aston Fields
Little Hereford
Boraston
Lindridge
Menithwood
Pensax
Dunley
Chadwick
Elmley Lovett
Bryan's Green
Stoke Heath
Burford
Newnham
Rochford
Eardiston
Abberley
Lincomb
Norchard
Elmbridge
Stoke Prior
Tenbury Wells
Kyrewood
Upper Rochford
Stockton on Teme
Abberley Common
The Burf
Astley
Crossway Green
Cutnall Green
Upton Warren
Berrington
Callows Grave
Hanley William
Orleton
Elms Green
Noutard's Green
Comhampton
Dunhampton
Broad Alley
Webbs of Wychbold
Wychbold
Middleton on the Hill
St Michaels
Hanley Child
Stanford on Teme
Stanford Bridge
Great Witley
Redmarley
Frog Pool
Sytchampton
Northampton
Doverdale
Hampton Lovett
Rashwood
Astwood
Miles Hope
Broadheath
Sapey Common
Woodbury Hill
Witley Court
Sankyn's Green
Shrawley
Uphampton
Ombersley
Oldfield
Droitwich
Sharpway Gate
Leysters
Kyre Park
Stoke Bliss
Upper Sapey
Shelsley Walsh
Little Witley
Holt Fleet
Hadley
Hanbury Hall
Hanbury
Bank Street
Sweet Green
Shelsley Beauchamp
Holt Heath
Holt
Sinton
Salwarpe
Hadzor
Grafton
Wolferlow
Three Gates
Clifton upon Teme
Ockeridge
Oakall Green
Grimley
Chatley
Ladywood
Goosehill Green
Whyle
Bockleton
Kyre Green
Collington
Harpley
Hill Side
Sinton Green
Hawford
Hawford Dovecote
Martin Hussingtree
Dunhampstead
Brough Green
Hatfield
Thornbury
Martley
Wichenford
Moseley
Fernhill Heath
Oddingley
Phepson
Pudleston
Old Church
Tedstone Wafer
Tedstone Delamere
Berrow Green
Dovecote
Shoulton
Hallow
Northwick
Hindlip
Himbleton
Earls Common
Steen's Bridge
Grendon Green
Edwyn Ralph
Edvin Loach
Horsham
Wants Green
Tibberton
Sale Green
Huddington
Docklow
Bredenbury
Sandy Cross
Whitbourne
Collins Green
Lower Broadheath
WORCESTER
Warndon
Crowle Green
Grafton Flyford
Humber
Marston Stannett
Bromyard Downs
Brockhampton Estate
Knightwick
Broad Green
Upper Broadheath
Rainbow Hill
Trotshill
Crowle
Broughton Hackett
Risbury
Hegdon Hill
Bromyard
Bringsty Common
Lulsley
Broadwas
Ravenhills Green
Leigh Court Barn
Henwick
Newtown
Spetchley
Churchill
Upton Snodsbury
Bowley
Pencombe
Suckley Green
Alfrick
Brockamin
Rushwick
Leigh
Upper Wick
St Johns
Cherry Orchard
Whittington
White Ladies Aston
Munderfield Row
Stanford Bishop
Linley Green
Bransford
Lower Wick
Little Cowarne
Stoke Cross
Munderfield Stocks
Acton Beauchamp
Suckley
Alfrick Pound
Smith End Green
Leigh Sinton
Bowling Green
Powick
Norton
Peopleton
Maund Bryan
Ullingswick
Paunton
Acton Green
Longley Green
Callow End
Pole Elm
Hatfield
Littleworth
Pinvin
Pool Head
Stoke Lacy
Bishop's Frome
Evesbatch
Storridge
Lower Howsell
Deblin's Green
Kempsey
Green Street
Stoulton
Hawbridge
Drakes Broughton
Upper Town
Felton
Moreton Jeffries
Panks Bridge
Stony Cross
Stifford's Bridge
Upper Howsell
Newland
Draycott
Napleton
Pirton
Stonehall
Preston Wynne
Burley Gate
Much Cowarne
Five Bridges
Halmond's Frome
Cradley
Malvern Link
Great Malvern
Madresfield
Kerswell Green
Wadborough
Ramsden
Pershore
Ocle Pychard
Lower Egleton
Castle Frome
Fromes Hill
Ridgeway Cross
West Malvern
Guarlford
Rhydd
Clifton
Sutton St Nicholas
Newtown
Upper Egleton
Stretton Grandison
Mathon
Ham Green
Norbridge
Birch Green
High Green
Wick
Withington Marsh
Westhide
Catley
Pow Green
Storeyard Green
South End
Severn Stoke
Croome Park
Besford
Defford
Pensham
Withington
Shucknall
Monkhide
Yarkhill
Bosbury
Colwall
Upper Wyche
Lower Wyche
Three Counties
Hanley Swan
Hanley Castle
Kinnersley
Dunstall Common
Birlingham
Lower Town
Canon Frome
Swinmore Common
Coddington
Staplow
Malvern Wells
Gilbert's End
Earl's Croome
Baughton
Woodmancote
Great Comberton
Hagley
Weston Beggard
Ashperton
Loxter
Upper Welland
Hook Bank
Tiltridge
Upton upon Severn
Holly Green
Strensham
Eckington
Elmley Castle
Bartestree
Dormington
Mosley
Wellington Heath
Little Malvern
Welland
Ryall
Naunton
Upper Strensham
Bredon's Norton
Newbridge
Bredon Hill
41
51
0 1 2 3 4 5 miles
0 1 2 3 4 5 6 7 8 kilometres

Aldridge
Walsall
Sutton Coldfield
West Bromwich
Birmingham
Solihull
Coleshill
Kingsbury
Atherstone
Hinckley
Nuneaton
Bedworth
Coventry
Kenilworth
Warwick
Leamington Spa
Redditch
Studley
Alcester
Stratford-upon-Avon
Bidford-on-Avon
Wellesbourne
Evesham
Shipston on Stour
Knowle
Dorridge
Balsall Common
Meriden
Alvechurch
Inkberrow
Dordon
Baddesley Ensor
Hartshill
Bulkington
Stoneleigh
Radford Semele
Ashorne
Moreton Morrell
Tiddington
Alveston
Wilmcote
Henley-in-Arden
Lapworth
Hockley Heath
Tanworth in Arden
Earlswood
Bickenhill
Elmdon
Hampton in Arden
Berkswell
Fillongley
Corley
Keresley
Binley
Baginton
Wolston
Ryton-on-Dunsmore
Harbury
Bishop's Itchington
Gaydon
Kineton
Ettington
Alderminster
Mickleton
Honington
Long Compton

Atherstone
Mancetter
Ratcliffe Culey
Sibson
Upton
Shenton
Cheney
Stapleton
Bosworth Battlefield
Kirkby Mallory
Mallory Park
Earl Shilton
Thurlaston
Enderby
Aylestone
Glen Parva
Wigston
Oadby
Great Glen
Blaby
Countesthorpe
Whetstone
Narborough
Littlethorpe
Cosby
Huncote
Potters Marston
Croft
Barwell
Elmesthorpe
Stoney Stanton
Sapcote
Hinckley
Burbage
Sketchley
Aston Flamville
Dadlington
Witherley
Fenny Drayton
Higham on the Hill
Stoke Golding
Wykin
Hartshill
Oldbury
Ridge Lane
Ansley
Galley Common
Stockingford
NUNEATON
Attleborough
Weddington
Burton Hastings
Smockington
Shelford
Wolvey
Wolvey Heath
Copston Magna
Wibtoft
Claybrooke Magna
Frolesworth
Wigston Parva
Sharnford
Leire
Broughton Astley
Primethorpe
Sutton in the Elms
Dunton Bassett
Ashby Parva
Ullesthorpe
Bitteswell
Lutterworth
Magna Park
Cotesbach
Shawell
Misterton
Walcote
Kimcote
Walton
Gilmorton
Peatling Parva
Ashby Magna
Willoughby Waterleys
Peatling Magna
Arnesby
Fleckney
Kilby
Foston
Newton Harcourt
Kibworth Harcourt
Kibworth Beauchamp
Saddington
Smeeton Westerby
Shearsby
Bruntingthorpe
Mowsley
Laughton
Gumley
Lubenham
Marston Trussell
Theddingworth
Husbands Bosworth
North Kilworth
South Kilworth
Sibbertoft
Welford
Stanford on Avon
Swinford
Stanford Hall
Naseby
Cold Ashby
Thornby
Winwick
Yelvertoft
Clay Coton
Lilbourne
Catthorpe
Clifton upon Dunsmore
Newton
Brownsover
Hillmorton
RUGBY
Bilton
New Bilton
Dunchurch
Cawston
Thurlaston
Draycote
Draycote Water
Toft
Kites Hardwick
Barby
Kilsby
Crick
West Haddon
Guilsborough
Hollowell
Coton Manor
Coton
Ravensthorpe
Teeton
East Haddon
Holdenby House
Watford
Watford Gap
Long Buckby
Ashby St Ledgers
Welton
Great Brington
Little Brington
Althorp Park
Whilton
Norton
Brockhall
Daventry
Dodford
Flore
Upper Heyford
Nether Heyford
Weedon
Stowehill
Bugbrooke
Rothersthorpe
Upper Stowe
Church Stowe
Farthingstone
Litchborough
Pattishall
Eastcote
Astcote
Cold Higham
Grimscote
Maidford
Blakesley
Foxley
Greens Norton
Woodend
Bradden
Towcester
Abthorpe
Slapton
Wappenham
Helmdon
Silverstone
Syresham
Whitfield
Biddlesden
Radstone
Crowfield
Brackley Hatch
Culworth
Weedon Lois
Milthorpe
Weston
Sulgrave
Greatworth
Marston St Lawrence
Thorpe Mandeville
Farthinghoe
Halse
Chipping Warden
Edgcote
Plumpton
Moreton Pinkney
Canons Ashby
Adstone
Woodford Halse
Byfield
Eydon
West Farndon
Aston le Walls
Charwelton
Preston Capes
Fawsley
Badby
Newnham
Little Everdon
Great Everdon
Hellidon
Upper Catesby
Lower Catesby
Staverton
Flecknoe
Lower Shuckburgh
Nethercote
Wolfhampcote
Braunston
Willoughby
Grandborough
Woolscott
Sawbridge
Broadwell
Stockton
Tomlow
Napton on the Hill
Chapel Green
Priors Marston
Priors Hardwick
Upper Boddington
Lower Boddington
Westhorp
Wormleighton
Southam
Ladbroke
Long Itchington
Bascote
Bascote Heath
Ufton
Harbury
Bishop's Tachbrook
Chesterton
Chesterton Green
Bishop's Itchington
Lighthorne
Lighthorne Heath
Moreton Morrell
Moreton Paddox
Heritage Motor Centre
Gaydon
Chadshunt
Northend
Burton Dassett
Fenny Compton
Avon Dassett
Claydon
Farnborough
Mollington
Cropredy
Wardington
Upper Wardington
Williamscot
Chacombe
Great Bourton
Little Bourton
Hanwell
Middleton Cheney
Thenford
Overthorpe
Banbury
Warkworth
Drayton
Wroxton
Balscote
Shenington
Alkerton
Horley
Hornton
Shotteswell
Warmington
Arlescote
Ratley
Edgehill
Radway
Kineton
Little Kineton
Butlers Marston
Pillerton Hersey
Pillerton Priors
Oxhill
Whatcote
Upper Tysoe
Middle Tysoe
Lower Tysoe
Upton House
Winderton
Shutford
Compton Verney
Combrook
Walton
Wellesbourne
Wellesbourne Mountford
Newbold Pacey
Ashorne
Wasperton
Barford
Longbridge
Warwick
LEAMINGTON SPA
Milverton
Old Milverton
Radford Semele
Whitnash
Offchurch
Cubbington
Hunningham
Eathorpe
Wappenbury
Weston under Wetherley
Princethorpe
Stretton-on-Dunsmore
Bourton on Dunsmore
Frankton
Marton
Birdingbury
Leamington Hastings
Hill
Wolston
Brandon
Church Lawford
Long Lawford
Kings Newnham
Bretford
Binley Woods
Binley
Ryton-on-Dunsmore
Baginton
Stoneleigh
Stareton
Bubbenhall
Ashow
Kenilworth
Leek Wootton
COVENTRY
Willenhall
Tollbar End
Stivichall
Earlsdon
Canley
Westwood Heath
Kirby Corner
Burton Green
Crackley
Allesley
Radford
Foleshill
Longford
Holbrooks
Keresley
Ash Green
Corley
Corley Moor
Corley Ash
Goodyers End
Exhall
Bedworth
Hawkesbury
Aldermans Green
Potters Green
Henley Green
Wyken
Walsgrave on Sowe
Coombe Abbey
Ansty
Shilton
Hopsford
Barnacle
Bulkington
Ryton
Weston in Arden
Marston Jabbet
Bramcote
Withybrook
Monks Kirby
Brockhurst
Newnham Paddox
Street Ashton
Stretton under Fosse
Pailton
Newbold Revel
Easenhall
Brinklow
Churchover
Harborough Magna
Newbold on Avon
Willey
Cloudesley Bush
Griff
Arley
Astley
Bermuda
Arbury Hall
Gun Hill
Wood End
Fillongley
Ballards Green
Devitts Green
Pickford
Pickford Green
Eastern Green
Tile Hill
M1
M6
M45
M40
M69
A5
A45
A46
A426
A428
A444
A4304
A5199
A14
A423
A452
A361
A43
A6
B4112
B4114
B4455
B4429
B4027
B4029
B4036
B4037
B4525
B4100
B4086
B4087
B4035
Mile and kilometre scale

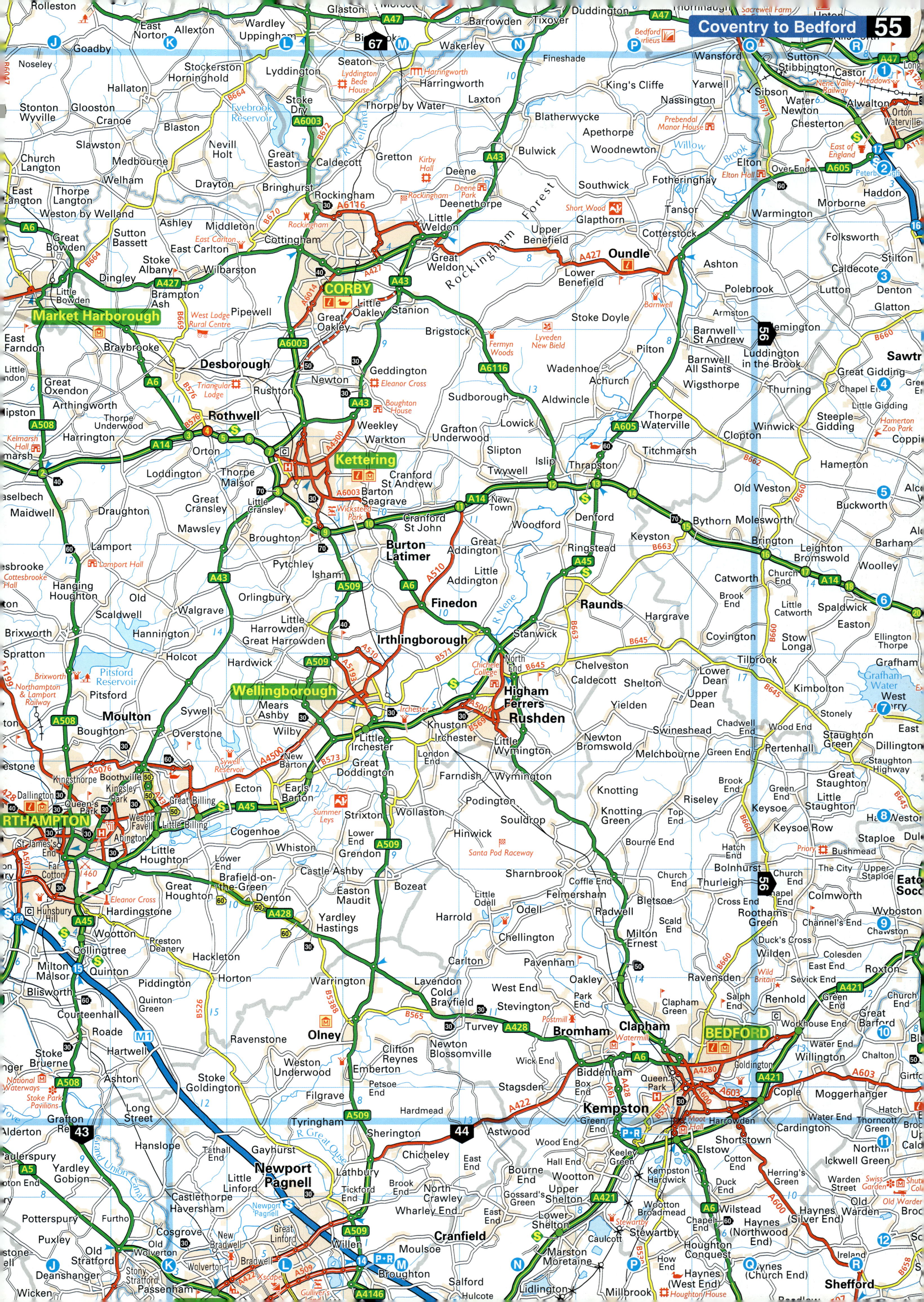
Market Harborough
CORBY
Kettering
Wellingborough
BEDFORD
Desborough
Rothwell
Oundle
Burton Latimer
Finedon
Irthlingborough
Higham Ferrers
Rushden
Raunds
Thrapston
Olney
Newport Pagnell
Kempston
Bromham
Clapham
Moulton
Rockingham Forest
Rockingham
Uppingham
Barrowden
Wansford
Castor
Alwalton
King's Cliffe
Brigstock
Geddington
Weekley
Warkton
Cranford St Andrew
Great Addington
Woodford
Denford
Ringstead
Stanwick
Chelveston
Yielden
Swineshead
Pertenhall
Kimbolton
Great Staughton
Little Staughton
Keysoe
Riseley
Knotting
Sharnbrook
Odell
Harrold
Carlton
Pavenham
Oakley
Turvey
Lavendon
Stevington
Wollaston
Podington
Hinwick
Bozeat
Grendon
Earls Barton
Ecton
Sywell
Overstone
Pitsford
Brixworth
Lamport
Hanging Houghton
Maidwell
Draughton
Arthingworth
Braybrooke
Great Oxenden
Harrington
Orton
Loddington
Thorpe Malsor
Great Cransley
Broughton
Pytchley
Isham
Orlingbury
Walgrave
Hannington
Holcot
Hardwick
Mears Ashby
Wilby
Great Doddington
Strixton
Yardley Hastings
Denton
Castle Ashby
Easton Maudit
Hackleton
Horton
Piddington
Quinton
Roade
Hartwell
Ashton
Stoke Goldington
Ravenstone
Weston Underwood
Emberton
Clifton Reynes
Newton Blossomville
Sherington
Chicheley
Lathbury
Hanslope
Tyringham
Cranfield
Moulsoe
Broughton
Salford
Stewartby
Shelton
Elstow
Cardington
Cople
Willington
Great Barford
Renhold
Ravensden
Wilden
Colmworth
Bolnhurst
Thurleigh
Milton Ernest
Bletsoe
Radwell
Felmersham
Souldrop
Wymington
Newton Bromswold
Melchbourne
Covington
Tilbrook
Catworth
Spaldwick
Molesworth
Brington
Bythorn
Keyston
Clopton
Titchmarsh
Thorpe Waterville
Aldwincle
Wadenhoe
Pilton
Barnwell
Polebrook
Lutton
Hemington
Luddington in the Brook
Great Gidding
Steeple Gidding
Winwick
Hamerton
Old Weston
Buckworth
Leighton Bromswold
Barham
Woolley
Easton
Stow Longa
Ellington Thorpe
Grafham
Grafham Water
West Perry
Stonely
Dillington
Staughton Highway
Staploe
Bushmead
Wyboston
Chawston
Roxton
Sudborough
Lowick
Slipton
Twywell
Islip
Grafton Underwood
Stanion
Great Oakley
Little Oakley
Pipewell
Rushton
Newton
Cottingham
Middleton
East Carlton
Wilbarston
Ashley
Stoke Albany
Dingley
Brampton Ash
Weston by Welland
Sutton Bassett
Great Bowden
Welham
Medbourne
Slawston
Drayton
Bringhurst
Great Easton
Caldecott
Gretton
Deene
Deenethorpe
Weldon
Laxton
Bulwick
Blatherwycke
Apethorpe
Woodnewton
Southwick
Glapthorn
Fotheringhay
Tansor
Cotterstock
Elton
Warmington
Nassington
Yarwell
Harringworth
Seaton
Lyddington
Stoke Dry
Wakerley
Duddington
Tixover
Glaston
Wardley
Allexton
Rolleston
Goadby
Noseley
Hallaton
Stonton Wyville
Glooston
Cranoe
Blaston
Nevill Holt
Stockerston
Horninghold
Church Langton
Thorpe Langton
East Langton
Little Bowden
East Farndon
Great Billing
Little Billing
Cogenhoe
Whiston
Brafield-on-the-Green
Great Houghton
Little Houghton
Hardingstone
Wootton
Collingtree
Milton Malsor
Blisworth
Courteenhall
Stoke Bruerne
Grafton Regis
Yardley Gobion
Potterspury
Old Stratford
Deanshanger
Passenham
Cosgrove
Castlethorpe
Haversham
Little Linford
Gayhurst
Filgrave
Astwood
Stagsden
Biddenham
Wootton
Marston Moretaine
Lidlington
Millbrook
Haynes
Shefford
Ireland
Old Warden
Northill
Ickwell Green
Moggerhanger
Chalton
Fineshade
Sibson
Water Newton
Chesterton
Haddon
Morborne
Folksworth
Stilton
Caldecote
Denton
Glatton
Sawtry
Coppingford
Alconbury

PETERBOROUGH
Whittlesey
North Side
Eldernell
Coates
Eastrea
Turves
West Fen
Westry
March
Chainbridge
Newark
Longthorpe
Castor
Ailsworth
Upton
Sutton
Stibbington
Wansford
Sibson
Water Newton
Alwalton
Chesterton
Orton Longueville
Orton Waterville
Woodston
Stanground
Old Fletton
Hampton
Farcet
Yaxley
Norman Cross
Farcet Fen
Whittlesey Mere
Pondersbridge
Chapelbridge
White Fen
Wimblington
Eastwood
Benwick
Doddington
Primrose Hill
Ramsey Mereside
Ramsey St Mary's
Ramsey Forty Foot
Chatteris
Langwood
Ramsey Heights
Ramsey
Bury
Tick Fen
Horseley Fen
King's Cliffe
Yarwell
Nassington
Prebendal Manor House
Woodnewton
Fotheringhay
Elton
Elton Hall
Over End
Haddon
Morborne
Warmington
Tansor
Cotterstock
Oundle
Ashton
Polebrook
Folksworth
Stilton
Caldecote
Holme
Holme Fen
Denton
Glatton
Lutton
Barnwell
Hemington
Barnwell St Andrew
Barnwell All Saints
Luddington in the Brook
Pilton
Wigsthorpe
Thurning
Great Gidding
Little Gidding
Chapel End
Coppingford
Green End
Sawtry
Conington
Woodwalton Fen
Church End
Upwood
Wood Walton
Great Raveley
Little Raveley
Wistow
Warboys
Fenton
Pidley
Somersham
Chatteris Fen
America
Thorpe Waterville
Titchmarsh
Clopton
Winwick
Steeple Gidding
Hamerton
Hamerton Zoo Park
Monks Wood
Upton
Alconbury Weston
Alconbury
Little Stukeley
Great Stukeley
Wennington
Abbots Ripton
Broughton
Kings Ripton
Old Hurst
Woodhurst
Colne
Wood End
Bluntisham
Earith
Old Weston
Buckworth
Barham
Molesworth
Bythorn
Keyston
Brington
Leighton Bromswold
Woolley
Catworth
Church End
Little Catworth
Spaldwick
Easton
Ellington
Ellington Thorpe
Brampton
Huntingdon
Hinchingbrooke
Sapley
St Peter's Hill
Hartford
Wyton
Houghton
Houghton Mill
Hemingford Abbots
Hemingford Grey
St Ives
Needingworth
Holywell
Ouse Fen
Over
Willingham
Hargrave
Covington
Stow Longa
Tilbrook
Kimbolton
Grafham
Grafham Water
Grafham Exhibition Centre
West Perry
East Perry
Stonely
Buckden
Stirtloe
Godmanchester
Offord Cluny
Offord D'Arcy
Fenstanton
Fen Drayton
Swavesey
Rampton
Cottenham
Longstanton
Boxworth End
Lower Dean
Upper Dean
Shelton
Yelden
Swineshead
Chadwell End
Pertenhall
Staughton Green
Dillington
Staughton Highway
Diddington
Duck End
Papworth St Agnes
Hilton
Conington
Elsworth
Boxworth
Lolworth
Oakington
Histon
Melchbourne
Green End
Great Staughton
Little Staughton
Southoe
Great Paxton
Graveley
Papworth Everard
Knapwell
Bar Hill
Girton
Dry Drayton
Knotting
Riseley
Keysoe
Keysoe Row
Hail Weston
Little Paxton
St Neots
Toseland
Yelling
Croxton
Caxton Gibbet
Madingley
Staploe
Duloe
Eaton Ford
Eaton Socon
Eynesbury
Bolnhurst
Bushmead
Thurleigh
Colmworth
Wyboston
Chawston
Little Barford
Abbotsley
Eltisley
Caxton
Cambourne
Bourn
Caldecote Highfields
Hardwick
Coton
CAMBRIDGE
Bletsoe
Radwell
Milton Ernest
Roxton
Tempsford
Waresley
Great Gransden
Little Gransden
Longstowe
Kingston
Toft
Comberton
Barton
Ravensden
Renhold
Great Barford
Gamlingay Cinques
Gamlingay
Waresley and Gransden Wood
Hatley St George
Great Eversden
Little Eversden
Haslingfield
Harlton
Clapham
BEDFORD
Willington
Blunham
Everton
Cockayne Hatley
East Hatley
Arrington
Croydon
Wimpole
Wimpole Hall & Home Farm
Orwell
Harston
Hauxton
Kempston
Cople
Moggerhanger
Sandy
Potton
Beeston
Wrestlingworth
Wendy
Barrington
Newton
Foxton
Shepreth
Cardington
Northill
Upper Caldecote
Lower Caldecote
Sutton
Tadlow
Eyeworth
Whaddon
Meldreth
Fowlmere
Melbourn
Shortstown
Elstow
Ickwell Green
Biggleswade
Dunton
Great Green
Kneesworth
Bassingbourn
Wilstead
Haynes
Old Warden
Shuttleworth Collection
Swiss Garden
Newton
Guilden Morden
Abington Pigotts
Litlington
Royston
Steeple Morden
Stewartby
Houghton Conquest
Southill
Langford
Edworth
Ashwell
Hinxworth
Stanford
Clifton
Astwick
Millbrook
A1(M)
A1
A14
A47
A15
A605
A141
A142
A1123
A428
A1198
A421
A6
A603
A600
A10
A505
A1303
M11
0 1 2 3 4 5 miles
0 1 2 3 4 5 6 7 8 kilometres

Three Holes
Nordelph
Fordham
Wretton
Stoke Ferry
Oxburgh Hall
Whittington
Foulden
Hilborough
Euximoor Fen
Upwell Fen
Hilgay
Wissington
Bodney
Beckett End
Euximoor Drove
Iron Bridge
Ten Mile Bank
R Wissey
Northwold
Christchurch
Lakesend
Old Bedford River
New Bedford River
Hilgay Fen
Brookville
Tipp's End
Methwold Hythe
Methwold
Cranwich
Ickburgh
Upwell Fen
Welney
Southery
Great Ouse
Stonea
Wildfowl & Wetlands Trust
Southery Fens
Methwold Fens
Queens Ground
Mundford
Gold Hill
Brandon Creek
Feltwell
Thetford Forest Park
Manea
Brandon Bank
Little Ouse
Weeting
Castle
Grime's Graves
Purls Bridge
Littleport Bridge
Hockwold Fens
Hockwold cum Wilton
Santon Downham
Croxton
Welches Dam
Pymoor
Burnt Fen
Little Ouse River
Brandon
Town Street
High Lodge Forest Centre
Oxlode
Littleport
Shippea Hill Station
Sedge Fen
Warren Lodge
Little Downham
Chettisham
Thetford
Coveney
Prickwillow
Lakenheath
Wardy Hill
Queen Adelaide
River Lark
Undley
Witcham
Ely
Kennyhill
Elveden Forest
Middle Fen
Mildenhall Fen
Beck Row
Wilde Street
Elveden
Wentworth
Witchford
Stuntney
Great Fen
Eriswell
Elveden War Memorial
Barnham
RAF Mildenhall
Holywell Row
Broad Hill
Isleham Fen
Thistley Green
West Row
Wilburton
Barway
Little Thetford
Stretham
Soham Cotes
Isleham
Mildenhall
Icklingham
Soham Mere
Priory Church
Worlington
Barton Mills
Anglo-Saxon Village Reconstruction
Soham
Freckenham
Tuddenham
Lackford Green
West Stow
Brockley
Ampton
River
Wicken Fen
Downfield
Fordham
Red Lodge
Herringswell
Cavenham
Lackford
Culford
Ingham
Timworth
Upware
Wicken
New River
Chippenham
Flempton
Hengrave
Timworth Green
Chittering
River Bank
North Street
Landwade
Kennett
Fornham All Saints
Fornham St Martin
Denny Abbey
Snailwell
Risby
Green End
Burwell
Kentford
Needham Street
Lower Green
Higham
Waterbeach
Reach
Exning
Packhorse Bridge
Burthorpe Green
Westley
Bury St Edmunds
Landbeach
Moulton
Upper Green
Barrow
Clayhithe
Commercial End
Swaffham Prior
Newmarket
Gazeley
Denham End
Great Saxham
Little Saxham
Milton
Lode
Anglesey Abbey
R Kennett
Ickworth House
Blackthorpe
Horningsea
Swaffham Bulbeck
National Stud
Ashley
Dalham
Horringer
Green End
Stow-cum-Quy
Cheveley
Denham
Nowton
Chesterton
Bottisham
Dunstall Green
High Green
Sicklesmere
Fen Ditton
Broad Green
Hargrave
Chevington
Pinford End
Cambridge
Frog End
Wooditton
Ousden
Hawstead
Teversham
Little Wilbraham
Stetchworth
Saxon Street
Back Street
Lady's Green
Whepstead
Hawstead Green
Great Welnetham
Church End
Great Wilbraham
Six Mile Bottom
Dullingham
Little Ditton
Upend
Lidgate
Depden Green
Chedburgh
Bradfield Combust
Ditton Green
Dullingham Ley
Kirtling
Baxter's Green
Stonecross Green
Mickley Green
Cherry Hinton
Fulbourn
Westley Waterless
Burrough End
Sascombe
Kirtling Green
Meeting Green
Depden
Gulling Green
Burrough Green
Boyden End
Ashfield Green
Rede
Melon Green
Stanningfield
Brinkley
Attleton Green
Thorns
Wandlebury
Cowlinge
Wickhambrook
Clopton Green
Brockley Green
Harrow Green
Willingham Green
Lambfair Green
Wickham Street
Lawshall
Weston Colville
Great Bradley
Pound Green
Stradishall
Hawkedon
Somerton
Cross Green
Great Shelford
West Wratting
Hobbles Green
Cock & End
Audley End
Shimpling Street
Carlton
Little Bradley
Farley Green
Denston
Stansfield
Hartest
Gifford's Hall
Stapleford
Weston Green
Little Thurlow Green
Lower Street
River Glem
Little Shelford
R Granta
Balsham
Carlton Green
Little Thurlow
Sowley Green
Assington Green
Upper Street
Boxted
Shimpling
Babraham
Temple End
Great Thurlow
Fenstead End
Bridge Street
Sawston
Little Abington
Chilford Hundred
West Wickham
Babel Green
Hundon
Brook Street
Stanstead
The Spike
Great Abington
Hildersham
Streetly End
Withersfield
Great Wratting
Barnardiston
Poslingford
Sue Ryder Foundation
Glemsford
Kentwell Hall
Pampisford
Mount Pleasant
Duxford Chapel
Linton
Horseheath
Hanchet End
Little Wratting
Keddington
Brockley Green
Chilton Street
Nether Hall
Cavendish
Pentlow
Long Melford
Duxford
Zoological Gardens
Cardinal's Green
Bartlow
Mill Green
Burton End
Haverhill
Calford Green
Boyton End
Clare
Clare Castle
Pentlow Street
Foxearth
Acton
Duxford Imperial War Museum (Aircraft)
Hinxton
Hadstock
Shudy Camps
Nosterfield End
Hazel Stub
Stoke by Clare
Liston
Ickleton
Great Chesterford
Steventon End
Castle Camps
Sturmer
Wixoe
Church Street
Newman's Green
Little Chesterford
Camps End
Pale Green
New England
Ovington
Belchamp St Paul
Borley
Ashdon
Helions Bumpstead
Wiggens Green
Baythorne End
Ashen
Belchamp Otten
Borley Green
Sudbury
Little Walden
Steeple Bumpstead
Birdbrook
Tilbury Green
Knowl Green
Belchamp Walter
Ballingdon
Elmdon
Strethall
Water End
Olmstead Green
Ridgewell
Tilbury Juxta Clare
Little Yeldham
Puttock End
Bulmer Tye
Radwinter End
Smith's Green
Finkle Green
Chrishall
Catmere
Littlebury
Saffron Walden
Chapelend
Stambourne
Bulmer
Middleton
A10
A11
A14
A134
A142
A143
A505
A1065
A1101
A1123
A1303
A1304
A1307
A1092
B1094
B1098
B1100
B1093
B1411
B1160
B1112
B1382
B1102
B1104
B1085
B1506
B1063
B1061
B1052
B1054
B1057
B1106
B1107
B1064
B1065
B1066
B1184
B1108
58
69
45
46

Watton
Wymondham
Attleborough
Thetford
Brandon
Diss
Bury St Edmunds
Stowmarket
Needham Market
Long Melford
Sudbury
Hadleigh
Lavenham
Hilborough
Little Cressingham
Toney
Foulden
Beckett End
Bodney
Merton
Griston
Caston
Scoulton
Rockland St Peter
Little Ellingham
Deopham
Morley St Botolph
Silfield
Wreningham
Northwold
Methwold
Cranwich
Ickburgh
Mundford
Thompson
Stow Bedon
Breckles
Great Hockham
East Wretham
Stonebridge
Shropham
Snetterton
Eccles Road
Larling
Quidenham
Wilby
Banham
Kenninghall
Old Buckenham
New Buckenham
Carleton Rode
Bunwell
Tibenham
Aslacton
Tivetshall St Margaret
Gissing
Winfarthing
Shelfanger
Burston
Shimpling
Dickleburgh
Weeting
Santon Downham
Croxton
Bridgham
East Harling
Brettenham
Shadwell
Garboldisham
North Lopham
South Lopham
Fersfield
Bressingham
Roydon
Palgrave
Scole
Rushford
Gasthorpe
Knettishall
Smallworth
Blo Norton
Redgrave
Wortham
Euston
Barnham
Elveden
Coney Weston
Hopton
Market Weston
Thelnetham
Hinderclay
Botesdale
Rickinghall
Thrandeston
Stuston
Oakley
Brome
Eye
Fakenham Magna
Barningham
Sapiston
Honington
Bardwell
Hepworth
Wattisfield
Stanton
Mellis
Yaxley
Braiseworth
Icklingham
Tuddenham
Lackford
Cavenham
Flempton
Hengrave
Culford
West Stow
Brockley
Ampton
Ingham
Timworth
Troston
Ixworth Thorpe
Ixworth
Great Livermere
Langham
West Street
Walsham le Willows
Crowland
Finningham
Westhorpe
Gislingham
Thornham Magna
Wickham Skeith
Cotton
Bacton
Mendlesham
Stoke Ash
Occold
Thorndon
Rishangles
Fornham All Saints
Fornham St Martin
Risby
Great Barton
Pakenham
Thurston
Norton
Elmswell
Stowlangtoft
Hunston
Badwell Ash
Great Ashfield
Haughley
Wetherden
Old Newton
Gipping
Higham
Barrow
Denham
Westley
Little Saxham
Great Saxham
Horringer
Rushbrooke
Blackthorpe
Beyton
Woolpit
Tostock
Hessett
Drinkstone
Rougham
Dagworth
Onehouse
Harleston
Combs
Stowupland
Creeting St Mary
Coddenham
Hemingstone
Barham
Claydon
Henley
Chevington
Hargrave
Hawstead
Whepstead
Chedburgh
Depden
Rede
Sicklesmere
Bradfield St George
Bradfield St Clare
Bradfield Combust
Rattlesden
Buxhall
Great Finborough
Gedding
Felsham
Cockfield
Stanningfield
Hitcham
Brettenham
Wattisham
Battisford
Ringshall
Barking
Great Bricett
Offton
Somersham
Nedging
Naughton
Bildeston
Kettlebaston
Chelsworth
Monks Eleigh
Brent Eleigh
Preston
Alpheton
Shimpling
Boxted
Hartest
Somerton
Hawkedon
Stradishall
Denston
Stansfield
Glemsford
Cavendish
Clare
Pentlow
Foxearth
Borley
Liston
Acton
Little Waldingfield
Great Waldingfield
Milden
Lindsey
Kersey
Aldham
Elmsett
Whatfield
Flowton
Bramford
Sproughton
Burstall
Hintlesham
Washbrook
Copdock
Chattisham
Belstead
Belchamp Walter
Belchamp St Paul
Belchamp Otten
Ballingdon
Great Cornard
Little Cornard
Newton
Boxford
Groton
Edwardstone
Polstead
Layham
Raydon
Great Wenham
Little Wenham
Whitton
Castle Hill
Chantry
Poslingford
Hundon
Ovington
Mount Pleasant
Thetford Forest Park
Peddars Way & Norfolk Coast Path
Little Ouse River
River Waveney
River Lark
River Glem
River Stour
A11
A14
A134
A143
A1066
A1065
A1088
A1075
A1101
A140
A1120
A1071
A1092
B1108
B1106
B1111
B1113
B1115
B1078
B1077
B1066
B1065
B1064
B1063
B1115
5 miles
8 kilometres

LOWESTOFT
Lowestoft Ness
Corton
Gunton
Oulton
Oulton Broad
Kirkley
Pakefield
Carlton Colville
Kessingland
Kessingland Beach
Benacre Ness
Benacre
Wrentham
Covehithe
South Cove
Suffolk Heritage Coast
Sole Bay
Reydon
Southwold
Walberswick
Dunwich
Grey Friars
Westleton
Minsmere
Eastbridge
Sizewell
Leiston
Aldringham
Thorpe Ness
Thorpeness
Aldeburgh
Aldeburgh Bay
River Alde
Orford
Orford Ness
Orfordness-Havergate
River Ore
North Weir Point
Hollesley Bay
Hollesley
Shingle Street
Bawdsey
Alderton
Woodbridge
Sutton Hoo
Martlesham Heath
Martlesham
IPSWICH
Kesgrave
Brightwell
Bucklesham
Levington
Kirton
Falkenham
River Deben
Melton
Ufford
Rendlesham
Wickham Market
Framlingham
Saxmundham
Yoxford
Halesworth
Bungay
Beccles
Harleston
Fressingfield
Laxfield
Wenhaston
Blythburgh
Wangford
Brampton
Worlingham
Gillingham
Ellingham
Ditchingham
Earsham
Flixton
Homersfield
Mendham
Metfield
Weybread
Hoxne
Stradbroke
Wilby
Dennington
Badingham
Peasenhall
Sibton
Heveningham
Ubbeston Green
Huntingfield
Cratfield
Walpole
Bramfield
Thorington
Darsham
Middleton
Theberton
Kelsale
Knodishall
Friston
Snape
The Maltings
Iken
Tunstall
Sudbourne
Chillesford
Butley
Eyke
Bromeswell
Campsea Ash
Blaxhall
Little Glemham
Marlesford
Parham
Easton
Kettleburgh
Brandeston
Earl Soham
Monk Soham
Cretingham
Otley
Charsfield
Dallinghoo
Pettistree
Clopton
Bredfield
Grundisburgh
Burgh
Hasketon
Great Bealings
Little Bealings
Playford
Culpho
Swilland
Ashbocking
Somerleyton
Blundeston
Herringfleet
Haddiscoe
Toft Monks
Aldeby
Wheatacre
Burgh St Peter
River Waveney
Thurlton
Loddon
Hales
Raveningham
Stockton
Geldeston
Barsham
Ringsfield
Redisham
Sotterley
Henstead
Rushmere
Mutford
Gisleham
Barnby
North Cove
Shadingfield
Frostenden
Uggeshall
Blyford
Holton
Spexhall
Wissett
Chediston
Rumburgh
St James South Elmham
St Cross South Elmham
Alburgh
Denton
Starston
Pulham Market
Tasburgh
Hempnall
Woodton
Hedenham
Seething
Mundham
Brooke
Bergh Apton
Chedgrave
Fritton
St Olaves
A12
A14
A140
A143
A144
A145
A146
A1094
A1095
A1120
A1152
A1214
Suffolk Coast
Suffolk Wildlife Park
Pleasurewood Hills
Somerleyton Hall & Gardens
Fritton Lake Countryworld
Leiston Abbey
Framlingham Castle
Orford Castle
Hen Reedbeds
Lighthouse

CAERNARFON
BAY
LLEYN
PENINSULA
72
Morfa Dinlle
Llanwnda
Dinas Dinlle
Llandwrog
Groeslon
Glynllifon
Carmel
Slateworks
Cilgwyn
Penygroes
Talysarn
A499
Pontlyfni
Aberdesach
Llanllyfni
Tai'n Lôn
Nebo
Clynnog-fawr
Capeluchaf
Nasareth
Gyrn-gôch
Pant Glas
522
Y GYRN-DDU
Lleyn Heritage Coast
Trefor
A487
564
YR EIFL
Tre'r Ceiri
Llanaelhaearn
Trwyn y Grolech
Bryncir
Garn-Dolbe
Glan-Dwyfach
Llithfaen
B4417
B4411
St Cybi's Well
Carreg Ddu
Porth Nefyn
Pistyll
Llwyndyrys
Pencaenewydd
Llangybi
Morfa Nefyn
Nefyn
Rhoslan
Afon Dwyfawr
Porth Dinllaen
Groesffordd
Fron
B4354
Y Ffor
Llanarmon
Pentre
Edern
Rhos-fawr
Llanystumdwy
Chwilog
Bodfuan
Porth Ysgaden
Rhos-y-llan
Llannor
R. Erch
Pennarth Fawr Medieval House
Criccieth
Castle
A497
Abererch
Tudweiliog
Dinas
371
Efailnewydd
Carn Fadrum
Porth Colman
B4415
Denio
Pen-ychain
Bryn-mawr
Llaniestyn
Rhyd-y-clafdy
Pwllheli
Garnfadryn
Penrhos
Pen-y-graig
Llangwnnadl
Meyllteyrn
Llanbedrog
Sarn
Botwnnog
Mynytho
Bryncroes
B4413
Nanhoron
Trwyn Llanbedrog
Porthor
Llandegwning
Rhydlios
Rhoshirwaun
St Tudwal's Road
Plas yn Rhiw
Llangian
Anelog
Penycaerau
Y Rhiw
Abersoch
Llanengan
Aberdaron
Llanfaelrhys
Sarn Bach
Porth Neigwl or Hell's Mouth
Uwchmynydd
Porth Ysgo
Bwlchtocyn
Marchros
St Tudwal's Island East
St Tudwal's Island West
Aberdaron Bay
Bardsey Sound
Porth Ceiriad
Lleyn Heritage Coast
St Mary's
BARDSEY ISLAND
A
B
C
D
E
F
G
H
1
2
3
4
5
6
7
8
9
10
11
12
0 1 2 3 4 5 miles
0 1 2 3 4 5 6 7 8 kilometres

Betws Garmon
MOEL EILIO
Snowdon Mountain Railway
Pass of Llanberis
Gwastadnant
GLYDER FAWR
GLYDER FACH
National Mountain Centre
Capel Curig
Gwydyr
Pont Cyfyng
Betws-y-Coed
Forest
Y Stablau
Conwy Valley Railway
Nebo
MOEL SEISIOG
MOEL LLYN
Llyn Alwen
Llyn Cwellyn
MYNYDD MAWR
SNOWDON
Pen-y-pass
Llyn Llydaw
Pen-y-Gwryd
MOEL-SIABOD
Pont-y-pant
Capel Garmon
Burial Chamber
Fairy Glen
Rhyd-Ddu
Llyn Gwynant
Dolwyddelan Castle
Dolwyddelan
Ty'n-y-Coed Uchaf
Rhydlanfair
Alwen Reservoir
YR ARAN
Glanaber
Pentre-bont
Park
Ty Mawr Wybrnant
Pentrefoelas
Cefn-brith
Hafod y Llan
Nant Gwynant
Penmachno
Woollen Mill
Rhyd-lydan
Glasfryn
Welsh Highland Railway
Tŷ Isaf
Beddgelert
Sygun Copper Mine
Gelli Iago
Llechwedd Slate Caverns
Ysbyty Ifan
Cerrigydrudion
MOEL HEBOG
Nantmor
Rhiwbryfdir
Blaenau Ffestiniog
Cwm Penmachno
Carrog
Llyn Conwy
River Conwy
Llanfihangel-y-pennant
Tan-y-grisiau
MOELWYN MAWR
Bethania
Congl-y-wal
MOEL DDU
Croesor
MOELWYN BACH
Hydro-electric Power Station
Tan-y-Grisiau Reservoir
CARNEDD Y-FILAST
Golan
Afon Glaslyn
Rhyd-y-sarn
Ffestiniog
Afon Serw
Afon Gelyn
Prenteg
Rhyd
Ffestiniog Railway
Tan-y-Bwlch
ARENIG FACH
Garreg
Llanfrothen
Penmorfa
Tremadog
Wern
Maentwrog
Ciltalgarth
Glan-yr-afon
Porthmadog
Penrhyndeudraeth
Gellilydan
Llyn Celyn
National Whitewater Centre
Fron-goch
Sarna
Cefn-ddwysarn
Toll
Gwaith Powdwr
Llandecwyn
Amphitheatre
Afon Tryweryn
Llidiardau
Minffordd
Portmeirion
Llyn Arenig Fawr
Rhiwlas
Morfa Bychan
Borth-y-Gest
Bryn-bwbach
Llyn Trawsfynydd
ARENIG FAWR
Rhyd-uchaf
Traeth Bach
Talsarnau
Trawsfynydd
Bala
Llanfor
Harlech Point
Llanfihangel-y-traethau
Rhos-y-g
Morfa Harlech
MOEL YSGYFARNOGOD
SNOWDONIA
Parc
Llyn Tegid
Bala Lake Railway
Harlech
Bronaber
Rhiw Goch
Afon Lliw
Llangower
Harlech Castle
Llanuwchllyn
Llanfair
Bryn-Eden
Afon Mawddach
NATIONAL
Pont Rhyd-sarn
Pandy
RHINOG FAWR
Llandanwg
Llanbedr
Pentre Gwynfryn
Coed-y-Brenin Forest Park
MOEL-Y-GEIFR
Ty-nant
Shell Island
Morfa Dyffryn
Coed-y-Brenin
Y LLETHR
RHOBELL FAWR
PARK
Afon Gamlan
Ganllwyd
Coed Ystumgwern
MOELFRE
Rhaeadr Ddu (Waterfall)
Llanenddwyn
Dyffryn Ardudwy
Afon Ysgethin
Cors-y-Gedol
DIFFWYS
Burial Chamber
Llanfachreth
Rhydymain
ARAN FAWDDWY
Llanddwywe
Tal-y-bont
Llanelltyd
Cymer Abbey
Bontddu
Llanaber
Caerdeon
Brithdir
Llanymawddwy
Cutiau
Penmaenpool
Caerynwch
Dolgellau
Barmouth
Afon Mawddach
Barmouth Bridge
Dyffrydan
WAEN OER
TIR RHIWIOG
Llanerch
Dinas-Mawddwy
Barmouth Bay
Fairbourne & Barmouth Steam Railway
Arthog
CADER IDRIS
Minllyn
Meirion Mill
Pont Minllyn
Cwm-Cewydd
Fairbourne
Mallwyd
Friog
Clipiau
Tal-y-llyn
Aberllefenni
Aberangell
CARNEDD WEN
Llwyngwril
Llanfihangel-y-pennant
Castell y Bere
Tal-y-llyn
Corris Uchaf
Railway Museum
Corris
King Arthur's Labyrinth & Craft Centre
Cwm Llinau
Afon Dysynni
Llangelynin
Abergynolwyn
Dol-fôr
Rhoslefain
Esgairgeiliog
Cemmaes
Peniarth
Dolgoch
Tal-y-Llyn Railway
Cemmaes Road
Pentre-celyn
Llanegryn
Pantperthog
Centre for Alternative Technology
Pandy
Ton fanau
Bryncrug
Dolgoch Falls
TAREN HENDRE
Commins Coch
Pentre-Maw
Machynlleth
Aber Dysynni
Pandy
Llanwrin
Machinations
Llanbrynmair
Abergwydol
Ynysymaengwyn
Rhyd-yr-onnen
Darowen
Tafolwern
Dolfach
Abercegir
Dovey Valley
Pennal
Penegoes
Talywern
Llan
Tywyn
Talerddig
Cwrt
Forge
Melin-byrhedyn
Bont-Dolgadfan
Derwenlas
MOELFRE
Pennant
Sarn
Glaspwll
Pantglas
Aberhosan
BRYN AMLWG
Glandyfi
Aberdyfi

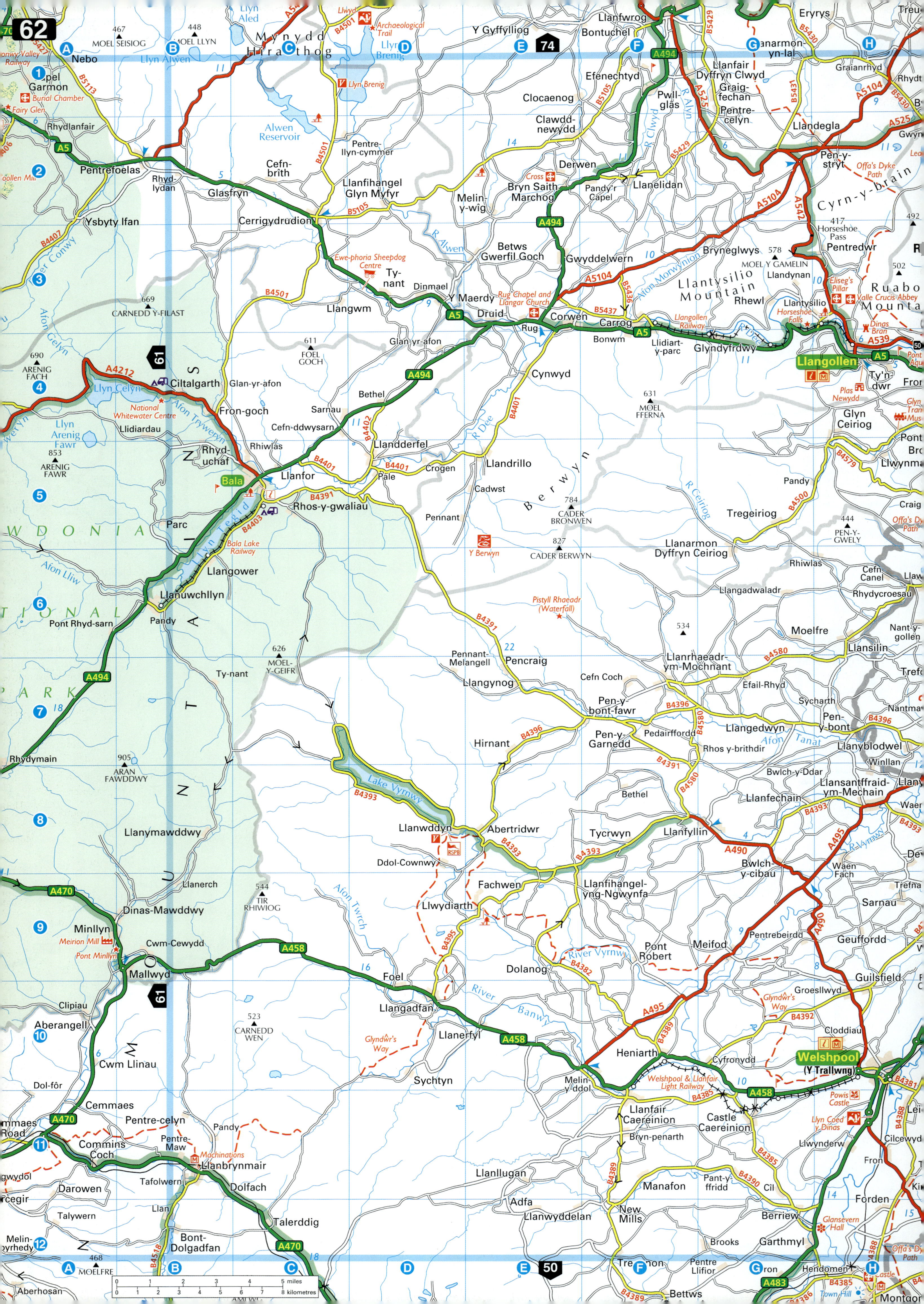
62
74
61
50
Nebo
Mynydd Hiraethog
Y Gyffylliog
Llanfwrog
Bontuchel
Eryrys
Llanarmon-yn-Ial
Graianrhyd
Efenechtyd
Llanfair Dyffryn Clwyd
Graig-fechan
Pentre-celyn
Pwll-glâs
Clocaenog
Clawdd-newydd
Llandegla
Pen-y-stryt
Offa's Dyke Path
Cyrn-y-brain
Alwen Reservoir
Llyn Brenig
Archaeological Trail
Pentre-llyn-cymmer
Cefn-brith
Llanfihangel Glyn Myfyr
Derwen
Llanelidan
Bryn Saith Marchog
Pandy'r Capel
Melin-y-wig
Rhydlanfair
Pentrefoelas
Rhyd-lydan
Glasfryn
Cerrigydrudion
Ysbyty Ifan
Betws Gwerfil Goch
Gwyddelwern
Bryneglwys
Llandynan
Pentredwr
Horseshoe Pass
Llantysilio Mountain
Rhewl
Llantysilio
Ruabon Mountain
Eliseg's Pillar
Valle Crucis Abbey
Horseshoe Falls
Dinas Bran
Ewe-phoria Sheepdog Centre
Ty-nant
Dinmael
Y Maerdy
Rug Chapel and Llangar Church
Druid
Corwen
Carrog
Rug
Bonwm
Llidiart-y-parc
Glyndyfrdwy
Llangollen Railway
Llangollen
Ty'n-dwr
Plas Newydd
Glyn Ceiriog
Llangwm
Glan-yr-afon
CARNEDD Y-FILAST
FOEL GOCH
ARENIG FACH
Ciltalgarth
Llyn Celyn
National Whitewater Centre
Fron-goch
Bethel
Sarnau
Cefn-ddwysarn
Cynwyd
MOEL FFERNA
Llyn Arenig Fawr
ARENIG FAWR
Llidiardau
Rhyd-uchaf
Rhiwlas
Llandderfel
Crogen
Llandrillo
Bala
Llanfor
Pale
Rhos-y-gwaliau
Cadwst
Berwyn
CADER BRONWEN
CADER BERWYN
Pennant
Y Berwyn
R. Ceiriog
Tregeiriog
Pandy
PEN-Y-GWELY
Llanarmon Dyffryn Ceiriog
SNOWDONIA NATIONAL PARK
Parc
Llyn Tegid
Bala Lake Railway
Llangower
Llanuwchllyn
Pont Rhyd-sarn
Rhiwlas
Cefn Canel
Llangadwaladr
Rhydycroesau
Pistyll Rhaeadr (Waterfall)
Moelfre
MOEL-Y-GEIFR
Ty-nant
Pennant-Melangell
Pencraig
Llanrhaeadr-ym-Mochnant
Llansilin
Cefn Coch
Efail-Rhyd
Llangynog
Pen-y-bont-fawr
Sycharth
Pen-y-bont
Hirnant
Pen-y-Garnedd
Pedairffordd
Llangedwyn
Rhos y-brithdir
Llanyblodwel
Rhydymain
ARAN FAWDDWY
Lake Vyrnwy
Bethel
Bwlch-y-Ddar
Llansantffraid-ym-Mechain
Llanfechain
Llanymawddwy
Llanwddyn
Abertridwr
Tycrwyn
Llanfyllin
Ddol-Cownwy
Bwlch-y-cibau
Waen Fach
Llanerch
TIR RHIWIOG
Fachwen
Llanfihangel-yng-Ngwynfa
Dinas-Mawddwy
Llwydiarth
Minllyn
Meirion Mill
Pont Minllyn
Cwm-Cewydd
Pont Robert
Meifod
Pentrebeirdd
Sarnau
Geuffordd
Guilsfield
Mallwyd
Foel
Dolanog
River Vyrnwy
Clipiau
Llangadfan
River Banwy
Groesllwyd
Glyndŵr's Way
Aberangell
CARNEDD WEN
Llanerfyl
Heniarth
Cyfronydd
Cloddiau
Welshpool (Y Trallwng)
Cwm Llinau
Sychtyn
Melin-y-ddol
Welshpool & Llanfair Light Railway
Powis Castle
Dol-fôr
Cemmaes
Pentre-celyn
Llanfair Caereinion
Castle Caereinion
Pandy
Pentre-Maw
Machinations
Bryn-penarth
Llwynderw
Commins Coch
Llanbrynmair
Darowen
Tafolwern
Dolfach
Llanllugan
Manafon
Pant-y-ffridd
Cil
Forden
Talywern
Llan
Talerddig
Adfa
Llanwyddelan
New Mills
Berriew
Glansevern Hall
Bont-Dolgadfan
Brooks
Garthmyl
MOELFRE
Tregynon
Pentre Llifior
Hendomen
Aberhosan
Bettws
Montgomery
A5
A494
A5104
A4212
A470
A458
A490
A495
A483
A525
A542
A539
B4501
B5105
B4401
B4402
B4391
B4403
B4396
B4580
B4393
B4395
B4382
B4389
B4390
B4385
B4392
B4500
B4579
B4580
B4518
0 1 2 3 4 5 miles
0 1 2 3 4 5 6 7 8 kilometres

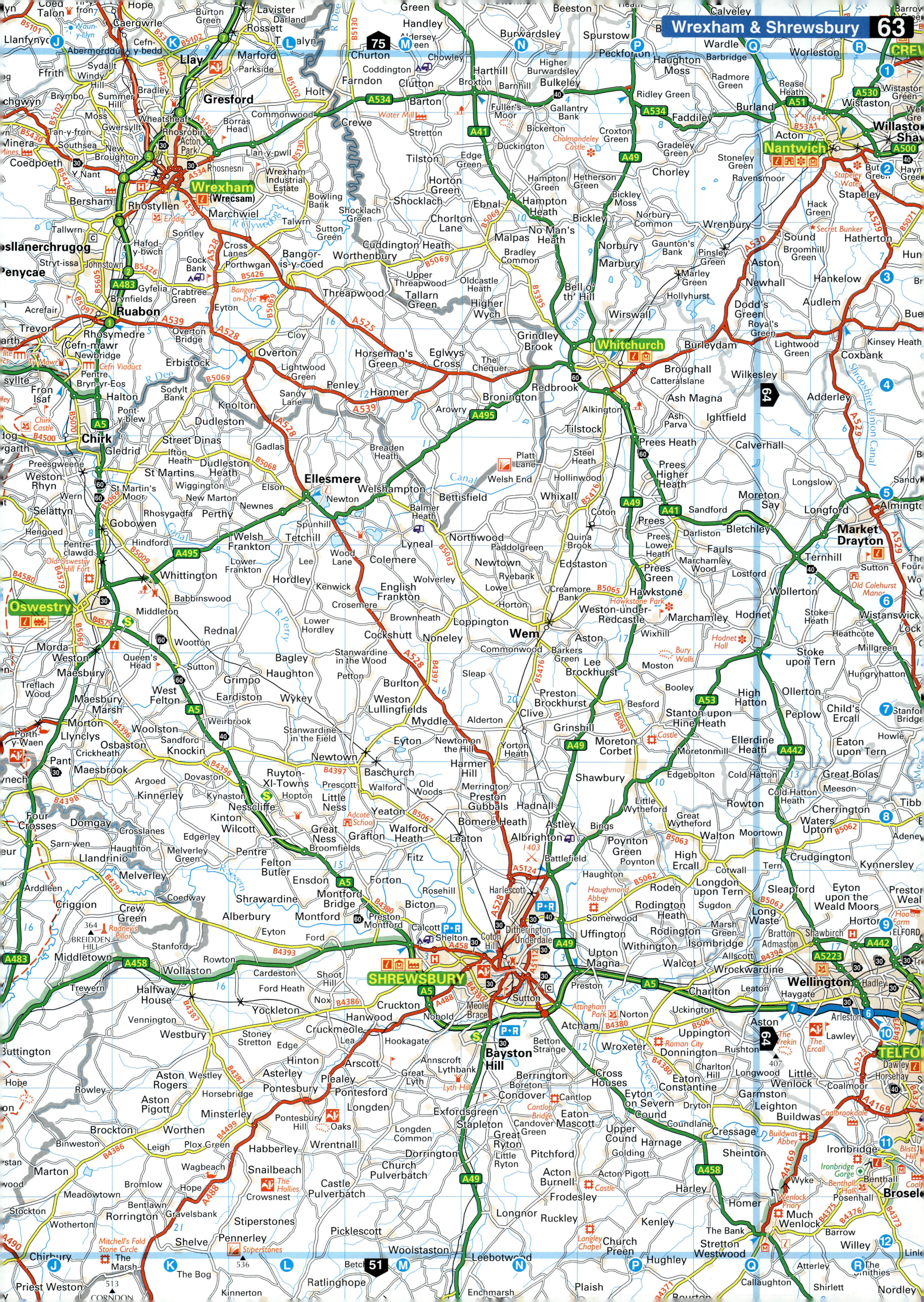
Wrexham
(Wrecsam)
Gresford
Ruabon
Chirk
Oswestry
Ellesmere
Whitchurch
Nantwich
Market Drayton
Wem
Shrewsbury
Wellington
Telford
Bayston Hill
Overton
Hanmer
Malpas
Audlem
Hodnet
Shawbury
Pontesbury
Much Wenlock
Ironbridge
Atcham
Condover
Dorrington
Baschurch
Nesscliffe
Whittington
Prees
Tilstock
Redbrook
Bronington
Welshampton
Cockshutt
Loppington
Grinshill
Clive
Ercall
Llay
Holt
Farndon
Churton
Tilston
Bangor-is-y-coed
Worthenbury
Penley
Rhosllanerchrugog
Johnstown
Cefn-mawr
St Martins
Gobowen
Weston Rhyn
Llanymynech
Knockin
Ruyton-XI-Towns
Montford Bridge
Ford
Westbury
Minsterley
Longden
Church Pulverbatch
Acton Burnell
Cressage
Harley
Sheinton
Buildwas
Leighton
Wroxeter
Upton Magna
Withington
Rodington
Uffington
Hadnall
Stanton upon Hine Heath
Moreton Corbet
Childs Ercall
High Ercall
Crudgington
Wistanswick
Hinstock
Cheswardine
Woore
Wrenbury
Norbury
Marbury
Bickley
Hampton Heath
No Man's Heath
Cholmondeley Castle
Broxton
Barton
Clutton
Coddington
Handley
Beeston
Burwardsley
Spurstow
Peckforton
Haughton Moss
Faddiley
Burland
Acton
Willaston
Wistaston
Stapeley
Hatherton
Hankelow
Buerton
Calverhall
Ightfield
Moreton Say
Adderley
Ternhill
Stoke upon Tern
Longford
Sutton
Lee Brockhurst
Preston Brockhurst
Edstaston
Hawkstone
Weston-under-Redcastle
Marchamley
Myddle
Burlton
Petton
Harmer Hill
Albrighton
Battlefield
Leaton
Bomere Heath
Walford Heath
Yeaton
Fitz
Forton
Bicton
Shelton
Meole Brace
Sutton
Berrington
Cross Houses
Eaton Constantine
Uppington
Rushton
Walcot
Charlton
Wrockwardine
Admaston
Lawley
Dawley
Coalbrookdale
Broseley
Willey
Stretton Westwood
Kenley
Church Preen
Hughley
Plaish
Longnor
Leebotwood
Woolstaston
Ratlinghope
Picklescott
Stiperstones
Snailbeach
Habberley
Pontesford
Hanwood
Cruckmeole
Cruckton
Yockleton
Rowton
Wollaston
Halfway House
Middletown
Trewern
Criggion
Crew Green
Alberbury
Shrawardine
Melverley
Llandrinio
Kinnerley
Maesbrook
Morton
Llynclys
Maesbury
Treflach Wood
Morda
Trefonen
Weston
Sweeney
Sarn-wen
Four Crosses
Priest Weston
Chirbury
Marton
Worthen
Brockton
Wotherton
Rorrington
Shelve
Pennerley
Hope
Gravelsbank
Meadowtown
Bromlow
Binweston
Leigh
Aston Rogers
Aston Pigott
Rowley
Buttington
Halton
Pentre
Bryn-yr-Eos
Froncysyllte
Trevor
Acrefair
Rhosymedre
Erbistock
Sodylt Bank
Dudleston Heath
Street Dinas
Welsh Frankton
Lower Frankton
Hordley
Tetchill
Colemere
Lyneal
Bettisfield
Welsh End
Whixall
Northwood
Newtown
Wolverley
English Frankton
Crosemere
Noneley
Alderton
Burlton
Sleap
Stanwardine in the Wood
Weston Lullingfields
Little Ness
Great Ness
Grafton
Kinton
Wilcott
Felton Butler
Edgerley
Pentre
Ensdon
Montford
Preston Montford
Calcott
Emstrey
Atcham
Norton
Betton Strange
Pitchford
Cantlop
Ryton
Frodesley
Ruckley
Longnor
Acton Pigott
Golding
Harnage
Cound
Eaton Mascott
Exfordsgreen
Stapleton
Annscroft
Lythbank
Great Lyth
Hookagate
Arscott
Pulverbatch
Castle Pulverbatch
Hinton
Asterley
Plealey
Minsterley
Crowsnest
Wrentnall
Cothercott
Westley
Horsebridge
Stoney Stretton
Edge
Nox
Shoot Hill
Cardeston
Ford Heath
Vennington
Hayford
Rorrington
Bentlawnt
Wagbeach
Plox Green
Lee
Cockshutt
Kenwick
Brownheath
Commonwood
Aston
Barkers Green
Booley
Moston
Wixhill
Besford
Bings
Poynton
Poynton Green
Haughton
Roden
Rodington Heath
Isombridge
Allscott
Longdon upon Tern
Sugdon
Cotwall
Sleapford
Long Waste
Bratton
Shawbirch
Horton
Preston upon the Weald Moors
Eyton upon the Weald Moors
Kynnersley
Tibberton
Meeson
Great Bolas
Cold Hatton
Cold Hatton Heath
Waters Upton
Cherrington
Ellerdine Heath
Ellerdine
Rowton
Edgebolton
Moortown
Walton
Great Wytheford
Little Wytheford
Astley
Hadnall
Merrington
Preston Gubbals
Old Woods
Walford
Yorton Heath
Eaton upon Tern
Howle
Peplow
Hungryhatton
Ollerton
High Hatton
Bletchley
Fauls
Sandford
Darliston
Prees Lower Heath
Prees Green
Lostford
Wollerton
Hodnet
Stoke Heath
Heathcote
Millgreen
Child's Ercall
Almington
Crewe
Nantwich

63
76
52
63
CREWE
Nantwich
Whitchurch
Haslington
Alsager
Kidsgrove
Audley
NEWCASTLE-UNDER-LYME
Hanley
STOKE-ON-TRENT
Stone
STAFFORD
Market Drayton
Newport
Gnosall
Eccleshall
Penkridge
Wellington
TELFORD
Shifnal
Albrighton
Codsall
WOLVERHAMPTON
Broseley
Ironbridge
Much Wenlock
Madeley
Dawley
Willaston
Shavington
Wybunbury
Stapeley
Audlem
Hankelow
Buerton
Woore
Madeley
Keele
Betley
Barthomley
Weston
Chorlton
Hough
Wrenbury
Aston
Newhall
Burleydam
Wilkesley
Adderley
Norton in Hales
Loggerheads
Ashley
Mucklestone
Maer
Whitmore
Baldwin's Gate
Hanchurch
Trentham
Barlaston
Meir
Blythe Bridge
Longton
Fenton
Burslem
Tunstall
Biddulph
Rudyard
Leek
Chapel Chorlton
Swynnerton
Yarnfield
Cotes Heath
Millmeece
Croxton
Sugnall
Cheswardine
Hinstock
Child's Ercall
Hodnet
Wistanswick
Ternhill
Stoke upon Tern
High Offley
Woodseaves
Knightley
Norbury
Forton
Ranton
Derrington
Haughton
Church Eaton
Bradley
Dunston
Acton Trussell
Brewood
Coven
Featherstone
Essington
Kingswood
Pattingham
Perton
Worfield
Beckbury
Ryton
Kemberton
Sutton Maddock
Coalport
Lilleshall
Muxton
Donnington
Trench
Hadley
Oakengates
Priorslee
Church Aston
Edgmond
Tibberton
Crudgington
High Ercall
Rodington
Withington
Wrockwardine
Charlton
Wroxeter
Uppington
Eaton Constantine
Cressage
Sheinton
Harley
Kenley
Homer
Leighton
Buildwas
Garmston
Little Wenlock
Lawley
Aston
Arleston
Haygate
Sleapford
Eyton upon the Weald Moors
Preston upon the Weald Moors
Kynnersley
Waters Upton
Great Bolas
Cold Hatton
Peplow
Ollerton
Hatton
Rowton
Ellerdine Heath
Moreton Corbet
Stanton upon Hine Heath
Marchamley
Hawkstone
Wollerton
Prees
Prees Heath
Ightfield
Ash Magna
Whixall
Weston-under-Redcastle
Lostford
Fauls
Darliston
Sandford
Moreton Say
Longford
Almington
Hales
Chipnall
Outlands
Great Soudley
Little Soudley
Goldstone
Knighton
Shebdon
Adbaston
Tunstall
Weston Jones
Sambrook
Pickstock
Puleston
Chetwynd
Edgmond Marsh
Outwoods
Moreton
Orslow
High Onn
Wheaton Aston
Lapley
Stretton
Gailey
Hatherton
Shareshill
Four Ashes
Bishop's Wood
Kiddemore Green
Tong
Tong Norton
Weston-under-Lizard
Blymhill
Sheriffhales
Woodcote
Great Chatwell
Brineton
Marston
Whiston
Mitton
Levedale
Bednall
Sandon
Salt
Hopton
Marston
Weston
Chebsey
Norton Bridge
Aston-by-Stone
Walton
Little Stoke
Oulton
Moddershall
Fulford
Hilderstone
Cresswell
Stallington
Dresden
Lightwood
Rough Close
Caverswall
Weston Coyney
Werrington
Bucknall
Hulme
Cellarhead
Milton
Baddeley Edge
Bagnall
Brown Edge
Endon
Stanley
Stockton Brook
Norton in the Moors
Smallthorne
Chell
Goldenhill
Talke
Butt Lane
Red Street
Chesterton
Wolstanton
Porthill
Silverdale
Knutton
Seabridge
Butterton
Acton
Shelton under Harley
Stableford
Beech
Tittensor
Hanford
Trent Vale
M6
M54
A5
A41
A442
A518
A519
A529
A525
A53
A51
A34
A500
A50
A520
A449
A454
A4169
A458
A49
A530
A534
A5223
B5062
B5063
B5026
B5415
B5405
B4379
B4380
B4373
B4176

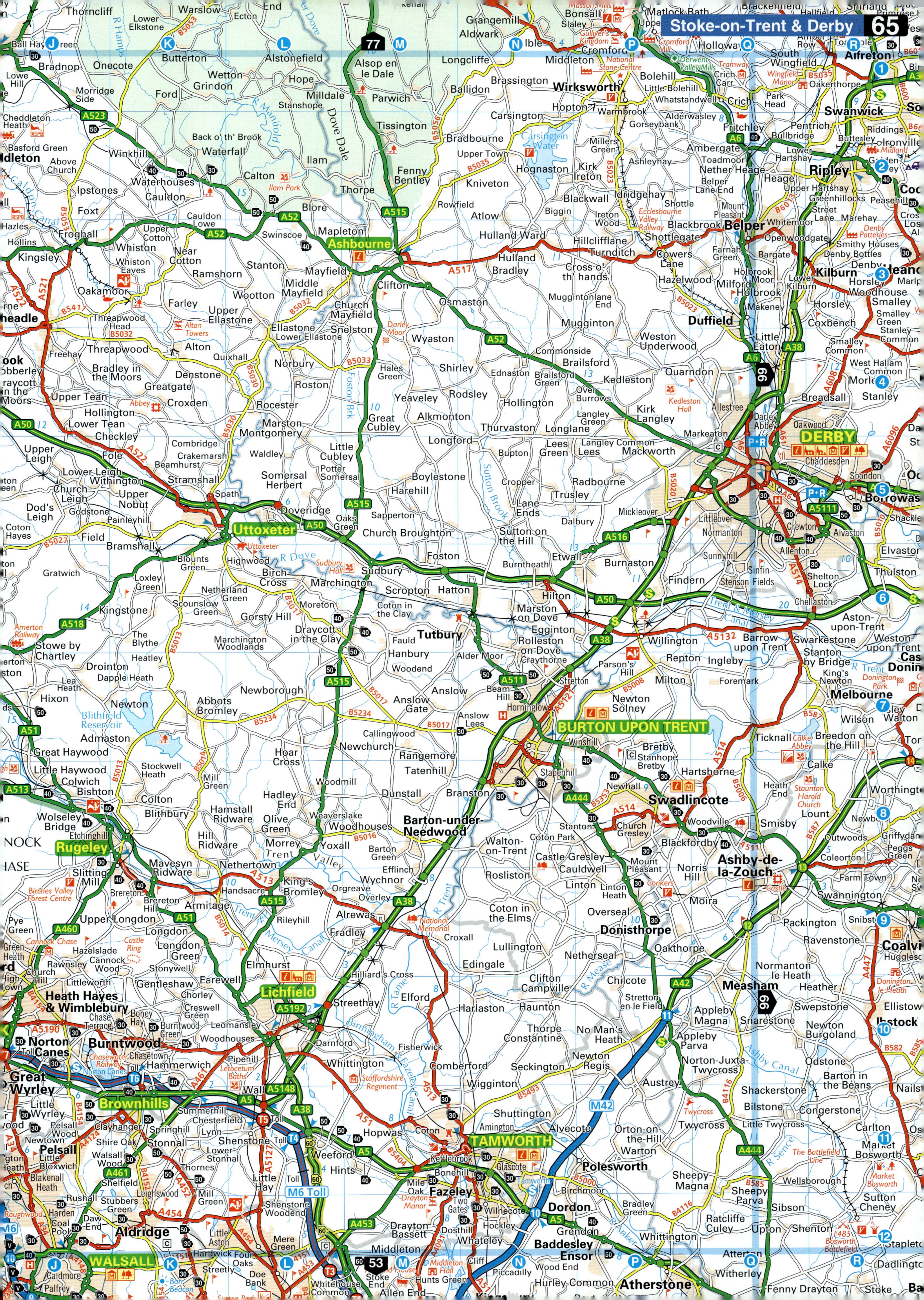
Ashbourne
Uttoxeter
DERBY
BURTON UPON TRENT
Swadlincote
Ashby-de-la-Zouch
Rugeley
Lichfield
TAMWORTH
WALSALL
Brownhills
Aldridge
Burntwood
Belper
Ripley
Alfreton
Wirksworth
Tutbury
Barton-under-Needwood
Measham
Atherstone
Polesworth
Fazeley
Melbourne
Duffield
Kilburn
Swanwick
Heath Hayes & Wimblebury
Norton Canes
Great Wyrley
Pelsall
Dordon
Baddesley Ensor
Donisthorpe
Matlock Bath
A52
A50
A38
A515
A5
A513
A514
A511
A444
A42
A453
A6
A61
A5111
A516
M42
M6 Toll
Dove Dale
Carsington Water
Blithfield Reservoir
Alton Towers
Sudbury Hall
Calke Abbey
Kedleston Hall
Tamworth Castle
Staunton Harold Church

Matlock Bath
Wessington
Alfreton
South Normanton
Kirkby in Ashfield
Rainworth
Blidworth
Kirklington
Farnsfield
Southwell
Edingley
Halam
Cromford
Holloway
South Wingfield
Pinxton
Ravenshead
Blidworth Bottoms
Haywood Oaks
SHERWOOD FOREST
Swanwick
Somercotes
Selston
Newstead
Papplewick
Halloughton
Oxton
Ambergate
Ripley
Codnor
Hucknall
Calverton
Thurgarton
Epperstone
Belper
Eastwood
Bestwood Village
Woodborough
Gonalston
NOTTINGHAM
Lowdham
Heanor
Kilburn
Arnold
Lambley
Burton Joyce
Duffield
Ilkeston
Carlton
Gedling
Shelford
East Bridgford
Newton
Stoke Bardolph
Saxondale
Stapleford
Beeston
West Bridgford
Radcliffe on Trent
DERBY
Ockbrook
Borrowash
Breaston
Long Eaton
Ruddington
Cotgrave
Clipston
Owthorpe
Keyworth
Stanton on the Wolds
Kinoulton
Hickling
Widmerpool
Kegworth
Castle Donington
Melbourne
Swarkestone
Willington
Repton
BURTON UPON TRENT
Swadlincote
Ashby-de-la-Zouch
Shepshed
Loughborough
Quorn
Sileby
Mountsorrel
Coalville
Whitwick
Measham
Ibstock
Markfield
Birstall
Syston
East Goscote
Groby
Ratby
LEICESTER
Kirby Muxloe
Desford
Market Bosworth
Atherstone
Oadby
Wigston
Enderby
Blaby
Narborough
Whetstone
M1
A38
A52
A6
A42
A50
A46
A453
A60
A606
A612
A6097
A614
A511
A512
A47
A444
A447
A5132
M42
M69

North Muskham
Little Carlton
Winthorpe
Langford
Disney
Carlton-le-Moorland
Navenby
Scopwick
Timberland
Hockerton
South Muskham
Nottinghamshire
Stapleford
79
Wellingore
Rowston
Thorpe Tilney
Walcott
Kelham
A617
A6065
Aircraft
Ashby de la Launde
Billinghay
Averham
Beacon Hill
Coddington
Beckingham
Brant Broughton
Welbourn
Digby
Staythorpe
Newark-on-Trent
A17
Bloxholm
Dorrington
Rolleston
Farndon
New Balderton
Balderton
Barnby in the Willows
Stragglethorpe
Leadenham
Ruskington
Fiskerton
Hawton
East Stoke
Fernwood
Fenton
B1188
Thorpe
Claypole
Fulbeck
RAF College (Cranwell)
Cranwell
Anwick
Hazelford
Stubton
Caythorpe
B1429
Leasingham
R Slea
R Trent
R Devon
Elston
Brandon
B1209
Cotham
Syerston
A1
Dry Doddington
Frieston
North Rauceby
Holdingham
Evedon
Ewerby Thorpe
Ewerby
Kirkby la Thorpe
Howell
Flintham
A46
Hough-on-the-Hill
A607
Normanton
Sleaford
Sibthorpe
Long Bennington
Gelston
Carlton Scroop
South Rauceby
Asgarby
Shelton
Staunton in the Vale
Westborough
Hougham
Sudbrook
Ancaster
B6403
B1517
Quarrington
Screveton
Hawksworth
Marston
A153
A15
Heckington
Flawborough
Kilvington
Foston
Honington
Wilsford
Little Green
Thoroton
Alverton
Barkston
Silk Willoughby
Burton Pedwardine
Great Hale
Little Hale
Normanton
Syston
Kelby
Swarby
Orston
Allington
Belton
Belton House
Culverthorpe
Aswarby
Scredington
Helpringham
Aslockton
Whatton
Bottesford
Belvoir
Great Gonerby
Heydour
Oasby
Aisby
Aunsby
Osbournby
Spanby
Elton
A52
Sedgebrook
Londonthorpe
B1394
Sutton
Gonerby Hill Foot
Manthorpe
Welby
Dembleby
Scott Willoughby
Swaton
Muston
Barrowby
Newton
Bridge End
Granby
Vale of Belvoir
Grantham
New Somerby
Haceby
Walcot
Threekingham
Barnstone
Redmile
Braceby
Horbling
Langar
Belvoir
Barkestone-le-Vale
Woolsthorpe
Ropsley
Sapperton
Pickworth
Billingborough
Plungar
Grantham Canal
Belvoir Castle
Denton
Harlaxton
Little Ponton
B1174
Old Somerby
Humby
Folkingham
Birthorpe
Sempringham
Harston
Hanby
Laughton
Pointon
Stathern
Stroxton
Great Ponton
Boothby Pagnell
B1176
Knipton
Harby
Croxton Kerrial
Hungerton
Scotland
Lenton
Aslackby
Milthorpe
Branston
Ingoldsby
Graby
Hose
Wyville
Bitchfield
Keisby
Rippingale
Dowsby
B1397
Eastwell
Eaton
A607
Bassingthorpe
Hawthorpe
Hall
Easton
R Witham
Stoke Rochford
Irnham
Goadby Marwood
Bescaby
Saltby
Skillington
Burton Coggles
Kirkby Underwood
Dunsby
Waltham on the Wolds
Bulby
Stainfield
Wycomb
Sproxton
Woolsthorpe Manor
Corby Glen
A151
Hacconby
Holwell
Chadwell
Woolsthorpe-by-Colsterworth
Colsterworth
Hanthorpe
Morton
Scalford
Stonesby
Birkholme
Elsthorpe
Ab Kettleby
Buckminster
Stainby
Twyford
Grimsthorpe
Dyke
North Witham
Swayfield
Swinstead
Edenham
Melton Mowbray
Coston
B676
Sewstern
Gunby
Scottlethorpe
Bourne
Thorpe Arnold
Freeby
Garthorpe
Creeton
Eastgate
Twenty
Saxby
A6006
Wyfordby
South Witham
Castle Bytham
Little Bytham
R Glen
Tongue End
Brentingby
Stapleford
Wymondham
Cribbs Meadow
Lound
Northorpe
Witham on the Hill
Toft
Ankle Hill
R Eye
Thistleton
Eye Kettleby
Burton Lazars
Edmondthorpe
Clipsham
Careby
Thurlby
A606
Teigh
Market Overton
Stretton
Manthorpe
Obthorpe
B6047
Little Dalby
Whissendine
Barrow
Greetham
Aunby
Great Dalby
Ashwell
Rutland
Pickworth
Carlby
A6121
Baston
Cross Drain
Leesthorpe
Cottesmore
Braceborough
Kirby Bellars
Shillingthorpe
Thorpe Satchville
Burrough Hill
Essendine
Market Deeping
Pickwell
Rutland Falconry & Owl Centre
Exton
A1
Open Air Theatre
Greatford
Langtoft
Barholm
Burrough on the Hill
Cold Overton
Ranksborough
Langham
B668
Ryhall
Towngate
Somerby
Barleythorpe
Vale of Catmose
Burley
Little Casterton
Belmesthorpe
West Deeping
Horsegate
Deeping Gate
Knossington
Whitwell
Tickencote
Empingham
Great Casterton
Tallington
Castle End
Marefield
Oakham
Ingthorpe
Northfields
Stamford
Maxey
Owston
Egleton
Upper Hambleton
Rutland Water
A606
Tinwell
A1175
Uffington
Lowesby
Braunston
Burghley
Bainton
Etton
Halstead
Normanton
Prior's Coppice
Brooke
Ketton
Wothorpe
Pilsgate
Ashton
Tilton on the Hill
River Chater
Manton
Edith Weston
Lyndon
Aldgate
Geeston
B1443
Barnack
Helpston
North Luffenham
Easton-on-the-Hill
Hills & Holes
Ufford
Wing
Ridlington
A6003
Southorpe
Skeffington
Loddington
Maze
Pilton
Collyweston
Wittering
Preston
South Luffenham
Castor Hanglands
Marholm
A47
Belton
Morcott
A43
Duddington
Thornhaugh
Sacrewell Farm & Country Centre
Upton
Tugby
Rolleston
Ayston
Glaston
Barrowden
Tixover
Allexton
East Norton
Wardley
Uppingham
Bisbrooke
Bedford Purlieus
Ailsworth
Goadby
Wakerley
Wansford
Sutton
Fineshade
Seaton
Stibbington
Castor
Nene Valley Railway
Ferry Meadows
Noseley
Stockerston
Horninghold
Lyddington
Lyddington Bede House
Harringworth
Harringworth
55
King's Cliffe
Yarwell
Sibson
Hallaton

Scopwick
Kirkby Green
Timberland
Tattershall
Coningsby
Tumby Woodside
New Bolingbroke
Sticknev
New Leake
Thorpe Tilney
Tattershall Castle
Tattershall College
Moor Side
Ashby de la Launde
Rowston
Walcott
Tattershall Bridge
Battle of Britain Memorial Flight
80
Medlam
Eastville
Hawthorn Hill
New York
East Fen
Dogdyke
Sandy Bank
Carrington
Digby
Billinghay
Scrub Hill
Bunker's Hill
West
Fen
Lade Bank
Chapel Hill
Hundle Houses
Northlands
Wrangle Common
Bloxholm
Dorrington
Haven Bank
Leake Common Side
North Kyme
Sibsey Fenside
Ruskington
R Witham
Sibsey Trader Windmill
Sibsey
Holland Fen
Frithville
Gipsey Bridge
Wrangle
RAF College (Cranwell)
Cranwell
Anwick
Fishtoft Drove
Old Leake
South Kyme
High Ferry
Leasingham
R Slea
Hurn's End
Langrick
Frith Bank
Evedon
Ewerby Thorpe
Hilldyke
Leverton
North Rauceby
Holdingham
Ewerby
Kirkby la Thorpe
Amber Hill
Anton's Gowt
Long Hedges
Benington
Lucasgate
Sleaford
Howell
Brothertoft
Haltoft End
Benington Sea End
South Rauceby
Asgarby
East Heckington
Holland Fen
Boston
Willoughby Hills
Butterwick
Brand End
Quarrington
Heckington
The Pearoom
Hubbert's Bridge
Freiston
Great Hale
Swineshead Bridge
Wyberton West
Tamworth Green
Silk Willoughby
Burton Pedwardine
Little Hale
North End
Frampton West End
Fishtoft
67
Swarby
Kirton Holme
Wyberton East
Scrane End
Aswarby
Scredington
Helpringham
Swineshead
Kirton End
Frampton
Heydour
Aisby
Aunsby
Bicker Gauntlet
Drayton
Blackjack
The Haven
Osbournby
Spanby
Bicker Bar
Fishmere End
Kirton
Sandholme
Dembleby
Scott Willoughby
Swaton
Bicker
Asperton
Skeldyke
Newton
Bridge End
Northorpe
Wigtoft
Seadyke
Haceby
Threekingham
Donington
Sutterton
Algarkirk
Walcot
Horbling
Burtoft
Church End
Quadring Eaudike
Sapperton
Billingborough
Donington Southing
Pitcher Row
Pickworth
Birthorpe
Fosdyke
Holbeach St Matthew
Humby
Folkingham
Sempringham
Quadring
Fosdyke Bridge
Hanby
Laughton
Pointon
Westhorpe
Gosberton
R Welland
Holbeach St Mark's
Lenton
Aslackby
Milthorpe
Risegate
Wargate
Ingoldsby
South Forty Foot Drain
Holbeach Marsh
Graby
Gosberton Clough
Surfleet Seas End
Keisby
Dowsby
Moulton Seas End
Saracen's Head
Holbeach Bank
Rippingale
Surfleet
Holbeach Hurn
Hawthorpe
Halesgate
Gedney Dyke
Irnham
Kirkby Underwood
Crossgate
Penny Hill
Dunsby
Pinchbeck
Holbeach Clough
Loosegate
Fleet Hargate
Bulby
Corby Glen
Stainfield
Hacconby
Pinchbeck Bars
Pinchbeck West
Springfields
Weston
Chapelgate
Hanthorpe
Morton
Mill Green
Moulton
Whaplode
Holbeach
Fleet
Gedney
Elsthorpe
Grimsthorpe
Dyke
Spalding
Fulney
Gedney Broadgate
Swinstead
Edenham
Pode Hole
Scottlethorpe
Bourne
Twenty
Little London
Austendike
Sutton Crosses
Creeton
Eastgate
Cuckoo Bridge
Fen End
Weston Hills
Tongue End
Little Bytham
Moulton Chapel
Holbeach St Johns
Sutton St James
Tydd St Mary
Lound
Witham on the Hill
Northorpe
R Glen
Cowbit
Toft
Careby
Thurlby
Deeping St Nicholas
Peak Hill
Tydd St Giles
Manthorpe
Deeping Fen
Bedford
Level
Aunby
Obthorpe
Brotherhouse Bar
Carlby
Hop Pole
Cross Drain
Sutton St Edmund
Baston
Braceborough
Whaplode Drove
Wilsthorpe
New River
Essendine
Holbeach Drove
Fitton End
Open Air Theatre
Greatford
Langtoft
Market Deeping
Shepeau Stow
Gedney Hill
Gorefield
Ryhall
Barholm
Towngate
Leverington
Belmesthorpe
Horsegate
Frognall
Dowsdale
West Deeping
Deeping St James
Crowland
Guanockgate
Tallington
Castle End
Deeping Gate
Throckenhalt
Wisbech St Mary
Great Casterton
Stamford
Northfields
Northborough
Parson Drove
Uffington
Maxey
Morris Fen
Murrow
Tholomas Drove
Burghley
Bainton
Etton
Peakirk
Pilsgate
Ashton
Glinton
Newborough
Thorney Toll
Barnack
Helpston
Eye Green
Thorney
Guyhirn Gull
Guyhirn
Hills & Holes
Ufford
Easton-on-the-Hill
Werrington
Eye
Wittering
Southorpe
Castor Hanglands
Marholm
Gunthorpe
Paston
Walton
Ring's End
Thornhaugh
Sacrewell Farm & Country Centre
New England
Dogsthorpe
Stone Bridge Corner
River Nene
Moreton Leam
Upton
Newark
North Side
Chainbridge
Bedford Purlieus
Ailsworth
PETERBOROUGH
Eldernell
West Fen
Wansford
Sutton
Stibbington
Longthorpe
Flag Fen Bronze Age Centre
Whittlesey
56
Westry
King's Cliffe
Castor
New Fletton
Woodston
Old Fletton
Stanground
Eastrea
Norwoodside
March
Badgeney

THE WASH
Wainfleet St Mary
Wainfleet All Saints
Gibraltar Point
Friskney Eaudike
81
70
57
Brancaster Bay
Holkham Bay
Scolt Head Island
Peddars Way & Norfolk Coast Path
Holme Dunes
Holme next the Sea
Brancaster
Brancaster Staithe
Burnham Norton
Burnham Overy Staithe
Old Hunstanton
Thornham
Titchwell
Branodunum Roman Fort
Burnham Deepdale
Burnham Market
Burnham Overy
Burnham Thorpe
Holkham Hall
Hunstanton
Ringstead
New Holkham
Creake Abbey
North Creake
Summerfield
Heacham
Norfolk Lavender
Docking
Stanhoe
Waterden
Sedgeford
South Creake
Southgate
Snettisham
Park Farm
Southgate
Fring
Bircham Newton
Barmer
Sydersone
Ingoldisthorpe
Shernborne
Great Bircham
Bircham Tofts
Wicken Green Village
Sculthorpe
Dersingham
Doddshill
Anmer
Tattersett
Dunton
Coxford
Dersingham Bog
Wolferton
Sandringham
West Newton
Houghton Hall
New Houghton
West Rudham
Broomsthorpe
Tatterford
East Rudham
Babingley River
Flitcham
Helhoughton
East Raynham
Hillington
Harpley
Little Massingham
West Raynham
South Raynham
Castle Rising
North Wootton
Congham
Great Massingham
Weasenham St Peter
Roydon
Grimston
South Wootton
Weasenham All Saints
Great Ouse
The Wash
Sutton
Sutton Bridge
Little London
Terrington St Clement
Walpole Cross Keys
Gaywood
Bawsey
Pott Row
Gayton
Rougham
Clenchwarton
African Violet Centre
West Lynn
Fairstead
King's Lynn
Brow-of-the-Hill
Ashwicken
Gayton Thorpe
Tydd Gote
Walpole St Andrew
Hay Green
Tilney All Saints
Tilney High End
Four Gotes
Walpole St Peter
Saddle Bow
Fair Green
East Winch
East Walton
West Acre
Castle Acre
West Lexham
East Lexham
Ingleborough
West Winch
Middleton
Newton
River Nene
St John's Highway
Tilney St Lawrence
North Runcton
Blackborough End
West Bilney
Priory
West Walton
Rattan Row
Wiggenhall St Germans
Pentney
South Acre
Little Dunham
Walpole Highway
Terrington St John
Wiggenhall St Mary the Virgin
Setchey
Narborough
West Walton Highway
Lordsbridge
Watlington
Wormegay
River Nar
Great Palgrave
Sporle
Wisbech
St John's Fen End
Wiggenhall St Mary Magdalen
Tottenhill
Marham
Ecotech Discovery Centre
Walsoken
New Walsoken
Runcton Holme
South Runcton
Shouldham
Swaffham
Necton
Marshland St James
Thorpland
Shouldham Thorpe
Holme Hale
Chequers Corner
North Pickenham
Emneth
Gaultree
Emneth Hungate
Middle Level Drain
Stowbridge
Stow Bardolph
Fincham
Elm
Holly End
West Head
Wimbotsham
Barton Bendish
Beachamwell
South Pickenham
Stradsett
Cockley Cley
Friday Bridge
Outwell
Stow Bardolph Fen
Downham Market
Crimplesham
Barroway Drove
Bexwell
Eastmoor
Iceni Village
Great Cressingham
Laddus Fen
Upwell
Denver
Boughton
West Dereham
Wereham
Oxborough
Gooderstone
Three Holes
Nordelph
Hilborough
Fordham
Oxburgh Hall
Euximoor Fen
Wretton
Whittington
Little Cressingham
Upwell Fen
Stoke Ferry
Foulden
Beckett End
Bodney
Euximoor Drove
Iron Bridge
Old Bedford River
Wissington
Ten Mile Bank
Wissey
Northwold
River Wissey
Christchurch
Lakesend
Hilgay
Brookville
A52
A17
A47
A10
A1101
A1122
A134
A148
A149
A1078
A1065
B1155
B1153
B1454
B1355
B1440
B1439
B1145
B1077
B1108
B1112
B1094
B1098
B1412
B1198

A
B
C
D
E
F
G
H
1
2
3
Brancaster Bay
Holkham Bay
North Norfolk Heritage Coast
Blakeney Point
Blakeney Point
Scolt Head Island
Peddars Way & Norfolk Coast Path
Brancaster
Brancaster Staithe
Burnham Norton
Burnham Overy Staithe
Holkham
Wells-next-the-sea
Morston Marshes
Morston
Blakeney
Guildhall
Cley Marshes
Cley next the Sea
Muckleburgh Collection
Sheringham
Titchwell
Branodunum Roman Fort
Burnham Deepdale
Burnham Market
B1155
Burnham Overy
Holkham Hall
Burnham Thorpe
A149
Warham St Mary
Stiffkey
Cockthorpe
Wiveton
Langham
Newgate
Glandford
Salthouse
Weybourne
Sheringham Park
Kelling
Upper Sheringham
Beeston Regis
A1082
High Kelling
Bodham
North Norfolk Railway
A148
Aylmerton
4
B1153
B1155
B1355
Warham All Saints
Westgate
Wighton
New Holkham
Creake Abbey
North Creake
B1105
Wells & Walsingham Light Railway
The Shrine of Our Lady
Binham Priory & Market Cross
Copy's Green
Binham
Field Dalling
B1156
Saxlingham
Letheringsett
R Glaven
Holt
West Beckham
East Beckham
Gresham
Lower Green
Sharrington
Little Thornage
Baconsthorpe Castle
Holt Lowes
Docking
Stanhoe
B1155
South Creake
Waterden
Little Walsingham
Great Walsingham
Hindringham
Bale
Brinton
B1110
Thornage
Hempstead
Bessingham
Baconsthorpe
5
B1153
69
Fring
Bircham Newton
Barmer
Southgate
North Barsham
West Barsham
Houghton St Giles
Great Snoring
Thursford
East Barsham
Thursford
Hunworth
Edgefield Green
Plumstead
Plumstead Green
Thurgarton
Matlask
Gunthorpe
B1354
Stody
Briningham
Edgefield
Little Barningham
Wickmere
B1149
B1155
Syderstone
R Stiffkey
Barney
Great Bircham
Bircham Tofts
Wicken Green Village
Little Snoring
A148
Croxton
Melton Constable
Briston
B1354
Mannington Gardens
Calthorpe
Wolterton Park
Swanton Novers
Craymere Beck
Saxthorpe
Itteringham
B1454
Sculthorpe
Kettlestone
Fulmodeston
6
B1153
Houghton Hall
Tattersett
Dunton
Coxford
Shereford
Fakenham
Pensthorpe Waterfowl Park
Hindolveston
Corpusty
Ingworth
Nethergate
New Houghton
West Rudham
Broomsthorpe
Hempton
Stibbard
Thurning
Norton Corner
Oulton
Blickling
Silvergate
B1146
Little Ryburgh
East Rudham
Tatterford
Toftrees
Wood Norton
B1110
Oulton Street
Flitcham
A148
East Raynham
Great Ryburgh
A1067
Heydon
Aylsham
Harpley
Helhoughton
Colkirk
R Wensum
Guist
Guestwick
Wood Dalling
B1149
7
Little Massingham
West Raynham
Oxwick
Foulsham
Salle
Southgate
South Raynham
Hamrow
Gateley
Twyford
Themelthorpe
Great Massingham
Weasenham St Peter
Whissonsett
Horningtoft
B1110
Broom Green
Bintree
Foxley Wood
Reepham
Cawston
Eastgate
Potthorpe
Brisley
North Elmham Chapel
Foxley
B1145
Whitwell Street
Wellingham
Tittleshall
North Elmham
Billingford
Weasenham All Saints
Stanfield
East Bilney
Bawdeswell
Great Witchingham
Brandiston
Rougham
B1145
Old Beetley
B1110
Worthing
B1145
Sparham
Norfolk Wildlife Park
Swannington
8
B1145
Mileham
B1146
B1147
Sparhamill
Alderford
Felthorpe
Gayton Thorpe
A1065
Litcham
Beetley
Lyng
A1067
Lenwade
Dinosaur Adventure Park
Bittering
Swanton Morley
Mill Street
Upgate
West Lexham
East Lexham
Gressenhall
Elsing
Morton on the Hill
Attlebridge
Castle Acre
Beeston
Hoe
Woodgate
Primrose Green
West Acre
Castle
Newton
Woodgate
Longham
Gressenhall Green
Northall Green
Peaseland Green
Greensgate
R Wensum
Priory
Gressenhall
B1147
Weston Longville
9
South Acre
Little Dunham
Great Dunham
Crane's Corner
Sparrow Green
Dereham
Etling Green
North Tuddenham
Hockering
Ringland
Taverham
A47
Great Fransham
Wendling
Scarning
Dereham
Mattishall
Mattishall Burgh
Costessey
69
Great Palgrave
Sporle
Little Fransham
Hulver Street
Toftwood
Clint Green
East Tuddenham
Honingham
Easton
A47
Ecotech Discovery Centre
Daffy Green
Westfield
Yaxham
South Green
Welborne
Royal Norfolk Showground
10
A1122
Swaffham
Necton
West End
Ivy Todd
East Bradenham
Whinburgh
Colton
Marlingford
Bowthorpe
Holme Hale
West Bradenham
Shipdham
A1075
Brandon Parva
R Yare
Barford
Bawburgh
North Pickenham
Garvestone
Runhall
B1108
Thuxton
Coston
Barnham Broom
Great Melton
Little Melton
Crowshill
B1135
Reymerston
High Common
Danemoor Green
Wramplingham
Lynch Green
B1077
South Pickenham
Mid Norfolk Railway
Carleton Forehoe
High Green
Beachamwell
11
Ashill
Saham Hills
Cranworth
Southburgh
Kimberley
Hethersett
Cockley Cley
Iceni Village
A1065
Woodrising
Hardingham
Crownthorpe
Kidd's Moor
B1172
Ovington
Hackford
Great Cressingham
Carbrooke
Hingham
B1108
Wicklewood
Gooderstone
R Wissey
Saham Toney
Watton Green
East Carleton
Oxburgh Hall
Hilborough
Little Cressingham
Watton
B1108
Scoulton
Deopham
Morley St Botolph
Wymondham
Mulbarton
12
Foulden
Beckett End
B1108
Bodney
Merton
A1075
Griston
B1077
Northacre
Little Ellingham
Deopham Green
Suton
A11
Silfield
Wreningham
Rockland St Peter
Bow Street
Stallan Comm
B1172
Ashwellthorpe
Topcroft
58
134
Northwold
Caston
Great Ellingham
Spooner Row
Fundenhall
Flordon
Thompson
Rockland
0 1 2 3 4 5 miles
0 1 2 3 4 5 6 7 8 kilometres

Great Yarmouth
NORWICH
CAISTER
LOWESTOFT
GREAT YARMOUTH STATION
Superstore
Gospel Hall
Magistrates Court
St Nicholas
Nursery
Priory Centre
Jobcentre Plus
Kingdom Hall
Police Station
St Nicholas School
Market
Market Gates
Louis Tussauds
Regent Bowl
St Mary's
Joyland
Britannia Pier
River Yare
Meeting House
Victoria Arcade
Town Hall
Elizabethan House
Memorial
St George's Park
Pirates Cove
Salvation Army
Norfolk Nelson
The Tolhouse
Viewing Tower
Marina Leisure Centre
Hippodrome Circus
St Georges School
Surgery
Amazonia
The Jetty
Time & Tide
Old Cemetery
New Cemetery
Recreation Ground
East Runton
Cromer
Norfolk Shire Horse Centre
Overstrand
Sidestrand
Felbrigg
Felbrigg Hall
Northrepps
Trimingham
Crossdale Street
Metton
Southrepps
Gimingham
Roughton
Hanworth
Mundesley
Stow Mill
Alby Hill
Thorpe Market
Lower Street
Trunch
Knapton
Paston
Bradfield
Bacton
Antingham
Old Hall Street
Edingthorpe
Walcott
Suffield
Colby
Swafield
Pollard Street
North Walsham
Edingthorpe Green
Witton
Ridlington
Happisburgh
Banningham
Spa Common
Ridlington Street
Whimpwell Green
Tungate
Meeting House Hill
Crostwight
Happisburgh Common
Eccles on Sea
Hempstead
Felmingham
Honing
Blickling Hall
Tuttington
Skeyton Corner
Westwick
Lessingham
Ingham Corner
Sea Palling
Briggate
East Ruston
Waxham
Burgh next Aylsham
Bengates
Skeyton
Worstead
Ingham
Stalham
Calthorpe Street
Bure Valley Railway
Swanton Abbott
Sloley
Dilham
Stalham Green
Frankfort
Hickling
Oxnead
Lamas
Smallburgh
Low Street
Horsey Corner
Brampton
Scottow
Fairstead
Pennygate
Barton Turf
Wood Street
Sutton
Hickling Green
Horsey
Little Hautbois
Hickling Heath
Hill Common
Hickling Broad
Horsey Windpump
Westgate Street
Buxton
Sco Ruston
Tunstead
Crowgate Street
Neatishead
Barton Broad
Catfield
Catfield Common
Stratton Strawless
St James
Irstead
East Somerton
Potter Heigham
West Somerton
Sharp Green
Winterton-on-Sea
Waterloo
Horstead
Coltishall
Threehammer Common
Ludham
Martham
Hainford
Frettenham
Belaugh
Hoveton
Johnson's Street
Bastwick
Cess
Hemsby Hole
Hemsby
Wroxham
Newport
Horsford
Newton St Faith
Hillside
Upper Street
Horning
Repps
Ormesby Broad
Scratby
Ormesby St Margaret
Crostwick
Bure Marshes
Rollesby
Burgh St Margaret
Broadland Conservation Centre
Thurne
California
Woodbastwick
Ormesby St Michael
Horsham St Faith
Spixworth
Rackheath
Salhouse
Ranworth
Pilson Green
Clippesby
Caister-on-Sea
Drayton
Norwich Aviation
New Rackheath
Little Plumstead
Fairhaven
Cargate Green
Billockby
Filby
Old Catton
Panxworth
South Walsham
Thrigby
Mautby
Hellesdon
Sprowston
Thorpe End
Town Green
Burlingham Green
Upton
Thrigby Hall
West End
Caister
West Caister
NORWICH
Blofield Heath
Great Plumstead
Hemblington
Acle
Stokesby
New Costessey
Thorpe St Andrew
North Burlingham
Runham
Witton
Stracey Arms Windpump
Blofield
Lingwood
Damgate
Earlham
Brundall
Strumpshaw
Beighton
Tunstall
THE BROADS
Runham
Whitlingham
Postwick
Norfolk Ski Centre
South Burlingham
Moulton St Mary
Halvergate
New Lakenham
River Yare
GREAT YARMOUTH
Eaton
Trowse Newton
Kirby Bedon
Surlingham
Buckenham
Freethorpe
Southtown
Burgh Castle
Old Lakenham
Bramerton
Hassingham
Wickhampton
Arminghall
Southwood
Berney Arms Windmill
Burgh Castle
Bradwell
Keswick
Framingham Pigot
Rockland St Mary
Cantley
Freethorpe Common
Gorleston on Sea
East Port
Caistor St Edmund
Caistor Roman Town
Framingham Earl
Claxton
Limpenhoe
Belton
Dunston
Upper Stoke
Hellington
Yelverton
Ashby St Mary
Carleton St Peter
Langley Street
Witton Green
Pettitts Crafts & Animal Adventure Park
Poringland
Reedham
Browston Green
Hardley Street
Mill Common
Alpington
Hobland Hall
Swainsthorpe
Stoke Holy Cross
Howe
Thurton
Nogdam End
Fritton
Fritton Lake Countryworld
Bracon Ash
Bergh Apton
Lower Thurlton
St Olave's Priory
Hopton on Sea
Hawe's Green
Shotesham
Chedgrave
Lound
Newton Flotman
Saxlingham Thorpe
Stubbs
Brooke
Loddon
Norton Subcourse
Thurlton
St Olaves
Saxlingham Nethergate
Mundham
Hales
Thorpe
Herringfleet
Somerleyton Hall & Gardens
Blundeston
Corton
Kirstead
Seething
Raveningham
Haddiscoe
Somerleyton
Pleasurewood Hills
59

A
B
C
D
E
F
G
H
1
2
3
4
5
6
7
8
9
10
11
12
The Skerries
CARMEL HEAD
North Anglesey Heritage Coast
Wylfa Head
Cemaes Bay
Porth Wen
Bull Bay
Amlwch
Point Lynas
Cemlyn Bay
Hen Borth
Cemaes
Llanbadrig
Bull Bay
Llaneilian
Burwen
Pentrefelin
Pengorffwysfa
Tregele
A5025
Rhosbeirio
Bodewryd
Nebo
Llanfairynghornwy
Llanfechell
Penysarn
Cerrig
Llanfflewyn
Rhosgoch
Gadfa
Dulas Bay
Dublin
Holyhead Bay
Church Bay
Llanrhyddlad
Carreglefn
Rhosybol
City Dulas
Dublin
Dún Laoghaire
(Apr-Sept)
Llanbabo
Capel Parc
Llyn Alaw
Brynrefail
Rhôs Lligwy
Llanfaethlu
B5111
Din Lligwy
Porth Tywynmawr
Llanddeusant
Gwredog
Llandyfrydog
North Stack
Breakwater Quarry
Llanfwrog
Stryd-y-Facsen
Elim
Llantrisant
Maenaddwyn
Gogarth Bay
Llaingoch
Holyhead
(Caergybi)
Afon Alaw
Llanerchymedd
Hebron
Bachau
South Stack
Holyhead Mountain Hut Group
Penrhos-Feilw
Llanfachraeth
Llanfigael
Pen-llyn
B5112
Capel Coch
Brynteg
Tynygongl
Holyhead Mountain Heritage Coast
South Stack
Kingsland
Penrhos
Llanynghenedl
Llyn Llywenan
A N G L E S E Y
Tregaian
Llanbedrgoch
Penrhyn Mawr
Porth Dafarch
Trefignath
A5
Presaddfed
B5109
Llechcynfarwy
B5111
Valley
A5025
Bodedern
Trefor
B5110
Llanddyfnan
Trearddur Bay
A55
Caergeiliog
B5112
Llangwyllog
B4545
Four Mile Bridge
Llanfihangel yn Nhowyn
Bryngwran
Llynfaes
Rhosmeirch
B5109
HOLY ISLAND
Bodffordd
Cefni Reservoir
Talwrn
Llanfair-yn-Neubwll
Llechylched
Gwalchmai
Oriel Ynys Môn
Rhoscefn
Capel Gwyn
Anglesey
Heneglwys
Llangefni
Rhoscolyn
RSPB
Plas Cymyran
A4080
A5
A5114
Ceint
B5420
Rhoscolyn Head
Ty Newydd
Dothan
A55
Cymyran Bay
Pencarnisiog
Cerrigceinwen
Penmynydd
Rhosneigr
Llanfaelog
Bryn Du
Din Dryfol
Llangristiolus
A4080
Ty Croes
B4422
Hen Blas
Pentre Berw
Llanfa
Barclodiad y Gawres
Bethel
Capel Mawr
Gaerwen
Porth Trecastell
Afon Cefni
Trefdraeth
B4419
Bryn Celli Ddu
Aberffraw
Llangadwaladr
Malltraeth
Llanddaniel Fab
Anglesey Circuit
Hermon
Llangaffo
Bodowyr Burial Chamber
Afon Braint
Bodorgan
A4080
Caer Leb
A4080
Y Felin
Brynsiencyn
Llanidan
Aberffraw Bay
B4421
B4419
Castell Bryn Gwyn
Dwyran
Newborough
Anglesey Sea Zoo
Aberffraw Bay Heritage Coast
Pen-lôn
Foel Farm Park
A487
Malltraeth Bay
Waterloo Port
Menai
Caernarfon
A4086
Llanddwyn Island
Caernarfon Castle
Segontium
Llanddwyn Bay
Abermenai Point
Welsh Highland Railway
Gypsy Wood
A4085
Foryd Bay
Bontnewydd
Saron
C A E R N A R F O N
Airworld
Llanwnda
Morfa Dinlle
Rhostry
Dinas Dinlle
Llandwrog
60
Groeslon
Glynllifon
Carmel
Slateworks
Cilgwyn
B A Y
0 1 2 3 4 5 miles
0 1 2 3 4 5 6 7 8 kilometres

Llandudno
Llandudno Bay
The Grand Hotel
Great Orme Tramway
War Memorial
South Parade
The Promenade
Gloddaeth Avenue
Town Hall
St John's
Victoria
Our Lady Star of the Sea
Holy Trinity
Medical Centre
The Parade
Mostyn Broadway
Conwy Archive Service
Mostyn Gallery
Parc Llandudno Retail Park
Swimming Pool
Venue Cymru
St Paul's
Llandudno Station
Police Station
Magistrates Court
Mostyn Champneys Retail Park
Ysgol Tudno
Fire & Ambulance Station
Bowling Alley
Superstore
Ysgol Craig Y Don
Ysgol Ffordd Dyffryn
Ysgol Morfa Rhianedd
Ysgol John Bright
Llandudno FC
Deganwy
Betws-y-Coed
Seawatch Centre
Great Orme Heritage Coast
Great Ormes Head
Little Ormes Head
Puffin Island
Penmon Priory, Cross & Dovecote
Black Point
Penmon
Red Wharf Bay
Benllech
Llanddona
Pentraeth
Llangoed
Beaumaris
Beaumaris Castle
Gaol & Courthouse
Llansadwrn
Llandegfan
Menai Bridge (Porthaethwy)
Bangor
Penrhyn
Llandygai
Conwy Bay
Llandudno
Deganwy
Penrhyn Bay
Rhôs-on-Sea
Colwyn Bay (Bae Colwyn)
Abergele Roads
Llandudno Junction
Conwy
Conwy Castle
Penmaenmawr
Dwygyfylchi
Penmaenan
Capelulo
Henryd
Llanfairfechan
Abergwyngregyn
Aber Waterfall
Snowdonia National Park
Llansanffraid Glan Conwy
Abergele
Llanddulas
Llysfaen
Dolwen
Betws-yn-Rhos
Llanfair Talhaiarn
Rowen
Ty'n-y-Groes
Tal-y-Cafn
Eglwysbach
Vale of Conwy
Bodnant
Llanbedr-y-Cennin
Tal-y-Bont
Dolgarrog
Pont Dolgarrog
Llyn Eigiau
Bethesda
Rachub
Tregarth
Llanllechid
Gerlan
Ogwen Bank
Afon Caseg
Trefriw
Trefriw Woollen Mill
Llanrwst
Llanddoget
Gwydir Castle
Llanrhychwyn
Llyn Crafnant
Llyn Cowlyd
Llyn Geirionydd
Gwydyr Forest
Capel Curig
National Mountain Centre
Pont Cyfyng
Betws-y-Coed
Nebo
Capel Garmon
Gwytherin
Llangernyw
Llansannan
Pandy Tudur
Hafodunos
River Elwy
Llyn Aled
Mynydd Hiraethog
Llyn Ogwen
Nant Peris
Pass of Llanberis
Llanberis
Dinorwic
Snowdon Mountain Railway
Dolbadarn Castle
Welsh Slate Museum
Electric Mountain
Llyn Padarn
Brynrefail
Cwm-y-glo
Deiniolen
Waunfawr
Betws Garmon
Pen-y-Gwryd
Pen-y-pass
Pont-y-pant
Conwy Valley Railway
Moel Siabod
Carnedd Llewelyn
Carnedd Dafydd
Y Garn
Y Tryfan
Glyder Fawr
Glyder Fach
Elidir Fawr
Foel-Fras
Tal-y-Fan
Moel Wnion
Y Drosgl
Moel Seisiog
Moel Llyn
A55
A5
A470
A4086
A548
A547
A544
A543
61
74

Liverpool
SOUTHPORT
M57, M58
ST HELENS M62, MANCHESTER
WIDNES, RUNCORN
LEEDS STREET
GREAT CROSSHALL ST
LONDON ROAD
LIME STREET STATION
LIVERPOOL CENTRAL STATION
MOORFIELDS STATION
JAMES ST STATION
River Mersey
Museum of Liverpool
Merseyside Maritime Museum
Tate Liverpool
Piermaster's House
The Cavern Quarter
St John's Shopping Centre
St George's Hall
Walker Art Gallery
World Museum
John Moores University
Liverpool One
FACT
The Bluecoat Gallery
QUEENSWAY (BIRKENHEAD TUNNEL)
Dublin
(Mar-Oct)
Douglas
Belfast
(Nov-Mar)
Douglas
LIVERPOOL BAY
Hoylake
Royal Liverpool
Hilbre Island
Middle Eye
Little Eye
Red Rocks Marsh
West Kirby
Grange
Caldy
Thurstaston
Great Meols
Point of Ayr
Talacre
River Dee
Little Ormes Head
Penrhyn Bay
Rhôs-on-Sea
Colwyn Bay (Bae Colwyn)
Llandudno Junction
Kinmel Bay
Abergele Roads
Rhyl
Prestatyn
Gronant
Gwespyr
Llanasa
Picton
Ffynnongroyw
Mostyn
Gwaenysgor
Meliden
Trelogan
Axton
Glan-y-don
Towyn
Pensarn
Abergele
Llanddulas
Rhuddlan
Dyserth
Trelawnyd
Cwm
Bodelwyddan
St George
St Asaph
Tremeirchion
Whitford
Greenfield
Holywell (Treffynnon)
Bagillt
Flint (Y Fflint)
Pantasaph
Caerwys
Afon-wen
Bodfari
Trefnant
Llannefydd
Henllan
Denbigh (Dinbych)
Llangernyw
Llansannan
Betws-yn-Rhos
Llanfair Talhaiarn
Dolwen
Llysfaen
Mochdre
Old Colwyn
Bryn-y-Maen
Llansanffraid Glan Conwy
Eglwysbach
Trofarth
Dawn
Glascoed
Groesffordd Marli
Pentre Isaf
Cefn Berain
Hafodunos
Vale of Clwyd
Clwydian Range
Afon Elwy
River Elwy
Moel Famau
Llangwyfan
Llandyrnog
Nannerch
Northop
Rhosesmor
Halkyn
Mold (Yr Wyddgrug)
Gwernaffield
Cilcain
Llanferres
Ruthin (Rhuthun)
Llanbedr-Dyffryn-Clwyd
Rhewl
Llanynys
Gellifor
Pentre Llanrhaeadr
Nantglyn
Bylchau
Gwytherin
Pandy Tudur
Llanfwrog
Bontuchel
Y Gyffylliog
Efenechtyd
Llanarmon-yn-Ial
Eryrys
Graianrhyd
Llyn Aled
Llyn Brenig
Mynydd Hiraethog
Moel Seisiog 467
Moel Llyn 448
Nebo
Capel Garmon
Burial Chamber
Conwy Valley Railway
A55
A548
A547
A525
A541
A543
A544
A494
B5381
B5382
B5429
62
73
0 1 2 3 4 5 miles
0 1 2 3 4 5 6 7 8 kilometres

LIVERPOOL
BIRKENHEAD
WALLASEY
BOOTLE
CROSBY
Formby
Ormskirk
Skelmersdale
WIGAN
ST HELENS
WARRINGTON
WIDNES
RUNCORN
ELLESMERE PORT
CHESTER
Maghull
Kirkby
Knowsley
Prescot
Huyton
Halewood
Speke
Bebington
Neston
Connah's Quay
Hawarden
Buckley (Bwcle)
Frodsham
Helsby
Northwich
Winsford
Tarporley
Standish
Orrell
Up Holland
Billinge
Haydock
Golborne
Newton-le-Willows
Leigh
Tyldesley
Atherton
Hindley
Westhoughton
Ince-in-Makerfield
Ashton-in-Makerfield
Culcheth
Risley
Woolston
Lymm
Burtonwood
Rainford
Burscough
Parbold
Coppull
Adlington
Horwich
Aspull
Abram
Weaverham
Cuddington
Kelsall
Tarvin
Saltney
Broughton
Mold
Lower Whitley
Comberbatch
Great Budworth
Sandiway
Delamere Forest Park
River Mersey
Manchester Ship Canal
John Lennon
Knowsley Safari Park

83
84
75
64
Richard
Limbrick
Belmont
Rivington
Egerton
Dimple
Chapeltown
Turton Bottoms
Hawkshaw
Nuttall
Summerseat
Red Lumb
Wolstenholme
Norden
Healey
Syke
Shawclough
Dearnley
Smallbridge
Littleborough
Smithy Bridge
Rakewood
Hollingworth Lake
Coppull
Adlington
Coppull Moor
Grimeford Village
Horwich
Dunscar
Eagley
Tottington
Affetside
Greenmount
Walmersley
ROCHDALE
Bamford
Firgrove
Milnrow
Higher Ogden
Horrocks Fold
Montcliffe
Barrow Bridge
Bottom o' th' Moor
Astley Bridge
Bradshaw
Woolfold
Walshaw
Limefield
BURY
Hooley Bridge
Crimble
Sudden
Lower Place
Newhey
Blackrod
Red Rock
Standish
Shevington Moor
Shevington
Standish Lower Ground
Boar's Head
Marylebone
Scot Lane End
Haigh
Aspull
Lostock Hall Fold
Chew Moor
Lostock Junction
Hunger Hill
Halliwell
BOLTON
Breightmet
Darcy Lever
Harwood
Harwood Lee
Ainsworth
Elton
Redvales
Heywood
Balderstone
Hopwood
Castleton
Slattocks
Burnedge
Shaw
Crompton Fold
Clough Grains Bar
Royton
Heyside
Moorside
Thurston Clough
WIGAN
Scholes
Kitt Green
Orrell
New Springs
Cooper Turning
Four Gates
Pennington Green
Westhoughton
Chequerbent
Deane
Daubhill
Farnworth
Burnden
Moses Gate
Little Lever
Radcliffe
Whitefield
Besses o' th' Barn
Unsworth
Birch
Top of Hebers
Langley
Sinister
Chadderton Fold
Chadderton
Austerlands
Grotton
Pemberton
Ince-in-Makerfield
Hindley
Hindley Green
Platt Bridge
Daisy Hill
Water's Nook
Hulton Lane Ends
Edgefold
New Bury
Kearsley
Prestolee
Outwood
Ringley
Stand
Prestwich
MIDDLETON
OLDHAM
Pitses
Park Bridge
Bryn
Bryn Gates
Abram
Bickershaw
Tamer Lane End
Atherton
Howe Bridge
Shakerley
Little Hulton
Walkden
Clifton
Pendlebury
Sedgley Park
Blackley
Crumpsall
Failsworth
Three Sisters
Tyldesley
Leigh
Astley
Higher Folds
Ellenbrook
Roe Green
Swinton
Wardley
Cheetham Hill
Harpurhey
Moston
Newton Heath
Woodhouses
Bardsley
Ashton-in-Makerfield
Plank Lane
Stubshaw Cross
Dover
Pennington Flash
Lowton Common
Lowton
Boothstown
Worsley
Monton
Broughton
Charlestown
Strangeways
Miles Platting
Ashton-under-Lyne
Droylsden
MANCHESTER
Golborne
Haydock
Blackbrook
Lately Common
Glazebury
Astley Green
Patricroft
Eccles
Barton upon Irwell
SALFORD
Weaste
Ardwick
Openshaw
Audenshaw
Guide Bridge
Dukinfield
Earlestown
Lane Head
Town of Lowton
Kenyon
Fowley Common
Culcheth
Irlam
Crofts Bank
Davyhulme
Urmston
TRAFFORD PARK
Old Trafford
Hulme
Rusholme
Gorton
Denton
Hyde
Godley
Mottram
Collins Green
Newton-le-Willows
Vulcan Village
New Lane End
Croft
Little Town
Eaves Brow
Glazebrook
Lower Irlam
Flixton
Stretford
Chorlton-cum-Hardy
Fallowfield
Levenshulme
Reddish
Haughton Green
Woolley
Gee Cross
Hattersley
Burtonwood
Winwick
Locking Stumps
Risley
Cadishead
Carrington
Partington
Ashton upon Mersey
Sale
Withington
Didsbury
Burnage
Heaton Chapel
Heaton Norris
South Reddish
Romiley
Werneth
Bredbury
Sankey Valley
Houghton Green
Hulme
Orford
Fearnhead
Birchwood
Hollins Green
Lane End
Brooklands
Wythenshawe Hall
Northenden
Heaton Mersey
STOCKPORT
Compstall
WARRINGTON
Padgate
Woolston
Warburton
Mossbrow
Sinderland Green
Broadheath
Timperley
Cheadle
Heaviley
Offerton
Marple
Paddington
Martinscroft
Oughtrington
Heatley
Dunham Town
Altrincham
Gatley
Cheadle Hulme
Adswood
Davenport
Stepping Hill
Hazel Grove
Sankey Bridges
Thelwall
Statham
Rush Green
Dunham Woodhouses
Davenport Green
Bowdon
Hale
Halebarns
Heald Green
Windlehurst
Higher Walton
Lymm
Grappenhall
Little Bollington
Dunham Massey
Ringway
Manchester Airport
Wythenshawe
Disley
Moore
Walton Hall
Stockton Heath
Appleton Thorn
Broomedge
High Legh
Rostherne
Ashley
Thorns Green
Heyhead
Styal
Quarry Bank Mill
Hollinlane
Handforth
Smithy Green
Bramhall
Poynton
High Lane
Keckwick
Hatton
Stretton
Swarton Heath
Hulse Heath
Hoo Green
Mere
Bucklow Hill
Tatton Park
Morley
Morley Green
Wilmslow
Dean Row
Woodford
Skellorn Green
Booth Green
Adlington
Hockley
Wardsend
Lyme Park
Daresbury
Lower Stretton
Preston on the Hill
Norcott Brook
Preston Brook
Arley Hall
Arley
Over Tabley
Tabley Hill
Mobberley
Davenport Green
Lindow End
Rows of Trees
Mottram St Andrew
Whiteley Green
Pott Shrigley
Bollington
Sutton Weaver
Aston Heath
Aston
Dutton
Higher Whitley
Lower Whitley
Frandley
Antrobus
Bate Heath
Gib Hill
Moss End
Great Budworth
Cross Town
Knutsford
Knolls Green
Great Warford
Alderley Edge
Hough
Hare Hill
Prestbury
Bollington Cross
Kerridge
Rainow
Tytherington
Comberbach
Higher Marston
Pickmere
Higher Wincham
Toft
Ollerton
Marthall
Nether Alderley
Kerridge-end
Acton Bridge
Little Leigh
Marbury
Anderton
Wincham
Lion Salt Works
Lostock Gralam
Smithy Green
Plumley
Chelford
Snelson
Monks Heath
Henbury
Broken Cross
Macclesfield
Higher Hurdsfield
Kingsley
Crowton
Barnton
Marston
Northwich
Onston
Weaverham
Rudheath
Broken Cross
Lostock Green
Lower Peover
Over Peover
Peover Heath
Swan Green
Boots Green
Capesthorne Hall
Withington Green
Siddington
Warren
Gurnett
Langley
Tegg's Nose
Cookson Green
Commonside
Norley
Bryn
Flaxmere
Cuddington
Gorstage
Hartford
Leftwich
Allostock
Blackden Heath
Jodrell Bank
Goostrey
Windyharbour
Hodgehill
Gawsworth
Sutton Lane Ends
Oakgrove
Highlane
Wildboarclough
Blakemere
Sandiway
Davenham
Mere Heath
Moulton
Lach Dennis
Rudheath Woods
Puddinglake
Twemlow Green
Lower Withington
Cranage
Kermincham
Gleadsmoss
Marton
Rode Heath
North Rode
Delamere
Whitegate
Foxwist Green
Bostock Green
Byley
Holmes Chapel
Swettenham
Bosley
Wincle
Danebridge
Quarrybank
Cotebrook
Marton
Kilnhouses
Salterswall
Littler
Wharton
Sproston Green
Sandlow Green
Brereton Heath
Newsbank
Hulme Walfield
Eaton
Little Budworth
Oulton Park
Winsford
Middlewich
Brereton Green
Congleton
Havannah
Key Green
Utkinton
Hebden Green
School Green
Leahead
Illidge Green
Smethwick Green
Buglawton
Woodhouse Green
Eaton
Rushton
Bradwall Green
Elworth
Arclid Green
Brookhouse Green
Astbury
Timbersbrook
Rushton Spencer
Tarporley
Rhuddall Heath
Four Lane Ends
Tilstone Fearnall
Lee Green
Wettenhall
Wimboldsley
Moston Green
Sandbach
Hightown
Whitemoor
Tiverton
Alpraham
Church Minshull
Warmingham
Minshull Vernon
Ettiley Heath
Overton Green
Smallwood
Spen Green
Brownlow Heath
Little Moreton Hall
Mossley
Newtown
Poolfold
Biddulph Grange Garden
Rudyard Reservoir
Tilstone Bank
Barrets Green
Calveley
Bunbury
Cholmondeston
Bradfield Green
Coppenhall Moss
Wheelock
Hassall Green
Fourlanes End
Kent Green
Gillow Heath
Biddulph
Biddulph Moor
Rudyard
Barrow's Green
Lakemore
Winterley
Hassall
Day Green
Rode Heath
Thurlwood
Mow Cop
Robin Hill
Wardle
Aston-juxta Mondrum
Maw Green
Wheelock Heath
Scholar Green
The Bank
Mow Cop (folly)
Brown Lees
Lask Edge
Horton
Peckforton
Haughton Moss
Barbridge
Worleston
CREWE
Haslington
Alsager
Church Lawton
Mount Pleasant
Harriseahead
Newchapel
Blackwood Hill
Longsdon
Ridley Green
Crewe Green
Oakhanger
Packmoor
Endon
M6
M61
M60
M62
M602
M56
M66
A627(M)
A6
A57
A50
A556
A34
A54
A49
A51
A530
A533
A534
A523
A536
A537
A559
A580
A579
A560
A555
miles
kilometres

PEAK DISTRICT
NATIONAL PARK
PEAK DISTRICT NATIONAL PARK
HIGH PEAK
ROAD CLOSED SAT/SUN/ BH MON
Howden Moors
Howden Reservoir
Derwent Reservoir
Ladybower Reservoir
Winscar Reservoir
Redmires Reservoir
Holme Moss
Saddleworth Moor
Close Moor
Pennine Way
FEATHERBED MOSS
BLEAKLOW HILL
MARGERY HILL
FEATHERBED TOP
KINDER SCOUT
THE PEAK
BLACK HILL
LOSE HILL
WIN HILL
HIGH NEB
BROWN KNOLL
HOB TOR
AXE EDGE
THE ROACHES
SHINING TOR
Goyt Valley
R Alport
R Noe
R Derwent
R Dove
R Wye
R Manifold
R Hamps
River Dove
Meltham
Marsden
Holmfirth
Holmbridge
Holme
Hepworth
Huddersfield
Honley
Brockholes
Kirkburton
Shelley
Skelmanthorpe
Denby Dale
Penistone
Langsett
Stocksbridge
Deepcar
Wharncliffe Side
Oughtibridge
Bradfield
Low Bradfield
Dungworth
Stannington
SHEFFIELD
Ecclesall
Chapeltown
Rotherham
BARNSLEY
Royston
Cudworth
Wombwell
Hoyland
Hoyland Nether
Wath upon Dearne
Darton
Mapplewell
Dodworth
Silkstone
Silkstone Common
Thurgoland
Oxspring
Glossop
Hadfield
Tintwistle
Crowden
Woodhead
Charlesworth
Simmondley
Old Glossop
Snake Pass Inn
Snake Pass
Hayfield
Little Hayfield
New Mills
Birch Vale
Chinley
Whaley Bridge
Chapel-en-le-Frith
Edale
Barber Booth
Hope
Castleton
Aston
Thornhill
Bamford
Hathersage
Hathersage Booths
Grindleford
Froggatt
Calver
Curbar
Baslow
Eyam
Stoney Middleton
Foolow
Great Hucklow
Little Hucklow
Bradwell
Tideswell
Wormhill
Miller's Dale
Litton
Wardlow
Peak Forest
Sparrowfit
Dove Holes
Combs
Buxton
Harpur Hill
Burbage
Taddington
Chelmorton
Flagg
Monyash
Sheldon
Ashford in the Water
Bakewell
Hassop
Pilsley
Edensor
Beeley
Rowsley
Stanton in Peak
Youlgreave
Middleton
Over Haddon
Darley Dale
Matlock
Matlock Bath
Cromford
Wirksworth
Winster
Elton
Birchover
Hartington
Longnor
Crowdecote
Earl Sterndale
Flash
Hollinscloth
Warslow
Alstonefield
Hulme End
Ecton
Wetton
Grindon
Onecote
Dronfield
Chesterfield
CHESTERFIELD
Old Brampton
Holymoorside
Wingerworth
Tupton
Clay Cross
Ashover
Kelstedge
Alfreton
South Wingfield
Holloway
Lea
Tansley
Wessington
Staveley
Mosborough
Eckington
Totley
Dore
Holmesfield
Wigley
Chatsworth
Haddon Hall
Arbor Low Stone Circle
Lathkill Dale
Magpie Mine
Peak Cavern
Blue John Cavern
Speedwell Cavern
Treak Cliff Cavern
Peveril Castle
Eyam Moor
Chestnut Centre
Poole's Cavern
Solomon's Temple
Heights of Abraham
Peak Railway
Crich Tramway
Monk Bretton Priory
Elsecar Workshops
Yorkshire Sculpture Park
Kirklees Light Railway
Cannon Hall Open Farm
Wyming Brook
Blacka Moor
Longshaw Estate
Hob Hurst's House
Nine Ladies
Market House
Gulliver's Kingdom
Masson Mills
Cromford Mill
Standedge Experience
Linacre Reservoirs
Ogston Reservoir
A628
A616
A57
A6187
A6013
A625
A623
A6
A619
A621
A515
A5270
A5004
A624
A6015
A6024
A635
A629
A61
A6102
A6135
A632
A617
A615
A5012
A53
A54
A537
A6020
M1
M62
A637
A633
A6195
A6096
A6178
A630

78
85
86
77
66
BARNSLEY
DONCASTER
ROTHERHAM
SHEFFIELD
CHESTERFIELD
MANSFIELD
Worksop
Matlock
Hemsworth
Royston
Cudworth
Wombwell
Hoyland Nether
Wath upon Dearne
Mexborough
Conisbrough
Swinton
Rawmarsh
Thurnscoe
Goldthorpe
Askern
Hatfield
Armthorpe
Bessacarr
Thorne
Stainforth
Adwick Le Street
South Elmsall
South Kirkby
Maltby
Tickhill
Bawtry
Harworth
Bircotes
Wickersley
Thurcroft
Dinnington
Aughton
Aston
Killamarsh
Mosborough
Eckington
Dronfield
Staveley
Clowne
Bolsover
Shirebrook
Market Warsop
Edwinstowe
Ollerton
Clay Cross
North Wingfield
Sutton in Ashfield
Kirkby in Ashfield
South Normanton
Alfreton
Pinxton
Chapeltown
Bramley
New Rossington
Brimington
Holmewood
Ravenshead
Blidworth
Carlton in Lindrick
Retford
0 1 2 3 4 5 miles
0 1 2 3 4 5 6 7 8 kilometres

SCUNTHORPE
Gainsborough
LINCOLN
Crowle
Epworth
Brigg
Broughton
Kirton in Lindsey
Market Rasen
Nettleham
Washingborough
Branston
North Hykeham
Waddington
Skellingthorpe
Saxilby
Humberhead Peatlands
Luddington
Flixborough
Normanby Hall
Saints
Bonby
Wootton
Ulceby
Amcotts
Flixborough Stather
Risby
Appleby
Dragonby
Worlaby
Elsham
Habrough
Low Santon
Melton Ross
Croxton
Kirmington
Brocklesby
Ealand
Keadby
Gunness
Crosby
Burringham
Brumby
Wressle
Barnetby le Wold
Humberside
Great Limber
Sandtoft
Grey Green
Althorpe
Derrythorpe
Ashby
Bottesford
Yaddlethorpe
Holme
Castlethorpe
Wrawby
Bigby
Westgate
Belton
Beltoft
Carrhouse
Church Town
West Butterwick
East Butterwick
Somerby
Searby
Owmby
Grasby
Clixby
Scawby
Sturton
Messingham
Howsham
Epworth Turbary
Old Rectory
Haxey Carr
Low Burnham
Kelfield
Susworth
Scotterthorpe
Manton
Hibaldstow
Cadney
North Kelsey Beck
North Kelsey
Caistor
Cabourne
Upperthorpe
Owston Ferry
Scotter
Gainsthorpe Medieval Village
Redbourne
Nettleton
Haxey
East Lound
Nethergate
East Ferry
Scotton
North End
Moortown
South Kelsey
Graiseloud
Wildsworth
Laughton
Northorpe
Brandy Wharf
Thornton le Moor
Holton le Moor
Thoresway
Gunthorpe
R Idle
West Stockwith
Grayingham
Waddingham
Snitterby
Normanby le Wold
Misterton
East Stockwith
Blyton
Blyborough
North Owersby
South Owersby
Claxby
Walkerith
Pilham
Aisby
Willoughton
Atterby
Kingerby
Usselby
Walkeringham
Gringley on the Hill
Morton
R Trent
Corringham
Yawthorpe
R Eau
Bishop Norton
Kirkby
Osgodby
Walesby
Chesterfield Canal
Hemswell
Hemswell Cliff
Spital in the Street
Bishopbridge
Middle Rasen
West Rasen
Wiseton
Beckingham
Harpswell
Caenby
Glentham
Toft next Newton
Springthorpe
Sturgate
Normanby
Saundby
Heapham
Glentworth
Owmby
Newton by Toft
Linwood
Bole
Lea
Upton
R Till
Saxby
Newtoft
Knaith Park
East Firsby
Buslingthorpe
Legsby
North Wheatley
Fillingham
Kexby
Faldingworth
Knaith
Sturton le Steeple
Willingham by Stow
Ingham
Spridlington
Friesthorpe
Lissington
Bleasby
North Leverton with Habblesthorpe
Fenton
Coates
Cold Hanworth
Gate Burton
Hackthorn
Welham
Littleborough
Marton
Stow
Cammeringham
Snarford
Wickenby
Holton cum Beckering
West Torrington
Little Gringley
Trent Port
Thorpe le Fallows
Brattleby
Grove
South Leverton
Ryland
Swinthorpe
Snelland
Cottam
Brampton
Sturton by Stow
Aisthorpe
Fulnetby
Treswell
Scampton
Welton
Dunholme
Rand
Stainton by Langworth
Sundown Adventureland
Torksey
Bransby
Wragby
Rampton
Nether Headon
Woodbeck
North Carlton
Scothern
Lincolnshire
Bullington
Stokeham
Laneham
South Carlton
Sudbrooke
Langworth
Langton by Wragby
Headon
Church Laneham
Fenton
Upton
East Drayton
Laughterton
Kettlethorpe
Burton
Apley
Askham
Riseholme
North Greetwell
Barlings
Kingthorpe
Fossdyke Navigation
Dunham
Toll
Markham Moor
Ragnall
Newton on Trent
Broadholme
Burton Waters
Reepham
Low Barlings
Bardney Limewoods
Stainfield
Darlton
North Clifton
Thorney
Cherry Willingham
Fiskerton
East Markham
Fledborough
Jerusalem
R Witham
Tuxford
High Marnham
South Clifton
Harby
Wigsley
New Boultham
Canwick
Branston Booths
Bardney
Skegby
Birchwood
Hartsholme
Swanpool Garden Suburb
Boultham
Heighington
Low Marnham
Spalford
Doddington
Normanton on Trent
Eagle Moor
Bracebridge Heath
Potterhanworth Booths
Weston
Grassthorpe
Sutton on Trent
Weecar
Eagle
Whisby
Road Transport
Swallow Beck
Hykeham Moor
Bracebridge Low Fields
Moorhouse
Girton
North Scarle
Potterhanworth
Besthorpe
Eagle Barnsdale
Thorpe on the Hill
Ossington
Sots Hole
Nocton
Wasps Nest
Carlton-on-Trent
South Scarle
Morton Hall
South Hykeham
Metheringham Delph
Norwell Woodhouse
Dunston
Cromwell
Swinderby
Haddington
Harmston
Aubourn
Norwell
Dolls
Collingham
Witham St Hughs
Thurlby
Metheringham
Caunton
Bassingham
Coleby
Martin
Blankney
Bathley
Holme
Timberland Dyke
Knapthorpe
North Muskham
Brough
Norton Disney
Boothby Graffoe
Scopwick
Kirkby Green
Little Carlton
Langford
Winthorpe
Carlton-le-Moorland
Navenby
Timberland
South Muskham
Nottinghamshire
Stapleford
Thorpe Tilney
Hockerton
R Brant
Wellingore
Kelham
Aircraft
Ashby de la Launde
Rowston
Averham
Brant
Digby
Billinghay
Upton
Walcott
Wrangham

87
79
68
HUMBER
GRIMSBY
Immingham
Cleethorpes
Humberston
SPURN HEAD
Spurn Heritage C
Kilnsea
Rotterdam (Europoort)
Zeebrugge
The Jungle
Pleasure Island
Wootton
Ulceby
Ulceby Skitter
Habrough
Croxton
Kirmington
Melton Ross
Elsham
Stallingborough
Brocklesby
Keelby
Healing
Great Coates
West Marsh
Little Coates
Old Clee
Thrunscoe
Nunsthorpe
Scartho
Humberside
Great Limber
Barnetby le Wold
Wrawby
Brigg
Bigby
Somerby
Searby
Owmby
Grasby
Howsham
Clixby
Riby
Aylesby
Bradley
Laceby
Irby upon Humber
Waltham
Waltham Windmill
New Waltham
Holton le Clay
Tetney Lock
Tetney
North End
Swallow
Caistor
Cabourne
North Kelsey
North Kelsey Beck
Barnoldby le Beck
Brigsley
Ashby cum Fenby
Beelsby
Hatcliffe
Cuxwold
Nettleton
Rothwell
West Ravendale
East Ravendale
Grainsby
Waithe
North Thoresby
North Cotes
Marshchapel
Eskham
Donna Nook
Grainthorpe
North Somercotes
North End
South Kelsey
Moortown
Thornton le Moor
Holton le Moor
Croxby
Thoresway
Thorganby
Swinhope
Wold Newton
Churchthorpe
West End
Fulstow
Canal
Lincolnshire Wolds Railway
Covenham St Bartholomew
Conisholme
Church End
Normanby le Wold
Brookenby
Ludborough
North Oversby
South Owersby
Kingerby
Usselby
Claxby
Stainton le Vale
Binbrook
North Ormsby
Covenham St Mary
South Somercotes
Skidbrooke
Norton
Kirkby
Osgodby
Walesby
Kirmond le Mire
Utterby
Little Grimsby
Yarburgh
Alvingham
Saltfleet
St Clem
Bishopbridge
Glentham
Toft next Newton
West Rasen
Middle Rasen
Market Rasen
Tealby
North Willingham
Ludford
Great Tows
THE WOLDS
Kelstern
North Elkington
Fotherby
Keddington Corner
Keddington
North Cockerington
South Cockerington
North End
Owmby
Newton by Toft
Newtoft
Linwood
Sixhills
Burgh on Bain
South Elkington
Welton le Wold
Little Welton
Louth
Stewton
Grimoldby
Manby
Great Carlton
Little Carlton
Buslingthorpe
Faldingworth
Legsby
Bleasby
Hainton
Hallington
Raithby
Legbourne
North Reston
South Reston
Gayton le Marsh
Spridlington
Cold Hanworth
Snarford
Friesthorpe
Lissington
South Willingham
East Torrington
West Torrington
Biscathorpe
Donington on Bain
Withcall
Maltby
Tathwell
Haugham
Little Cawthorpe
Tothill
Withern
Wickenby
Holton cum Beckering
Benniworth
East Barkwith
West Barkwith
R Bain
Market Stainton
Stenigot
Cadwell Park
Mucton
Authorpe
Woodthorpe
Ryland
Swinthorpe
Snelland
Fulnetby
Rand
Dunholme
Stainton by Langworth
Panton
Wragby
Goulceby
Ranby
Sotby
Cawkwell
Asterby
Maidenwell
Burwell
Belleau
Claythorpe
Watermill & Wildfowl Gardens
Aby
Thoresby
Scothern
Sudbrooke
Langworth
Bullington
Langton by Wragby
Hatton
Great Sturton
Low Langton
Scamblesby
Farforth
Oxcombe
Ruckland
Walmsgate
Worlaby
Ketsby
White Pit
Swaby
South Thoresby
Haugh
Nettleham
North Greetwell
Barlings
Apley
Kingthorpe
Baumber
Hemingby
Belchford
Little London
South Ormsby
Calceby
Rigsby
Reepham
Cherry Willingham
Fiskerton
Low Barlings
Stainfield
Bardney Limewoods
Minting
Fulletby
Tetford
Salmonby
Brinkhill
Driby
Well
Mawthorpe
Ulceby
Furzehills
Gautby
Wispington
Edlington
Thimbleby
West Ashby
Horncastle
Low Toynton
Somersby
Bag Enderby
Ashby Puerorum
Harrington
Langton
Sutterby
Dalby
R Witham
Washingborough
Branston Booths
Heighington
Branston
Bardney
Bucknall
Langton
High Toynton
Greetham
Scrafield
Hagworthingham
Aswardby
Sausthorpe
Partney
Grebby
Horsington
Old Woodhall
Thornton
Martin
Mareham on the Hill
Winceby
Snipe Dales
Lusby
Mavis Enderby
Raithby
Spilsby
R Lymn
Potterhanworth Booths
Potterhanworth
Southrey
Stixwould
Hameringham
Asgarby
Scrivelsby
Hareby
Hundleby
Halton Holegate
Reeds Beck
Dalderby
Roughton
Old Bolingbroke
Moorby
Nocton
Sots Hole
Wasps Nest
Woodhall Spa
Haltham
Miningsby
West Keal
Bolingbroke Castle
Toynton All Saints
Northcote
Halton Fenside
Dunston
Car Dyke
Metheringham Delph
Kirkstead
Woodhall Spa
Kirkby on Bain
Wood Enderby
Wilksby
East Kirkby
Hagnaby
East Keal
Toynton St Peter
Lincolnshire Aviation
Keal Cotes
Toynton Fen Side
Metheringham
Blankney
Martin Dales
Toft Hill
Revesby
Stickford
Martin
Timberland Delph
Tattershall Thorpe
Mareham le Fen
Tumby
Scopwick
Kirkby Green
Timberland
Tattershall
Tattershall Castle
Tattershall College
Coningsby
Battle of Britain Memorial Flight
Tumby Woodside
Moor Side
New Bolingbroke
Stickney
New Leake
Midville
Eastville
Thorpe Tilney
Rowston
Walcott
Tattershall Bridge
Ashby de la Launde
Dogdyke
Hawthorn Hill
New York
Scrub Hill
Sandy Bank
Bunker's Hill
Medlam
Carrington
East Fen
West Fen
Lade Bank
A15
A160
A180
M180
A18
A1173
A46
A16
A1098
B1219
A1031
B1203
B1225
A1103
A631
A157
B1202
A153
A158
B1399
A155
B1191
B1192
B1190
B1188
B1178
B1189
A1104
A1028
B1200
B1520
B1183
B1195
B1434
B1205
B1206
B1210
B1211
A1136
B1201
A1084
0 1 2 3 4 5 miles
0 1 2 3 4 5 6 7 8 kilometres

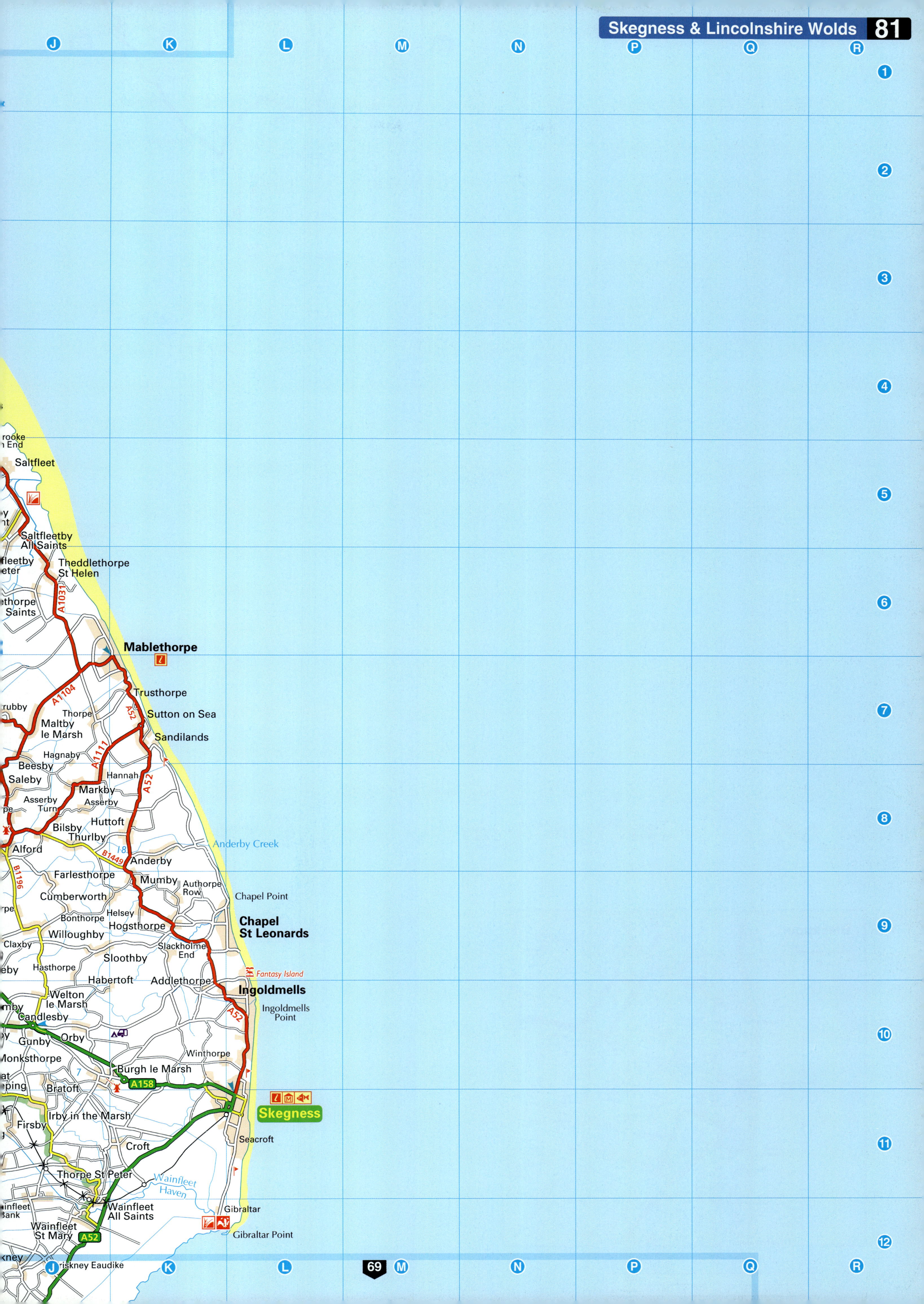
J
K
L
M
N
P
Q
R
1
2
3
4
5
6
7
8
9
10
11
12
Saltfleet
Saltfleetby
All Saints
Theddlethorpe
St Helen
A1031
Mablethorpe
Trusthorpe
A1104
Thorpe
Maltby
le Marsh
A52
Sutton on Sea
Sandilands
Hagnaby
Beesby
Saleby
A1111
Hannah
Asserby
Turn
Markby
Asserby
Huttoft
Bilsby
Thurlby
Alford
B1449
Anderby
Anderby Creek
B1196
Farlesthorpe
Mumby
Authorpe
Row
Cumberworth
Chapel Point
Bonthorpe
Helsey
Hogsthorpe
Chapel
St Leonards
Willoughby
Claxby
Slackholme
End
Sloothby
Hasthorpe
Fantasy Island
Habertoft
Addlethorpe
Ingoldmells
Welton
le Marsh
Ingoldmells
Point
Candlesby
Gunby
Orby
Monksthorpe
Winthorpe
Burgh le Marsh
A158
Bratoft
Skegness
Irby in the Marsh
Firsby
Seacroft
Croft
Thorpe St Peter
Wainfleet
Haven
Wainfleet
All Saints
Gibraltar
Wainfleet
St Mary
A52
Gibraltar Point
Friskney Eaudike
69

88
89
A
B
C
D
E
F
G
H
1
2
3
4
5
6
7
8
9
10
11
12
North Walney
Dalton-in-Furness
Urswick
Scales
Baycliff
Hawcoat
Newton
Stainton with Adgarley
Furness Abbey
Bow Bridge
Watermill
Aldingham
BARROW-IN-FURNESS
North Scale
Dendron
Gleaston
Roose
Leece
Newbiggin
Vickerstown
Barrow Island
A590
A5087
Roosebeck
Biggar
ISLE OF WALNEY
Roa Island
Rampside
Sheep Island
Piel Castle
Foulney Island
Piel Island
Piel Bar
Hilpsford Point
South Walney
Douglas
Fleetwood
Rossall Point
River Wyre
A587
B5268
A585
Cleveleys
Thornton
Norcross
Little Bispham
Norbreck
Churchtown
Bispham
Carleton
A584
B5124
Warbreck
A586
North Shore
Hoohill
BLACKPOOL
Model Village
Great Marton
South Shore
Common Edge
B5262
B5261
A5230
Blackpool
St Anne's
B5233
Royal Lytham & St Annes
Fairhaven
Lytham St Anne's
SOUTHPORT
New Pleasureland
P+R
RSPB
The Royal Birkdale
Birkdale
A5267
Ainsdale-on-Sea
Ainsdale
Blackpool
0 200 m
FLEETWOOD
LANCASTER
BLACKPOOL NORTH STATION
PROMENADE
Metropole Hotel
Grundy Art Gallery
Jobcentre Plus
Sacred Heart
TALBOT ROAD
North Pier
Travelodge
St John the Evangelist
Medical Centre
Sports Barn
CHURCH STREET
COOKSON ST
Salvation Army
St John's School
Grand
Winter Gardens
Medical Centre
Meeting House
Tower Festival Headland
The Blackpool Tower
Houndshill
Council Offices
Register Office
St John Ambulance
Spiritualist
Kingdom Hall
ALBERT ROAD
CORONATION STREET
Blackpool & Fylde College
Coral Island
Lifeboat Station
Sea Life
Market
Police Station
County Court
Madame Tussauds Blackpool
Magistrates' Court
Central Pier
CENTRAL DRIVE
LYTHAM ST ANNES
PRESTON (M55)
0 1 2 3 4 5 miles
0 1 2 3 4 5 6 7 8 kilometres

MORECAMBE BAY
Morecambe
Heysham
Lancaster
Carnforth
Bolton le Sands
Hest Bank
Slyne
Halton
Caton
Galgate
Garstang
Forest of Bowland
Calder Fell
Abbeystead
Dolphinholme
Slaidburn
Newton-in-Bowland
Dunsop Bridge
Whitewell
Chipping
Longridge
Longridge Fell
Clitheroe
Whalley
Waddington
Sawley
Preesall
Pilling
Stalmine
Hambleton
Poulton-le-Fylde
Singleton
Kirkham
Freckleton
Warton
Lytham
PRESTON
BLACKBURN
Great Harwood
Clayton-le-Moors
Rishton
Oswaldtwistle
Accrington
Haslingden
Darwen
Leyland
Chorley
Bamber Bridge
Higher Walton
Longton
Tarleton
Croston
Eccleston
Euxton
Coppull
Adlington
Horwich
Rivington
Egerton
Edgworth
Ramsbottom
Tottington
Helmshore
Rufford
Mawdesley
Scarisbrick
Burscough Bridge
High Bentham
Low Bentham
Clapham
Austwick
Wray
Hornby
Wennington
Melling
Arkholme
Kirkby Lonsdale
Over Kellet
Nether Kellet
M6
M55
M65
M61
A6
A59
A565
A683
A687
A65
A56
A666
A671
A680
A677
A584
A583
A585
A588
A586
A589
A581
WARD'S STONE 560
HAWTHORNTHWAITE FELL 478
WHINS BROW 477
TOTRIDGE FELL 497
FAIRSNAPE FELL 511
PARLICK 432
GREAT HARLOW 488
BRADFORD FELL 396
River Ribble
River Lune
Lancaster Canal

90
91
83
76
77
Horton in Ribblesdale
Pen-y-ghent
Arncliffe
Kettlewell
Great Whernside
Hawkswick
Arncliffe Cote
Kilnsey
Conistone
Conistone Moor
Meugher
Ramsgill
Gouthwaite Reservoir
Lofthouse
Stean
Bouthwaite
Wath
Heathfield
Bridgehouse Gate
Greenhow Hill
Grimwith Reservoir
Stump Cross Caverns
Grassington
Threshfield
Linton
Hebden
Burnsall
Thorpe
Threapland
Cracoe
Appletreewick
Skyreholme
Simon's Seat
Drebley
Parcevall Hall
Barden Tower
Rylstone
Hetton
Flasby
Winterburn
Eshton
Malham
Malham Tarn
Malham Cove
National Park Centre
Kirkby Malham
Hanlith
Airton
Calton
Otterburn
Bell Busk
Hellifield
Long Preston
Wigglesworth
Tosside
Rathmell
Mearbeck
Town Head
Settle
Giggleswick
Langcliffe
Stackhouse
Stainforth
Little Stainforth
Feizor
Austwick
Clapham
Newby
Wharfe
Helwith Bridge
Higher Studfold
Studfold
Lawkland
Lawkland Green
Ingleborough
Stocks Reservoir
Halton West
Swinden
Nappa
Coniston Cold
Gargrave
Thorlby
Stirton
Embsay
Eastby
Halton East
Bolton Abbey
Bolton Priory
Bolton Bridge
Draughton
Embsay & Bolton Abbey Steam Railway
Skipton
Beamsley
Langbar
Addingham
Nesfield
Middleton
Denton
Ilkley
Ben Rhydding
Burley in Wharfedale
Burley Wood Head
West End Outdoor Centre
Blubberhouses
Fewston Reservoir
Paythorne
Forest Becks
Newsholme
Horton
Gisburn
West Marton
East Marton
Bank Newton
Broughton
Elslack
Carleton
High Bradley
Low Bradley
Cringles
Silsden
Swartha
Brunthwaite
Rombalds Moor
Holden
Bolton by Bowland
Sawley
Grindleton
Rimington
Downham
Chatburn
Worston
Clitheroe
Pendleton
Pendle Hill
Barley
Roughlee
Newchurch in Pendle
Barrowford
Nelson
Colne
Barnoldswick
Bracewell
Salterforth
Kelbrook
Earby
Thornton-in-Craven
Lothersdale
Cononley
Kildwick
Glusburn
Sutton-in-Craven
Cross Hills
Steeton
Eastburn
Keighley
Cowling
Ickornshaw
Foulridge
Laneshaw Bridge
Wycoller
Trawden
Keighley Moor
Oldfield
Haworth
Stanbury
Oxenhope
Cullingworth
Wilsden
Bingley
Harden
Denholme
Thornton
Queensbury
Halifax
Elland
Brighouse
Huddersfield
Whalley
Sabden
Higham
Padiham
Burnley
Brierfield
The Forest of Trawden
Boulsworth Hill
Widdop
Wadsworth Moor
Worsthorne
Hurstwood
Heptonstall Moor
Heptonstall
Hebden Bridge
Mytholmroyd
Todmorden
Walsden
Littleborough
Milnrow
Rishworth Moor
Ripponden
Sowerby Bridge
Clayton-le-Moors
Church
Accrington
Oswaldtwistle
Haslingden
Rawtenstall
Bacup
Whitworth
Ramsbottom
Edenfield
Tottington
Edgworth

Ripon
HARROGATE
Knaresborough
Wetherby
Otley
Guiseley
Yeadon
LEEDS
BRADFORD
Pudsey
Morley
Rothwell
Garforth
Castleford
Pontefract
Knottingley
WAKEFIELD
Dewsbury
Batley
Mirfield
Ossett
Horbury
Normanton
Featherstone
Tadcaster
Sherburn in Elmet
Easingwold
Haxby
Boroughbridge
Kippax
Cleckheaton
Heckmondwike
Liversedge
Bramhope
Boston Spa
Walton
Crofton
Ackworth Moor Top
Hemsworth
Kirkburton
Skelmanthorpe
Dishforth
Kirby Hill
Aldborough
Great Ouseburn
Tholthorpe
Alne
Tollerton
Linton-on-Ouse
Shipton
Wigginton
Nether Poppleton
Upper Poppleton
Hessay
Knapton
Rufforth
Long Marston
Bilton
Askham Bryan
Askham Richard
Bishopthorpe
Copmanthorpe
Acaster Malbis
Appleton Roebuck
Acaster Selby
Cawood
Ulleskelf
Church Fenton
Barkston Ash
South Milford
Monk Fryston
Hambleton
Brayton
Thorpe Willoughby
Birkin
Beal
Kellington
West Haddlesey
Eggborough
Whitley
Darrington
Womersley
Little Smeaton
Kirk Smeaton
Norton
Askern
Pannal
Spofforth
Kirkby Overblow
Sicklinghall
Harewood
Collingham
Bramham
Aberford
Saxton
Micklefield
Ledsham
Fairburn
Brotherton
Ferrybridge
Methley
Oulton
Stanley
Sandal Magna
Netherton
Flockton
Emley
Lepton
Kirkheaton
Huddersfield
Holmfirth
Wilsill
Pateley Bridge
Summerbridge
Darley
Birstwith
Hampsthwaite
Killinghall
Ripley
Burnt Yates
Kettlesing
Fewston
Beckwithshaw
Leathley
Pool
Arthington
Weardley
Bardsey
East Keswick
Scarcroft
Thorner
Shadwell
Sand Hills
Horsforth
Rawdon
Farsley
Tong
Drighlington
Gildersome
Birstall
Gomersal
Thornhill
Crigglestone
Notton
Woolley
Royston
Ryhill
Havercroft
South Hiendley
Fitzwilliam
Wragby
Badsworth
Upton
North Elmsall
South Elmsall
Skelbrooke
Haywood
Sutton
Campsall
Fountains Abbey
Studley Royal Park
Newby Hall
Harlow Carr
Bramham Park
Temple Newsam
Nostell Priory
Lotherton Hall
Yorkshire Sculpture Park
National Coal Mining Museum
Kirklees Light Railway
Middleton Railway
A1(M)
M1
M62
M621
M606
A1
A19
A59
A61
A64
A65
A168
A658
A660
A661
A162
A63
A638
A628
A645
A639
A642
A655
A636
A637
A6038
B6265
B6165
B1224
B1223
B1222
R Nidd
R Wharfe
R Ouse
R Aire
R Calder
R Went
Eccup Reservoir
Swinsty Res

86
92
93
85
78
79
Howardian Hills
Brandsby
Coulton
Scackleton
Appleton-le-Street
Swinton
Broughton
Malton
Old Malton
Norton
Wintringham
Newton
Settrington
Helperthorpe
West Lutton
East Lutton
Stearsby
Crayke
Easingwold
Skewsby
Dalby
Whenby
Terrington
Coneysthorpe
Castle Howard
Ganthorpe
Welburn
Bulmer
High Hutton
Low Hutton
Whitewall Corner
North Grimston
Duggleby
Kirby Grindalythe
Stillington
Farlington
Sheriff Hutton
Thornton-le-Clay
Whitwell-on-the-Hill
Firby
Kirkham
Kennythorpe
Langton
Birdsall
Wharram-le-Street
Sledmere
Huby
Sutton-on-the-Forest
Sutton Park
West Lilling
Foston
Barton Hill
Crambe
Priory
Westow
Burythorpe
Leavening
Wharram Percy Deserted Medieval Village
Towthorpe
Burdale
Raisthorpe
Aldro
Acklam
Howsham
Barton-le-Willows
Flaxton
Strensall
Harton
Bossall
Leppington
Scrayingham
Claxton
Thixendale
Fimber
Fridaythorpe
Wetwang
Kirby Underdale
Buttercrambe
Sand Hutton
Wigginton
Towthorpe
Haxby
Skelton
Haxby Gates
Earswick
Huntington
New Earswick
East Huntington
Stockton on the Forest
Upper Helmsley
Bugthorpe
Painsthorpe
Skirpenbeck
Yorkshire Wolds Way
Huggate
Tibthorpe
Youlthorpe
Bishop Wilton
Gowthorpe
Fangfoss
Great Givendale
Gate Helmsley
Stamford Bridge
1066
Full Sutton
Warthill
Holtby
Hopgrove
Poppleton
Upper Poppleton
Rawcliffe
Clifton
YORK
Murton
Dunnington
Low Catton
High Catton
Yorkshire Museum of Farming
Spittal
Meltonby
Bolton
Millington
North Dalton
Knapton
Acomb
Holgate
Osbaldwick
South Bank
Dringhouses
Nunthorpe
Fulford
Heslington
Kexby
Wilberfoss
Yapham
Kilnwick Percy
Warter
Middleton on the Wolds
Askham Bryan
Yorkshire Air Museum
Barmby Moor
Newton upon Derwent
Pocklington
Burnby Hall
Nunburnholme
Bishopthorpe
Copmanthorpe
Crockey Hill
Elvington
Sutton upon Derwent
Allerthorpe
Hayton
Burnby
Londesborough
Holme on the Wolds
Acaster Malbis
Naburn
Colton
Deighton
Wheldrake
Storwood
Thornton
Melbourne
South Dalton
Thicket Priory
Bielby
Thorpe le Street
Shiptonthorpe
Goodmanham
Etton
Appleton Roebuck
Escrick
West Cottingwith
East Cottingwith
Everingham
Market Weighton
Gardham
Acaster Selby
Holme Green
Thorganby
Seaton Ross
Harswell
Sancton
Bishop Burton
Stillingfleet
Ryther
Moor End
Little Skipwith
Skipwith
Ellerton
Aughton
Laytham
Water End
Holme upon Spalding Moor
North Newbald
Cawood
Kelfield
Riccall
North Duffield
Harlthorpe
Foggathorpe
Highfield
Bubwith
Sand Hole
North Cliffe
South Cliffe
South Newbald
Wistow
Barlby
Osgodby
Lund
Menthorpe
Gunby
Willitoft
Breighton
Gribthorpe
Spaldington
Bursea
Hotham
High Hunsley
Thorpe Willoughby
Selby
Brayton
Cliffe
South Duffield
Wressle
North Cave
Everthorpe
Rowley
Riplingham
Hemingbrough
Brind
Cavil
Portington
Hive
Sandholme
Gilberdyke
Scalby
Newport
West End
South Cave
Eastrington
Newland
Bennetland
Staddlethorpe
Ellerker
Brantingham
Gateforth
Barmby on the Marsh
Newsholme
Howden
Knedlington
Burn
Barlow
Long Drax
Asselby
Balkholme
Green Oak
Bellasize
Elloughton
Welton
Brough
Melton
Birkin
Chapel Haddlesey
West Haddlesey
Camblesforth
Drax
Boothferry
Kilpin Pike
Kilpin
Broomfleet
Beal
Kellington
Temple Hirst
Hirst Courtney
Drax Hales
Airmyn
Hook
Skelton
Laxton
Blacktoft
Faxfleet
Newland
Saltmarshe
Goole
Yokefleet
Whitton
Hut Green
Hensall
Carlton
Rawcliffe
Reedness
Little Reedness
Whitgift
Ousefleet
Winteringham
Read's Island
Snaith
Waterways
Julians Bower
Walcot
Alkborough
West Halton
Whitley
Gowdall
High Eggborough
Old Goole
Swinefleet
Adlingfleet
Ferriby Sluice
Great Heck
West Cowick
East Cowick
Rawcliffe Bridge
Dutch River
Pollington
Goole Fields
Fockerby
Coleby
The Showground
Aire and Calder Navigation
Balne
Garthorpe
Winterton
Burton upon Stather
Thealby
Walden Stubbs
Eskholme
Normanby
Normanby Hall
Roxby
Topham
Sykehouse
Pincheon Green
Eastoft
Luddington
Fenwick
Wormley Hill
Norton
Moorends
Flixborough
Risby
Fosterhouses
Humberhead Peatlands
Amcotts
Appleby
Askern
Moss
Kirkhouse Green
Waterside
Flixborough Stather
Dragonby
Low Santon
Sutton
Haywood
Thorne
Crowle
Ealand
R Ouse
R Derwent
R Foulness
R Went
R Don
R Trent
Selby Canal
A64
A166
A1079
A614
A1034
A163
A19
A1036
A1237
A59
A63
A1041
A1238
A645
A161
A1077
A1430
M62
M18
B1248
B1253
B1251
B1252
B1363
B1246
B1228
B1247
B1222
B1223
B1230
B1392
B1216
5 miles
8 kilometres

Foxholes
Wold Newton
Burton Fleming
Grindale
Buckton
Bempton
North Landing
Selwicks Bay
FLAMBOROUGH HEAD
Lighthouse
Flamborough
Marton
Sewerby
Bondville Miniature Village
Thwing
Octon
Langtoft
Rudston
Monolith
Boynton
Bessingby
Carnaby
Bridlington
Hilderthorpe
BRIDLINGTON BAY
Cottam
Haisthorpe
Thornholme
Kilham
Burton Agnes
Norman Manor House
Ruston Parva
Harpham
Lowthorpe
Fraisthorpe
Nafferton
Little Kelk
Gransmoor
Driffield
Little Driffield
Great Kelk
Lissett
Barmston
Gembling
Ulrome
Wansford
Kirkburn
Southburn
Skerne
Cruckley Animal Farm
Foston on the Wolds
Castle
Skipsea
Brigham
Beeford
Upton
Skipsea Brough
Hutton
Cranswick
Hutton Cranswick
North Frodingham
Rotsea
Dunnington
Atwick
Watton
Kilnwick
Hempholme
Nunkeeling
Bewholme
Honeysuckle Farm
Hornsea
Hornsea Mere
Beswick
Burshill
Lockington
Brandesburton
Seaton
Thorpe
Aike
Scorborough
Rolston
Sigglesthorpe
Goxhill
Catwick
Little Catwick
Leven
New Arram
Arram
Mappleton
Mappleton Sands
Leconfield
Little Hatfield
Great Hatfield
Long Riston
Great Cowden
Beverley
Routh
Rise
Tickton
Molescroft
North End
Arnold
Withernwick
New Ellerby
Meaux
Weel
Skirlaugh
Marton
Mount Pleasant
Aldbrough
Old Ellerby
West Newton
Woodmansey
East Newton
Bentley
Wawne
Thearne
Burton Constable Hall
Flinton
Swine
Garton
Dunswell
Grimston
Coniston
Thirtleby
Fitling
Skidby
Ganstead
Sproatley
Humbleton
Hilston
Wyton
Bransholme
Owstwick
Cottingham
Sutton-on-Hull
Bilton
Lelley
Eppleworth
Newland
Stoneferry
Elstronwick
Danthorpe
North End
Tunstall
Willerby
Burton Pidsea
Roos
Waxholme
Kirk Ella
East End
Preston
Marfleet
West End
Anlaby
East Ella
West Ella
International Ferry Terminal
Hedon
Rimswell
Owthorne
Haven Side
Burstwick
West End
Withernsea
KINGSTON UPON HULL
Northfield
Hessle
North Ferriby
South Field
East End
Thorngumbald
Halsham
Paull
Fort Paull
Keyingham
Hollym
Ryehill
Ottringham
Humber Bridge
Far Ings
Barton Waterside
New Holland
North End
Winestead
Holmpton
Barton-upon-Humber
Barrow Haven
Patrington
Out Newton
Goxhill
Patrington Haven
St Peter's Church
Barrow-upon-Humber
East Halton
RIVER HUMBER
Welwick
South Ferriby
South End
Easington
Weeton
Sunk Island
Skeffling
South End
Thornton Abbey & Gatehouse
Horkstow
North Killingholme
Thornton Curtis
Immingham Dock
South Killingholme
Spurn Heritage Coast
Burnham
Kilnsea
Wootton
Bonby
Ulceby Skitter
Immingham
Ulceby
Habrough
Elsham
Croxton
Kirmington
Stallingborough
Spurn Heritage Coast
GRIMSBY

A
B
C
D
E
F
G
H
1
2
3
4
5
6
7
8
9
10
11
12
Seaton
Camerton
Great Clifton
97
Bridgefoot
Brigham
A66
Cockermouth
Embleton
Wyt'G
Mill
High Side
Scarness
931
SKIDDAW
North Side
Greysouthen
Workington
Stainburn
Little Clifton
Eaglesfield
Lakeland Sheep & Wool Centre
Armaside
Mirehouse
Little Crosthwaite
Millbeck
Moss Bay
Mossbay
Westfield
Salterbeck
High Harrington
Harrington
Grayson Green
A596
A595
Winscales
Branthwaite
Deanscales
Dean
Ullock
Pardshaw
Low Lorton
Mosser Mains
High Lorton
Thackthwaite
B5292
552
LORDS SEAT
Thornthwaite
Whinlatter
318
Whinlatter Pass
A66
Great Crosthwaite
A591
Portinscale
Braithwaite
790
GRISEDALE PIKE
770
HOBCARTON PIKE
Distington
Common End
B5306
Gilgarran
Pica
Kidburngill
Mockerkin
Waterend
Lowca
Parton
Howgate
Low Moresby
Brownrigg
R Keekle
A5086
Lamplugh
Loweswater
572
851
GRASMOOR
Stair
Swinside
Derwent Water
Little Town
Moresby Parks
Arlecdon
Asby
Rowrah
Kirkland
Whitehaven
Kells
Saltom Bay
Hensingham
Frizington
High Leys
Winder
Crummock Water
Buttermere
Grange
Lodore Falls
Bowder Stone
Borrow
Hassness
Gatesgarth
DALE HEAD
754
356
Honister Pass
B5289
Rost
Seatoller
Sto
B5295
B5294
Cleator Moor
Moor Row
Ennerdale Bridge
615
636
Ennerdale Water
Buttermere
806
HIGH STILE
River Liza
River Ehen
Mirehouse
Sandwith
Sandwith Newtown
B5345
Rottington
Bigrigg
Cleator
St Bees Head
RSPB
St Bees Head Heritage Coast
St Bees
Egremont
River Calder
533
LANK RIGG
892
PILLAR
Seathwaite
LAKE DISTRICT
798
HAYCOCK
802
KIRK FELL
899
GREAT GABLE
780
GLARAMARA
Wilton
Carleton
Thornhill
Coulderton
Middletown
Haile
Worm Gill
River Bleng
691
SEATALLAN
Wasdale Head
NATIONAL
910
GREAT END
978
SCAFELL PIKE
964
SCAFELL
902
BOW FELL
Nethertown
Beckermet
Blackbeck
Braystones
Calder Bridge
Ponsonby
Wast Water
Burnmoor Tarn
PARK
CUMBRIA
PIKE OF
R Ehen
Cross
Wellington
Nether Wasdale
R Irt
R Mite
Calder
Gosforth
B5343
Santon
Santon Bridge
393
Hardknott Pass
Hardknott Fort
Boot
Beckfoot
Eskdale Green
Eskdale
Seascale
Hallsenna Moor
Drigg
Holmrook
652
HARTER FELL
Cockley Beck
Furness
Muncaster Mill
Ravenglass and Eskdale Railway
River Esk
Devoke Water
River Duddon
Seathwaite Tarn
Saltcoats
Ravenglass
Roman Bath House
Muncaster
A595
Hall Dunnerdale
Seathwaite
Broad Oak
Newbiggin
Waberthwaite
573
WHITFELL
Ulpha
Corney
Loganbeck
Beckfoot
Broughton Mills
A593
Hycemoor
Selker Bay
Lower Hawthwaite
Duddon Bridge
Broughton Tower
Swinside Stone Circle
Hyton
Bootle
Broughton-in-Furness
Wreaks End
Annaside
600
BLACK COMBE
A595
Hallthwaites
Lady Hall
Foxfield
Grizebeck
Gutterby Spa
Whitbeck
The Green
Arnaby
Bridge End
Chapels
Wall End
Kirkby-in-Furness
Beck Side
Whicham
Silecroft
The Hill
A5093
Sand Side
Soutergate
Kirksanton
Millom
A595
Steel Green
Borwick Rails
RSPB
Ulverston
Haverigg
Haverigg Point
Askam in Furness
Ireleth
Pennington
Marton
Lindal in Furness
A590
South Lakes Animal Park
Sandscale Haws
Little Urswick
North Walney
Dalton-in-Furness
Newton
Stainton with Adgarley
Hawcoat
Furness Abbey
Bow Bridge
BARROW-IN-FURNESS
Dendron
Gleaston
North Scale
Roose
82
0 1 2 3 4 5 miles
0 1 2 3 4 5 6 7 8 kilometres

Penrith
Windermere
Kendal
Kirkby Lonsdale
Ambleside
Grasmere
Glenridding
Patterdale
Ullswater
Haweswater
Hawkshead
Bowness-on-Windermere
Grange-over-Sands
Sedbergh
Shap
Tebay
Appleby-in-Westmorland
Carnforth
Staveley
Coniston Water
Windermere
Grizedale Forest Park
Newby Bridge
Ulverston
Milnthorpe
Arnside
Brampton
Orton
Kirkstone Pass
Helvellyn
Pooley Bridge
Eamont Bridge
Clifton
Lowther
Askham
Bampton
Morecambe
M6
A6
A66
A591
A590
A685
A683
A65
A592
A684
A5092
A5084
A593
A6070
A687

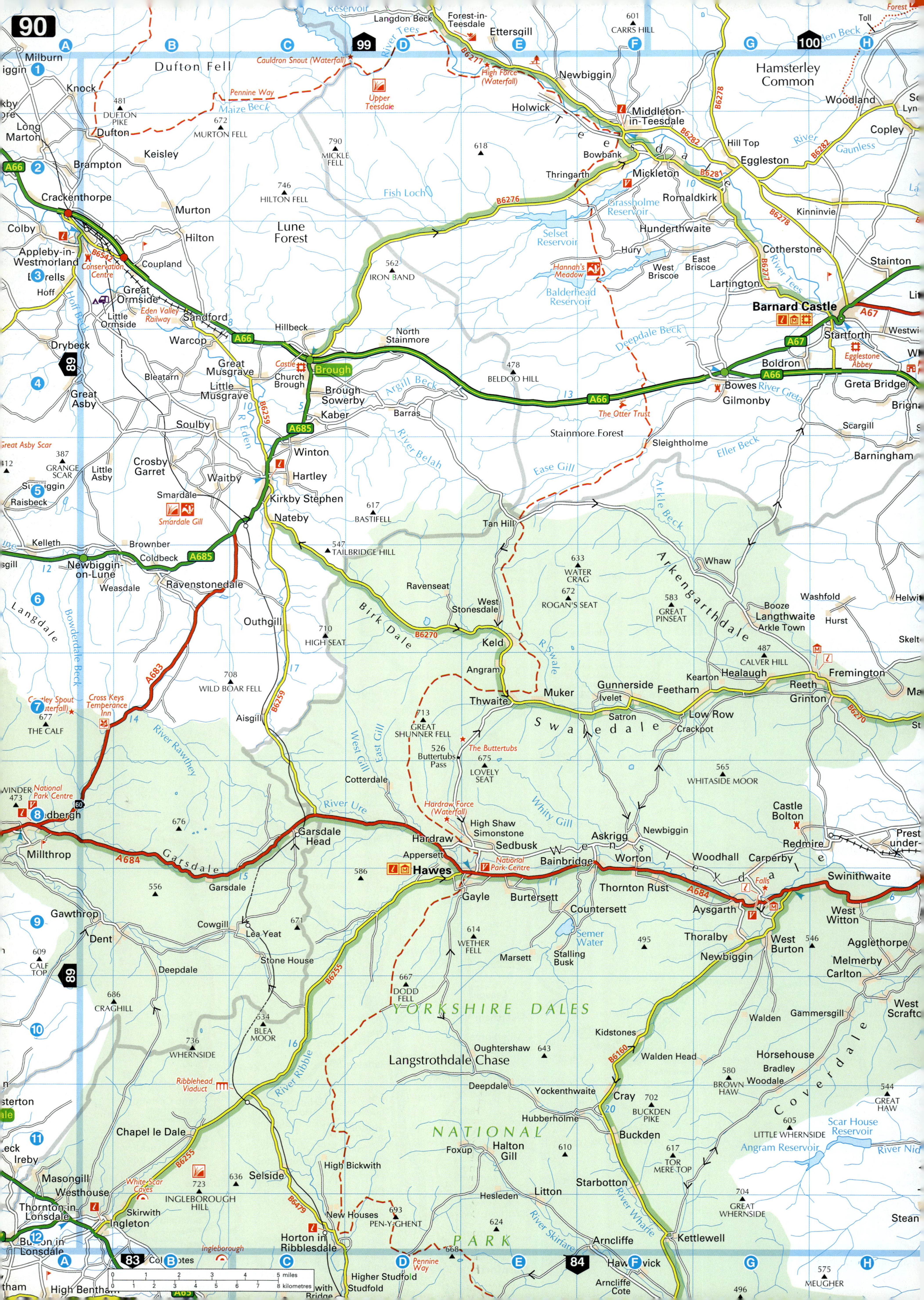

99
100
89
83
84
A
B
C
D
E
F
G
H
1
2
3
4
5
6
7
8
9
10
11
12
Milburn
Knock
Dufton Fell
Cauldron Snout (Waterfall)
Langdon Beck
Forest-in-Teesdale
Ettersgill
River Tees
601
CARRS HILL
Hamsterley Common
Woodland
Toll
Pennine Way
Maize Beck
481
DUFTON PIKE
Dufton
672
MURTON FELL
Upper Teesdale
B6277
High Force (Waterfall)
Newbiggin
Holwick
Middleton-in-Teesdale
B6278
B6282
Hill Top
Eggleston
Copley
River Gaunless
Long Marton
Keisley
790
MICKLE FELL
618
Bowbank
Teesdale
A66
Brampton
Thringarth
Mickleton
B6281
Crackenthorpe
746
HILTON FELL
Fish Loch
B6276
Romaldkirk
Kinninvie
Murton
Lune Forest
Grassholme Reservoir
Selset Reservoir
Hunderthwaite
Colby
Hilton
Appleby-in-Westmorland
B6542
Conservation Centre
Coupland
562
IRON BAND
Hury
Hannah's Meadow
West Briscoe
East Briscoe
Cotherstone
Stainton
Balderhead Reservoir
Lartington
River Tees
Hoff
Great Ormside
Little Ormside
Eden Valley Railway
Hoff Beck
Sandford
Barnard Castle
A67
Warcop
Hillbeck
North Stainmore
Deepdale Beck
Startforth
Drybeck
Great Musgrave
Castle
Church Brough
Brough
478
BELDOO HILL
Boldron
Egglestone Abbey
Bleatarn
Little Musgrave
Brough Sowerby
Argill Beck
Bowes
River Greta
Greta Bridge
Great Asby
Kaber
Barras
The Otter Trust
Gilmonby
B6259
A685
R Eden
Soulby
Stainmore Forest
Scargill
Great Asby Scar
387
GRANGE SCAR
Little Asby
Crosby Garret
Winton
River Belah
Sleightholme
Eller Beck
Barningham
Hartley
Waitby
Ease Gill
Raisbeck
Smardale
Kirkby Stephen
Arkle Beck
Smardale Gill
617
BASTIFELL
Nateby
Tan Hill
Kelleth
Brownber
547
TAILBRIDGE HILL
Whaw
Newbiggin-on-Lune
Coldbeck
633
WATER CRAG
Weasdale
Ravenstonedale
Arkengarthdale
Ravenseat
672
ROGAN'S SEAT
583
GREAT PINSEAT
Washfold
Langdale
West Stonesdale
Booze
Langthwaite
Arkle Town
Hurst
Outhgill
Birk Dale
B6270
710
HIGH SEAT
Keld
487
CALVER HILL
Bowderdale Beck
R Swale
Angram
Kearton
Healaugh
Fremington
708
WILD BOAR FELL
A683
Gunnerside
Feetham
Reeth
Thwaite
Muker
Ivelet
Grinton
Cross Keys Temperance Inn
677
THE CALF
Aisgill
713
GREAT SHUNNER FELL
Satron
Low Row
Swaledale
Crackpot
River Rawthey
West Gill
East Gill
526
Buttertubs Pass
The Buttertubs
675
LOVELY SEAT
565
WHITASIDE MOOR
National Park Centre
473
Cotterdale
Castle Bolton
Sedbergh
676
River Ure
Hardraw Force (Waterfall)
Whitty Gill
High Shaw
Simonstone
Askrigg
Newbiggin
Redmire
Garsdale Head
Hardraw
Sedbusk
Millthrop
A684
Garsdale
Appersett
Bainbridge
Worton
Woodhall
Carperby
Wensleydale
586
Hawes
National Park Centre
Falls
Swinithwaite
556
Garsdale
Gayle
Burtersett
Thornton Rust
Aysgarth
West Witton
Gawthrop
Countersett
Dent
Cowgill
671
Lea Yeat
614
WETHER FELL
Semer Water
495
Thoralby
West Burton
546
Agglethorpe
609
CALF TOP
Marsett
Stalling Busk
Newbiggin
Melmerby
Carlton
Stone House
Deepdale
B6255
667
DODD FELL
686
CRAGHILL
YORKSHIRE DALES
West Scrafton
Walden
Gammersgill
Kidstones
534
BLEA MOOR
736
WHERNSIDE
Oughtershaw
643
Langstrothdale Chase
B6160
Walden Head
Horsehouse
Bradley
Coverdale
580
BROWN HAW
Woodale
Ribblehead Viaduct
Deepdale
Yockenthwaite
Cray
702
BUCKDEN PIKE
544
GREAT HAW
River Ribble
Hubberholme
605
LITTLE WHERNSIDE
Scar House Reservoir
Chapel le Dale
NATIONAL
Buckden
Foxup
Halton Gill
610
617
TOR MERE TOP
Angram Reservoir
River Nidd
Ireby
White Scar Caves
636
Selside
High Bickwith
Masongill
Westhouse
723
INGLEBOROUGH HILL
Starbotton
Hesleden
Litton
River Wharfe
704
GREAT WHERNSIDE
Thornton-in-Lonsdale
Ingleton
Skirwith
B6479
New Houses
693
PEN-Y-GHENT
624
River Skirfare
PARK
Stean
Burton in Lonsdale
Ingleborough
Horton in Ribblesdale
668
Arncliffe
Kettlewell
Pennine Way
Hawkswick
Higher Studfold
Studfold
Arncliffe Cote
575
MEUGHER
496
High Bentham
5 miles
8 kilometres

Bishop Auckland
Shildon
Newton Aycliffe
Sedgefield
Billingham
STOCKTON-ON-TEES
MIDDLESBROUGH
DARLINGTON
Yarm
Hurworth-on-Tees
Stokesley
Richmond
Scotch Corner
Hipswell
Catterick
Leyburn
Bedale
Northallerton
Thirsk
Sowerby
Masham
Ripon
Middleton Tyas
Middleton St George
Croft-on-Tees
Great Ayton
Osmotherley
Staindrop
Barnard Castle
River Swale
River Tees
River Ure
Cod Beck Reservoir
Leighton Reservoir
Roundhill Reservoir
Black Hambleton
The Hambleton Hills
Cleveland Way
A1(M)
A19
A66
A67
A167
A684
A6108
A168
A689
A170
A172

92
101
A
B
C
D
E
F
G
H
1
2
3
4
5
6
7
8
9
10
11
12
Hartlepool Bay
Summerhill
Seaton Carew
Owton Manor
Greatham
Graythorpe
Hartlepool Power Station Visitor Centre
Tees Bay
Newton Bewley
Billingham
Coatham Marsh
Coatham
Redcar
Warrenby
Marske-by-the-Sea
Saltburn-by-the-Sea
Cowpen Bewley
Norton Hill
Teesport
Port Clarence
River Tees
Kirkleatham
Old Hall
Yearby
New Marske
Upleatham
Saltburn Smugglers
New Brotton
Hummersea Scar
Brotton
Carlin How
Skinningrove
Upton
Boulby
Staithes
Heritage Centre
Port Mulgrave
Toll
South Bank
Grangetown
North Ormesby
Lazenby
Lackenby
Wilton
Eston
Skelton
New Skelton
North Skelton
Kilton
Loftus
Liverton Mines
Dalehouse
Easington
Hinderwell
Runswick Bay
North Yorkshire and Cleveland Heritage Coast
MIDDLESBROUGH
Teesside Park
Normanby
Acklam
Nature's World
Ormesby
Ormesby Hall
Dunsdale
Tockets
Boosbeck
Lingdale
Kilton Thorpe
Margrove Park
Woodhill
Liverton
Stanghow
Roxby
Newton Mulgrave
Borrowby
Runswick
Kettleness
Goldsborough
Overdale Wyke
Marton
Handale
Ellerby
Stainton
Hemlington
Nunthorpe
Pinchinthorpe
Guisborough Forest
Guisborough
Hutton Lowcross
Cleveland Way
Moorsholm
Scaling
Gerrick
Scaling Dam
Mickleby
Lythe
Sandsend
Sandsend Wyke
Thornton
Maltby
Newby
Nunthorpe Village
Newton under Roseberry
322
ROSEBERRY TOPPING
West Barnby
East Barnby
Raithwaite
Dunsley
Hilton
Tanton
Langbaurgh
Great Ayton
Captain Cook Monument
Commondale
Ugthorpe
Newholm
Seamer
Middleton-on-Leven
Little Ayton
Kildale
The Moors Centre
301
Danby
Stonegate
Hutton Mulgrave
Ruswarp
Briggswath
Stokesley
Easby
Aislaby
Sleights
Ugglebarnby
Braworth
River Leven
Battersby
Castleton
Ainthorpe
Lealholm
Lealholm Side
Egton
Iburndale
Rudby
Sexhow
Great Busby
Kirkby
Ingleby Greenhow
Baysdale Abbey
River Esk
The Green
Esk Dale
Grosmont
Sneaton
Enterpen
Great Broughton
Westerdale
Danby Bottom
Glaisdale
Egton Bridge
Littlebeck
Carlton-in-Cleveland
Street
Key Green
Faceby
NORTH YORK MOORS
Beck Hole
Whorlton
Urra
454
URRA MOOR
382
Heathwaite
Seave Green
326
PIKE HILL
Goathland
369
Chop Gate
Cod Beck Reservoir
Cockayne
Church Houses
NATIONAL PARK
North Yorkshire Moors Railway
292
Mount Grace Priory
Osmotherley
Low Bell End
Wheeldale Roman Road
394
Thorgill
NORTH YORK MOORS
Rosedale
Rosedale Abbey
Newtondale Forest Drive
Bilsdale
338
Low Mill
Bransdale
290
Stape
Hole of Horcum
399
BLACK HAMBLETON
Fangdale Beck
River Seven
North Riding Forest Park
Silton
River Rye
Farndale
Hartoft End
Levisham
Bridestones (Rock Formation)
Lastingham
Newton Dale
Dalby Forest Drive
319
Gillamoor
Newton-on-Rawcliffe
Hawnby
Hutton-le-Hole
Spaunton
Lockton
Cleveland Way
Fadmoor
Appleton-le-Moors
Cawthorn
239
The Hambleton Hills
Knowle
Cropton
North Riding
Boltby
Old Byland
Carlton
Kirkbymoorside
Keldholme
Friars' Hill
Wrelton
Aislaby
Dalby Forest
Rievaulx Terrace & Temples
River Riccal
Pockley
Rievaulx
Beadlam
Nawton
Kirkby Mills
Sinnington
Middleton
New Bridge
Thirlby
Sutton Bank
Cold Kirby
Wombleton
Keld Head
Castle
Rievaulx Abbey
Scawton
R. Rye
Helmsley
River Dove
Great Edstone
Marton
Pickering
Wilton
Duncombe Park
Thornton le Dale
Balk
White Horse
Sproxton
Harome
Normanby
Allerston
Bagby
High Kilburn
Oldstead
Muscoates
Flamingo Land
Little Barugh
Nunnington Hall
Salton
Great Barugh
Kilburn
Wass
Oswaldkirk
West Ness
Kirby Misperton
High Marishes
Little Thirkleby
Byland Abbey
Ampleforth
Nunnington
East Ness
Brawby
Low Marishes
Shandy Hall
Ampleforth
Little Habton
Hutton Sessay
Coxwold
Gilling East
Stonegrave
Butterwick
River Derwent
Carlton Husthwaite
Newburgh Priory
Cawton
Great Habton
Ryton
West Knapton
Knapton
Birdforth
Husthwaite
Hovingham
Fryton
Slingsby
Barton-le-Street
Scampston
Yearsley
River Rye
Eden Camp
Rillington
Thormanby
Oulston
Amotherby
Broughton
Thorpe Bassett
Wintringham
Coulton
Scackleton
Appleton-le-Street
Old Malton
Brandsby
Swinton
Newton
Scagglethorpe
Raskelf
Howardian Hills
Malton
85
Stearsby
Dalby
Terrington
Coneysthorpe
86
Norton
Settrington
Crayke
Easingwold
Whenby
Ganthorpe
Castle Howard
Whitewall
A689
A178
A1185
B1275
A1046
A66
A19
A1032
B1380
A172
A174
A171
A1042
B1269
A1085
B1268
A173
B1292
B1365
B1366
B1266
A169
B1257
A170
B1363
A64
B1248
B1258
B1415
5 miles
8 kilometres

J
K
L
M
N
P
Q
R
1
2
3
4
5
6
7
8
9
10
11
12
Middlesbrough
TRANSPORTER BRIDGE
Police HQ
BRIDGE STREET W
MIDDLESBROUGH STATION
Middlesbrough College
Hill Street
Superstore
Cannon Park Ind Est
Travelodge
Town Hall
Thistle Hotel
Empire
Leisure Park
The Mall
Council Offices
Register Office
Combined Court Centre
MIMA Art Gallery
All Saints
TEESPORT
Newport Primary School
Sikh Temple
Newport South Business Park
University of Teesside
Salvation Army
Christadelphian Hall
Surgery
Abingdon Primary School
STOCKTON
Ayresome Primary School
Archibald Primary School
Sacred Heart RC Primary School
Surgery
Ambulance Station
Dorman
RC Church of the Sacred Heart
Albert Park
Boathouse
Fire Station
Clairville Stadium
St Joseph's RC Primary School
STOKESLEY
WHITBY
Bowls Centre
North Bay
Castle Hill
Castle
Coastguard Station
St Mary's
Friarage School
YMCA
Council Offices
Lifeboat Station
Old Harbour
Lighthouse
Balmoral Centre
Town Hall
Magistrates' Court
Police Sta
Stephen Joseph
SCARBOROUGH STATION
Brunswick Centre
Olympia Scarborough
Grand Hotel
Rotunda Art Gallery
Woodend Creative Workspace
Yorkshire Coast College
South Bay
PICKERING MALTON
FILEY
Scarborough
Whitby
Saltwick Bay
Abbey
Stainsacre
High Hawsker
Low Hawsker
Ness Point or North Cheek
Robin Hood's Bay
Raw
Fylingthorpe
Robin Hood's Bay
Old Peak or South Cheek
A171
Ravenscar
Staintondale
Shire Horse Centre
Hayburn Wyke
Harwood Dale
Cloughton Newlands
Cloughton
Cloughton Wyke
Cromer Point
Burniston
A165
Broxa
Silpho
Cleveland Way
Suffield
Langdale End
Hackness
Scalby
Newby
Scarborough
Wrench Green
Everley
Sea Cut
Castle
Forest Park
Falsgrave
Hatherleigh Deep Sea Trawler
Oliver's Mount
River Derwent
Bee Dale
A170
West Ayton
East Ayton
A165
Cayton Bay
Sawdon
Irton
Eastfield
Osgodby
Hutton Buscel
Ruston
Seamer
Crossgates
B1261
High Killerby
The Wyke
Snainton
Wykeham
Cayton
Brompton-by-Sawdon
B1261
Lebberston
Filey Brigg
Gristhorpe
A1039
A64
R. Hertford
Filey
Folkton
Muston
Willerby
A1039
Flixton
West Flotmanby
Filey Bay
Staxton
Sherburn
Ganton
Yorkshire Wolds Way
Hunmanby
East Heslerton
Potter Brompton
Fordon
Reighton
Flamborough Head Heritage Coast
Speeton
B1229
Bempton Cliffs
Thornwick Bay
Foxholes
Wold Newton
Burton Fleming
Buckton
Bempton
North Landing
Butterwick
A165
Grindale
Selwicks Bay
Helperthorpe
86
87
B1249
Weaverthorpe
Thwing
Octon
Marton
B1259
Lighthouse
FLAMBOROUGH HEAD
B1255
Flamborough

A
B
C
D
E
F
G
H
104
1
2
3
4
5
6
7
8
9
10
11
12
Bennane Head
Colmonell
River Stinchar
A77
B734
B7044
Heronsford
Water of Tig
Ballantrae
437
BENERAIRD
321
CARLOCK HILL
387
ALTIMEG HILL
Belfast
Larne
Larne
(Mar-Oct)
Currarie Port
Glen App
Milleur Point
Corsewall Point
Lady Bay
Barnhills
Portencalzie
Glenwhilly
Laggan Standing
Kirkcolm
B738
Cairnryan
Penwhirn Reservoir
Main Water of Luce
Cross Water of Luce
Ervie
Loch Connell
A718
B798
Low Barbeth
Beoch Burn
Braid Fell
A77
Low Salchrie
New Luce
Knocknain
Leswalt
B7043
Loch Ryan
Innermessan
A751
Castle of St John
A77
Black Loch
Castle Kennedy
White Loch
164
CRAIG FELL
Chlenry
Balgracie
Stranraer
Aird
Auchnotteroch
Castle Kennedy
A75
Portslogan
Broadsea Bay
B738
Glenluce Abbey
Glenwhan
Dunragit
Glenluce
Whitecrook
THE RHINNS OF GALLOWAY
Lochans
181
CAIRN PAT
Kildrochet House
Piltanton Burn
Black Head
B7077
B7084
Ringdoo Point
A716
Portpatrick
A77
Stoneykirk
B7084
Stairhaven
North Milmain
B7042
Mull of
Sandhead
Cairngarroch
Kirkmadrine Stones
Money Head
Ardwell
High Ardwell
Ardwell Bay
Ardwell House
Chapel Rossan
Drumbreddon
Balgowan
LUCE
Logan
Port Logan Bay
Port Logan
B7065
A716
Garrochtrie
Clanyard Bay
Kilstay
Laggantalluch Head
Kirkmaiden
Drummore
Barncorkrie
High Drummore
Killiness Point
Drumnaglaur
Maryport
B7041
Cardryne
Cardrain
West Cairngaan
MULL OF GALLOWAY
0 1 2 3 4 5 miles
0 1 2 3 4 5 6 7 8 kilometres

Galloway
Forest Park
104
96
781
KIRRIEREOCH HILL
842
MERRICK
813
CORSERINE
716
MILFIRE
Loch Dungeon
Loch Moan
Loch Enoch
346
GARWALL HILL
Loch Neldricken
Silver Flowe
Muck Water
Duisk River
Barrhill
Feoch Burn
Lochton
River Cree
Water of Minnoch
Glen Trool Lodge
Bruce Memorial
Loch Trool
Loch Dee
Knocksheen
Garroch
Blawquhairn
St John's Town of Dalry
A713
A762
B7000
B7075
380
BENNAN
Bruce's Stone
New Galloway
Clatteringshaws Forest & Wildlife Centre
Clatteringshaws Loch
A714
Glentrool Village
Glen Trool
Creebank
Bargrennan
716
LAMACHAN HILL
675
LARG HILL
654
MILLFORE
Drumlamford
Loch Dornal
305
BENBRAKE HILL
Loch Maberry
B7027
Loch Ochiltree
Southern Upland Way
Knowe
River Bladnoch
Black Burn
184
URRALL FELL
440
GARLICK HILL
Galloway Deer Range
A712
402
ROUND FELL
471
FELL OF FLEET
Black Water of Dee
325
CAIRN EDWARD
Mossc
G A L L O W A Y
Penkill Burn
Loch Grannoch
Loch Fleet
208
AUCHENCLOY HILL
Loch Skerrow
271
ARTFIELD FELL
Carseriggan
Challoch
R. Cree
Minnigaff
710
CAIRNSMORE OF FLEET
Barfad
214
CULVENNAN FELL
Newton Stewart
Creebridge
Kirroughtree
Big Water of Fleet
Loch Ronald
Shennanton
Palnure
335
WHITE TOP OF CULREACH
Big Water of Fleet
Little Water of Fleet
Tarf Water
B735
B733
A75
Craighlaw
Kirkcowan
Baltersan
Upper Ruscoe
Loch Whinyeon
361
BENGRAY
Causeway End
Gem Rock
B796
Fleet Valley
Creetown
60
Dernaglar Loch
R. Bladnoch
Clugston
Torhouse Stone Circle
B7052
Kirkmabreck
455
CAIRNHARROW
Skyre Burn
Anwoth
Gatehouse of Fleet
Cardoness Castle
B727
Littleton
A747
Fell Loch
THE
B733
Wigtown
Bladnoch
Carsluith
Cairnholy Chambered Cairns
Castle Loch
B7005
Kirwaugh
MACHARS
Carsluith Castle
Girthon
Mochrum Loch
Water of Malzie
Braehead
Ravenshall Point
Mossyard
Fleet Bay
Lennox Plunton
Comp
henmalg
inniness
Auchenmalg Bay
Culshabbin
B7005
B7085
Kirkinner
Orchardton Bay
Margrie
Gledpark
Chapel Finian (ruin)
Barrachan
Whauphill
B7004
Islands of Fleet
Culscadden
Borgue
Little Airies
A746
Kirkandrews
Elrig
Druchtag Motte
Sorbie
Wigtown Bay
Garlieston
Mochrum
Drumtrodden Cup & Ring
Pouton
Borness
Balmangan
Drumtrodden Standing Stones
Drummoddie
Broughton Mains
Cruggleton Bay
Ringdoo Point
Port William
Big Balcraig
B7063
B A Y
'Wren's Egg' Standing Stones
B7021
Priory
Barsalloch Fort
Monreith
Whithorn Story
Barsalloch Point
Whithorn
Rispain Camp
Point of Leg
Portyerrock
St Ninian's Cave
Isle of Whithorn
Kidsdale
St Ninian's Chapel (ruin)
Cutcloy
BURROW HEAD
J
K
L
M
N
P
Q
R
1
2
3
4
5
6
7
8
9
10
11
12

A
B
C
D
E
F
G
H
1
2
3
4
5
6
7
8
9
10
11
12
105
95
813
CORSERINE
716
MILFIRE
Loch Dungeon
Silver Flowe
Loch Dee
Glenhoul
Black Water
385
WETHER HILL
Craigneston
Glencrosh
Blackwood
431
BOGRIE HILL
Skelston
Snade
Lag
Sundaywell
Dunscore
Throughgate
B729
Loch Urr
Loch Howie
B7000
A702
A713
Blawquhairn
Knocksheen
Garroch
St John's Town of Dalry
Bogue
B7075
A762
Stepford
392
SKEOCH HILL
Drumpark
380
BENNAN
Balmaclellan
A712
Bruce's Stone
New Galloway
281
LARGLEAR HILL
Corsock
Shawhead
Clatteringshaws Loch
Clatteringshaws Forest & Wildlife Centre
MILLFORE
Black Water of Dee
Ironmacannie
325
CAIRN EDWARD
Eastlands
A75
Lochfoot
Crocketford
Galloway Deer Range
402
ROUND FELL
471
FELL OF FLEET
Knockvennie Smithy
B794
Auchenreoch Loch
Milton Loch
Lochrutton Loch
Mossdale
Airds of Kells
Milton
Loch Grannoch
Loch Fleet
208
AUCHENCLOY HILL
Loch Skerrow
Loch Ken
RSPB
Loch Roan
Walbutt
Kirkpatrick Durham
Springholm
Drumcoltran Tower
Beeswing
Old Bridge of Urr
710
CAIRNSMORE OF FLEET
Woodhall Loch
Crossmichael
Hardgate
Kirkgunzeon
334
LOTUS HILL
Haugh of Urr
Redcastle
A711
Clarebrand
B795
Laurieston
Glenlochar
Townhead of Greenlaw
Hillowton
Urr Water
Glaisters Burn
Big Water of Fleet
Little Water of Fleet
335
WHITE TOP OF CULREACH
Threave Castle
A745
Edingham
Castle Douglas
Loch Whinyeon
Longwood
Threave Garden
Carlingwark Loch
Little Knox
Dalbeattie
Upper Ruscoe
B796
367
BENGRAY
Bridge of Dee
Rhonehouse
Creetown
Fleet Valley
Skyre Burn
Gelston
A710
B793
B736
Craigley
Barlochan
Palnackie
Ringford
Airieland
Barnbarroch
Fairgirth
Kirkmabreck
455
CAIRNHARROW
Anwoth
Cardoness Castle
Gatehouse of Fleet
B727
Littleton
River Dee
343
SCREEL HILL
Orchardton Tower
Kippford or Scaur
Mote of Mark
Drumburn
Sandyhills
Carsluith
Cairnholy Chambered Cairns
Carsluith Castle
390
BENGAIRN
Tongland
Colvend
East Stewartry Coast
Rockcliffe
Portling
Girthon
Twynholm
Little Sypland
Compstonend
Ravenshall Point
Mossyard
Fleet Bay
Lennox Plunton
A755
Wildlife Park
Whinnie Liggate
Castlehill Point
Kirkchrist
MacLellan's Castle
Auchencairn
Auchencairn Bay
Heston Island
Margrie
Gledpark
Kirkcudbright
Culnaightrie
Balcary
Balcary Point
Islands of Fleet
Culscadden
Borgue
Mutehill
Kirkandrews
Wigtown Bay
Dundrennan
Rascarrel
Kirkcudbright Bay
A711
Orroland
Dundrennan Abbey
Garlieston
Borness
Balmangan
Cruggleton Bay
Ringdoo Point
Ross
Balmae
Netherlaw
Abbey Head
B7004
B7063
Little Ross
Portyerrock
Isle of Whithorn
St Ninian's Chapel (ruin)
BURROW HEAD
5 miles
8 kilometres

High Auldgirth
Auldgirth
Dalswinton
Townhead
Parkgate
Nethermill
106
Jardine Hall
Templand
Nethercleuch
Ae Bridgend
Cumrue
Shieldhill
Millhousebridge
Corrie
CAULDKINERIG
New Langholm
Auchencairn
Duncow
Marjoriebanks
Applegarth Town
Amisfield Town
Tinwald
Lochmaben
Lockerbie
Bankshill
319 GRANGE FELL
Holywood
Kirkton
Holywood Village
Locharbriggs
Lochmaben Castle
Greenhill
Tundergarth
Bigholms
252 COLLIN HAGS
Twelve Apostles
Lincluden Collegiate Church
Newbridge
Heath Hall
Hightae
Torthorwald
Roman Camp
Waterbeck
Terregles
Lochside
Lincluden
Roucan
240 CARTHAT HILL
Solwaybank
Maxwell Town
Collin
Kettleholm
Middlebie
Evertow
Cargenbridge
Dumfries
Greenlea
Racks
Dalton
Ecclefechan
Milltow
Hoddom Cross
A74(M)
Eaglesfield
Chapelknowe
Timpanheck
Islesteps
Kingholm Quay
Thomas Carlyle's Birthplace
Kirtlebridge
Merkland Cross
Mouswald
Carrutherstown
Hoddom Mains
Bonshaw Tower
Robgill Tower
Lochober Loch
Kirkconnell Flow
Kelton
Brydekirk
Kirkpatrick-Fleming
Conheath
Kelhead
Creca
Glencaple
Bankend
Clarencefield
Ruthwell Cross
Hollee
Springfield
Kirkconnell
Annan
Gretna Green
Kinharvie
Nith Estuary
Ruthwell
Corn Mill
Sweetheart Abbey
Shearington
Savings Bank
Cummertrees
Howes
Eastriggs
Rigg
Gretna
New Abbey
Ingleston
Bowhouse
Caerlaverock Castle
Powfoot
Blackshaw
Wildlife & Wetlands Trust Centre
Newbie
Dornock
Redkirk Point
Loch Kindar
Torduff Point
Rockcliffe Cross
569 CRIFFELL
Bowness-on-Solway
Port Carlisle
Carse Bay
Rockcliffe
Glasson
Hadrian's Wall Path
Kirkbean
Carsethorn
Bowness Common
Drumburgh
Boustead Hill
Burgh by Sands
Easton
North End
SOLWAY FIRTH
Cardurnock
Longcroft
Longburgh
West End
Monkhill
Drumburgh Moss
Borron Point
Grune Point
Anthorn
Whitrigg
Fingland
Thurstonfield
Moorhouse
Arbigland
Angerton
Mainsriddle
Skinburness
Moricambe Bay
Kirkbride
Whitrigglees
Finglandrigg Woods
Gill Foot Bay
Studholme
Kirkbampton
Bow
Loaningfoot
Powhill
Laythes
Little Bampton
Oughterby
Little Orton
Southerness
Newton Arlosh
Wampool
East Cote
Border
Salt Coates
Southerness Point
Silloth
Calvo
Great Orton
Causewayhead
Seaville
Blackdyke
Brownrigg
Wedholme Flow
Aikton
Biglands
Wiggonby
Newby
Moss Side
Gamelsby
Orton Rigg
Blitterlees
Raby
Thornby
Woodhouses
Kingside Hill
Abbey Town
Drumleaning
Moorhouse
Baldwin
Whinnow
Holm Cultram
Wolsty
Kelsick
Oulton
Micklethwaite
Dockray
Crofton
Thursby
Beckfoot
Dundraw
Lessonhall
Pelutho
Highlaws
Moor Row
Aikhead
East Curthwaite
Newtown
Waverbridge
Aldoth
Wheyrigg
Wigton
West Curthwaite
Blencogo
Tarns
Waverton
Holme St Cuthbert
Highmoor
Howrigg
Bromfield
Parkgate
Mawbray
Mealrigg
High Scales
Red Dial
Brackenthwaite
Dubmill Point
Salta
Waterside
Rosley
Langrigg
Edderside
New Cowper
Low Row
Bolton Low Houses
Westward
Westnewton
Welton
Yearngill
Crookdake
Bolton New Houses
Grassgarth
Allonby
Watchill
Fletchertown
Allonby Bay
Brocklebank
Aspatria
Hayton
Baggrow
Mealsgate
Harriston
Blennerhasset
343 FAULDS BROW
Ratten Row
Sebergham
Prospect
Oughterside
Kirkland Guards
Boltongate
Caldbeck
Arkleby
Torpenhow
Sandale
Whelpo
Allerby
Threapland
Upton
Crosscanonby
Parsonby
Plumbland
Bothel
Whitrigg
Ireby
Hesket Newmarket
Crosby
Crosby Villa
Bullgill
Aughertree
Fell Side
Gilcrux
Fort
River Ellen
High Ireby
Uldale
Nether Row
Greengill
Branthwaite
Maryport
Dearham
Ruthwaite
Low Row
447 BINSEY
Longlands
Ellenborough
Townhead
Tallentire
Sunderland
High Row
Risehow
Bewaldeth
Fothergill
Woodside
Blindcrake
Trotters World of Animals
Orthwaite
Bridekirk
663 CARROCK FELL
Flimby
Broughton Moor
High Bewaldeth
Redmain
R Derwent
710 KNOTT
Standingstone
Dovenby
Kilnhill
St Helens
Little Broughton
Bassenthwaite
Great Broughton
Papcastle
North Row
Mosedale
Siddick
High Seaton
Chapel
690 GREAT CALVA
River Caldew
Camerton
Embleton
High Side
703 BOWSCALE FELL
Seaton
Cockermouth
Scarness
Great Clifton
Brigham
Wythop Mill
North Side
Bridgefoot
Greysouthen
931 SKIDDAW
Workington
Stainburn
Little Clifton
Eaglesfield
88
Lakeland Sheep & Wool Centre
Mirehouse
Armaside
Little Crosthwaite
868 SADDLEBACK
Bassenthwaite Lake
Mossbay
A76
A75
A709
A780
A711
A710
B725
B724
B7020
B723
B7076
B7068
B722
B6357
B6357
B7076
A6071
B721
B5307
B5302
B5300
B5301
A596
B5299
A595
A591
A594
B5291
A66

107
97
89
Corrie
Craigcleuch
Newcastleton
Langholm
New Langholm
Malcolm Memorial
Skipper's Bridge
Under Burnmouth
Kershopefoot
Bankshill
Tundergarth
Bigholms
Caulside
Baileyhead
Claygate
Harelaw
Warwicksland
Nook
Waterbeck
Solwaybank
Hollows
Rowanburn
Canonbie
Pentonbridge
Sleetbeck
Catlowdy
Blackpool Gate
Oakshaw Ford
Roadhead
Bewcastle
Roman Camp
Middlebie
Evertown
Milltown
Woodhouselees
Timpanheck
Scuggate
Haggbeck
Ecclefechan
Hoddom Cross
Eaglesfield
Chapelknowe
Carwinley
Lyneholmford
Thomas Carlyle's Birthplace
Merkland Cross
Scotsdike
Kirtlebridge
Bonshaw Tower
Robgill Tower
Hoddom Mains
Netherby
Stapleton
Kirkpatrick-Fleming
Creca
Hollee
Springfield
Longtown
Kirkcambeck
Annan
Gretna Green
Gretna
Prior Rigg
Boltonfellend
Howes
Eastriggs
Rigg
Kirklinton
Hetherside
Hethersgill
Nickies Hill
Triermain
Dornock
Redkirk Point
Sandysike
Skitby
Newbie
Westlinton
Smithfield
Walton
Hadrian's Wall Path
Banks
Torduff Point
Scaleby
Scalebyhill
Burtholme
Lanercost Priory
Todhills
Newtown
Bowness-on-Solway
Rockcliffe Cross
Laversdale
Low Row
Port Carlisle
Blackford
Rockcliffe
Barclose
Longpark
Oldwall
Brampton
Irthington
Milton
Glasson
Hadrian's Wall Path
Wallhead
Walby
Harker
Solway Aviation
Hallbankgate
Drumburgh
Boustead Hill
Burgh by Sands
Beaumont
Bowness Common
Easton
North End
Low Crosby
High Crosby
Kingstown
Low Gettbridge
Cargo
Grinsdale
Houghton
Newby East
Edmond Castle
Kirkhouse
Talkin Tarn
Farlam
Longcroft
Drumburgh Moss
Longburgh
West End
Monkhill
Linstock
Little Corby
Whitrigg
Anthorn
Fingland
Kirkandrews upon Eden
Knowlefield
Warwick Bridge
Corby Hill
Hayton
Talkin
Forest Head
Angerton
Thurstonfield
Moorhouse
Stanwix
Burnrigg
Kirkbride
Whitrigglees
Finglandrigg Woods
Kirkbampton
Bow
Stainton
Belle Vue
CARLISLE
Warwick-on-Eden
How Mill
Powhill
Studholme
Fenton
Laythes
Little Bampton
Oughterby
Little Orton
Morton
Harraby
Scotby
Heads Nook
Faugh
Castle Carrock
Newton Arlosh
Salt Coates
Wampool
Great Orton
Wetheral
Great Corby
Wetheral Priory Gatehouse
Seaville
Wedholme Flow
Aikton
Newby West
Upperby
Brownrigg
Biglands
Wiggonby
Newby Cross
Cummersdale
Blackwell
Carleton
Cumwhinton
Cumwhitton
Moss Side
Gamelsby
Orton Rigg
Baldwinholme
Raby
Thornby
Woodhouses
Drumleaning
Whinnow
Cardewlees
Durdar
Brisco
483 CUMREW FELL
Abbey Town
Holm Cultram
Moorhouse
Kelsick
Oulton
Thursby
Cotehill
Hornsbygate
Cumrew
Micklethwaite
Dockray
Crofton
Dalston
Ratten Row
Burthwaite
Scalesceugh
Hornsby
Newbiggin
Lessonhall
Dundraw
Moor Row
Aikhead
East Curthwaite
Green Head
Buckabank
Wreay
Holmwrangle
Waverbridge
Wigton
West Curthwaite
Cumdivock
Bridge End
Unthank
Wheyrigg
Blencogo
Waverton
Highmoor
Hawksdale
Foulbridge
Croglin
Parkgate
Howrigg
Raughton
Aiketgate
Towngate
Ainstable
High Scales
Red Dial
Brackenthwaite
Gaitsgill
Low Hesket
Nunclose
Scale Houses
Waterside
Rosley
Raughton Head
Mellguards
Southwaite
Armathwaite
Bolton Low Houses
Low Row
Westward
Welton
Nether Welton
Skiprigg
Stockdalewath
High Hesket
Crookdake
Grassgarth
Thethwaite
Ruckcroft
Dale
Bolton New Houses
Ivegill
Old Town
Baronwood
Watchill
Fletchertown
Brocklebank
Low Braithwaite
High Bankhill
Staffield
Baggrow
Mealsgate
Middlesceugh
Blennerhasset
Boltongate
Sebergham
Kirkoswald
Kirkland Guards
Sandale
FAULDS BROW
Whelpo
Ratten Row
Caldbeck
Sowerby Row
Thomas Close
Calthwaite
Torpenhow
Newlands
Morton
Lazonby
Upton
Southernby
Hesket Newmarket
Hutton End
Fieldhead
Bothel
Whitrigg
Ireby
Aughertree
Glassonby
247 LAZONBY FELL
Salkeld Dykes
Great Salkeld
Long Meg and her Daughters
Fell Side
Nether Row
Millhouse
Brackleymoor
Plumpton
High Ireby
Uldale
Branthwaite
Haltcliff Bridge
New Rent
Little Salkeld
Hunsonby
Ruthwaite
Low Row
High Row
Lamonby
Unthank
Hutton-in-the-Forest
Plumpton Head
Sunderland
447 BINSEY
Longlands
Ellonby
Skelton
Winskill
Bewaldeth
Langwathby
Trotters World of Animals
High Bewaldeth
Orthwaite
663 CARROCK FELL
Hutton Roof
Little Blencow
Catterlen
Kilnhill
710 KNOTT
Johnby
Laithes
Bassenthwaite
Great Blencow
Edenhall
North Row
Chapel
Mosedale
Bowscale
Newton Reigny
Thacka Beck
Penrith
Embleton
High Side
690 GREAT CALVA
703 BOWSCALE FELL
Mungrisdale
357 BERRIER HILL
Greystoke
Castle
Scarness
Gill
Newbiggin
Mayburgh Henge
Carleton
Brougham Castle
931 SKIDDAW
Berrier
Motherby
Countess Pillar
Oasis Whinfell Park
Mirehouse
Tarn Moss
Penruddock
Stainton
Eamont Bridge
868 SADDLEBACK
Scales
Dalemain
Rheged Discovery Centre
Yanwath
Border Forest
Liddesdale
Wilson's Pike
513 GLENDHU HILL
275 BLINKBONNY HEIGHT
404 TINNIS HILL
450 CAULDKINE RIG
HART FELL
319 GRANGE FELL
252 COLLIN HAGS
355 BARRON'S PIKE
Solway Firth
River Esk
River Lyne
R Eden
R Irthing
River Gelt
River Caldew
R Ive
Roe Beck
Chalk Beck
R Petteril
R Eamont
R Derwent
Bassenthwaite Lake
Wauchope Water
Tarras Water
Kirtle Water
Water of Milk
R Sark
Carlisle
M6
A7
A74(M)
A75
A6071
A689
A69
A595
A596
A6
A591
A66
A686
B7068
B6318
B6357
B720
B722
B723
B725
B7076
B721
B5307
B5302
B5305
B5299
B6263
B6413
B6412
B5288
B5291
0 1 2 3 4 5 miles
0 1 2 3 4 5 6 7 8 kilometres

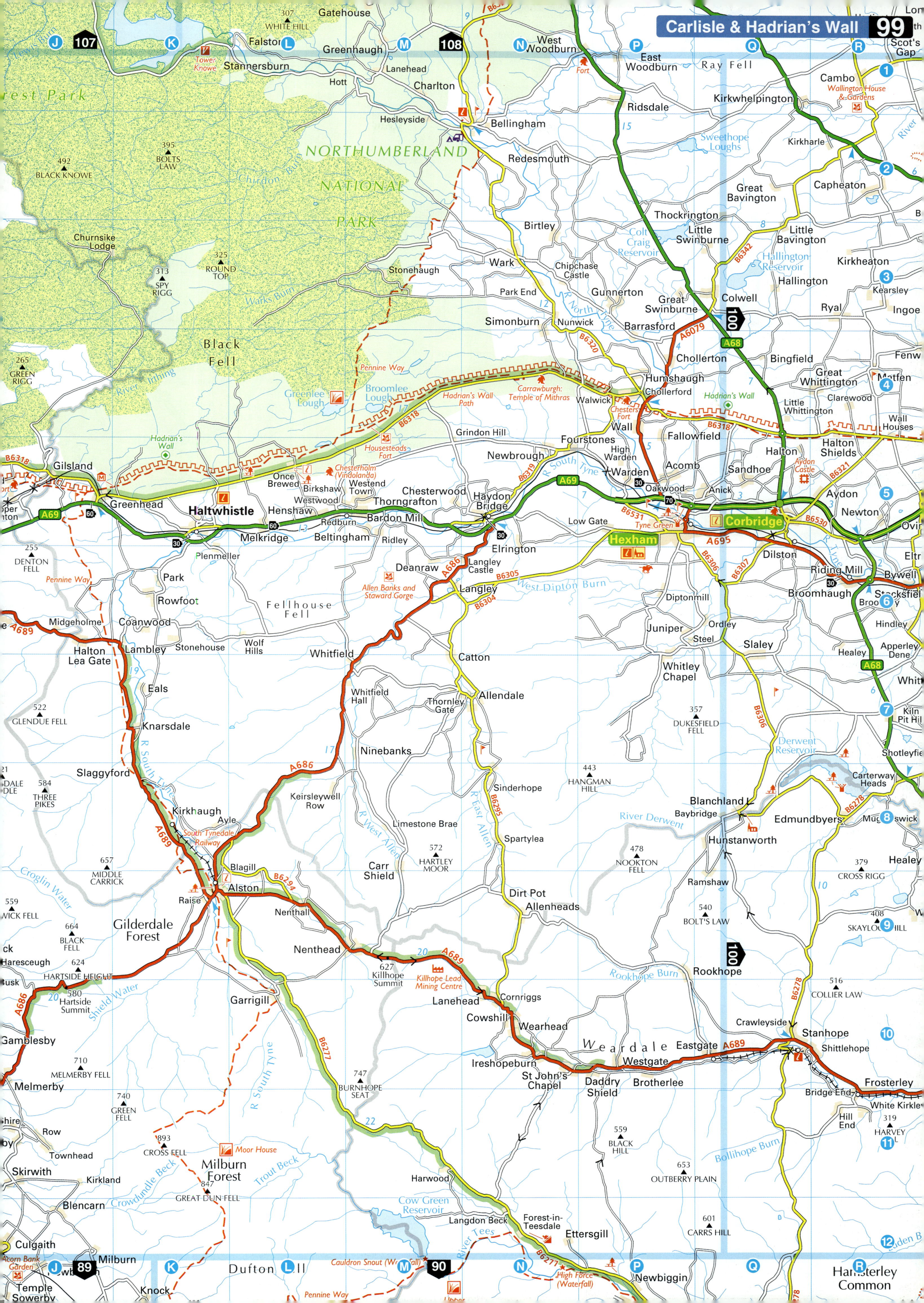
107
108
100
89
90
Gatehouse
307 WHITE HILL
Falstone
Tower Knowe
Stannersburn
Greenhaugh
Lanehead
Hott
Charlton
West Woodburn
East Woodburn
Fort
Ray Fell
Cambo
Wallington House & Gardens
Scot's Gap
Kirkwhelpington
Ridsdale
Hesleyside
Bellingham
Sweethope Loughs
Kirkharle
River
NORTHUMBERLAND
NATIONAL
PARK
Redesmouth
492 BLACK KNOWE
395 BOLTS LAW
Chirdon Burn
Great Bavington
Capheaton
Thockrington
Little Swinburne
Colt Craig Reservoir
Little Bavington
Hallington Reservoir
Hallington
Kirkheaton
Kearsley
Birtley
Churnsike Lodge
313 SPY RIGG
325 ROUND TOP
Stonehaugh
Wark
Chipchase Castle
Gunnerton
Great Swinburne
Colwell
Ryal
Ingoe
Warks Burn
Park End
R. North Tyne
Simonburn
Nunwick
Barrasford
A6079
A68
B6320
Black Fell
265 GREEN RIGG
River Irthing
Pennine Way
Greenlee Lough
Broomlee Lough
Chollerton
Bingfield
Great Whittington
Fenwick
Matfen
Humshaugh
Chollerford
Hadrian's Wall Path
Carrawburgh: Temple of Mithras
Walwick
Chesters Fort
Hadrian's Wall
Little Whittington
Clarewood
Wall Houses
B6318
Housesteads Fort
Grindon Hill
Fourstones
Wall
Fallowfield
Halton
Halton Shields
High Warden
Newbrough
Acomb
Sandhoe
Aydon Castle
B6321
Gilsland
Once Brewed
Chesterholm (Vindolanda)
Birkshaw
Westend Town
Chesterwood
B6319
R. South Tyne
Warden
Oakwood
Anick
Aydon
Newton
Greenhead
Haltwhistle
Henshaw
Westwood
Thorngrafton
Haydon Bridge
A69
Tyne Green
B6531
Corbridge
B6530
Ovington
Melkridge
Redburn
Bardon Mill
Beltingham
Ridley
Low Gate
Hexham
A695
Dilston
Riding Mill
Bywell
Eltringham
255 DENTON FELL
Plenmeller
Elrington
Langley Castle
Deanraw
A686
B6306
B6307
Broomhaugh
Stocksfield
Broomley
Park
Rowfoot
Allen Banks and Staward Gorge
B6305
Langley
West Dipton Burn
B6304
Diptonmill
Hindley
Midgeholme
A689
Coanwood
Fellhouse Fell
Juniper
Ordley
Steel
Slaley
Healey
Apperley Dene
Halton Lea Gate
Lambley
Stonehouse
Wolf Hills
Whitfield
Catton
Whitley Chapel
Whittonstall
Eals
Whitfield Hall
Thornley Gate
Allendale
522 GLENDUE FELL
Knarsdale
357 DUKESFIELD FELL
Kiln Pit Hill
Ninebanks
Derwent Reservoir
Shotley Bridge
R. South Tyne
Slaggyford
584 THREE PIKES
443 HANGMAN HILL
Sinderhope
Carterway Heads
Blanchland
Baybridge
River Derwent
Edmundbyers
B6278
Kirkhaugh
Keirsleywell Row
Ayle
South Tynedale Railway
R. West Allen
Limestone Brae
R. East Allen
Spartylea
Hunstanworth
657 MIDDLE CARRICK
572 HARTLEY MOOR
478 NOOKTON FELL
379 CROSS RIGG
Croglin Water
Blagill
B6294
Carr Shield
Ramshaw
Raise
Alston
Dirt Pot
Allenheads
559 WICK FELL
664 BLACK FELL
Gilderdale Forest
Nenthall
540 BOLT'S LAW
408 SKAYLOCK HILL
Nenthead
Haresceugh
624 HARTSIDE HEIGHT
627 Killhope Summit
Killhope Lead Mining Centre
Rookhope Burn
Rookhope
580 Hartside Summit
Shield Water
Garrigill
Lanehead
Cornriggs
516 COLLIER LAW
Cowshill
Wearhead
Crawleyside
Stanhope
Shittlehope
Gamblesby
Weardale
Eastgate
Westgate
B6277
710 MELMERBY FELL
747 BURNHOPE SEAT
Ireshopeburn
St John's Chapel
Daddry Shield
Brotherlee
Frosterley
Bridge End
White Kirkley
Melmerby
740 GREEN FELL
R. South Tyne
Row
893 CROSS FELL
559 BLACK HILL
Hill End
319 HARVEY
Townhead
Moor House
Milburn Forest
Trout Beck
Bollihope Burn
Skirwith
Kirkland
Crowdundle Beck
847 GREAT DUN FELL
Harwood
653 OUTBERRY PLAIN
Blencarn
Cow Green Reservoir
Langdon Beck
Forest-in-Teesdale
Ettersgill
601 CARRS HILL
River Tees
Culgaith
Acorn Bank Garden
Milburn
Dufton
Cauldron Snout (Waterfall)
High Force (Waterfall)
Newbiggin
Hamsterley Common
Temple Sowerby
Knock
Pennine Way

West Woodburn
East Woodburn
Ray Fell
Hartington
Rothley
Longwitton
Scot's Gap
Hart Burn
River Font
Pigdon
Newton Underwood
Pegswood
Ashington
Morpeth
Bothal
Sheepwash
North Seaton
Ridsdale
Kirkwhelpington
Cambo
Wallington House & Gardens
Hartburn
Meldon Park
Throphill
Mitford
Hepscott
Scotland Gate
Bomarsund
West Sleekburn
Middleton
Wansbeck
High Angerton
Low Angerton
Meldon
Molesden
Clifton
Choppington
Nedderton
Bedlington
East Sleekburn
Sweethope Loughs
Kirkharle
Bolam
Bolam Lake
Edington
Whalton
Tranwell
Stannington Station
Cowpen
Bebside
Newsham
Great Bavington
Capheaton
Harnham
Saltwick
Plessey Woods
East Hartford
New Delaval
Thockrington
Little Swinburne
Colt Crag Reservoir
Little Bavington
Hallington Reservoir
Bradford
Belsay
Belsay Hall, Castle & Gardens
Ogle
Stannington
Shotton
Shankhouse
Cramlington
East Cramlington
New Hartley
Birtley
Chipchase Castle
Gunnerton
Great Swinburne
Colwell
Hallington
Kirkheaton
Kearsley
Ingoe
Black Heddon
Milbourne
Higham Dykes
River Blyth
Berwick Hill
Brenkley
Big Waters
Mason
Seaton Burn
Annitsford
Seghill
North Tyne
Nunwick
Barrasford
Ryal
Heugh
Ponteland
Dinnington
Brunswick Village
Dudley
Wide Open
Burradon
Camperdown
Killingworth
Chollerton
Bingfield
Great Whittington
Fenwick
Stamfordham
Dalton
Darras Hall
Prestwick
Newcastle
Hazlerigg
Woolsington
Humshaugh
Chollerford
Hadrian's Wall
Little Whittington
Clarewood
Matfen
Hawkwell
River Pont
Eachwick
High Callerton
Black Callerton
Kenton Bankfoot
Kenton
Forest Hall
Walwick
Chesters Fort
Wall
Fallowfield
Wall Houses
Harlow Hill
Hadrian's Wall Path
Rudchester
North Walbottle
Fawdon
Gosforth
South Gosforth
Longbenton
Fourstones
High Warden
Warden
Acomb
Halton
Halton Shields
Aydon Castle
Sandhoe
Houghton
Heddon-on-the-Wall
Throckley
Westerhope
Jesmond
Wallsend
South Tyne
Oakwood
Anick
Aydon
Horsley
George Stephenson's Birthplace
Tyne Riverside
Walbottle
Newburn
NEWCASTLE UPON TYNE
Heaton
Walker
Byker
Low Gate
Hexham
Tyne Green
Corbridge
Newton
Ovington
Ovingham
Wylam
Castle
Clara Vale
Ryton
Crawcrook
Stella
Scotswood
Elswick
Felling
Dilston
West Wylam
Ryton Woodside
Blaydon
Metro Centre
Dunston
Eltringham
Cherryburn
Prudhoe
Riding Mill
Bywell
West Mickley
Mickley Square
Prestclose Wood
Greenside
Winlaton
Derwent Walk
Whickham
GATESHEAD
West Dipton Burn
Diptonhill
Broomhaugh
Stocksfield
Broomley
Painshawfield
High Mickley
Coalburns
Barlow
Winlaton Mill
Team Valley
Low Fell
Wrekenton
Juniper
Ordley
Steel
Hindley
New Ridley
Hedley on the Hill
Leadgate
High Spen
Highfield
Sunniside
Street Gate
Bowes Railway Museum
Slaley
Healey
Apperley Dene
Chopwell
Rowland's Gill
Gibside
Lamesley
Springwell
Whitley Chapel
Blackhall Mill
Derwentcote Steel Furnace
Sheep Hill
Marley Hill
Byermoor
Tanfield Railway
Angel of the North
Birtley
Portobello
Whittonstall
Hamsterley
Burnopfield
Kibblesworth
Newlands
Hobson
Causey Arch
Tanfield
Washington
357 DUKESFIELD FELL
Kiln Pit Hill
Ebchester
High Westwood
Tantobie
Tanfield Lea
Open Air
High Urpeth
Ouston
Fatfield
Medomsley
Beamish
Perkinsville
Shotley Bridge
Shotleyfield
Dipton
White-le-Head
Stanley
West Pelton
Pelton
Pelton Fell
River Wear
Shiney
Derwent Reservoir
443 HANGMAN HILL
Carterway Heads
Benfieldside
Bridgehill
Blackhill
Harelaw
Catchgate
Oxhill
The Middles
Grange Villa
Newfield
Chester-le-Street
Houghton Gate
Leadgate
Annfield Plain
South Moor
Quaking Houses
Blanchland
Baybridge
River Derwent
Consett
Crookhall
Iveston
Craghead
Allensford
Templetown
Delves
Greencroft Hall
Maiden Law
Holmside
Waldridge
Waldridge Fell
Chester Moor
Great Lumley
Hunstanworth
Edmundbyers
Muggleswick
Castleside
Knitsley
Ornsby Hill
Burnhope
Edmondsley
Nettlesworth
Plawsworth
Finchale Priory
Leamside
478 NOOKTON FELL
379 CROSS RIGG
Healeyfield
Rowley
Newbiggin
Lanchester
Sacriston
Kimblesworth
Witton Gilbert
Pity Me
Ramshaw
East Butsfield
River Browney
Diggerland
Langley Park
Framwellgate Moor
Allenheads
540 BOLT'S LAW
408 SKAYLOCK HILL
Waskerley
West Butsfield
Cornsay
Satley
Cornsay Colliery
Quebec
Esh
Bearpark
Crook Hall
Gilesgate Moor
Rookhope
Rookhope Burn
516 COLLIER LAW
Waskerley Beck
Esh Winning
Ushaw Moor
New Brancepeth
Broompark
Durham
Hedleyhope Fell
Waterhouses
Langley Moor
Brandon
High Stoop
Inkerman
East Hedleyhope
Meadowfield
Shincliffe
Crawleyside
Stanhope
Shittlehope
Weardale
Eastgate
Westgate
St John's Chapel
Daddry Shield
Brotherlee
Tow Law
Sunniside
Stanley Crook
Bowburn
Frosterley
Upper Town
Billy Row
Brancepeth
Sunderland Bridge
Bridge End
White Kirkley
Wolsingham
Thornley
Roddymoor
Oakenshaw
Croxdale
Hett
Hill End
319 HARVEY HILL
River Wear
Crook
Helmington Row
Willington
Page Bank
Tudhoe
559 BLACK HILL
Fir Tree
Rumby Hill
Sunny Brow
Tod Hills
Byers Green
Mount Pleasant
Bollihope Burn
Weardale Railway
Howden-le-Wear
Spennymoor
653 OUTBERRY PLAIN
St Johns
Newfield
Middlestone Moor
North Close
Bedburn
North Bitchburn
High Grange
Binchester Blocks
Middlestone
Kirk Merrington
Hamsterley Forest
Witton le Wear
Hunwick
Auckland Castle
Leasingthorne
Forest-in-Teesdale
601 CARRS HILL
Toll
Hamsterley
Witton
Witton Park
Toronto
Ettersgill
Euden Beck
Escomb
Coundon
High Etherley
Coundon Grange
Chilton
Hamsterley Common
Toft Hill
Bishop Auckland
South Church
Eldon
Rushyford
High Force (Waterfall)
Morley
St Helen Auckland
Old Eldon
0 1 2 3 4 5 miles
0 1 2 3 4 5 6 7 8 kilometres

Newbiggin-by-the-Sea
109
Blyth
North Blyth
Seaton Sluice
Seaton Delaval
Hartley
St Mary's Lighthouse
Whitley Bay
Cullercoats
Monkseaton
Tynemouth
Tynemouth Priory & Castle
North Shields
SOUTH SHIELDS
IJmuiden
Int. Ferry Terminal
Tyne Tunnel
Westoe
Harton
Marsden Bay
Marsden
Souter Lighthouse
Souter Point
Whitburn
Whitburn Bay
Cleadon
West Boldon
Boldon Colliery
East Boldon
Hylton
Fulwell
Southwick
Roker
Seaburn
Monkwearmouth
Castletown
SUNDERLAND
South Hylton
Pennywell
Wildfowl & Wetlands Trust
Offerton
Hendon
Grangetown
Penshaw Monument
Penshaw
High Newport
Tunstall
Herrington
New Silksworth
Ryhope
Durham Heritage Coast
New Herrington
Philadelphia
Newbottle
Houghton-le-Spring
Bournmoor
Seaton
Seaham
Hetton-le-Hole
Murton
Parkside
Dalton-le-Dale
East Rainton
Dalton Park
Cold Hesledon
Low Moorsley
South Hetton
Hawthorn
Easington Lane
Pittington
Easington Colliery
Hallgarth
High Haswell
Haswell
Easington
Littletown
Little Thorpe
Sherburn
Haswell Plough
Shotton Colliery
Peterlee
Sherburn Hill
Ludworth
Horden
Shadforth
Thornley
Shotton
Blackhall Colliery
Old Cassop
Cassop Colliery
Wheatley Hill
Castle Eden
Blackhall Rocks
Old Quarrington
Quarrington Hill
Blackhall
Hesleden
Wingate
Station Town
Kelloe
Town Kelloe
Hart Station
Coxhoe
Trimdon Grange
Hutton Henry
Sheraton
Hart
Trimdon Colliery
South Wingate
Cornforth
Trimdon
High Throston
The Headland
Historic Quay
Elwick
HARTLEPOOL
Hurworth Burn
Dalton Piercy
Fishburn
River Skerne
Hartlepool Bay
Summerhill
Bishop Middleham
Hardwick Hall
Brierton
Butterwick
Seaton Carew
Sedgefield
Embleton
Owton Manor
91
92
Bradbury
Greatham
Graythorpe
Wynyard
Tees Bay
Port of Tyne
Tynemouth
Meadow Well
Percy Main
Howdon Road
Wet'n'Wild Water Park
Royal Quays Outlet Shopping Centre
Premier Inn
East Howdon
International Passenger Terminal
River Tyne
Jarrow
Sunderland
500 m
Newcastle upon Tyne
Royal Victoria Infirmary
Newcastle University
Leazes Park
Sports Direct Arena (Newcastle United FC)
Civic Centre
Northumbria University
Eldon Square
Monument
Grainger Market
Laing Art Gallery
New Bridge St
The Gate
Newcastle Central Station
Westgate Road
Neville Street
Life Science Centre
Black Gate
Castle Keep
Millennium Bridge
Gateshead Quays
The Sage
Hexham, Blaydon
Gateshead
Metro station
Sunderland
South Shields
River Wear
Superstore
Livingstone Rd
St Mary's Way
West Wear Street
Sunderland Station
The Bridges
University of Sunderland (City Campus)
Chester Road
Burn Park Road
Stockton Road
Park
Mowbray Gardens
Sunderland Museum & Winter Gardens
Civic Centre & Register Office
Peel St
Salem Rd
Hudson Road School
Sunderland High School
Durham
Teesside (A19)
Chester-le-Street

Port Ellen
A846
Ardbeg
Lagavulin
Laphroaig
Texa
Rudha na Gainmhich
165
MAOL BUIDHE
THE OA
110
111
Kilnaughton Bay
Lower Killeyan
Risabus
Kinnabus
Loch Kinnabus
American Monument
MULL OF OA
Rudha nan Leacan
Port Ellen - Kennacraig
Cara
Glenacardoch Point
Bellochantuy Bay
Machrihanish Bay
Machrihanish
Drumlemble
Earadale Point
385
THE STATE
446
CNOC MOY
Dalsmeran
Glen Breackerie
Strone Glen
BEINN NA LICE
428
Carskey
MULL OF KINTYRE
Borgadale
Isle of Man
0 1 2 3 4 5 miles
0 1 2 3 4 5 6 7 8 kilometres
POINT OF AYRE
Ayres
Rue Point
Port Cranstal
Cranstal
The Lhen
Cronk y Bing
Bride
Shellag Point
Jurby Head
Jurby
Andreas
Sandygate
Regaby
The Cronk
St Jude's
Ballachurry Fort
The Grove
Close Sartfield
Sulby
Ramsey Bay
Ramsey (Rhumsaa)
Curraghs
Sulby R
Ballaugh
Orrisdale
Orrisdale Head
Cronk Sumark
Churchtown
Manx Electric Railway
Port e Vullen
Glen Auldyn
ISLE OF MAN
Ravensdale
Ancient Crosses
Maughold
Maughold Head
Dreemskerry
561
NORTH BARRULE
Corrany
Ballajora
Ballafayle
Cashtal yn Ard
Kirk Michael
Cooildarry
488
Block Eary
620
SNAEFELL
462
SLIEAU LHEAN
Glen Mona
Sulby Reservoir
Barregarrow
The Bungalow
Snaefell Mountain Railway
Laxey Wheel
Dhoon Bay
Knocksharry
Peel Castle
St Patrick's Isle
Peel (Purt ny-Hinshey)
Cronk-y-Voddy
R Neb
ELLAN
545
BEINN Y PHOTT
Laxey
King Orry's Grave
487
COLDEN
Millennium Way
Ballalheannagh
Old Laxey
Laxey Head
Laxey Bay
Contrary Head
Corrins Folly
Tynwald Hill
R Dhoo
VANNIN
479
SLIEAU RUY
Cregny Baa
Patrick
St John's
Greeba
Baldwin
Baldrine
Cloven Stones
Clay Head
Waterfall
Glen Maye
TT Circuit
Manx Electric Railway
Onchan (Kiondroghad)
Lower Foxdale
Crosby
Glen Vine
Strang
Castleward
Groudle Glen Railway
Onchan Head
Niarbyl
Dalby
Foxdale
Eairy
Union Mills
Cronkbourne
Belfast
Norse Houses
Round Table
Niarbyl Bay
483
SOUTH BARRULE
DOUGLAS (DOOLISH)
(Apr-Sept)
Dalby Mountain
437
CRONK NY ARREY LAA
Braaid
Heysham
Closeclark
Brough Fort
St Marks
Douglas Head
(Mar-Oct)
Liverpool
Ballamodha
Millennium Way
(Nov-Mar)
Fleshwick Bay
Grenaby
Santon
Port Soderick
Ballakilpheric
Ballakelly
(Apr-Sept)
Birkenhead
Ballafesson
Silverdale Glen
Isle of Man Steam Railway
Milners Tower
Bradda Head
Colby
Ballabeg
Rushen Abbey
Santon Head
Port Erin
Cronk ny Merriu
Dublin
Marine Interpretation Centre
Ballasalla
Howe
Castletown
Isle of Man (Ronaldsway)
The Sound
Meayll Circle
Port St Mary
Derbyhaven
Hango Hill
Derby Fort
CALF OF MAN
Cregneash
Close ny Chollagh
Scarlett
Calf Sound
Spanish Head
Scarlett Point
Castletown Bay
Herring Tower
Dreswick Point
Caigher Point
Manx Heritage site

Tayinloan
Grogport
Barmollack
Pirnmill
Penrioch
North Arran
CAISTEAL ABHAIL
Corrie
354 CRUACH NAN GABHAR
Whitefarland
715 BEINN BHARRAIN
Loch Tanna
Glen Iorsa
874 GOATFELL
Muasdale
Carradale Water
Imachar
Balliekine
792 BEINN NUIS
Glen Rosa
Merkland Point
Carradale
Belloch
Barr Water
Bridgend
Dippen
Carradale House
Iorsa Water
Brodick Castle, Garden & Country Club
Brodick Bay
MacAlister Clan
454 BEINN AN TUIRC
Torrisdale
Carradale Point
Carradale Bay
ARRAN
Brodick
Strathwhillan
319
Cleongart
408 BORD MOR
Machrie Bay
Auchagallon Stone Circle
Machrie
Corriegills
512 A'CHRUACH
Clauchlands Point
Saddell
Tormore
Machrie Moor Stone Circles
Bellochantuy
Saddell Bay
Moss Farm Road Stone Circle
Balmichael
503 BEINN BHREAC
Lamlash
Margnaheglish
Balmichael
Lamlash Bay
Holy Island
396 SGREADAN HILL
Ugadale
Torbeg
Shiskine
Cordon
Tangy Loch
Blackwaterfoot
Auchencairn
Kingscross
Knockenkelly
Drumadoon Bay
Kilpatrick
Kilpatrick Dun
Glen Scorrodale
Carn Ban
Whiting Bay
Glen Lussa
Brown Head
Peninver
Ardnacross Bay
Glen Ashdale
Largymore
Corriecravie
Kilmory Water
Kilmichael
Torr a' Chaisteal Fort
Sliddery
Largybeg
Dippen Head
Dippen
Campbeltown
Kilmory
Lagg
Torrylin Cairn
Bennan
Kildonan
Campbeltown Loch
Island Davarr
Bennan Head
Pladda
Kilkerran
Kildalloig
352 BEINN GHUILEAN
Achinhoan
Ru Stafnish
Conie Glen
Glen Kerran
Cattadale
Polliwilline Bay
Southend
Macharioch
Dunaverty
Sanda Sound
Sheep Island
Sanda Island
340 Ailsa Craig
Bennane Head
KINTYRE
KILBRANNAN SOUND
A83
B842
B843
B879
B880
A841

FIRTH
OF
CLYDE
Irvine
Bay
Ayr
Bay
Ardrossan
Horse Isle
Saltcoats
Stevenston
Kilwinning
Dalgarven
Ardeer
Irvine
Dreghorn
Springside
Kilmaurs
Stewarton
Fenwick
Crosshouse
Gatehead
Drybridge
Dundonald
Gailes
Barassie
Troon
Loans
Symington
Monkton
Prestwick
New Prestwick
Ayr
Wallacetown
Whitletts
Doonfoot
Alloway
Heads of Ayr
Fisherton
Dunure
Culroy
Minishant
Dalrymple
Maybole
Maidens
Turnberry
Kirkoswald
Crosshill
Kirkmichael
Straiton
Dailly
Old Dailly
Girvan
Woodland
Pinmore
Pinwherry
Barr
Lendalfoot
Colmonell
Bennane Head
Tarbolton
Mossblown
Annbank
Coylton
Patna
Waterside
Dalquhairn
Tallaminnock
Loch Bradan
Galloway
Corrie
Corriegills
Clauchlands Point
Strathwhillan
Holy Island
Lamlash Bay
Cordon
Kingscross
Whiting Bay
Largymore
Largybeg
Dippen Head
Kildonan
Ailsa Craig
Larne
CARRICK
A77
A78
A71
A719
A713
A714
113
103
95

113
114
106
96
Strathaven
Carnduff
361 LAIRDS SEAT
Draffan
Blackwood
Nemphlar
Sandford
Kirkmuirhill
Auchenheath
Kirkfieldbank
Lanark
New Lanark
World Heritage Village
Falls of Clyde
Caldermill
Boghead
Brocketsbrae
Lesmahagow
Hawksland
New Trows
Auchlochan
Stockbriggs
Douglas Water
Drumalbin
Waterside
Polbaith Burn
Glen Water
Avon Water
Kype Water
Logan Water
River Nethan
Drumclog
Newmilns
Darvel
Greenholm
Priestland
Spirit of Scotland
Dungavel
Galston
Middleyard
Auchmillan
Mauchline
Haugh
Catrine
Sorn
Limmerhaugh
Muirkirk
Kames
River Ayr
Glenbuck
Carmacoup
Glespin
Coalburn
Bellfield
Rigside
Happendon
Uddington
405 ROBERT LAW
Cameronians Regimental Memorial
Douglas West
St Bride's Church
Douglas
Crawfordjohn
Balgray
Glespin Burn
Duneaton Water
Lettershaw
Snar Water
Nether Whitecleuch
WELLGRAIN DOD
Wanlock Water
Leadhills
Lead Mining
Wanlockhead Beam Engine
Wanlockhead
732 GREEN LOWTHER
725 LOWTHER HILL
Lowther Hills
335 MILL RIG
461 AUCHINGILLOCH
522 NUTBERRY HILL
492 PRIESTHILL HEIGHT
383 DISTINKHORN
408 MID HILL
466 MIDDLEFIELD LAW
593 CAIRN TABLE
440 DRYRIGS HILL
497 WARDLAW HILL
562
Gass Water
Glenmuir Water
478 MOUNT STEWART
Spango Water
Fingland
450 HALFMERK HILL
503 COCKER HILL
Meikle Carco
Kirkland
Cronberry
Lugar
Lugar Water
Ochiltree
Auchinleck
Holmhead
Logan
Laigh Glenmuir
Cumnock
Palmerston
Garrallan
Skares
Roadside
Sinclairston
363 CARSGAILOCH HILL
Mansfield
Dalgig
River Nith
Connel Park
Bankglen
Craigbank
New Cumnock
Kirkconnel
Kelloholm
Newtown
Sanquhar
Kello Water
Ulzieside
Mennock
594 HARE HILL
Blackcraig
700 BLACKCRAIG
464 BENBEOCH
568 ENOCH HILL
High Pennyvenie
Dalmellington
Euchan Water
450 CLOUD HILL
River Nith
Enterkin Burn
Enterkinfoot
Durisdeermill
Durisdeer
Gateslack
East Morton
Mossdale
536
478
Polgown
475 COUNTAM
554 CAIRNKINNA HILL
Cleuch-head
697 WINDY STANDARD
Drumlanrig
Morton Loch
Morton Castle
Loch Doon
Drumjohn
Bow Burn
796 CAIRNSMORE OF CARSPHAIRN
598 COLT HILL
Big Carlae
Old Auchenbrack
Auchenhessnane
Carronbridge
Tibbers
Shinnel Water
Scaur Water
Nithsdale
Burnhead
Penpont
Thornhill
Closeburn
Benbuie
337 BENNAN
Keir Mill
Camp
Closeburn
Southern Upland Way
Water of Ken
532 CORNHARROW HILL
Stenhouse
Tynron
Park
Kirkpatrick
622
Carsphairn
Garryhorn Burn
Water of Deugh
Knowehead
Moniaive
Kirkland
Maxwelton
Keir Hills
695 MEAUL
Polmaddy Burn
Glenhoul
Black Water
385 WETHER HILL
Glencrosh
Craigneston
Blackwood
813 CORSERINE
716 MILLFIRE
431 BOGRIE HILL
Skelston
Sundaywell
Dunscore
Lag
Throughgate
A71
A70
A76
A713
A702
A73
A743
A719
M74
B743
B745
B7086
B7018
B7078
B7037
B744
B705
B713
B7036
B7083
B741
B729
B740
B797
B731
B7000

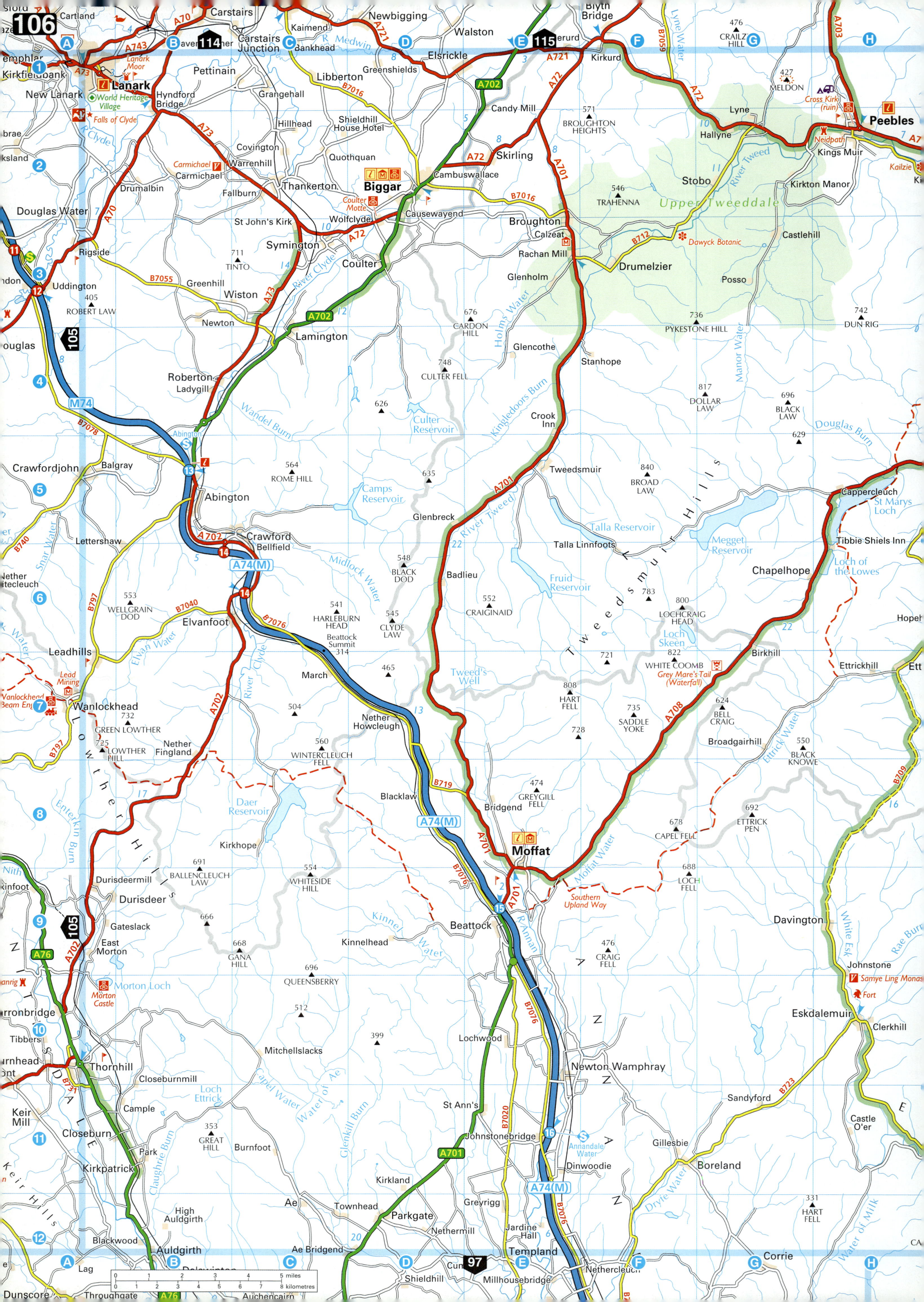
114
115
105
97
Cartland
Carstairs
Carstairs Junction
Kaimend
Bankhead
Newbigging
Walston
Blyth Bridge
Kirkurd
Elsrickle
Lanark
Lanark Moor
Kirkfieldbank
New Lanark
World Heritage Village
Falls of Clyde
Hyndford Bridge
Pettinain
Grangehall
Libberton
Greenshields
Hillhead
Shieldhill House Hotel
Covington
Quothquan
Carmichael
Warrenhill
Drumalbin
Fallburn
Thankerton
Biggar
Coulter Motte
Cambuswallace
Candy Mill
Skirling
Broughton
Calzeat
Rachan Mill
Causewayend
Wolfclyde
Symington
Coulter
St John's Kirk
Douglas Water
Rigside
Uddington
ROBERT LAW
TINTO
Greenhill
Wiston
Newton
Lamington
Roberton
Ladygill
Abington
Crawfordjohn
Balgray
Lettershaw
Crawford
Bellfield
Elvanfoot
Leadhills
Lead Mining
Wanlockhead
GREEN LOWTHER
LOWTHER HILL
Nether Fingland
WELLGRAIN DOD
Lowther Hills
Daer Reservoir
Kirkhope
Durisdeermill
Durisdeer
BALLENCLEUCH LAW
Gateslack
East Morton
Morton Loch
Morton Castle
GANA HILL
QUEENSBERRY
Thornhill
Closeburnmill
Cample
Closeburn
Park
Kirkpatrick
GREAT HILL
Burnfoot
Loch Ettrick
High Auldgirth
Blackwood
Auldgirth
Lag
Dunscore
Throughgate
Auchencairn
Ae
Ae Bridgend
Townhead
Parkgate
Kirkland
Nethermill
Mitchellslacks
Capel Water
Water of Ae
Glenkill Burn
Claughrie Burn
Keir Mill
Keir Hills
Tibbers
Nithsdale
Wandel Burn
ROME HILL
Camps Reservoir
Glenbreck
BLACK DOD
Midlock Water
HARLEBURN HEAD
Beattock Summit
CLYDE LAW
March
Nether Howcleugh
WINTERCLEUCH FELL
Blacklaw
WHITESIDE HILL
Kinnel Water
Kinnelhead
Beattock
Moffat
Bridgend
GREYGILL FELL
Southern Upland Way
Lochwood
Newton Wamphray
St Ann's
Johnstonebridge
Annandale Water
Dinwoodie
Greyrigg
Jardine Hall
Templand
Millhousebridge
Shieldhill
Nethercleugh
CULTER FELL
CARDON HILL
Culter Reservoir
Glencothe
Holms Water
Kingledoors Burn
Crook Inn
Tweedsmuir
River Tweed
Badlieu
Tweed's Well
CRAIGINAID
Talla Reservoir
Talla Linnfoots
Fruid Reservoir
BROAD LAW
Tweedsmuir Hills
HART FELL
SADDLE YOKE
WHITE COOMB
Grey Mare's Tail (Waterfall)
LOCHCRAIG HEAD
Loch Skeen
Megget Reservoir
Chapelhope
Cappercleuch
St Marys Loch
Tibbie Shiels Inn
Loch of the Lowes
Birkhill
Ettrickhill
BELL CRAIG
Broadgairhill
BLACK KNOWE
ETTRICK PEN
CAPEL FELL
LOCH FELL
Moffat Water
CRAIG FELL
Davington
Eskdalemuir
Clerkhill
Samye Ling Monastery
Fort
Johnstone
White Esk
Sandyford
Castle O'er
Gillesbie
Boreland
Dryfe Water
HART FELL
Corrie
Water of Milk
Broughton Heights
Stanhope
Drumelzier
Dawyck Botanic
Glenholm
Upper Tweeddale
TRAHENNA
Stobo
Hallyne
Lyne
Kings Muir
Kirkton Manor
Castlehill
Posso
PYKESTONE HILL
DUN RIG
Manor Water
DOLLAR LAW
BLACK LAW
Douglas Burn
MELDON
Cross Kirk (ruin)
Neidpath
Peebles
Kailzie
CRAILZIE HILL
Lyne Water
Carmichael
A70
A73
A743
A721
A72
A702
A701
A708
A74(M)
M74
A76
B7016
B7055
B7078
B740
B797
B7040
B7076
B719
B7020
B712
B7059
B723
B709
B731
0 1 2 3 4 5 miles
0 1 2 3 4 5 6 7 8 kilometres

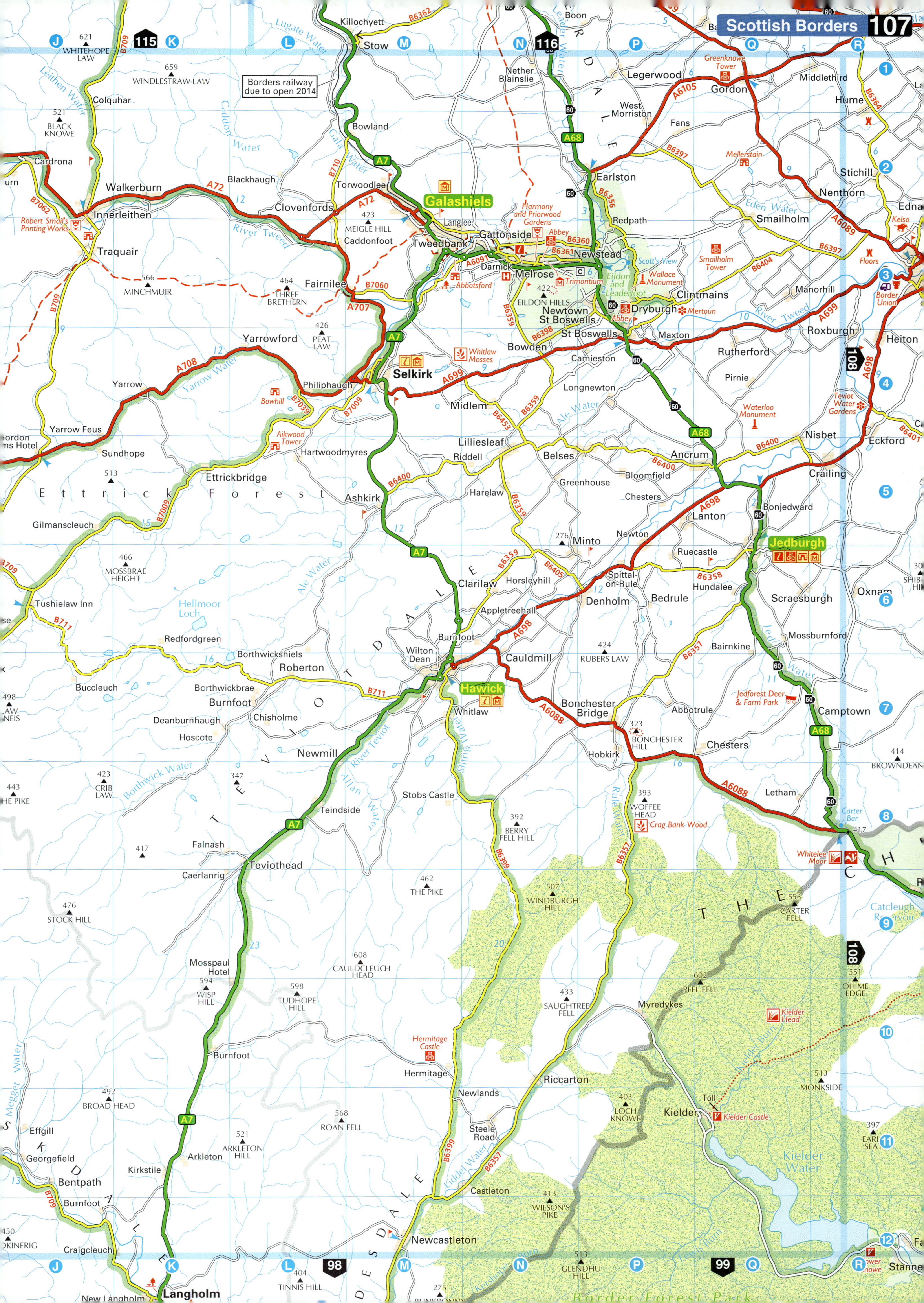

Killochyett
Stow
Lugate Water
621 WHITEHOPE LAW
115
116
659 WINDLESTRAW LAW
Borders railway due to open 2014
Leithen Water
Colquhar
521 BLACK KNOWE
Caddon Water
Gala Water
Bowland
Boon
Nether Blainslie
Leader Water
LAUDERDALE
Legerwood
West Morriston
Fans
Greenknowe Tower
Gordon
Middlethird
Hume
Cardrona
Walkerburn
Blackhaugh
Torwoodlee
Galashiels
Clovenfords
Innerleithen
Robert Smail's Printing Works
Traquair
River Tweed
423 MEIGLE HILL
Caddonfoot
Langlee
Tweedbank
Gattonside
Harmony and Priorwood Gardens
Abbey
Newstead
Redpath
Earlston
Mellerstain
Stichill
Nenthorn
Ednam
Eden Water
Smailholm
Kelso
Floors
Smailholm Tower
Scott's View
Wallace Monument
Darnick
Melrose
Abbotsford
Trimontium
Eildon and Leaderfoot
422 EILDON HILLS
Newtown St Boswells
Dryburgh Abbey
Mertoun
Clintmains
Manorhill
Border Union
566 MINCHMUIR
464 THREE BRETHERN
Fairnilee
426 PEAT LAW
Yarrowford
Yarrow Water
Yarrow
Philiphaugh
Bowhill
Selkirk
Whitlaw Mosses
Bowden
St Boswells
Camieston
Maxton
Rutherford
Roxburgh
Heiton
Pirnie
Teviot Water Gardens
Longnewton
Midlem
Ale Water
Waterloo Monument
Yarrow Feus
Dryhope
Sundhope
Aikwood Tower
Hartwoodmyres
Lilliesleaf
Riddell
Belses
Ancrum
Nisbet
Eckford
Bloomfield
Greenhouse
Chesters
Crailing
513
Ettrickbridge
Ettrick Forest
Ashkirk
Harelaw
Lanton
Bonjedward
Gilmanscleuch
276 Minto
Newton
Ruecastle
Jedburgh
466 MOSSBRAE HEIGHT
Clarilaw
Horsleyhill
Spittal-on-Rule
Hundalee
Oxnam
Tushielaw Inn
Hellmoor Loch
Appletreehall
Denholm
Bedrule
Scraesburgh
Redfordgreen
Burnfoot
424 RUBERS LAW
Bairnkine
Mossburnford
Borthwickshiels
Wilton Dean
Cauldmill
Roberton
TEVIOTDALE
Jedforest Deer & Farm Park
Buccleuch
Borthwickbrae
Hawick
Burnfoot
Whitlaw
Bonchester Bridge
323 BONCHESTER HILL
Abbotrule
Camptown
Chisholme
Deanburnhaugh
Hoscote
Chesters
Hobkirk
414 BROWNDEAN
Newmill
River Teviot
Slitrig Water
Borthwick Water
423 CRIB LAW
347
443 THE PIKE
Allan Water
Stobs Castle
Teindside
393 WOFFEE HEAD
Crag Bank Wood
Letham
Carter Bar
Rule Water
392 BERRY FELL HILL
417
Whitelee Moor
Falnash
Teviothead
Caerlanrig
462 THE PIKE
507 WINDBURGH HILL
THE CHEVIOT HILLS
553 CARTER FELL
476 STOCK HILL
Catcleugh Reservoir
608 CAULDCLEUCH HEAD
Mosspaul Hotel
594 WISP HILL
598 TUDHOPE HILL
433 SAUGHTREE FELL
602 PEEL FELL
551 OH ME EDGE
Myredykes
Kielder Head
Hermitage Castle
Burnfoot
Hermitage
Riccarton
Kielder Burn
513 MONKSIDE
Newlands
Toll
403 LOCH KNOWE
Kielder
Kielder Castle
492 BROAD HEAD
568 ROAN FELL
Effgill
521 ARKLETON HILL
Steele Road
397 EARL SEAT
Georgefield
Arkleton
Liddel Water
Kielder Water
Kirkstile
Bentpath
ESKDALE
Castleton
413 WILSON'S PIKE
Burnfoot
LIDDESDALE
Newcastleton
450 ...KINERIG
Craigcleuch
Meggat Water
513 GLENDHU HILL
Tower Knowe
Stannersburn
404 TINNIS HILL
98
99
108
Kershope Burn
Lewis Burn
275
New Langholm
Langholm
Border Forest Park
A7
A68
A72
A699
A698
A6088
A6091
A6105
A6089
A708
A707
B709
B7062
B710
B7060
B6362
B6397
B6356
B6360
B6361
B6359
B6398
B6404
B6453
B6400
B7009
B7039
B711
B6405
B6358
B6357
B6399
B6364
B6401

Greenlaw
Upsettlington
Shoreswood
West Allerdean
Ancroft
Simprim
Leitholm
Felkington
Grindon
Haggerston
Berrington
Beal
Middlethird
Lambden
Shellacres
Grindonrigg
Hume
Eccles
Duddo
Bowsden
Lennel
Donaldson's Lodge
The Hirsel
Coldstream
Cornhill-on-Tweed
Castle
Etal
Heatherslaw Light Railway
Heatherslaw Corn Mill
Lady Waterford Hall
Birgham
Lowick
West Kyloe
Fenwick
Fenham
Stichill
Carham
Wark
West Learmouth
Buckton
Nenthorn
Ednam
Shidlaw
Branxton
Crookham
Ford
Detchant
Holburn
East Learmouth
1513
Kelso
Hadden
Flodden
Kimmerston
St Cuthbert's Cave
Middleton
Pressen
Hetton Steads
Sprouston
Floors
Kelso
Thornington
Howtel
Milfield
Fenton
North Hazelrigg
Manorhill
Border Union
Lempitlaw
Mindrum
Pawston
Nesbit
Doddington
South Hazelrigg
Kilham
Newtown
Easter Softlaw
Roxburgh
Lanton
West Horton
East Horton
Heiton
Yeavering
Coupland
Shotton
Kirknewton
Akeld
Chatton
Yeavering Bell
Humbleton
Wooler
Teviot Water Gardens
Frogden
Kirk Yetholm
Hethpool
Town Yetholm
Earle
Haugh Head
Wild Cattle Park
Ros Castle
NORTHUMBERLAND
Primsidemill
Middleton Hall
Newtown
Chillingham
Lilburn Tower
Caverton Mill
Nisbet
Eckford
Linton
Pennine Way
North Middleton
Hepburn
Morebattle
Crailing
Preston Hill
South Middleton
The Curr
Bonjedward
NATIONAL PARK
Old Bewick
The Schil
Ilderton
Gateshaw
Jedburgh
The Cheviot
Roddam
Mowhaugh
Wooperton
New Bewick
Shibden Hill
Hownam
Oxnam
Scraburgh
Dunmoor Hill
River Breamish
Beanley
Chatto
Brandon
Powburn
Mossburnford
Branxton
Hartside
Ingram
Windy Gyle Hill
Fawdon
Glanton
Cushat Law
Cochrane Pike
Glanton Pike
Shawdon Hill
Great Ryle
Bolton
Jed Water
Camps
Deer Park
Camptown
Prendwick
Little Ryle
Whittingham
Thrunton
Carlcroft
Barrow Burn
Browndean
Blindburn
Alnham
River Alwin
Shillhope Law
Yetlington
Elilaw
Scrainwood
Letham
Biddlestone
Shillmoor
Carter Bar
Netherton
Long Crag
Newton
Alwinton
Burradon
Lorbottle
Hungry Law
Linshiels
High Trewhitt
Whitelee Moor
Harbottle
Cartington
Ramshope
Black Kip
Sharperton
Carter Fell
Holystone
Flotterton
Warton
Snitter
Cragside House
Catcleugh Reservoir
NORTHUMBERLAND
River Coquet
Rothbury
Byrness
Corby Pike
Thropton
Hepple
Whitton
Longframlington
Great Tosson
Newtown
NATIONAL
Oh Me Edge
The Beacon
Swindon
Bickerton
Lordenshaws
Camp
Kielder Head
River Rede
Rochester
Tosson Hill
Rothbury Forest
Hindhope Law
Horsley
PARK
Forestburn Gate
Pennine Way
Monkside
Dough Crag
1388
Otterburn
Elsdon
Fontburn Reservoir
Earls Seat
Otterburn Mill
Raylees
Kielder Water
Highgreen Manor
Troughend
Black Middens Bastle House
Rothley Lakes
Netherwitton
Gatehouse
White Hill
Hartington
Longwitton
Rothley
Falstone
West Woodburn
Scot's Gap
Hart Burn
Tower Knowe
Stannersburn
Greenhaugh
East Woodburn
Rayshill
Cambo
Hartburn
Lanehead
Fort
Charlton
Wallington House & Gardens
Kirkwhelpington
CHEVIOT HILLS
A697
A698
A699
A6089
A6112
A68
A696
B6460
B6461
B6364
B6350
B6397
B6396
B6352
B6436
B6401
B6437
B6354
B6525
B6353
B6351
B6348
B6349
B6346
B6341
B6342
B6343
B6320
116
117
107
99
100
0 1 2 3 4 5 miles
0 1 2 3 4 5 6 7 8 kilometres

J
117
K
L
M
N
P
Q
R
1
2
3
4
5
6
7
8
9
10
11
12
HOLY ISLAND
Holy Island
Lindisfarne Castle
Lindisfarne Priory
Castle Point
Guile Point
CAUSEWAY FLOODED AT HIGH TIDE
Longstone Lighthouse
FARNE ISLANDS
Staple Sound
Inner Sound
North Northumberland Heritage Coast
Elwick
Ross
Low Middleton
Easington
Budle Bay
Bamburgh
B1342
Budle
Waren Mill
B1340
Outchester
Spindlestone
Burton
New Shoreston
Seahouses
Bradford
B1341
Bellshill
Elford
North Sunderland
Lucker
Adderstone
Warenford
Newham
Beadnell
A1
Swinhoe
Chathill
Beadnell Bay
Newstead
Tughall
Ellingham
Preston
Preston Pele Tower
Newton-by-the-Sea
Brunton
Embleton & Newton Links
Brownieside
Doxford
Christon Bank
Embleton
Embleton Bay
North Charlton
Fallodon
B6347
B1339
Dunstan Steads
Dunstanburgh Castle
West Ditchburn
South Charlton
Dunstan
Craster
Eglingham
B6341
Rock
Rennington
Stamford
Howick Hall
Howick
Cullernose Point
B1340
Broxfield
Littlehoughton
Longhoughton
East Bolton
B6346
Denwick
Boulmer
River Aln
Abberwick
Alnwick
Broome Park
Hawkhill
Seaton Point
Lesbury
Hipsburn
Bilton
Alnmouth
Castle
Alnmouth Bay
Bilton Banks
High Buston
Edlingham
A1068
Shilbottle
Low Buston
Birling
260
GLANTLEES HILL
Newton-on-the-Moor
Warkworth Castle & Hermitage
Warkworth
Amble
Coquet Island
Swarland
Guyzance
Gloster Hill
North Togston
High Hauxley
A697
Old Swarland
Acklington
Togston
North End
Radcliffe
Felton
B6345
East Thirston
Broomhill
B6344
South Broomhill
B1330
West Thirston
Weldon Bridge
Red Row
Druridge Bay
Eshott
Druridge Bay
West Chevington
Helm
Druridge
Causey Park
Stobswood
Widdrington
North Northumberland Heritage Coast
Longhorsley
Causey Park Bridge
Widdrington Station
Cresswell
Earsdon
B1337
A1068
Tritlington
Ulgham
Ellington
Fenrother
Linton
Lynemouth
Stanton
Hebron
A189
Beacon Point
River Font
Longhirst
Woodhorn
Woodhorn Demesne
Pigdon
Ashington
Pegswood
A197
North Seaton
Newbiggin-by-the-Sea
Newton Underwood
Bothal
Wansbeck Riverside
Mitford
Morpeth
100
A196
Sheepwash
Stakeford
Guide Post
North Seaton Colliery
Molesden
Hepscott
Scotland
West Sleekburn
101

A
B
C
D
E
F
G
H
1
2
3
4
5
6
7
8
9
10
11
12
COLONSAY
Kilchatt
Garva
Oronsay
Dubh Eilean
ORONSAY
ISLAY
Nave Island
Ardnave Point
Gortantaoid Point
Ton Mhòr
Kilnave
Sanaigmore
Eilean Mòr
Loch Gorr
Rudha Lamanais
Lecht Gruinart
Loch Gruinart
RSPB
B8018
B8017
Gruinart
Gleann Mòr
Saligo Bay
Loch Gorm
Coul Point
Sunderland
Kilchoman
Machir Bay
A847
Bridgend
Gartach
Loch Indaal
Bruichladdich
Bowmore
Kilchiaran Bay
RHINNS OF ISLAY
15
Port Charlotte
231
BEINN TART A'MHILL
River Laggan
Lossit Bay
Nereabolls
Duich R
A846
B8016
Rudha na Faing
Portnahaven
Port Wemyss
Orsay
RHINNS POINT
Laggan Bay
Glenegedale
Islay
Rudha Mòr
Kintra
165
MAOL BUIDHE
THE OA
Risabus
Killeyan
Kinnabus
Kilnaughton Bay
0 1 2 3 4 5 miles
0 1 2 3 4 5 6 7 8 kilometres

102

J
K
119
L
M
N
P
120
Q
R
CRUACH SCARBA
Ardfern
Gulf of Corryvreckan
Eilean Dubh
Balnahard
Rudh' a' Geodha
Kiloran Bay
Kiloran
B8086
Scalasaig
Machrins
B8085
Rudha Bàn
Eilean Ghurdmail
Colonsay-Port Askaig
JURA
Glengarrisdale Bay
295 CRUACH NA SEILCHEIG
Glendebadel Bay
364 BEN GARRISDALE
Lealt Burn
Corpach Bay
Lussa River
466 BEINN BHREAC
Glen Grundale
Shian Bay
453 RAINBERG MÒR
Ardlussa
Lussa Point
Lussagiven
A846
Loch Righ Mòr
Rudh' ant-Sàilein
Loch Tarbert
Rudha' a' Mhàil
Rudha Bholsa
363 SGARBH BREAC
506 SCRINADLE
398 BEINN TARSUINN
Jura Forest
784 BEINN AN OIR
734
Paps of Jura
Loch a' Chnuic Bhric
Bunnahabhain
316 GUIR-BHEINN
Jura
24
Knockrome
Ardfernal
Sound of Islay
Port Askaig
Kiells
Finlaggan
Feolin Ferry
560 GLASS BHEINN
529 DUBHA BHEINN
Keils
Craighouse
Small Isles
342 BRAT BHEINN
Rudha na Gaillich
Loch Ballygrant
Ballygrant
Loch Lossit
A846
266 BEINNE DUBH
Cabrach
Am Fraoch Eilean
Brosdale Island
Rudha na Tràille
429 SGÒRR NAM FAOILEANN
471
Kilennan Burn
McArthur's Head
490 BEINN BHEIGEIR
Port Askaig - Kennacraig
Rudha Liath
Ardtalla
454 BEINN URARAIDH
Loch Uaraidh
Claggain Bay
Kintour
Kilcalton Cross
Ardmore Point
346 BEINN SHOLUM
Eilean a' Chuirn
Port Ellen - Kennacraig
Rudha na Gainmhich
Ardbeg
A846
Lagavulin
Laphroaig
Texa
102
Aird
Loch Craignish
Craignish Point
Island Macaskin
Slockav
Temple Wood Stone Circles
Ri Cruin
Poltal
Loch Crinan
Crinan
Kilmahumaig
B8025
Bellanoch
Barnluasgan
112
SOUND OF JURA
Carsaig Bay
Tayvallich
Achnamara
Knapdale
Taynish
Kilmichael of Inverlussa
466 CRUACH LUSACH
B8025
Loch Sween
Keills Chapel
Kilbride
Castle Sween
Loch na Cille
Danna Island
Lochead
Achahoish
St Cormac's Chapel
Ellary
Kilmory Knap Chapel
Kilmory
Kilmory Bay
Loch Caolisport
Ormsary
Point of Knap
Druimdrishaig
480 DUBH CHREAG
Loch nan Torran
Cretshengan
Coulaghailtro
Kilberry Sculptured Stones
Kilberry
Kilberry Head
213 CRUACH AIRDE
Keppoch Point
Torinturk
Tiretigan
B8024
Loch Stornoway
Kilchamai
West Loch Tarbert
Ardpatrick
112
Portachoillan
Clachan
Ronachan Point
Ronachan
Loch Ciaran
Loch Garasdale
Kinerarach
Tarbert
Sound of Gigha
GIGHA
247 CRUACH MHIC GOUGAIN
CNOC-AN T-SAMHLAIDH
Rhunahaorine Point
Ardminish
Rhunahaorine
Achamore
38
Tayinloan
Cara
103
354
1
2
3
4
5
6
7
8
9
10
11
12

120
121
111
103
Ardfern
En Mhic Chrion
Ford
Fincharn
Loch Leacann
Auchindrain
Strachur
Aird
Loch Craignish
Island Macaskin
Carnassarie Castle
Glebe Cairn
Kilmartin
Kilmartin House
Slockavullin
Temple Wood Stone Circles
The Nether Largie Cairns
Dunchraigaig Cairn
Ri Cruin Cairn
Poltalloch
Loch Leathan
Loch Gaineamhach
CRUACH MHIC FHIONNLARDH
BEINN LAOIGH
Gleann Airidh
Furnace
Sandhole
Crarae
Crarae Garden
Minard
Tullochgorm
Newton
Castle Lachlan
Balliemore
Invernoaden
Glenbranter
CRUACH NAN CAPULL
BEINN BHEULA
Loch Eck
Loch Crinan
Crinan
Kilmahumaig
Bellanoch
Moine Mhor
Kilmichael Glassary Inscribed Stone
Kilmichael Glassary
Dunadd Fort
River Add
Crinan Canal
Cup & Ring
Cairnbaan
Barnluasgan
Loch Glashan
Asknish
Lochgair
Middle Kames
Barnacarry
CRUACH AN LOCHAIN
Dunans Castle
BEINN BHEAG
Whistlefield Inn
Argyll Forest Park
BEINN MHOR
Sligrachan
Carrick Castle
Cam Loch
Achnamara
Lochgilphead
Kilmory Woodland Park
Loch Gilp
Carrick
Loch Fyne
River Ruel
CRUACH CHUILCEACHAN
Glenmassen
Glen Massen
CLACH BHEINN
BEINN RUADH
Ardentinny
Benmore
STRONCHULLIN HILL
Knapdale
Taynish
Kilmichael of Inverlussa
Ardrishaig
Shirvan
Largiemore
Kilmodan Sculptured Stones
Glendaruel
CRUACH NAN CUILEAN
Loch Tarsan
SGORACH MÒR
Glen Lean
Rashfield
Ardbeg
BEINN BHEAG
CRUACH LUSACH
Brenfield
Otter Ferry
Stronafian
Clachaig
Sandbank
Ardnadam
Holy Loch
Glenkin
Fearnoch
CRUACH NAN CAPULL
Glenstriven
Lochead
Kilfinan Bay
Kilfinan
Drum
Loch Riddon
BEINN BHREAC
Dunoon
BISHOP'S SEAT
Achahoish
Erines
SLIABH GAOIL
Kyles of Bute
Port Driseach
Ardentraive
Colintraive
BEINN BHREAC
Loch Striven
Ardhallow
Ormsary
Stonefield Castle Hotel
Auchenlochan
Tighnabruaich
Rhubodach
Altgaltraig
KILMARNOCK HILL
Ardyne Burn
BEINN RUADH
Dunan
DUBH CHREAG
Glenan Bay
Kames
Millhouse
BUTE
Knockdow
Innellan
Wemyss Bay
An Tairbeart
Glenralloch
Tarbert
West Tarbert
Portavadie
Blair's Ferry
CNOC NA CARRAIGE
KAMES HILL
Ardmaleish
Ardyne Point
Port Bannatyne
Kilbride
St Colmac
Toward
Toward Quay
Skelmorlie
CRUACH AN T SORCHAIN
Kilbride Bay
Ardlamont
Ardlamont Bay
Kildavaig
Kildavanan
Ettrick Bay
Ardbeg
Castle
Bogany Point
Rothesay
Torinturk
CNOC A' BHAILE-SHOIS
Kennacraig
Ardlamont Point
St Mary's Chapel (ruin)
Ardencraig
Ascog
Loch Ascog
Ballanlay
Meikle Kilmory
Kerrycroy
Knock Castle
Whitehouse
Kilchamaig
West Loch Tarbert
Loch Fada
Inchmarnock
Midpark
Mount Stuart
Portachoillan
Castle
Chapel
Skipness
Skipness Point
Bruchag
GREAT CUMBRAE ISLAND
Millport
Clachan
Claonaig
Ardscalpsie Bay
Kingarth
Stravanan Bay
Kilchattan Bay
Kilchattan
St Blane's Church
Sound of Bute
Loch Ciaran
Loch Garasdale
Cock of Arran
Garrochty
Fairlie Roads
Garroch Head
Hunterston Power Station
Crossaig
Lochranza
Castle
Catacol
Glen Chalmadale
Little Cumbrae Island
CNOC-AN T-SAMHLAIDH
Cour Bay
Cour
Glen Catacol
Portencross
Farland Head
Kilbrannan Sound
Sannox
Penrioch
North Arran
CAISTEAL ABHAIL
Grogport
Pirnmill
Loch Tanna
Corrie
Barmolloch
0 1 2 3 4 5 miles
0 1 2 3 4 5 6 7 8 kilometres
A83
A815
A886
A885
A816
A841
A844
B8002
B840
B8025
B841
B8000
B8024
B8003
B836
B8001
B842
B875
B878
B881
B896
B899

Lochgoilhead
Loch Goil
Arddarroch
Portincaple
Whistlefield
Garelochhead
Rockville
Greenfield
Glen Douglas
Inverbeg
Rowardennan
BEN LOMOND
Ben Lomond
Queen Elizabeth Forest Park
Kinlochard
Loch Ard
Aberfoyle
Port of Menteith
Lake of Menteith
Inchmahome Priory
Dykehead
Gartmore
Dalmary
Arnprior
Buchlyvie
Balfron
Fintry
Killearn
Gartness
Croftamie
Drymen
Buchanan Smithy
Milton of Buchanan
Balmaha
Luss
Inchlonaig
Aldochlay
Loch Lomond
LOCH LOMOND AND THE TROSSACHS NATIONAL PARK
Glen Luss
Glen Fruin
Inchmurrin
Gartocharn
Arden
Cross Keys
Coulport
Shandon
Clynder
Rhu
Rosneath
Cove
Kilcreggan
Strone
Helensburgh
Hill House
Craigendoran
Balloch
Balloch Castle
Mill of Haldane
Archencarroch
Jamestown
Alexandria
Bonhill
Renton
Cardross
Ardmore
Firth of Clyde
Gourock
GREENOCK
Port Glasgow
Kilpatrick Hills
Dumbarton
Dumbarton Castle
Milton
Bowling
Old Kilpatrick
Duntocher
Erskine Bridge
Erskine
CLYDEBANK
Bearsden
Milngavie
Mugdock
Dumgoyne
Blanefield
Strathblane
Lennoxtown
CAMPSIE FELLS
Bishopbriggs
GLASGOW
Springburn
Rutherglen
Renfrew
Kilmacolm
Bishopton
Houston
Craigends
Crosslee
Bridge of Weir
Kilbarchan
Johnstone
Elderslie
Linwood
PAISLEY
Barrhead
Neilston
Newton Mearns
Eaglesham
Clarkston
Thornliebank
Giffnock
Pollokshields
Largs
Fairlie
Kilbirnie
Beith
Lochwinnoch
Howwood
Castle Semple Loch
Dalry
West Kilbride
Kilwinning
Ardrossan
Stewarton
Dunlop
Uplawmoor
Lugton
Fenwick
Waterside
CUNNINGHAME
Auldhouse
Thorntonhall

122 123 113 105 106

FIRTH OF FORTH
EDINBURGH
Kinross
Loch Leven
Kennoway
Leslie
Glenrothes
Leven
Methil
Buckhaven
East Wemyss
West Wemyss
Kirkcaldy
Kinghorn
Burntisland
Aberdour
Cowdenbeath
Lochgelly
Kelty
Cardenden
Dunfermline
Rosyth
Inverkeithing
North Queensferry
South Queensferry
Dalgety Bay
Forth Road Bridge
Forth Railway Bridge
Inchkeith
Cramond Island
Kirkliston
Broxburn
Linlithgow
Livingston
Musselburgh
Prestonpans
Cockenzie and Port Seton
Tranent
Dalkeith
Bonnyrigg
Loanhead
Penicuik
Gorebridge
Carlops
West Linton
Pentland Hills
Moorfoot Hills
Borders railway due to open 2014

116
125
115
107
108
Lundin Mill
Colinsburgh
Newton of Balcormo
Cellardyke
Anstruther
Fisheries
Drumeldrie
Lower Largo
Lundin Links
Kilconquhar
Pittenweem
St Monans
Leven
Innerleven
Largo Bay
Earlsferry
Elie
Methil
Buckhaven
Isle of May
F O R T H
Fidra
Craigleith
Bass Rock
Eyebroughy
North Berwick
Scottish Seabird
Tantallon Castle
Dirleton Castle & Gardens
Dirleton
Muirfield
Gullane Bay
Gullane Point
Gullane
Fenton Barns
NORTH BERWICK LAW
187
Cleghornie
Whitekirk
Kingston
Aberlady Bay
Craigelaw Point
Aberlady
Luffness
Drem
Prora
East Fortune
St Baldred's Cradle
Tyne Mouth
Belhaven Bay
Belhaven
Dunbar
Tyninghame
John Muir
Preston Mill & Phantassie Doocot
Museum of Flight
Markle
East Linton
Motor
Chesters Hill Fort
Ballencrieff
Spittal
Gosford Bay
Athelstaneford
West Barns
Broxburn
Barns Ness
East Barns
Chapel Point
Skateraw
1650
Cockenzie and Port Seton
Seton Collegiate Church
Preston Market Cross
Longniddry
Huntington
Haddington
Hailes Castle
Traprain
Spott
Doonhill Homestead
Seton Mains
Elvingston
Pitcox
Thorntonloch
St Martin's Kirk (ruin)
Traprain Law
Luggate Burn
Stenton
The Brunt
Dry Burn
Innerwick
Crowhill
1745
Tranent
Gladsmuir
Lauderdale Aisle St Mary's Church
Papple
Reed Point
Cove
Pease Bay
Dunglass Collegiate Church
Wallyford
Macmerry
Lennoxlove
Morham
Garvald
Nunraw Abbey
319 COCKLAW HILL
397 BRANSLY HILL
Oldhamstocks
Cockburnspath
New Winton
Elphinstone
Ormiston Market Cross
Samuelston
Boggs Holdings
Ormiston
Bolton
Crossgatehall
River Tyne
Pencaitland
Gifford
Danskine
Cousland
Ecclaw
East Saltoun
West Saltoun
HILLS
Monynut Water
Bothwell Water
391 HEART LAW
Long Newton
Longyester
463 SPARTLETON
Southern Upland Way
Butterdean
Gilchriston
Pathhead
St Agnes
Eye Water
Vogrie
Newlandrig
Crichton
Crichton Castle
Humbie
Fala Dam
Fala
Blegbie
Whiteadder Reservoir
528 LAMMER LAW
MEIKLE SAYS LAW 533
Cranshaws
Abbey St Bathans
Quixwood
Ellemford
Edin's Hall Broch
325 COCKBURN LAW
Soutra Summit 363
509 CRIB LAW
513 SEENES LAW
467 MEIKLE LAW
495 HUNT LAW
Whitchester
394 DUN LAW
380 TURF LAW
L A M M E R M U I R
Southern Upland Way
Longformacus
Primrosehill
Gilston
Soonhope Burn
448 HOGS LAW
399 DIRRINGTON GREAT LAW
Cumledge
Edrom
Manderston
Heriot
Oxton
Carfraemill
Watch Water
Wedderlie Burn
Duns
Gavinton
383 COLLIE LAW
L A U D E R D A L E
Polwarth
Nisbet Hill
Blythe
Westruther
Spottiswoode
Fogo
425 DUN LAW
Fountainhall
Thornydykes
Borders railway due to open 2014
Torquhan
Lauder
Thirlestane
Thirlestane
Houndslow
Charterhall
Boon
Bassendean
Greenlaw
Blackadder Water
Killochyett
Lugate Water
Stow
Leader Water
Greenknowe Tower
Nether Blainslie
Legerwood
Gordon
Middlethird
Lambden
Leitholm
TRAW LAW
A1
A7
A68
A697
A6105
A6112
A6089
A6093
A6137
A198
A199
A1087
B6355
B6368
B6369
B6370
B6371
B6363
B6414
B6367
B6458
B6362
B6456
B6460
B6461
B6365
B6471
B1377
B1343
B1347
B1345
B1407
B942
B941
B709
0 1 2 3 4 5 miles
0 1 2 3 4 5 6 7 8 kilometres

Fast Castle Head
196
BROWN RIG
Coldingham Loch
ST ABB'S HEAD
St Abbs
Coldingham
Coldingham Bay
A1107
B6438
Houndwood
Heugh Head
Cairncross
Eyemouth
262
B6355
A1
Reston
Ayton
Burnmouth
B6438
Auchencrow
Lamberton
B6437
B6355
Chirnside
Marshall Meadows Bay
Foulden
North Northumberland Heritage Coast
Chirnsidebridge
Foulden Tithe Barn
1333
Broadhaugh
Edington
Whiteadder Water
A6105
Berwick-upon-Tweed
Allanton
Hutton
Castle
Barracks
B6437
Paxton
Town Ramparts
Blackadder
B6460
B6461
Tweedmouth
B6460
Paxton
Spittal
Whitsome
Hilton
Loanend
East Ord
Huds Head
A1167
B6437
Horndean
Horncliffe
Scremerston
B6461
Murton
Unthank
Ladykirk
Castle
A1
Thornton
Swinton
B6470
Norham
A698
Cheswick
Upsettlington
West Allerdean
CAUSEWAY FLOODED AT HIGH TIDE
Shoreswood
B6354
Simprim
Grindon
Ancroft
Goswick
Felkington
River Tweed
B6525
Haggerston
B6437
HOLY ISLAND
Holy Island
ellacres
Grindonrigg
108
Berrington
109
Beal
Bowsden

A
B
C
D
E
F
G
H
126
1
2
3
4
5
6
7
8
9
10
11
12
Arnabost
Grishipoll
Clabhach
Loch Cliad
B8071
Hogh Bay
Ballyhaugh
Arinagour
Totronald
Feall Bay
Arileod
Coll
Acha
B8070
Eilean Ornsay
Uig
RSPB
COLL
Calgary Point
Crossapol Bay
Gunna
Loch Breachacha
Rudha Fàsachd
Caoles
Rudha Dubh
V
Rudha Port Bhiosd
Clachan Mor
Balephetrish Bay
B8069
Loch Bhasapoll
B8068
Ruaig
Haugh Bay
Ballevullin
Cornoigmore
Kenovay
Gott Bay
Tiree
Kilkenneth
Moss
B8065
Scarinish
Middleton
Heylipoll
Crossapoll
TIREE
Hynish Bay
Barrapoll
B8067
Balemartine
Loch a' Phuill
Mannel
Rinn Thorbhais
Balephuil Bay
Hynish
Bac Mòr or Dutchmans Cap
Bac Beag
Soa Island
0 1 2 3 4 5 miles
0 1 2 3 4 5 6 7 8 kilometres

J
K
L
M
N
P
Q
R
126
127
111
120
1
2
3
4
5
6
7
8
9
10
11
12
Ardslignish
Glenborrodale
RSPB
Carna
Oronsay
Auliston Point
Ardmore Point
Sorne Point
Quinish Point
Glengorm Castle
Tobermory
Calve Island
Coll - Oban
Caliach Point
292
'S AIRDE BEINN
Drimnin
Loch Teacuis
571
BEINN LADAIN
437
BEINN BHUIDHE
550
SITHEAN NA RAPLAICH
Loch Arienas
Calgary
Dervaig
Achnadrish House
B8073
B849
A848
Calgary Bay
Ensay
342
CÀRN MÒR
444
SPEINNE MÒR
Loch Frisa
Treshnish Point
Sound of Mull
Fuinary
A884
Rudh' a' Chaoil
Burg
Glen Aros
Aros
Lochaline
Fladda
Fanmore
390
CNOC AN DÀ CHINN
Glenaros House
Loch Tuath
Ballygown
Salen
Fishnish Point
Fishnish Pier
Lunga
TRESHNISH ISLES
Eas Fors (Waterfall)
333
BEINN NAN CÀRN
Killiechronan
B8035
A849
Gometra
ULVA
Oskamull
Gruline
Macquarie Mausoleum
408
BEINN NAN LUS
Glen Forsa
Scallastle
Eorsa
Loch na Keal
Loch Bà
ISLE OF MULL
636
BEINN MHEADHON
591
BEINN A' GHRÀIG
766
DUN DA GHAOITHE
Staffa
Little Colonsay
Inch Kenneth
Inchkenneth Chapel (ruin)
Fingal's Cave
Loch na Keal, Isle of Mull
Balnahard
966
BEN MORE
704
CRUACHAN DEARG
519
BEIN NA SREINE
Strathcoil
491
CREACH BHEINN
Aird of Kinloch
Glen More
Fossil Tree
Burg
Loch Fuaran
717
BEN BUIE
698
BEN CREACH
IONA
Iona Abbey & Nunnery
Rudha nan Cearc
Kintra
Baile Mòr
MacLean's Cross
Fionnphort
Loch Scridain
Pennycross
Pennyghael
503
BEINN NA CROISE
Lochbuie
Loch Uisg
Loch Spelve
Aridhglas
Sound of Iona
Loch na Lathaich
Leidle Water
Loch Buie
337
St Columba Exhibition Centre
Bunessan
Loch Assapol
376
CRUACHAN MIN
376
BEINN CHREAGACH
Carsaig
Rudha Dubh
377
DRUIM FADA
ROSS OF MULL
Erraid
Uisken
Ardchiavaig
Malcolm's Point
Rudha nam Braithrean
FIRTH
Rudha Ardalanish
Torran Rocks
Colonsay - Oban
Garbh Eileach
Eilean Dubh Mòr
GARVELLACHS
Monastery & Beehive Cells
Eileach an Naoimh
LUNGA
SCARBA
448
Eilean Dubh

Glenborrodale
Laga
RSPB
Carna
Oronsay
Drimnin
437 BEINN BHUIDHE
550 SÌTHEAN NA RAPLAICH
Loch Teacuis
571 BEINN LADAIN
522 MEALL A' CHOISE
Loch Arienas
Glen Dubh
Acharn
Gleann Geal
Claggan
Larachbeg
339 MEALL DAMH
Rannoch River
Achranich
Loch Aline
Loch Tearnait
Lochaline
Fuinary
Sound of Mull
Aros
Salen
A849
Fishnish Point
Fishnish Pier
464 GLAIS BHEINN
514 AN SLEAGHOCH
Rudha an Ridire
B8035
Gruline
Macquarie Mausoleum
408 BEINN NAN LUS
Glen Forsa
ISLE OF MULL
Loch Ba
591 BEINN A' GHRÀIG
636 BEINN MHEADHON
766 DUN DA GHAOITHE
Scallastle Bay
Altcreich
Craignure
Duart Bay
Duart Point
Torosay
Duart
Lochdonhead
Lochdon
Gorten
Loch Don
Grass Point
704 CRUACHAN DEARG
Strathcoil
Glen More
247 CARN BAN
698 BEN CREACH
717 BEN BUIE
Loch Fuaran
Loch Spelve
Croggan
503 BEINN NA CROISE
Lochbuie
Loch Uisg
337 MAOL BAN
Loch Buie
377 DRUIM FADA
Carsaig
Rudha Dubh
FIRTH OF LORNE
Colonsay - Oban
Insh Island
Clachan
Clachan-Seil
SEIL
Ellenabeich
Easdale
Balvicar
B844
B8003
Cuan
Seil Sound
Garbh Eileach
Cullipool
Torsa
Degnish
Eilean Dubh Mòr
LUING
GARVELLACHS
Monastery & Beehive Cells
Eileach an Naoimh
LUNGA
Toberonochy
Scarba, Lunga and the Garvellachs
Sound of Luing
Shuna Sound
SHUNA
Shuna Point
SCARBA
448 CRUACH SCARBA
Gulf of Corryvreckan
339 GEÀRR CHREAG
Camasine
Woodend
Strontian
A861
Achnalea
Ardnastang
Camasschoirce
Liddesdale
A884
Glen Tarbert
Inversanda
620 GLAS BHEINN
853 CREACH BHEINN
Lochuisge
651 BEINN NA CILLE
B8043
Loch a' Choire
738 BEINN MHEADHOIN
568 SGURR A BHUIC
Shuna Island
Portnacroish
Appin
Port Ramsay
Port Appin
Inverfolla
LOCH LINNHE
Clachan
Eriska
North Shian
LISMORE
B8045
Lynn of Lorne
South Shian
Loch Creran
Achnacroish
Barcaldine
A828
Scottish Sea Life Sanctuary
Kilcheran
Bernera Island
Lynn of Lorn
Kiel Crofts
Benderloch
Ledaig
BENDERLOCH
Ardmucknish Bay
Dunstaffnage Castle
Dunstaffnage Chapel (ruin)
Black Crofts
North Connel
Connel
Achaleven
A85
Dunbeg
Ganavan Bay
Dunollie Castle
McCaig's Tower
Oban
(An t-Oban)
KERRERA
Clenamacrie
River Lonan
Glen Lonan
Gallanachbeg
Gallanachmore
Ariogan
Loch Nell
Sound of Kerrera
Rudha Seanach
Lerags
Kilmore
515 BEINN GHLAS
Ardentallen
Loch Feochan
A816
Kilninver
356 AN CREACHAN
482 BEINN DEARG
Loch Scamadale
Loch Tralaig
Lochavich
Loch Avich
Melfort
Kilmelford
Barnline Stables
Dalavich
Loch Melfort
Newyork
Arduaine
Gleann Domhain
Glen Liever
Craobh Haven
Craigdhu
Inverliever Lodge
Braevallich
B840
Kintraw
Ardfern
B8002
En Mhic Chrion
En Righ
Ford
Fincharn
458 CRUACH MHIC FHIONNLARDH
Carnassarie Castle
Aird
Loch Gainneamhach
127
128
119
111
112
A B C D E F G H
1 2 3 4 5 6 7 8 9 10 11 12
0 1 2 3 4 5 miles
0 1 2 3 4 5 6 7 8 kilometres

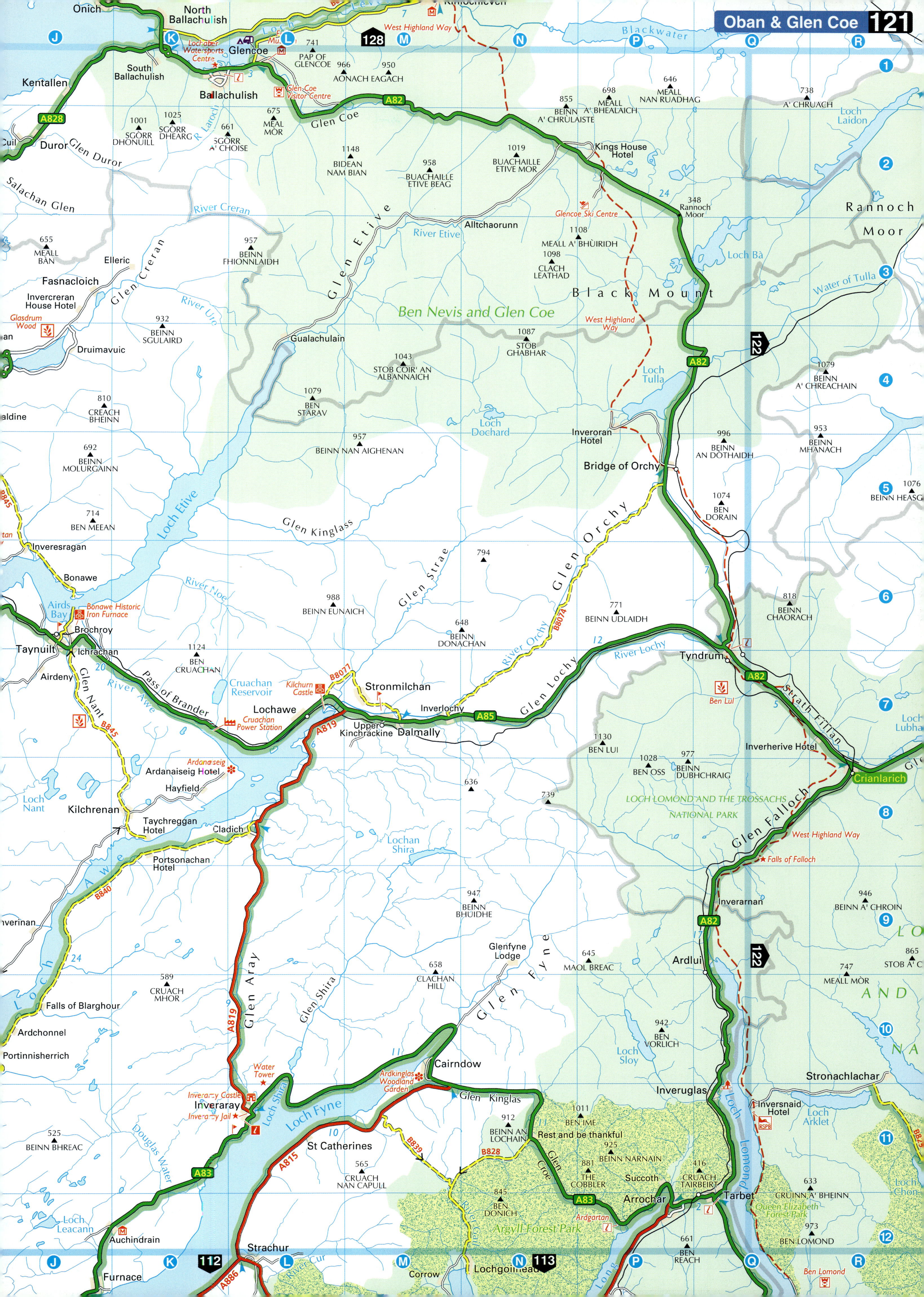
Onich
North Ballachulish
Glencoe
Lochaber Watersports Centre
PAP OF GLENCOE
741
West Highland Way
128
Blackwater
South Ballachulish
Ballachulish
Kentallen
Glen-Coe Visitor Centre
966 AONACH EAGACH
950
A82
A828
Glen Coe
1001 SGÒRR DHONUILL
1025 SGÒRR DHEARG
661 SGÒRR A' CHOISE
675 MEAL MÒR
855 BEINN A' CHRULAISTE
698 MEALL A' BHEALAICH
646 MEALL NAN RUADHAG
738 A' CHRUACH
Loch Laidon
Duror
Glen Duror
1148 BIDEAN NAM BIAN
958 BUACHAILLE ETIVE BEAG
1019 BUACHAILLE ETIVE MOR
Kings House Hotel
Salachan Glen
River Creran
Glen Etive
River Etive
Alltchaorunn
Glencoe Ski Centre
348 Rannoch Moor
Rannoch Moor
655 MEALL BÀN
957 BEINN FHIONNLAIDH
1108 MEALL A' BHÙIRIDH
1098 CLACH LEATHAD
Loch Bà
Elleric
Fasnacloich
Glen Creran
Black Mount
Water of Tulla
Invercreran House Hotel
River Ure
Ben Nevis and Glen Coe
Glasdrum Wood
932 BEINN SGULAIRD
West Highland Way
1087 STOB GHABHAR
122
Gualachulain
Druimavuic
1043 STOB COIR' AN ALBANNAICH
Loch Tulla
1079 BEINN A' CHREACHAIN
810 CREACH BHEINN
1079 BEN STARAV
Loch Dochard
Inveroran Hotel
996 BEINN AN DOTHAIDH
953 BEINN MHANACH
692 BEINN MOLURGAINN
957 BEINN NAN AIGHENAN
Bridge of Orchy
1076 BEINN HEASG
714 BEN MEEAN
Loch Etive
Glen Kinglass
1074 BEN DORAIN
Glen Orchy
Inveresragan
794
Bonawe
River Noe
988 BEINN EUNAICH
Glen Strae
771 BEINN UDLAIDH
818 BEINN CHAORACH
Airds Bay
Bonawe Historic Iron Furnace
B8074
Brochroy
648 BEINN DONACHAN
Taynuilt
Ichrachan
1124 BEN CRUACHAN
River Orchy
River Lochy
Tyndrum
Airdeny
Glen Nant
Pass of Brander
Cruachan Reservoir
Kilchurn Castle
B8077
Stronmilchan
Glen Lochy
Ben Lui
Strath Fillan
River Awe
Lochawe
Cruachan Power Station
Inverlochy
A85
Upper Kinchrackine
Dalmally
A819
1130 BEN LUI
Inverherive Hotel
B845
Ardanaiseig
Ardanaiseig Hotel
1028 BEN OSS
977 BEINN DUBHCHRAIG
Crianlarich
Hayfield
636
739
Loch Nant
Kilchrenan
LOCH LOMOND AND THE TROSSACHS NATIONAL PARK
Taychreggan Hotel
Cladich
Glen Falloch
Lochan Shira
West Highland Way
Portsonachan Hotel
Falls of Falloch
Loch Awe
B840
947 BEINN BHUIDHE
Inverarnan
946 BEINN A' CHROIN
A82
Glenfyne Lodge
645 MAOL BREAC
Ardlui
865 STOB A' C
Glen Aray
658 CLACHAN HILL
747 MEALL MÒR
589 CRUACH MHOR
Glen Shira
Glen Fyne
Falls of Blarghour
942 BEN VORLICH
Ardchonnel
Portinnisherrich
Cairndow
Loch Sloy
Water Tower
Ardkinglas Woodland Garden
Stronachlachar
Inveraray Castle
Inveraray
Inveraray Jail
Glen Kinglas
Inveruglas
1011 BEN IME
Inversnaid Hotel
Loch Arklet
Loch Shira
Loch Fyne
912 BEINN AN LOCHAIN
Rest and be thankful
525 BEINN BHREAC
St Catherines
925 BEINN NARNAIN
Loch Lomond
Douglas Water
B839
B828
Glen Croe
881 THE COBBLER
416 CRUACH TAIRBEIRT
Succoth
A815
565 CRUACH NAN CAPULL
633 CRUINN A' BHEINN
A83
845 BEN DONICH
A83
Arrochar
Tarbet
Queen Elizabeth Forest Park
Loch Leacann
Argyll Forest Park
Ardgartan
973 BEN LOMOND
Auchindrain
661 BEN REACH
Strachur
112
River Cur
113
Corrow
Lochgoilhead
Loch Long
Ben Lomond
Furnace
A886

Blackwater Reservoir
129
130
Rannoch Station
Dunan
B846
Bridge of Ericht
Killichonan
Forest Park
Loch Rannoch
Kinloch Rannoch
Drumchast'
Finnart
Inverhadden
Carie
Bridge of Gaur
Camghouran
Tay Forest Park
Loch Eigheach
Loch Laidon
738 A' CHRUACH
646 MEALL NAN RUADHAG
698 MEALL A' BHEALAICH
Kings House Hotel
348 Rannoch Moor
Rannoch Moor
Loch Bà
Water of Tulla
Black Mount
West Highland Way
Loch Rannoch and Glen Lyon
745 MEALL A' MHUIC
824 BEINN DEARG
1027 CARN GORM
1042 CARN MAIRG
931 MEALL BUIDHE
860 CAM CHREAG
Loch an Daimh
Glen Lyon
Bridge of Balgie
River Lyon
121
A82
Loch Tulla
1079 BEINN A' CHREACHAIN
780 MEALL LUAIDHE
924 MEALL A' CHOIRE LEITH
1116 MEALL GARBH
1000 MEALL GREIGH
Inveroran Hotel
996 BEINN AN DOTHAIDH
953 BEINN MHANACH
Loch Lyon
908 BEINN NAN OIGHREAG
1214 BEN LAWERS
Lochan na Làirige
Bridge of Orchy
1038 MEALL GHAORDIE
1076 BEINN HEASGARNICH
1074 BEN DORAIN
Ben Lawers
Lawers
A827
Orchy
River Lochay
Milton Morenish
Morenish
Ardeonaig
Falls of Lochay
Moirlanich Longhouse
Finlarig
Glen Lochay
Killin
Breadalbane Folklore Centre
Falls of Dochart
818 BEINN CHAORACH
937 BEINN CHEATHAICH
771 BEINN UDLAIDH
682 RUADH MHEALL
River Lochy
Tyndrum
A82
BREADALBANE
Auchlyne
Ben Lui
Strath Fillan
Loch Lubhair
A85
River Dochart
Glen Dochart
Glen Beich
671 SRON MHOR
1130 BEN LUI
1028 BEN OSS
977 BEINN DUBHCHRAIG
Inverherive Hotel
Crianlarich
1171 BEN MORE
778 MEALL AN FHIODHAIN
Dalveich
Loch Earn
LOCH LOMOND AND THE TROSSACHS NATIONAL PARK
1164 STOBINIAN
Lochearnhead
Ardvorlich
Glen Falloch
West Highland Way
A84
Glen Vorlich
Falls of Falloch
Balquhidder
Auchtubh
Craigruie
Kingshouse Hotel
Loch Voil
Loch Doine
985 BEN VORLICH
975 STUC A' CHROIN
Inverarnan
946 BEINN A' CHROIN
Ballimore
Strathyre
645 MEALL AN FHOIDHAIN
Ardlui
865 STOB A' CHOIN
747 MEALL MÒR
LOCH LOMOND AND THE TROSSACHS NATIONAL PARK
818 BENVANE
630 MEALL ODHAR
Ardchullarie More
942 BEN VORLICH
671 MEALL CALA
Loch Lubnaig
Loch Sloy
Queen Elizabeth Forest Park
Stronachlachar
Loch Katrine
876 BEN LEDI
Glen Finglas Reservoir
Kilmahog Woollen Mill
Inveruglas
Loch Lomond
Inversnaid Hotel
Loch Arklet
RSPB
B829
The Trossachs
Sir Walter Scott
Trossachs Pier
Falls of Leny
Kilmahog
Callander (Calasraid)
Brig o'Turk
Coilantogle
Upper Drumbane
BEINN NARNAIN
881 THE COBBLER
416 CRUACH TAIRBEIRT
Succoth
700 BEINN BHREAC
729 BEN VENUE
Loch Achray
Lendrick
A821
Rob Roy and Trossachs
A84
A83
Arrochar
Tarbet
633 CRUINN A' BHEINN
Queen Elizabeth Forest Park
Loch Chon
Loch Drunkie
Loch Venachar
A81
Menteith Hills
427 BEINN DEARG
Drumvaich
B8032
Ardgartan
973 BEN LOMOND
Altskeith Hotel
B822
661 BEN REACH
Kinlochard
113
Milton
Queen Elizabeth Forest Park
Aberfoyle
Port of Menteith
Ruskie
114
Thornhill
Inchmahome Priory
Goodie Water
Loch Ard
0 1 2 3 4 5 miles
0 1 2 3 4 5 6 7 8 kilometres

Killiecrankie
Tay Forest Park
Tressait
B8019
B846
Dunalastair
Dunalastair Water
Loch Tummel
Tummel Bridge
Foss
Daloist
Frenich
Queen's View
Moulin
Kinnaird
Kirkmichael
Blacklunans
Loch Broom
Faskally Wayside Centre
Pitlochry
(Baile Chloichridh)
Edradour Distillery
Dunfallandy Stone
Strath Ardle
Ballintuim
1081
SCHIEHALLION
780
FARRAGON HILL
780
MEALL TAIRNEACHAN
Loch Derculich
Strathtay
Dalcapon
561
CRAIG NAM MIAL
479
A924
A93
Loch Glassie
Derculich
Grandtully
A827
Tulliemet
Glengoulandie Deer Park
Edradynate
Logierait
Ballinluig
A9
Balnaguard
B846
B898
Kindallachan
Loch Ordie
Loch Benachally
Bridge of Cally
St Mary's
Coshieville
Camserney
Menzies
Weem
Dull
Keltneyburn
Dewars
Aberfeldy
River Tay
Kincraigie
Guay
Dowally
509
DEUCHARY HILL
Fortingall
Croftmoraig Stone Circle
532
GRANDTULLY HILL
Tay Forest Park
Dalguise
Loch Skiach
Kenmore
Fearnan
Acharn
Loch Kennard
A826
B898
River Tay
Butterstone
Achalader
Dunkeld Town
Loch of the Lowes
A923
Cathedral
Dunkeld
Concraigie
Clunie
Craigie
The Crannog Centre
Ballinloan Burn
Little Dunkeld
Inver
Birnam
Lethendy
Spittalfield
B947
The Hermitage
Loch Tay
616
MEALL DUBH
Leckbuie
713
BEINN BHREAC
Glen Quaich
Trochry
A984
Caputh
Gellyburn
Meikle
River Tay
A822
Strath Braan
Kinclaven
River Quaich
Loch Freuchie
Meikle Obney
Murthly
B867
BREADALBANE
864
SRÒN A' CHAOINEIDH
802
MEALL NAM FUARAN
Achnafauld
Amulree
Obney
Waterloo
Glen Shee
Balquharn
Bankfoot
Airntully
Perthshire
B9099
Balholm
River Almond
666
MEALL REAMHAR
879
929
BEN CHONZIE
Loch Lednock
Stanley
Harrietfield
B8063
Newmiln
Downhill
Moneydie
Luncarty
Colenden
Glen Almond
Buchanty
River Almond
Dalcrue
Redgorton
Invergeldie
Loch Turret
445
CNOC BEITHE
Pitcairngreen
Scone Palace
Glen Lednock
Funtullich
Glen Turret
Methven
Almondbank
Monzie
Keillour
A822
Fillans
A85
Lord Melville's Monument
Deil's Caldron (Waterfall)
Falls of Turret
Sculptured Stone
Fowlis Wester
West Huntingtower
Huntingtower Castle
Bridgend
Quoig
Distillery
Hosh
Gilmerton
A85
Perth
Branklyn Garden
River Earn
Comrie
Tibbermore
The Ross
Dalginross
Baird Monument
Crieff
Madderty
Welltree
M90
Clathymore
St David's
Clathy
Findo Gask
Aberdalgie
MONCREIFFE HILL
221
Glen Artney
Balloch
Auchingarrich Wildlife Centre
B8062
Ardunie Roman Signal Station
Muir o'Fauld Roman Signal Station
Craigend
River Earn
Forgandenny
Innerpeffray Library
Old Church & Tower
Innerpeffray Chapel (ruin)
Kirkton
Trinity Gask
A9
B935
Kintillo
Drummond Castle
A822
Denfield
Ichruin
Muthill
River Earn
Kinkell Bridge
Baldinnies
Forteviot
B934
Aberuthven
St Serf's Church
B9141
533
BEN CLACH
Mill of Drummond
Tullibardine Chapel
Dunning
Langside
Auchterarder
A824
B8062
A823
Muirton
B827
Knaik Water
A822
Path of Condie
Abbots Deuglie
Glenfarg Reservoir
Glenfarg
Gleneagles
Blackhall Camps
475
CORB LAW
Braco
Allan Water
Blackford
Duncrievie
Strathallan
Greenloaning
486
STEELE'S KNOWE
497
INNERDOUNY HILL
Drunzie
Middleton
Tillyrie
B8033
Glen Eagles
OCHIL HILLS
B934
River Devon
Glen Devon
Milnathort
Kinbuck
A9
Burnfoot
Glendevon
Dalqueich
Burleigh Castle
456
LENDRICK HILL
Carnbo
Ashfield
Burn of Cambus
632
BLAIRDENON HILL
Castlehill Reservoir
Kinross
A922
Buchany
Yetts o'Muckhart
A91
Doune
A820
B8033
645
TARMANGIE HILL
Pool of Muckhart
Drum
Kinross House
B826
Doune Castle
B824
Dunblane
720
BENCLEUCH
Castle Campbell
Crook
M90
Meldrum
648

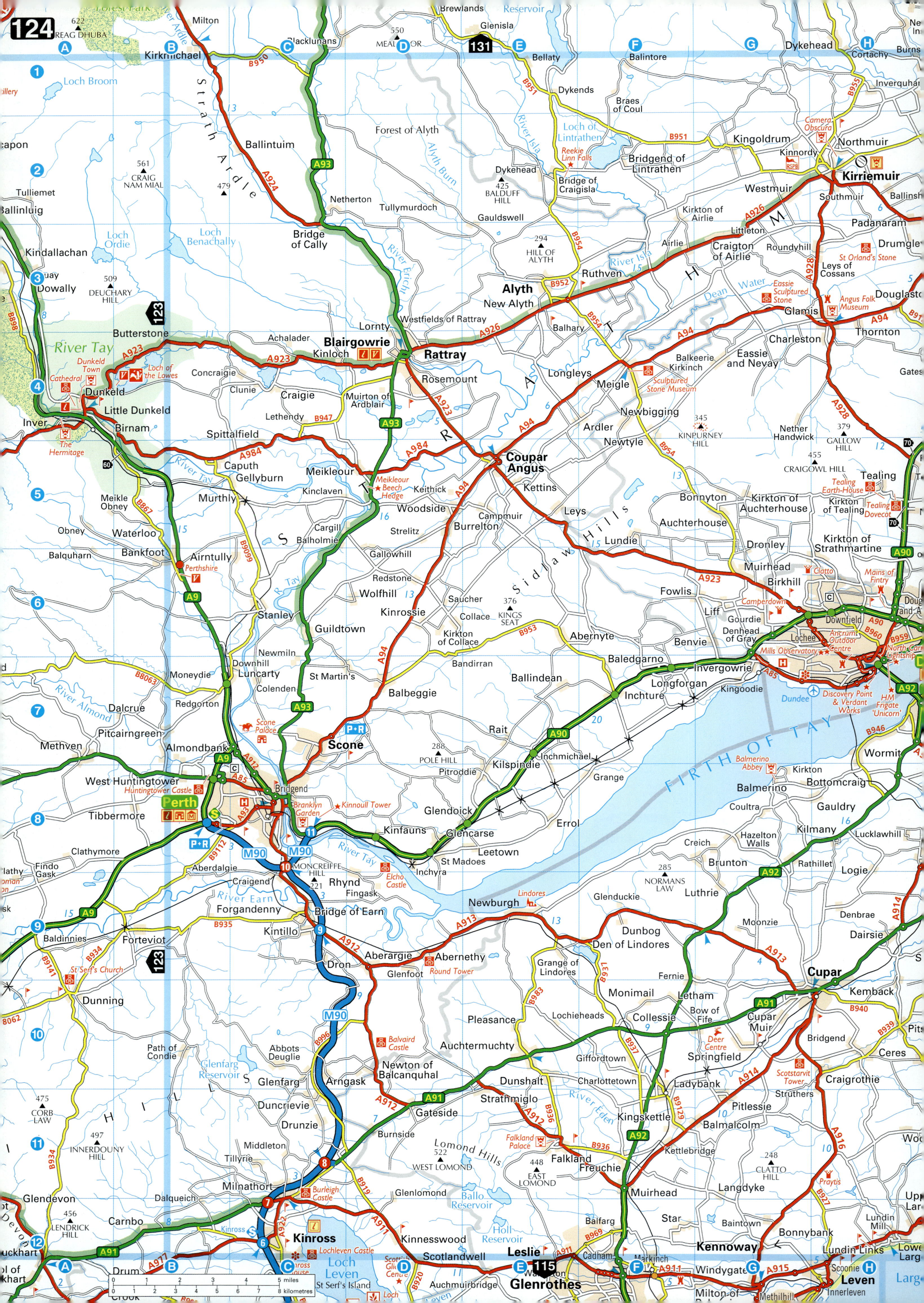
Milton
Kirkmichael
Blacklunans
Brewlands
Reservoir
Glenisla
131
Bellaty
Balintore
Dykehead
Cortachy
Strath Ardle
Loch Broom
Forest of Alyth
Alyth Burn
River Isla
Dykends
Braes of Coul
Loch of Lintrathen
Reekie Linn Falls
Kingoldrum
Camera Obscura
Northmuir
Kinnordy
Kirriemuir
Bridgend of Lintrathen
Ballintuim
561 CRAIG NAM MIAL
479
Tulliemet
Ballinluig
Netherton
Tullymurdoch
Dykehead
425 BALDUFF HILL
Bridge of Craigisla
Westmuir
Southmuir
Padanaram
Gauldswell
Kirkton of Airlie
Loch Ordie
Loch Benachally
Bridge of Cally
River Ericht
294 HILL OF ALYTH
Littleton
Airlie
Craigton of Airlie
Roundyhill
Drumgley
Kindallachan
509 DEUCHARY HILL
Dowally
Alyth
New Alyth
Ruthven
River Isla
Leys of Cossans
St Orland's Stone
Dean Water
Eassie Sculptured Stone
Glamis
Angus Folk Museum
Douglastown
Thornton
Butterstone
River Tay
Dunkeld Town
Cathedral
Loch of the Lowes
Achalader
Blairgowrie
Kinloch
Lornty
Westfields of Rattray
Rattray
Rosemount
Balhary
Longleys
Meigle
Balkeerie
Kirkinch
Eassie and Nevay
Charleston
Sculptured Stone Museum
Dunkeld
Little Dunkeld
Inver
Birnam
The Hermitage
Concraigie
Clunie
Craigie
Lethendy
Muirton of Ardblair
Newbigging
Ardler
Newtyle
345 KINPURNEY HILL
Nether Handwick
379 GALLOW HILL
455 CRAIGOWL HILL
Spittalfield
Caputh
Gellyburn
River Tay
Meikleour
Meikleour Beech Hedge
Kinclaven
Keithick
Coupar Angus
Kettins
Tealing
Tealing Earth-House
Kirkton of Tealing
Tealing Dovecot
Meikle Obney
Murthly
Woodside
Cargill
Balholmie
Campmuir
Burrelton
Leys
Bonnyton
Kirkton of Auchterhouse
Auchterhouse
Obney
Waterloo
Strelitz
Sidlaw Hills
Lundie
Dronley
Kirkton of Strathmartine
Balquharn
Bankfoot
Airntully
Perthshire
Gallowhill
Redstone
Muirhead
Birkhill
Claypotts Castle
Mains of Fintry
Wolfhill
Kinrossie
Saucher
Collace
376 KINGS SEAT
Kirkton of Collace
Fowlis
Liff
Camperdown
Gourdie
Denhead of Gray
Benvie
Lochee
Downfield
Stanley
Guildtown
Abernyte
Baledgarno
Camperdown Outdoor Centre
Mills Observatory
North Carr Lightship
Newmiln
Downhill
Luncarty
Moneydie
Colenden
St Martin's
Bandirran
Ballindean
Invergowrie
Longforgan
Inchture
Kingoodie
Dundee
Discovery Point & Verdant Works
HM Frigate 'Unicorn'
River Almond
Dalcrue
Redgorton
Pitcairngreen
Scone Palace
Balbeggie
Rait
Methven
Almondbank
Scone
288 POLE HILL
Pitroddie
Kilspindie
Inchmichael
Grange
FIRTH OF TAY
Wormit
Balmerino Abbey
Kirkton
Bottomcraig
Balmerino
West Huntingtower
Huntingtower Castle
Perth
Bridgend
Branklyn Garden
Kinnoull Tower
Glendoick
Errol
Coultra
Gauldry
Tibbermore
Kinfauns
Glencarse
Hazelton Walls
Kilmany
Lucklawhill
Clathymore
M90
MONCREIFFE HILL
River Tay
Elcho Castle
Leetown
St Madoes
Inchyra
Creich
Brunton
Rathillet
Findo Gask
Aberdalgie
Craigend
221
Rhynd
Fingask
285 NORMANS LAW
Logie
River Earn
Forgandenny
Bridge of Earn
Newburgh
Lindores
Glenduckie
Luthrie
Moonzie
Denbrae
Dairsie
Baldinnies
Forteviot
Kintillo
Aberargie
Abernethy
Round Tower
Glenfoot
Dron
Grange of Lindores
Dunbog
Den of Lindores
Fernie
Cupar
Kemback
St Serf's Church
Dunning
Monimail
Letham
Bow of Fife
Collessie
Cupar Muir
Pleasance
Lochieheads
Pitscottie
Path of Condie
Abbots Deuglie
Balvaird Castle
Auchtermuchty
Giffordtown
Deer Centre
Springfield
Bridgend
Ceres
Glenfarg Reservoir
Glenfarg
Arngask
Newton of Balcanquhal
Dunshalt
Charlottetown
Ladybank
Scotstarvit Tower
Craigrothie
Struthers
475 CORB LAW
Duncrievie
Gateside
Strathmiglo
River Eden
Kingskettle
Pitlessie
Balmalcolm
Drunzie
Burnside
497 INNERDOUNY HILL
Middleton
Lomond Hills
522 WEST LOMOND
Falkland Palace
448 EAST LOMOND
Falkland
Freuchie
Kettlebridge
248 CLATTO HILL
Tillyrie
Praytis
Glendevon
Milnathort
Dalqueich
Glenlomond
Burleigh Castle
Ballo Reservoir
Muirhead
Langdyke
456 LENDRICK HILL
Carnbo
Kinross
Balfarg
Star
Baintown
Bonnybank
Lundin Mill
Kinnesswood
Holl Reservoir
Lochleven Castle
Scotlandwell
Leslie
Cadham
Markinch
Kennoway
Lundin Links
Drum
Loch Leven
St Serf's Island
Auchmuirbridge
115
Glenrothes
Windygates
Scoonie
Leven
Innerleven
Methilhill
Milton of
A93
A924
B950
A926
B951
B954
B952
A94
A923
A984
B947
A9
A912
A85
B935
B934
M90
A91
B996
A977
B919
A911
A913
A92
A90
A914
B940
B939
A916
B936
B937
B9129
B969
A915
B920
B8063
B9099
B867
B9112
B953
A928
B946
B960
B959
5 miles
8 kilometres

Fern
Careston
Maison Dieu Chapel (ruin)
Trinity
Hillside
Brechin
Brechin Castle & Pictavia
Dun
House of Dun
Montrose
Air Station
Montrose Basin
Caledonian Railway
Haughs of Kinnaird
Barnhead
Maryton
Scurdie Ness
Ferryden
Craig
Usan
Noran Water
River South Esk
Tannadice
Murthill
Doocot
Finavon
Netherton
Crosston
Oathlaw
Sculptured Stones
Aberlemno
Battledykes
Mains of Melgunds
Farnell
Westerton of Rossie
Kemp's Castle
Lunanhead
Restenneth Priory
Reswallie
Forfar Loch
Forfar
Kingsmuir
Burnside
Dunnichen
Bowriefauld
Letham
Pitmuies
Guthrie
Bolshan
Wuddy Law
Glasterlaw
Kinnell
Braehead
Boddin Point
Lunan
Lunan Bay
Lunan Water
Friockheim
Boysack
Inverkeilor
Red Head
Craichie
Leysmill
Chapelton
Cauldcots
Letham Grange
Colliston
Redford
Marywell
Inverarity
Whigstreet
Greystone
Kirkbuddo
Carmyllie
Hatton
Condor
St Vigeans
Auchmithie
Carlingheugh Bay
The Deil's Head
Gallowfauld
Hayhillock
Elliot Water
Arbroath
Arbirlot
Bonnington
Crombie
Carrot Hill
Monikie
Kirkton of Monikie
Craigton
Muirdrum
Wellbank
Newbigging
Carlungie Earth House
Ardestie Earth-House
Kellas
Murroes
Upper Victoria
Barry Mill
Barry
East Haven
Panbride
West Haven
Carnoustie
Baldovie
Claypotts Castle
Monifieth
Barnhill
Broughty Ferry
Broughty Castle
Dundee
Buddon Ness
Tayport
Tentsmuir Point
Newport-on-Tay
Scottish National Golf Centre
Leuchars
RAF Leuchars
St Andrews Bay
Guardbridge
River Eden
Kincaple
St Andrews
Castle
Botanic Garden
Craigtoun
Brownhills
Boarhills
Kingsbarns
Cameron Reservoir
Dunino
Balcomie Links
Fife Ness
Radernie
Baldinnie
Peat Inn
Lathones
Kingsmuir
Scotland's Secret Bunker
Crail
Largoward
Lochty
Carnbee
Kellie Castle
Easter Pitkierie
Arncroach
Wester Pitkierie
Kilrenny
Cellardyke
Colinsburgh
Newton of Balcormo
Fisheries
Anstruther
Pittenweem
Kilconquhar
St Monans
Drumeldrie
Earlsferry
Elie
Dundee
St Andrews
A92
A90
A94
A932
A933
A934
A935
A926
A91
A915
A917
A930
B9127
B961
B978
B9128
B9113
B9134
B940
B941
B942
B939
B9131
B945
B9171

134
119
118
Loch Brittle
894
GARS BHEINN
225
CEANN NA BEINNE
Rudh' an Dùnain
Soay Sound
139
BEINN BHREAC
Mol-chlach
SOAY
Rudh' Aonghais
CUILLIN SOUND
CANNA
210
CÀRN A' GHAILL
A'Chill
Canna Harbour
Garrisdale Point
Sanday
Sound of Canna
Rudha Shamhnan Insir
302
MULLACH MÓR
Rudha na Roinne
Kinloch
Loch Scresort
A Bhrideanach
570
ORVAL
RÙM
810
ASKIVAL
763
SGÙRR NAN GILLEAN
Rudha nam Meirleach
The Small Isles
Oigh-sgeir
Sound of Rum
Bay of Laig
Laig
Rudha an Fhasaidh
EIGG
393
AN SGÙRR
Sound of Eigg
Eilean nan Each
MUCK
Port Mor
Sanna Point
Sanna Bay
Sanna Bay
Portuairk
Achnaha
Ardnamurchan Point
Achosnich
B8007
342
BEINN NA SEILG
Bagh a Chaisteil (Castlebay)
Loch Baghasdail (Lochboisdale)
Eilean Mòr
Rudha Mòr
Rudha Sgor-innis
Bousd
Sorisdale
B8072
Cliad Bay
COLL
Arnabost
Grishipoll
B8071
Arinagour
Coll - Oban
Ardmore Point
Sorne Point
Glengorm Castle
Quinish Point
5 miles
8 kilometres

Kirkibost
B8083
Loch Slapin
300 BEINN NAN CÀRN
Heast
135
Loch Scavaig
344 BEN MEABOST
Suisnish
Rudha Suisnish
Loch Eishort
Drumfearn
561 BEINN NA SEAMRAIG
BEN ASLAK
Glenelg Bay
Eilanreach
Glenelg Brochs
Glean Beag
Balvraid
Elgol
Glasnakille
298 SGORACH BREAC
Duisdalemore
Isleornsay
Loch na Dal
Ornsay
Sandaig Island
974 BEINN SGRITHEAL
773 BEINN NAN CAORACH
Tokavaig
Ord River
Strathaird Point
Rudha Buidhe
Loch Hourn
Arnisdale
Glen Arnisdale
Corran
Tarskavaig
Tarskavaig Bay
Achnacloich
Loch nam Uamph
Teangue
Knock
Ferrindonald
Kilmore
Kilbeg
Knock Bay
SOUND OF SLEAT
Rudh' Ard Slisneach
614
709 DRUM FADA
Inverguseran
784 BEINN NA CAILLICH
Barrisdale Bay
Glen Guseran
Clan Donald
A851
Ardvasar
Armadale
Calligarry
Airor
518 DRUIM NA CLUAIN-AIRIDHE
1019 LADHAR BHEINN
128
Sandaig
Knoydart
KNOYDART
Aird of Sleat
Sandaig Bay
Inverie
940 LUINNE BHEINN
Loch an Dubh-Lochain
Ard Thurinish
Point of Sleat
Rudha Raonuill
Inverie Bay
Courteachan
Mallaig (Malaig)
Mallaigvaig
547 CÀRN A'GHOBHAIR
Loch Nevis
854 BEINN BHUIDHE
1039 SGURR NA CICHE
Glasnacardoch Bay
Loch an Nostaire
437 SGURR BHUIDHE
Beoraidbeg
Morar
Bracorina
Bracora
Kylesmorar
859 SGURR NAH-AIDE
723 SGARR BREAC
Tarbet
Swordland
Glenancross
Loch Morar
B8008
A830
Lettermorar
503 CÀRN A' MHADAIDH-RUAIDH
716 AN STAC
Meoble
949 SGURR NAN COIREACHAN
Eilean Ighe
Bunacaimb
Back of Keppoch
Loch nan Ceall
Arisaig
Luinga Mhòr
600 SIDHEAN MOR
River Meoble
710 MEITH BHEINN
Kildonnan
Rudh' Arisaig
103 CRUACH DOIRE
Druimindarroch
Arisaig House
Prince Charlie's Cairn
Kinlochnanuagh
Loch Beoriad
633
796 SGURR AN UTHA
Glen Finnan
Eilean Chathastail
Loch nan Uamh
Polnish
Lochailort
Inveraitort
Loch Eilt
A830
Glenfinnan
Glenfinnan Monument
Sound of Arisaig
Rudha Chaolais
Ardnish
Loch Ailort
A861
877 ROIS-BHEINN
882 BEINN ODHAR BHEAG
Smearisary
Glenuig
712
664 BEINN GAIRE
718 MEALL NAM DAM
Eilean Shona
Loch Shiel
Rudha Aird Druimnich
Kinlochmoidart
Glen Forsian
Scamodale
758 MEALL MÒR
Ockle Point
Loch Moidart
Tioram
239 BEINN BHREAC
Ardmolich
Brunery
Glen Moidart
754 SGOR AN TARMACHAIN
Morar, Moidart and Ardnamurchan
MOIDART
Kilmory
Ockle
Ardtoe
Shielfoot
Dalnabreck
Loch Shiel
Glen Hurich
356 BEINN BHREAC
B8044
Blain
Dalelia
Branault
Kentra
Mingarrypark
Loch Doilet
888 SGURR DHOMHNUILL
436 MEALL NAN CON
Arevegaig
Polloch
ARDNAMURCHAN
Acharacle
Claish Moss
437
SUNART
Loch Mudle
A861
846 BEINN RESIPOL
Kilchoan
Salen
Resipole
Ariundle Oakwood
Mingary
527 BEN HIANT
Glenbeg
512 BEN LAGA
B8007
Loch Sunart
Anaheilt
884 GARBH BHEINN
Glencripesdale
Glenborrodale
Laga
339 GEARR CHREAG
Woodend
Strontian
Achnalea
Ardslignish
Camasine
Ardnastang
A861
Camasachoirce
Glen Tarbert
Carna
Oronsay
Aulist Point
119
120
Liddesdale
A884
620
853

Glenelg
Balvraid
Glenelg Brochs
Glean Beag
BEINN A' CHAOINICH
Moyle
Mam Ratagan
Shiel Bridge
FIVE SISTERS
Glen Shiel
Kintail
BEN ATTOW
136
SGURR FHUARAN
CISTE DHUBH
MULLACH FRAOCH-CHOIRE
AONACH SHASUINN
A'CHRALAIG
SQÙRR A'BHEALAICH
SGURR NAN CONBHAIREAN
River Doe
THE SADDLE
BEINN SGRITHEAL
BEINN NAN CAORACH
SGURR NA SGINE
A87
Cluanie Inn
Cluanie Lodge
Loch Cluanie
Ceannacroc Lodge
Loch Hourn
Arnisdale
Glen Arnisdale
Corran
DRUM FADA
Kinloch Hourn
AONACH AIR CHRITH
CREAG A'MHAIM
SGURR A MHAORAICH
Barrisdale Bay
GLEOURAICH
SPIDEAN MIALACH
Glenquoich Forest
Loch Loyne
Glen Loyne
LADHAR BHEINN
127
Knoydart
KNOYDART
LUINNE BHEINN
Loch an Dubh-Lochain
Loch Quoich
Glen Garry
Inchlaggan
Glen Garry
Tomdoun
Greenfield
River Garry
GAIRICH
Glen Kingie
River Kingie
SGURR MÒR
GLAS BHEINN
BEINN BHUIDHE
SGURR NA CICHE
Glengarry Forest
MEALL BLÀIR
SGURR MHURLAGAIN
Loch Blair
MEALL COIRE NAN SAOBHAIDH
Kylesmorar
SGARR BREAC
SGURR NAH-AIDE
Glen Dessarry
Murlaggan
Caonich
Loch Arkaig
Gleann Cia-aig
Glen Pean
Ardechive
AN STAC
Meoble
MEITH BHEINN
SGURR NAN COIREACHAN
SGÙRR THUILM
GULVAIN
Glen Mallie
Clunes
Achnacarry
Clan Cameron
Bunarkaig
MEALL A' PHUBUILL
BEINN BHAN
Great Glen Way
B8005
A82
Loch Beoriad
SGURR AN UTHA
Glen Finnan
Gleann Dubhlighe
Gleann Fionnlighe
Glen Loy
Gairlochy
Stronenaba
B8004
Loch Eilt
A830
Glenfinnan
Glenfinnan Visitor Centre
Glenfinnan Monument
STOB A' GHRIANAIN
Strone
Brackletter
Commando Memorial
Spean Bridge
Killiechonate
DRUIM FADA
Muirshearlich
Kinlocheil
Locheilside Station
Fassfern
Drimsallie
Loch Eil
River Loy
Torcastle
Nevis Range
BEINN ODHAR BHEAG
Garvan
Duisky
Blaich
A861
Treasures of the Earth
Neptune's Staircase (Locks)
Corpach
Banavie
Caol
B8006
River Lundy
SGÙRR FINNISG-AIG
Inverlochy Castle
Glen Garvan
MEALL NAM DAMH
Camusnagaul
Trislaig
Fort William
(An Gearasdan)
Loch Shiel
Scamodale
MEALL MÒR
Cona Glen
STOB COIRE A'CHEARCAILL
Auchintore
Glen Nevis House
AONACH MÒR
BEN NEVIS
AONACH BEAG
SGOR AN TARMACHAIN
Druimarbin
Loch Linnhe
Glen Nevis
Glen Hurich
Loch Doilet
Conaglen House
Blarmachfoldach
SGURR DHOMHNUILL
Glen Scaddle
Inverscaddle Bay
Coruanan
Achriabhach
Ben Nevis and Glen Coe
SUNART
Blàr a' Chaorainn
SGÙRR A'MHAIM
STOB BAN
BEINN NA GUCAIG
AM BODACH
NA GRUAGAICHEAN
BINNEIN MÒR
Ariundle Oakwood
Glen Gour
Ardgour
Clovulin
Corran
Mamore Forest
MAM NA GUALAINN
Anaheilt
Strontian
Achnalea
GARBH BHEINN
Onich
North Ballachulish
B863
Kinlochleven
West Highland Way
Ardnastang
Glen Tarbert
Inversanda
Lochaber Watersports Centre
Glencoe
Folk Museum
PAP OF GLENCOE
121
AONACH EAGACH
120
South Ballachulish
Kentallen
Glen Coe
0 1 2 3 4 5 miles
0 1 2 3 4 5 6 7 8 kilometres

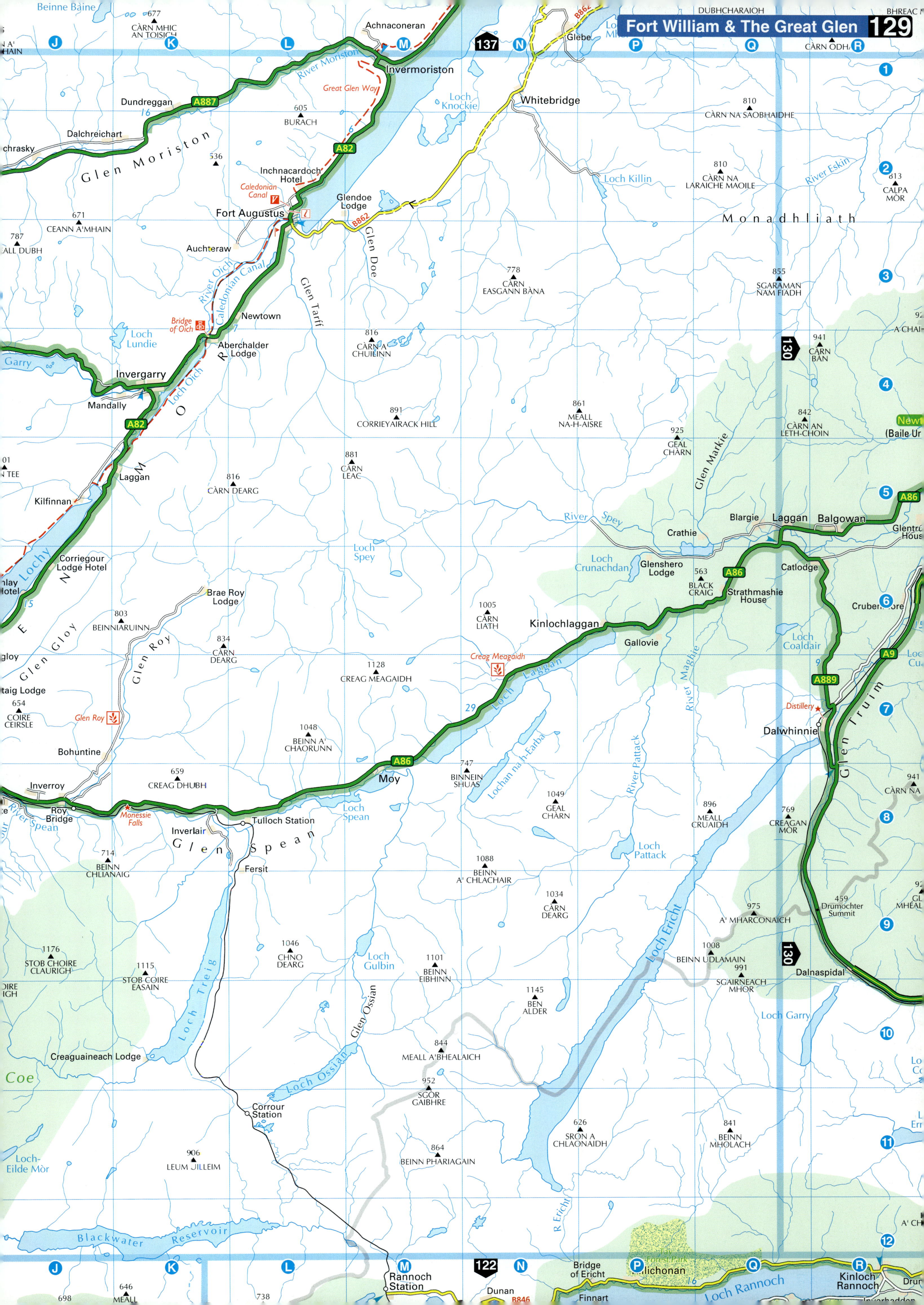

Beinne Bàine
677
CÀRN MHIC AN TOISICH
Achnaconeran
137
Glebe
B862
DUBHCHARAIOH
BHREAC
CÀRN ODHA
Invermoriston
River Moriston
Great Glen Way
Dundreggan
A887
605
BURACH
Loch Knockie
Whitebridge
810
CÀRN NA SAOBHAIDHE
Dalchreichart
chrasky
Glen Moriston
536
A82
Inchnacardoch Hotel
Caledonian Canal
Glendoe Lodge
Fort Augustus
B862
Loch Killin
810
CÀRN NA LARAICHE MAOILE
River Eskin
813
CALPA MÒR
Monadhliath
671
CEANN A'MHAIN
787
Auchteraw
Glen Doe
778
CÀRN EASGANN BÀNA
855
SGARAMAN NAM FIADH
River Oich
Caledonian Canal
Glen Tarff
Newtown
Bridge of Oich
Loch Lundie
816
CÀRN A' CHUILINN
941
CÀRN BÀN
130
Aberchalder Lodge
Garry
Invergarry
Loch Oich
Mandally
891
CORRIEYAIRACK HILL
861
MEALL NA-H-AISRE
842
CÀRN AN LETH-CHOIN
(Baile Ùr
925
GEAL CHÀRN
Glen Markie
Laggan
881
CÀRN LEAC
816
CÀRN DEARG
Kilfinnan
River Spey
Blargie
Laggan
Balgowan
A86
Crathie
Loch Spey
Loch Crunachdan
Glenshero Lodge
563
BLACK CRAIG
Catlodge
Strathmashie House
Corriegour Lodge Hotel
Loch Lochy
Brae Roy Lodge
1005
CÀRN LIATH
Kinlochlaggan
Gallovie
803
BEINNIARUINN
Glen Gloy
Glen Roy
834
CÀRN DEARG
Creag Meagaidh
1128
CREAG MEAGAIDH
Loch Coaldair
A9
A889
River Maghie
Distillery
Dalwhinnie
Glen Truim
654
COIRE CEIRSLE
Glen Roy
1048
BEINN A' CHAORUNN
Loch Laggan
Lochan na h-Earba
River Pattack
Bohuntine
659
CREAG DHUBH
A86
Moy
747
BINNEIN SHUAS
1049
GEAL CHÀRN
896
MEALL CRUAIDH
769
CREAGAN MÒR
941
CÀRN NA
Inverroy
Roy Bridge
River Spean
Monessie Falls
Inverlair
Tulloch Station
Loch Spean
Glen Spean
Loch Pattack
714
BEINN CHLIANAIG
Fersit
1088
BEINN A' CHLACHAIR
1034
CÀRN DEARG
459
Drumochter Summit
975
A' MHARCONAICH
1176
STOB CHOIRE CLAURIGH
1115
STOB COIRE EASAIN
Loch Treig
1046
CHNO DEARG
Loch Gulbin
1101
BEINN EIBHINN
Loch Ericht
1008
BEINN UDLAMAIN
991
SGAIRNEACH MHOR
130
Dalnaspidal
1145
BEN ALDER
Loch Garry
Glen Ossian
844
MEALL A'BHEALAICH
Creaguaineach Lodge
Coe
Loch Ossian
952
SGÒR GAIBHRE
Corrour Station
626
SRON A CHLAONAIDH
841
BEINN MHOLACH
Loch-Eilde Mòr
906
LEUM UILLEIM
864
BEINN PHARIAGAIN
R. Ericht
Blackwater Reservoir
Rannoch Station
122
Bridge of Ericht
Forest Park
Kinloch Rannoch
Loch Rannoch
646
MEALL
698
738
Dunan
B846
Finnart

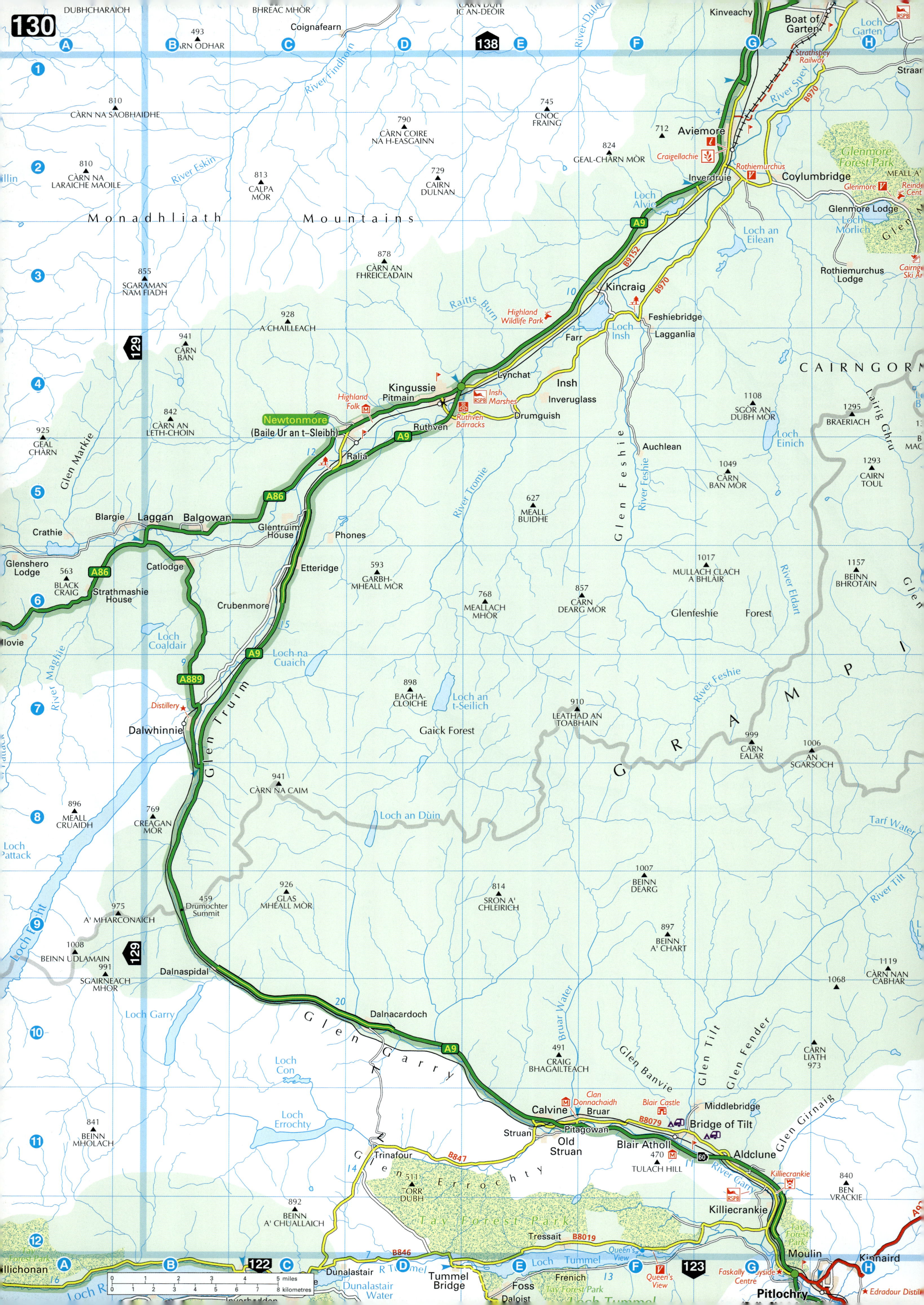
DUBHCHARAIOH
BHREAC MHÒR
493
ARN ODHAR
Coignafearn
138
Kinveachy
Boat of Garten
Loch Garten
RSPB
Strathspey Railway
Straan
A
B
C
D
E
F
G
H
1
2
3
4
5
6
7
8
9
10
11
12
River Findhorn
River Dulnain
810
CÀRN NA SAOBHAIDHE
790
CÀRN COIRE NA H-EASGAINN
745
CNOC FRAING
712
Aviemore
River Spey
B970
Glenmore Forest Park
810
CÀRN NA LARAICHE MAOILE
River Eskin
813
CALPA MÒR
729
CAIRN DULNAN
824
GEAL-CHÀRN MÒR
Craigellachie
Inverdruie
Rothiemurchus
Coylumbridge
Glenmore
MEALL A'
Reindeer Centre
Monadhliath
Mountains
Loch Alvie
A9
Glenmore Lodge
Loch Morlich
Loch an Eilean
Glen More
878
CÀRN AN FHREICEADAIN
855
SGARAMAN NAM FIADH
B9152
Rothiemurchus Lodge
Cairngorm Ski Area
Kincraig
B970
Raitts Burn
Highland Wildlife Park
928
A' CHAILLEACH
Feshiebridge
Loch Insh
Lagganlia
Farr
129
941
CÀRN BÀN
Lynchat
CAIRNGORM
Insh
Kingussie
Pitmain
Insh Marshes
Inveruglass
Highland Folk
Ruthven Barracks
Drumguish
1108
SGÒR AN DUBH MÒR
1295
BRAERIACH
Lairig Ghru
842
CÀRN AN LETH-CHOIN
Newtonmore
(Baile Ur an t-Sleibh)
Ruthven
A9
Loch Einich
925
GEAL CHÀRN
Glen Markie
Ralia
Auchlean
MAC
A86
River Tromie
Glen Feshie
River Feshie
1049
CÀRN BAN MÒR
1293
CAIRN TOUL
627
MEALL BUIDHE
Blargie
Laggan
Balgowan
Crathie
Glentruim House
Phones
Glenshero Lodge
563
BLACK CRAIG
A86
Catlodge
Etteridge
593
GARBH-MHEALL MÒR
1017
MULLACH CLACH A' BHLAIR
1157
BEINN BHROTAIN
River Eidart
Strathmashie House
768
MEALLACH MHÒR
857
CÀRN DEARG MÒR
Crubenmore
Glenfeshie
Forest
Glen
Loch Coaldair
llovie
A9
Loch na Cuaich
A889
River Mashie
898
BAGHA-CLOICHE
Loch an t-Seilich
River Feshie
Distillery
910
LEATHAD AN TOABHAIN
Dalwhinnie
Gaick Forest
Glen Truim
999
CÀRN EALAR
1006
AN SGARSOCH
GRAMPIAN
941
CÀRN NA CAIM
896
MEALL CRUAIDH
769
CREAGAN MÒR
Loch an Dùin
Tarf Water
Loch Pattack
1007
BEINN DEARG
River Tilt
926
GLAS MHEALL MÒR
814
SRÒN A' CHLEIRICH
459
Drumochter Summit
975
A' MHARCONAICH
897
BEINN A' CHAT
Loch Ericht
1008
BEINN UDLAMAIN
129
991
SGAIRNEACH MHOR
Dalnaspidal
1119
CÀRN NAN GABHAR
1068
Loch Garry
Bruar Water
Dalnacardoch
Glen Garry
A9
CÀRN LIATH
973
491
CRAIG BHAGAILTEACH
Glen Banvie
Glen Tilt
Glen Fender
Loch Con
Loch Errochty
Clan Donnachaidh
Calvine
Bruar
Blair Castle
Middlebridge
Glen Girnaig
B8079
Bridge of Tilt
841
BEINN MHÒLACH
Struan
Pitagowan
Old Struan
Blair Atholl
470
TULACH HILL
Aldclune
Trinafour
B847
River Garry
Killiecrankie
Glen Errochty
840
BEN VRACKIE
511
TORR DUBH
892
BEINN A' CHUALLAICH
Tay Forest Park
Killiecrankie
Tressait
B8019
B846
Loch Tummel
Queen's View
Moulin
Kinnaird
illichonan
Loch Rannoch
122
123
Dunalastair
R Tummel
Tummel Bridge
Foss
French
Tay Forest Park
Queen's View
Faskally Wayside Centre
Pitlochry
Edradour Distillery
Dunalastair Water
Dalchosnie
Loch Tummel
5 miles
8 kilometres

Milton
Delnabo
Dorback Lodge
River Nethy
606 CARN TUADHAM
803 CÀRN MÒR
656 MOSS HILL
Belnacraig
Kirkton of Glenbuchat
Glenbuchat Castle
Glenkindie
Towie
718 THE SOCACH
637 Lecht Summit
Lecht Ski Area
Strathdon
Bellabeg
Forbestown
Roughpark
821 GEAL CHÀRN
803 CARN BHEADHAIR
792 CARN EALASAID
710 CRAIG VEANN
Heughhead
Boltenston
Garchory
Milltown
Cock Bridge
Corgarff Castle
Corgarff
730 MAIM SUIM
741 BIG GARVOUN
River Avon
CAIRNGORMS NATIONAL PARK
Glen Avon
713 THE BRUACH
749 MONA GOWAN
1245 CAIRN GORM
829 BROWN COW HILL
744 CARN A' BHACAIN
872 MORVEN
Logie Coldstone
Loch Builg
1083 BEINN A CHAORRUINN
1196 NORTH TOP
1171 BEN AVON
River Gairn
MOUNTAINS
Muir of Dinnet
Candacraig
Cambus o' May
1084 CARN EAS
900 CULARDOCH
743 GEALLAIG HILL
Bridge of Gairn
Milton of Tullich
Coilacriech
1177 SOUTH TOP
930 BEINN BHREAC
Glen Derry
Balmoral Castle
Crathie
River Dee
Ballater
Pannanich Wells
Littlemill
618 MEALL GORM
Easter Balmoral
Balnacroft
Birkhall
531 BLACK C
Inver
Glen Lui
Linn of Dee
Quoich Water
Mar Lodge Estate
Allanaquoich
Braemar
Keiloch
600 CREAG NAN GALL
596 THE COYLES OF MUICK
699 CAIRN LEUCHAN
Water of Tanar
813 SGOR MÒR
Inverey
Glen Gelder
859 MORRONE HILL
Balmoral Forest
River Muick
Glen Muick
816 CARN LIATH
938 MOUNT KEEN
1154 LOCHNAGAR
720 FASHEILACH
Clunie Water
Loch Callater
1045 CAIRN TAGGART
Spittal of Glenmuick
Loch Muick
919 CARN BHAC
Glen Ey
886 SGOR MOR
Glen Clunie Lodge
996 BROAD CAIRN
Glen Mark
Baddoch Burn
1018 CÀRN AN TUIRC
832 EASTERBALLOCH
Glen Lee
Loch Lee
Glenshee Ski Area
Gleann Mòr
932 THE CAIRNWELL
670
1067 GLAS MAOL
Glen Doll
831 LAIR OF ALDARARIE
1050 GLAS TULAICHEAN
River Isla
Corrie Fee
896 BEN TIRRAN
739
928 MAYAR
946 DRIESH
Clova
Glen Lochsie
861 CARN AIT
805 BEN GULABIN
649 CAIRN OF BAMS
Glen Clova
867 MEALL A' CHOIRE BHUIDHE
Spittal of Glenshee
807 MONAMEANOCH
755 FINBRACKS
Rottal Lodge
903 BEN VUIRICH
Gleann Fearnach
Glen Shee
792 MEALL UAINE
700 DUCHRAY HILL
740 BADENDUN HILL
603 CAIRN DAUNIE
Glen Damff
Runtaleave
Cormuir
Glen Prosen
508
Presnerb
Glen Finlet
Pitcarity
River South Esk
490 NAKED TAM
Straloch
Enochdhu
Clackavoid
744 MOUNT BLAIR
Folda
Glencally
Tay Forest Park
River Ardle
Bridge of Brewlands
Backwater Reservoir
Glenisla
Glenquie
622 CREAG DHUBA
Milton
Blacklunans
550 MEALL MOR
Kirkmichael
Dykehead
Newmill
Inshewan
Burnside
Loch Broom
Dykends
Cortachy
Inverquharity
A939
A944
A97
A93
B976
B972
B9119
B955
B951
B950
139
132
124
J
K
L
M
N
P
Q
R

Kildrummy Castle
Kildrummy
Milltown
Montgarrie
Haughton House
Alford Valley Railway
Alford
Whitehouse
Keig
River Don
Pitfichie
Monymusk
Craigearn
Pitmunie
Belnacraig
Kirkton of Glenbuchat
Glenbuchat Castle
Bellabeg
Strathdon
Forbestown
Roughpark
Heughhead
Glenkindie
Towie
Sinnarhard
Muir of Fowlis
Kirkton of Tough
Tillyfourie
Cushnie
Boltenstone
Ordhead
Sauchen
Leochel-Cushnie
Craigievar Castle
BROOM HILL
PRESSENDY
BENAQUHALLIE
Corsindae
Comers
Tillybirloch
Marionburgh
Barmekin
Migvie
Crossroads
Tornaveen
MONA GOWAN
Tarland
Culsh Earth-House
CRAIGUCH
Lumphanan
Findrack House
Drumlasie
Logie Coldstone
Corrachree
Peel Ring of Lumphanan
Milltown of Learney
Landerb
MORVEN
Tomnaverie Stone Circle
Milton of Auchinhove
Coull
Auchlossan
HILL OF FARE
Ordie
Loch Davan
Torphins
Milltown of Campfield
Muir of Dinnet
Loch Kinord
Kincardine O'Neil
Mid Beltie
Candacraig
Cambus o' May
Dinnet
Aboyne
Brathens
Drumfrennie
Bridge of Gairn
Milton of Tullich
River Dee
Birsemore
Potarch
Upper Lochton
The Neuk
Coilacriech
Pannanich Wells Hotel
Birse
Marywell
Bridge of Canny
Banchory
Littlemill
Ballater
Glen Tanar
Bridge of Feugh
Royal Deeside Railway
BLACK CRAIG
TOM'S CAIRN
Bauld
SCOLTY HILL
Birkhall
Glen Tanar
CARNFERG
Finzean
Waulkmill
Strachan
Water of Tanar
THE COYLES OF MUICK
CAIRN LEUCHAN
CLACHAN YELL
HILL OF DUCHERY
Water of Feugh
Water of Aven
Glen Muick
River Muick
COCK CAIRN
PETER HILL
KERLOCH
MOUNT KEEN
HILL OF CAT
MOUNT SHADE
CLACHNABEN
Glen Dye
Bridge of Dye
FASHEILACH
Spittal of Glenmuick
MOUNT BATTOCK
Water of Dye
LEACHIE
Glen Mark
Water of Tarf
Glen Tennet
HILL OF FINGRAY
GOYLE HILL
Cairn O'Mount
Invermark
Tarfside
EASTERBALLOCH
Glen Lee
Loch Lee
Glenesk Folk
Auchenblae
FINELLA HILL
LAIR OF ALDARARIE
River North Esk
STURDY HILL
CRUYS
WEST KNOCK
BULG
Glen Esk
Mains of Balnakettle
Pittarrow
BEN TIRRAN
HILL OF WIRREN
Water of Saughs
Fettercairn
Mains of Haulkerton
Clova
Glen Clova
CAIRN OF BAMS
Hunthill Lodge
West Water
Gannachy
Bogmuir
FINBRACKS
Rottal Lodge
Edzell Castle & Garden
Sauchieburn
HILL OF GARBET
Bridgend
Balfield
Edzell
Edzell Woods
Luthermuir
Dykelands
Dunlappie
Brown Caterthun
White Caterthun
Glen Prosen
Pitcarity
River South Esk
NAKED TAM
Kirkton of Menmuir
Tigerton
Inchbare
Newtonmill
Marykirk
Craigo
Lochside
Logie Pert
Logie
Morphie
Auchnacree
Mains of Balhall
Little Brechin
Keithock
Glencally
Glenquiech
Shandford
Lochty
Maison Dieu Chapel (ruin)
Trinity
Hillside
Newmill of Inshewan
Fern
Careston
Brechin
House of Dun
Dun
Dykehead
Cortachy
Burnside
Noran Water
Tannadice
Brechin Castle & Pictavia
Caledonian Railway
Haughs of Kinnaird
Montrose
miles
kilometres

Newmachar
Whitecairns
Belhelvie
Balmedie
141
Kintore
Hatton of Fintray
Kinmundy
Cothal
Potterton
Cottown
Leylodge
Dyce Symbol Stones
Overton
Blackdog
Blackburn
Aberdeen
Dyce
Middleton Park
Denmore
Clinterty
Stoneywood
Kirkwall
Lerwick
Bucksburn
Bankhead
Bridge of Don
Skene House
Millbuie
Brimmond Hill
Northfield
Old Aberdeen
Loch of Skene
Westhill
Kingswells
Kittybrewster
Kirkton of Skene
Kingsford
Garlogie
Carnie
Elrick
ABERDEEN
Torry
Nigg Bay
Redhill
Cullerlie Stone Circle
Easter Ord
Blacktop
Ruthrieston
Mannofield
Benthoul
Cults
Bieldside
Kincorth
Milltimber
Nigg
Hardgate
Craigton
Milton of Murtle
Banchory-Devenick
Altens Haven
Cove Bay
Drum Castle
Charlestown
West Park
Peterculter
Kingcausie
Marywell
River Dee
Maryculter
Hillside
Auchlee
Findon
Durris
Denside
Portlethen
Woodlands
Cammachmore Bay
Downies
Cammachmore
Crossroads
Cookney
Newtonhill
Netherley
Skateraw
Muchalls
Doonie Point
Garron Point
Stonehaven Bay
Hill of Trusta
Kirktown of Fetteresso
Stonehaven
Elfhill
Dunnottar
Tannachie
New Mill
Drumlithie
Temple of Fiddes
Crawton
Fowlsheugh
Trelong Bay
Mondynes
Catterline
Kinneff
Todhead Point
Arbuthnott
Redmyre
Inverbervie
Bervie Bay
Gourdon
Redford
Benholm
Johnshaven
Bush
Milton Ness
St Cyrus
Aberdeen Harbour
Footdee
North Pier
Ferry Terminal
Aberdeen Station
Ferryhill
Torry
Aberdeen
Union Street
King Street
Union Square
Victoria Dock
Albert Basin
River Dee

A
B
C
D
E
F
G
H
1
2
3
4
5
6
7
8
9
10
11
12
North Duntulm
Duntulm
Kilmaluag
A855
Tairbeart (Tarbert)
Lùb Score
Skye Museum of Island Life
Flodigarry
Poldorais
Borneskitaig
Kilmuir
Heribusta
142
Kilvaxter
542
MEAL NA SUIREAMACH
Digg
Balgown
Brogaig
Loch nam Madadh (Lochmaddy)
Waternish Point
Linicro
Stenscholl
Totscore
464
BIODA BUIDHE
Trotternish
River Rha
Maligar
Ascrib Islands
Idrigill
Marishader
Uig
(Uige)
611
BEINN EDRA
River Conon
Uig Bay
283
BEN GEARY
Geary
Trumpan
Loch Snizort
Earlish
Ardmore Point
Gillen
Hallin
16
Peinlich
608
CREAG A' LAIN
A87
River Hinnisdal
DUNVEGAN HEAD
Isay
Mingay
Stein
Lusta
451
BEINN A' SGÀ
Loch Bay
214
BEN DIUBAIG
Greshornish House Hotel
Loch Greshornish
Kingsburgh
Loch Snizort Beag
Loch Dunvegan
Claigan
Romesdal
River Romesdal
Boreraig
Bay
22
Treaslane
Eyre
327
BEINN BHREAC
B886
Uig
Flashader
A850
Kensaleyre
River Haulton
Loch Pooltiel
Upperglen
Feriniquarrie
Totaig
Edinbane
Bernisdale
B8036
Oisgill Bay
Glendale
Milovaig
B884
Colbost
Dunvegan
A850
Tote
Carbost
Borve
Waterstein
Lephin
Colbost Croft
Toy
Dunvegan
Skeabost
Giant Angus MacAskill
Skinidin
Kilmuir
A864
Caroy River
265
BEN AKETIL
271
CRUACHAN BEINN A' CHEARCAILL
Uigshader
Drumuie
Neist Point
Lonmore
Moonen Bay
Roskhill
Glengrasco
469
HEALAVAL MORE
I
S
L
E
B885
Portree
Ramasaig
Orbost
Roag
Vatten
Seafield
Hoe Rape
Glen Ose
488
HEALAVAL BHEAG
Caroy
Harlosh
A863
417
BEINN NA GRÈINE
Loch
Hoe Point
Ose
Glenmore
368
BEINN NA BOINEID
Harlosh Island
Colbost Point
Loch Duagrich
Glenvarragill
Dun Beag
Bracadale
Tarner Island
Mugeary
Coillore
Struan
O
F
Loch Bracadale
Ullinish Lodge Hotel
Wiay
23
Idrigill Point
Oronsay
Loch Harport
Glen
Portnalong
439
ROINEVAL
Fiskavaig
B8009
S
Rudha nan Clach
Fernilea
369
ARNAVAL
Carbost
Drynoch
A863
K
Merkadale
Glen Drynoch
Y
Talisker Bay
Talisker
Sligachan
Glen Eynort
369
BEINN BHREAC
447
BEINN BHREAC
Grula
965
SGURR NAN GILLEAN
Loch Eynort
974
SGURR A' GHEADAIDH
434
AN CRUACHIN
Glenbrittle House
Cuillin Hills
1009
SGURR ALASDAIR
Bualintur
Loch Coruisk
894
GARS BHEINN
Loch Brittle
225
CEANN NA BEINNE
126
Rudh' an Dùnain
Soay Sound
139
BEINN
0 1 2 3 4 5 miles
0 1 2 3 4 5 6 7 8 kilometres

Longa Island
Loch Gairloch
Gairloch
Charlestown
Eilean Horrisdale
Port Henderson
B8056
Badachro
Opinan
South Erradale
MEALL AN DOIRENN
Loch Bad an Sgalaig
Loch Maree Hotel
Talladale
Eilean Flodigarry
Staffin Island
143
Redpoint
Staffin
Kilt Rock Waterfall
Ellishader
Red Point
Loch Ghaineamhach
Loch a' Ghobhainn
875 BAOSBHEINN
Loch na A-Oidhche
855
619 BEINN BHREAC
Loch a' Bhealaich
Valtos
Rudha nam Brathairean
Garros
Culnaknock
Loch a' Bhraige
Loch Torridon
Craig River
Rudha na Fearn
Fearnmore
Lower Diabaig
Loch Diabaig
985 BEINN ALLIGIN
914 BEINN DEARG
Lealt
Tote
A855
Òb Chuaig
Fearnbeg
136
Inveralligin
RONA
Arrina
Kenmore
Alligin Shuas
1024 LIATHACH
Torridon House
Torridon
Cuaig
Ardheslaig
Upper Loch Torridon
Callakille
Loch Shieldaig
Shieldaig
Countryside
Annat
Old Man of Storr
719 THE STORR
SOUND OF RAASAY
Eilean Tigh
Lonbain
492 AN GARBH-MHEALL
Wester Ross
493 CROIC-BHEINN
A896
Loch Damph
Loch Leathan
Eilean Fladday
902 BEINN DAMPH
933 MAOL CHEAN
Glenshieldaig Forest
Loch Fada
Manish Point
Loch Arnish
Torran
River Applecross
Loch Lundie
Arnish
INNER SOUND
A855
312
Brochel
Loch Coultrie
895 BEINN BHAN
730 SGURR A GHARAIDH
Applecross Bay
Applecross
Torvaig
RAASAY
Milton
626 Pass of the Cattle
774
SGÙRR A' CHAORACHAIN
Camusteel
Rassal Ashwood
Penifiler
412 BEN TIANAVAIG
Camusterrach
Bealach-Na-Ba
Aird Dhubh
Culduie
Kishorn
A896
Kirkton
Lochcarron
444 DÙN CAAN
Camastianavaig
Tianavaig Bay
Oskaig
Rudha na' Leac
Toscaig
River Toscaig
Loch Kishorn
Ardarroch
Achintraid
Slumbay
Ollach
B883
310 BEINN NA LEAC
Clachan
Kishorn Island
394 BAD A CHREAMHA
Strome
Inverarish
Caolas Mòr
Ardaneaskan
Ardnarff
The Braes
Eilean Meadhonach
Eilean Mòr
Loch Carron
Plockton
Stromeferry
A890
444 BEN LEE
Peinchorran
Suisnish Point
Eyre Point
Achmore
SCALPAY
CROWLIN ISLANDS
Sconser
Port-an-Eorna
67 Longay
Drumbuie
Duirinish
447 BEINN RAIMH
773 GLAMAIG
396 MULLACH NA CARN
Badicaul
Balmacara
Loch Long
A87
Loch Ainort
Dunan
Kyle of Lochalsh
(Caol Loch Aillse)
Auchtertyre
Conchra
Luib
Caolas Scalpay
27 Pabay
Skye Bridge
Lochalsh Woodland Garden
Nostie
Bundalloch
Carndu
564 GLAS BHEIN MHÒRN
Kyleakin
Kirkton
Ardelve
Eilean Donan
Dornie
A87
Broadford Bay
Loch Alsh
Keppoch
Cuillin Hills
732 BEINN NA CAILLICH
Corry
Lower Breakish
708 BEINN DEORG MHÒR
Broadford
Waterloo
Upper Breakish
Letterfearn
Loch Duich
B8083
Harrapool
Skulamus
732 SGURR NA COINNICH
Kyle Rhea
603 BEINN A' CHUIRN
927 BLAVEN
A851
Otter Haven
Bernera
Loch na Crèitheach
Torrin
Galltair
Kylerhea
605 BEN ASLAK
(Apr-Oct)
350 Mam Ratagan
Ratagan
Glenelg Bay
Glenelg
408 BEINN A' CHAOINICH
Moyle
300 BEINN NAN CARN
Eilanreach
Kirkibost
B8083
Loch Slapin
Heast
561 BEINN NA SEAMRAIG
Glenelg Brochs
Glen Beag
Balvraid
344 BEN MEABOST
Suisnish
127
Drumfearn
Rudha Suisnish
Loch Eishort
J K L M N P Q R
1 2 3 4 5 6 7 8 9 10 11 12

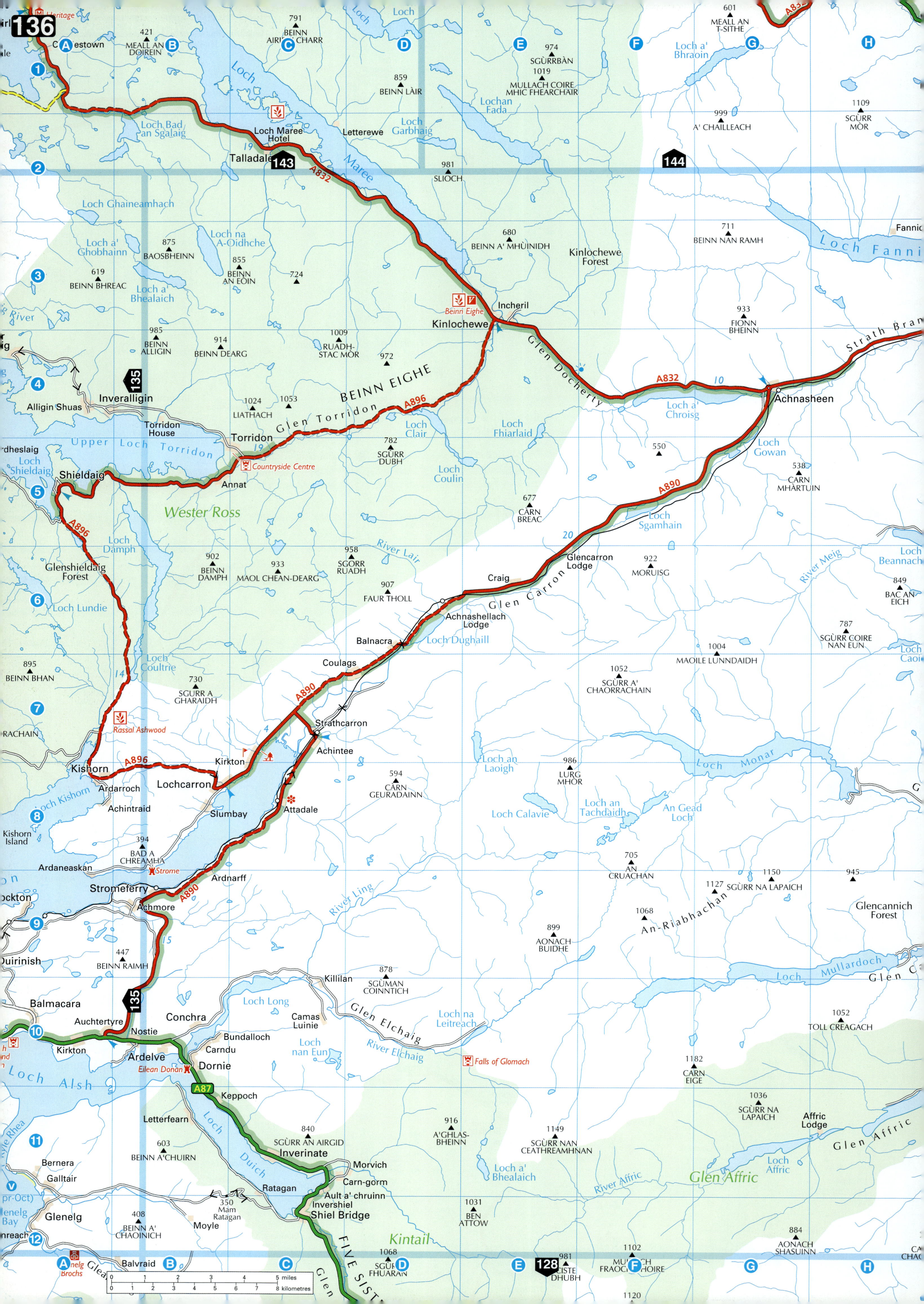
136
Heritage
Camestown
421
MEALL AN DOIREIN
791
BEINN AIRIGH CHARR
Loch
Loch
974
SGÙRR BÀN
1019
MULLACH COIRE MHIC FHEARCHAIR
601
MEALL AN T-SITHE
A832
Loch a' Bhraoin
859
BEINN LÀIR
Loch Maree
Lochan Fada
999
A' CHAILLEACH
1109
SGÙRR MÒR
Loch Bad an Sgalaig
Loch Maree Hotel
Letterewe
Loch Garbhaig
Talladale
143
144
A832
Maree
981
SLIOCH
Loch Ghaineamhach
Loch na A-Oidhche
680
BEINN A' MHÙINIDH
711
BEINN NAN RAMH
Fannich
Loch Fannich
Loch a' Ghobhainn
875
BAOSBHEINN
855
BEINN AN EOIN
724
619
BEINN BHREAC
Loch a' Bhealaich
Kinlochewe Forest
River
Beinn Eighe
Incheril
Kinlochewe
933
FIONN BHEINN
Strath Bran
985
BEINN ALLIGIN
914
BEINN DEARG
1009
RUADH-STAC MÒR
972
Glen Docherty
BEINN EIGHE
135
Inveralligin
Alligin Shuas
A896
1024
LIATHACH
1053
Glen Torridon
A832
10
Achnasheen
Loch a' Chroisg
Torridon House
Torridon
Loch Clair
Loch Fhiarlaid
Upper Loch Torridon
19
782
SGURR DUBH
550
Loch Gowan
rdheslaig
Loch Shieldaig
Shieldaig
Countryside Centre
Annat
Loch Coulin
538
CARN MHÀRTUIN
A890
Wester Ross
677
CARN BREAC
Loch Sgamhain
A896
Loch Damph
20
Loch Beannach
902
BEINN DAMPH
933
MAOL CHEAN-DEARG
958
SGORR RUADH
River Lair
Glencarron Lodge
922
MORUISG
River Meig
Glenshieldaig Forest
Craig
849
BAC AN EICH
907
FAUR THOLL
Glen Carron
Loch Lundie
Achnashellach Lodge
787
SGÙRR COIRE NAN EUN
Balnacra
Loch Dughaill
1004
MAOILE LUNNDAIDH
Loch Caoi
Loch Coultrie
Coulags
1052
SGURR A' CHAORRACHAIN
895
BEINN BHAN
14
730
SGURR A GHARAIDH
A890
Strathcarron
RACHAIN
Rassal Ashwood
4
Achintee
Loch an Laoigh
986
LURG MHOR
Loch Monar
Kishorn
A896
Kirkton
594
CARN GEURADAINN
Lochcarron
Ardarroch
Loch Kishorn
Achintraid
Slumbay
Attadale
Loch Calavie
Loch an Tachdaidh
An Gead Loch
Kishorn Island
394
BAD A CHREAMHA
Ardaneaskan
Strome
705
AN CRUACHAN
Ardnarff
1150
SGÙRR NA LAPAICH
945
1127
Stromeferry
ckton
A890
Achmore
River Ling
1068
An-Riabhachan
Glencannich Forest
899
AONACH BUIDHE
447
BEINN RAIMH
15
uirinish
878
SGÙMAN COINNTICH
Killilan
Loch Mullardoch
Glen Cannich
Balmacara
135
Loch Long
Camas Luinie
Conchra
Glen Elchaig
Loch na Leitreach
1052
TOLL CREAGACH
Auchtertyre
Nostie
Bundalloch
Carndu
Loch nan Eun
River Elchaig
Kirkton
Ardelve
Dornie
Falls of Glomach
Eilean Donan
1182
CARN EIGE
Loch Alsh
A87
Keppoch
1036
SGÙRR NA LAPAICH
Affric Lodge
Letterfearn
Loch Duich
Kyle Rhea
916
A' GHLAS-BHEINN
840
SGÙRR AN AIRGID
1149
SGÙRR NAN CEATHREAMHNAN
Glen Affric
603
BEINN A' CHUIRN
Invernate
Bernera
Morvich
Loch a' Bhealaich
Loch Affric
Galltair
Carn-gorm
River Affric
Glen Affric
Ratagan
Ault a' chruinn
350
Mam Ratagan
Inversheil
Shiel Bridge
1031
BEN ATTOW
Glenelg Bay
Glenelg
408
BEINN A' CHAOINICH
Moyle
Kintail
884
AONACH SHASUINN
Arnisdale
Balvraid
Glenelg Brochs
Glen
FIVE SISTERS
Glen
1068
SGÙRR FHUARAN
981
CISTE DHUBH
128
1102
MULLACH FRAOCH-CHOIRE
1120
5 miles
8 kilometres

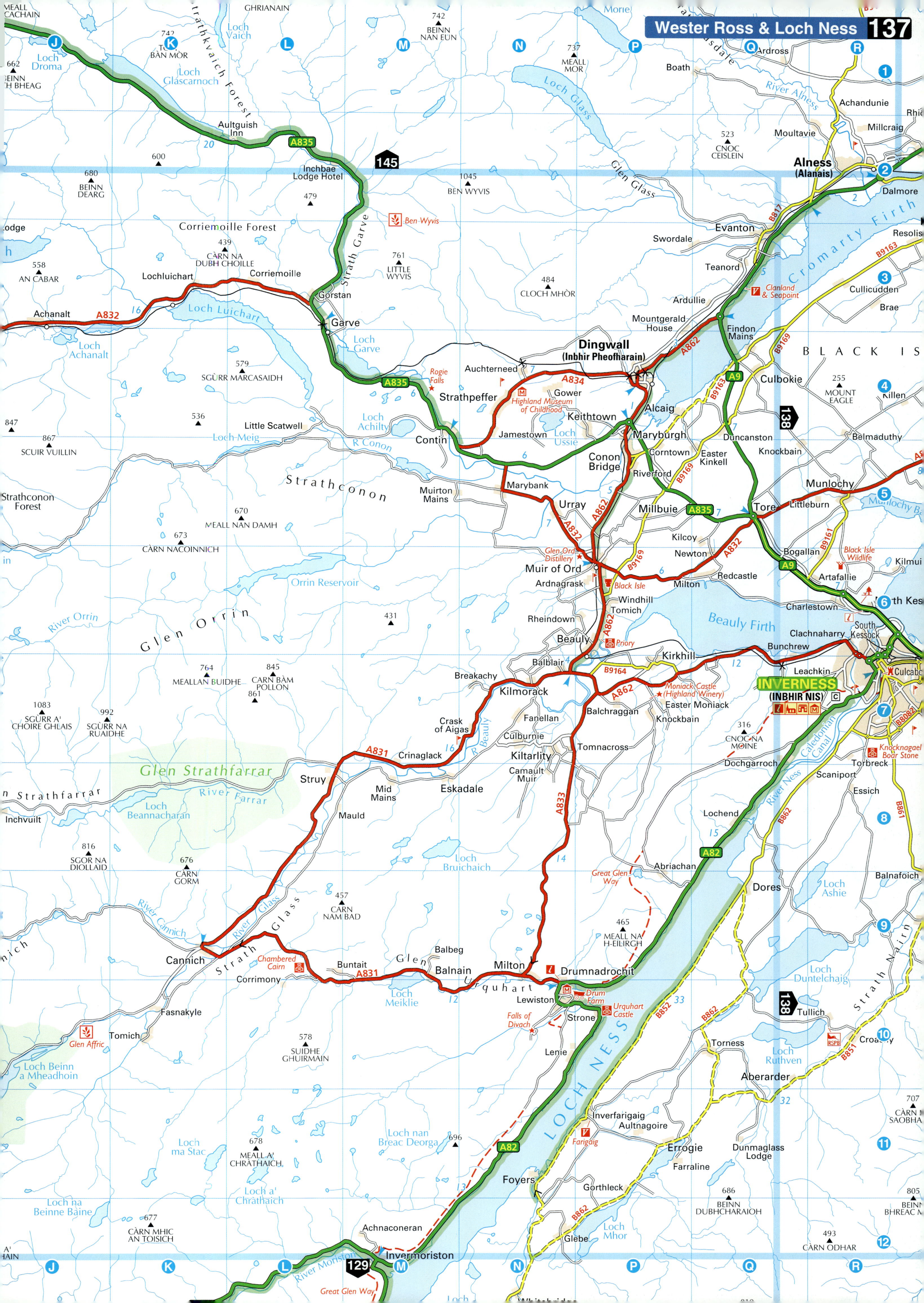

Loch Vaich
Loch Droma
Loch Glascarnoch
Strathvaich Forest
Aultguish Inn
A835
145
Inchbae Lodge Hotel
BEINN DEARG
BEN WYVIS
Ben Wyvis
Loch Glass
Glen Glass
Boath
Ardross
River Alness
Achandunie
Millcraig
Moultavie
CNOC CEISLEIN
Alness (Alanais)
Dalmore
Cromarty Firth
Evanton
Swordale
Teanord
Resolis
Clanland & Seapoint
Cullicudden
Brae
Corriemoille Forest
CÀRN NA DUBH CHOILLE
Corriemoille
Lochluichart
AN CABAR
Achanalt
A832
Loch Luichart
Loch Achanalt
Gorstan
Strath Garve
LITTLE WYVIS
CLOCH MHÒR
Garve
Loch Garve
SGÙRR MARCASAIDH
Ardullie
Mountgerald House
Findon Mains
Dingwall (Inbhir Pheofharain)
A862
A834
Auchterneed
Rogie Falls
Strathpeffer
Highland Museum of Childhood
Gower
Alcaig
Keithtown
Jamestown
Loch Ussie
Maryburgh
A9
Culbokie
BLACK ISLE
MOUNT EAGLE
Killen
138
Duncanston
Belmaduthy
Knockbain
Little Scatwell
Loch Meig
Loch Achilty
R Conon
Contin
SCUIR VUILLIN
Conon Bridge
Corntown
Easter Kinkell
Riverford
B9169
B9163
Strathconon
Strathconon Forest
Muirton Mains
Marybank
Urray
Millbuie
Tore
Littleburn
Munlochy
Munlochy Bay
MEALL NAN DAMH
CÀRN NACOINNICH
Kilcoy
Newton
Bogallan
B9161
Black Isle Wildlife
Glen Ord Distillery
Muir of Ord
Ardnagrask
Black Isle
Milton
Redcastle
Artafallie
Kilmuir
Orrin Reservoir
Windhill
Tomich
Charlestown
North Kessock
Rheindown
Beauly Firth
South Kessock
River Orrin
Glen Orrin
Beauly
Priory
Clachnaharry
Bunchrew
Balblair
Kirkhill
Leachkin
B9164
Culcabock
Breakachy
Kilmorack
Moniack Castle (Highland Winery)
INVERNESS (INBHIR NIS)
MEALLAN BUIDHE
CARN BÀM POLLOH
Balchraggan
Easter Moniack
SGÙRR A' CHOIRE GHLAIS
SGÙRR NA RUAIDHE
Fanellan
Knockbain
B8082
Crask of Aigas
R Beauly
Culburnie
CNOC NA MÒINE
Caledonian Canal
A831
Cringlack
Kiltarlity
Tomnacross
Dochgarroch
Knocknagael Boar Stone
Torbreck
Glen Strathfarrar
Stuy
Camault Muir
Scaniport
Strathfarrar
River Farrar
Mid Mains
Eskadale
River Ness
Essich
Inchvuilt
Loch Beannacharan
Mauld
A833
Lochend
B862
B861
SGOR NA DIOLLAID
CÀRN GORM
Loch Bruiachaig
Abriachan
A82
Balnafoich
Great Glen Way
Dores
Loch Ashie
CARN NAM BAD
River Cannich
River Glass
Strath Glass
MEALL NA H-EILRIGH
Strath Nairn
Cannich
Chambered Cairn
Buntait
Balbeg
Glen Urquhart
Balnain
Milton
Drumnadrochit
Corrimony
Loch Meiklie
Lewiston
Drum Farm
Urquhart Castle
Loch Duntelchaig
Fasnakyle
Falls of Divach
Strone
B852
Tullich
Glen Affric
Tomich
SUIDHE GHUIRMAIN
Lenie
Torness
Loch Ruthven
Croachy
B851
Loch Beinn a Mheadhoin
LOCH NESS
Aberarder
CARN SAOBHA
Loch nan Breac Deorga
Inverfarigaig
Aultnagoire
Loch ma Stac
MEALL A' CHRATHAICH
Farigaig
Errogie
Dunmaglass Lodge
Farraline
Loch a' Chrathaich
Foyers
Gorthleck
Loch na Beinne Baine
BEINN DUBHCHARAIOH
CÀRN MHIC AN TOISICH
Achnaconeran
Loch Mhor
Glebe
CÀRN ODHAR
Invermoriston
River Moriston
129
Great Glen Way

Ardross
River Alness
Achandunie
Moultavie
523
CNOC CEISLEIN
Millcraig
Rhicullen
Tomich
Achnagarron
Alness
(Alanais)
Dalmore
Delny
Kilmuir
Barbaraville
Balintraid
Saltburn
Invergordon
Pallchraggan
Kildary
Milton
Arabella
Fearn
Tullich
Hilton
Balintore
Shandwick Bay
Ankerville
Pitcalnie
Nigg
Nigg Bay
Nigg Ferry
(Jun-Oct)
Cromarty
Hugh Miller's Cottage
Newton
Navity
Upper Eathie
Cromarty Bay
Udale Bay
RSPB
Balblair
Resolis
Jemimaville
Allerton
Evanton
Swordale
Teanord
Ardullie
Mountgerald House
Clanland & Seapoint
Cullicudden
Brae
Cromarty Firth
Findon Mains
BLACK ISLE
255
MOUNT EAGLE
Culbokie
Killen
Raddery
Rosemarkie
Cathedral
Groam House
Fortrose
Fort George
Chanonry Point
Avoch
Whiteness Head
Nairn
(Inbhir Nàrann)
Tradespark
Ardersier
Moss-side
Househill
Boath Doocot
Auldearn
Foynesfield
Gollanfield
Culbin Forest
Kintes
Brodie Castle
Brodie
Whitemire
Conicavel
MORAY FIRTH
Alcaig
Maryburgh
Corntown
Riverford
Easter Kinkell
Duncanston
Knockbain
Belmaduthy
Munlochy
Munlochy Bay
Millbuie
Tore
Littleburn
Kilcoy
Newton
Redcastle
Milton
Bogallan
Black Isle Wildlife
Artafallie
Kilmuir
North Kessock
Charlestown
Beauly Firth
Clachnaharry
South Kessock
Bunchrew
Kirkhill
Leachkin
Moniack Castle (Highland Winery)
INVERNESS
(INBHIR NIS)
Easter Moniack
Knockbain
Culcabock
316
CNOC NA MOINE
Dochgarroch
Caledonian Canal
River Ness
Torbreck
Knocknagael Boar Stone
Scaniport
Essich
Milton of Leys
Fisherton
Castle Stuart
Easter Dalziel
Inverness (Dalcross)
Lochside
Clephanton
Cawdor
Piperhill
Righoul
Culcharry
Fornighty
Littlemill
Logie
Relu
Tornagrain
Croy
Newton
Cantraywood
River Nairn
Balloch
Culloden
Smithton
Resaurie
Culloden Battlefield & Visitor Centre
Clava Cairns
Culloden Viaduct
Kirkton of Barevan
Clunas
Redburn
Ardclach Bell Tower
Ferness
323
CÀRN MAOL
401
CÀRN A' CHRASGIE
Daviot House
Daviot
Drummossie Muir
548
BEINN BHUIDHE MHOR
609
CÀRN NAN TRI-TIGHEARNAN
Bridge of Dulsie
464
Lochindorb
Lochindorb Lodge
Lochend
Abriachan
Dores
Loch Ashie
Balnafoich
Loch Moy
Moy
River Findhorn
Farr
615
CÀRN NA H-EASGAINN
633
CÀRN AN T-SEAN-LIATHANAICH
Balvraid
Loch Duntelchaig
Strath Nairn
Tullich
Croachy
Torness
Loch Ruthven
Aberarder
Tomatin Distillery Visitor Centre
Findhorn Viaduct
Tomatin
Raigbeg
617
659
CÀRN GLAS-CHOIRE
485
CÀRN SGRIOB
600
BEINN BHREAC
603
CÀRN GLAC AN FICH
Findhorn Bridge
406
Slochd Summit
Clune
707
CÀRN NA SAOBHAIDH
Garbole
Strathdearn
Duthil
Bogroy
Carrbridge
Auchterblair
Landmark Forest Adventure Park
Drumuillie
Dunmaglass Lodge
Farraline
Erogie
Inverarnie
686
BEINN DUBHCHARAIDH
805
BEINN BHREAC MHÒR
617
CÀRN PHRIS MHÒIR
750
CÀRN DUH' IC AN-DEOIR
Dalnahaitnach
River Dulnain
Kinveachy
Boat of Garten
Loch Garten
Strathspey Railway
Coignafearn
493
CÀRN ODHAR
River Findhorn
146
137
130
A9
A96
A82
A832
A835
A862
A939
A938
A95
B817
B9175
B9163
B9169
B9160
B9161
B9092
B9006
B9039
B9091
B9090
B9101
B9177
B8082
B851
B861
B862
B852
B9154
B9007
B9153
0 1 2 3 4 5 miles
0 1 2 3 4 5 6 7 8 kilometres

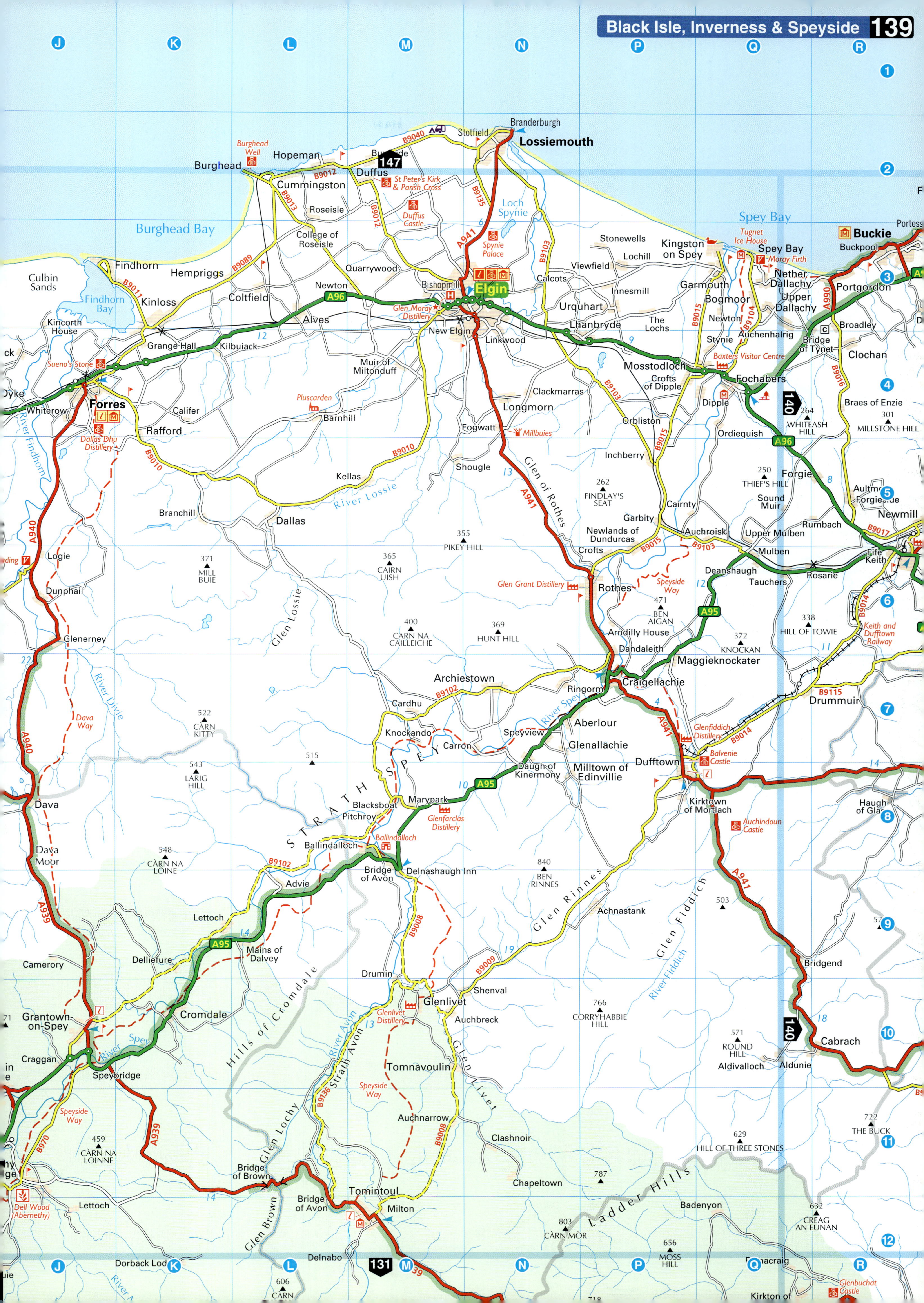
J
K
L
M
N
P
Q
R
Branderburgh
Stotfield
B9040
Lossiemouth
Burghead Well
Hopeman
Burghead
147
Duffus
B9012
Cummingston
St Peter's Kirk & Parish Cross
B9013
Roseisle
B9012
Duffus Castle
B9135
Loch Spynie
Spey Bay
Portessie
Burghead Bay
College of Roseisle
A941
Spynie Palace
B9103
Stonewells
Kingston on Spey
Tugnet Ice House
Buckie
Buckpool
Lochill
Spey Bay
Moray Firth
Culbin Sands
Findhorn
Hempriggs
B9089
Quarrywood
Viewfield
Calcots
Nether Dallachy
Portgordon
Findhorn Bay
B9011
Kinloss
Coltfield
Newton
A96
Bishopmill
Elgin
Innesmill
Garmouth
Upper Dallachy
A990
Urquhart
Bogmoor
B9015
Newton
B9104
Kincorth House
Alves
Glen Moray Distillery
Lhanbryde
The Lochs
Broadley
New Elgin
Stynie
Auchenhalrig
Bridge of Tynet
Grange Hall
Kilbuiack
Linkwood
Sueno's Stone
Muir of Miltonduff
Mosstodloch
Baxters Visitor Centre
Clochan
Crofts of Dipple
Fochabers
Dyke
Clackmarras
B9016
Whiterow
Forres
Califer
Pluscarden
Longmorn
Dipple
140
Braes of Enzie
Rafford
Barnhill
B9103
264 WHITEASH HILL
301 MILLSTONE HILL
River Findhorn
Dallas Dhu Distillery
Fogwatt
Millbuies
Orbliston
Ordiequish
A96
B9010
B9010
Shougle
Glen of Rothes
Inchberry
250 THIEF'S HILL
Forgie
Kellas
262 FINDLAY'S SEAT
Aultmore
Forgieside
River Lossie
Sound Muir
Branchill
Dallas
Cairnty
Newmill
Garbity
Rumbach
A940
355 PIKEY HILL
Newlands of Dundurcas
Auchroisk
Upper Mulben
B9017
371 MILL BUIE
365 CAIRN UISH
Crofts
B9015
B9103
Mulben
Fife Keith
Logie
Deanshaugh
Rosarie
Tauchers
Glen Grant Distillery
Rothes
Speyside Way
Dunphail
471 BEN AIGAN
A95
B9014
400 CARN NA CAILLEICHE
369 HUNT HILL
338 HILL OF TOWIE
Keith and Dufftown Railway
Glen Lossie
Arndilly House
372 KNOCKAN
Glenerney
Dandaleith
Maggieknockater
River Divie
Archiestown
Craigellachie
Ringorm
B9102
B9115
Cardhu
Drummuir
River Spey
Dava Way
522 CARN KITTY
Aberlour
Knockando
Speyview
Glenfiddich Distillery
B9014
A940
Carron
Glenallachie
A941
515
Balvenie Castle
543 LARIG HILL
STRATH SPEY
Daugh of Kinermony
Milltown of Edinvillie
Dufftown
A95
Dava
Marypark
Kirktown of Mortlach
Haugh of Glass
Blacksboat
Glenfarclas Distillery
Pitchroy
Auchindoun Castle
Dava Moor
Ballindalloch
548 CARN NA LOINE
Ballindalloch
B9102
Bridge of Avon
Delnashaugh Inn
840 BEN RINNES
Advie
A941
503
A939
Lettoch
Glen Rinnes
Achnastank
Glen Fiddich
B9008
A95
Mains of Dalvey
Camerory
Dellefure
Bridgend
Drumin
B9009
River Fiddich
Hills of Cromdale
Shenval
Glenlivet
766 CORRYHABBIE HILL
Grantown-on-Spey
Cromdale
River Avon
Glenlivet Distillery
Auchbreck
140
Cabrach
River Spey
Glen Livet
571 ROUND HILL
Craggan
Aldivalloch
Aldunie
Speybridge
Tomnavoulin
Strath Avon
Speyside Way
Speyside Way
B9136
Glen Lochy
Auchnarrow
722 THE BUCK
A939
459 CARN NA LOINNE
B970
B9008
Clashnoir
629 HILL OF THREE STONES
Bridge of Brown
787
Chapeltown
Ladder Hills
Tomintoul
Dell Wood (Abernethy)
Lettoch
Bridge of Avon
Milton
Badenyon
632 CREAG AN EUNAN
Glen Brown
803 CARN MÒR
656 MOSS HILL
Dorback Lodge
Delnabo
131
Fenacraig
606 CARN
Glenbuchat Castle
Kirkton of

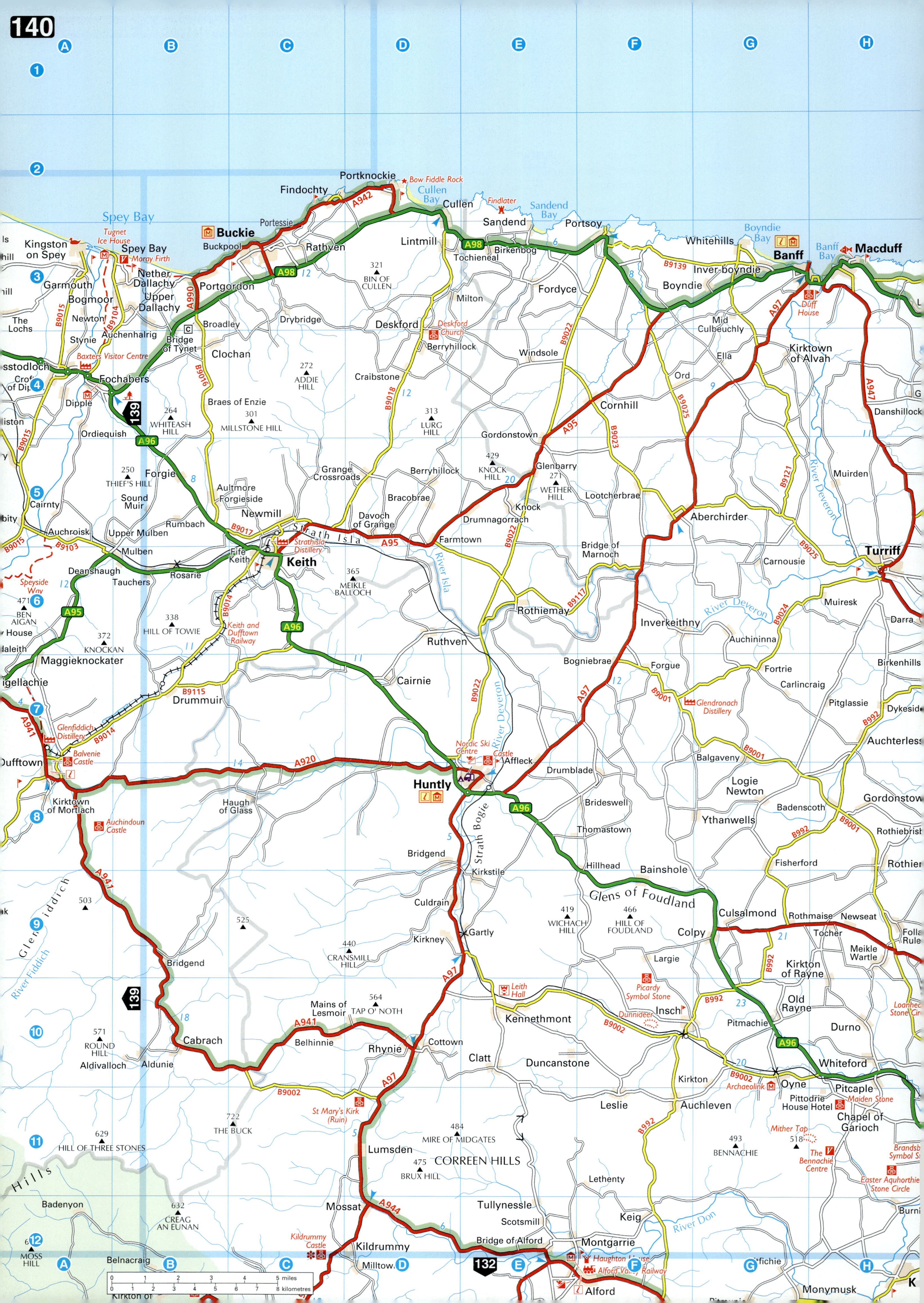
Spey Bay
Kingston on Spey
Tugnet Ice House
Spey Bay
Moray Firth
Garmouth
Bogmoor
Newton
Stynie
Auchenhalrig
The Lochs
Nether Dallachy
Upper Dallachy
Bridge of Tynet
Baxters Visitor Centre
Fochabers
Dipple
Ordiequish
Buckie
Buckpool
Portessie
Portgordon
Findochty
Portknockie
Bow Fiddle Rock
Cullen Bay
Cullen
Rathven
Lintmill
Findlater
Sandend Bay
Sandend
Portsoy
Birkenbog
Tochieneal
321 BIN OF CULLEN
Broadley
Drybridge
Clochan
Deskford
Deskford Church
Berryhillock
Milton
Fordyce
Windsole
Whitehills
Boyndie Bay
Banff
Banff Bay
Macduff
Inver-boyndie
Boyndie
Duff House
Mid Culbeuchly
Kirktown of Alvah
Ella
Ord
272 ADDIE HILL
Craibstone
Braes of Enzie
301 MILLSTONE HILL
264 WHITEASH HILL
313 LURG HILL
Cornhill
Danshillock
Gordonstown
429 KNOCK HILL
Glenbarry
271 WETHER HILL
Knock
Lootcherbrae
Aberchirder
Muirden
River Deveron
250 THIEF'S HILL
Forgie
Sound Muir
Cairnty
Aultmore
Forgieside
Newmill
Grange Crossroads
Berryhillock
Bracobrae
Davoch of Grange
Drumnagorrach
Auchroisk
Upper Mulben
Rumbach
Mulben
Strath Isla
Strathisla Distillery
Fife Keith
Keith
Farmtown
Bridge of Marnoch
Carnousie
Turriff
Deanshaugh
Tauchers
Rosarie
Speyside Way
471 BEN AIGAN
365 MEIKLE BALLOCH
River Isla
Rothiemay
River Deveron
Inverkeithny
Muiresk
Darra
338 HILL OF TOWIE
372 KNOCKAN
Keith and Dufftown Railway
Auchininna
Maggieknockater
Ruthven
Bogniebrae
Forgue
Fortrie
Birkenhills
Carlincraig
Cairnie
Drummuir
Glendronach Distillery
Pitglassie
Dykeside
Glenfiddich Distillery
Balvenie Castle
Dufftown
Nordic Ski Centre
Castle
Huntly
Affleck
Drumblade
Balgaveny
Logie Newton
Auchterless
Kirktown of Mortlach
Haugh of Glass
Brideswell
Badenscoth
Gordonstown
Auchindoun Castle
Strath Bogie
Thomastown
Ythanwells
Rothiebrisbane
Bridgend
Kirkstile
Hillhead
Bainshole
Fisherford
Rothienorman
Glen Fiddich
River Fiddich
503
525
Culdrain
Glens of Foudland
419 WICHACH HILL
466 HILL OF FOUDLAND
Culsalmond
Rothmaise
Newseat
Colpy
Tocher
Gartly
Kirkney
440 CRANSMILL HILL
Largie
Meikle Wartle
Bridgend
Picardy Symbol Stone
Kirkton of Rayne
Leith Hall
Old Rayne
564 TAP O' NOTH
Mains of Lesmoir
Kennethmont
Dunnideer
Insch
Pitmachie
Durno
571 ROUND HILL
Cabrach
Belhinnie
Rhynie
Cottown
Clatt
Duncanstone
Whiteford
Aldivalloch
Aldunie
Kirkton
Archaeolink
Oyne
Pitcaple
Maiden Stone
Pittodrie House Hotel
Chapel of Garioch
St Mary's Kirk (Ruin)
Leslie
Auchleven
722 THE BUCK
629 HILL OF THREE STONES
484 MIRE OF MIDGATES
Mither Tap
518
493 BENNACHIE
The Bennachie Centre
Lumsden
475 BRUX HILL
CORREEN HILLS
Lethenty
Easter Aquhorthies Stone Circle
Badenyon
632 CREAG AN EUNAN
Mossat
Tullynessle
Scotsmill
Keig
River Don
Kildrummy Castle
Kildrummy
Bridge of Alford
Montgarrie
Haughton House
Alford Valley Railway
MOSS HILL
Belnacraig
Milltown
Alford
Monymusk
A98
A942
A990
A96
A95
A97
A947
A920
A941
A944
B9015
B9104
B9016
B9018
B9022
B9023
B9025
B9139
B9121
B9017
B9103
B9014
B9115
B9117
B9024
B9001
B992
B9002
139
132
0 1 2 3 4 5 miles
0 1 2 3 4 5 6 7 8 kilometres

J
K
L
M
N
P
Q
R
1
2
3
4
5
6
7
8
9
10
11
12
Troup Head
Cullykhan Bay
Rosehearty
Castle Lighthouse & Museum
Kinnaird Head
Sandhaven
Pittulie
Fraserburgh
Gamrie Bay
Crovie
Pennan
Aberdour Bay
Craigiefold
Peathill
Kirktown
Fraserburgh Bay
Cairnbulg
Inverallochy
Gardenstown
Silverford
Dubford
Protstonhill
Percyhorner
Coburby
Pitblae
Maggie's Hoosie
Whitelinks Bay
Mid Ardlaw
B9031
B9033
St Combs
Gamrie
New Aberdour
Boyndlie
B9032
Memsie
A90
A98
Clenerty
Minnonie
Memsie Cairn
Rathen
Crofts of Savoch
Netherbrae
221
BRACKLAMORE HILL
Newburgh
Lonmay
A981
Rattray Head
Loch of Strathbeg
234
WAUGHTON HILL
Crimond
Blackhill
B9105
New Pitsligo
B9093
Strichen
A952
Fintry
New Byth
New Leeds
Bonnykelly
Leys
Garmond
B9027
Denhead
Backfolds
Kirktown
St Fergus
Fetterangus
Cuminestown
A950
Rora
Deer Abbey
Dunshillock
River Ugie
B9170
Maud
B9106
Aden
Mintlaw
Longside
Inverugie
Buchanhaven
Peterhead
New Deer
B9029
Old Deer
A950
Howe of Teuchar
Blackhill of Clackriach
Inverquhomery
Peterhead Bay
Slacks of Cairnbanno
A948
B9028
Drymuir
Bulwark
Stuartfield
Millbreck
Nether Kinmundy
Hillhead of Cocklaw
A982
Burnhaven
Nethermuir
Knaven
Clola
Buchan Ness
North Millbrex
Kinnadie
B9030
Blackhill
Stirling
Boddam
Gourdas
Auchnagatt
Lendrum Terrace
A947
Cottown of Gight
Cairnorrie
Lethenty
Kinknockie
Brownhill
Fyvie Castle
Inkhorn
Longhaven
Fyvie
R. Ythan
Ardallie
B9005
Coldwells
Bullers of Buchan
Woodhead
Haddo
Auchiries
Methlick
Hatton
North Haven
Muirtack
Arthrath
Slains
Cruden Bay
R. Ythan
B9170
Haddo House
Bogbrae
Chapel Hill
Earlsford
St Katherines
Barthol Chapel
Bay of Cruden
A975
Ythanbank
Birness
Wedderlairs
Whinnyfold
The Skares
Cross of Jackston
Auchedly
Altar Tomb of William Forbes
Tulloch
Tarves
Artrochie
Kinharrachie
Ythsie
Ellon
P+R
Craigdam
Esslemont
Kirkton of Logie Buchan
Kirktown of Slains
A920
Tolquhon Castle
B999
A920
Collieston
Daviot
Oldmeldrum
Pitmedden Garden
Pitmedden
Forvie
Carnbrogie
Logierieve
B9000
Housieside
B9001
Udny Green
B9000
Newburgh
Kirktown of Bourtie
Udny Station
Whiterashes
Woodland
Pettymuk
Foveran
Cultercullen
Inverurie
Tillygreig
Nether Crimond
A975
B993
Port Elphinstone
Straloch
Delfrigs
Reisque
Causeyend
Kinmuck
Kinkell Church
Newmachar
B979
Balmedie
Whitecairns
Belhelvie
Kinmundy
Hatton of Fintray
B977
133
R. Don
Kintore
B994
Dyce Symbol
Potterton

see page 152 for Western Isles
Fladda-chùain
Eilean Trodday
Rudha Hunish
North Duntulm
Duntulm
Kilmaluag
A855
Tairbeart (Tarbert)
Lùb Score
Skye Museum of Island Life
Flodigarry
Poldorais
Eilean Flodigarry
Borneskitaig
Heribusta
Kilmuir
Kilvaxter
542
MEAL NA SUIREAMACH
Digg
Staffin Bay
Staffin Island
Balgown
134
Brogaig
135
ternish Point
Stenscholl
Staffin
Linicro
Totscore
464
BIODA BUIDHE
Kilt Rock Waterfall
Ellishader
Trotternish
River Rha
Maligar
Ascrib Islands
Idrigill
Marishader
Valtos
River Conon
Uig Bay
(Uige)
BEINN EDRA
Garros
Rudha nam Brathai
Culnaknock
Loch a' Bhra
0 1 2 3 4 5 miles
0 1 2 3 4 5 6 7 8 kilometres
283

Baddidarrach
Inverkirkaig
Rhu Coigach
Eilean Mòr
Enard Bay
Rubha Mòr
Reiff
Achnahaird
Altandhu
Eilean Mullagrach
Isle Ristol
Loch Osgaig
Polbain
Glas-leac Mòr
SUMMER ISLES
Achiltibuie
Tanera Beg
Badentarbat Bay
Polglass
Steornabhagh (Stornoway)
Tanera Mòr
Ben mor Coigach
Horse Island
Horse Sound
Glas-leac Beag
Achduart
652
BEN MOR COIGACH
Culnacraig
Eilean Dubh
Priest Island
Leac Dhonn
Isle Martin
Greenstone Point
Cailleach Head
Rudha Beag
Scoraig
Annat Bay
Mellon Udrigle
Stattic Point
Rhireavach
635
BEINN GHOBHLACH
GRUINARD ISLAND
Badluachrach
Little Loch Broom
Foura
A832
Gruinard Bay
Badrallach
Rudha Reidh
Cove
Laide
Mellon Charles
Ormiscaig
Badcaul
Aultbea
Ardessie
Camusnagaul
296
AN CUAIDH
B8057
Gruinard
764
SAIL MHOR
Dundonnell
Melvaig
ISLE OF EWE
Little Gruinard River
Gruinard River
Lochan Gaineamhaich
Aultgrishin
Loch Ewe
Loch Fada
347
CREAG-MHEAL BEAG
Inverasdale
Strathnasheallag Forest
293
CNOC BREAC
Naast
1062
AN TEALLACH
Inverewe Garden
Loch na Sealga
B8021
681
BEINN A' CHAISGEIN BEAG
North Erradale
250
MEALL NA MEINE
Londubh
Poolewe
Fionn
Wester Ross
906
BEINN DEARG MHOR
Big Sand
Strath
A832
Smithstown
Longa Island
Lonemore
Auchtercairn
Heritage
Dubh Loch
Loch
791
BEINN AIRIDH CHARR
Loch Gairloch
Gairloch
421
MEALL AN DOIREIN
Eilean Horrisdale
Charlestown
974
SGÙRRBÀN
Port Henderson
B8056
Loch
1019
MULLACH COIRE MHIC FHEARCHAIR
859
BEINN LÀIR
Badachro
Opinan
Lochan Fada
South Erradale
Loch Bad an Sgalaig
Loch Maree Hotel
Letterewe
Loch Garbhaig
Talladale
Maree
981
SLIOCH
Redpoint
A832
Loch Ghaineamhach
Red Point
680
BEINN A' MHÙINIDH
Loch a' Ghobhainn
875
BAOSBHEINN
Loch na A-Oidhche
Kinlochewe Forest
855
BEINN AN EOIN
724
619
BEINN BHREAC
Loch a' Bhealaich
Loch Torridon
Beinn Eighe
Incheril
Craig River
Rudha na Fearn
985
1009
Kinlochewe

Baddidarrach
Lochinver
Soyea Island
Loch Inver
539
BEINN GHARBH
Inchnadamph
148
Strathan
Assynt - Coigach
Inverkirkaig
998
BEN MORE ASSYNT
Loch na Gainimh
847
CANISP
Stronchrubie
Rhu Coigach
River Kirkaig
Fionn Loch
732
SUILVEN
713
BREABAG
Eilean Mòr
Enard Bay
River Loanan
814
Loch Awe
Rubha Mòr
Reiff
Achnahaird
Càm Loch
Loch Sionascaig
Altandhu
849
CUL MÒR
Loch Veyatie
Ledmore Junction
A837
Eilean Mullagrach
Loch Osgaig
Isle Ristol
143
Polbain
612
STAC POLLAIDH
Knockan
Elphin
Loch Urigill
Glas-leac Mòr
SUMMER ISLES
Achiltibuie
769
CUL BEAG
Knockan Cliff
Knockan Crag
307
CNOC NA GLAS CHOILLE
Tanera Beg
Badentarbat Bay
Polglass
Loch Lurgainn
Ben mor Coigach
Cromalt Hills
Steornabhagh (Stornoway)
Tanera Mòr
COIGACH
Glas-leac Beag
Horse Island
Horse Sound
Achduart
652
BEN MORE COIGACH
Drumrunie Lodge
Culnacraig
Eilean Dubh
Loch a' Chroisg
Priest Island
Strathcanaird
Rappach
Strath Canaird
408
NA DROMANNAN
Leac Dhonn
A835
Cailleach Head
Isle Martin
Rudha Beag
Ardmair
Annat Bay
Scoraig
Stattic Point
Morefield
Rhireavach
Ullapool (Ulapul)
Loch Achall
Glen Achall
635
BEINN GHOBHLACH
Loch an Daimh
GRUINARD ISLAND
Badluachrach
Little Loch Broom
558
BEINN EILIDEACH
Strath Mulzie
A832
Laide
Gruinard Bay
Badrallach
Badcaul
Loch Broom
677
MEALL NAM BRADHAN
Leckmelm
642
MEALL DUBH
Ardessie
Camusnagaul
Gruinard
764
SÀIL MHÒR
Ardcharnich
Ardindrean
Loch a' Choire Mhòir
Little Gruinard River
Gruinard River
Dundonnell
Lochan Gaineamhaich
Letters
647
CÀRN MÒR
347
CREAG-MHEAL BEAG
Inverlael
Loch Fada
Strathnasheallag Forest
River Lael
1062
AN TEALLACH
507
CÀRN BHIORAIN
Croftown
Glean
681
BEINN A' CHAISGEIN BEAG
Loch na Sealga
R Broom
250
MEALL NA MEINE
1081
BEINN DEARG
906
BEINN DEARG MHOR
Fionn Loch
Wester Ross
Braemore
387
CÀRN BREAC BEAG
Corrieshalloch Gorge
Falls of Measach
Loch Coire Làir
Dubh Loch
618
MEALL LEACACHAIN
791
BEINN AIRIDH CHARR
601
MEALL AN T-SITHE
742
TOM BÀN MÒR
974
SGÙRRBÀN
Loch a' Bhraoin
Loch Droma
Loch Maree
1019
MULLACH COIRE MHIC FHEARCHAIR
859
BEINN LÀIR
662
BEINN LIATH BHEAG
Lochan Fada
1109
SGÙRR MÒR
Loch Maree Hotel
Letterewe
Loch Garbhaig
999
A' CHAILLEACH
Talladale
981
SLIOCH
136
600
680
BEINN DEARG
137
Loch na A-Oidhche
680
BEINN A' MHÙINIDH
711
BEINN NAN RAMH
Fannich Lodge
Loch Fannich
855
BEINN AN EOIN
724
Kinlochewe Forest
558
AN CABAR
Lochluichart
Incheril
933
FIONN BHEINN
Achanalt
A832
0 1 2 3 4 5 miles
0 1 2 3 4 5 6 7 8 kilometres

Overscaig Hotel
Ben Armine Forest
Loch Shin
Strath Tirry
Shinness
Achnairn
Colaboll
Duchally
Glen Muic
Glen Cassley
River Cassley
435 BEN SCREAVIL
476 BEINN SGEIREACH
544 BEINN AN EÒIN
364
510 MAOVALLY
Loch na Claise Mòire
River Oykel
402 CNOC A' CHOIRE
Ferrycroft Countryside Centre
Lairg
Tomich
Torrobull
323 BEN DOULA
Loch Craggie
Loch Beannach
317 SITHEAN ACHADH NAN EUN
462 MEALIAN LIATH MOR
Glas-loch Mòr
River Brora
293 CNOC LEAMHNACHD
Dalreavoch Lodge
River B
A838
A836
A839
A837
B864
A949
A9
A835
B817
B9176
B9163
Rosehall
Oykel Bridge Hotel
Doune
Strath Oykel
Glen Einig
Achany
Altass
Linsidemore
Falls of Shin
Inveran
Invershin
Culrain
Kyle of Sutherland
313 CREAGAN GLAS
333 MEALL EACHAINN
Loch Buidhe
Rogart
Torboll
Sleasdairidh
349 BEINN DONUILL
River Evelix
Cambusavie Platform
Badninish
Achvaich
Rearquhar
Birichin
Astle
Evelix
493 BEINN ULBHAIDH
412 CREAG LOISGTE
463 BREAC BHEINN
506 MEALL DHEIRGIDH
Brealangwell Lodge
701 CARN A' CHOIN DEIRG
Giasha Burn
Croick
Strathcarron
Lower Gledfield
Dounie
Bonar Bridge
Loch Migdale
Spinningdale
Clashmore
Ardgay
Kincardine
Upper Ardchronie
River Carron
Glencalvie Forest
634 CÀRN BHREN
Whiteface
Dornoch Firth
Ferrytown
Cuthill
Ardmore
Cambuscurrie Bay
Ferry Point
Struie Hill
Edderton
477 BEINN CLACH AN FHEADAIN
Morangie
Glenmorangie Distillery
838 CÀRN CHUINNEAG
710 BEINN THARSUINN
Crom Loch
628
602 CÀRN CAS NAN GABHAR
Aultnamain Inn
284
Tain (Baile Dhubhthaich)
EASTER ROSS
692 BEINN THARSUINN
Loch a' Chaorunn
379 CNOC AN T-SABHAIL
771 MEALL A' GHRIANAIN
Loch Vaich
Loch Morie
742 BEINN NAN EUN
Newfield
737 MEALL MOR
Strath Rusdale
Ardross
Ballchraggan
Kildary
Boath
Loch Glass
River Alness
Achandunie
Delny
Kilmuir
Milton
Barbaraville
Rhicullen
Millcraig
Tomich
Aultguish Inn
Moultavie
523 CNOC CEISLEIN
Achnagarron
Balintraid
Nigg Bay
Alness (Alanais)
Saltburn
Invergordon
Dalmore
Inchbae Lodge Hotel
1045 BEN WYVIS
Glen Glass
479
Ben Wyvis
Strath Garve
Evanton
Swordale
Balblair
Resolis
Cromarty Firth
Udale Bay
Cromarty Bay
439 CÀRN NA ...BH CHOILLE
761 LITTLE WYVIS
Corriemoille
Teanord
Jemimaville
Allerton
484 CLOCH MHÒR
Clanland & Seapoint
Cullicudden
Ardullie
Brae
Gorstan
Garve
Mountgerald House
Findon
Loch Luichart
A832
149
146
137
138
J K L M N P Q R

Ben Armine Forest
Glas-loch Mòr
462 MEALLAN LIATH MOR
Strath Skinsdale
337 CNOC NA H-INNSE MOIRE
421 CNOC NAN CRÙBAG MÒR
150
Kildonan Lodge
Strath of Kildonan
416 BEINN DUBHAIN
Kildonan
A897
Torrish
River Helmsdale
624 BEINN DHORAIN
591 BEINN NA MEILICH
Glen Loth
Lothmore
Lothbeg
Gartymore
Portgower
A836
Loch Beannach
317 SITHEAN ACHADH NAN EUN
River Brora
293 CNOC LEAMHNACHD
Black Water
Balnacoil Lodge
Strath Brora
539 COL-BHEINN
145
Ferrycroft Countryside Centre
Loch Craggie
323 BEN DOULA
Dalreavoch Lodge
Loch Brora
Lairg
Tomich
Torrobull
A839
Loch Horn
520 BEN HORN
Dalchalm
Brora
Golspie Burn
378 CAGAR FEOSAIG
Rogart
313 CREAGAN GLAS
446 BEN LUNDIE
383 BEN BHRAGGIE
Backies
Carn Liath
Doll
A9
Dunrobin Castle
Rhives
Golspie
B864
333 MEALL EACHAINN
Falls of Shin
Loch Buidhe
Torboll
Sleasdairidh
349 BEINN DONUILL
Cambusavie Platform
Loch Fleet
Skelbo
Skelbo Street
Badninish
River Evelix
Achvaich
Fourpenny
Embo
A836
Kyle of Sutherland
Rearquhar
Birichin
Astle
Embo Street
B9168
Pitgrudy
Lower Gledfield
Bonar Bridge
Evelix
A949
Loch Migdale
Spinningdale
Clashmore
Camore
Dornoch
Kincardine
Upper Ardchronie
Historylinks
Whiteface
Dornoch Firth
Cuthill
Ferrytown
Ardmore
Struie Hill
Cambuscurrie Bay
Ferry Point
Innis Mhor
Tarbat Ness
Brucefield
Wilkhaven
Edderton
477 BEINN CLACH AN FHEADAIN
Glenmorangie Distillery
Morangie
Portmahomack
Inver
Rockfield
Aultnamain Inn
284
Tain (Baile Dhubhthaich)
Arboll
B9165
Toulvaddie
Lochslin
692 BEINN THARSUINN
379 CNOC AN T-SABHAIL
Loch Eye
Hill of Fearn
Rhynie
Balmuchy
Hilton of Cadboll Chapel (ruin)
B9176
Newfield
Fearn
Tullich
B9166
Hilton
Balintore
Strath Rusdale
Ardross
Ballchraggan
Arabella
Shandwick
Shandwick Bay
Kildary
Ankerville
Milton
B9175
River Alness
Achandunie
Kilmuir
Pitcalnie
Delny
Barbaraville
Rhicullen
Nigg
Moultavie
Millcraig
Tomich
Nigg Bay
523 CNOC CEISLEIN
Achnagarron
Balintraid
Alness (Alanais)
Saltburn
Nigg Ferry
Invergordon
Dalmore
B817
(Jun-Oct)
138
Cromarty
Evanton
Balblair
Cromarty Firth
Resolis
Udale Bay
Cromarty Bay
Hugh Miller's Cottage
Newton
B9163
Navity
Teanord
Jemimaville
Allerton
Clanland & Seaport
Cullicudden
Ardullie
Upper Eathie
Moray Firth
A832
Findon
Culbin
0 1 2 3 4 5 miles
0 1 2 3 4 5 6 7 8 kilometres

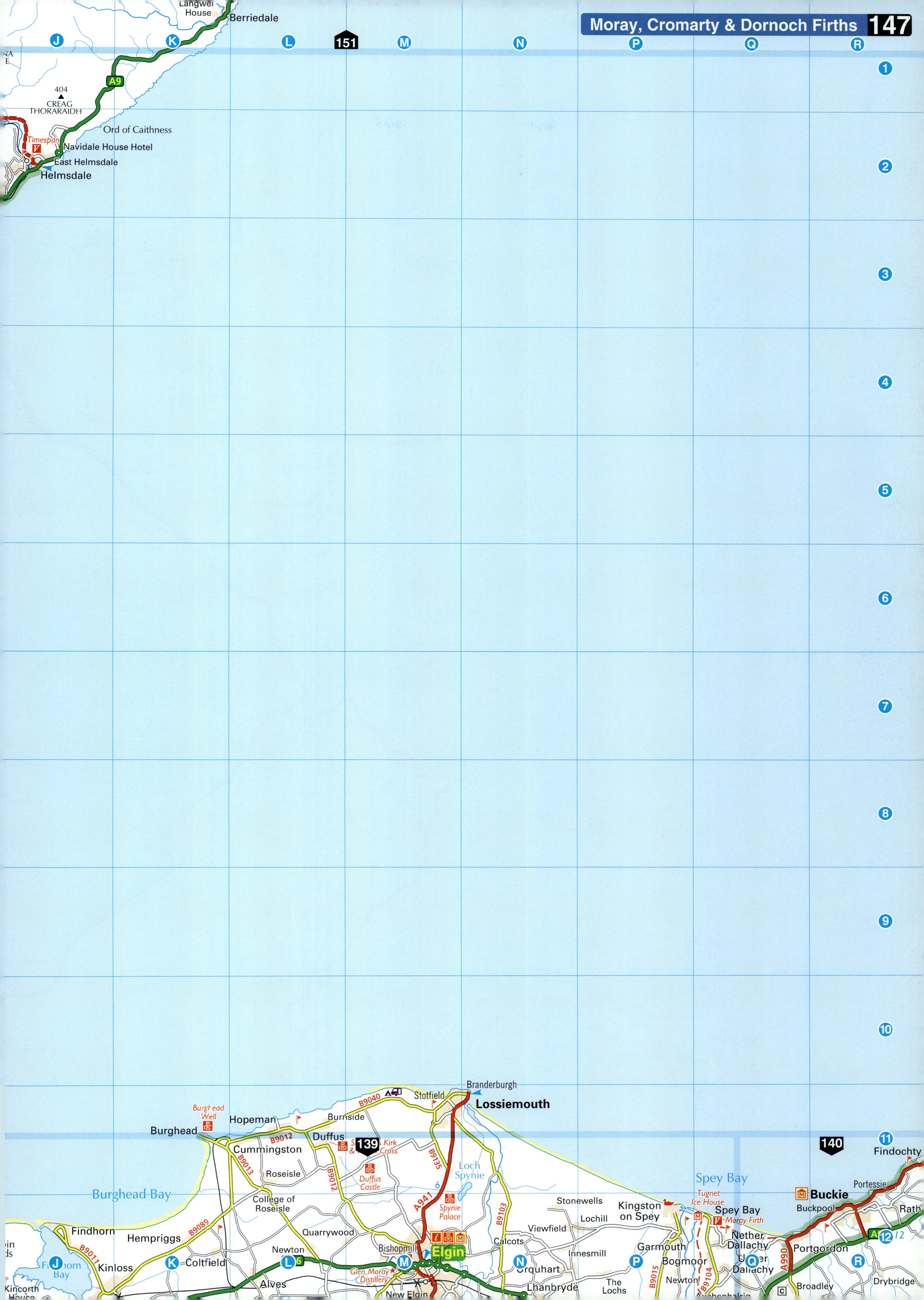
151
J
K
L
M
N
P
Q
R
1
2
3
4
5
6
7
8
9
10
11
12
Langwell House
Berriedale
A9
404
CREAG THORARAIDH
Ord of Caithness
Timespan
Navidale House Hotel
East Helmsdale
Helmsdale
Branderburgh
Stotfield
Lossiemouth
B9040
Burghead Well
Hopeman
Burnside
Burghead
B9012
Duffus
139
Kirk Cross
Cummingston
B9013
B9135
Loch Spynie
Roseisle
B9012
Duffus Castle
Burghead Bay
College of Roseisle
A941
Spynie Palace
B9103
Stonewells
Kingston on Spey
Lochill
Spey Bay
Tugnet Ice House
Spey Bay
Moray Firth
Findhorn
B9089
Quarrywood
Viewfield
Nether Dallachy
Hempriggs
Calcots
Garmouth
Upper Dallachy
Newton
Bishopmill
Elgin
Innesmill
Bogmoor
A990
Portgordon
B9011
Kinloss
Coltfield
Glen Moray Distillery
Urquhart
B9015
Newton
B9104
Findhorn Bay
Alves
New Elgin
Lhanbryde
The Lochs
Broadley
Drybridge
Kincorth House
140
Findochty
Portessie
Buckie
Buckpool
Rath

A
B
C
D
E
F
G
H
1
2
3
4
5
6
7
8
9
10
11
12
CAPE WRATH
Cléit Dhubh
371
SGRIBHIS-BHEINN
297
CNOC A GHIUBHAIS
300
MAOVALLY
THE PARPH
457
FASHVEN
Sandwood Bay
Loch Airigh na Beinne
Sandwood Loch
485
CREAG RIABACH
468
BEINN DEARG MHÒR
464
MEALL NA MOINE
331
GHLAS-BHEINN
Rudh' an Fhir Leithe
Strath Shinary
Sheigra
Balchreick
Blairmore
Oldshoremore
521
FARVEALL
355
AN SOCACH
773
BEINN SPIONNAIDH
801
CRANSTACKIE
Kinlochbervie
Loch Clash
Badcall
B801
Loch Inchard
Achriesgill
A838
Strath Dionard
River Dionard
Rhiconich
Loch na Claise Càrnaich
Rudha Ruadh
908
FOINAVEN
Skerricha
Fanagmore
Tarbet
Loch Laxford
Foindle
HANDA ISLAND
North-west Sutherland
Loch na Tuadh
786
ARKLE
Laxford Bridge
River Laxford
Scourie Bay
A894
Scourie
Scourie More
Loch Stack
721
BEN STACK
SÀBHAL
Badcall
Strath Stack
Achfary
386
BEN AUSKAIRD
333
BEN SCREAVIE
800
Badcall Bay
Loch a' Mhuilinn
Rudh' a' Mhucard
Loch More
419
BEN STROME
Loch an Leathaid Bhuain
Point of Stoer
OLDANY ISLAND
Eddrachillis Bay
Old Man of Stoer
Culkein Drumbeg
Kylestrome
Kinloch
Loch a' Chàirn Bhàin
Kylesku
Culkein
Clashnessie Bay
Oldany
Drumbeg
Loch Glendhu
Glen Dhu
Unapool
Achnacarnin
Nedd
B869
525
BEINN AIRD DA LOCH
613
MEALL AN FHEUR
Clashmore
Loch Poll
Glen Leirg
Loch an Leothaid
776
SAIL GHORM
Loch Glencoul
Clashnessie
809
QUINAG
792
BEINN LEOID
Stoer
Clachtoll
Bay of Clachtoll
Loch Beannach
Eas a' Chuall Aluinn (Waterfall)
774
GLAS BHEINN
Achmelvich Bay
Achmelvich
Rhicarn
A837
Loch Assynt
Ardvreck
Baddidarrach
539
BEINN GHARBH
Lochinver
Inchnadamph
Soyea Island
Loch Inver
Assynt - Coigach
Strathan
Inverkirkaig
144
998
BEN MORE ASSYNT
Loch na Gainimh
847
Stronchrubie
Loanan
0 1 2 3 4 5 miles
0 1 2 3 4 5 6 7 8 kilometres

Faraid Head
Sango Bay
Smoo Cave
Durness
Sangomore
Smoo
Keoldale
Sangobeg
Eilean Hoan
Whiten Head
Loch Meadaidh
423 MEALL MEADHONACH
Loch Eriboll
Laid
230 BEN ARNABOLL
A838
408 BEN HUTIG
Strathan
Rabbit Islands
Eilean Nan Ròn
Neave Island
Talmine
Melness
Midtown
Tongue Bay
Kyle of Tongue
Skerray
Achtoty
Torrisdale
Torrisdale Bay
Farr Bay
Farr
Farr Point
Kirtomy Point
Ardmore Point
Armadale
Armadale Bay
Kirtomy
Swordly
Strathy
A836
Scullomie
Coldbackie
Bettyhill
Invernaver
Achina
Borgie
Loch Meadie
228 BEINN NAM BO
262 DRUIM NAN CLIAR
Tongue
310 MEALL LEATHAD NA CRAOIBHE
River Borgie
Skelpick
Skelpick Burn
Strath Naver
Loch Mòr na Caorach
Loch nan Clach
Strath Beag
520 AN LEAN-CHÀRN
Loch Hope
Kinloch
318 CNOC CRAGGIE
Loch Craggie
Loch na Seilg
Kyle of Tongue
598 MEALLAN LIATH
927 BEN HOPE
River Hope
527 BEINN STUMANADH
213 CNOC MALPELLY
B871
763 BEN LOYAL
Loch an Deerie
Loch Loyal
Loyal Lodge
Loch Strathy
335 MEALL BAD NA CUAICHE
463 FEINNE-BHEINN NHOR
Strath More
Dun Dornaigil Broch
557 CNOC NAN CUILEAN
Loch Syre
River Naver
Syre
345 CNOC NAM TRI-CHLACH
Loch Cro
Glen Golly
656 CNOC AN DÀIMH MÒR
294 POLE HILL
404 BEINN MHADADH
Loch Meadie
259 BEINN ROSAIL
Loch à Chl
757 CARN AN TIONAIL
B873
590 BEN GRIAM MOR
Strath Naver
Loch Naver
230 MEALL A' BHROLLAICH
270 BEADAIG
River Mallart
Loch Coire na Saidhe Duibhe
Altnaharra
Loch Rimsdale
Loch nan Clàr
Loch Badanloch
873 BEN HEE
680 MEALL AN LIATH MOR
Loch a' Ghorm-choire
Loch an Altan Fheàrna
Loch Truderscaig
River
472 MEALL AN FHUARAIN
959 BEN KLIBRECK
Strath Bagastie
Loch Choire Forest
694 CREAG N-IOLAIRE
434 CNOC AN LIATH-BHAID MHÒIR
Loch Fiag
Fiag Lodge
Glen Fiag
Loch Choire
713 CREAG MHOR
Loch a' Bhealaich
Borrobol Forest
372 CNOC A' GHRIAMA
Crask Inn
346 CNOC A' GHIUBHAIS
364 CNOC NA BREUN-CHOILLE
Overscaig Hotel
Gorm-loch Mòr
Ben Armine Forest
Strath Skinsdale
Glas-loch Mòr
150
145

A
B
C
D
E
F
G
H
1
2
3
4
5
6
7
8
9
10
11
12
149
146
Strathy Point
Strathy Bay
Melvich Bay
Sandside Bay
Upper Dounreay
Isauld
Armadale Bay
Ardmore Point
Kirtomy Point
Eilean Nan Ròn
Rabbit Islands
Neave Island
Farr Point
Brawl
Strathy Inn
Baligill
Portskerra
Bighouse
Strathy
Melvich
Reay
Achvarasdal
A836
15
Armadale
Kirtomy
Swordly
Farr
Torrisdale Bay
Farr Bay
Tongue Bay
Skerray
Achtoty
Torrisdale
Bettyhill
Scullomie
Invernaver
Achina
Talmine
Melness
Midtown
Kyle of Tongue
Coldbackie
Borgie
13
Tongue
Loch Meadie
River Strathy
185 BEINN RUADH
242 BEINN RATHA
Loch na Seilge
229 BEINN RUADH
228 BEINN NAM BO
Upper Bighouse
Skelpick
Skelpick Burn
River Borgie
310 MEALL LEATHAD NA CRAOIBHE
A897
Dalhalvaig
Strath Halladale
Strath Naver
Loch Mòr na Caorach
290 BEINN NAM BAD MHÒR
Trantlemore
Trantelbeg
243 CNOC AN FHOARAIN BHÀIN
318 CNOC CRAGGIE
Loch Craggie
12
Loch nan Clach
213 CNOC BAD AIREACH NA GAOITHE
Loch Tuim Ghlais
184 CREAG NA CRICHE
17
527 BEINN STUMANADH
213 CNOC MALPELLY
Dyke Water
763 BEN LOYAL
Loch Loyal
B871
203 CNOC PREAS A'MHADAIDH
Loyal Lodge
Loch Strathy
335 MEALL BAD NA CUAICHE
21
280 SLETILL HILL
557 CNOC NAN CUILEAN
Loch Syre
River Naver
217 CNOC A' BHREUN BHAID
Halladale River
345 CNOC NAM TRI-CHLACH
Loch Cròcach
Syre
Forsinard
275 CNOC NAN GALL
294 POLE HILL
404 BEINN MHADADH
588 BEN GRIAM BEG
Rumsdale Water
259 BEINN ROSAIL
337 MEAL A' BHEALAICH
Loch Druim a' Chliabhain
590 BEN GRIAM MOR
16
B873
Loch an Ruathair
230 ALL A' BHROLLAICH
Strath Naver
Loch Naver
270 BEADAIG
River Mallart
Loch Rimsdale
Loch nan Clàr
440
KNOCKFIN HEIGHTS
432
Loch Badanloch
Loch Arichlinie
317 CNOC LOCH MHADADH
Loch an Altan Fhearna
Loch Truderscaig
River Helmsdale
Kinbrace
Kinbrace Burn
437 CNOC COIRE NA FEARNA
959 BEN KLIBRECK
Loch Choire Forest
694 CREAG N-IOLAIRE
434 CNOC AN LIATH-BHAID MHÒIR
202 CNOC DAIL-CHAIRN
518 CNOC AN EIREANNAICH
Loch Choire
713 CREAG MHOR
Borrobol Forest
Strath Free
Suisgill Burn
Loch Ascaig
Loch a' Bhealaich
364 CNOC NA BREUN-CHOILLE
388 CREAG NAM FIADH
Learable Hill Cairns, Stone Row & Stone Circles
554 CREAG SCALABSDALE
Gorm-loch Mòr
Kildonan Lodge
Strath of Kildonan
Ben Armine Forest
Kildonan
416 BEINN DUBHAIN
Strath Skinsdale
337
0 1 2 3 4 5 miles
0 1 2 3 4 5 6 7 8 kilometres

PENTLAND FIRTH
Langaton Point
Nethertown
ISLAND OF STROMA
Uppertown
Mell Head
DUNNET HEAD
127
St John's Point
Inner Sound
St Margaret's Hope
Stromness
Briga Head
Scarfskerry
Castle of Mey
Gills Bay
Huna
DUNCANSBY HEAD
121 DUNNET HILL
Brough
St John's Loch
Rattar
Loch Mey
Mey
Gills
Kirkstyle
Muckle Stack
John o' Groats
Stacks of Duncansby
Brims Ness
Holborn Head
West Dunnet
Dunnet Bay
Dunnet
Barrock
Canisbay
St Mary's Chapel (ruin)
Scrabster
Crosskirk
Thurso Bay
Inkstack
Brabstermire
Thurso
Castlehill
Murkle
Loch Heilen
Skirza
Bridge of Forss
Skiall
Castletown
Greenland
Gill Burn
Freswick
Freswick Bay
Ness Head
Achreamie
Lythmore
Olrig House
Slickly
Cnoc Freiceadain Long Cairns
Forss Water
Glengolly
Weydale
Tain
Auckengill
Shebster
Westfield
Hilliclay
Bowermadden
Kirk Burn
Broch
Nybster
Sortat
Lyth
Bower
Brough Head
Sordale
Howe
Loch Calder
Roadside
Knockdee
Loch Scarmclate
Halcro
Burn of Lyth
Mireland
Keiss
Broubster
Clayock
Gillock
Kirk
Halkirk
Shurrery
Georgemas Junction Station
Loch of Wester
Sinclair Bay
Shurrery Lodge
Scotscalder Station
Loch Watten
Killimster
Harpsdale
176 SPITTAL HILL
Castle Girnigoe & Sinclair
Noss Head
Dorrery
Loch Shurrery
Olgrinmore
Watten
Reiss
Winless
Spittal
River Thurso
Wick River
Sibster
Ackergill
160
132 DRUIM A' CHRACAIRNIE
Bilbster
Staxigoe
Mybster
Loch of Toftingall
Wick
Janetstown
Papigoe
Westerdale
Haster
Milton
Wick Bay
Old Wick
Newton
South Head
Castle of Old Wick
Strath Beg
Badlipster
Achairn Burn
Whiterow
136 BEINN CHÀITEAG
Tannach
Loch Hempriggs
Thrumster
145 BALLHARN HILL
Grey Cairns of Camster
Loch Ruard
Loch More
Sarclet
212 HILL OF YARROWS
Loch of Yarrows
Loch Stemster
Achavanich
248 STEMSTER HILL
Loch Sand
Loch an Thulachan
Loch Rangag
Strathmore Water
Cairn o'Get
Ulbster
Whaligoe
Dalnawillan Lodge
226 COIRE NA BEINN
Roster
Whaligoe Steps
Bruan
348 BEN ALISKY
Hill o'Many Stanes
287 BEN-A-CHIELT
Upper Lybster
Mid Clyth
Halberry Head
264 CNOCAN CONACHREAG
Swiney
Clyth Ness
Occumster
Houstry
Invershore
Lybster
Lybster Bay
Land-hallow
Forse
Smerral
Latheron
Dunbeath Water
Latheronwheel
Janetstown
Berriedale Water
Laidhay Croft
484 MAIDEN PAP
Braemore
Dunbeath
Knockally
626 SCARABEN
Ramscraigs
Borgue
Langwell Forest
Newport
Langwell House
Berriedale
404
A9
A99
A836
A882
B855
B874
B870
B876
147

## FERRY SERVICES

### Western Isles

Lewis is linked by ferry to the mainland at Ullapool, with daily sailings. There are ferry services from Harris (Tairbeart) and North Uist (Loch nam Madadh) to Uig on Skye. Harris and North Uist are connected by a ferry service between An t-Ob (Leverburgh) and Berneray, and then causeway to Otternish. South Uist and Barra are served by ferry services from Oban and a ferry service operates between Eriskay and Barra and another causeway links South Uist to Eriskay. Berneray, North Uist, Benbecula, South Uist and Erishkay are all connected by causeways.

### Shetland Islands

The main service is from Aberdeen on the mainland to the island port of Lerwick. A service from Kirkwall (Orkney) to Lerwick is also available. Shetland Islands Council operates an inter-island car ferry service.

### Orkney Islands

The main service is from Scrabster on the Caithness coast to Stromness and there is a further service from Gills (Caithness) to St Margaret's Hope on South Ronaldsay. A service from Aberdeen to Kirkwall provides a link to Shetland at Lerwick. Inter-island car ferry services are also operated (advance reservations recommended).

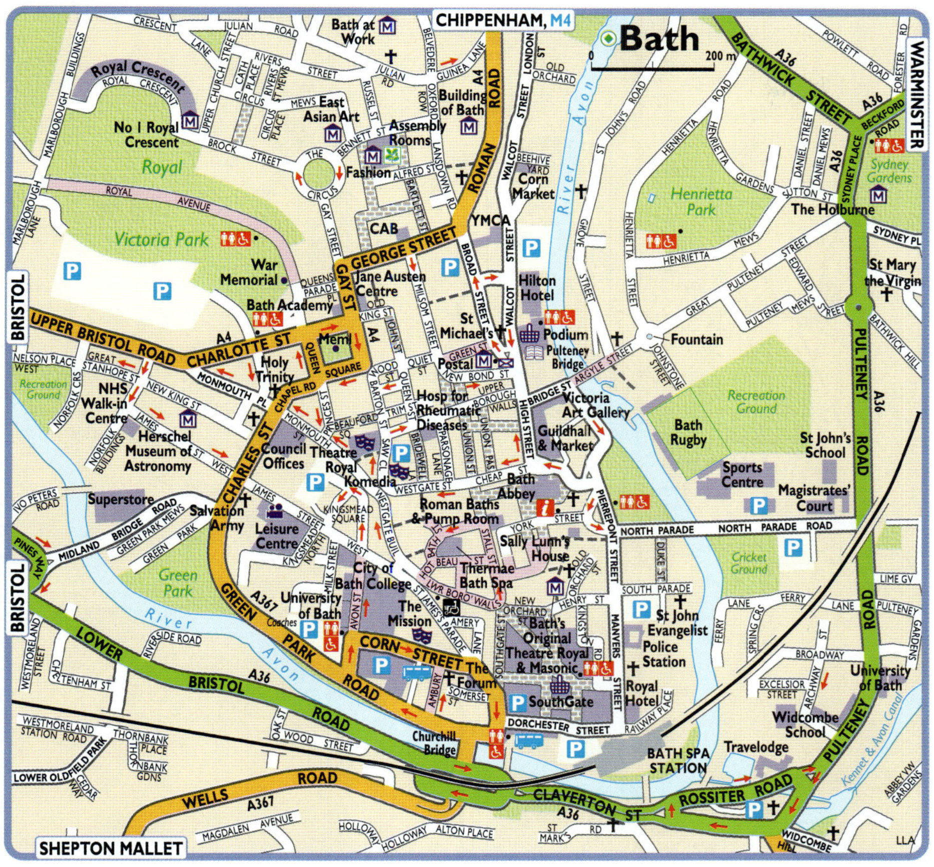
Bath
200 m
CHIPPENHAM, M4
WARMINSTER
BRISTOL
SHEPTON MALLET
Royal Crescent
No I Royal Crescent
Royal Victoria Park
Bath at Work
East Asian Art
Building of Bath
Assembly Rooms
Fashion
Corn Market
YMCA
Henrietta Park
The Holburne
Sydney Gardens
St Mary the Virgin
War Memorial
Bath Academy
Jane Austen Centre
GEORGE STREET
Hilton Hotel
Podium
Pulteney Bridge
Fountain
Recreation Ground
Bath Rugby
UPPER BRISTOL ROAD
CHARLOTTE ST
Holy Trinity
NHS Walk-in Centre
Herschel Museum of Astronomy
Council Offices
Theatre Royal
Komedia
Hosp for Rheumatic Diseases
Victoria Art Gallery
Guildhall & Market
St John's School
Sports Centre
Magistrates Court
Superstore
Salvation Army
Leisure Centre
Roman Baths & Pump Room
Bath Abbey
Sally Lunn's House
NORTH PARADE
PULTENEY ROAD
Cricket Ground
Green Park
University of Bath
City of Bath College
The Mission
Thermae Bath Spa
Bath's Original Theatre Royal & Masonic
St John Evangelist
Police Station
Royal Hotel
University of Bath
Widcombe School
Travelodge
LOWER BRISTOL ROAD
CORN STREET
GREEN PARK ROAD
Forum
SouthGate
Churchill Bridge
BATH SPA STATION
WELLS ROAD
CLAVERTON ST
ROSSITER ROAD
A36
A367
A4
A431
LLA

Birmingham
200 m
A38(M), M6, LICHFIELD
DUDLEY, SMETHWICK
BROMSGROVE, REDDITCH
St Chad's Cathedral
ST CHADS QUEENSWAY
Thistle Birmingham Hotel
St Paul's
Birmingham Childrens
Police Station
Aston University
Sikh Temple
Travelodge
BT Tower
BIRMINGHAM SNOW HILL STATION
Police HQ
Law Courts
Juvenile Court
Crown Court
Queen Elizabeth Law Courts
St John's Ambulance
Quaker Meeting House
The Minories
GREAT CHARLES STREET QUEENSWAY
University College Birmingham
Birmingham & Midland Institute
School of Art
Art Gallery
Birmingham Council House
Waterhall Gallery of Modern Art
Town Hall
Birmingham Cathedral
Martineau Place
Priory Walk
Carling Academy
The Square
Saturday Bridge
Queensway Tunnel
Paradise Forum
Memorial
War Memorial
Birmingham Repertory (The REP)
International Convention Centre
Birmingham City University (Adrian Boult Hall)
Piccadilly Arcade
Travelodge
The Burlington Hotel
Britannia Hotel
Pavilions
MOOR ST STATION
Regency Wharf
Crowne Plaza Hotel
BIRMINGHAM NEW STREET STATION
The Pallasades
Bullring
St Martin in the Bullring
London College of Business
Premier Inn
Jurys Inn Hotel
City of Birmingham Symphony Orchestra (CBSO)
Register Office
The Mailbox
Ramada Hotel
The Cube
The Old Rep
Alexandra
Radisson Hotel
Holiday Inn
Market
St Martin's Rag Market
South Birmingham College
Horticulture Market
SUFFOLK STREET QUEENSWAY
A38
B4284
A4400
LLA

Bradford
200 m
KEIGHLEY
SHIPLEY
LEEDS
HALIFAX
HUDDERSFIELD
WAKEFIELD
Forster Square Retail Park
HAMM STRASSE
Manningham Lane Retail Park
Forster Square Retail Park
St Patrick's Friary
Register Office
FORSTER SQUARE STATION
BARKEREND RD
St Mary's
Oastler
Midland Hotel
Bradford Cathedral
Kirkgate Centre
Area due for development
Sikh Temple
WOW Academy
Jurys Inn
Bradford College
City Hall
St George's Hall
The Law Courts
CAB
Jobcentre Plus
Playhouse
HALL INGS
LEEDS ROAD
Government Offices
Alhambra
The Studio
Magistrates' Court
Hilton Hotel
Great Victoria Hotel
The Leisure Exchange
Holiday Inn Express
Bradford College
University of Bradford
Delius Centre
BRADFORD INTERCHANGE STATION
National Media Museum
Council Offices
Police Station
Police HQ
St James Wholesale Market
MORLEY STREET
MANCHESTER ROAD
WESTGATE
GODWIN ST
PRINCES WAY
A650
A647
A641
A6181
A658
LLA

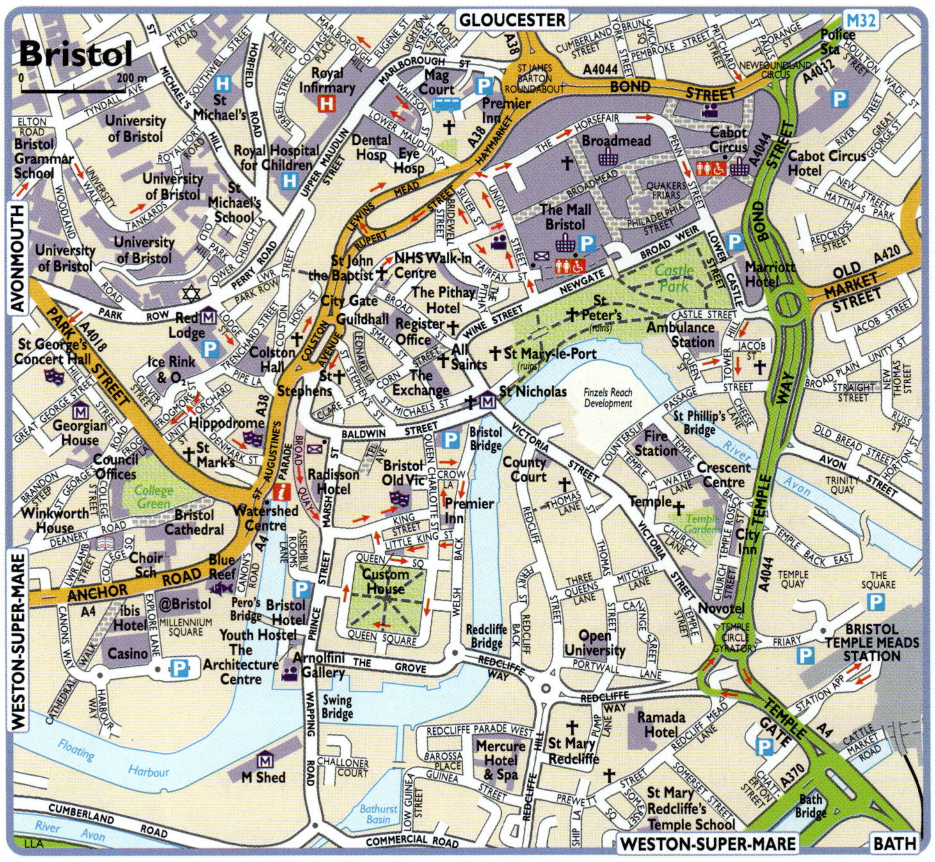
Bristol
200 m
GLOUCESTER
M32
AVONMOUTH
WESTON-SUPER-MARE
BATH
University of Bristol
Bristol Grammar School
St Michael's
Royal Infirmary
Royal Hospital for Children
Dental Hosp
Eye Hosp
Mag Court
Premier Inn
BOND STREET
Broadmead
Cabot Circus
Cabot Circus Hotel
The Mall Bristol
NHS Walk-in Centre
The Pithay
Hotel
Castle Park
St Peter's
Marriott Hotel
St George's Concert Hall
Colston Hall
Guildhall
Register Office
All Saints
St Mary-le-Port
Ambulance Station
Hippodrome
St Nicholas
Finzels Reach Development
Fire Station
St Philip's Bridge
Georgian House
Council Offices
Radisson Hotel
Bristol Old Vic
County Court
Premier Inn
Temple
Crescent Centre
College Green
Bristol Cathedral
Watershed Centre
Custom House
Winkworth House
Choir Sch
Blue Reef
ANCHOR ROAD
Ibis Hotel
@Bristol
Pero's Bridge
Youth Hostel
The Architecture Centre
Arnolfini Gallery
Redcliffe Bridge
Open University
Novotel
BRISTOL TEMPLE MEADS STATION
Casino
Swing Bridge
Floating Harbour
M Shed
Ramada Hotel
Mercure Hotel & Spa
St Mary Redcliffe
St Mary Redcliffe's Temple School
Bath Bridge
Bathurst Basin
CUMBERLAND ROAD
COMMERCIAL ROAD
River Avon
TEMPLE WAY
A4044
A4032
A420
A370
A4
A38
LLA

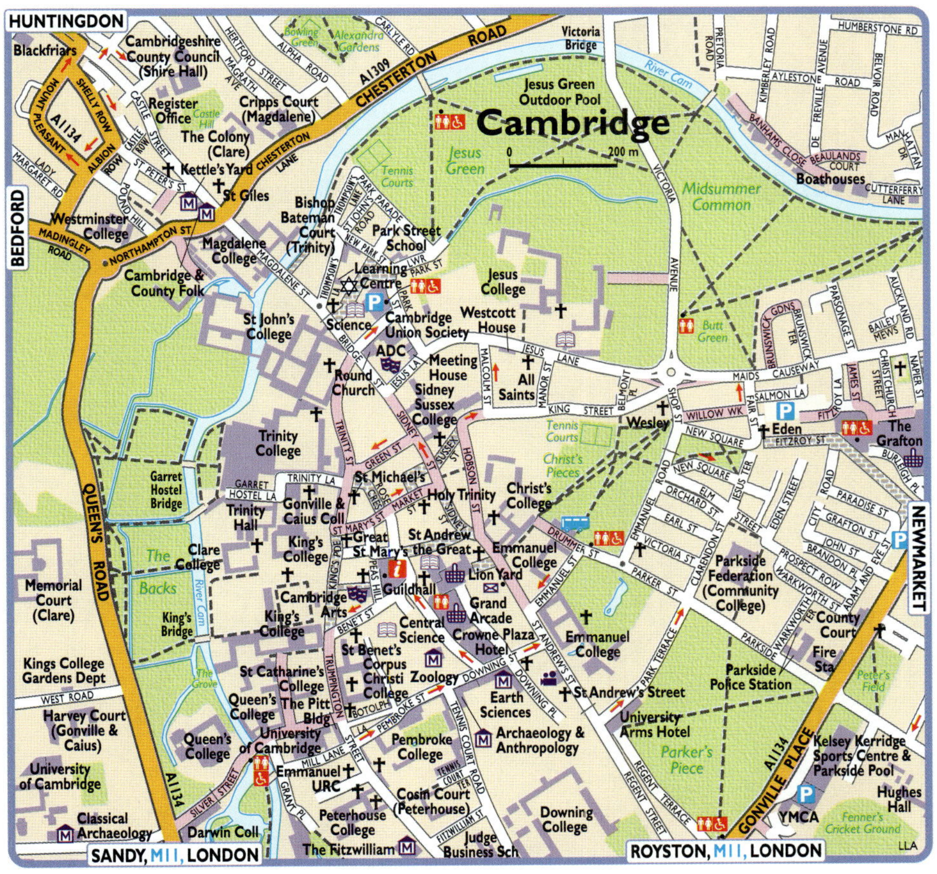
Cambridge
200 m
HUNTINGDON
BEDFORD
NEWMARKET
SANDY, M11, LONDON
ROYSTON, M11, LONDON
Blackfriars
Cambridgeshire County Council (Shire Hall)
Register Office
Cripps Court (Magdalene)
CHESTERTON ROAD
Victoria Bridge
Jesus Green Outdoor Pool
The Colony (Clare)
Kettle's Yard
St Giles
Jesus Green
Midsummer Common
Boathouses
Westminster College
Bishop Bateman Court (Trinity)
Magdalene College
Park Street School
Cambridge & County Folk
Jesus College
St John's College
Cambridge Union Society
Westcott House
Round Church
Sidney Sussex College
Meeting House
All Saints
Trinity College
Wesley
Eden
The Grafton
Garret Hostel Bridge
Trinity Hall
St Michael's
Holy Trinity
Christ's College
Gonville & Caius Coll
Great St Mary's
St Andrew the Great
Emmanuel College
Clare College
King's College
Guildhall
Lion Yard
Grand Arcade
Parkside Federation (Community College)
Memorial Court (Clare)
The Backs
King's Bridge
Cambridge Arts
Central Science
Crowne Plaza Hotel
Emmanuel College
County Court
Fire Sta
Kings College Gardens Dept
St Catharine's College
St Benet's
Corpus Christi College
Zoology
Parkside Police Station
Harvey Court (Gonville & Caius)
Queen's College
The Pitt Bldg
Earth Sciences
St Andrew's Street
University Arms Hotel
Parker's Piece
Kelsey Kerridge Sports Centre & Parkside Pool
University of Cambridge
Emmanuel URC
Pembroke College
Archaeology & Anthropology
Hughes Hall
Classical Archaeology
Darwin Coll
Peterhouse College
Coslin Court (Peterhouse)
Downing College
YMCA
Fenner's Cricket Ground
The Fitzwilliam
Judge Business Sch
QUEEN'S ROAD
GONVILLE PLACE
A1134
A1303
A1309
LLA

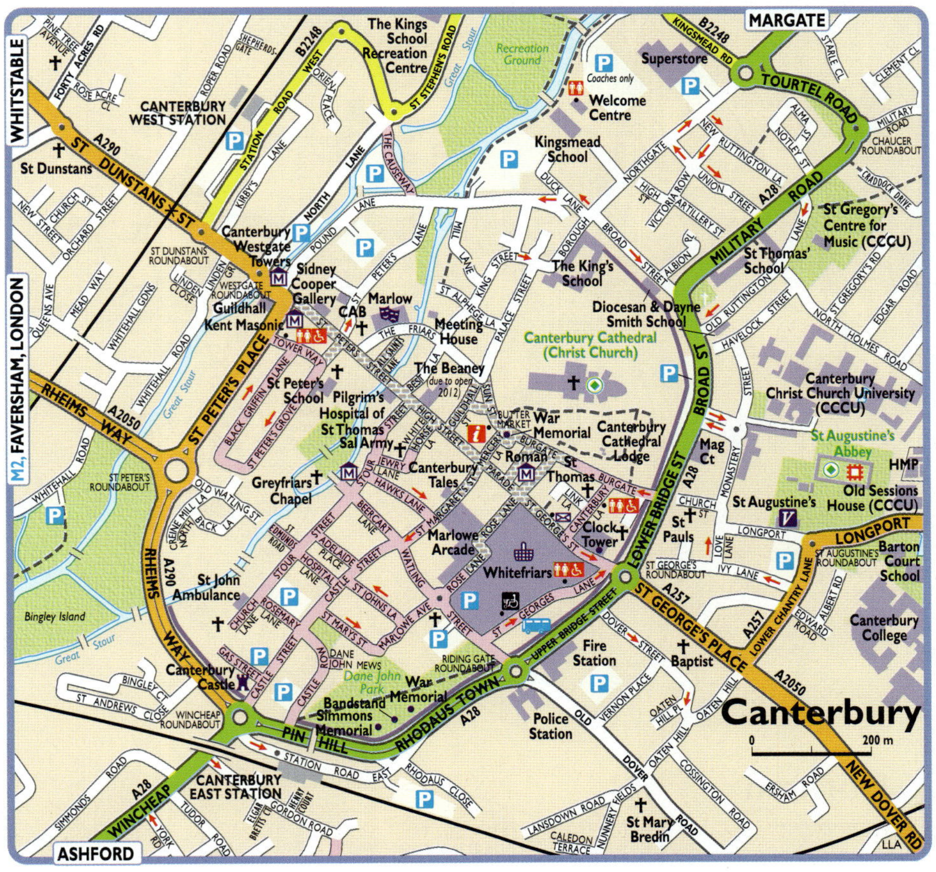
Canterbury
200 m
WHITSTABLE
MARGATE
M2, FAVERSHAM, LONDON
ASHFORD
The Kings School Recreation Centre
Recreation Ground
Superstore
TOURTEL ROAD
CANTERBURY WEST STATION
ST DUNSTANS ST
St Dunstans
Coaches only
Welcome Centre
Kingsmead School
MILITARY ROAD
St Gregory's Centre for Music (CCCU)
St Thomas' School
Canterbury Westgate Towers
Sidney Cooper Gallery
Guildhall
Kent Masonic
Marlow
CAB
The King's School
Diocesan & Payne Smith School
Canterbury Cathedral (Christ Church)
Meeting House
The Beaney
St Peter's School
Pilgrim's Hospital of St Thomas
Sal Army
War Memorial
Canterbury Cathedral Lodge
Canterbury Christ Church University (CCCU)
St Augustine's Abbey
HMP
Roman
St Thomas
Canterbury Tales
Greyfriars Chapel
Marlowe Arcade
Clock Tower
St Paul's
St Augustine's House
Old Sessions House (CCCU)
LONGPORT
Barton Court School
Whitefriars
St John Ambulance
Bingley Island
Great Stour
Fire Station
St George's Place
Baptist
Canterbury College
Canterbury Castle
Dane John Gardens
Bandstand
Dane John Memorial
War Memorial
Police Station
RHODAUS TOWN
PIN HILL
CANTERBURY EAST STATION
St Mary Bredin
WINCHEAP
RHEIMS WAY
ST PETERS PLACE
BROAD ST
NEW DOVER RD
A28
A290
A2050
A257
LLA

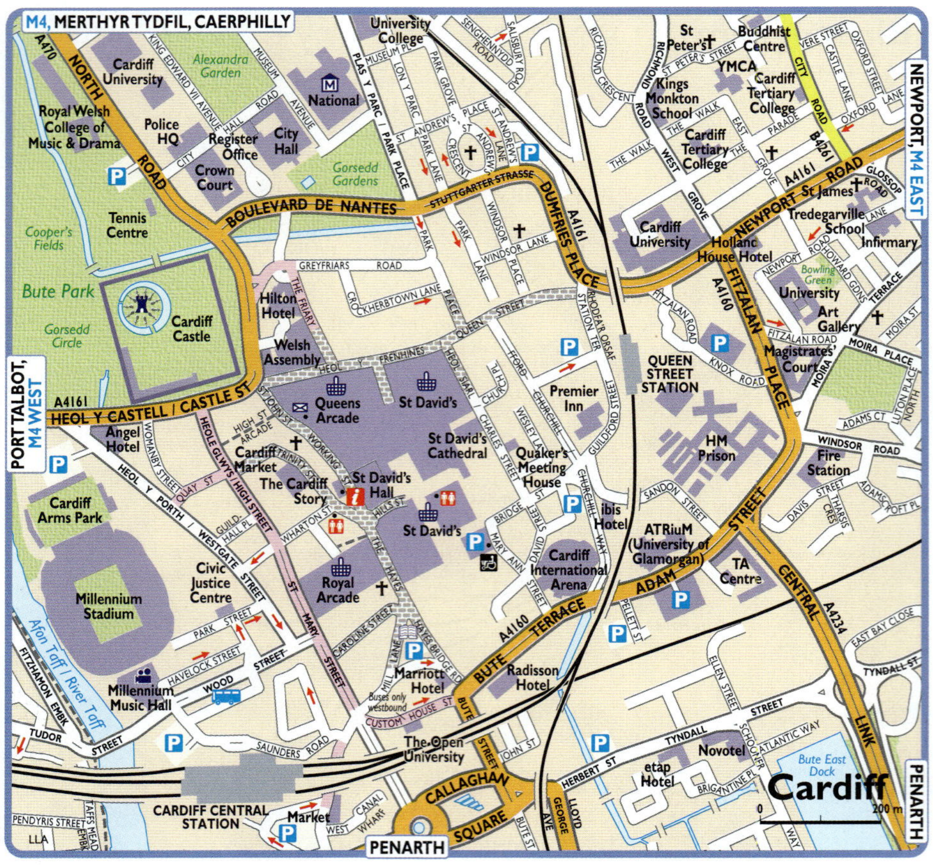
Cardiff
M4, MERTHYR TYDFIL, CAERPHILLY
NEWPORT, M4 EAST
PORT TALBOT, M4 WEST
PENARTH
PENARTH
0 200 m
LLA

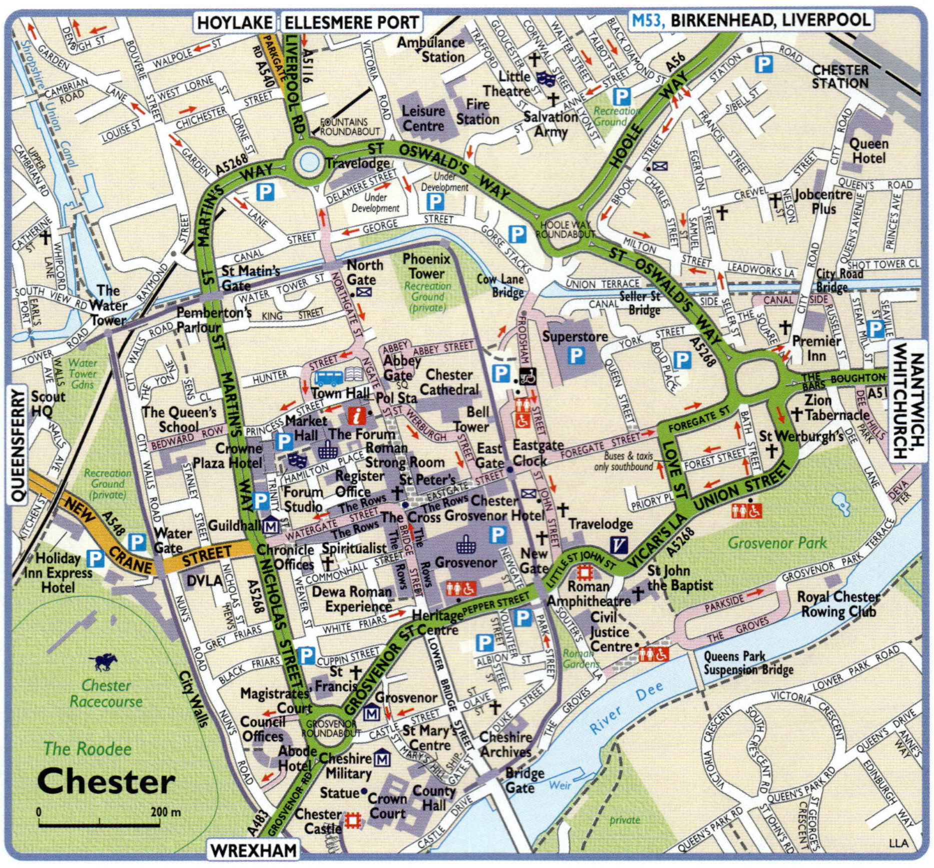
Chester
HOYLAKE
ELLESMERE PORT
M53, BIRKENHEAD, LIVERPOOL
NANTWICH, WHITCHURCH
QUEENSFERRY
WREXHAM
0 200 m
LLA

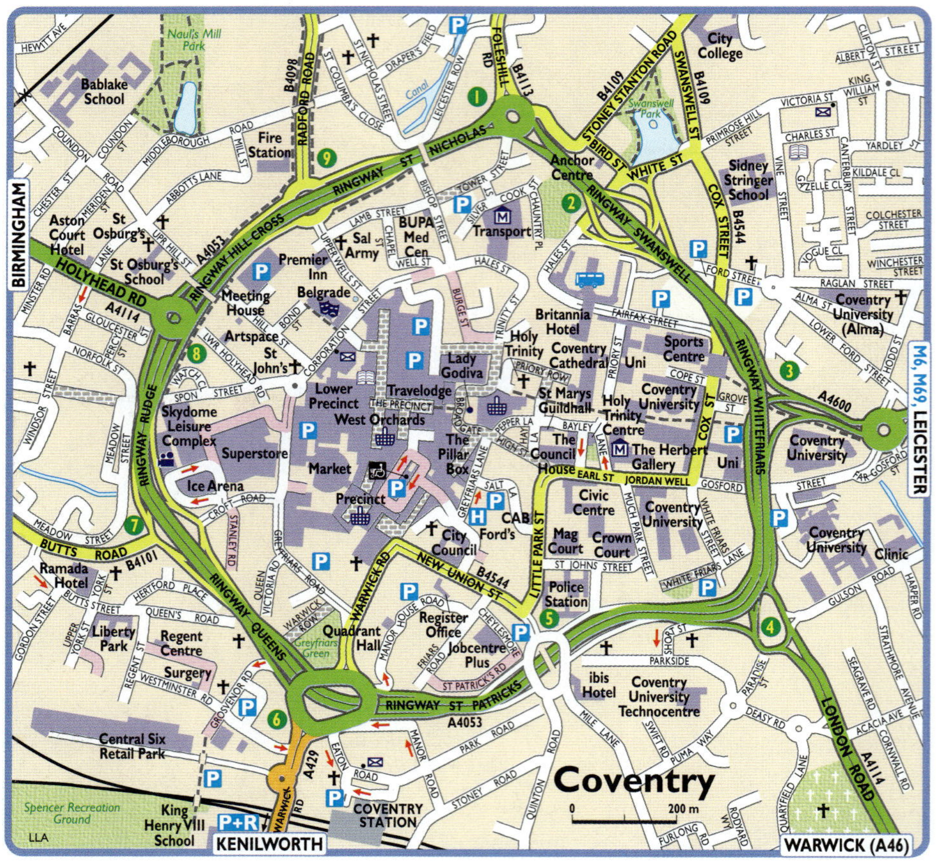
Coventry
BIRMINGHAM
M6, M69, LEICESTER
KENILWORTH
WARWICK (A46)
0 200 m
LLA

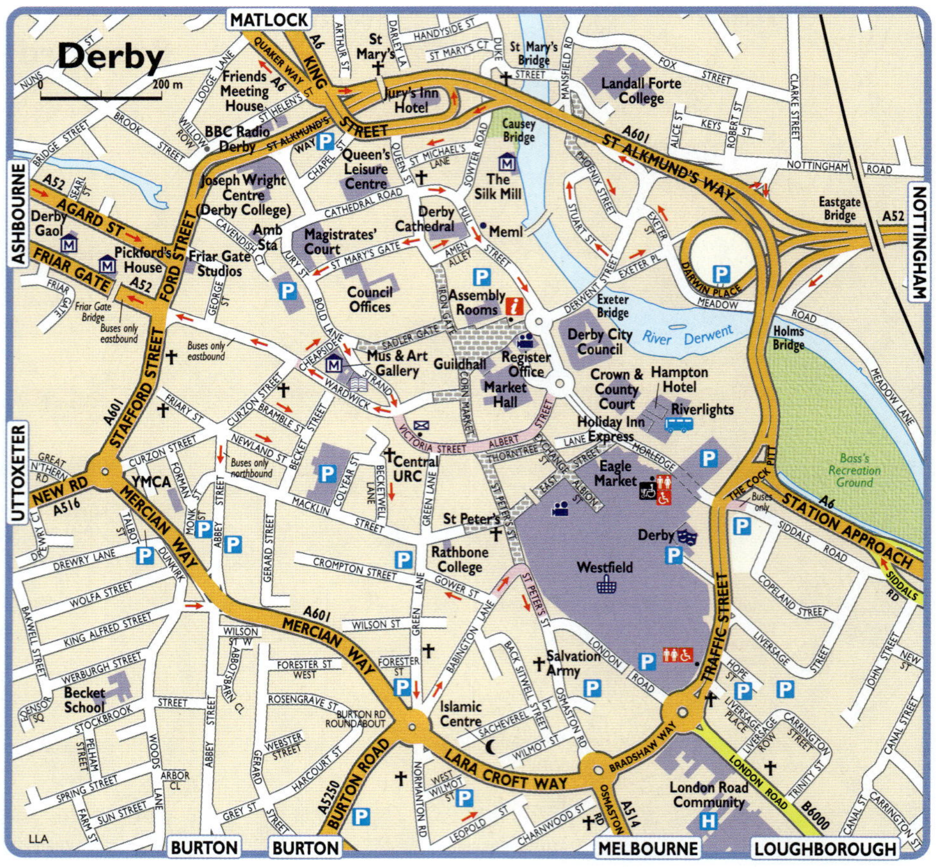
Derby
MATLOCK
ASHBOURNE
NOTTINGHAM
UTTOXETER
BURTON
BURTON
MELBOURNE
LOUGHBOROUGH
0 200 m
LLA

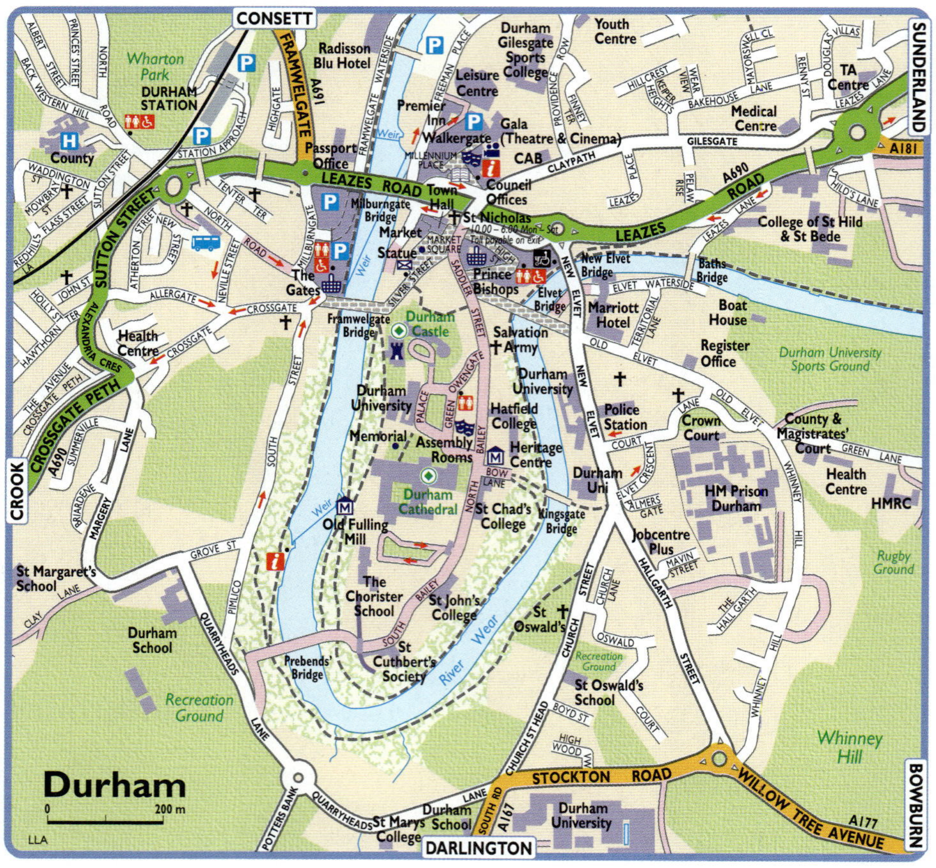
Durham
CONSETT
SUNDERLAND
CROOK
BOWBURN
DARLINGTON
0 200 m
LLA

Edinburgh
LEITH
(A1) BERWICK-UPON-TWEED
KILMARNOCK, LANARK
FORTH ROAD BRIDGE
PEEBLES, JEDBURGH
0 200 m
LLA

Glasgow
MILNGAVIE
M8
COATBRIDGE CARLISLE
KILMARNOCK
CARMUNNOCK, GOVANHILL

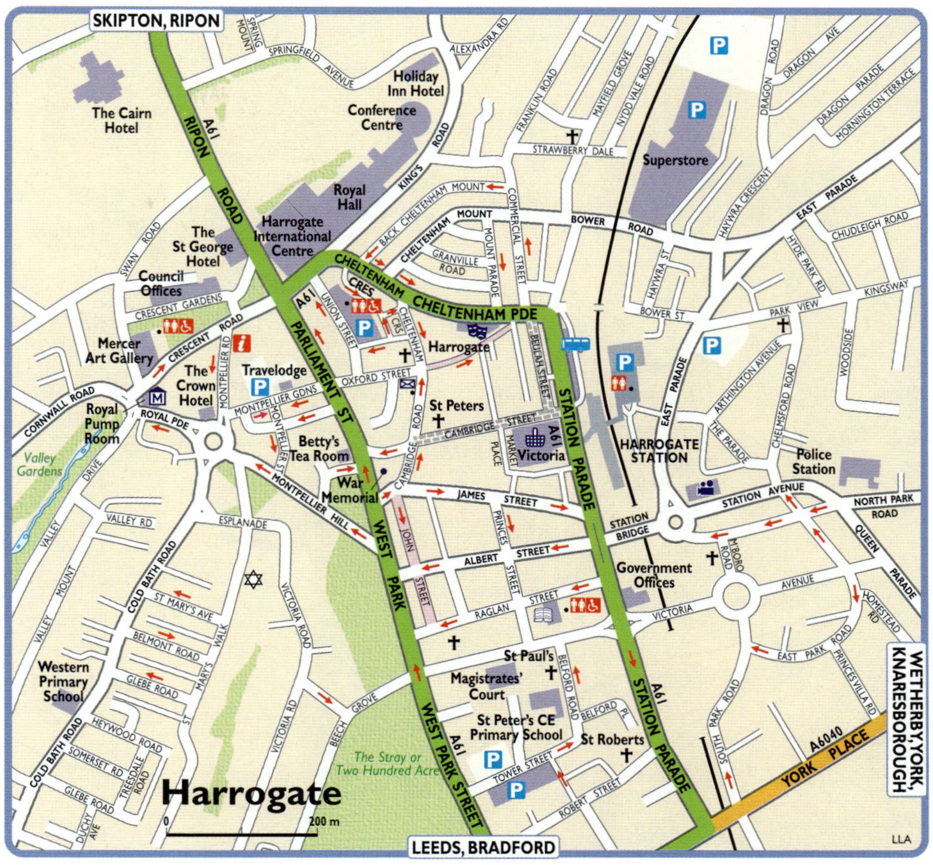
Harrogate
SKIPTON, RIPON
WETHERBY, YORK, KNARESBOROUGH
LEEDS, BRADFORD

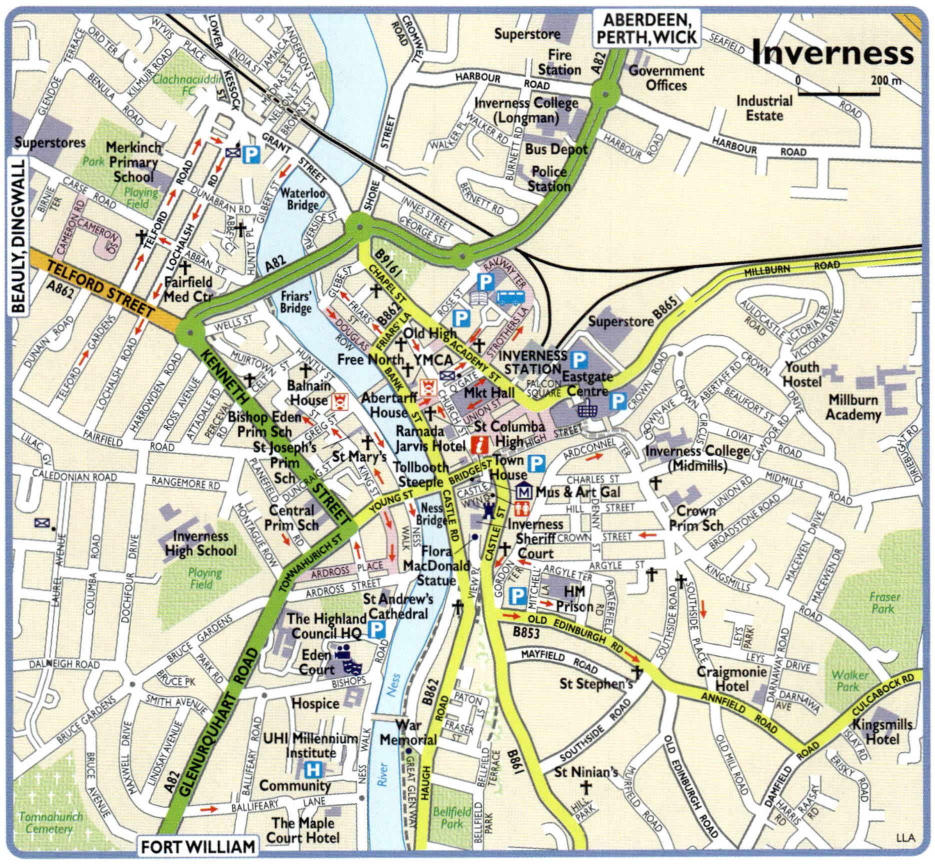
Inverness
ABERDEEN, PERTH, WICK
BEAULY, DINGWALL
FORT WILLIAM

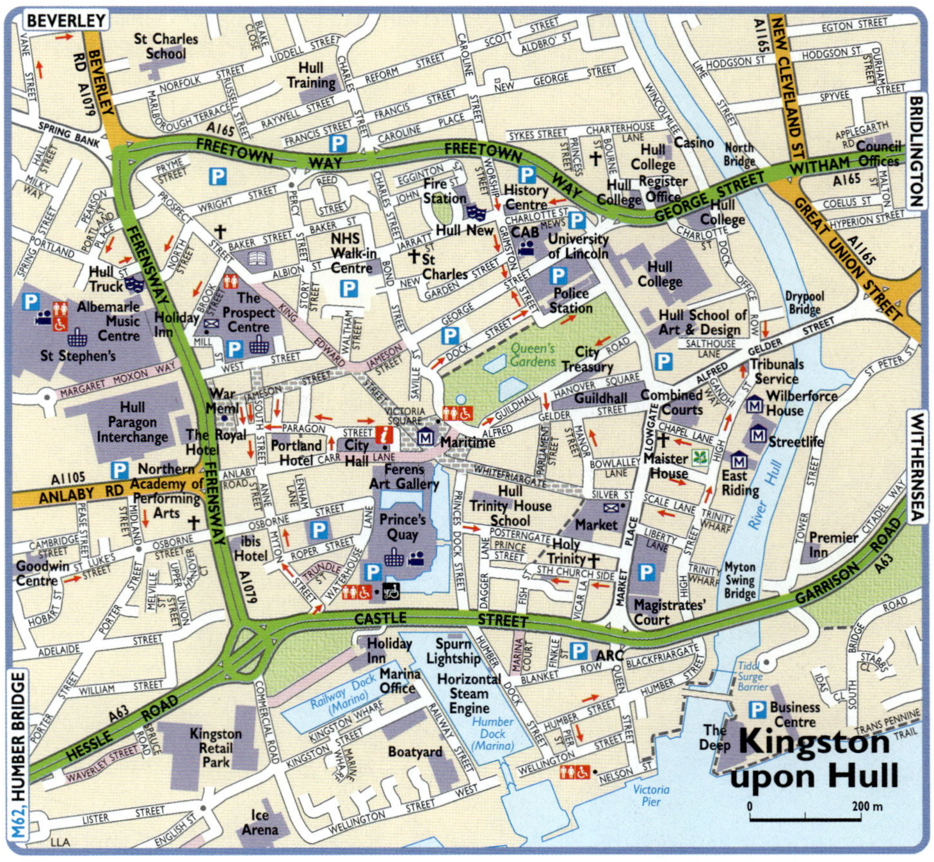
Kingston upon Hull
BEVERLEY
BRIDLINGTON
WITHERNSEA
M62, HUMBER BRIDGE

Leeds
SKIPTON
HARROGATE, WETHERBY
BRADFORD
YORK
M621, M1
M1
Loop traffic

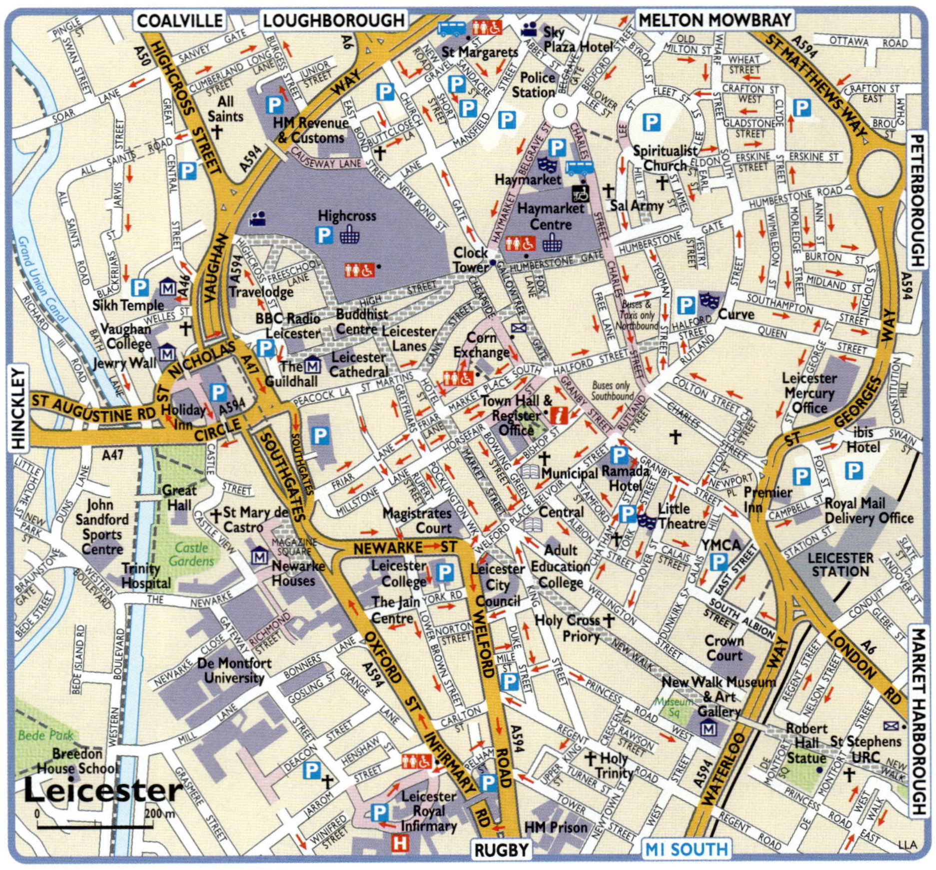
Leicester
COALVILLE
LOUGHBOROUGH
MELTON MOWBRAY
PETERBOROUGH
HINCKLEY
MARKET HARBOROUGH
RUGBY
M1 SOUTH

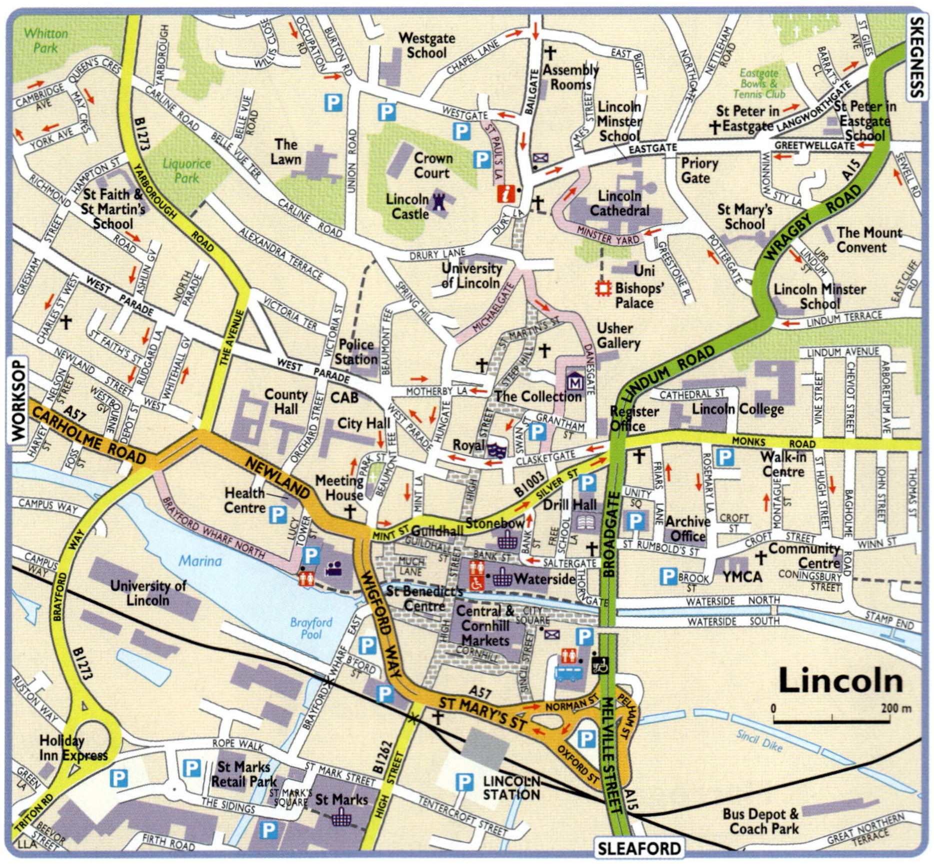
Lincoln
SKEGNESS
WORKSOP
SLEAFORD
0 200 m

Central London
CAMDEN
MARYLEBONE
KNIGHTSBRIDGE
CITY
CHELSEA
Strand
St James's
River Thames
0 200 m

Manchester
BURY
CHEETHAM HILL
MIDDLETON
LOWER BROUGHTON
PRESTON, BOLTON
LEEDS, ROCHDALE, OLDHAM
ALTRINCHAM
STOCKPORT
M60
0 200 m

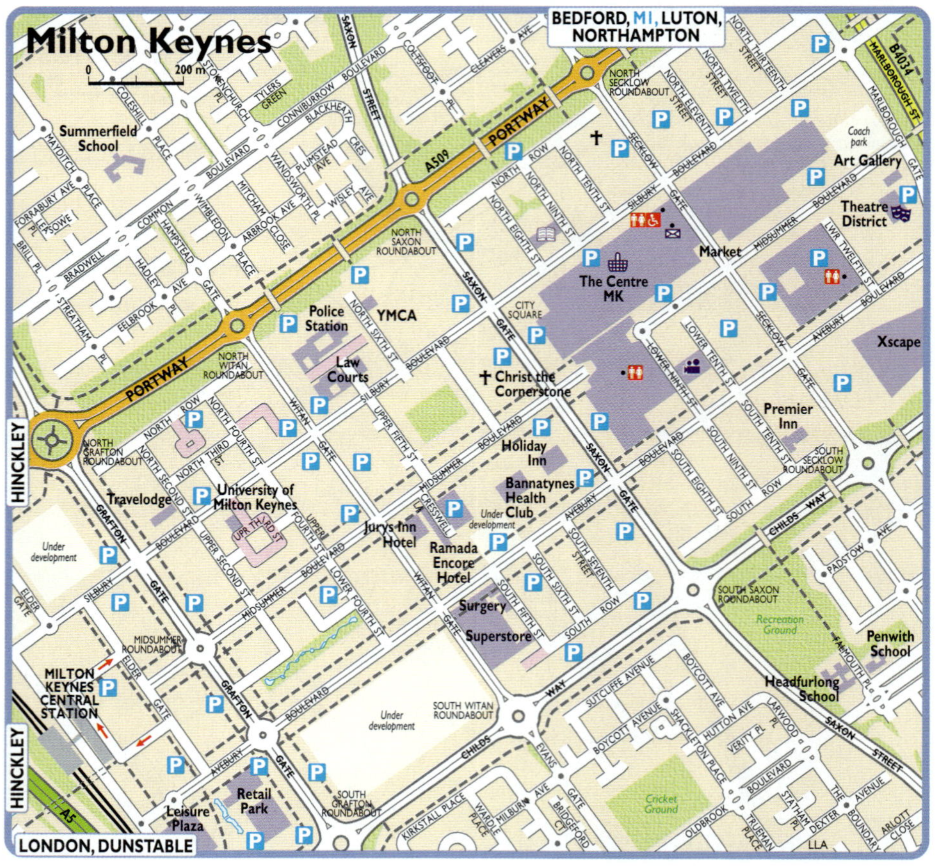
Milton Keynes
BEDFORD, M1, LUTON, NORTHAMPTON
HINCKLEY
LONDON, DUNSTABLE
0 200 m

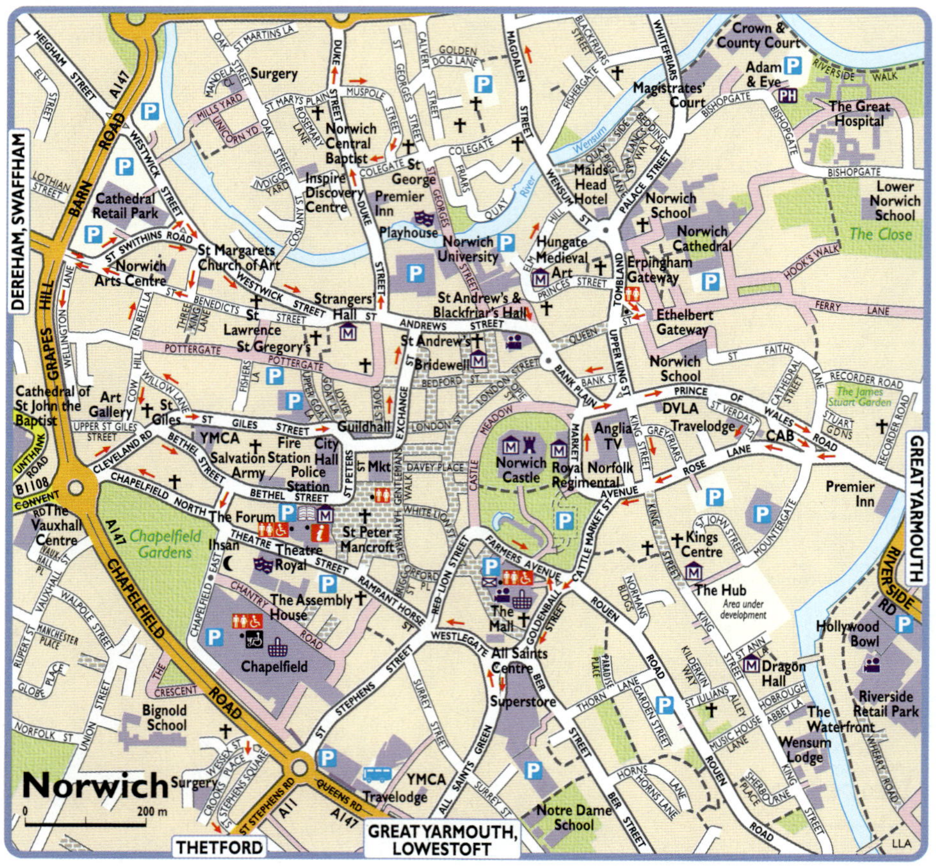
Norwich
DEREHAM, SWAFFHAM
GREAT YARMOUTH
THETFORD
GREAT YARMOUTH, LOWESTOFT
0 200 m

Nottingham
MANSFIELD
M1 (NORTH), MATLOCK
SOUTHWELL
DERBY, M1, LONG EATON
M1 (SOUTH), BIRMINGHAM
LOUGHBOROUGH, MELTON
0 200 m

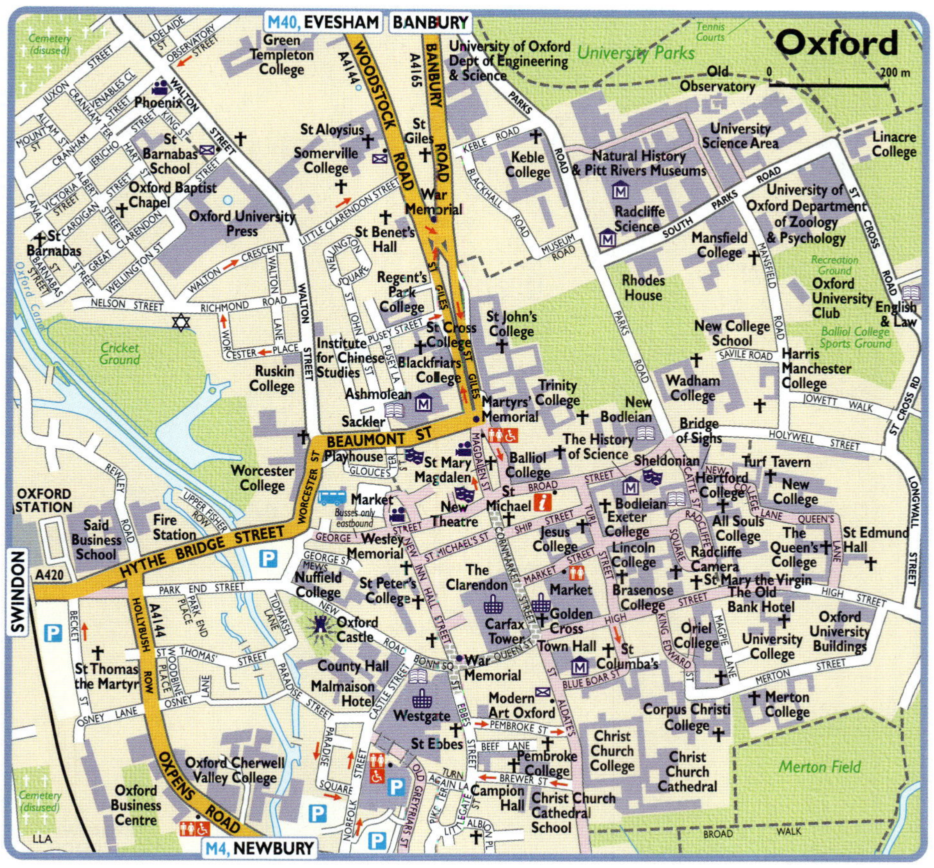
Oxford
M40, EVESHAM
BANBURY
SWINDON
M4, NEWBURY

Peterborough
SLEAFORD
LEICESTER
WISBECH
WHITTLESEY, RAMSEY
CORBY, LONDON

Portsmouth
M275, M27
Portsmouth Harbour

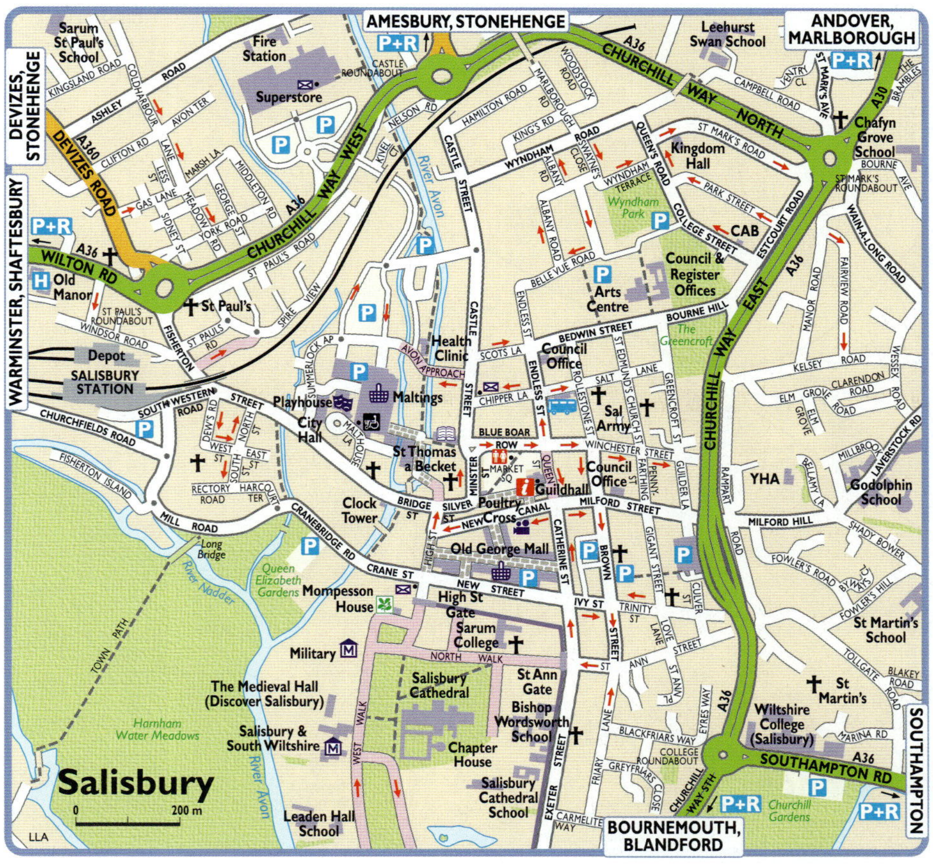
Salisbury
AMESBURY, STONEHENGE
ANDOVER, MARLBOROUGH
DEVIZES, STONEHENGE
WARMINSTER, SHAFTESBURY
SOUTHAMPTON
BOURNEMOUTH, BLANDFORD

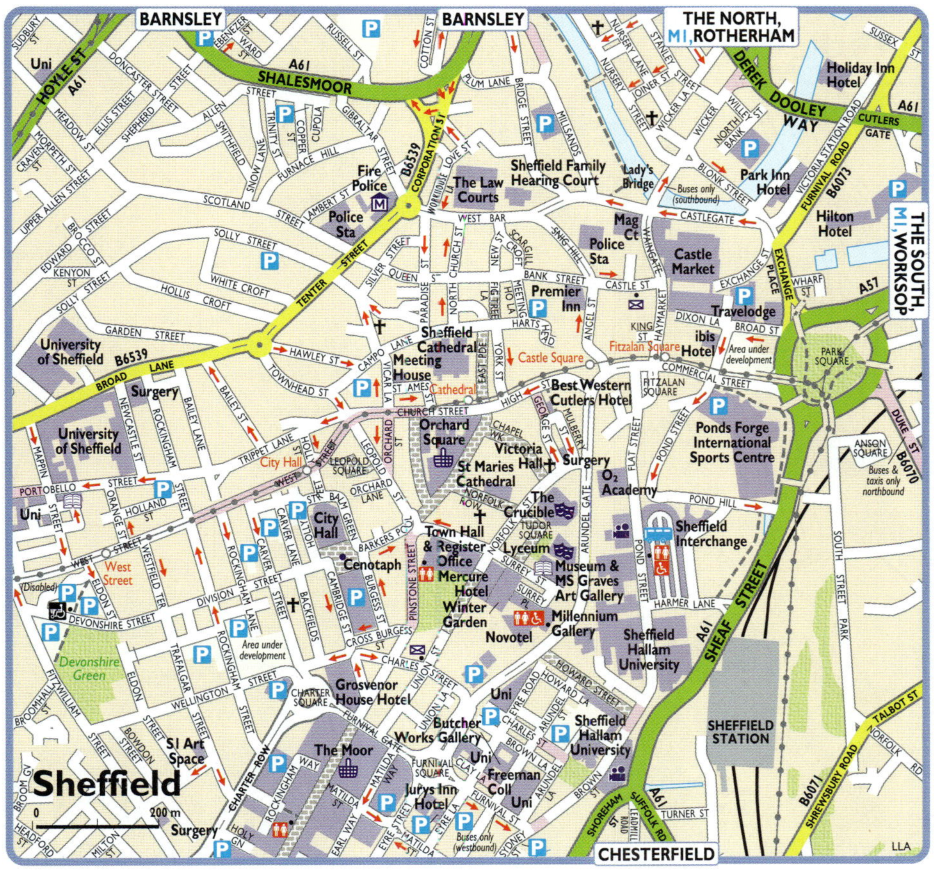
Sheffield
BARNSLEY
BARNSLEY
THE NORTH, M1, ROTHERHAM
THE SOUTH, M1, WORKSOP
CHESTERFIELD

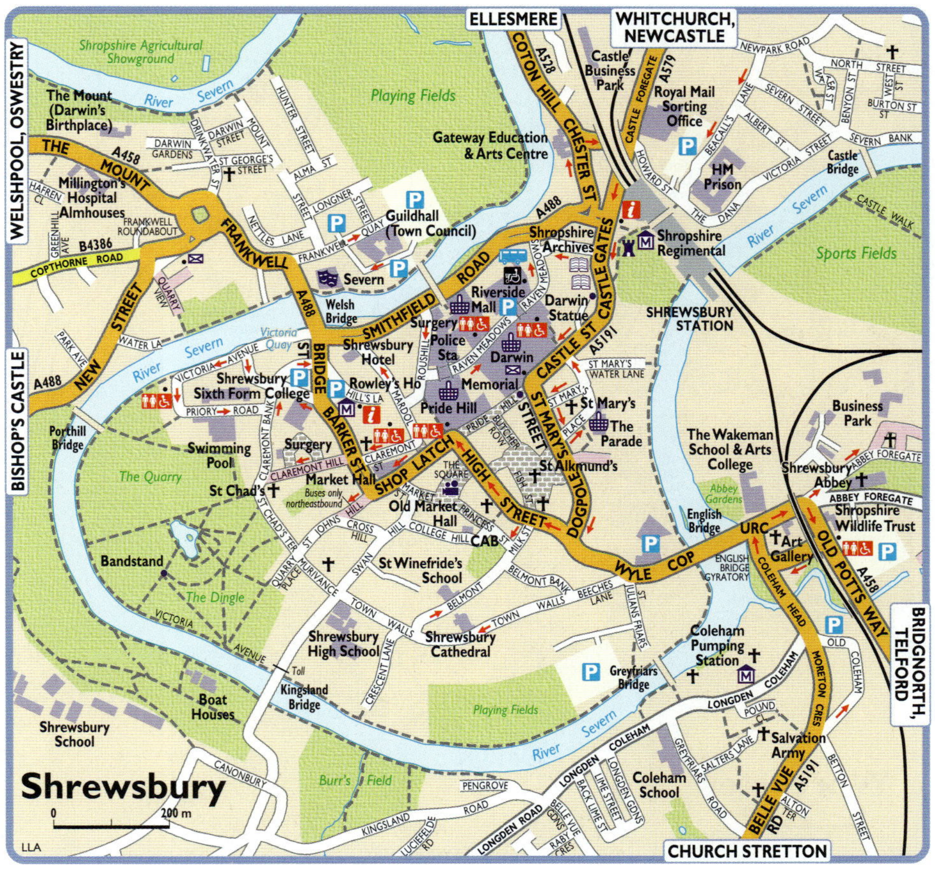
Shrewsbury
ELLESMERE
WHITCHURCH, NEWCASTLE
WELSHPOOL, OSWESTRY
BISHOP'S CASTLE
BRIDGNORTH, TELFORD
CHURCH STRETTON

Southampton
WINCHESTER, LONDON, (M3)
FAREHAM, PORTSMOUTH
FAREHAM
THE WEST, (A33), (M271)
River Test
200 m
LLA

Stratford-upon-Avon
HENLEY
(M40), WARWICK
ALCESTER, WORCESTER
BIDFORD
BROADWAY, SHIPSTON
BANBURY
200 m
LLA

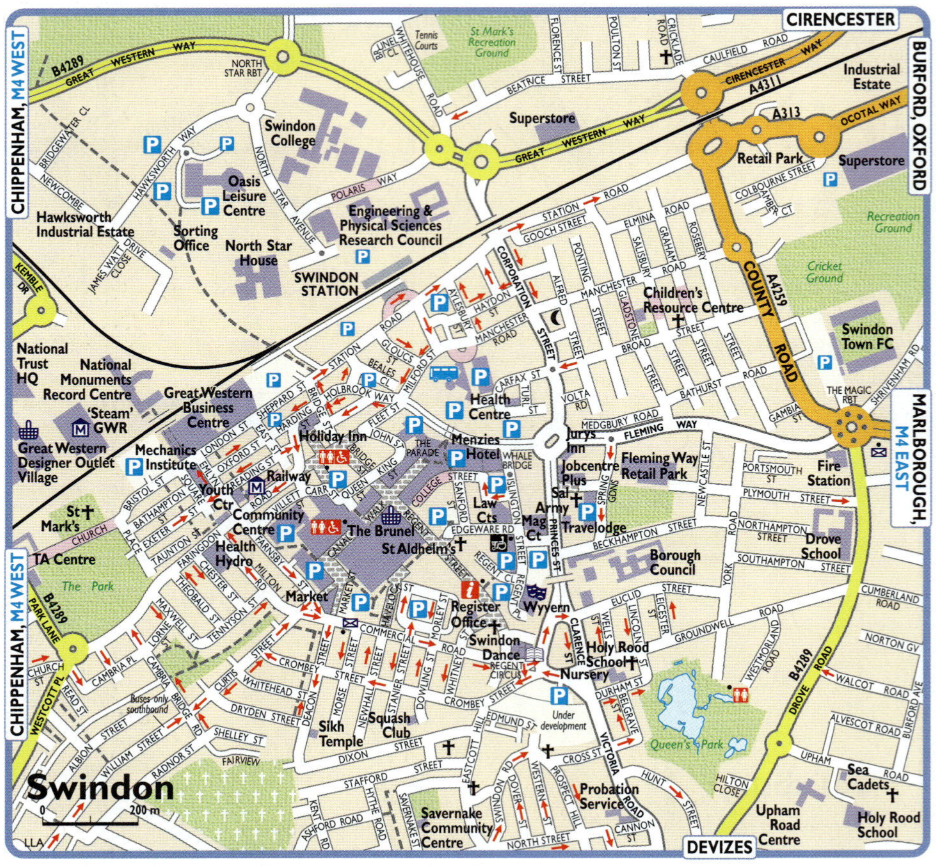
Swindon
CIRENCESTER
BURFORD, OXFORD
MARLBOROUGH, M4 EAST
CHIPPENHAM, M4 WEST
DEVIZES
200 m
LLA

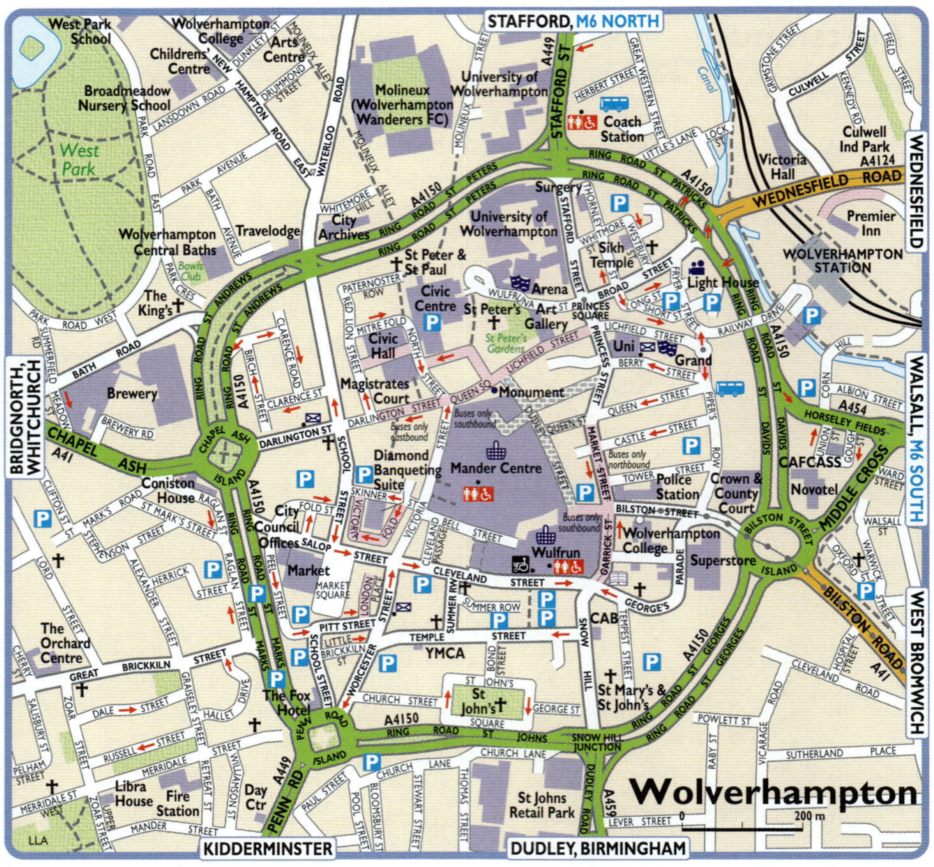
Wolverhampton
STAFFORD, M6 NORTH
WEDNESFIELD
WALSALL, M6 SOUTH
WEST BROMWICH
BRIDGNORTH, WHITCHURCH
KIDDERMINSTER
DUDLEY, BIRMINGHAM
200 m
LLA

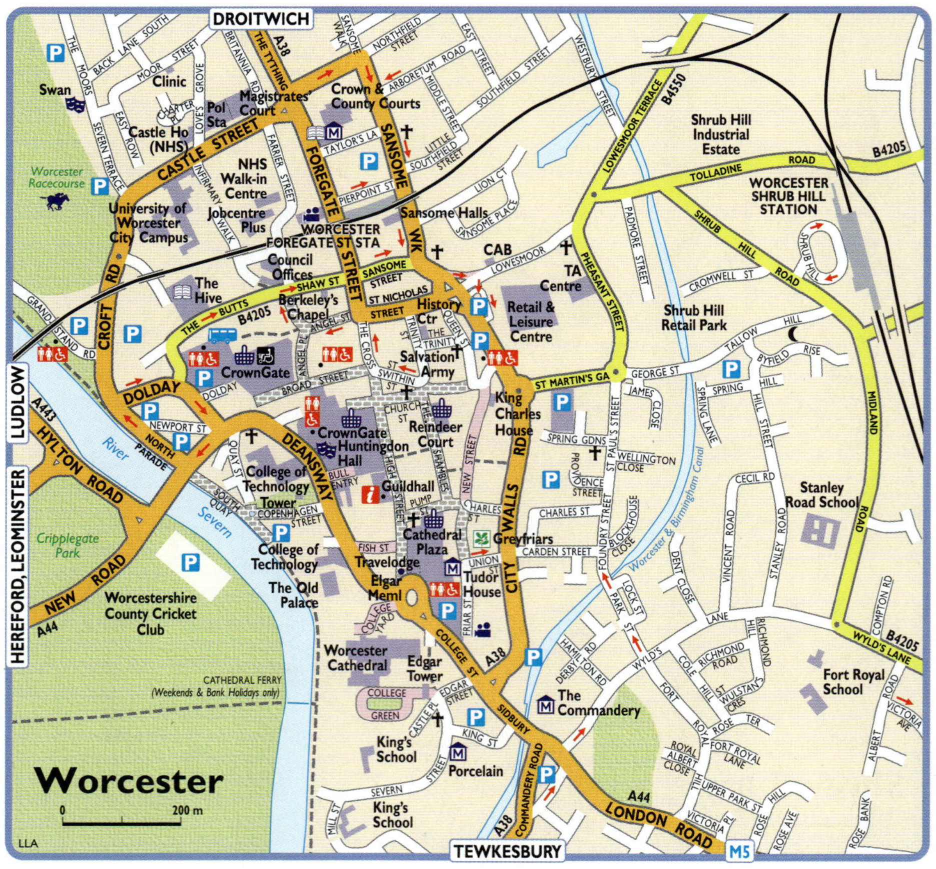
Worcester
DROITWICH
TEWKESBURY
M5
LUDLOW
HEREFORD, LEOMINSTER
200 m
LLA

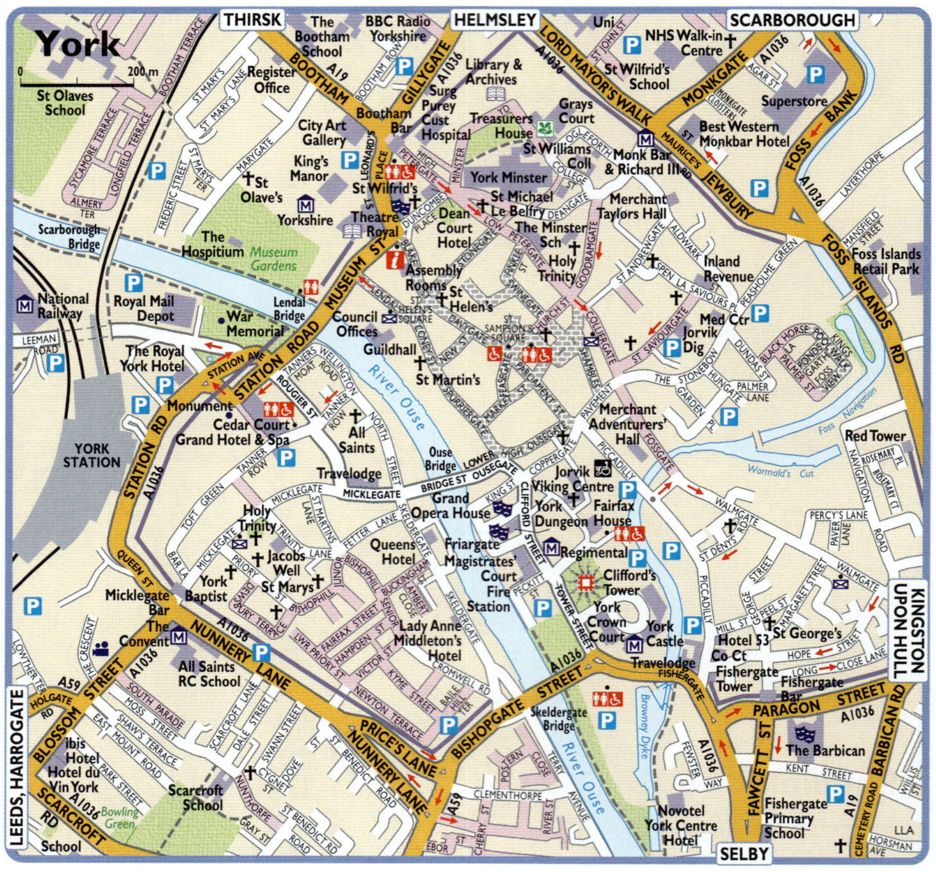
York
THIRSK
HELMSLEY
SCARBOROUGH
KINGSTON UPON HULL
SELBY
LEEDS, HARROGATE
200 m
LLA

# M25 London orbital motorway

Refer also to atlas pages 32–33

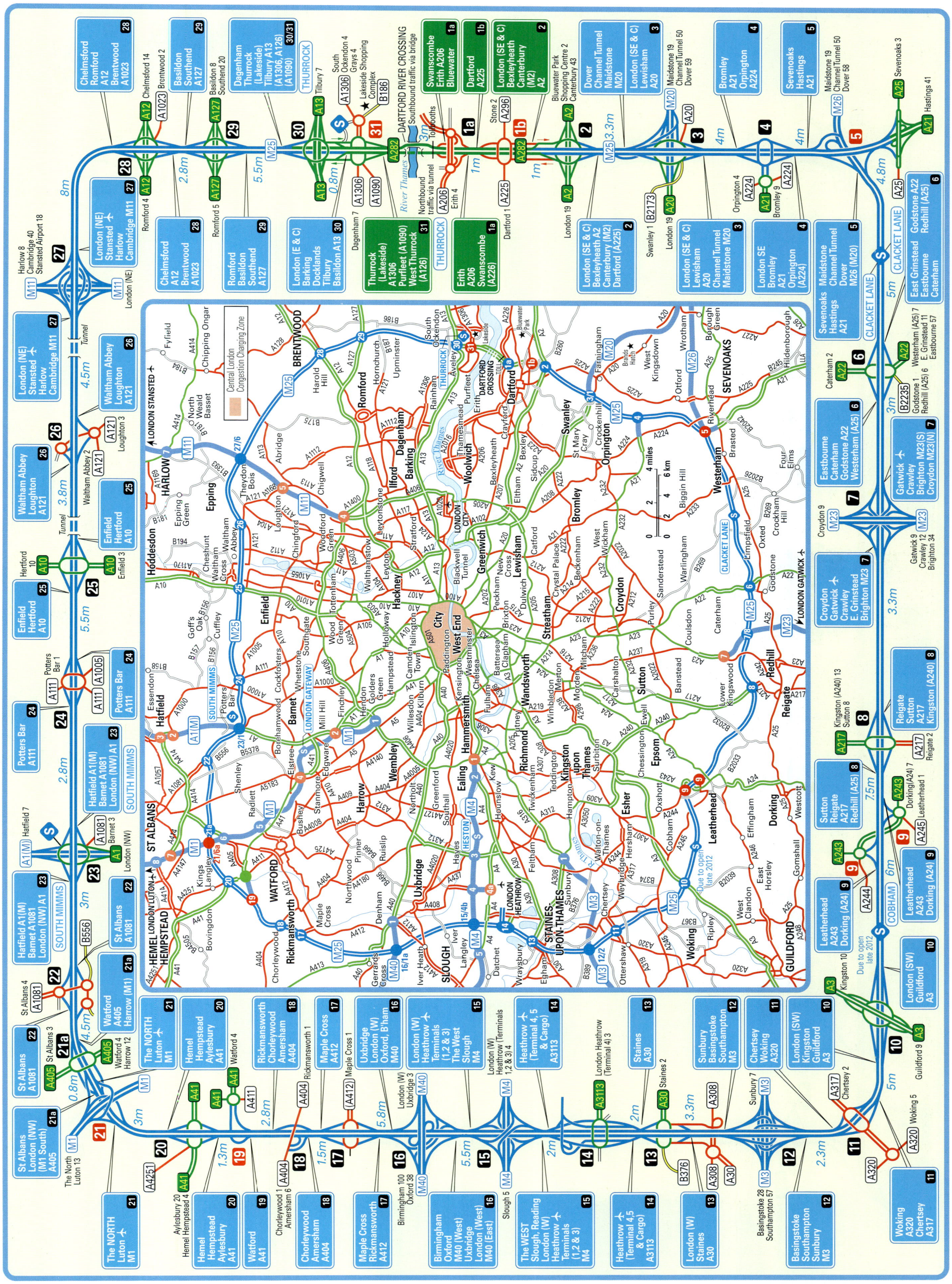

# M6 Toll Motorway

Refer also to atlas pages 53, 64–65

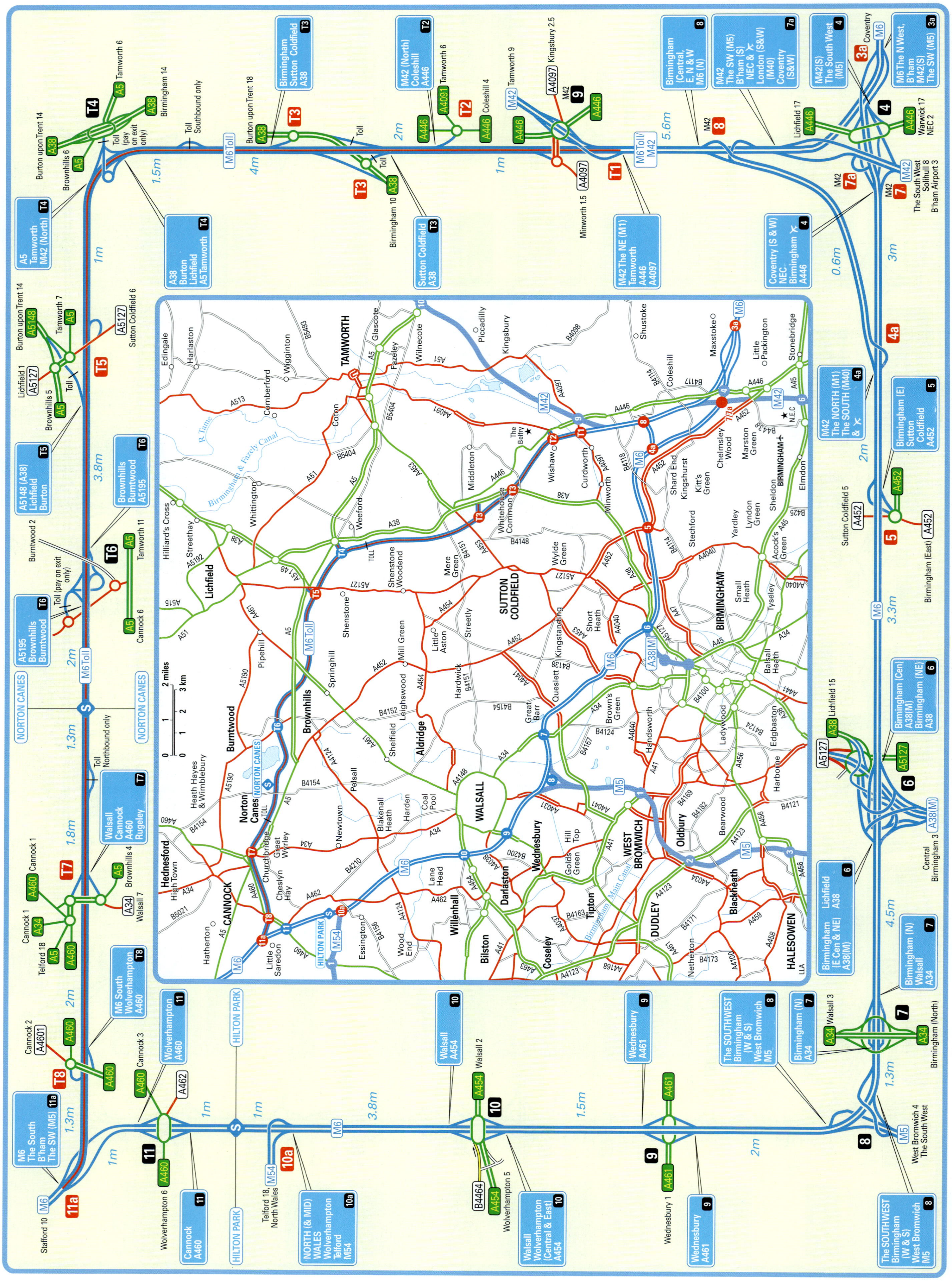

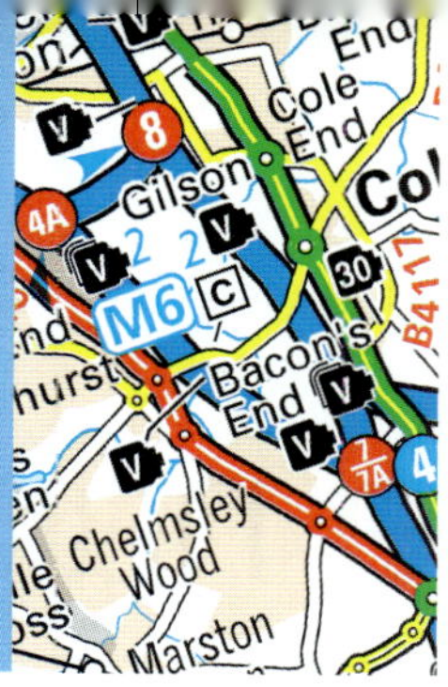


# Restricted junctions

Motorway and Primary Route junctions which have access or exit restrictions are shown on the map pages thus:

## M1 London - Leeds

| Junction | Northbound | Southbound |
|---|---|---|
| 2 | Access only from A1 *(northbound)* | Exit only to A1 *(southbound)* |
| 4 | Access only from A41 *(northbound)* | Exit only to A41 *(southbound)* |
| 6A | Access only from M25 (no link from A405) | Exit only to M25 (no link from A405) |
| 7 | Access only from A414 | Exit only to A414 |
| 17 | Exit only to M45 | Access only from M45 |
| 19 | Exit only to M6 *(northbound)* | Access only from M6 |
| 21A | Exit only, no access | Access only, no exit |
| 23A | Access only from A42 | No restriction |
| 24A | Access only, no exit | Exit only, no access |
| 35A | Exit only, no access | Access only, no exit |
| 43 | Exit only to M621 | Access only from M621 |
| 48 | Exit only to A1(M) *(northbound)* | Access only from A1(M) *(southbound)* |

## M2 Rochester - Faversham

| Junction | Westbound | Eastbound |
|---|---|---|
| 1 | No exit to A2 *(eastbound)* | No access from A2 *(westbound)* |

## M3 Sunbury - Southampton

| Junction | Northeastbound | Southwestbound |
|---|---|---|
| 8 | Access only from A303, no exit | Exit only to A303, no access |
| 10 | Exit only, no access | Access only, no exit |
| 14 | Access from M27 only, no exit | No access to M27 *(westbound)* |

## M4 London - South Wales

| Junction | Westbound | Eastbound |
|---|---|---|
| 1 | Access only from A4 *(westbound)* | Exit only to A4 *(eastbound)* |
| 4A | No exit to A4 *(westbound)* | No restriction |
| 21 | Exit only to M48 | Access only from M48 |
| 23 | Access only from M48 | Exit only to M48 |
| 25 | Exit only, no access | Access only, no exit |
| 25A | Exit only, no access | Access only, no exit |
| 29 | Exit only to A48(M) | Access only from A48(M) |
| 38 | Exit only, no access | No restriction |
| 39 | Access only, no exit | No access or exit |

## M5 Birmingham - Exeter

| Junction | Northeastbound | Southwestbound |
|---|---|---|
| 10 | Access only, no exit | Exit only, no access |
| 11A | Access only from A417 *(westbound)* | Exit only to A417 *(eastbound)* |
| 18 | Exit only, no access | Access only, no exit |
| 18A | Exit only to M49 | Access only from M49 |
| 29 | No restriction | Access only from A30 *(westbound)* |

## M6 Toll Motorway

| Junction | Northwestbound | Southeastbound |
|---|---|---|
| T1 | Access only, no exit | No access or exit |
| T2 | No access or exit | Exit only, no access |
| T3 | Staggered junction, follow signs - access only from A38 *(northbound)* | Staggered junction follow signs - access only from A38 *(southbound)* |
| T5 | Access only, no exit | Exit only to A5148 *(northbound)*, no access |
| T7 | Exit only, no access | Access only, no exit |
| T8 | Exit only, no access | Access only, no exit |

## M6 Rugby - Carlisle

| Junction | Northbound | Southbound |
|---|---|---|
| 3A | Exit only to M6 Toll | Access only from M6 Toll |
| 4A | Access only from M42 *(southbound)* | Exit only to M42 |
| 5 | Exit only, no access | Access only, no exit |
| 10A | Exit only to M54 | Access only from M54 |
| 11A | Access only from M6 Toll | Exit only to M6 Toll |
| with M56 (jct 20A) | No restriction | Access only from M56 *(eastbound)* |
| 20 | Access only, no exit | No restriction |
| 24 | Access only, no exit | Exit only, no access |
| 25 | Exit only, no access | Access only, no exit |
| 29 | No direct access, use adjacent slip road to jct 29A | No direct exit, use adjacent slip road from jct 29A |
| 29A | Access only, no exit | Exit only, no access |
| 30 | Access only from M61 | Exit only to M61 |
| 31A | Exit only, no access | Access only, no exit |
| 45 | Exit only, no access | Access only, no exit |

## M8 Edinburgh - Bishopton

| Junction | Westbound | Eastbound |
|---|---|---|
| 8 | No access from M73 *(southbound)* or from A8 *(eastbound)* & A89 | No exit to M73 *(northbound)* or to A8 *(westbound)* & A89 |
| 9 | Access only, no exit | Exit only, no access |
| 13 | Access only from M80 *(southbound)* | Exit only to M80 *(northbound)* |
| 14 | Access only, no exit | Exit only, no access |
| 16 | Exit only to A804 | Access only from A879 |
| 17 | Exit only to A82 | No restriction |
| 18 | Access only from A82 *(eastbound)* | Exit only to A814 |
| 19 | No access from A814 *(westbound)* | Exit only to A814 *(westbound)* |
| 20 | Exit only, no access | Access only, no exit |
| 21 | Access only, no exit | Exit only to A8 |
| 22 | Exit only to M77 *(southbound)* | Access only from M77 *(northbound)* |
| 23 | Exit only to B768 | Access only from B768 |
| 25 | No access or exit from or to A8 | No access or exit from or to A8 |
| 25A | Exit only, no access | Access only, no exit |
| 28 | Exit only, no access | Access only, no exit |
| 28A | Exit only to A737 | Access only from A737 |

## M9 Edinburgh - Dunblane

| Junction | Northwestbound | Southeastbound |
|---|---|---|
| 1A | Exit only to M9 spur | Access only from M9 spur |
| 2 | Access only, no exit | Exit only, no access |
| 3 | Exit only, no access | Access only, no exit |
| 6 | Access only, no exit | Exit only to A905 |
| 8 | Exit only to M876 *(southwestbound)* | Access only from M876 *(northeastbound)* |

## M11 London - Cambridge

| Junction | Northbound | Southbound |
|---|---|---|
| 4 | Access only from A406 *(eastbound)* | Exit only to A406 |
| 5 | Exit only, no access | Access only, no exit |
| 9 | Exit only to A11 | Access only from A11 |
| 13 | Exit only, no access | Access only, no exit |
| 14 | Exit only, no access | Access only, no exit |

## M20 Swanley - Folkestone

| Junction | Northwestbound | Southeastbound |
|---|---|---|
| 2 | Staggered junction; follow signs - access only | Staggered junction; follow signs - exit only |
| 3 | Exit only to M26 *(westbound)* | Access only from M26 *(eastbound)* |
| 5 | Access only from A20 | For access follow signs - exit only to A20 |
| 6 | No restriction | For exit follow signs |
| 11A | Access only, no exit | Exit only, no access |

## M23 Hooley - Crawley

| Junction | Northbound | Southbound |
|---|---|---|
| 7 | Exit only to A23 *(northbound)* | Access only from A23 *(southbound)* |
| 10A | Access only, no exit | Exit only, no access |

## M25 London Orbital Motorway

| Junction | Clockwise | Anticlockwise |
|---|---|---|
| 1B | No direct access, use slip road to Jct 2. Exit only | Access only, no exit |
| 5 | No exit to M26 *(eastbound)* | No access from M26 |
| 19 | Exit only, no access | Access only, no exit |
| 21 | Access only from M1 *(southbound)*. Exit only to M1 *(northbound)* | Access only from M1 *(southbound)*. Exit only to M1 *(northbound)* |
| 31 | No exit (use slip road via jct 30), access only | No access (use slip road via jct 30), exit only |

## M26 Sevenoaks - Wrotham

| Junction | Westbound | Eastbound |
|---|---|---|
| with M25 (jct 5) | Exit only to clockwise M25 *(westbound)* | Access only from anticlockwise M25 *(eastbound)* |
| with M20 (jct 3) | Access only from M20 *(northwestbound)* | Exit only to M20 *(southeastbound)* |

## M27 Cadnam - Portsmouth

| Junction | Westbound | Eastbound |
|---|---|---|
| 4 | Staggered junction; follow signs - access only from M3 *(southbound)*. Exit only to M3 *(northbound)* | Staggered junction; follow signs - access only from M3 *(southbound)*. Exit only to M3 *(northbound)* |
| 10 | Exit only, no access | Access only, no exit |
| 12 | Staggered junction; follow signs - exit only to M275 *(southbound)* | Staggered junction; follow signs - access only from M275 *(northbound)* |

## M40 London - Birmingham

| Junction | Northwestbound | Southeastbound |
|---|---|---|
| 3 | Exit only, no access | Access only, no exit |
| 7 | Exit only, no access | Access only, no exit |
| 8 | Exit only to M40/A40 | Access only from M40/A40 |
| 13 | Exit only, no access | Access only, no exit |
| 14 | Access only, no exit | Exit only, no access |
| 16 | Access only, no exit | Exit only, no access |

## M42 Bromsgrove - Measham

| Junction | Northeastbound | Southwestbound |
|---|---|---|
| 1 | Access only, no exit | Exit only, no access |
| 7 | Exit only to M6 *(northwestbound)* | Access only from M6 *(northwestbound)* |
| 7A | Exit only to M6 *(southeastbound)* | No access or exit |
| 8 | Access only from M6 *(southeastbound)* | Exit only to M6 *(northwestbound)* |

## M45 Coventry - M1

| Junction | Westbound | Eastbound |
|---|---|---|
| Dunchurch (unnumbered) | Access only from A45 | Exit only, no access |
| with M1 (jct 17) | Access only from M1 *(northbound)* | Exit only to M1 *(southbound)* |

## M53 Mersey Tunnel - Chester

| Junction | Northbound | Southbound |
|---|---|---|
| 11 | Access only from M56 *(westbound)*. Exit only to M56 *(eastbound)* | Access only from M56 *(westbound)*. Exit only to M56 *(eastbound)* |

## M54 Telford

| Junction | Westbound | Eastbound |
|---|---|---|
| with M6 (jct 10A) | Access only from M6 *(northbound)* | Exit only to M6 *(southbound)* |

## M56 North Cheshire

| Junction | Westbound | Eastbound |
|---|---|---|
| 1 | Access only from M60 *(westbound)* | Exit only to M60 *(eastbound)* & A34 *(northbound)* |
| 2 | Exit only, no access | Access only, no exit |
| 3 | Access only, no exit | Exit only, no access |
| 4 | Exit only, no access | Access only, no exit |
| 7 | Exit only, no access | No restriction |
| 8 | Access only, no exit | No access or exit |
| 15 | Exit only to M53 | Access only from M53 |

## M57 Liverpool Outer Ring Road

| Junction | Northwestbound | Southeastbound |
|---|---|---|
| 3 | Access only, no exit | Exit only, no access |
| 5 | Access only from A580 *(westbound)* | Exit only, no access |

## M58 Liverpool - Wigan

| Junction | Westbound | Eastbound |
|---|---|---|
| 1 | Exit only, no access | Access only, no exit |

## M60 Manchester Orbital

| Junction | Clockwise | Anticlockwise |
|---|---|---|
| 2 | Access only, no exit | Exit only, no access |
| 3 | No access from M56 | Access only from A34 *(northbound)* |
| 4 | Access only from A34 *(northbound)*. Exit only to M56 | Access only from M56 *(eastbound)*. Exit only to A34 *(southbound)* |
| 5 | Access and exit only from and to A5103 *(northbound)* | Access and exit only from and to A5103 *(southbound)* |
| 7 | No direct access, use slip road to jct 8. Exit only to A56 | Access only from A56. No exit - use jct 8 |
| 14 | Access from A580 *(eastbound)* | Exit only to A580 *(westbound)* |
| 16 | Access only, no exit | Exit only, no access |
| 20 | Exit only, no access | Access only, no exit |
| 22 | No restriction | Exit only, no access |
| 25 | Exit only, no access | No restriction |
| 26 | No restriction | Exit only, no access |
| 27 | Access only, no exit | Exit only, no access |

## M61 Manchester - Preston

| Junction | Northwestbound | Southeastbound |
|---|---|---|
| 3 | No access or exit | Exit only, no access |
| with M6 (jct 30) | Exit only to M6 *(northbound)* | Access only from M6 *(southbound)* |

## M62 Liverpool - Kingston upon Hull

| Junction | Westbound | Eastbound |
|---|---|---|
| 23 | Access only, no exit | Exit only, no access |
| 32A | No access to A1(M) (southbound) | No restriction |

## M65 Preston - Colne

| Junction | Northeastbound | Southwestbound |
|---|---|---|
| 9 | Exit only, no access | Access only, no exit |
| 11 | Access only, no exit | Exit only, no access |

## M66 Bury

| Junction | Northbound | Southbound |
|---|---|---|
| with A56 | Exit only to A56 *(northbound)* | Access only from A56 *(southbound)* |
| 1 | Exit only, no access | Access only, no exit |

## M67 Hyde Bypass

| Junction | Westbound | Eastbound |
|---|---|---|
| 1 | Access only, no exit | Exit only, no access |
| 2 | Exit only, no access | Access only, no exit |
| 3 | Exit only, no access | No restriction |

## M69 Coventry - Leicester

| Junction | Northbound | Southbound |
|---|---|---|
| 2 | Access only, no exit | Exit only, no access |

## M73 East of Glasgow

| Junction | Northbound | Southbound |
|---|---|---|
| 2 | No access from or exit to A89. No access from M8 *(eastbound)*. | No access from or exit to A89. No exit to M8 *(westbound)* |

## M74 and A74(M) Glasgow - Gretna

| Junction | Northbound | Southbound |
|---|---|---|
| 3 | Exit only, no access | Access only, no exit |
| 3A | Access only, no exit | Exit only, no access |
| 7 | Access only, no exit | Exit only, no access |
| 9 | No access or exit | Exit only, no access |
| 10 | No restrictions | Access only, no exit |
| 11 | Access only, no exit | Exit only, no access |
| 12 | Exit only, no access | Access only, no exit |
| 18 | Exit only, no access | Access only, no exit |

## M77 South of Glasgow

| Junction | Northbound | Southbound |
|---|---|---|
| with M8 (jct 22) | No exit to M8 *(westbound)* | No access from M8 *(eastbound)* |
| 4 | Access only, no exit | Exit only, no access |
| 6 | Access only, no exit | Exit only, no access |
| 7 | Access only, no exit | No restriction |

## M80 Glasgow - Stirling

| Junction | Northbound | Southbound |
|---|---|---|
| 4A | Exit only, no access | Access only, no exit |
| 6A | Access only, no exit | Exit only, no access |
| 8 | Exit only to M876 *(northeastbound)* | Access only from M876 *(southwestbound)* |

## M90 Forth Road Bridge - Perth

| Junction | Northbound | Southbound |
|---|---|---|
| 2A | Exit only to A92 *(eastbound)* | Access only from A92 *(westbound)* |
| 7 | Access only, no exit | Exit only, no access |
| 8 | Exit only, no access | Access only, no exit |
| 10 | No access from A912. No exit to A912 *(southbound)* | No access from A912 *(northbound)*. No exit to A912 |

## M180 Doncaster - Grimsby

| Junction | Westbound | Eastbound |
|---|---|---|
| 1 | Access only, no exit | Exit only, no access |

## M606 Bradford Spur

| Junction | Northbound | Southbound |
|---|---|---|
| 2 | Exit only, no access | No restriction |

## M621 Leeds - M1

| Junction | Clockwise | Anticlockwise |
|---|---|---|
| 2A | Access only, no exit | Exit only, no access |
| 4 | No exit or access | No restriction |
| 5 | Access only, no exit | Exit only, no access |
| 6 | Exit only, no access | Access only, no exit |
| with M1 (jct 43) | Exit only to M1 *(southbound)* | Access only from M1 *(northbound)* |

## M876 Bonnybridge - Kincardine Bridge

| Junction | Northeastbound | Southwestbound |
|---|---|---|
| with M80 (jct 5) | Access only from M80 *(northbound)* | Exit only to M80 *(southbound)* |
| with M9 (jct 8) | Exit only to M9 *(eastbound)* | Access only from M9 *(westbound)* |

## A1(M) South Mimms - Baldock

| Junction | Northbound | Southbound |
|---|---|---|
| 2 | Exit only, no access | Access only, no exit |
| 3 | No restriction | Exit only, no access |
| 5 | Access only, no exit | No access or exit |

## A1(M) East of Leeds

| Junction | Northbound | Southbound |
|---|---|---|
| 41 | No access to M62 *(eastbound)* | No restriction |
| 43 | Access only from M1 *(northbound)* | Exit only to M1 *(southbound)* |

## A1(M) Scotch Corner - Newcastle upon Tyne

| Junction | Northbound | Southbound |
|---|---|---|
| 57 | Exit only to A66(M) *(eastbound)* | Access only from A66(M) *(westbound)* |
| 65 | No access Exit only to A194(M) & A1 *(northbound)* | No exit Access only from A194(M) & A1 *(southbound)* |

## A3(M) Horndean - Havant

| Junction | Northbound | Southbound |
|---|---|---|
| 1 | Access only from A3 | Exit only to A3 |
| 4 | Exit only, no access | Access only, no exit |

## A48(M) Cardiff Spur

| Junction | Westbound | Eastbound |
|---|---|---|
| 29 | Access only from M4 *(westbound)* | Exit only to M4 *(eastbound)* |
| 29A | Exit only to A48 *(westbound)* | Access only from A48 *(eastbound)* |

## A66(M) Darlington Spur

| Junction | Westbound | Eastbound |
|---|---|---|
| with A1(M) (jct 57) | Exit only to A1(M) *(southbound)* | Access only from A1(M) *(northbound)* |

## A194(M) Newcastle upon Tyne

| Junction | Northbound | Southbound |
|---|---|---|
| with A1(M) (jct 65) | Access only from A1(M) *(northbound)* | Exit only to A1(M) *(southbound)* |

## A12 M25 - Ipswich

| Junction | Northeastbound | Southwestbound |
|---|---|---|
| 13 | Access only, no exit | No restriction |
| 14 | Exit only, no access | Access only, no exit |
| 20A | Exit only, no access | Access only, no exit |
| 20B | Access only, no exit | Exit only, no access |
| 21 | No restriction | Access only, no exit |
| 23 | Exit only, no access | Access only, no exit |
| 24 | Access only, no exit | Exit only, no access |
| 27 | Exit only, no access | Access only, no exit |
| with A120 (unnumbered) | Exit only, no access | Access only, no exit |
| 29 | Access only, no exit | Exit only, no access |
| Dedham & Stratford St Mary (unnumbered) | Exit only | Access only |

## A14 M1 - Felixstowe

| Junction | Westbound | Eastbound |
|---|---|---|
| With M1/M6 (jct19) | Exit only to M6 and M1 *(northbound)* | Access only from M6 and M1 *(southbound)* |
| 4 | Exit only, no access | Access only, no exit |
| 31 | Access only from A1307 | Exit only, to A1307 |
| 34 | Access only, no exit | Exit only, no access |
| 36 | Exit only to A11 | Access only from A11 |
| 38 | Access only from A11 | Exit only to A11 |
| 39 | Exit only, no access | Access only, no exit |
| 61 | Access only, no exit | Exit only, no access |

## A55 Holyhead - Chester

| Junction | Westbound | Eastbound |
|---|---|---|
| 8A | Exit only, no access | Access only, no exit |
| 23A | Access only, no exit | Exit only, no access |
| 24A | Exit only, no access | No access or exit |
| 33A | Exit only, no access | No access or exit |
| 33B | Exit only, no access | Access only, no exit |
| 36A | Exit only to A5104 | Access only from A5104 |

# Index to place names

This index lists places appearing in the main-map section of the atlas in alphabetical order. The reference before each name gives the atlas page number and grid reference of the square in which the place appears. The map shows counties, unitary authorities and administrative areas, together with a list of the abbreviated name forms used in the index.

The top 100 places of tourist interest are indexed in **red**, (or **green** if a World Heritage site), motorway service areas in **blue** and airports in blue *italic*.

## Scotland

| | |
|---|---|
| Abers | **Aberdeenshire** |
| Ag & B | **Argyll and Bute** |
| Angus | **Angus** |
| Border | **Scottish Borders** |
| C Aber | **City of Aberdeen** |
| C Dund | **City of Dundee** |
| C Edin | **City of Edinburgh** |
| C Glas | **City of Glasgow** |
| Clacks | **Clackmannanshire (1)** |
| D & G | **Dumfries & Galloway** |
| E Ayrs | **East Ayrshire** |
| E Duns | **East Dunbartonshire (2)** |
| E Loth | **East Lothian** |
| E Rens | **East Renfrewshire (3)** |
| Falk | **Falkirk** |
| Fife | **Fife** |
| Highld | **Highland** |
| Inver | **Inverclyde (4)** |
| Mdloth | **Midlothian (5)** |
| Moray | **Moray** |
| N Ayrs | **North Ayrshire** |
| N Lans | **North Lanarkshire (6)** |
| Ork | **Orkney Islands** |
| P & K | **Perth & Kinross** |
| Rens | **Renfrewshire (7)** |
| S Ayrs | **South Ayrshire** |
| Shet | **Shetland Islands** |
| S Lans | **South Lanarkshire** |
| Stirlg | **Stirling** |
| W Duns | **West Dunbartonshire (8)** |
| W Isls | **Western Isles (Na h-Eileanan an Iar)** |
| W Loth | **West Lothian** |

## Wales

| | |
|---|---|
| Blae G | **Blaenau Gwent (9)** |
| Brdgnd | **Bridgend (10)** |
| Caerph | **Caerphilly (11)** |
| Cardif | **Cardiff** |
| Carmth | **Carmarthenshire** |
| Cerdgn | **Ceredigion** |
| Conwy | **Conwy** |
| Denbgs | **Denbighshire** |
| Flints | **Flintshire** |
| Gwynd | **Gwynedd** |
| IoA | **Isle of Anglesey** |
| Mons | **Monmouthshire** |
| Myr Td | **Merthyr Tydfil (12)** |
| Neath | **Neath Port Talbot (13)** |
| Newpt | **Newport (14)** |
| Pembks | **Pembrokeshire** |
| Powys | **Powys** |
| Rhondd | **Rhondda Cynon Taff (15)** |
| Swans | **Swansea** |
| Torfn | **Torfaen (16)** |
| V Glam | **Vale of Glamorgan (17)** |
| Wrexhm | **Wrexham** |

## England

| | |
|---|---|
| BaNES | **Bath & N E Somerset (18)** |
| Barns | **Barnsley (19)** |
| Bed | **Bedford** |
| Birm | **Birmingham** |
| Bl w D | **Blackburn with Darwen (20)** |
| Bmouth | **Bournemouth** |
| Bolton | **Bolton (21)** |
| Bpool | **Blackpool** |
| Br & H | **Brighton & Hove (22)** |
| Br For | **Bracknell Forest (23)** |
| Bristl | **City of Bristol** |
| Bucks | **Buckinghamshire** |
| Bury | **Bury (24)** |
| C Beds | **Central Bedfordshire** |
| C Brad | **City of Bradford** |
| C Derb | **City of Derby** |
| C KuH | **City of Kingston upon Hull** |
| C Leic | **City of Leicester** |
| C Nott | **City of Nottingham** |
| C Pete | **City of Peterborough** |
| C Plym | **City of Plymouth** |
| C Port | **City of Portsmouth** |
| C Sotn | **City of Southampton** |
| C Stke | **City of Stoke-on-Trent** |
| C York | **City of York** |
| Calder | **Calderdale (25)** |
| Cambs | **Cambridgeshire** |
| Ches E | **Cheshire East** |
| Ches W | **Cheshire West and Chester** |
| Cnwll | **Cornwall** |
| Covtry | **Coventry** |
| Cumb | **Cumbria** |
| Darltn | **Darlington (26)** |
| Derbys | **Derbyshire** |
| Devon | **Devon** |
| Donc | **Doncaster (27)** |
| Dorset | **Dorset** |
| Dudley | **Dudley (28)** |
| Dur | **Durham** |
| E R Yk | **East Riding of Yorkshire** |
| E Susx | **East Sussex** |
| Essex | **Essex** |
| Gatesd | **Gateshead (29)** |
| Gloucs | **Gloucestershire** |
| Gt Lon | **Greater London** |
| Halton | **Halton (30)** |
| Hants | **Hampshire** |
| Hartpl | **Hartlepool (31)** |
| Herefs | **Herefordshire** |
| Herts | **Hertfordshire** |
| IoS | **Isles of Scilly** |
| IoW | **Isle of Wight** |
| Kent | **Kent** |
| Kirk | **Kirklees (32)** |
| Knows | **Knowsley (33)** |
| Lancs | **Lancashire** |
| Leeds | **Leeds** |
| Leics | **Leicestershire** |
| Lincs | **Lincolnshire** |
| Lpool | **Liverpool** |
| Luton | **Luton** |
| M Keyn | **Milton Keynes** |
| Manch | **Manchester** |
| Medway | **Medway** |
| Middsb | **Middlesbrough** |
| NE Lin | **North East Lincolnshire** |
| N Linc | **North Lincolnshire** |
| N Som | **North Somerset (34)** |
| N Tyne | **North Tyneside (35)** |
| N u Ty | **Newcastle upon Tyne** |
| N York | **North Yorkshire** |
| Nhants | **Northamptonshire** |
| Norfk | **Norfolk** |
| Notts | **Nottinghamshire** |
| Nthumb | **Northumberland** |
| Oldham | **Oldham (36)** |
| Oxon | **Oxfordshire** |
| Poole | **Poole** |
| R & Cl | **Redcar & Cleveland** |
| Readg | **Reading** |
| Rochdl | **Rochdale (37)** |
| Rothm | **Rotherham (38)** |
| Rutlnd | **Rutland** |
| S Glos | **South Gloucestershire (39)** |
| S on T | **Stockton-on-Tees (40)** |
| S Tyne | **South Tyneside (41)** |
| Salfd | **Salford (42)** |
| Sandw | **Sandwell (43)** |
| Sefton | **Sefton (44)** |
| Sheff | **Sheffield** |
| Shrops | **Shropshire** |
| Slough | **Slough (45)** |
| Solhll | **Solihull (46)** |
| Somset | **Somerset** |
| St Hel | **St Helens (47)** |
| Staffs | **Staffordshire** |
| Sthend | **Southend-on-Sea** |
| Stockp | **Stockport (48)** |
| Suffk | **Suffolk** |
| Sundld | **Sunderland** |
| Surrey | **Surrey** |
| Swindn | **Swindon** |
| Tamesd | **Tameside (49)** |
| Thurr | **Thurrock (50)** |
| Torbay | **Torbay** |
| Traffd | **Trafford (51)** |
| W & M | **Windsor and Maidenhead (52)** |
| W Berk | **West Berkshire** |
| W Susx | **West Sussex** |
| Wakefd | **Wakefield (53)** |
| Warrtn | **Warrington (54)** |
| Warwks | **Warwickshire** |
| Wigan | **Wigan (55)** |
| Wilts | **Wiltshire** |
| Wirral | **Wirral (56)** |
| Wokham | **Wokingham (57)** |
| Wolves | **Wolverhampton (58)** |
| Worcs | **Worcestershire** |
| Wrekin | **Telford & Wrekin (59)** |
| Wsall | **Walsall (60)** |

## Channel Islands & Isle of Man

| | |
|---|---|
| Guern | **Guernsey** |
| Jersey | **Jersey** |
| IoM | **Isle of Man** |

## A

22 F9 **Abbas Combe** Somset
52 D7 **Abberley** Worcs
52 D7 **Abberley Common** Worcs
46 H8 **Abberton** Essex
53 J10 **Abberton** Worcs
109 J7 **Abberwick** Nthumb
45 Q9 **Abbess Roding** Essex
9 M3 **Abbey** Devon
50 E6 **Abbey-Cwm-Hir** Powys
77 Q7 **Abbeydale** Sheff
40 E5 **Abbey Dore** Herefs
76 H12 **Abbey Green** Staffs
21 L9 **Abbey Hill** Somset
116 G9 **Abbey St Bathans** Border
83 M4 **Abbeystead** Lancs
97 N8 **Abbey Town** Cumb
83 P10 **Abbey Village** Lancs
33 N6 **Abbey Wood** Gt Lon
107 P7 **Abbotrule** Border
18 H10 **Abbots Bickington** Devon
65 K7 **Abbots Bromley** Staffs
10 E7 **Abbotsbury** Dorset
77 J6 **Abbot's Chair** Derbys
124 C10 **Abbots Deuglie** P & K
18 H8 **Abbotsham** Devon
5 P3 **Abbotskerswell** Devon
44 F11 **Abbots Langley** Herts
5 N7 **Abbotsleigh** Devon
28 H7 **Abbots Leigh** N Som
56 E9 **Abbotsley** Cambs
53 J9 **Abbots Morton** Worcs
56 E5 **Abbots Ripton** Cambs
53 K10 **Abbot's Salford** Warwks
25 J6 **Abbotstone** Hants
24 F8 **Abbotswood** Hants
24 H7 **Abbots Worthy** Hants
24 E5 **Abbotts Ann** Hants
11 N5 **Abbott Street** Dorset
51 L5 **Abcott** Shrops
51 P3 **Abdon** Shrops
41 K8 **Abenhall** Gloucs
48 G8 **Aberaeron** Cerdgn
27 N2 **Aberaman** Rhondd
61 P10 **Aberangell** Gwynd
37 Q3 **Aber-arad** Carmth
138 B10 **Aberarder** Highld
124 D9 **Aberargie** P & K
48 H8 **Aberarth** Cerdgn
26 H4 **Aberavon** Neath
38 A3 **Aber-banc** Cerdgn
27 R2 **Aberbargoed** Caerph
40 B11 **Aberbeeg** Blae G
39 P11 **Abercanaid** Myr Td
28 B3 **Abercarn** Caerph
36 G4 **Abercastle** Pembks
61 P11 **Abercegir** Powys
129 K4 **Aberchalder Lodge** Highld
140 F5 **Aberchirder** Abers
39 Q7 **Aber Clydach** Powys
39 K9 **Abercraf** Powys
27 K3 **Abercregan** Neath
27 N2 **Abercwmboi** Rhondd
37 P2 **Abercych** Pembks
27 P3 **Abercynon** Rhondd
124 B9 **Aberdalgie** P & K
39 N11 **Aberdare** Rhondd
60 B7 **Aberdaron** Gwynd
133 M3 **Aberdeen** C Aber
133 L2 ***Aberdeen Airport*** C Aber
133 L3 **Aberdeen Crematorium** C Aber
60 G2 **Aberdesach** Gwynd
115 M4 **Aberdour** Fife
27 J2 **Aberdulais** Neath
49 K1 **Aberdyfi** Gwynd
39 P2 **Aberedw** Powys
36 F4 **Abereiddy** Pembks
60 F5 **Abererch** Gwynd
27 P2 **Aberfan** Myr Td
123 L3 **Aberfeldy** P & K
72 F10 **Aberffraw** IoA
49 L5 **Aberffrwd** Cerdgn
85 N8 **Aberford** Leeds
113 Q1 **Aberfoyle** Stirlg
27 L5 **Abergarw** Brdgnd
39 J11 **Abergarwed** Neath
40 D9 **Abergavenny** Mons
74 C8 **Abergele** Conwy
38 D3 **Aber-giar** Carmth
38 E5 **Abergorlech** Carmth
49 Q10 **Abergwesyn** Powys
38 C7 **Abergwili** Carmth
61 N11 **Abergwydol** Powys
27 L3 **Abergwynfi** Neath
73 L9 **Abergwyngregyn** Gwynd
61 L10 **Abergynolwyn** Gwynd
50 E2 **Aberhafesp** Powys
49 P1 **Aberhosan** Powys
27 L5 **Aberkenfig** Brdgnd
116 B5 **Aberlady** E Loth
125 K2 **Aberlemno** Angus
61 N10 **Aberllefenni** Gwynd
40 A4 **Aberllynfi** Powys
139 N7 **Aberlour** Moray
49 L6 **Aber-Magwr** Cerdgn
49 J9 **Aber-meurig** Cerdgn
75 J12 **Abermorddu** Flints
50 G2 **Abermule** Powys
37 R6 **Abernant** Carmth
39 N11 **Aber-nant** Rhondd
124 D9 **Abernethy** P & K
124 E6 **Abernyte** P & K
48 D10 **Aberporth** Cerdgn
60 E6 **Abersoch** Gwynd
40 C11 **Abersychan** Torfn
27 N7 **Aberthin** V Glam
40 B11 **Abertillery** Blae G
27 Q4 **Abertridwr** Caerph
62 E8 **Abertridwr** Powys
39 Q10 **Abertysswg** Caerph
123 N9 **Aberuthven** P & K
39 N6 **Aberyscir** Powys
49 K4 **Aberystwyth** Cerdgn
49 K4 **Aberystwyth Crematorium** Cerdgn
31 K3 **Abingdon-on-Thames** Oxon
14 G2 **Abinger Common** Surrey
14 F1 **Abinger Hammer** Surrey
55 K8 **Abington** Nhants
106 B5 **Abington** S Lans
45 K3 **Abington Pigotts** Cambs
106 B5 **Abington Services** S Lans
14 G7 **Abingworth** W Susx
67 J7 **Ab Kettleby** Leics
53 J10 **Ab Lench** Worcs
42 C10 **Ablington** Gloucs
23 P4 **Ablington** Wilts
77 M7 **Abney** Derbys
65 J2 **Above Church** Staffs
132 E5 **Aboyne** Abers
75 Q3 **Abram** Wigan
137 P9 **Abriachan** Highld
33 N3 **Abridge** Essex
114 E6 **Abronhill** N Lans
29 L7 **Abson** S Glos
43 N2 **Abthorpe** Nhants
80 H8 **Aby** Lincs
86 A6 **Acaster Malbis** C York
85 R7 **Acaster Selby** N York
84 A9 **Accrington** Lancs
84 A9 **Accrington Crematorium** Lancs
118 G2 **Acha** Ag & B
112 A6 **Achahoish** Ag & B
124 C4 **Achalader** P & K
120 H6 **Achaleven** Ag & B
152 e3 **Acha Mor** W Isls
137 J3 **Achanalt** Highld
145 P10 **Achandunie** Highld
145 N5 **Achany** Highld
127 M10 **Acharacle** Highld
120 D3 **Acharn** Highld
123 K4 **Acharn** P & K
151 M8 **Achavanich** Highld
144 C4 **Achduart** Highld
148 G8 **Achfary** Highld
126 E3 **A'Chill** Highld
144 C3 **Achiltibuie** Highld
150 C4 **Achina** Highld
103 K6 **Achinhoan** Ag & B
136 C7 **Achintee** Highld
135 Q8 **Achintraid** Highld
148 C11 **Achmelvich** Highld
135 Q9 **Achmore** Highld
152 e3 **Achmore** W Isls
148 C10 **Achnacarnin** Highld
128 G7 **Achnacarry** Highld
127 K3 **Achnacloich** Highld
137 M12 **Achnaconeran** Highld
120 F4 **Achnacroish** Ag & B
119 M2 **Achnadrish House** Ag & B
123 M5 **Achnafauld** P & K
146 C11 **Achnagarron** Highld
126 H10 **Achnaha** Highld
144 C2 **Achnahaird** Highld
145 M3 **Achnairn** Highld
127 Q12 **Achnalea** Highld
112 A4 **Achnamara** Ag & B
136 G4 **Achnasheen** Highld
136 D6 **Achnashellach Lodge** Highld
139 P9 **Achnastank** Moray
126 H10 **Achosnich** Highld
120 D3 **Achranich** Highld
151 J3 **Achreamie** Highld
128 G10 **Achriabhach** Highld
148 F6 **Achriesgill** Highld
149 P4 **Achtoty** Highld
55 P4 **Achurch** Nhants
146 C6 **Achvaich** Highld
150 H4 **Achvarasdal** Highld
151 Q6 **Ackergill** Highld
91 R3 **Acklam** Middsb
86 E3 **Acklam** N York
52 E1 **Ackleton** Shrops
109 L9 **Acklington** Nthumb
85 N10 **Ackton** Wakefd
85 N12 **Ackworth Moor Top** Wakefd
71 M10 **Acle** Norfk
53 L4 **Acock's Green** Birm
35 P9 **Acol** Kent
85 R5 **Acomb** C York
99 P5 **Acomb** Nthumb
21 K10 **Acombe** Somset
40 G5 **Aconbury** Herefs
84 B10 **Acre** Lancs
63 J3 **Acrefair** Wrexhm
64 B2 **Acton** Ches E
11 N9 **Acton** Dorset
32 H6 **Acton** Gt Lon
51 K4 **Acton** Shrops
64 F4 **Acton** Staffs
46 F3 **Acton** Suffk
52 F7 **Acton** Worcs
52 C10 **Acton Beauchamp** Herefs
75 Q8 **Acton Bridge** Ches W
63 P11 **Acton Burnell** Shrops
52 C10 **Acton Green** Herefs
63 K2 **Acton Park** Wrexhm
63 P11 **Acton Pigott** Shrops
52 B2 **Acton Round** Shrops
51 M3 **Acton Scott** Shrops
64 H8 **Acton Trussell** Staffs
29 N6 **Acton Turville** S Glos
64 E6 **Adbaston** Staffs
22 D9 **Adber** Dorset
66 F4 **Adbolton** Notts
43 K4 **Adderbury** Oxon
64 C4 **Adderley** Shrops
109 J4 **Adderstone** Nthumb
114 H8 **Addiewell** W Loth
84 G5 **Addingham** C Brad
43 Q6 **Addington** Bucks
33 L9 **Addington** Gt Lon
34 B10 **Addington** Kent
33 L9 **Addiscombe** Gt Lon
32 F9 **Addlestone** Surrey
32 F9 **Addlestonemoor** Surrey
81 K10 **Addlethorpe** Lincs
64 C8 **Adeney** Wrekin
44 F10 **Adeyfield** Herts
62 E12 **Adfa** Powys
51 L6 **Adforton** Herefs
35 M11 **Adisham** Kent
42 F6 **Adlestrop** Gloucs
86 F11 **Adlingfleet** E R Yk
76 G7 **Adlington** Ches E
75 Q1 **Adlington** Lancs
65 K7 **Admaston** Staffs
64 B9 **Admaston** Wrekin

## B

69 Q3 Brancaster Staithe Norfk
100 G10 Brancepeth Dur
139 K5 Branchill Moray
68 G3 Brand End Lincs
147 N11 Branderburgh Moray
87 L6 Brandesburton E R Yk
59 K8 Brandeston Suffk
41 L6 Brand Green Gloucs
7 M4 Brandis Corner Devon
70 H8 Brandiston Norfk
100 G10 Brandon Dur
67 M3 Brandon Lincs
108 G6 Brandon Nthumb
57 Q3 Brandon Suffk
54 C5 Brandon Warwks
57 M3 Brandon Bank Norfk
57 L2 Brandon Creek Norfk
70 G10 Brandon Parva Norfk
92 C12 Brandsby N York
79 P4 Brandy Wharf Lincs
2 C9 Brane Cnwll
46 B6 Bran End Essex
11 P6 Branksome Poole
11 P6 Branksome Park Poole
24 G5 Bransbury Hants
79 M8 Bransby Lincs
9 M7 Branscombe Devon
52 E10 Bransford Worcs
12 C5 Bransgore Hants
87 L8 Bransholme C KuH
52 C5 Bransley Shrops
53 K6 Branson's Cross Worcs
67 K6 Branston Leics
79 P10 Branston Lincs
65 N8 Branston Staffs
79 Q10 Branston Booths Lincs
13 J8 Branstone IoW
67 M1 Brant Broughton Lincs
47 K5 Brantham Suffk
88 E2 Branthwaite Cumb
98 C10 Branthwaite Cumb
86 H9 Brantingham E R Yk
78 G3 Branton Donc
108 G6 Branton Nthumb
85 N3 Branton Green N York
108 E2 Branxton Nthumb
75 N11 Brassey Green Ches W
65 N1 Brassington Derbys
33 N11 Brasted Kent
33 N11 Brasted Chart Kent
132 G5 Brathens Abers
81 J10 Bratoft Lincs
79 N7 Brattleby Lincs
20 E4 Bratton Somset
23 K3 Bratton Wilts
64 B9 Bratton Wrekin
7 N6 Bratton Clovelly Devon
19 M6 Bratton Fleming Devon
22 F7 Bratton Seymour Somset
45 M6 Braughing Herts
45 M7 Braughing Friars Herts
54 E7 Braunston Nhants
67 L10 Braunston Rutlnd
66 F11 Braunstone Leics
19 J6 Braunton Devon
92 E11 Brawby N York
150 E3 Brawl Highld
92 A5 Braworth N York
32 C6 Bray W & M
55 J4 Braybrooke Nhants
30 B5 Braydon Wilts
30 A4 Braydon Brook Wilts
30 B5 Braydon Side Wilts
19 N6 Brayford Devon
16 B8 Bray's Hill E Susx
7 L10 Bray Shop Cnwll
88 D5 Braystones Cumb
85 K5 Braythorn N York
86 B9 Brayton N York
32 C6 Braywick W & M
32 C7 Braywoodside W & M
7 K6 Brazacott Cnwll
17 M1 Breach Kent
34 E9 Breach Kent
44 G7 Breachwood Green Herts
63 M5 Breaden Heath Shrops
66 B4 Breadsall Derbys
29 L2 Breadstone Gloucs
51 J9 Breadward Herefs
2 F9 Breage Cnwll
137 N7 Breakachy Highld
32 F4 Breakspear Crematorium Gt Lon
145 M6 Brealangwell Lodge Highld
41 J10 Bream Gloucs
23 P9 Breamore Hants
28 D11 Brean Somset
152 c3 Breanais W Isls
84 F10 Brearley Calder
85 L3 Brearton N York
152 e3 Breascleit W Isls
152 e3 Breasclete W Isls
66 D5 Breaston Derbys
38 D6 Brechfa Carmth
132 F12 Brechin Angus
58 D2 Breckles Norfk
39 P6 Brecon Powys
39 N7 Brecon Beacons National Park
76 G5 Bredbury Stockp
16 E7 Brede E Susx
51 Q9 Bredenbury Herefs
59 K10 Bredfield Suffk
34 F10 Bredgar Kent
34 D10 Bredhurst Kent
41 Q4 Bredon Worcs
41 P5 Bredon's Hardwick Worcs
41 Q4 Bredon's Norton Worcs
40 D3 Bredwardine Herefs
66 C7 Breedon on the Hill Leics
114 H9 Breich W Loth
76 D2 Breightmet Bolton
86 D8 Breighton E R Yk
40 G4 Breinton Herefs
29 R8 Bremhill Wilts
19 N7 Bremridge Devon
16 B2 Brenchley Kent
7 L3 Brendon Devon
19 P4 Brendon Devon
20 G6 Brendon Hill Somset
112 B5 Brenfield Ag & B
152 c3 Brenish W Isls
100 G3 Brenkley N u Ty
58 D11 Brent Eleigh Suffk
32 H7 Brentford Gt Lon
67 K8 Brentingby Leics
21 M3 Brent Knoll Somset
5 L5 Brent Mill Devon
45 N5 Brent Pelham Herts
33 Q4 Brentwood Essex
16 H5 Brenzett Kent
16 H5 Brenzett Green Kent
65 K9 Brereton Staffs
76 E10 Brereton Green Ches E
76 E10 Brereton Heath Ches E
65 K9 Brereton Hill Staffs
152 t7 Bressay Shet
58 G4 Bressingham Norfk
58 G4 Bressingham Common Norfk
65 P7 Bretby Derbys
65 P7 Bretby Crematorium Derbys
54 C5 Bretford Warwks
42 C3 Bretforton Worcs
83 L11 Bretherton Lancs
152 t6 Brettabister Shet
58 D4 Brettenham Norfk
58 E10 Brettenham Suffk
77 M8 Bretton Derbys
75 K11 Bretton Flints
45 Q7 Brewers End Essex
33 L12 Brewer Street Surrey
64 G10 Brewood Staffs
11 K6 Briantspuddle Dorset
45 Q6 Brick End Essex
45 L10 Brickendon Herts
44 G11 Bricket Wood Herts
77 P7 Brick Houses Sheff
46 C5 Brickkiln Green Essex
41 R3 Bricklehampton Worcs
102 f2 Bride IoM
97 M11 Bridekirk Cumb
37 N2 Bridell Pembks
7 P7 Bridestowe Devon
140 F8 Brideswell Abers
8 F7 Bridford Devon
35 L11 Bridge Kent
88 G10 Bridge End Cumb
98 D8 Bridge End Cumb
5 L7 Bridge End Devon
100 C11 Bridge End Dur
46 B5 Bridge End Essex
68 C5 Bridge End Lincs
97 L12 Bridgefoot Cumb
45 N4 Bridge Green Essex
22 D8 Bridgehampton Somset
85 M1 Bridge Hewick N York
100 E8 Bridgehill Dur
84 H2 Bridgehouse Gate N York
13 K4 Bridgemary Hants
64 D3 Bridgemere Ches E
140 D8 Bridgend Abers
103 L2 Bridgend Ag & B
110 H9 Bridgend Ag & B
132 E10 Bridgend Angus
27 L6 Bridgend Brdgnd
48 B11 Bridgend Cerdgn
89 L4 Bridgend Cumb
106 E8 Bridgend D & G
5 J7 Bridgend Devon
124 H10 Bridgend Fife
140 B9 Bridgend Moray
124 C8 Bridgend P & K
115 J6 Bridgend W Loth
124 F2 Bridgend of Lintrathen Angus
140 E12 Bridge of Alford Abers
114 E2 Bridge of Allan Stirlg
139 L11 Bridge of Avon Moray
139 M8 Bridge of Avon Moray
122 F3 Bridge of Balgie P & K
131 M12 Bridge of Brewlands Angus
139 L11 Bridge of Brown Highld
124 C3 Bridge of Cally P & K
132 G5 Bridge of Canny Abers
124 E2 Bridge of Craigisla Angus
96 E6 Bridge of Dee D & G
133 M2 Bridge of Don C Aber
138 G7 Bridge of Dulsie Highld
132 G7 Bridge of Dye Abers
124 C9 Bridge of Earn P & K
122 E1 Bridge of Ericht P & K
132 H5 Bridge of Feugh Abers
151 J3 Bridge of Forss Highld
131 Q5 Bridge of Gairn Abers
122 E1 Bridge of Gaur P & K
140 F6 Bridge of Marnoch Abers
121 P5 Bridge of Orchy Ag & B
130 F11 Bridge of Tilt P & K
140 B4 Bridge of Tynet Moray
152 r6 Bridge of Walls Shet
113 M8 Bridge of Weir Rens
19 M10 Bridge Reeve Devon
7 K4 Bridgerule Devon
51 L1 Bridges Shrops
40 F3 Bridge Sollers Herefs
58 C10 Bridge Street Suffk
7 L7 Bridgetown Cnwll
20 E7 Bridgetown Somset
75 M9 Bridge Trafford Ches W
29 K8 Bridge Yate S Glos
58 E3 Bridgham Norfk
52 D2 Bridgnorth Shrops
21 L6 Bridgwater Somset
21 M6 Bridgwater Services Somset
87 M2 Bridlington E R Yk
10 D6 Bridport Dorset
41 J7 Bridstow Herefs
84 C8 Brierfield Lancs
78 C2 Brierley Barns
41 J8 Brierley Gloucs
51 N9 Brierley Herefs
52 G3 Brierley Hill Dudley
101 L12 Brierton Hartpl
89 J2 Briery Cumb
79 P2 Brigg N Linc
71 L7 Briggate Norfk
92 H5 Briggswath N York
89 J2 Brigham Cumb
97 M12 Brigham Cumb
87 K4 Brigham E R Yk
84 H10 Brighouse Calder
12 G8 Brighstone IoW
77 P11 Brightgate Derbys
42 H11 Brighthampton Oxon
77 P5 Brightholmlee Sheff
8 B5 Brightley Devon
16 B6 Brightling E Susx
47 K8 Brightlingsea Essex
15 K10 Brighton Br & H
3 M4 Brighton Cnwll
75 K4 Brighton le Sands Sefton
114 G6 Brightons Falk
31 J6 Brightwalton W Berk
31 J6 Brightwalton Green W Berk
31 J7 Brightwalton Holt W Berk
47 N3 Brightwell Suffk
31 N3 Brightwell Baldwin Oxon
31 M4 Brightwell-cum-Sotwell Oxon
31 N3 Brightwell Upperton Oxon
90 H4 Brignall Dur
122 F11 Brig o'Turk Stirlg
80 E3 Brigsley NE Lin
89 M9 Brigsteer Cumb
55 N4 Brigstock Nhants
43 N9 Brill Bucks
2 H8 Brill Cnwll
51 J11 Brilley Herefs
51 N7 Brimfield Herefs
51 P7 Brimfield Cross Herefs
78 C9 Brimington Derbys
8 E9 Brimley Devon
41 Q9 Brimpsfield Gloucs
31 L9 Brimpton W Berk
31 M9 Brimpton Common W Berk
41 P11 Brimscombe Gloucs
75 J7 Brimstage Wirral
77 Q7 Brincliffe Sheff
86 D9 Brind E R Yk
22 C5 Brindham Somset
152 r6 Brindister Shet
83 N10 Brindle Lancs
64 E9 Brineton Staffs
55 L2 Bringhurst Leics
52 C9 Bringsty Common Herefs
56 B5 Brington Cambs
70 F5 Briningham Norfk
66 H2 Brinkely Notts
80 G9 Brinkhill Lincs
57 M9 Brinkley Cambs
54 D5 Brinklow Warwks
30 B5 Brinkworth Wilts
83 N11 Brinscall Lancs
21 P3 Brinscombe Somset
28 F10 Brinsea N Som
66 D2 Brinsley Notts
40 F3 Brinsop Herefs
78 C6 Brinsworth Rothm
70 F5 Brinton Norfk
152 k3 Brinyan Ork
98 E8 Brisco Cumb
70 D8 Brisley Norfk
29 J8 Brislington Bristl
16 G3 Brissenden Green Kent
29 J8 Bristol Bristl
28 G9 Bristol Airport N Som
28 H7 Bristol Zoo Bristl
70 F6 Briston Norfk
5 J4 Brisworthy Devon
84 C11 Britannia Lancs
23 P8 Britford Wilts
39 Q11 Brithdir Caerph
61 N8 Brithdir Gwynd
34 C10 British Legion Village Kent
26 H3 Briton Ferry Neath
31 N4 Britwell Salome Oxon
5 Q5 Brixham Torbay
5 J6 Brixton Devon
33 K7 Brixton Gt Lon
23 J5 Brixton Deverill Wilts
55 J6 Brixworth Nhants
42 G10 Brize Norton Oxon
42 G10 Brize Norton Airport Oxon
52 G7 Broad Alley Worcs
30 D4 Broad Blunsdon Swindn
77 J5 Broadbottom Tamesd
13 P4 Broadbridge W Susx
14 G4 Broadbridge Heath W Susx
42 D4 Broad Campden Gloucs
84 G11 Broad Carr Calder
23 M8 Broad Chalke Wilts
84 C10 Broad Clough Lancs
9 J5 Broadclyst Devon
113 L6 Broadfield Inver
37 M9 Broadfield Pembks
135 L11 Broadford Highld
16 C3 Broad Ford Kent
14 G6 Broadford Bridge W Susx
106 G7 Broadgairhill Border
58 E8 Broadgrass Green Suffk
57 N8 Broad Green Cambs
46 F7 Broad Green Essex
52 E9 Broad Green Worcs
53 J6 Broad Green Worcs
117 J10 Broadhaugh Border
36 G8 Broad Haven Pembks
76 E6 Broadheath Traffd
52 C7 Broadheath Worcs
9 L4 Broadhembury Devon
5 N3 Broadhempston Devon
57 L5 Broad Hill Cambs
30 C7 Broad Hinton Wilts
79 M9 Broadholme Lincs
16 E7 Broadland Row E Susx
38 B10 Broadlay Carmth
31 J10 Broad Layings Hants
45 M10 Broadley Essex
84 C12 Broadley Lancs
140 B3 Broadley Moray
45 M10 Broadley Common Essex
42 D2 Broad Marston Worcs
10 H7 Broadmayne Dorset
64 F2 Broad Meadow Staffs
25 K4 Broadmere Hants
41 K8 Broadmoor Gloucs
37 L9 Broadmoor Pembks
8 D4 Broadnymett Devon
88 F8 Broad Oak Cumb
10 C5 Broadoak Dorset
15 R6 Broad Oak E Susx
16 E7 Broad Oak E Susx
41 L9 Broadoak Gloucs
25 N3 Broad Oak Hants
40 G7 Broad Oak Herefs
35 L10 Broad Oak Kent
75 P5 Broad Oak St Hel
75 L12 Broadoak Wrexhm
59 K5 Broad Road Suffk
46 C9 Broad's Green Essex
35 Q9 Broadstairs Kent
40 G11 Broadstone Mons
11 N6 Broadstone Poole
51 P3 Broadstone Shrops
16 F7 Broad Street E Susx
45 Q8 Broad Street Essex
17 K3 Broad Street Kent
34 E11 Broad Street Kent
34 D8 Broad Street Medway
30 C10 Broad Street Wilts
46 F9 Broad Street Green Essex
30 C7 Broad Town Wilts
52 D9 Broadwas Worcs
45 J7 Broadwater Herts
14 G10 Broadwater W Susx
52 F5 Broadwaters Worcs
37 Q8 Broadway Carmth
38 B10 Broadway Carmth
36 G8 Broadway Pembks
21 M10 Broadway Somset
59 M5 Broadway Suffk
42 C4 Broadway Worcs
41 J9 Broadwell Gloucs
42 E6 Broadwell Gloucs
42 F10 Broadwell Oxon
54 D7 Broadwell Warwks
10 G8 Broadwey Dorset
10 C4 Broadwindsor Dorset
8 B3 Broadwood Kelly Devon
7 M7 Broadwoodwidger Devon
40 D3 Brobury Herefs
135 K6 Brochel Highld
121 J6 Brochroy Ag & B
83 L7 Brock Lancs
52 E10 Brockamin Worcs
25 K9 Brockbridge Hants
59 J5 Brockdish Norfk
52 G6 Brockencote Worcs
12 E4 Brockenhurst Hants
105 Q2 Brocketsbrae S Lans
58 G7 Brockford Green Suffk
58 G7 Brockford Street Suffk
54 G8 Brockhall Nhants
14 H1 Brockham Surrey
41 Q6 Brockhampton Gloucs
42 B7 Brockhampton Gloucs
13 M3 Brockhampton Hants
41 J5 Brockhampton Herefs
52 C9 Brockhampton Estate Herefs
10 H3 Brockhampton Green Dorset
77 M2 Brockholes Kirk
77 Q10 Brockhurst Derbys
54 D4 Brockhurst Warwks
98 C9 Brocklebank Cumb
80 C1 Brocklesby Lincs
28 G9 Brockley N Som
58 B6 Brockley Suffk
46 C2 Brockley Green Suffk
58 B9 Brockley Green Suffk
98 F11 Brockleymoor Cumb
52 G3 Brockmoor Dudley
7 N6 Brockscombe Devon
31 K10 Brock's Green Hants
51 K3 Brockton Shrops
51 P2 Brockton Shrops
63 K11 Brockton Shrops
64 D11 Brockton Shrops
64 F6 Brockton Staffs
28 H2 Brockweir Gloucs
25 K8 Brockwood Park Hants
41 P8 Brockworth Gloucs
6 E11 Brocton Cnwll
64 H8 Brocton Staffs
103 Q3 Brodick N Ayrs
138 H4 Brodie Moray
78 E2 Brodsworth Donc
134 H2 Brogaig Highld
44 D4 Brogborough C Beds
29 Q4 Brokenborough Wilts
76 G9 Broken Cross Ches E
76 C9 Broken Cross Ches W
23 J3 Brokerswood Wilts
75 K7 Bromborough Wirral
58 H5 Brome Suffk
58 H5 Brome Street Suffk
59 L10 Bromeswell Suffk
97 N9 Bromfield Cumb
51 N5 Bromfield Shrops
55 P10 Bromham Bed
29 Q9 Bromham Wilts
77 Q4 Bromley Barns
52 G3 Bromley Dudley
33 M8 Bromley Gt Lon
52 D2 Bromley Shrops
33 M9 Bromley Common Gt Lon
47 J6 Bromley Cross Essex
16 H3 Bromley Green Kent
63 K11 Bromlow Shrops
34 D8 Brompton Medway
91 P7 Brompton N York
93 J10 Brompton-by-Sawdon N York
91 L7 Brompton-on-Swale N York
20 H7 Brompton Ralph Somset
20 E7 Brompton Regis Somset
41 K7 Bromsash Herefs
41 L5 Bromsberrow Gloucs
41 L5 Bromsberrow Heath Gloucs
52 H6 Bromsgrove Worcs
64 E8 Bromstead Heath Staffs
52 C9 Bromyard Herefs
52 C9 Bromyard Downs Herefs
61 M6 Bronaber Gwynd
49 L7 Bronant Cerdgn
51 P3 Broncroft Shrops
48 E11 Brongest Cerdgn
63 N4 Bronington Wrexhm
39 Q5 Bronllys Powys
38 B7 Bronwydd Carmth
40 B3 Bronydd Powys
63 J5 Bronygarth Shrops
73 P8 Bron-y-Nant Crematorium Conwy
37 P8 Brook Carmth
24 D10 Brook Hants
24 E7 Brook Hants
12 F8 Brook IoW
17 J2 Brook Kent
14 D3 Brook Surrey
14 F2 Brook Surrey
71 K12 Brooke Norfk
67 L11 Brooke Rutlnd
80 D5 Brookenby Lincs
55 Q8 Brook End Bed
56 C11 Brook End C Beds
55 Q6 Brook End Cambs
44 C3 Brook End M Keyn
113 N8 Brookfield Rens
31 M3 Brookhampton Oxon
22 E8 Brookhampton Somset
24 D10 Brook Hill Hants
74 E10 Brook House Denbgs
83 M2 Brookhouse Lancs
78 E6 Brookhouse Rothm
76 E11 Brookhouse Green Ches E
77 J6 Brookhouses Derbys
16 H5 Brookland Kent
76 E5 Brooklands Traffd
45 J11 Brookmans Park Herts
62 G12 Brooks Powys
66 H9 Brooksby Leics
35 N9 Brooks End Kent
14 G6 Brooks Green W Susx
33 Q4 Brook Street Essex
16 G4 Brook Street Kent
58 B11 Brook Street Suffk
15 K5 Brook Street W Susx
41 N9 Brookthorpe Gloucs
57 P1 Brookville Norfk
32 D11 Brookwood Surrey
44 H3 Broom C Beds
78 D5 Broom Rothm
53 K10 Broom Warwks
59 M2 Broome Norfk
51 L4 Broome Shrops
52 G5 Broome Worcs
76 D6 Broomedge Warrtn
109 J7 Broome Park Nthumb
14 G6 Broomer's Corner W Susx
14 F7 Broomershill W Susx
46 C9 Broomfield Essex
34 E11 Broomfield Kent
35 M9 Broomfield Kent
21 K7 Broomfield Somset
63 M8 Broomfields Shrops
86 G9 Broomfleet E R Yk
70 E7 Broom Green Norfk
32 D9 Broomhall W & M
100 C6 Broomhaugh Nthumb
78 C3 Broom Hill Barns
11 P4 Broom Hill Dorset
66 E3 Broom Hill Notts
109 L9 Broomhill Nthumb
52 G5 Broom Hill Worcs
64 B3 Broomhill Green Ches E
100 D6 Broomley Nthumb
100 G10 Broompark Dur
41 L5 Broom's Green Gloucs
70 C6 Broomsthorpe Norfk
35 J10 Broom Street Kent
146 G4 Brora Highld
64 C11 Broseley Shrops
68 E9 Brotherhouse Bar Lincs
99 P10 Brotherlee Dur
68 E3 Brothertoft Lincs
85 P10 Brotherton N York
92 E3 Brotton R & Cl
151 J5 Broubster Highld
90 C4 Brough Cumb
77 M7 Brough Derbys
86 H10 Brough E R Yk
151 M2 Brough Highld
79 L12 Brough Notts
152 t5 Brough Shet
63 P4 Broughall Shrops
152 u3 Brough Lodge Shet
90 C4 Brough Sowerby Cumb
106 E3 Broughton Border
44 B9 Broughton Bucks
56 F5 Broughton Cambs
75 K11 Broughton Flints
24 E7 Broughton Hants
83 M8 Broughton Lancs
44 C4 Broughton M Keyn
79 N2 Broughton N Linc
84 D5 Broughton N York
92 F12 Broughton N York
55 L5 Broughton Nhants
43 J4 Broughton Oxon
76 F3 Broughton Salfd
64 E5 Broughton Staffs
27 L8 Broughton V Glam
54 E2 Broughton Astley Leics
89 J10 Broughton Beck Cumb
29 P9 Broughton Gifford Wilts
52 H8 Broughton Green Worcs
52 G9 Broughton Hackett Worcs
88 G9 Broughton-in-Furness Cumb
95 N9 Broughton Mains D & G
88 H8 Broughton Mills Cumb
97 L11 Broughton Moor Cumb
42 F11 Broughton Poggs Oxon
88 G9 Broughton Tower Cumb
125 J7 Broughty Ferry C Dund
88 H11 Brow End Cumb
90 B5 Brownber Cumb
25 K5 Brown Candover Hants
83 J12 Brown Edge Lancs
64 G1 Brown Edge Staffs
75 M10 Brown Heath Ches W
63 M6 Brownheath Shrops
141 L8 Brownhill Abers
125 K9 Brownhills Fife
65 K11 Brownhills Wsall
109 K5 Brownieside Nthumb
31 M10 Browninghill Green Hants
64 G1 Brown Lees Staffs
76 F11 Brownlow Heath Ches E
88 D3 Brownrigg Cumb
97 N7 Brownrigg Cumb
11 N7 Brownsea Island Dorset
53 K2 Brown's Green Birm
18 F8 Brownsham Devon
41 P11 Browns Hill Gloucs
54 E5 Brownsover Warwks
5 L6 Brownston Devon
58 F8 Brown Street Suffk
69 N8 Brow-of-the-Hill Norfk
71 P11 Browston Green Norfk
93 J8 Broxa N York
45 L10 Broxbourne Herts
116 F6 Broxburn E Loth
115 K7 Broxburn W Loth
109 K6 Broxfield Nthumb
45 Q6 Broxted Essex
63 N1 Broxton Ches W
15 N8 Broyle Side E Susx
151 P8 Bruan Highld
130 F11 Bruar P & K
146 G8 Brucefield Highld
112 G9 Bruchag Ag & B
75 M11 Bruera Ches W
42 F7 Bruern Abbey Oxon
110 G9 Bruichladdich Ag & B
59 L7 Bruisyard Suffk
59 L7 Bruisyard Street Suffk
79 M2 Brumby N Linc
77 L11 Brund Staffs
71 L10 Brundall Norfk
59 K7 Brundish Suffk
59 K6 Brundish Street Suffk
127 N10 Brunery Highld
2 E7 Brunnion Cnwll
51 L4 Brunslow Shrops
100 G4 Brunswick Village N u Ty
85 K10 Bruntcliffe Leeds
84 F6 Brunthwaite C Brad
54 G3 Bruntingthorpe Leics
124 G8 Brunton Fife
109 K5 Brunton Nthumb
30 F11 Brunton Wilts
8 C3 Brushford Devon
20 E8 Brushford Somset
22 F6 Bruton Somset
52 G7 Bryan's Green Worcs
11 L3 Bryanston Dorset
32 B2 Bryant's Bottom Bucks
97 N4 Brydekirk D & G
2 b1 Bryher IoS
63 J1 Brymbo Wrexhm
22 C10 Brympton Somset
26 E2 Bryn Carmth
75 Q9 Bryn Ches W
27 J4 Bryn Neath
51 J4 Bryn Shrops
75 P3 Bryn Wigan
38 H9 Brynamman Carmth
37 L3 Brynberian Pembks
27 J4 Brynbryddan Neath
61 K5 Bryn-bwbach Gwynd
27 N6 Bryncae Rhondd
27 L5 Bryncethin Brdgnd
60 H3 Bryncir Gwynd
26 H2 Bryn-coch Neath
60 C6 Bryncroes Gwynd
61 K11 Bryncrug Gwynd
72 E9 Bryn Du IoA
61 M6 Bryn-Eden Gwynd
62 G3 Bryneglwys Denbgs
63 K3 Brynfields Wrexhm
74 G9 Brynford Flints
75 Q3 Bryn Gates Wigan
27 N5 Bryn Golau Rhondd
72 F8 Bryngwran IoA
40 E10 Bryngwyn Mons
50 G10 Bryngwyn Powys
37 K3 Bryn-Henllan Pembks
48 E10 Brynhoffnant Cerdgn
83 J9 Bryning Lancs
28 B2 Brynithel Blae G
40 B9 Brynmawr Blae G
60 D5 Bryn-mawr Gwynd
27 L5 Brynmenyn Brdgnd
26 F4 Brynmill Swans
27 N6 Brynna Rhondd
62 F11 Bryn-penarth Powys
73 J11 Brynrefail Gwynd
72 H6 Brynrefail IoA
27 N6 Brynsadler Rhondd
62 E2 Bryn Saith Marchog Denbgs
72 H10 Brynsiencyn IoA
72 H7 Brynteg IoA
75 J10 Bryn-y-bal Flints
73 P8 Bryn-y-Maen Conwy
63 J4 Bryn-yr-Eos Wrexhm
134 G11 Bualintur Highld
74 G8 Buarth-draw Flints
54 B6 Bubbenhall Warwks
86 D8 Bubwith E R Yk
107 J7 Buccleuch Border
113 N3 Buchanan Smithy Stirlg
141 Q6 Buchanhaven Abers
123 N7 Buchanty P & K
123 J12 Buchany Stirlg
113 Q2 Buchlyvie Stirlg
98 D8 Buckabank Cumb
56 D7 Buckden Cambs
90 F11 Buckden N York
71 M11 Buckenham Norfk
9 L5 Buckerell Devon
5 M3 Buckfast Devon
5 M3 Buckfastleigh Devon
115 Q2 Buckhaven Fife
40 G8 Buckholt Mons
7 M5 Buckhorn Devon
22 G8 Buckhorn Weston Dorset
33 M3 Buckhurst Hill Essex
140 C3 Buckie Moray
43 P5 Buckingham Bucks
44 C9 Buckland Bucks
5 L8 Buckland Devon
42 C4 Buckland Gloucs
12 E5 Buckland Hants
45 L5 Buckland Herts
17 P2 Buckland Kent
30 H3 Buckland Oxon
33 J12 Buckland Surrey
18 H9 Buckland Brewer Devon
44 C10 Buckland Common Bucks
22 G3 Buckland Dinham Somset
7 N3 Buckland Filleigh Devon
8 D10 Buckland in the Moor Devon
4 H3 Buckland Monachorum Devon
10 G4 Buckland Newton Dorset
10 G8 Buckland Ripers Dorset
21 L10 Buckland St Mary Somset
5 M7 Buckland-Tout-Saints Devon
31 L8 Bucklebury W Berk
12 G5 Bucklers Hard Hants
47 M3 Bucklesham Suffk
75 J11 Buckley Flints
53 M7 Buckley Green Warwks
76 D7 Bucklow Hill Ches E
67 L7 Buckminster Leics
64 G3 Bucknall C Stke
80 D10 Bucknall Lincs
43 M6 Bucknell Oxon
51 K6 Bucknell Shrops
140 C3 Buckpool Moray
133 L2 Bucksburn C Aber
18 G9 Buck's Cross Devon
14 F4 Bucks Green W Susx
83 M11 Buckshaw Village Lancs
32 F2 Bucks Hill Herts
25 P5 Bucks Horn Oak Hants
18 G8 Buck's Mills Devon
93 N12 Buckton E R Yk
51 L6 Buckton Herefs
108 H2 Buckton Nthumb
56 C5 Buckworth Cambs
78 G9 Budby Notts
64 D2 Buddileigh Staffs
7 J4 Bude Cnwll
4 E5 Budge's Shop Cnwll
9 J5 Budlake Devon
109 J3 Budle Nthumb
9 K8 Budleigh Salterton Devon
15 N6 Budlett's Common E Susx
3 J8 Budock Water Cnwll
64 C3 Buerton Ches E
54 H9 Bugbrooke Nhants
5 P6 Bugford Devon
76 G11 Buglawton Ches E
3 P3 Bugle Cnwll
22 H8 Bugley Dorset
86 E4 Bugthorpe E R Yk
64 B11 Buildwas Shrops
50 E10 Builth Road Powys
50 E10 Builth Wells Powys
44 D9 Bulbourne Herts
23 N7 Bulbridge Wilts
67 Q7 Bulby Lincs
23 Q5 Bulford Wilts
24 C5 Bulford Camp Wilts
63 P1 Bulkeley Ches E
54 C3 Bulkington Warwks
29 Q10 Bulkington Wilts
18 H10 Bulkworthy Devon
91 P8 Bullamoor N York
72 G5 Bull Bay IoA
66 B2 Bullbridge Derbys
32 C8 Bullbrook Br For
45 J10 Bullen's Green Herts
41 M8 Bulley Gloucs
97 M10 Bullgill Cumb
40 G4 Bullinghope Herefs
24 G5 Bullington Hants
80 B8 Bullington Lincs
35 L9 Bullockstone Kent
45 K8 Bull's Green Herts
59 N2 Bull's Green Norfk
46 E4 Bulmer Essex
86 C2 Bulmer N York
46 E4 Bulmer Tye Essex
34 B5 Bulphan Thurr
9 M7 Bulstone Devon
44 E11 Bulstrode Herts
16 D9 Bulverhythe E Susx
141 M7 Bulwark Abers
66 E3 Bulwell C Nott
55 N2 Bulwick Nhants
45 M10 Bumble's Green Essex
127 M6 Bunacaimb Highld
128 H7 Bunarkaig Highld
75 P12 Bunbury Ches E
75 P12 Bunbury Heath Ches E
138 B6 Bunchrew Highld
14 G8 Buncton W Susx
136 B10 Bundalloch Highld
119 L8 Bunessan Ag & B
59 L3 Bungay Suffk
68 E1 Bunker's Hill Lincs
111 J6 Bunnahabhain Ag & B
66 F6 Bunny Notts
137 L9 Buntait Highld
45 L6 Buntingford Herts
58 G2 Bunwell Norfk
58 H2 Bunwell Hill Norfk
65 N5 Bupton Derbys
77 K9 Burbage Derbys
54 D2 Burbage Leics
30 F10 Burbage Wilts
51 K8 Burcher Herefs
16 B4 Burchett's Green E Susx
32 B6 Burchett's Green W & M
23 N7 Burcombe Wilts
31 M3 Burcot Oxon
52 H6 Burcot Worcs
52 D2 Burcote Shrops
44 B8 Burcott Bucks
44 C7 Burcott Bucks
86 G3 Burdale N York
46 F5 Bures Essex
42 F9 Burford Oxon
51 P7 Burford Shrops
119 L4 Burg Ag & B
58 G5 Burgate Suffk
25 N7 Burgates Hants
44 G5 Burge End Herts
15 K7 Burgess Hill W Susx
59 J10 Burgh Suffk
98 C6 Burgh by Sands Cumb
71 P11 Burgh Castle Norfk
31 K10 Burghclere Hants
139 L2 Burghead Moray
31 N8 Burghfield W Berk
31 N9 Burghfield Common W Berk
33 J10 Burgh Heath Surrey
16 C5 Burgh Hill E Susx
40 G3 Burghill Herefs
5 K8 Burgh Island Devon
81 J10 Burgh le Marsh Lincs
71 J7 Burgh next Aylsham Norfk
80 D6 Burgh on Bain Lincs
71 N9 Burgh St Margaret Norfk
59 P2 Burgh St Peter Norfk
78 E1 Burghwallis Donc
34 C10 Burham Kent
25 M9 Buriton Hants
63 Q2 Burland Ches E
6 E10 Burlawn Cnwll
41 P11 Burleigh Gloucs
20 G10 Burlescombe Devon
11 J6 Burleston Dorset
5 N7 Burlestone Devon
12 C4 Burley Hants
67 L10 Burley Rutlnd
51 N4 Burley Shrops
63 Q4 Burleydam Ches E
41 J2 Burley Gate Herefs
84 H6 Burley in Wharfedale C Brad
12 C4 Burley Lawn Hants
12 C4 Burley Street Hants
84 H6 Burley Wood Head C Brad
71 M10 Burlingham Green Norfk
51 J9 Burlingjobb Powys
64 E10 Burlington Shrops
63 M7 Burlton Shrops
17 K4 Burmarsh Kent
42 F4 Burmington Warwks
86 B9 Burn N York
76 F5 Burnage Manch
65 P6 Burnaston Derbys
89 N3 Burnbanks Cumb
114 F9 Burnbrae N Lans
86 F6 Burnby E R Yk
77 Q4 Burn Cross Sheff
14 E10 Burndell W Susx
76 D2 Burnden Bolton
76 G2 Burnedge Rochdl
89 N7 Burneside Cumb
91 M9 Burneston N York
29 K9 Burnett BaNES
107 L7 Burnfoot Border
107 N6 Burnfoot Border
106 C11 Burnfoot D & G
107 J12 Burnfoot D & G
107 K10 Burnfoot D & G
123 P12 Burnfoot P & K
32 D6 Burnham Bucks
87 K11 Burnham N Linc
69 Q3 Burnham Deepdale Norfk
45 J8 Burnham Green Herts
70 B4 Burnham Market Norfk
70 B3 Burnham Norton Norfk
34 G3 Burnham-on-Crouch Essex
21 M3 Burnham-on-Sea Somset
70 B4 Burnham Overy Norfk
70 C3 Burnham Overy Staithe Norfk
70 C4 Burnham Thorpe Norfk
141 Q7 Burnhaven Abers
105 Q10 Burnhead D & G
140 H12 Burnhervie Abers
64 E12 Burnhill Green Staffs
100 F8 Burnhope Dur
113 M11 Burnhouse N Ayrs
93 K8 Burniston N York
84 C8 Burnley Lancs
84 B9 Burnley Crematorium Lancs
117 L9 Burnmouth Border
82 H6 Burn Naze Lancs
123 J12 Burn of Cambus Stirlg
100 F7 Burnopfield Dur
98 F7 Burnrigg Cumb
84 F3 Burnsall N York
124 H1 Burnside Angus
125 K3 Burnside Angus
124 D11 Burnside Fife
147 L11 Burnside Moray
115 K6 Burnside W Loth
125 J6 Burnside of Duntrune Angus
32 E11 Burntcommon Surrey
65 N6 Burntheath Derbys
47 J6 Burnt Heath Essex
31 M7 Burnt Hill W Berk
3 J7 Burnthouse Cnwll
91 J2 Burnt Houses Dur
115 N4 Burntisland Fife
15 P5 Burnt Oak E Susx
65 K10 Burntwood Staffs
65 K10 Burntwood Green Staffs
85 K3 Burnt Yates N York
21 K10 Burnworthy Somset
32 E12 Burpham Surrey
14 E9 Burpham W Susx
100 H4 Burradon N Tyne
108 F8 Burradon Nthumb
152 u2 Burrafirth Shet
2 H7 Burras Cnwll
4 F3 Burraton Cnwll
152 t4 Burravoe Shet
89 R3 Burrells Cumb
124 D5 Burrelton P & K
9 Q3 Burridge Devon
19 L6 Burridge Devon
13 J3 Burridge Hants
91 L9 Burrill N York
79 L2 Burringham N Linc
19 M10 Burrington Devon
51 M6 Burrington Herefs
28 G10 Burrington N Som
57 M9 Burrough End Cambs
57 M9 Burrough Green Cambs
67 J10 Burrough on the Hill Leics
89 Q11 Burrow Lancs
20 E5 Burrow Somset
21 M7 Burrow Bridge Somset
32 D9 Burrowhill Surrey
14 F2 Burrows Cross Surrey
26 C4 Burry Swans
26 C4 Burry Green Swans
26 C2 Burry Port Carmth
75 M2 Burscough Lancs
75 M1 Burscough Bridge Lancs
86 E8 Bursea E R Yk
87 K5 Burshill E R Yk
12 H3 Bursledon Hants
64 F2 Burslem C Stke
47 K3 Burstall Suffk
10 C4 Burstock Dorset
58 H4 Burston Norfk
64 H6 Burston Staffs
15 K3 Burstow Surrey
87 N9 Burstwick E R Yk
90 E9 Burtersett N York
98 G5 Burtholme Cumb
57 P8 Burthorpe Green Suffk
98 E8 Burthwaite Cumb
3 M3 Burthy Cnwll
21 N4 Burtle Hill Somset
68 E5 Burtoft Lincs
75 K9 Burton Ches W
75 N11 Burton Ches W
10 G6 Burton Dorset
12 B6 Burton Dorset
79 N9 Burton Lincs
109 K3 Burton Nthumb
37 J9 Burton Pembks
21 K4 Burton Somset
22 C10 Burton Somset
22 H7 Burton Wilts
29 N6 Burton Wilts
87 L3 Burton Agnes E R Yk
10 D7 Burton Bradstock Dorset
67 N7 Burton Coggles Lincs
87 M8 Burton Constable Hall E R Yk
54 C10 Burton Dassett Warwks
45 P7 Burton End Essex
46 B3 Burton End Suffk
93 M12 Burton Fleming E R Yk
53 P5 Burton Green Warwks
75 K12 Burton Green Wrexhm

## C

22 E8 Compton Pauncefoot Somset
10 F6 Compton Valence Dorset
53 P10 Compton Verney Warwks
115 J3 Comrie Fife
123 K8 Comrie P & K
128 E10 Conaglen House Highld
136 B10 Conchra Highld
124 C4 Concraigie P & K
83 K4 Conder Green Lancs
41 Q4 Conderton Worcs
42 D6 Condicote Gloucs
114 D6 Condorrat N Lans
63 N11 Condover Shrops
41 N8 Coney Hill Gloucs
14 G6 Coneyhurst Common W Susx
86 D1 Coneysthorpe N York
85 N3 Coneythorpe N York
58 E5 Coney Weston Suffk
25 P7 Conford Hants
7 K9 Congdon's Shop Cnwll
66 B11 Congerstone Leics
69 N7 Congham Norfk
76 F11 Congleton Ches E
61 M3 Congl-y-wal Gwynd
28 F9 Congresbury N Som
64 G9 Congreve Staffs
97 K4 Conheath D & G
138 H5 Conicavel Moray
80 D12 Coningsby Lincs
56 D3 Conington Cambs
56 F7 Conington Cambs
78 E4 Conisbrough Donc
80 H4 Conisholme Lincs
89 J7 Coniston Cumb
87 M8 Coniston E R Yk
84 D4 Coniston Cold N York
84 E2 Conistone N York
75 J10 Connah's Quay Flints
120 G6 Connel Ag & B
105 L7 Connel Park E Ayrs
2 F6 Connor Downs Cnwll
137 P5 Conon Bridge Highld
84 E6 Cononley N York
64 H2 Consall Staffs
100 E8 Consett Dur
91 K8 Constable Burton N York
84 B10 Constable Lee Lancs
3 J8 Constantine Cnwll
6 C10 Constantine Bay Cnwll
137 M4 Contin Highld
73 N8 Conwy Conwy
34 G9 Conyer Kent
58 C7 Conyer's Green Suffk
16 C9 Cooden E Susx
7 M3 Cookbury Devon
7 M4 Cookbury Wick Devon
32 C5 Cookham W & M
32 B5 Cookham Dean W & M
32 C5 Cookham Rise W & M
53 K9 Cookhill Worcs
59 L5 Cookley Suffk
52 F5 Cookley Worcs
31 P4 Cookley Green Oxon
133 L6 Cookney Abers
15 M8 Cooksbridge E Susx
52 G7 Cooksey Green Worcs
47 L8 Cook's Green Essex
58 E10 Cooks Green Suffk
64 H3 Cookshill Staffs
6 F11 Cooksland Cnwll
46 B10 Cooksmill Green Essex
75 P9 Cookson Green Ches W
14 G6 Coolham W Susx
34 D7 Cooling Medway
34 D7 Cooling Street Medway
2 G6 Coombe Cnwll
3 K6 Coombe Cnwll
3 M4 Coombe Cnwll
8 F8 Coombe Devon
8 H10 Coombe Devon
9 L6 Coombe Devon
29 M3 Coombe Gloucs
25 L9 Coombe Hants
23 P3 Coombe Wilts
23 P8 Coombe Bissett Wilts
8 G10 Coombe Cellars Devon
25 L9 Coombe Cross Hants
41 P6 Coombe Hill Gloucs
11 K8 Coombe Keynes Dorset
5 Q3 Coombe Pafford Torbay
14 H9 Coombes W Susx
51 L8 Coombes-Moor Herefs
22 G7 Coombe Street Somset
52 H3 Coombeswood Dudley
45 N11 Coopersale Common Essex
45 N11 Coopersale Street Essex
33 P12 Cooper's Corner Kent
15 N6 Coopers Green E Susx
44 H9 Coopers Green Herts
35 P10 Cooper Street Kent
76 B2 Cooper Turning Bolton
14 F8 Cootham W Susx
47 K3 Copdock Suffk
46 G7 Copford Green Essex
85 M3 Copgrove N York
152 t4 Copister Shet
56 B11 Cople Bed
84 G10 Copley Calder
90 H2 Copley Dur
76 H4 Copley Tamesd
77 M8 Coplow Dale Derbys
85 R6 Copmanthorpe C York
64 E6 Copmere End Staffs
83 K7 Copp Lancs
7 J5 Coppathorne Cnwll
64 G8 Coppenhall Staffs
76 D12 Coppenhall Moss Ches E
2 F7 Copperhouse Cnwll
52 D5 Coppicegate Shrops
56 C5 Coppingford Cambs
16 G1 Coppins Corner Kent
8 E4 Copplestone Devon
83 M12 Coppull Lancs
75 P1 Coppull Moor Lancs
14 H6 Copsale W Susx
83 P8 Copster Green Lancs
54 D3 Copston Magna Warwks
35 N10 Cop Street Kent
33 M2 Copthall Green Essex
53 M5 Copt Heath Solhll
85 M1 Copt Hewick N York
7 K6 Copthorne Cnwll
15 K3 Copthorne W Susx
66 D9 Copt Oak Leics
70 D4 Copy's Green Norfk
24 E10 Copythorne Hants
46 H3 Coram Street Suffk
33 Q5 Corbets Tey Gt Lon
13 a3 Corbiere Jersey
100 C5 Corbridge Nthumb
55 M3 Corby Nhants
67 P7 Corby Glen Lincs
98 F7 Corby Hill Cumb
103 Q4 Cordon N Ayrs
77 P8 Cordwell Derbys
52 B6 Coreley Shrops
32 C5 Cores End Bucks
21 K9 Corfe Somset
11 M8 Corfe Castle Dorset
11 N5 Corfe Mullen Dorset
51 N4 Corfton Shrops
131 P3 Corgarff Abers
25 K9 Corhampton Hants
16 B3 Corks Pond Kent
53 P4 Corley Warwks
53 P3 Corley Ash Warwks
53 P4 Corley Moor Warwks
53 P3 Corley Services Warwks
131 P11 Cormuir Angus
46 F3 Cornard Tye Suffk
8 C7 Corndon Devon
83 K8 Corner Row Lancs
88 F8 Corney Cumb
101 J11 Cornforth Dur
140 F4 Cornhill Abers
108 D2 Cornhill-on-Tweed Nthumb
84 D10 Cornholme Calder
46 B4 Cornish Hall End Essex
118 D3 Cornoigmore Ag & B
99 N10 Cornriggs Dur
100 F9 Cornsay Dur
100 F9 Cornsay Colliery Dur
137 P5 Corntown Highld
27 L7 Corntown V Glam
42 F6 Cornwell Oxon
5 K5 Cornwood Devon
5 P5 Cornworthy Devon
128 F9 Corpach Highld
70 G6 Corpusty Norfk
132 D3 Corrachree Abers
127 Q2 Corran Highld
128 E11 Corran Highld
102 f4 Corrany IoM
97 P1 Corrie D & G
103 Q1 Corrie N Ayrs
103 N5 Corriecravie N Ayrs
103 Q3 Corriegills N Ayrs
129 J6 Corriegour Lodge Hotel Highld
137 L3 Corriemoille Highld
137 L10 Corrimony Highld
79 L5 Corringham Lincs
34 C5 Corringham Thurr
61 N10 Corris Gwynd
61 M10 Corris Uchaf Gwynd
113 J1 Corrow Ag & B
135 L11 Corry Highld
8 B5 Corscombe Devon
10 D4 Corscombe Dorset
41 M6 Corse Gloucs
41 N5 Corse Lawn Gloucs
29 P8 Corsham Wilts
132 G3 Corsindae Abers
23 J4 Corsley Wilts
22 H4 Corsley Heath Wilts
96 F3 Corsock D & G
29 L9 Corston BaNES
29 Q5 Corston Wilts
115 M7 Corstorphine C Edin
61 K7 Cors-y-Gedol Gwynd
132 B12 Cortachy Angus
59 Q1 Corton Suffk
23 K5 Corton Wilts
22 E9 Corton Denham Somset
128 E10 Coruanan Highld
62 E3 Corwen Denbgs
10 F7 Coryates Dorset
7 N8 Coryton Devon
34 C6 Coryton Thurr
54 F2 Cosby Leics
52 H2 Coseley Dudley
64 E11 Cosford Shrops
43 R3 Cosgrove Nhants
13 L4 Cosham C Port
37 K10 Cosheston Pembks
123 K3 Coshieville P & K
66 D4 Cossall Notts
66 D4 Cossall Marsh Notts
66 G9 Cossington Leics
21 M5 Cossington Somset
70 H9 Costessey Norfk
66 F7 Costock Notts
67 L8 Coston Leics
70 F11 Coston Norfk
42 H11 Cote Oxon
21 M4 Cote Somset
75 P10 Cotebrook Ches W
98 F8 Cotehill Cumb
89 M9 Cotes Cumb
66 F8 Cotes Leics
64 F5 Cotes Staffs
54 E4 Cotesbach Leics
64 F5 Cotes Heath Staffs
21 J8 Cotford St Luke Somset
66 G5 Cotgrave Notts
133 L1 Cothal Abers
67 K3 Cotham Notts
21 J7 Cothelstone Somset
90 G3 Cotherstone Dur
31 K2 Cothill Oxon
9 N4 Cotleigh Devon
66 D3 Cotmanhay Derbys
56 H9 Coton Cambs
54 H6 Coton Nhants
63 P5 Coton Shrops
64 E8 Coton Staffs
64 H6 Coton Staffs
65 M11 Coton Staffs
64 F7 Coton Clanford Staffs
65 J5 Coton Hayes Staffs
63 N9 Coton Hill Shrops
65 M6 Coton in the Clay Staffs
65 N9 Coton in the Elms Derbys
65 P8 Coton Park Derbys
42 A10 Cotswolds
5 N4 Cott Devon
24 G5 Cottage End Hants
83 L8 Cottam Lancs
79 K8 Cottam Notts
57 J7 Cottenham Cambs
90 D8 Cotterdale N York
45 K6 Cottered Herts
53 K5 Cotteridge Birm
55 P3 Cotterstock Nhants
54 H6 Cottesbrooke Nhants
67 M9 Cottesmore Rutlnd
87 K8 Cottingham E R Yk
55 L3 Cottingham Nhants
84 H8 Cottingley C Brad
85 K9 Cottingley Hall Crematorium Leeds
43 M5 Cottisford Oxon
58 G7 Cotton Suffk
44 F3 Cotton End Bed
84 D7 Cotton Tree Lancs
133 J1 Cottown Abers
140 D10 Cottown Abers
141 K8 Cottown of Gight Abers
4 G4 Cotts Devon
63 Q8 Cotwall Wrekin
64 H5 Cotwalton Staffs
4 A5 Couch's Mill Cnwll
41 J7 Coughton Herefs
53 K8 Coughton Warwks
111 Q8 Coulaghailtro Ag & B
136 D7 Coulags Highld
88 C5 Coulderton Cumb
132 D4 Coull Abers
113 J4 Coulport Ag & B
33 K10 Coulsdon Gt Lon
23 L3 Coulston Wilts
106 D3 Coulter S Lans
14 D7 Coultershaw Bridge W Susx
21 K5 Coultings Somset
92 D12 Coulton N York
124 G8 Coultra Fife
63 P11 Cound Shrops
63 P11 Coundlane Shrops
100 G12 Coundon Dur
91 L1 Coundon Grange Dur
90 E9 Countersett N York
23 P5 Countess Wilts
46 F5 Countess Cross Essex
8 H7 Countess Wear Devon
54 F2 Countesthorpe Leics
19 P3 Countisbury Devon
124 E5 Coupar Angus P & K
83 N9 Coup Green Lancs
90 B3 Coupland Cumb
108 F4 Coupland Nthumb
112 B11 Cour Ag & B
17 K4 Court-at-Street Kent
127 M5 Courteachan Highld
55 J10 Courteenhall Nhants
38 E7 Court Henry Carmth
35 J4 Courtsend Essex
21 K6 Courtway Somset
115 Q7 Cousland Mdloth
16 B4 Cousley Wood E Susx
113 J5 Cove Ag & B
116 H7 Cove Border
20 E9 Cove Devon
25 Q2 Cove Hants
143 L7 Cove Highld
133 M4 Cove Bay C Aber
59 P5 Cove Bottom Suffk
59 Q4 Covehithe Suffk
64 G11 Coven Staffs
57 J4 Coveney Cambs
80 G5 Covenham St Bartholomew Lincs
80 G5 Covenham St Mary Lincs
64 G11 Coven Heath Staffs
53 Q5 Coventry Covtry
54 B6 Coventry Airport Warwks
3 J11 Coverack Cnwll
2 G8 Coverack Bridges Cnwll
91 J9 Coverham N York
55 Q6 Covington Cambs
106 C2 Covington S Lans
89 Q11 Cowan Bridge Lancs
16 A8 Cowbeech E Susx
68 E8 Cowbit Lincs
27 N7 Cowbridge V Glam
77 K9 Cowdale Derbys
15 N3 Cowden Kent
115 L3 Cowdenbeath Fife
15 N2 Cowden Pound Kent
15 N2 Cowden Station Kent
65 P3 Cowers Lane Derbys
12 H5 Cowes IoW
91 Q9 Cowesby N York
24 D8 Cowesfield Green Wilts
15 J6 Cowfold W Susx
90 C9 Cowgill Cumb
58 F7 Cow Green Suffk
29 J4 Cowhill S Glos
114 F3 Cowie Stirlg
86 H2 Cowlam E R Yk
8 G5 Cowley Devon
41 Q8 Cowley Gloucs
32 F6 Cowley Gt Lon
43 L11 Cowley Oxon
83 N11 Cowling Lancs
84 E6 Cowling N York
91 L9 Cowling N York
57 N10 Cowlinge Suffk
85 J12 Cowmes Kirk
84 C11 Cowpe Lancs
100 H2 Cowpen Nthumb
91 Q2 Cowpen Bewley S on T
13 M3 Cowplain Hants
99 N10 Cowshill Dur
28 G10 Cowslip Green N Som
85 N5 Cowthorpe N York
51 L6 Coxall Herefs
64 C4 Coxbank Ches E
66 B3 Coxbench Derbys
22 C6 Coxbridge Somset
59 M4 Cox Common Suffk
6 H5 Coxford Cnwll
70 C6 Coxford Norfk
52 E3 Coxgreen Staffs
34 C12 Coxheath Kent
101 J11 Coxhoe Dur
22 C5 Coxley Somset
85 K11 Coxley Wakefd
22 C4 Coxley Wick Somset
7 M10 Coxpark Cnwll
33 Q3 Coxtie Green Essex
92 B11 Coxwold N York
27 M6 Coychurch Brdgnd
27 M6 Coychurch Crematorium Brdgnd
104 H6 Coylton S Ayrs
130 G2 Coylumbridge Highld
27 L5 Coytrahen Brdgnd
53 K7 Crabbs Cross Worcs
11 Q3 Crab Orchard Dorset
15 J6 Crabtree W Susx
63 K3 Crabtree Green Wrexhm
89 Q2 Crackenthorpe Cumb
6 G5 Crackington Haven Cnwll
64 F2 Crackley Staffs
53 P6 Crackley Warwks
64 E10 Crackleybank Shrops
90 F7 Crackpot N York
84 E3 Cracoe N York
20 H11 Craddock Devon
45 N7 Cradle End Herts
52 H4 Cradley Dudley
41 L2 Cradley Herefs
52 H3 Cradley Heath Sandw
39 N5 Cradoc Powys
4 E6 Crafthole Cnwll
44 C8 Crafton Bucks
89 M12 Crag Foot Lancs
139 J10 Craggan Highld
85 K7 Cragg Hill Leeds
100 G8 Craghead Dur
39 L7 Crai Powys
140 D4 Craibstone Moray
125 K3 Craichie Angus
125 N2 Craig Angus
136 E6 Craig Highld
105 L7 Craigbank E Ayrs
115 N10 Craigburn Border
38 G11 Craigcefnparc Swans
107 K12 Craigcleuch D & G
141 K10 Craigdam Abers
120 F11 Craigdhu Ag & B
132 H2 Craigearn Abers
139 P7 Craigellachie Moray
124 C9 Craigend P & K
113 N7 Craigend Rens
113 L5 Craigendoran Ag & B
113 N8 Craigends Rens
95 K6 Craighlaw D & G
111 L8 Craighouse Ag & B
124 C4 Craigie P & K
104 H3 Craigie S Ayrs
141 M3 Craigiefold Abers
96 F6 Craigley D & G
38 H10 Craig Llangiwg Neath
115 M7 Craiglockhart C Edin
115 P7 Craigmillar C Edin
63 J5 Craignant Shrops
105 N12 Craigneston D & G
114 D10 Craigneuk N Lans
114 D8 Craigneuk N Lans
120 D5 Craignure Ag & B
132 H11 Craigo Angus
27 M7 Craig Penllyn V Glam
124 H10 Craigrothie Fife
122 E9 Craigruie Stirlg
46 C4 Craig's End Essex
125 K5 Craigton Angus
133 K4 Craigton C Aber
113 P10 Craigton E Rens
113 Q8 Craigton Crematorium C Glas
124 G3 Craigton of Airlie Angus
38 H11 Craig-y-Duke Neath
39 K8 Craig-y-nos Powys
125 M11 Crail Fife
107 R5 Crailing Border
79 J4 Craiselound N Linc
91 L9 Crakehall N York
91 Q12 Crakehill N York
65 K5 Crakemarsh Staffs
86 D2 Crambe N York
100 H3 Cramlington Nthumb
115 M6 Cramond C Edin
115 M6 Cramond Bridge C Edin
24 F9 Crampmoor Hants
76 D10 Cranage Ches E
64 F5 Cranberry Staffs
23 N10 Cranborne Dorset
32 C8 Cranbourne Br For
16 D4 Cranbrook Kent
16 D3 Cranbrook Common Kent
77 P3 Crane Moor Barns
70 D9 Crane's Corner Norfk
44 D3 Cranfield C Beds
18 G9 Cranford Devon
32 G7 Cranford Gt Lon
55 M5 Cranford St Andrew Nhants
55 M5 Cranford St John Nhants
41 P9 Cranham Gloucs
33 Q5 Cranham Gt Lon
53 L10 Cranhill Warwks
75 N4 Crank St Hel
14 F3 Cranleigh Surrey
58 F6 Cranmer Green Suffk
12 F7 Cranmore IoW
22 F5 Cranmore Somset
55 J2 Cranoe Leics
59 L7 Cransford Suffk
116 F9 Cranshaws Border
102 f2 Cranstal IoM
87 J5 Cranswick E R Yk
3 K2 Crantock Cnwll
67 P2 Cranwell Lincs
57 P2 Cranwich Norfk
70 E11 Cranworth Norfk
120 E11 Craobh Haven Ag & B
4 H3 Crapstone Devon
112 E2 Crarae Ag & B
149 L11 Crask Inn Highld
137 N7 Crask of Aigas Highld
109 L6 Craster Nthumb
40 C4 Craswall Herefs
64 G10 Crateford Staffs
59 L5 Cratfield Suffk
133 J5 Crathes Abers
132 H5 Crathes Castle Abers
131 N5 Crathie Abers
129 Q5 Crathie Highld
91 Q5 Crathorne N York
51 M4 Craven Arms Shrops
100 E5 Crawcrook Gatesd
75 N3 Crawford Lancs
106 C5 Crawford S Lans
106 A5 Crawfordjohn S Lans
24 G6 Crawley Hants
42 H9 Crawley Oxon
15 K3 Crawley W Susx
15 L3 Crawley Down W Susx
100 C10 Crawleyside Dur
84 B10 Crawshawbooth Lancs
133 L8 Crawton Abers
46 G8 Craxe's Green Essex
90 F11 Cray N York
33 P7 Crayford Gt Lon
85 R1 Crayke N York
70 F6 Craymere Beck Norfk
34 C4 Crays Hill Essex
31 N6 Cray's Pond Oxon
65 N7 Craythorne Staffs
20 F10 Craze Lowman Devon
31 R6 Crazies Hill Wokham
20 C9 Creacombe Devon
121 J4 Creagan Inn Ag & B
152 b8 Creag Ghoraidh W Isls
152 b8 Creagorry W Isls
129 K10 Creaguaineach Lodge Highld
63 N6 Creamore Bank Shrops
54 H6 Creaton Nhants
97 P4 Creca D & G
40 F3 Credenhill Herefs
8 F5 Crediton Devon
95 L3 Creebank D & G
95 M5 Creebridge D & G
11 M8 Creech Dorset
21 L8 Creech Heathfield Somset
21 L8 Creech St Michael Somset
3 M5 Creed Cnwll
33 N6 Creekmouth Gt Lon
34 G3 Creeksea Essex
58 G9 Creeting St Mary Suffk
67 P8 Creeton Lincs
95 N6 Creetown D & G
102 b7 Cregneash IoM
102 e5 Cregny Baa IoM
50 F10 Cregrina Powys
124 G8 Creich Fife
27 P6 Creigiau Cardif
4 G6 Cremyll Cnwll
63 Q11 Cressage Shrops
77 M9 Cressbrook Derbys
37 L9 Cresselly Pembks
32 B4 Cressex Bucks
46 D7 Cressing Essex
109 M11 Cresswell Nthumb
37 K9 Cresswell Pembks
64 H4 Cresswell Staffs
78 E9 Creswell Derbys
65 K10 Creswell Green Staffs
59 J8 Cretingham Suffk
111 Q8 Cretshengan Ag & B
64 D1 Crewe Ches E
63 M2 Crewe Ches W
76 C12 Crewe Crematorium Ches E
64 D1 Crewe Green Ches E
63 K9 Crew Green Powys
10 C3 Crewkerne Somset
33 K2 Crews Hill Station Gt Lon
66 B5 Crewton C Derb
122 C8 Crianlarich Stirlg
49 J10 Cribyn Cerdgn
60 H4 Criccieth Gwynd
65 Q1 Crich Derbys
65 Q1 Crich Carr Derbys
115 Q9 Crichton Mdloth
28 G4 Crick Mons
54 F6 Crick Nhants
39 P3 Crickadarn Powys
10 B3 Cricket St Thomas Somset
63 J7 Crickheath Shrops
40 B8 Crickhowell Powys
30 C4 Cricklade Wilts
33 J5 Cricklewood Gt Lon
85 Q11 Cridling Stubbs N York
123 L8 Crieff P & K
3 P2 Criggan Cnwll
63 J9 Criggion Powys
85 L12 Crigglestone Wakefd
76 F1 Crimble Rochdl
141 P4 Crimond Abers
69 M11 Crimplesham Norfk
42 F2 Crimscote Warwks
137 M8 Crinaglack Highld
112 A2 Crinan Ag & B
114 E10 Crindledyke N Lans
71 J11 Cringleford Norfk
84 F5 Cringles C Brad
37 M7 Crinow Pembks
2 D7 Cripplesease Cnwll
23 N11 Cripplestyle Dorset
16 D6 Cripp's Corner E Susx
138 B10 Croachy Highld
6 F10 Croanford Cnwll
33 P9 Crockenhill Kent
31 P5 Crocker End Oxon
14 C9 Crockerhill W Susx
8 E6 Crockernwell Devon
40 H8 Crocker's Ash Herefs
23 J5 Crockerton Wilts
96 G4 Crocketford D & G
86 B6 Crockey Hill C York
33 N12 Crockham Hill Kent
16 A2 Crockhurst Street Kent
47 J6 Crockleford Heath Essex
21 M10 Crock Street Somset
27 K3 Croeserw Neath
36 F4 Croes-goch Pembks
38 B3 Croes-lan Cerdgn
61 L3 Croesor Gwynd
38 B8 Croesyceiliog Carmth
28 D3 Croesyceiliog Torfn
28 D4 Croes-y-mwyalch Torfn
40 D11 Croes-y-pant Mons
54 E1 Croft Leics
81 K11 Croft Lincs
76 B5 Croft Warrtn
113 P4 Croftamie Stirlg
2 G7 Croft Mitchell Cnwll
98 C8 Crofton Cumb
85 M11 Crofton Wakefd
30 F10 Crofton Wilts
91 M5 Croft-on-Tees N York
144 F8 Croftown Highld
139 P6 Crofts Moray
76 E4 Crofts Bank Traffd
139 P4 Crofts of Dipple Moray
141 P4 Crofts of Savoch Abers
26 D3 Crofty Swans
62 D5 Crogen Gwynd
120 D7 Croggan Ag & B
98 H9 Croglin Cumb
145 L7 Croick Highld
138 E2 Cromarty Highld
115 J4 Crombie Fife
139 K10 Cromdale Highld
45 K6 Cromer Herts
71 J4 Cromer Norfk
77 P12 Cromford Derbys
29 L4 Cromhall S Glos
29 L4 Cromhall Common S Glos
152 f4 Cromor W Isls
76 H2 Crompton Fold Oldham
79 K11 Cromwell Notts
105 L5 Cronberry E Ayrs
25 N4 Crondall Hants
102 e6 Cronkbourne IoM
102 d4 Cronk-y-Voddy IoM
75 N6 Cronton Knows
89 M7 Crook Cumb
100 F11 Crook Dur
97 P9 Crookdake Cumb
75 P2 Crooke Wigan
41 J8 Crooked End Gloucs
104 H2 Crookedholm E Ayrs
30 G8 Crooked Soley Wilts
77 Q6 Crookes Sheff
100 E8 Crookhall Dur
108 E2 Crookham Nthumb
31 L9 Crookham W Berk
25 N3 Crookham Village Hants
106 E4 Crook Inn Border
89 N10 Crooklands Cumb
115 J1 Crook of Devon P & K
65 N5 Cropper Derbys
43 K2 Cropredy Oxon
66 F10 Cropston Leics
42 A3 Cropthorne Worcs
92 F9 Cropton N York
66 H5 Cropwell Bishop Notts
66 H5 Cropwell Butler Notts
152 f1 Cros W Isls
152 f3 Crosbost W Isls
97 M10 Crosby Cumb
102 d5 Crosby IoM
79 M1 Crosby N Linc
75 K4 Crosby Sefton
90 B5 Crosby Garret Cumb
89 Q4 Crosby Ravensworth Cumb
97 M10 Crosby Villa Cumb
22 D4 Croscombe Somset
63 M6 Crosemere Shrops
77 L1 Crosland Edge Kirk
84 H12 Crosland Hill Kirk
21 N2 Cross Somset
112 B11 Crossaig Ag & B
118 D4 Crossapoll Ag & B
40 F8 Cross Ash Mons
16 D2 Cross-at-Hand Kent
14 E9 Crossbush W Susx
97 L10 Crosscanonby Cumb
2 H4 Cross Coombe Cnwll
71 J4 Crossdale Street Norfk
55 Q9 Cross End Bed
46 F5 Cross End Essex
83 J11 Crossens Sefton
84 G7 Cross Flatts C Brad
115 K4 Crossford Fife
114 E12 Crossford S Lans
7 L7 Crossgate Cnwll
68 E7 Crossgate Lincs
64 H5 Crossgate Staffs
115 Q7 Crossgatehall E Loth
113 M12 Crossgates E Ayrs
115 L3 Crossgates Fife
85 M8 Cross Gates Leeds
93 L10 Crossgates N York
50 F7 Crossgates Powys
83 M3 Crossgill Lancs
7 M7 Cross Green Devon
85 L9 Cross Green Leeds
64 G11 Cross Green Staffs
58 B10 Cross Green Suffk
58 C9 Cross Green Suffk
58 E10 Cross Green Suffk
37 N6 Crosshands Carmth
38 E9 Cross Hands Carmth
105 J4 Crosshands E Ayrs
37 L8 Cross Hands Pembks
66 C2 Cross Hill Derbys
115 M2 Crosshill Fife
104 F8 Crosshill S Ayrs
84 F6 Cross Hills N York
104 G2 Crosshouse E Ayrs
52 C2 Cross Houses Shrops
63 P10 Cross Houses Shrops
15 Q6 Cross in Hand E Susx
48 F9 Cross Inn Cerdgn
49 J8 Cross Inn Cerdgn
37 L9 Cross Inn Pembks
27 P6 Cross Inn Rhondd
113 L4 Cross Keys Ag & B
28 B4 Crosskeys Caerph
29 P8 Cross Keys Wilts
151 J3 Crosskirk Highld
89 K9 Crosslands Cumb
12 H7 Cross Lane IoW
52 D2 Cross Lane Head Shrops
2 H10 Cross Lanes Cnwll
3 J6 Cross Lanes Cnwll
85 Q2 Cross Lanes N York
63 K8 Crosslanes Shrops
63 L3 Cross Lanes Wrexhm
113 N8 Crosslee Rens
85 J11 Crossley Kirk
96 E5 Crossmichael D & G
39 Q7 Cross Oak Powys
141 J9 Cross of Jackston Abers
65 P3 Cross o' th' hands Derbys
15 J6 Crosspost W Susx
132 E3 Crossroads Abers
133 J5 Crossroads Abers
59 J5 Cross Street Suffk
125 K2 Crosston Angus
76 D8 Cross Town Ches E
40 F8 Crossway Mons
50 E9 Crossway Powys
28 H3 Crossway Green Mons
52 F7 Crossway Green Worcs
11 J7 Crossways Dorset
37 M3 Crosswell Pembks
89 L8 Crosthwaite Cumb
83 L11 Croston Lancs
71 K9 Crostwick Norfk
71 L6 Crostwight Norfk
34 A11 Crouch Kent
35 J10 Crouch Kent
33 K5 Crouch End Gt Lon
23 N8 Croucheston Wilts
10 H3 Crouch Hill Dorset
15 N2 Crough House Green Kent
43 L5 Croughton Nhants
141 K3 Crovie Abers
12 B4 Crow Hants
2 G7 Crowan Cnwll
15 P4 Crowborough E Susx
15 P4 Crowborough Town E Susx
21 J6 Crowcombe Somset
77 L10 Crowdecote Derbys
77 K4 Crowden Derbys
7 P5 Crowden Devon
24 H9 Crowdhill Hants
33 Q10 Crowdleham Kent
77 M3 Crow Edge Barns
31 Q2 Crowell Oxon
56 F9 Crow End Cambs
43 N3 Crowfield Nhants
58 H9 Crowfield Suffk
58 H9 Crowfield Green Suffk
71 L8 Crowgate Street Norfk
33 Q3 Crow Green Essex
116 G6 Crowhill E Loth
41 K6 Crow Hill Herefs
77 Q8 Crowhole Derbys
16 D8 Crowhurst E Susx
15 M1 Crowhurst Surrey
15 M1 Crowhurst Lane End Surrey
68 E10 Crowland Lincs
58 F6 Crowland Suffk
2 E8 Crowlas Cnwll
79 K1 Crowle N Linc
52 G9 Crowle Worcs
52 G9 Crowle Green Worcs
31 N4 Crowmarsh Gifford Oxon
59 K6 Crown Corner Suffk
4 G5 Crownhill C Plym
44 B4 Crownhill Crematorium M Keyn
14 D2 Crownpits Surrey
70 G11 Crownthorpe Norfk
2 G8 Crowntown Cnwll
2 C9 Crows-an-Wra Cnwll
46 C6 Crow's Green Essex
70 D11 Crowshill Norfk
4 C3 Crow's Nest Cnwll
63 L11 Crowsnest Shrops
32 B9 Crowthorne Wokham
75 P9 Crowton Ches W
65 M9 Croxall Staffs
80 D4 Croxby Lincs
100 H11 Croxdale Dur
65 K4 Croxden Staffs
32 F3 Croxley Green Herts
75 L4 Croxteth Lpool
56 E8 Croxton Cambs
80 B1 Croxton N Linc
58 C3 Croxton Norfk
70 E6 Croxton Norfk
64 E6 Croxton Staffs
64 E6 Croxtonbank Staffs
63 P2 Croxton Green Ches E
67 L6 Croxton Kerrial Leics
138 E6 Croy Highld
114 D6 Croy N Lans
19 J5 Croyde Devon
18 H5 Croyde Bay Devon
56 F10 Croydon Cambs
33 L9 Croydon Gt Lon
33 K9 Croydon Crematorium Gt Lon
130 C6 Crubenmore Highld
63 M10 Cruckmeole Shrops
63 M10 Cruckton Shrops
141 Q8 Cruden Bay Abers
64 B8 Crudgington Wrekin
29 Q4 Crudwell Wilts
7 P5 Cruft Devon
50 G6 Crug Powys
6 C9 Crugmeer Cnwll
38 G4 Crugybar Carmth
50 G4 Crug-y-byddar Powys
28 B3 Crumlin Caerph
4 B6 Crumplehorn Cnwll
76 F3 Crumpsall Manch
17 J1 Crundale Kent
37 J7 Crundale Pembks
37 N8 Crunwear Pembks
20 D11 Cruwys Morchard Devon
31 J11 Crux Easton Hants
10 F5 Cruxton Dorset
38 C9 Crwbin Carmth
32 C3 Cryers Hill Bucks
37 N4 Crymmych Pembks
39 J10 Crynant Neath
33 L8 Crystal Palace Gt Lon
135 N4 Cuaig Highld
120 E10 Cuan Ag & B
53 Q7 Cubbington Warwks
3 J3 Cubert Cnwll
77 N3 Cubley Barns
44 B7 Cublington Bucks
40 E4 Cublington Herefs
15 K6 Cuckfield W Susx
22 G8 Cucklington Somset
78 F9 Cuckney Notts
68 D8 Cuckoo Bridge Lincs
25 N5 Cuckoo's Corner Hants
75 L11 Cuckoo's Nest Ches W
43 M11 Cuddesdon Oxon
43 Q9 Cuddington Bucks
75 Q9 Cuddington Ches W
63 M3 Cuddington Heath Ches W
83 L8 Cuddy Hill Lancs
33 N10 Cudham Gt Lon
7 P9 Cudliptown Devon
11 P5 Cudnell Bmouth
78 C2 Cudworth Barns
10 B3 Cudworth Somset
75 P6 Cuerdley Cross Warrtn
31 N11 Cufaude Hants
45 K11 Cuffley Herts
121 J2 Cuil Highld
137 Q4 Culbokie Highld
20 C4 Culbone Somset
137 N7 Culburnie Highld
138 C7 Culcabock Highld
138 F6 Culcharry Highld
76 C5 Culcheth Warrtn
140 D9 Culdrain Abers
135 N8 Culduie Highld
58 B6 Culford Suffk
99 J12 Culgaith Cumb
31 L3 Culham Oxon
148 B10 Culkein Highld
148 D10 Culkein Drumbeg Highld
29 Q3 Culkerton Gloucs
140 D2 Cullen Moray
101 J4 Cullercoats N Tyne
133 J4 Cullerlie Abers
138 B3 Cullicudden Highld
84 G8 Cullingworth C Brad
134 H11 Cuillin Hills Highld
120 D10 Cullipool Ag & B
152 t2 Cullivoe Shet
138 D6 Culloden Highld
9 J3 Cullompton Devon
9 J3 Cullompton Services Devon
20 H10 Culm Davy Devon
51 N4 Culmington Shrops
20 H10 Culmstock Devon
144 D4 Culnacraig Highld
96 F8 Culnaightrie D & G
135 J3 Culnaknock Highld
59 J10 Culpho Suffk
145 N6 Culrain Highld
114 H4 Culross Fife
104 F7 Culroy S Ayrs
140 G9 Culsalmond Abers
95 N8 Culscadden D & G
95 K8 Culshabbin D & G
152 r7 Culswick Shet
141 M11 Cultercullen Abers
133 L4 Cults C Aber
34 B9 Culverstone Green Kent
67 P4 Culverthorpe Lincs
43 L2 Culworth Nhants
104 D8 Culzean Castle & Country Park S Ayrs
114 D6 Cumbernauld N Lans
114 D6 Cumbernauld Village N Lans
81 K9 Cumberworth Lincs
98 D8 Cumdivock Cumb
141 K6 Cuminestown Abers
116 H10 Cumledge Border
98 E7 Cummersdale Cumb
97 N5 Cummertrees D & G
139 L2 Cummingston Moray
105 K6 Cumnock E Ayrs
43 K11 Cumnor Oxon
98 G8 Cumrew Cumb
97 L1 Cumrue D & G
98 F7 Cumwhinton Cumb
98 G8 Cumwhitton Cumb
91 P12 Cundall N York
104 G1 Cunninghamhead N Ayrs
152 s8 Cunningsburgh Shet
124 G10 Cupar Fife
124 G10 Cupar Muir Fife
77 N9 Curbar Derbys
13 J2 Curbridge Hants
42 G10 Curbridge Oxon
25 J10 Curdridge Hants
53 M2 Curdworth Warwks
21 L10 Curland Somset
31 K8 Curridge W Berk
115 M8 Currie C Edin
21 M9 Curry Mallet Somset
21 N8 Curry Rivel Somset
16 E3 Curteis Corner Kent
16 C3 Curtisden Green Kent
5 M6 Curtisknowle Devon
2 H10 Cury Cnwll
132 D2 Cushnie Abers
21 K7 Cushuish Somset
40 C3 Cusop Herefs
95 N11 Cutcloy D & G
20 E5 Cutcombe Somset
84 C12 Cutgate Rochdl
146 D7 Cuthill Highld
61 L8 Cutiau Gwynd
45 Q5 Cutler's Green Essex
3 Q2 Cutmadoc Cnwll
4 E4 Cutmere Cnwll
52 G7 Cutnall Green Worcs
42 C6 Cutsdean Gloucs
85 N10 Cutsyke Wakefd
77 Q9 Cutthorpe Derbys
4 E4 Cuttivett Cnwll
31 N3 Cuxham Oxon
34 C9 Cuxton Medway
80 D3 Cuxwold Lincs
40 B10 Cwm Blae G
74 E8 Cwm Denbgs
27 J4 Cwmafan Neath
27 N2 Cwmaman Rhondd
38 E2 Cwmann Carmth
40 C10 Cwmavon Torfn
37 P5 Cwmbach Carmth
38 D11 Cwm-bach Carmth
40 A4 Cwmbach Powys
39 N11 Cwmbach Rhondd
50 D10 Cwmbach Llechrhyd Powys
50 C4 Cwmbelan Powys
28 C3 Cwmbran Torfn
49 M4 Cwmbrwyno Cerdgn
38 C11 Cwm Capel Carmth
28 B4 Cwmcarn Caerph
40 G10 Cwmcarvan Mons
40 B10 Cwm-celyn Blae G
61 Q9 Cwm-Cewydd Gwynd
37 Q2 Cwm-cou Cerdgn
39 Q7 Cwm Crawnon Powys
39 N11 Cwmdare Rhondd
38 F6 Cwmdu Carmth
40 A7 Cwmdu Powys
26 F3 Cwmdu Swans
38 B5 Cwmduad Carmth
38 F11 Cwm Dulais Swans
38 H5 Cwmdwr Carmth
27 K4 Cwmfelin Brdgnd
27 P2 Cwmfelin Myr Td
37 N7 Cwmfelin Boeth Carmth
28 B4 Cwmfelinfach Caerph
37 P5 Cwmfelin Mynach Carmth
38 B8 Cwmffrwd Carmth
39 J9 Cwmgiedd Powys
38 G9 Cwmgorse Carmth
38 E9 Cwmgwili Carmth
39 K10 Cwmgwrach Neath
37 R3 Cwmhiraeth Carmth
38 G6 Cwm-Ifor Carmth
49 Q10 Cwm Irfon Powys
38 D8 Cwmisfael Carmth
61 P10 Cwm Llinau Powys
38 H9 Cwmllynfell Neath
38 D9 Cwmmawr Carmth
37 Q3 Cwm Morgan Carmth
27 M3 Cwmparc Rhondd
37 R3 Cwmpengraig Carmth
61 N3 Cwm Penmachno Conwy
27 N2 Cwmpennar Rhondd
40 B7 Cwmrhos Powys
26 G2 Cwmrhydyceirw Swans
38 C2 Cwmsychbant Cerdgn
40 B10 Cwmtillery Blae G
39 J9 Cwm-twrch Isaf Powys
38 H9 Cwm-twrch Uchaf Powys
38 E9 Cwm-y-glo Carmth
73 J11 Cwm-y-glo Gwynd
40 D7 Cwmyoy Mons
49 N6 Cwmystwyth Cerdgn
61 M12 Cwrt Gwynd
48 H11 Cwrt-newydd Cerdgn
40 B8 Cwrt-y-gollen Powys
62 G10 Cyfronydd Powys
38 H11 Cylibebyll Neath
27 K3 Cymer Neath
27 N4 Cymmer Rhondd
39 J4 Cynghordy Carmth
38 D10 Cynheidre Carmth
27 K3 Cynonville Neath
62 E4 Cynwyd Denbgs
38 B6 Cynwyl Elfed Carmth


## D


5 Q3 Daccombe Devon
89 M1 Dacre Cumb
85 J3 Dacre N York
85 J3 Dacre Banks N York
99 P10 Daddry Shield Dur
43 N4 Dadford Bucks
54 C1 Dadlington Leics
26 D2 Dafen Carmth
70 E10 Daffy Green Norfk
33 P5 Dagenham Gt Lon
42 A10 Daglingworth Gloucs

44 E8 Dagnall Bucks
58 F8 Dagworth Suffk
104 E9 Dailly S Ayrs
5 P3 Dainton Devon
124 H9 Dairsie Fife
76 C3 Daisy Hill Bolton
85 K9 Daisy Hill Leeds
152 b10 Dalabrog W Isls
120 H10 Dalavich Ag & B
96 G6 Dalbeattie D & G
65 N5 Dalbury Derbys
102 b5 Dalby IoM
80 H9 Dalby Lincs
86 B1 Dalby N York
123 N2 Dalcapon P & K
146 G4 Dalchalm Highld
129 J2 Dalchreichart Highld
123 J9 Dalchruin P & K
123 Q7 Dalcrue P & K
80 E10 Dalderby Lincs
9 K8 Dalditch Devon
114 C9 Daldowie Crematorium C Glas
98 G9 Dale Cumb
66 C4 Dale Derbys
36 F9 Dale Pembks
89 J2 Dale Bottom Cumb
77 N11 Dale End Derbys
84 E6 Dale End N York
16 C5 Dale Hill E Susx
92 F3 Dalehouse N York
127 N10 Dalelia Highld
113 K12 Dalgarven N Ayrs
115 L4 Dalgety Bay Fife
105 K7 Dalgig E Ayrs
123 K8 Dalginross P & K
123 P3 Dalguise P & K
150 F6 Dalhalvaig Highld
57 N8 Dalham Suffk
152 b10 Daliburgh W Isls
115 Q8 Dalkeith Mdloth
139 L5 Dallas Moray
59 K9 Dallinghoo Suffk
16 B7 Dallington E Susx
55 J8 Dallington Nhants
91 K12 Dallow N York
121 M7 Dalmally Ag & B
113 P2 Dalmary Stirlg
105 J8 Dalmellington E Ayrs
115 L6 Dalmeny C Edin
138 C2 Dalmore Highld
113 P7 Dalmuir W Duns
127 M10 Dalnabreck Highld
130 D10 Dalnacardoch P & K
138 F11 Dalnahaitnach Highld
130 B9 Dalnaspidal P & K
151 J8 Dalnawillan Lodge Highld
123 K1 Daloist P & K
124 B12 Dalqueich P & K
104 F10 Dalquhairn S Ayrs
146 D3 Dalreavoch Lodge Highld
113 K11 Dalry N Ayrs
104 F7 Dalrymple E Ayrs
114 E11 Dalserf S Lans
102 H7 Dalsmeran Ag & B
98 D8 Dalston Cumb
33 L5 Dalston Gt Lon
97 J1 Dalswinton D & G
89 N11 Dalton Cumb
97 M3 Dalton D & G
75 N2 Dalton Lancs
91 J5 Dalton N York
91 Q11 Dalton N York
100 E4 Dalton Nthumb
78 D5 Dalton Rothm
88 H12 Dalton-in-Furness Cumb
101 K8 Dalton-le-Dale Dur
78 D5 Dalton Magna Rothm
91 M5 Dalton-on-Tees N York
78 D5 Dalton Parva Rothm
101 L12 Dalton Piercy Hartpl
122 G8 Dalveich Stirlg
130 B7 Dalwhinnie Highld
9 N5 Dalwood Devon
45 J6 Damask Green Herts
23 N10 Damerham Hants
71 M10 Damgate Norfk
58 F4 Dam Green Norfk
34 F9 Danaway Kent
46 D10 Danbury Essex
92 E5 Danby N York
92 E6 Danby Bottom N York
91 N7 Danby Wiske N York
139 P6 Dandaleith Moray
115 P7 Danderhall Mdloth
76 H10 Danebridge Ches E
45 L7 Dane End Herts
15 Q4 Danegate E Susx
15 M5 Danehill E Susx
66 F11 Dane Hills C Leic
70 F11 Danemoor Green Norfk
52 D2 Danesford Shrops
78 C11 Danesmoor Derbys
35 J11 Dane Street Kent
16 G3 Daniel's Water Kent
140 H4 Danshillock Abers
116 D8 Danskine E Loth
87 N8 Danthorpe E R Yk
53 L7 Danzey Green Warwks
65 K7 Dapple Heath Staffs
32 B10 Darby Green Hants
76 D2 Darcy Lever Bolton
40 B8 Dardy Powys
40 B9 Daren-felen Mons
33 Q8 Darenth Kent
75 P7 Daresbury Halton
78 C3 Darfield Barns
78 F8 Darfoulds Notts
35 K10 Dargate Kent
4 C3 Darite Cnwll
34 D9 Darland Medway
75 L12 Darland Wrexhm
52 H1 Darlaston Wsall
52 H1 Darlaston Green Wsall
85 J3 Darley N York
66 B4 Darley Abbey C Derb
77 P11 Darley Bridge Derbys
77 P11 Darley Dale Derbys
53 M6 Darley Green Solhll
44 G7 Darleyhall Herts
85 J3 Darley Head N York
42 F3 Darlingscott Warwks
91 M4 Darlington Darltn
91 M4 Darlington Crematorium Darltn
63 P5 Darliston Shrops
79 K9 Darlton Notts
65 L10 Darnford Staffs
107 N3 Darnick Border
61 P11 Darowen Powys
140 H6 Darra Abers
18 E9 Darracott Devon
19 J5 Darracott Devon
100 F4 Darras Hall Nthumb
85 P11 Darrington Wakefd
59 N6 Darsham Suffk
22 E4 Darshill Somset
33 P7 Dartford Kent
5 N4 Dartington Devon
8 C10 Dartmeet Devon
8 D9 Dartmoor National Park Devon
5 P6 Dartmouth Devon
77 P2 Darton Barns
105 K2 Darvel E Ayrs
16 C7 Darwell Hole E Susx
83 Q10 Darwen Bl w D
32 E7 Datchet W & M
45 K8 Datchworth Herts
45 K8 Datchworth Green Herts
76 C2 Daubhill Bolton
139 N7 Daugh of Kinermony Moray
30 A6 Dauntsey Wilts
139 J8 Dava Highld
76 C9 Davenham Ches W
76 G6 Davenport Stockp
76 F8 Davenport Green Ches E
76 E6 Davenport Green Traffd
54 F8 Daventry Nhants
115 M6 Davidson's Mains C Edin
6 H7 Davidstow Cnwll
34 B9 David Street Kent
106 H9 Davington D & G
34 H10 Davington Hill Kent
141 J10 Daviot Abers
138 D8 Daviot Highld
138 D7 Daviot House Highld
15 P7 Davis's Town E Susx
140 D5 Davoch of Grange Moray
76 D4 Davyhulme Traffd
65 J12 Daw End Wsall
15 J1 Dawesgreen Surrey
64 C10 Dawley Wrekin
8 H9 Dawlish Devon
9 J9 Dawlish Warren Devon
73 Q9 Dawn Conwy
21 K9 Daws Green Somset
34 E5 Daws Heath Essex
7 L8 Daw's House Cnwll
68 H6 Dawsmere Lincs
66 F3 Daybrook Notts
76 E12 Day Green Ches E
64 H6 Dayhills Staffs
52 H5 Dayhouse Bank Worcs
42 F6 Daylesford Gloucs
74 G9 Ddol Flints
62 D8 Ddol-Cownwy Powys
35 Q12 Deal Kent
88 E2 Dean Cumb
5 M4 Dean Devon
19 M4 Dean Devon
19 N4 Dean Devon
23 L10 Dean Dorset
24 G7 Dean Hants
25 J9 Dean Hants
84 C10 Dean Lancs
42 H7 Dean Oxon
22 F5 Dean Somset
33 Q8 Dean Bottom Kent
107 K7 Deanburnhaugh Border
5 M4 Deancombe Devon
43 K10 Dean Court Oxon
76 C2 Deane Bolton
25 J3 Deane Hants
23 L10 Dean End Dorset
77 P4 Dean Head Barns
84 F12 Deanhead Kirk
23 M9 Deanland Dorset
25 N11 Deanlane End W Susx
5 M4 Dean Prior Devon
99 M6 Deanraw Nthumb
76 G7 Dean Row Ches E
115 J7 Deans W Loth
88 E1 Deanscales Cumb
43 Q4 Deanshanger Nhants
139 Q6 Deanshaugh Moray
114 C1 Deanston Stirlg
34 D11 Dean Street Kent
97 L11 Dearham Cumb
84 D12 Dearnley Rochdl
59 K10 Debach Suffk
33 N3 Debden Essex
45 Q5 Debden Essex
45 Q5 Debden Green Essex
58 H8 Debenham Suffk
52 E11 Deblin's Green Worcs
115 J7 Dechmont W Loth
115 J7 Dechmont Road W Loth
43 K5 Deddington Oxon
47 J5 Dedham Essex
47 J5 Dedham Heath Essex
32 D7 Dedworth W & M
55 N2 Deene Nhants
55 N2 Deenethorpe Nhants
77 P4 Deepcar Sheff
32 C11 Deepcut Surrey
90 B9 Deepdale Cumb
90 E10 Deepdale N York
68 C10 Deeping Gate C Pete
68 C10 Deeping St James Lincs
68 D9 Deeping St Nicholas Lincs
41 P6 Deerhurst Gloucs
41 P6 Deerhurst Walton Gloucs
34 H9 Deerton Street Kent
41 Q3 Defford Worcs
39 L6 Defynnog Powys
73 N8 Deganwy Conwy
120 E10 Degnish Ag & B
86 B6 Deighton C York
91 P6 Deighton N York
73 K11 Deiniolen Gwynd
6 F8 Delabole Cnwll
75 P10 Delamere Ches W
141 M11 Delfrigs Abers
19 K8 Delley Devon
139 K9 Delliefure Highld
13 P4 Dell Quay W Susx
42 H9 Delly End Oxon
139 L12 Delnabo Moray
139 M9 Delnashaugh Inn Moray
146 D10 Delny Highld
77 J2 Delph Oldham
100 E8 Delves Dur
46 D5 Delvin End Essex
67 P5 Dembleby Lincs
3 N2 Demelza Cnwll
78 D4 Denaby Donc
78 E4 Denaby Main Donc
32 G12 Denbies Surrey
74 E10 Denbigh Denbgs
124 H9 Denbrae Fife
5 N3 Denbury Devon
66 C3 Denby Derbys
66 C3 Denby Bottles Derbys
77 N2 Denby Dale Kirk
30 H4 Denchworth Oxon
82 G1 Dendron Cumb
44 E4 Denel End C Beds
123 N9 Denfield P & K
55 N5 Denford Nhants
46 H11 Dengie Essex
32 F5 Denham Bucks
57 P8 Denham Suffk
59 J6 Denham Suffk
57 P8 Denham End Suffk
32 F5 Denham Green Bucks
59 J6 Denham Green Suffk
141 N5 Denhead Abers
125 J10 Denhead Fife
124 G6 Denhead of Gray C Dund
107 P6 Denholm Border
84 G8 Denholme C Brad
84 G8 Denholme Clough C Brad
60 F5 Denio Gwynd
25 L11 Denmead Hants
133 M2 Denmore C Aber
14 H5 Denne Park W Susx
59 K7 Dennington Suffk
114 E5 Denny Falk
114 E5 Dennyloanhead Falk
124 F9 Den of Lindores Fife
76 H2 Denshaw Oldham
133 K5 Denside Abers
17 M2 Densole Kent
57 P10 Denston Suffk
65 L4 Denstone Staffs
35 K10 Denstroude Kent
90 B9 Dent Cumb
56 C3 Denton Cambs
91 L3 Denton Darltn
15 N10 Denton E Susx
17 M1 Denton Kent
34 B7 Denton Kent
67 L6 Denton Lincs
84 H5 Denton N York
55 L9 Denton Nhants
59 K3 Denton Norfk
43 M11 Denton Oxon
76 G5 Denton Tamesd
69 L11 Denver Norfk
109 K7 Denwick Nthumb
70 F12 Deopham Norfk
70 F12 Deopham Green Norfk
57 P9 Depden Suffk
57 P9 Depden Green Suffk
33 L7 Deptford Gt Lon
23 M6 Deptford Wilts
66 B5 Derby C Derb
19 L6 Derby Devon
102 c7 Derbyhaven IoM
123 M2 Derculich P & K
70 E9 Dereham Norfk
27 Q2 Deri Caerph
7 K4 Derril Devon
35 M12 Derringstone Kent
64 G7 Derrington Staffs
7 L4 Derriton Devon
29 Q8 Derry Hill Wilts
79 K2 Derrythorpe N Linc
69 N6 Dersingham Norfk
119 M2 Dervaig Ag & B
62 E2 Derwen Denbgs
38 E7 Derwen Fawr Carmth
61 M12 Derwenlas Powys
88 H3 Derwent Water Cumb
38 F8 Derwydd Carmth
55 K4 Desborough Nhants
66 D11 Desford Leics
140 D3 Deskford Moray
108 H2 Detchant Nthumb
34 D10 Detling Kent
52 C3 Deuxhill Shrops
28 G3 Devauden Mons
49 M5 Devil's Bridge Cerdgn
53 P3 Devitts Green Warwks
30 B10 Devizes Wilts
4 G6 Devonport C Plym
114 G2 Devonside Clacks
3 K7 Devoran Cnwll
115 Q8 Dewarton Mdloth
11 J5 Dewlish Dorset
85 K11 Dewsbury Kirk
85 K10 Dewsbury Moor Kirk
85 K11 Dewsbury Moor Crematorium Kirk
62 H8 Deytheur Powys
28 H9 Dial N Som
14 C5 Dial Green W Susx
14 H7 Dial Post W Susx
10 C4 Dibberford Dorset
12 G3 Dibden Hants
12 G3 Dibden Purlieu Hants
53 L5 Dickens Heath Solhll
58 H4 Dickleburgh Norfk
42 B5 Didbrook Gloucs
31 L4 Didcot Oxon
31 L4 Didcot Railway Centre Oxon
56 D7 Diddington Cambs
51 N3 Diddlebury Shrops
40 F5 Didley Herefs
25 P9 Didling W Susx
29 N5 Didmarton Gloucs
76 F5 Didsbury Manch
5 L4 Didworthy Devon
67 Q1 Digby Lincs
134 H2 Digg Highld
77 J2 Diggle Oldham
75 N3 Digmoor Lancs
45 J8 Digswell Herts
45 J8 Digswell Water Herts
48 H9 Dihewyd Cerdgn
71 L7 Dilham Norfk
64 H3 Dilhorne Staffs
83 R9 Dill Hall Lancs
56 C7 Dillington Cambs
100 C5 Dilston Nthumb
23 J4 Dilton Wilts
23 J3 Dilton Marsh Wilts
51 L9 Dilwyn Herefs
83 Q12 Dimple Bolton
77 P11 Dimple Derbys
37 P4 Dinas Carmth
6 C10 Dinas Cnwll
60 D5 Dinas Gwynd
37 K3 Dinas Pembks
27 N4 Dinas Rhondd
60 G1 Dinas Dinlle Gwynd
61 Q9 Dinas-Mawddwy Gwynd
27 R8 Dinas Powys V Glam
22 D4 Dinder Somset
40 H4 Dinedor Herefs
40 F9 Dingestow Mons
75 L6 Dingle Lpool
16 E5 Dingleden Kent
55 K3 Dingley Nhants
137 P4 Dingwall Highld
62 D3 Dinmael Conwy
132 C5 Dinnet Abers
100 G4 Dinnington N u Ty
78 E6 Dinnington Rothm
21 N10 Dinnington Somset
73 K11 Dinorwic Gwynd
43 Q9 Dinton Bucks
23 M7 Dinton Wilts
106 E11 Dinwoodie D & G
18 F10 Dinworthy Devon
21 K9 Dipford Somset
31 Q11 Dipley Hants
103 L2 Dippen Ag & B
103 Q5 Dippen N Ayrs
25 P4 Dippenhall Surrey
7 N3 Dippermill Devon
7 N8 Dippertown Devon
139 Q4 Dipple Moray
104 D9 Dipple S Ayrs
5 M5 Diptford Devon
100 F7 Dipton Dur
99 P6 Diptonmill Nthumb
116 C4 Dirleton E Loth
99 N9 Dirt Pot Nthumb
51 J7 Discoed Powys
66 D7 Diseworth Leics
91 P12 Dishforth N York
76 H7 Disley Ches E
58 G4 Diss Norfk
50 E9 Disserth Powys
88 D2 Distington Cumb
88 D2 Distington Hall Crematorium Cumb
23 N7 Ditchampton Wilts
22 E6 Ditcheat Somset
59 L2 Ditchingham Norfk
15 L8 Ditchling E Susx
63 N9 Ditherington Shrops
29 N8 Ditteridge Wilts
5 P6 Dittisham Devon
34 C10 Ditton Kent
57 M9 Ditton Green Cambs
51 Q3 Ditton Priors Shrops
41 R5 Dixton Gloucs
40 G9 Dixton Mons
6 H5 Dizzard Cnwll
77 J2 Dobcross Oldham
4 C4 Dobwalls Cnwll
8 E7 Doccombe Devon
138 B7 Dochgarroch Highld
25 P5 Dockenfield Surrey
89 P11 Docker Lancs
69 P5 Docking Norfk
51 P9 Docklow Herefs
89 L2 Dockray Cumb
98 B8 Dockray Cumb
5 M8 Dodbrooke Devon
33 Q2 Doddinghurst Essex
56 H3 Doddington Cambs
34 G11 Doddington Kent
79 M9 Doddington Lincs
108 G3 Doddington Nthumb
52 B5 Doddington Shrops
8 F7 Doddiscombsleigh Devon
63 Q3 Dodd's Green Ches E
69 N6 Doddshill Norfk
4 D4 Doddy Cross Cnwll
54 G8 Dodford Nhants
52 H6 Dodford Worcs
29 M6 Dodington S Glos
21 J5 Dodington Somset
75 K11 Dodleston Ches W
19 K9 Dodscott Devon
113 P10 Dodside E Rens
65 J5 Dod's Leigh Staffs
77 P3 Dodworth Barns
77 Q3 Dodworth Bottom Barns
77 P3 Dodworth Green Barns
53 L1 Doe Bank Birm
78 D10 Doe Lea Derbys
68 D1 Dogdyke Lincs
85 J12 Dogley Lane Kirk
25 N3 Dogmersfield Hants
30 C5 Dogridge Wilts
68 D12 Dogsthorpe C Pete
9 J5 Dog Village Devon
62 E9 Dolanog Powys
50 G7 Dolau Powys
38 G3 Dolaucothi Carmth
60 H4 Dolbenmaen Gwynd
64 D6 Doley Staffs
62 B11 Dolfach Powys
50 F3 Dolfor Powys
61 P11 Dol-for Powys
73 N10 Dolgarrog Conwy
61 M8 Dolgellau Gwynd
61 L11 Dolgoch Gwynd
38 C5 Dol-gran Carmth
146 F4 Doll Highld
114 H2 Dollar Clacks
114 H2 Dollarfield Clacks
51 J7 Dolley Green Powys
49 M4 Dollwen Cerdgn
74 H9 Dolphin Flints
83 M4 Dolphinholme Lancs
115 K12 Dolphinton S Lans
19 L11 Dolton Devon
73 Q9 Dolwen Conwy
61 M2 Dolwyddelan Conwy
49 K3 Dolybont Cerdgn
50 H9 Dolyhir Powys
63 J8 Domgay Powys
108 D1 Donaldson's Lodge Nthumb
78 F3 Doncaster Donc
78 F3 Doncaster Carr Donc
78 H2 Doncaster North Services Donc
23 K8 Donhead St Andrew Wilts
23 K8 Donhead St Mary Wilts
115 L3 Donibristle Fife
20 H5 Doniford Somset
68 D5 Donington Lincs
80 E7 Donington on Bain Lincs
66 D7 Donington Park Services Leics
68 D5 Donington Southing Lincs
65 P9 Donisthorpe Leics
17 K4 Donkey Street Kent
32 D10 Donkey Town Surrey
42 E6 Donnington Gloucs
41 L5 Donnington Herefs
63 P10 Donnington Shrops
31 K8 Donnington W Berk
13 Q4 Donnington W Susx
64 D9 Donnington Wrekin
64 D9 Donnington Wood Wrekin
21 M10 Donyatt Somset
14 H5 Doomsday Green W Susx
104 F6 Doonfoot S Ayrs
131 K1 Dorback Lodge Highld
10 H6 Dorchester Dorset
31 M3 Dorchester Oxon
65 N12 Dordon Warwks
77 P7 Dore Sheff
137 Q9 Dores Highld
14 H1 Dorking Surrey
46 G4 Dorking Tye Suffk
15 M2 Dormans Land Surrey
15 M3 Dormans Park Surrey
41 J4 Dormington Herefs
53 J9 Dormston Worcs
42 E5 Dorn Gloucs
32 D6 Dorney Bucks
136 B10 Dornie Highld
146 E7 Dornoch Highld
97 P5 Dornock D & G
151 K6 Dorrery Highld
53 M6 Dorridge Solhll
67 Q2 Dorrington Lincs
63 N11 Dorrington Shrops
64 D4 Dorrington Shrops
53 L10 Dorsington Warwks
40 D3 Dorstone Herefs
43 P9 Dorton Bucks
65 N12 Dosthill Staffs
72 F9 Dothan IoA
10 C6 Dottery Dorset
4 B4 Doublebois Cnwll
29 P4 Doughton Gloucs
102 e6 Douglas IoM
105 Q4 Douglas S Lans
124 H6 Douglas and Angus C Dund
102 e6 Douglas Borough Crematorium IoM
113 J1 Douglas Pier Ag & B
124 H3 Douglastown Angus
105 R2 Douglas Water S Lans
105 Q3 Douglas West S Lans
22 E5 Doulting Somset
152 j4 Dounby Ork
145 L5 Doune Highld
114 D1 Doune Stirlg
104 C10 Dounepark S Ayrs
145 N7 Dounie Highld
4 H3 Dousland Devon
63 K8 Dovaston Shrops
66 D2 Dove Green Notts
77 K8 Dove Holes Derbys
97 M11 Dovenby Cumb
17 P2 Dover Kent
75 Q4 Dover Wigan
17 P2 Dover Castle Kent
47 N5 Dovercourt Essex
52 F7 Doverdale Worcs
65 L5 Doveridge Derbys
15 J1 Doversgreen Surrey
123 P3 Dowally P & K
83 K9 Dowbridge Lancs
42 B7 Dowdeswell Gloucs
39 P10 Dowlais Myr Td
7 Q3 Dowland Devon
21 M10 Dowlish Ford Somset
21 N10 Dowlish Wake Somset
30 C3 Down Ampney Gloucs
4 D6 Downderry Cnwll
33 M10 Downe Gt Lon
29 N3 Downend Gloucs
13 J7 Downend IoW
29 K7 Downend S Glos
31 K7 Downend W Berk
124 H6 Downfield C Dund
7 K10 Downgate Cnwll
7 L10 Downgate Cnwll
34 C3 Downham Essex
33 M8 Downham Gt Lon
84 B6 Downham Lancs
69 L11 Downham Market Norfk
41 P7 Down Hatherley Gloucs
22 D8 Downhead Somset
22 F4 Downhead Somset
6 B11 Downhill Cnwll
124 C7 Downhill P & K
75 L2 Downholland Cross Lancs
91 J7 Downholme N York
7 M7 Downicarey Devon
133 M5 Downies Abers
74 G8 Downing Flints
32 B3 Downley Bucks
8 D4 Down St Mary Devon
15 L9 Downs Crematorium Br & H
22 E3 Downside Somset
22 E4 Downside Somset
32 G10 Downside Surrey
4 H7 Down Thomas Devon
12 D6 Downton Hants
24 C9 Downton Wilts
68 C6 Dowsby Lincs
68 F10 Dowsdale Lincs
64 G7 Doxey Staffs
109 K5 Doxford Nthumb
29 L7 Doynton S Glos
28 B5 Draethen Caerph
114 E12 Draffan S Lans
86 G12 Dragonby N Linc
14 G6 Dragons Green W Susx
78 H5 Drakeholes Notts
52 F4 Drakelow Worcs
113 K11 Drakemyre N Ayrs
52 H11 Drakes Broughton Worcs
7 N10 Drakewalls Cnwll
84 F5 Draughton N York
55 J5 Draughton Nhants
86 C10 Drax N York
86 C10 Drax Hales N York
54 D6 Draycote Warwks
30 E7 Draycot Foliat Swindn
66 D5 Draycott Derbys
42 E4 Draycott Gloucs
52 E2 Draycott Shrops
21 Q3 Draycott Somset
22 D9 Draycott Somset
52 F11 Draycott Worcs
65 M6 Draycott in the Clay Staffs
64 H4 Draycott in the Moors Staffs
19 Q10 Drayford Devon
13 L4 Drayton C Port
55 L2 Drayton Leics
68 E4 Drayton Lincs
71 J9 Drayton Norfk
31 K3 Drayton Oxon
43 J3 Drayton Oxon
21 N8 Drayton Somset
52 G5 Drayton Worcs
65 M12 Drayton Bassett Staffs
44 C9 Drayton Beauchamp Bucks
65 M12 Drayton Manor Park Staffs
44 B6 Drayton Parslow Bucks
31 M3 Drayton St Leonard Oxon
84 F3 Drebley N York
102 f4 Dreemskerry IoM
36 H7 Dreen Hill Pembks
38 A4 Drefach Carmth
38 D9 Drefach Carmth
38 D3 Drefach Cerdgn
38 A4 Drefelin Carmth
104 F2 Dreghorn N Ayrs
17 M3 Drellingore Kent
116 C5 Drem E Loth
64 G4 Dresden C Stke
8 D6 Drewsteignton Devon
80 G9 Driby Lincs
87 J4 Driffield E R Yk
30 C2 Driffield Gloucs
30 C3 Driffield Cross Roads Gloucs
2 C9 Drift Cnwll
88 E7 Drigg Cumb
85 K9 Drighlington Leeds
119 P2 Drimnin Highld
10 C4 Drimpton Dorset
128 D8 Drimsallie Highld
86 A5 Dringhouses C York
58 E8 Drinkstone Suffk
58 E8 Drinkstone Green Suffk
10 F3 Drive End Dorset
45 J7 Driver's End Herts
65 J7 Drointon Staffs
52 G8 Droitwich Worcs
124 C9 Dron P & K
78 B8 Dronfield Derbys
77 Q8 Dronfield Woodhouse Derbys
104 H6 Drongan E Ayrs
124 G6 Dronley Angus
11 J3 Droop Dorset
78 C5 Dropping Well Rothm
25 K9 Droxford Hants
76 G4 Droylsden Tamesd
62 E3 Druid Denbgs
36 G7 Druidston Pembks
128 F10 Druimarbin Highld
121 J4 Druimavuic Ag & B
111 Q7 Druimdrishaig Ag & B
127 M7 Druimindarroch Highld
112 D6 Drum Ag & B
115 J1 Drum P & K
106 B2 Drumalbin S Lans
148 D10 Drumbeg Highld
140 F8 Drumblade Abers
94 F9 Drumbreddon D & G
135 P9 Drumbuie Highld
98 B6 Drumburgh Cumb
96 H7 Drumburn D & G
113 Q7 Drumchapel C Glas
122 H1 Drumchastle P & K
105 M2 Drumclog S Lans
125 J12 Drumeldrie Fife
106 F3 Drumelzier Border
127 M1 Drumfearn Highld
132 H5 Drumfrennie Abers
124 H3 Drumgley Angus
130 E4 Drumguish Highld
139 M10 Drumin Moray
105 J10 Drumjohn D & G
95 K3 Drumlamford S Ayrs
132 G3 Drumlasie Abers
98 B8 Drumleaning Cumb
103 J6 Drumlemble Ag & B
133 J8 Drumlithie Abers
95 M9 Drummoddie D & G
94 G11 Drummore D & G
140 B7 Drummuir Moray
137 N10 Drumnadrochit Highld
94 G11 Drumnaglaur D & G
140 E5 Drumnagorrach Moray
96 H2 Drumpark D & G
144 E4 Drumrunie Lodge Highld
104 E7 Drumshang S Ayrs
134 H6 Drumuie Highld
138 H11 Drumuillie Highld
122 H12 Drumvaich Stirlg
124 C11 Drunzie P & K
109 M10 Druridge Nthumb
75 J10 Drury Flints
89 Q4 Drybeck Cumb
140 C3 Drybridge Moray
104 G2 Drybridge N Ayrs
41 K8 Drybrook Gloucs
107 P3 Dryburgh Border
67 L3 Dry Doddington Lincs
56 G8 Dry Drayton Cambs
113 P3 Drymen Stirlg
141 L6 Drymuir Abers
134 G9 Drynoch Highld
31 K2 Dry Sandford Oxon
38 E7 Dryslwyn Carmth
34 C5 Dry Street Essex
63 P11 Dryton Shrops
141 J3 Dubford Abers
58 H7 Dublin Suffk
145 J2 Duchally Highld
44 F3 Duck End Bed
56 E8 Duck End Cambs
46 B5 Duck End Essex
46 B6 Duck End Essex
46 C7 Duckend Green Essex
63 N2 Duckington Ches W
42 H10 Ducklington Oxon
56 B9 Duck's Cross Bed
45 N4 Duddenhoe End Essex
115 P7 Duddingston C Edin
67 N12 Duddington Nhants
21 K9 Duddlestone Somset
15 N5 Duddleswell E Susx
52 C4 Duddlewick Shrops
108 F1 Duddo Nthumb
75 N10 Duddon Ches W
88 G9 Duddon Bridge Cumb
75 N10 Duddon Common Ches W
63 K4 Dudleston Shrops
63 L5 Dudleston Heath Shrops
52 H3 Dudley Dudley
100 H3 Dudley N Tyne
85 J9 Dudley Hill C Brad
52 H2 Dudley Port Sandw
52 C6 Dudnill Shrops
11 P5 Dudsbury Dorset
44 D9 Dudswell Herts
65 Q3 Duffield Derbys
27 K3 Duffryn Neath
139 P8 Dufftown Moray
139 M2 Duffus Moray
90 A2 Dufton Cumb
86 G2 Duggleby N York
135 P9 Duirinish Highld
127 M2 Duisdalemore Highld
128 D9 Duisky Highld
39 Q9 Dukestown Blae G
47 J3 Duke Street Suffk
76 H4 Dukinfield Tamesd
76 H4 Dukinfield Crematorium Tamesd
72 H6 Dulas IoA
22 D4 Dulcote Somset
9 K3 Dulford Devon
123 K3 Dull P & K
114 D6 Dullatur N Lans
57 M9 Dullingham Cambs
57 M9 Dullingham Ley Cambs
139 J11 Dulnain Bridge Highld
56 C8 Duloe Bed
4 C5 Duloe Cnwll
20 E8 Dulverton Somset
33 L7 Dulwich Gt Lon
113 M6 Dumbarton W Duns
42 B4 Dumbleton Gloucs
97 K3 Dumfries D & G
113 Q5 Dumgoyne Stirlg
25 K4 Dummer Hants
35 Q9 Dumpton Kent
132 G12 Dun Angus
123 J1 Dunalastair P & K
112 H7 Dunan Ag & B
135 K10 Dunan Highld
122 D1 Dunan P & K
103 J8 Dunaverty Ag & B
21 M5 Dunball Somset
116 F5 Dunbar E Loth
151 L10 Dunbeath Highld
120 G6 Dunbeg Ag & B
114 E1 Dunblane Stirlg
124 F9 Dunbog Fife
24 E8 Dunbridge Hants
137 Q4 Duncanston Highld
140 E10 Duncanstone Abers
8 G7 Dunchideock Devon
54 D6 Dunchurch Warwks
54 H10 Duncote Nhants
97 K2 Duncow D & G
124 C11 Duncrievie P & K
14 D7 Duncton W Susx
124 H7 Dundee C Dund
124 H7 *Dundee Airport* C Dund
124 H6 Dundee Crematorium C Dund
22 B7 Dundon Somset
104 G3 Dundonald S Ayrs
144 D7 Dundonnell Highld
97 P8 Dundraw Cumb
129 K1 Dundreggan Highld
96 F8 Dundrennan D & G
28 H9 Dundry N Som
133 J2 Dunecht Abers
115 K4 Dunfermline Fife
115 L4 Dunfermline Crematorium Fife
30 D3 Dunfield Gloucs
77 M3 Dunford Bridge Barns
34 G10 Dungate Kent
105 M2 Dungavel S Lans
23 K2 Dunge Wilts
17 K7 Dungeness Kent
77 P6 Dungworth Sheff
79 K9 Dunham Notts
75 M9 Dunham-on-the-Hill Ches W
52 G8 Dunhampstead Worcs
52 F7 Dunhampton Worcs
76 D6 Dunham Town Traffd
76 D6 Dunham Woodhouses Traffd
79 P8 Dunholme Lincs
125 K10 Dunino Fife
114 E4 Dunipace Falk
123 P4 Dunkeld P & K
29 L10 Dunkerton BaNES
9 M3 Dunkeswell Devon
85 L6 Dunkeswick N York
75 L9 Dunkirk Ches W
35 J10 Dunkirk Kent
29 M5 Dunkirk S Glos
30 A10 Dunkirk Wilts
33 R11 Dunk's Green Kent
132 F10 Dunlappie Angus
24 G3 Dunley Hants
52 E7 Dunley Worcs
113 M11 Dunlop E Ayrs
137 Q11 Dunmaglass Highld
6 F11 Dunmere Cnwll
114 G3 Dunmore Falk
151 M2 Dunnet Highld
125 K3 Dunnichen Angus
123 P10 Dunning P & K
86 C5 Dunnington C York
87 M5 Dunnington E R Yk
53 K10 Dunnington Warwks
84 B9 Dunnockshaw Lancs
34 D10 Dunn Street Kent
112 H6 Dunoon Ag & B
139 J6 Dunphail Moray
94 H7 Dunragit D & G
116 H10 Duns Border
77 N9 Dunsa Derbys
68 B7 Dunsby Lincs
76 D1 Dunscar Bolton
96 H1 Dunscore D & G
78 G2 Dunscroft Donc
92 C3 Dunsdale R & Cl
31 Q7 Dunsden Green Oxon
7 K3 Dunsdon Devon
14 E4 Dunsfold Surrey
8 F7 Dunsford Devon
124 E10 Dunshalt Fife
141 N6 Dunshillock Abers
78 D11 Dunsill Notts
92 H4 Dunsley N York
52 F4 Dunsley Staffs
44 B10 Dunsmore Bucks
83 P5 Dunsop Bridge Lancs
44 E7 Dunstable C Beds
65 M8 Dunstall Staffs
41 P3 Dunstall Common Worcs
57 P8 Dunstall Green Suffk
109 L6 Dunstan Nthumb
109 L5 Dunstan Steads Nthumb
20 F5 Dunster Somset
43 K6 Duns Tew Oxon
100 G6 Dunston Gatesd
79 Q11 Dunston Lincs
71 J11 Dunston Norfk
64 H8 Dunston Staffs
5 J6 Dunstone Devon
8 D9 Dunstone Devon
64 G8 Dunston Heath Staffs
78 G2 Dunsville Donc
87 K8 Dunswell E R Yk
115 K11 Dunsyre S Lans
7 M9 Dunterton Devon
42 H6 Dunthrop Oxon
41 R10 Duntisbourne Abbots Gloucs
41 R10 Duntisbourne Leer Gloucs
42 A10 Duntisbourne Rouse Gloucs
10 H3 Duntish Dorset
113 P7 Duntocher W Duns
44 B7 Dunton Bucks
45 J3 Dunton C Beds
70 C6 Dunton Norfk
54 E3 Dunton Bassett Leics
33 P11 Dunton Green Kent
34 B4 Dunton Wayletts Essex
142 D10 Duntulm Highld
104 E7 Dunure S Ayrs
26 F4 Dunvant Swans
134 D6 Dunvegan Highld
59 P6 Dunwich Suffk
64 H1 Dunwood Staffs
98 E8 Durdar Cumb
3 J9 Durgan Cnwll
100 H9 Durham Dur
100 H10 Durham Cathedral Dur
100 H10 Durham Crematorium Dur
100 H11 Durham Services Dur
91 P4 *Durham Tees Valley Airport* S on T
106 A9 Durisdeer D & G
106 A9 Durisdeermill D & G
85 L11 Durkar Wakefd
21 L6 Durleigh Somset
24 J10 Durley Hants
30 F9 Durley Wilts
25 J10 Durley Street Hants
35 N10 Durlock Kent
35 P9 Durlock Kent
41 K4 Durlow Common Herefs
84 E12 Durn Rochdl
149 J3 Durness Highld
140 H10 Durno Abers
121 J2 Duror Highld
120 H11 Durran Ag & B
14 G9 Durrington W Susx
23 P4 Durrington Wilts
133 J5 Durris Abers
29 M3 Dursley Gloucs
41 L7 Dursley Cross Gloucs
21 L7 Durston Somset
11 L3 Durweston Dorset
55 J8 Duston Nhants
138 H11 Duthil Highld
50 H5 Dutlas Powys
45 R6 Duton Hill Essex
7 L7 Dutson Cnwll
75 P8 Dutton Ches W
45 N2 Duxford Cambs
30 H2 Duxford Oxon
45 N2 Duxford Aircraft Museum Cambs
73 M8 Dwygyfylchi Conwy
72 G10 Dwyran IoA
133 L2 Dyce C Aber
46 C4 Dyer's End Essex
26 C2 Dyfatty Carmth
61 M9 Dyffrydan Gwynd
27 K3 Dyffryn Brdgnd
39 P11 Dyffryn Myr Td
27 P8 Dyffryn V Glam
61 K7 Dyffryn Ardudwy Gwynd
49 N4 Dyffryn Castell Cerdgn
39 K9 Dyffryn Cellwen Neath
68 B7 Dyke Lincs
138 H4 Dyke Moray
124 E2 Dykehead Angus
132 B12 Dykehead Angus
114 F9 Dykehead N Lans
114 A2 Dykehead Stirlg
132 H10 Dykelands Abers
124 E1 Dykends Angus
140 H7 Dykeside Abers
49 Q2 Dylife Powys
17 K5 Dymchurch Kent
41 L5 Dymock Gloucs
29 L7 Dyrham S Glos
115 P3 Dysart Fife
74 E8 Dyserth Denbgs

## E

53 J5 Eachway Worcs
100 E4 Eachwick Nthumb
83 K6 Eagland Hill Lancs
79 L10 Eagle Lincs
79 L10 Eagle Barnsdale Lincs
79 M10 Eagle Moor Lincs
91 P4 Eaglescliffe S on T
88 E1 Eaglesfield Cumb
97 P3 Eaglesfield D & G
113 Q11 Eaglesham E Rens
76 D1 Eagley Bolton
102 d6 Eairy IoM
78 H11 Eakring Notts
79 K1 Ealand N Linc
32 H6 Ealing Gt Lon
99 K7 Eals Nthumb
89 N1 Eamont Bridge Cumb
84 D6 Earby Lancs
83 P10 Earcroft Bl w D
52 D2 Eardington Shrops
51 L9 Eardisland Herefs
51 K11 Eardisley Herefs
63 L7 Eardiston Shrops
52 C7 Eardiston Worcs
56 G6 Earith Cambs
108 F4 Earle Nthumb
75 P5 Earlestown St Hel
31 Q8 Earley Wokham
71 J10 Earlham Norfk
71 J10 Earlham Crematorium Norfk
134 G4 Earlish Highld
55 L8 Earls Barton Nhants
46 F6 Earls Colne Essex
52 H9 Earls Common Worcs
41 P3 Earl's Croome Worcs
52 B5 Earlsditton Shrops
53 Q5 Earlsdon Covtry
16 B7 Earl's Down E Susx
116 C1 Earlsferry Fife
33 J8 Earlsfield Gt Lon
141 K9 Earlsford Abers
58 F7 Earl's Green Suffk
85 K11 Earlsheaton Kirk
54 D1 Earl Shilton Leics
59 J8 Earl Soham Suffk
77 K10 Earl Sterndale Derbys
107 P2 Earlston Border
104 G3 Earlston E Ayrs
58 G9 Earl Stonham Suffk
15 K1 Earlswood Surrey
53 L6 Earlswood Warwks
28 F3 Earlswood Common Mons
13 P5 Earnley W Susx

## F

## G

## H

63 L11 Habberley Shrops
52 E5 Habberley Worcs
84 B8 Habergham Lancs
81 J10 Habertoft Lincs
25 P9 Habin W Susx
80 C1 Habrough NE Lin
68 B7 Hacconby Lincs
67 P5 Haceby Lincs
59 L9 Hacheston Suffk
33 K9 Hackbridge Gt Lon
78 C7 Hackenthorpe Sheff
70 F11 Hackford Norfk
91 L8 Hackforth N York
64 C3 Hack Green Ches E
152 k4 Hackland Ork
55 K9 Hackleton Nhants
35 P11 Hacklinge Kent
52 G5 Hackman's Gate Worcs
93 K8 Hackness N York
21 M4 Hackness Somset
33 L5 Hackney Gt Lon
79 N7 Hackthorn Lincs
89 N2 Hackthorpe Cumb
33 Q5 Hacton Gt Lon
108 C3 Hadden Border
43 Q10 Haddenham Bucks
57 J5 Haddenham Cambs
116 C6 Haddington E Loth
79 M11 Haddington Lincs
59 N1 Haddiscoe Norfk
141 K8 Haddo Abers
56 C2 Haddon Cambs
77 L3 Hade Edge Kirk
77 J4 Hadfield Derbys
45 M8 Hadham Cross Herts
45 N7 Hadham Ford Herts
34 E5 Hadleigh Essex
47 J3 Hadleigh Suffk
46 H3 Hadleigh Heath Suffk
52 F8 Hadley Worcs
64 C10 Hadley Wrekin
65 L8 Hadley End Staffs
33 J3 Hadley Wood Gt Lon
34 B12 Hadlow Kent
15 P6 Hadlow Down E Susx
63 N8 Hadnall Shrops
100 B4 Hadrian's Wall Nthumb
45 Q3 Hadstock Essex
52 G8 Hadzor Worcs
16 F3 Haffenden Quarter Kent
73 Q10 Hafodunos Conwy
63 K3 Hafod-y-bwch Wrexhm
28 B2 Hafod-y-coed Blae G
28 B3 Hafodyrynys Caerph
84 C8 Haggate Lancs
98 F3 Haggbeck Cumb
152 s7 Haggersta Shet
108 G1 Haggerston Nthumb
19 L4 Haggington Hill Devon
114 E5 Haggs Falk
40 H3 Hagley Herefs
52 G4 Hagley Worcs
46 G4 Hagmore Green Suffk
80 G11 Hagnaby Lincs
81 J7 Hagnaby Lincs
80 G10 Hagworthingham Lincs
75 Q2 Haigh Wigan
83 M8 Haighton Green Lancs
88 D5 Haile Cumb
42 B6 Hailes Gloucs
45 L9 Hailey Herts
31 N5 Hailey Oxon
42 H9 Hailey Oxon
15 Q9 Hailsham E Susx
56 C8 Hail Weston Cambs
33 N4 Hainault Gt Lon
35 P9 Haine Kent
71 J8 Hainford Norfk
80 D7 Hainton Lincs
84 G7 Hainworth C Brad
87 L2 Haisthorpe E R Yk
36 H9 Hakin Pembks
66 H1 Halam Notts
115 L3 Halbeath Fife
20 F10 Halberton Devon
151 M4 Halcro Highld
89 N11 Hale Cumb
75 M7 Hale Halton
24 C9 Hale Hants
22 G8 Hale Somset
25 P4 Hale Surrey
76 E6 Hale Traffd
75 N7 Hale Bank Halton
76 E6 Halebarns Traffd
15 Q8 Hale Green E Susx
83 J6 Hale Nook Lancs
59 M1 Hales Norfk
64 D5 Hales Staffs
68 F7 Halesgate Lincs
65 M4 Hales Green Derbys
52 H4 Halesowen Dudley
35 L10 Hales Place Kent
16 B1 Hale Street Kent
34 F4 Halesville Essex
59 M5 Halesworth Suffk
75 M6 Halewood Knows
8 F10 Halford Devon
51 M4 Halford Shrops
42 F3 Halford Warwks
89 N9 Halfpenny Cumb
52 F2 Halfpenny Green Staffs
91 L10 Halfpenny Houses N York
38 F5 Halfway Carmth
39 K5 Halfway Carmth
78 C7 Halfway Sheff
31 J8 Halfway W Berk
14 D6 Halfway Bridge W Susx
63 K10 Halfway House Shrops
34 G8 Halfway Houses Kent
84 G10 Halifax Calder
113 N10 Halket E Ayrs
151 L5 Halkirk Highld
74 H9 Halkyn Flints
113 N10 Hall E Rens
66 D4 Hallam Fields Derbys
15 P7 Halland E Susx
55 K1 Hallaton Leics
29 K11 Hallatrow BaNES
98 H6 Hallbankgate Cumb
89 Q9 Hallbeck Cumb
85 L11 Hall Cliffe Wakefd
83 K9 Hall Cross Lancs
88 G7 Hall Dunnerdale Cumb
28 H6 Hallen S Glos
44 E3 Hall End Bed
44 F4 Hall End C Beds
78 C12 Hallfield Gate Derbys
101 J9 Hallgarth Dur
114 G5 Hall Glen Falk
53 L4 Hall Green Birm
134 D4 Hallin Highld
34 C9 Halling Medway
80 F6 Hallington Lincs
100 C3 Hallington Nthumb
76 C2 Halliwell Bolton
66 H2 Halloughton Notts
52 F9 Hallow Worcs
52 F9 Hallow Heath Worcs
5 N9 Hallsands Devon
45 M10 Hall's Green Essex
45 K6 Hall's Green Herts
88 G9 Hallthwaites Cumb
6 H7 Hallworthy Cnwll
106 G2 Hallyne Border
64 E2 Halmer End Staffs
52 C11 Halmond's Frome Herefs
41 L11 Halmore Gloucs
14 C9 Halnaker W Susx
75 L2 Halsall Lancs
43 M4 Halse Nhants
21 J8 Halse Somset
2 D7 Halsetown Cnwll
87 P9 Halsham E R Yk
19 K5 Halsinger Devon
46 E5 Halstead Essex
33 N10 Halstead Kent
67 J11 Halstead Leics
10 E3 Halstock Dorset
20 H6 Halsway Somset
98 D11 Haltcliff Bridge Cumb
87 J9 Haltemprice Crematorium E R Yk
80 E11 Haltham Lincs
68 G3 Haltoft End Lincs
44 C9 Halton Bucks
75 P7 Halton Halton
83 L2 Halton Lancs
85 M8 Halton Leeds
100 C5 Halton Nthumb
63 J4 Halton Wrexhm
84 F4 Halton East N York
80 H11 Halton Fenside Lincs
90 E11 Halton Gill N York
83 L2 Halton Green Lancs
80 H10 Halton Holegate Lincs
99 J6 Halton Lea Gate Nthumb
4 F4 Halton Quay Cnwll
100 C4 Halton Shields Nthumb
84 C4 Halton West N York
99 K5 Haltwhistle Nthumb
71 N10 Halvergate Norfk
5 N6 Halwell Devon
7 N5 Halwill Devon
7 N5 Halwill Junction Devon
9 N4 Ham Devon
29 K3 Ham Gloucs
41 R7 Ham Gloucs
32 H8 Ham Gt Lon
35 P11 Ham Kent
21 L8 Ham Somset
22 F4 Ham Somset
30 G9 Ham Wilts
31 R5 Hambleden Bucks
25 L10 Hambledon Hants
14 D3 Hambledon Surrey
12 H3 Hamble-le-Rice Hants
83 J7 Hambleton Lancs
85 Q9 Hambleton N York
83 J7 Hambleton Moss Side Lancs
21 N9 Hambridge Somset
29 K6 Hambrook S Glos
13 N3 Hambrook W Susx
22 H8 Ham Common Dorset
80 F10 Hameringham Lincs
56 C5 Hamerton Cambs
41 M3 Ham Green Herefs
16 F5 Ham Green Kent
34 E8 Ham Green Kent
28 H7 Ham Green N Som
53 J8 Ham Green Worcs
34 C10 Ham Hill Kent
114 D10 Hamilton S Lans
114 D10 Hamilton Services S Lans
10 F3 Hamlet Dorset
15 Q9 Hamlins E Susx
14 F9 Hammerpot W Susx
33 J6 Hammersmith Gt Lon
65 K10 Hammerwich Staffs
15 N3 Hammerwood E Susx
45 L11 Hammond Street Herts
22 H10 Hammoon Dorset
152 s8 Hamnavoe Shet
15 R10 Hampden Park E Susx
45 Q5 Hamperden End Essex
42 C8 Hampnett Gloucs
78 E2 Hampole Donc
11 P5 Hampreston Dorset
89 L10 Hampsfield Cumb
83 L4 Hampson Green Lancs
33 J5 Hampstead Gt Lon
31 L7 Hampstead Norreys W Berk
85 K3 Hampsthwaite N York
56 D2 Hampton C Pete
9 P5 Hampton Devon
32 G8 Hampton Gt Lon
35 L8 Hampton Kent
52 D3 Hampton Shrops
30 E4 Hampton Swindn
42 B3 Hampton Worcs
40 H4 Hampton Bishop Herefs
32 H8 Hampton Court Palace & Gardens Gt Lon
29 P2 Hampton Fields Gloucs
63 N2 Hampton Green Ches W
63 N2 Hampton Heath Ches W
53 M4 Hampton in Arden Solhll
52 D3 Hampton Loade Shrops
52 G7 Hampton Lovett Worcs
53 N9 Hampton Lucy Warwks
53 N7 Hampton Magna Warwks
53 N8 Hampton on the Hill Warwks
43 L8 Hampton Poyle Oxon
32 H8 Hampton Wick Gt Lon
24 D9 Hamptworth Wilts
70 D7 Hamrow Norfk
15 M8 Hamsey E Susx
33 L10 Hamsey Green Surrey
65 L8 Hamstall Ridware Staffs
53 K2 Hamstead Birm
12 F6 Hamstead IoW
31 J9 Hamstead Marshall W Berk
100 E12 Hamsterley Dur
100 E7 Hamsterley Dur
16 H4 Hamstreet Kent
22 D6 Ham Street Somset
28 E11 Hamwood N Som
11 N6 Hamworthy Poole
65 M6 Hanbury Staffs
52 H7 Hanbury Worcs
67 P6 Hanby Lincs
46 B2 Hanchet End Suffk
64 F4 Hanchurch Staffs
148 D7 Handa Island Highld
92 E4 Handale R & Cl
9 K5 Hand and Pen Devon
75 L10 Handbridge Ches W
15 J5 Handcross W Susx
76 F7 Handforth Ches E
75 P11 Hand Green Ches W
75 M12 Handley Ches W
78 B11 Handley Derbys
46 B11 Handley Green Essex
65 K9 Handsacre Staffs
53 K3 Handsworth Birm
78 C6 Handsworth Sheff
32 B4 Handy Cross Bucks
64 F4 Hanford C Stke
11 K3 Hanford Dorset
85 K10 Hanging Heaton Kirk
55 J6 Hanging Houghton Nhants
23 M6 Hanging Langford Wilts
15 K9 Hangleton Br & H
14 F10 Hangleton W Susx
29 K8 Hanham S Glos
64 C3 Hankelow Ches E
29 R4 Hankerton Wilts
16 A9 Hankham E Susx
64 G3 Hanley C Stke
41 N3 Hanley Castle Worcs
52 C7 Hanley Child Worcs
41 N3 Hanley Swan Worcs
52 C7 Hanley William Worcs
84 D3 Hanlith N York
63 M4 Hanmer Wrexhm
19 L7 Hannaford Devon
81 J8 Hannah Lincs
25 J2 Hannington Hants
55 K6 Hannington Nhants
30 E4 Hannington Swindn
30 E3 Hannington Wick Swindn
44 G5 Hanscombe End C Beds
44 A2 Hanslope M Keyn
68 B7 Hanthorpe Lincs
32 H6 Hanwell Gt Lon
43 J3 Hanwell Oxon
63 M10 Hanwood Shrops
32 G8 Hanworth Gt Lon
71 J5 Hanworth Norfk
105 Q3 Happendon S Lans
71 M6 Happisburgh Norfk
71 M6 Happisburgh Common Norfk
75 M9 Hapsford Ches W
84 B9 Hapton Lancs
58 H1 Hapton Norfk
5 N5 Harberton Devon
5 N5 Harbertonford Devon
35 K10 Harbledown Kent
53 J4 Harborne Birm
54 D5 Harborough Magna Warwks
108 E9 Harbottle Nthumb
5 M4 Harbourneford Devon
52 H7 Harbours Hill Worcs
12 B3 Harbridge Hants
12 B3 Harbridge Green Hants
54 B8 Harbury Warwks
67 J6 Harby Leics
79 L9 Harby Notts
8 G8 Harcombe Devon
9 M7 Harcombe Devon
9 Q5 Harcombe Bottom Devon
84 G7 Harden C Brad
65 J12 Harden Wsall
29 P7 Hardenhuish Wilts
133 J4 Hardgate Abers
96 G5 Hardgate D & G
85 K3 Hardgate N York
113 P7 Hardgate W Duns
14 E7 Hardham W Susx
83 J8 Hardhorn Lancs
70 F11 Hardingham Norfk
55 J9 Hardingstone Nhants
22 G3 Hardington Somset
10 D2 Hardington Mandeville Somset
10 D3 Hardington Marsh Somset
22 C11 Hardington Moor Somset
18 E9 Hardisworthy Devon
12 G4 Hardley Hants
71 M12 Hardley Street Norfk
55 M11 Hardmead M Keyn
90 D8 Hardraw N York
84 B11 Hardsough Lancs
78 D11 Hardstoft Derbys
13 K4 Hardway Hants
22 G6 Hardway Somset
44 A8 Hardwick Bucks
56 G9 Hardwick Cambs
55 L7 Hardwick Nhants
59 J3 Hardwick Norfk
42 H10 Hardwick Oxon
43 M6 Hardwick Oxon
78 D6 Hardwick Rothm
65 K12 Hardwick Wsall
41 M9 Hardwicke Gloucs
41 P6 Hardwicke Gloucs
46 G7 Hardy's Green Essex
15 Q8 Harebeating E Susx
80 G10 Hareby Lincs
84 G8 Hare Croft C Brad
32 F4 Harefield Gt Lon
47 K6 Hare Green Essex
32 A7 Hare Hatch Wokham
65 M5 Harehill Derbys
85 L8 Harehills Leeds
108 H6 Harehope Nthumb
107 N5 Harelaw Border
98 E3 Harelaw D & G
100 F7 Harelaw Dur
16 E3 Hareplain Kent
99 J9 Harescеugh Cumb
41 N9 Harescombe Gloucs
41 N9 Haresfield Gloucs
24 H7 Harestock Hants
33 P2 Hare Street Essex
45 M9 Hare Street Essex
45 M6 Hare Street Herts
85 L6 Harewood Leeds
40 H6 Harewood End Herefs
5 K5 Harford Devon
58 G2 Hargate Norfk
77 L8 Hargatewall Derbys
75 N11 Hargrave Ches W
55 P6 Hargrave Nhants
57 P8 Hargrave Suffk
98 E6 Harker Cumb
47 L5 Harkstead Suffk
65 N10 Harlaston Staffs
67 L6 Harlaxton Lincs
61 K6 Harlech Gwynd
63 N9 Harlescott Shrops
33 J6 Harlesden Gt Lon
78 E8 Harlesthorpe Derbys
5 N7 Harleston Devon
59 K4 Harleston Norfk
58 F8 Harleston Suffk
54 H8 Harlestone Nhants
84 C8 Harle Syke Lancs
78 B4 Harley Rothm
63 Q11 Harley Shrops
44 E5 Harlington C Beds
78 D3 Harlington Donc
32 F7 Harlington Gt Lon
134 E7 Harlosh Highld
45 N9 Harlow Essex
100 D4 Harlow Hill Nthumb
86 D8 Harlthorpe E R Yk
56 G10 Harlton Cambs
6 C9 Harlyn Cnwll
11 N8 Harman's Cross Dorset
91 J9 Harmby N York
45 J8 Harmer Green Herts
63 N8 Harmer Hill Shrops
32 F7 Harmondsworth Gt Lon
79 N11 Harmston Lincs
63 P11 Harnage Shrops
100 D2 Harnham Nthumb
30 C2 Harnhill Gloucs
33 P4 Harold Hill Gt Lon
36 G7 Haroldston West Pembks
152 u2 Haroldswick Shet
33 Q4 Harold Wood Gt Lon
92 D10 Harome N York
44 G9 Harpenden Herts
9 L7 Harpford Devon
87 K3 Harpham E R Yk
69 Q7 Harpley Norfk
52 C8 Harpley Worcs
54 H8 Harpole Nhants
151 L5 Harpsdale Highld
31 Q6 Harpsden Oxon
79 M6 Harpswell Lincs
76 F3 Harpurhey Manch
77 K9 Harpur Hill Derbys
98 E7 Harraby Cumb
19 L8 Harracott Devon
135 M11 Harrapool Highld
123 P7 Harrietfield P & K
34 F11 Harrietsham Kent
33 K5 Harringay Gt Lon
88 C2 Harrington Cumb
80 G9 Harrington Lincs
55 K5 Harrington Nhants
55 M1 Harringworth Nhants
152 d5 Harris W Isls
64 F1 Harriseahead Staffs
97 N10 Harriston Cumb
85 L4 Harrogate N York
85 L4 Harrogate Crematorium N York
55 N9 Harrold Bed
77 J2 Harrop Dale Oldham
32 H5 Harrow Gt Lon
7 M10 Harrowbarrow Cnwll
44 F2 Harrowden Bed
91 M3 Harrowgate Village Darltn
58 C9 Harrow Green Suffk
32 H5 Harrow on the Hill Gt Lon
32 H4 Harrow Weald Gt Lon
56 H10 Harston Cambs
67 L6 Harston Leics
86 F7 Harswell E R Yk
101 L11 Hart Hartpl
100 E1 Hartburn Nthumb
58 B10 Hartest Suffk
15 N4 Hartfield E Susx
56 E6 Hartford Cambs
76 B9 Hartford Ches W
20 E7 Hartford Somset
31 Q10 Hartfordbridge Hants
46 B8 Hartford End Essex
91 K5 Hartforth N York
23 J9 Hartgrove Dorset
63 N1 Harthill Ches W
114 G8 Harthill N Lans
78 E7 Harthill Rothm
77 L11 Hartington Derbys
108 G12 Hartington Nthumb
18 E8 Hartland Devon
18 E8 Hartland Quay Devon
52 F6 Hartlebury Worcs
101 M11 Hartlepool Hartpl
101 M12 Hartlepool Crematorium Hartpl
90 C5 Hartley Cumb
16 D4 Hartley Kent
33 R9 Hartley Kent
101 J3 Hartley Nthumb
33 R9 Hartley Green Kent
64 H6 Hartley Green Staffs
31 P10 Hartley Wespall Hants
31 Q11 Hartley Wintney Hants
34 E9 Hartlip Kent
92 F8 Hartoft End N York
86 D3 Harton N York
101 K5 Harton S Tyne
51 N3 Harton Shrops
41 M7 Hartpury Gloucs
85 J10 Hartshead Kirk
85 J10 Hartshead Moor Services Calder
64 F3 Hartshill C Stke
53 Q2 Hartshill Warwks
65 Q8 Hartshorne Derbys
108 F6 Hartside Nthumb
89 L4 Hartsop Cumb
101 M11 Hart Station Hartpl
20 H8 Hartswell Somset
55 K10 Hartwell Nhants
85 J3 Hartwith N York
114 F9 Hartwood N Lans
107 L5 Hartwoodmyres Border
34 B9 Harvel Kent
52 G6 Harvington Worcs
53 K10 Harvington Worcs
78 H5 Harwell Notts
31 K4 Harwell Oxon
47 N5 Harwich Essex
76 D2 Harwood Bolton
99 M11 Harwood Dur
93 K7 Harwood Dale N York
76 D1 Harwood Lee Bolton
45 J7 Harwood Park Crematorium Herts
78 G5 Harworth Notts
52 H4 Hasbury Dudley
14 E3 Hascombe Surrey
54 H5 Haselbech Nhants
10 D3 Haselbury Plucknett Somset
53 N7 Haseley Warwks
53 N7 Haseley Green Warwks
53 N6 Haseley Knob Warwks
53 L9 Haselor Warwks
41 N6 Hasfield Gloucs
36 G8 Hasguard Pembks
75 K2 Haskayne Lancs
59 K10 Hasketon Suffk
78 C9 Hasland Derbys
14 C4 Haslemere Surrey
84 B10 Haslingden Lancs
56 H10 Haslingfield Cambs
64 D1 Haslington Ches E
76 E12 Hassall Ches E
76 E12 Hassall Green Ches E
17 K2 Hassell Street Kent
71 M11 Hassingham Norfk
88 G3 Hassness Cumb
15 K7 Hassocks W Susx
77 N9 Hassop Derbys
14 C4 Haste Hill Surrey
151 P6 Haster Highld
81 J9 Hasthorpe Lincs
17 K2 Hastingleigh Kent
16 E9 Hastings E Susx
21 M10 Hastings Somset
16 E8 Hastings Borough Crematorium E Susx
45 N10 Hastingwood Essex
44 C9 Hastoe Herts
101 K9 Haswell Dur
101 K10 Haswell Plough Dur
56 C11 Hatch C Beds
21 M9 Hatch Beauchamp Somset
55 Q8 Hatch End Bed
32 G4 Hatch End Gt Lon
12 F4 Hatchet Gate Hants
44 G9 Hatching Green Herts
75 P9 Hatchmere Ches W
80 D4 Hatcliffe NE Lin
78 H2 Hatfield Donc
51 Q8 Hatfield Herefs
45 J10 Hatfield Herts
52 G10 Hatfield Worcs
45 Q8 Hatfield Broad Oak Essex
45 P8 Hatfield Heath Essex
46 D9 Hatfield Peverel Essex
78 H2 Hatfield Woodhouse Donc
30 H3 Hatford Oxon
24 E3 Hatherden Hants
7 Q4 Hatherleigh Devon
66 E8 Hathern Leics
42 D10 Hatherop Gloucs
77 N7 Hathersage Derbys
77 N7 Hathersage Booths Derbys
64 C3 Hatherton Ches E
64 H10 Hatherton Staffs
56 E10 Hatley St George Cambs
4 F4 Hatt Cnwll
77 J5 Hattersley Tamesd
25 L6 Hattingley Hants
141 P8 Hatton Abers
125 J4 Hatton Angus
65 N6 Hatton Derbys
32 G7 Hatton Gt Lon
80 D8 Hatton Lincs
51 M3 Hatton Shrops
75 Q7 Hatton Warrtn
53 N7 Hatton Warwks
75 M11 Hatton Heath Ches W
133 K1 Hatton of Fintray Abers
105 J5 Haugh E Ayrs
80 H8 Haugh Lincs
76 H1 Haugh Rochdl
80 G7 Haugham Lincs
114 A5 Haughhead E Duns
108 G4 Haugh Head Nthumb
58 F8 Haughley Suffk
58 F8 Haughley Green Suffk
140 C8 Haugh of Glass Moray
96 G5 Haugh of Urr D & G
125 M1 Haughs of Kinnaird Angus
78 H9 Haughton Notts
63 J8 Haughton Powys
52 C1 Haughton Shrops
63 L7 Haughton Shrops
63 P9 Haughton Shrops
64 D10 Haughton Shrops
64 F8 Haughton Staffs
76 H5 Haughton Green Tamesd
91 M3 Haughton le Skerne Darltn
75 P12 Haughton Moss Ches E
45 L7 Haultwick Herts
65 N10 Haunton Staffs
13 c1 Hautes Croix Jersey
56 H10 Hauxton Cambs
76 F10 Havannah Ches E
13 M3 Havant Hants
51 L10 Haven Herefs
68 E2 Haven Bank Lincs
87 M9 Haven Side E R Yk
13 J6 Havenstreet IoW
78 C1 Havercroft Wakefd
37 J7 Haverfordwest Pembks
46 B3 Haverhill Suffk
88 F11 Haverigg Cumb
33 P4 Havering-atte-Bower Gt Lon
44 B3 Haversham M Keyn
89 K10 Haverthwaite Cumb
91 R2 Haverton Hill S on T
28 G10 Havyat N Som
22 C6 Havyatt Somset
75 K10 Hawarden Flints
52 G10 Hawbridge Worcs
46 D7 Hawbush Green Essex
88 G12 Hawcoat Cumb
48 E11 Hawen Cerdgn
90 E9 Hawes N York
71 K12 Hawe's Green Norfk
52 F8 Hawford Worcs
107 M7 Hawick Border
9 Q5 Hawkchurch Devon
57 Q10 Hawkedon Suffk
16 E2 Hawkenbury Kent
23 J3 Hawkeridge Wilts
9 K7 Hawkerland Devon
29 M5 Hawkesbury S Glos
54 B4 Hawkesbury Warwks
29 M5 Hawkesbury Upton S Glos
53 P4 Hawkes End Covtry
76 H6 Hawk Green Stockp
109 L7 Hawkhill Nthumb
16 D5 Hawkhurst Kent
15 P7 Hawkhurst Common E Susx
17 M3 Hawkinge Kent
17 M3 Hawkinge Crematorium Kent
25 N7 Hawkley Hants
75 P3 Hawkley Wigan
20 D7 Hawkridge Somset
98 D8 Hawksdale Cumb
84 A12 Hawkshaw Bury
89 K7 Hawkshead Cumb
89 K7 Hawkshead Hill Cumb
105 Q2 Hawksland S Lans
46 B5 Hawkspur Green Essex
63 P6 Hawkstone Shrops
84 E1 Hawkswick N York
85 J7 Hawksworth Leeds
67 J3 Hawksworth Notts
34 E4 Hawkwell Essex
100 D4 Hawkwell Nthumb
32 B10 Hawley Hants
33 Q8 Hawley Kent
42 C7 Hawling Gloucs
92 B9 Hawnby N York
84 F8 Haworth C Brad
44 D10 Hawridge Bucks
58 C9 Hawstead Suffk
58 C9 Hawstead Green Suffk
101 K9 Hawthorn Dur
25 L6 Hawthorn Hants
27 Q5 Hawthorn Rhondd
32 B7 Hawthorn Hill Br For
68 D1 Hawthorn Hill Lincs
67 P7 Hawthorpe Lincs
67 K2 Hawton Notts
86 B4 Haxby C York
86 B4 Haxby Gates C York
79 K4 Haxey N Linc
79 J3 Haxey Carr N Linc
15 M2 Haxted Surrey
23 P3 Haxton Wilts
3 N4 Hay Cnwll
6 E10 Hay Cnwll
29 L9 Haycombe Crematorium BaNES
75 P4 Haydock St Hel
22 F3 Haydon BaNES
22 F10 Haydon Dorset
21 L8 Haydon Somset
99 N5 Haydon Bridge Nthumb
30 D5 Haydon Wick Swindn
4 E3 Haye Cnwll
32 G6 Hayes Gt Lon
33 M9 Hayes Gt Lon
32 F6 Hayes End Gt Lon
121 K8 Hayfield Ag & B
77 J6 Hayfield Derbys
64 B10 Haygate Wrekin
69 K8 Hay Green Norfk
125 K4 Hayhillock Angus
2 E7 Hayle Cnwll
52 H4 Hayley Green Dudley
13 M4 Hayling Island Hants
64 C2 Haymoor Green Ches E
8 E7 Hayne Devon
20 E10 Hayne Devon
44 F3 Haynes (Church End) C Beds
44 G3 Haynes (Northwood End) C Beds
44 G3 Haynes (Silver End) C Beds
44 F4 Haynes (West End) C Beds
40 B3 Hay-on-Wye Powys
36 H5 Hayscastle Pembks
36 H5 Hayscastle Cross Pembks
15 Q2 Haysden Kent
45 M6 Hay Street Herts
97 M10 Hayton Cumb
98 G7 Hayton Cumb
86 F6 Hayton E R Yk
79 J7 Hayton Notts
51 N4 Hayton's Bent Shrops
8 E9 Haytor Vale Devon
18 G10 Haytown Devon
15 L6 Haywards Heath W Susx
78 F1 Haywood Donc
40 G5 Haywood Herefs
66 G1 Haywood Oaks Notts
16 C8 Hazards Green E Susx
114 F12 Hazelbank S Lans
10 H3 Hazelbury Bryan Dorset
46 E11 Hazeleigh Essex
31 Q10 Hazeley Hants
67 J2 Hazelford Notts
76 G6 Hazel Grove Stockp
76 H4 Hazelhurst Tamesd
65 J9 Hazelslade Staffs
16 C3 Hazel Street Kent
46 B3 Hazel Stub Suffk
124 G8 Hazelton Walls Fife
65 Q3 Hazelwood Derbys
32 C3 Hazlemere Bucks
100 G4 Hazlerigg N u Ty
65 J3 Hazles Staffs
42 C8 Hazleton Gloucs
69 N5 Heacham Norfk
24 H7 Headbourne Worthy Hants
51 J9 Headbrook Herefs
16 E2 Headcorn Kent
85 L8 Headingley Leeds
43 L10 Headington Oxon
91 K3 Headlam Dur
114 G9 Headlesscross N Lans
53 J7 Headless Cross Worcs
25 P6 Headley Hants
31 L10 Headley Hants
32 H11 Headley Surrey
25 P6 Headley Down Hants
53 K5 Headley Heath Worcs
7 L4 Headon Devon
79 J8 Headon Notts
98 G7 Heads Nook Cumb
66 B2 Heage Derbys
85 P6 Healaugh N York
90 G7 Healaugh N York
76 F6 Heald Green Stockp
19 M4 Heale Devon
21 K9 Heale Somset
21 N8 Heale Somset
91 K10 Healey N York
100 C6 Healey Nthumb
84 D12 Healey Rochdl
85 K11 Healey Wakefd
100 D8 Healeyfield Dur
80 D2 Healing NE Lin
2 D8 Heamoor Cnwll
66 C3 Heanor Derbys
19 K6 Heanton Punchardon Devon
79 L6 Heapham Lincs
25 P6 Hearn Hants
54 C2 Heart of England Crematorium Warwks
114 G8 Heart of Scotland Services N Lans
34 F10 Hearts Delight Kent
19 P7 Heasley Mill Devon
135 L12 Heast Highld
78 D10 Heath Derbys
85 M11 Heath Wakefd
44 C6 Heath and Reach C Beds
14 G8 Heath Common W Susx
77 L11 Heathcote Derbys
64 C6 Heathcote Shrops
32 C3 Heath End Bucks
31 J10 Heath End Hants
66 B8 Heath End Leics
53 N8 Heath End Warwks
66 C10 Heather Leics
8 F9 Heathfield Devon
15 Q6 Heathfield E Susx
84 H2 Heathfield N York
21 J8 Heathfield Somset
43 L8 Heathfield Village Oxon
53 K6 Heath Green Worcs
97 K2 Heath Hall D & G
65 J10 Heath Hayes & Wimblebury Staffs
64 E9 Heath Hill Shrops
21 P4 Heath House Somset
32 F7 Heathrow Airport Gt Lon
9 N4 Heathstock Devon
52 E2 Heathton Shrops
64 H12 Heath Town Wolves
91 R6 Heathwaite N York
65 K7 Heatley Staffs
76 C6 Heatley Warrtn
76 C2 Heaton Bolton
84 H8 Heaton C Brad
83 K3 Heaton Lancs
100 H5 Heaton N u Ty
76 H11 Heaton Staffs
76 G5 Heaton Chapel Stockp
76 F5 Heaton Mersey Stockp
76 G5 Heaton Norris Stockp
75 L1 Heaton's Bridge Lancs
33 Q10 Heaverham Kent
76 G6 Heaviley Stockp
8 H6 Heavitree Devon
101 J5 Hebburn S Tyne
84 F3 Hebden N York
84 E9 Hebden Bridge Calder
76 B10 Hebden Green Ches W
45 K7 Hebing End Herts
37 N5 Hebron Carmth
72 G7 Hebron IoA
109 K11 Hebron Nthumb
31 P10 Heckfield Hants
59 J5 Heckfield Green Suffk
46 G7 Heckfordbridge Essex
68 C3 Heckington Lincs
85 J10 Heckmondwike Kirk
30 A9 Heddington Wilts
100 E5 Heddon-on-the-Wall Nthumb
59 L2 Hedenham Norfk
24 H10 Hedge End Hants
32 D5 Hedgerley Bucks
32 D5 Hedgerley Green Bucks
21 L7 Hedging Somset
100 D6 Hedley on the Hill Nthumb
65 J9 Hednesford Staffs
87 M9 Hedon E R Yk
32 C5 Hedsor Bucks
51 Q10 Hegdon Hill Herefs
152 s6 Heglibister Shet
91 L2 Heighington Darltn
79 P10 Heighington Lincs
52 E6 Heightington Worcs
108 B4 Heiton Border
5 M3 Hele Devon
9 J4 Hele Devon
19 K4 Hele Devon
21 J8 Hele Somset
7 J4 Helebridge Cnwll
8 E3 Hele Lane Devon
113 K5 Helensburgh Ag & B
104 G4 Helenton S Ayrs
3 J9 Helford Cnwll
3 J9 Helford Passage Cnwll
70 C7 Helhoughton Norfk
46 B3 Helions Bumpstead Essex
78 E5 Hellaby Rothm
6 F10 Helland Cnwll
6 F10 Hellandbridge Cnwll
30 H9 Hell Corner W Berk
7 K7 Hellescott Cnwll
71 J9 Hellesdon Norfk
2 D6 Hellesveor Cnwll
54 E9 Hellidon Nhants
84 C4 Hellifield N York
15 Q8 Hellingly E Susx
71 L11 Hellington Norfk
109 K10 Helm Nthumb
43 M3 Helmdon Nhants
77 L1 Helme Kirk
59 J9 Helmingham Suffk
100 F11 Helmington Row Dur
147 J2 Helmsdale Highld
84 B11 Helmshore Lancs
92 C10 Helmsley N York
85 N1 Helperby N York
86 H1 Helperthorpe N York
68 C4 Helpringham Lincs
68 C11 Helpston C Pete
75 N8 Helsby Ches W
81 K9 Helsey Lincs
2 G9 Helston Cnwll
6 F8 Helstone Cnwll
89 N2 Helton Cumb
90 H6 Helwith N York
84 B1 Helwith Bridge N York
71 L10 Hemblington Norfk
22 D6 Hembridge Somset
44 F10 Hemel Hempstead Herts
5 J5 Hemerdon Devon
86 C9 Hemingbrough N York
80 E9 Hemingby Lincs
78 C3 Hemingfield Barns
56 F6 Hemingford Abbots Cambs
56 F6 Hemingford Grey Cambs
58 H10 Hemingstone Suffk
66 D6 Hemington Leics
56 B4 Hemington Nhants
22 G3 Hemington Somset
47 N3 Hemley Suffk
92 A4 Hemlington Middsb
87 K5 Hempholme E R Yk
59 K2 Hempnall Norfk
59 K2 Hempnall Green Norfk
139 K3 Hempriggs Moray
46 B4 Hempstead Essex
34 D9 Hempstead Medway
70 G5 Hempstead Norfk
71 N6 Hempstead Norfk
41 N8 Hempsted Gloucs
70 D6 Hempton Norfk
43 J5 Hempton Oxon
71 P8 Hemsby Norfk
79 M5 Hemswell Lincs
79 N6 Hemswell Cliff Lincs
78 C1 Hemsworth Wakefd
21 J10 Hemyock Devon
28 H6 Henbury Bristl
76 G9 Henbury Ches E
5 M6 Hendham Devon
50 H1 Hendomen Powys
33 J4 Hendon Gt Lon
101 K7 Hendon Sundld
33 J4 Hendon Crematorium Gt Lon
2 H7 Hendra Cnwll
6 E9 Hendra Cnwll
27 M6 Hendre Brdgnd
74 G10 Hendre Flints
40 F9 Hendre Mons
38 E11 Hendy Carmth
72 G8 Heneglwys IoA
15 J7 Henfield W Susx
7 M6 Henford Devon
16 G3 Henghurst Kent
27 R3 Hengoed Caerph
50 H10 Hengoed Powys
63 J5 Hengoed Shrops
58 B7 Hengrave Suffk
45 Q6 Henham Essex
62 F10 Heniarth Powys
21 L8 Henlade Somset
10 H4 Henley Dorset
41 P8 Henley Gloucs
51 M3 Henley Shrops
51 P5 Henley Shrops
21 P7 Henley Somset
58 H10 Henley Suffk
14 C6 Henley W Susx
54 B4 Henley Green Covtry
53 M7 Henley-in-Arden Warwks
31 Q6 Henley-on-Thames Oxon
32 D11 Henley Park Surrey
16 C8 Henley's Down E Susx
34 B9 Henley Street Kent
38 A4 Henllan Cerdgn
74 D10 Henllan Denbgs
37 N6 Henllan Amgoed Carmth
28 C4 Henllys Torfn
44 H4 Henlow C Beds
8 F8 Hennock Devon
46 F4 Henny Street Essex
73 N9 Henryd Conwy
37 K5 Henry's Moat (Castell Hendre) Pembks
86 B10 Hensall N York
99 L5 Henshaw Nthumb
88 C3 Hensingham Cumb
59 P3 Henstead Suffk
24 H9 Hensting Hants
22 G9 Henstridge Somset
22 G9 Henstridge Ash Somset
22 G9 Henstridge Marsh Somset
43 Q11 Henton Oxon
22 C4 Henton Somset
52 F9 Henwick Worcs
7 K10 Henwood Cnwll
43 K11 Henwood Oxon
26 G3 Heol-las Swans
39 L7 Heol Senni Powys
27 M5 Heol-y-Cyw Brdgnd
108 H5 Hepburn Nthumb
108 G9 Hepple Nthumb
100 G1 Hepscott Nthumb
84 E9 Heptonstall Calder
77 M2 Hepworth Kirk
58 E6 Hepworth Suffk
36 G9 Herbrandston Pembks
40 G4 Hereford Herefs
40 G4 Hereford Crematorium Herefs
35 Q9 Hereson Kent
142 D11 Heribusta Highld
115 R10 Heriot Border
115 M7 Hermiston C Edin
107 M10 Hermitage Border
10 G3 Hermitage Dorset
31 L8 Hermitage W Berk
13 N4 Hermitage W Susx
77 Q3 Hermit Hill Barns
38 A5 Hermon Carmth
72 F10 Hermon IoA
37 N4 Hermon Pembks
35 L9 Herne Kent
35 L8 Herne Bay Kent
35 L9 Herne Common Kent
33 L7 Herne Hill Gt Lon
34 B11 Herne Pound Kent
19 L8 Herner Devon
35 J10 Hernhill Kent
4 C4 Herodsfoot Cnwll
35 N11 Heronden Kent
34 A4 Herongate Essex
94 G2 Heronsford S Ayrs
32 E3 Heronsgate Herts
25 L4 Herriard Hants
59 P1 Herringfleet Suffk
44 F3 Herring's Green Bed
57 N6 Herringswell Suffk
78 D5 Herringthorpe Rothm
101 J7 Herrington Sundld
35 M10 Hersden Kent
7 K3 Hersham Cnwll
32 G9 Hersham Surrey
16 B8 Herstmonceux E Susx
11 N9 Herston Dorset
152 k6 Herston Ork
45 L9 Hertford Herts
45 L9 Hertford Heath Herts
45 K9 Hertingfordbury Herts
83 K10 Hesketh Bank Lancs
83 N7 Hesketh Lane Lancs
98 D10 Hesket Newmarket Cumb
83 M12 Heskin Green Lancs
101 L10 Hesleden Dur
90 E11 Hesleden N York
78 G5 Hesley Donc
99 M2 Hesleyside Nthumb

## I



## J



## K

122 H1 Kinloch Rannoch P & K
139 K3 Kinloss Moray
74 D7 Kinmel Bay Conwy
141 K12 Kinmuck Abers
141 L12 Kinmundy Abers
102 B1 Kinnabus Ag & B
141 N7 Kinnadie Abers
123 N1 Kinnaird P & K
133 K9 Kinneff Abers
106 D9 Kinnelhead D & G
125 M3 Kinnell Angus
63 K8 Kinnerley Shrops
51 K10 Kinnersley Herefs
41 P3 Kinnersley Worcs
50 H8 Kinnerton Powys
51 L1 Kinnerton Shrops
75 K11 Kinnerton Green Flints
124 D12 Kinnesswood P & K
90 H2 Kinninvie Dur
124 G2 Kinnordy Angus
66 H6 Kinoulton Notts
124 C12 Kinross P & K
124 D6 Kinrossie P & K
124 C12 Kinross Services P & K
44 G8 Kinsbourne Green Herts
64 C4 Kinsey Heath Ches E
51 K7 Kinsham Herefs
41 Q4 Kinsham Worcs
85 N12 Kinsley Wakefd
11 P5 Kinson Bmouth
136 D12 Kintail Highld
30 H9 Kintbury W Berk
139 J4 Kintessack Moray
124 C9 Kintillo P & K
51 L6 Kinton Herefs
63 L8 Kinton Shrops
133 J1 Kintore Abers
111 K11 Kintour Ag & B
110 H11 Kintra Ag & B
119 K8 Kintra Ag & B
120 F11 Kintraw Ag & B
103 K2 Kintyre Ag & B
138 G12 Kinveachy Highld
52 F4 Kinver Staffs
91 M7 Kiplin N York
85 M9 Kippax Leeds
114 B2 Kippen Stirlg
96 G7 Kippford or Scaur D & G
16 B3 Kipping's Cross Kent
152 k5 Kirbister Ork
71 K11 Kirby Bedon Norfk
67 J8 Kirby Bellars Leics
59 M2 Kirby Cane Norfk
53 P5 Kirby Corner Covtry
47 M7 Kirby Cross Essex
66 E11 Kirby Fields Leics
86 G2 Kirby Grindalythe N York
85 N2 Kirby Hill N York
91 J5 Kirby Hill N York
91 Q9 Kirby Knowle N York
47 M7 Kirby le Soken Essex
92 F10 Kirby Misperton N York
66 E11 Kirby Muxloe Leics
91 P8 Kirby Sigston N York
86 E3 Kirby Underdale E R Yk
91 P9 Kirby Wiske N York
14 E5 Kirdford W Susx
151 N5 Kirk Highld
152 t8 Kirkabister Shet
96 C8 Kirkandrews D & G
98 D6 Kirkandrews upon Eden Cumb
98 C7 Kirkbampton Cumb
97 K6 Kirkbean D & G
78 G1 Kirk Bramwith Donc
97 P7 Kirkbride Cumb
91 L8 Kirkbridge N York
125 K4 Kirkbuddo Angus
107 J2 Kirkburn Border
86 H4 Kirkburn E R Yk
77 M1 Kirkburton Kirk
75 L4 Kirkby Knows
79 Q5 Kirkby Lincs
92 B5 Kirkby N York
91 M8 Kirkby Fleetham N York
80 B12 Kirkby Green Lincs
66 D1 Kirkby in Ashfield Notts
88 H10 Kirkby-in-Furness Cumb
68 B3 Kirkby la Thorpe Lincs
89 P11 Kirkby Lonsdale Cumb
84 D3 Kirkby Malham N York
66 D12 Kirkby Mallory Leics
91 L11 Kirkby Malzeard N York
92 E9 Kirkby Mills N York
92 E9 Kirkbymoorside N York
80 E11 Kirkby on Bain Lincs
85 L5 Kirkby Overblow N York
90 C5 Kirkby Stephen Cumb
89 Q2 Kirkby Thore Cumb
67 Q7 Kirkby Underwood Lincs
85 P7 Kirkby Wharf N York
66 E1 Kirkby Woodhouse Notts
115 P3 Kirkcaldy Fife
115 N2 Kirkcaldy Crematorium Fife
98 G4 Kirkcambeck Cumb
96 D8 Kirkchrist D & G
94 E4 Kirkcolm D & G
105 N7 Kirkconnel D & G
97 K5 Kirkconnell D & G
95 L6 Kirkcowan D & G
96 D8 Kirkcudbright D & G
75 K5 Kirkdale Lpool
85 N5 Kirk Deighton N York
87 J9 Kirk Ella E R Yk
105 R1 Kirkfieldbank S Lans
96 H5 Kirkgunzeon D & G
66 D4 Kirk Hallam Derbys
83 K9 Kirkham Lancs
86 D2 Kirkham N York
85 L10 Kirkhamgate Wakefd
85 P3 Kirk Hammerton N York
100 C2 Kirkharle Nthumb
99 K8 Kirkhaugh Nthumb
85 J11 Kirkheaton Kirk
100 C3 Kirkheaton Nthumb
137 P7 Kirkhill Highld
106 C8 Kirkhope S Lans
98 H6 Kirkhouse Cumb
78 G1 Kirkhouse Green Donc
135 K12 Kirkibost Highld
124 F4 Kirkinch P & K
95 M8 Kirkinner D & G
114 B6 Kirkintilloch E Duns
65 P2 Kirk Ireton Derbys
88 E3 Kirkland Cumb
99 J11 Kirkland Cumb
105 N7 Kirkland D & G
105 Q11 Kirkland D & G
106 D11 Kirkland D & G
97 N10 Kirkland Guards Cumb
65 P4 Kirk Langley Derbys
92 C2 Kirkleatham R & Cl
91 Q5 Kirklevington S on T
59 Q2 Kirkley Suffk
91 N10 Kirklington N York
78 H12 Kirklington Notts
98 E5 Kirklinton Cumb
115 L6 Kirkliston C Edin
95 N7 Kirkmabreck D & G
94 G11 Kirkmaiden D & G
100 H12 Kirk Merrington Dur
102 d4 Kirk Michael IoM
131 K12 Kirkmichael P & K
104 F8 Kirkmichael S Ayrs
105 P1 Kirkmuirhill S Lans
108 E4 Kirknewton Nthumb
115 L8 Kirknewton W Loth
140 D9 Kirkney Abers
114 F8 Kirk of Shotts N Lans
98 H10 Kirkoswald Cumb
104 D8 Kirkoswald S Ayrs
106 B11 Kirkpatrick D & G
96 F4 Kirkpatrick Durham D & G
98 C4 Kirkpatrick-Fleming D & G
78 G2 Kirk Sandall Donc
88 F10 Kirksanton Cumb
85 Q12 Kirk Smeaton N York
85 K8 Kirkstall Leeds
80 D11 Kirkstead Lincs
140 E9 Kirkstile Abers
107 K11 Kirkstile D & G
89 L5 Kirkstone Pass Inn Cumb
151 P2 Kirkstyle Highld
85 M11 Kirkthorpe Wakefd
140 G10 Kirkton Abers
97 K2 Kirkton D & G
124 G8 Kirkton Fife
135 Q10 Kirkton Highld
136 C7 Kirkton Highld
123 N9 Kirkton P & K
106 G2 Kirkton Manor Border
124 F3 Kirkton of Airlie Angus
124 G5 Kirkton of Auchterhouse Angus
138 F6 Kirkton of Barevan Highld
124 D6 Kirkton of Collace P & K
132 B1 Kirkton of Glenbuchat Abers
141 N10 Kirkton of Logie Buchan Abers
132 E11 Kirkton of Menmuir Angus
125 K5 Kirkton of Monikie Angus
140 H10 Kirkton of Rayne Abers
133 K3 Kirkton of Skene Abers
124 H6 Kirkton of Strathmartine Angus
124 H5 Kirkton of Tealing Angus
152 F2 Kirkton of Tough Abers
141 N3 Kirktown Abers
141 Q5 Kirktown Abers
140 G4 Kirktown of Alvah Abers
141 K10 Kirktown of Bourtie Abers
133 K7 Kirktown of Fetteresso Abers
139 P8 Kirktown of Mortlach Moray
141 P10 Kirktown of Slains Abers
106 F1 Kirkurd Border
152 k4 Kirkwall Ork
152 m5 Kirkwall Airport Ork
100 C1 Kirkwhelpington Nthumb
108 D4 Kirk Yetholm Border
80 B1 Kirmington N Linc
80 D5 Kirmond le Mire Lincs
112 H6 Kirn Ag & B
124 H2 Kirriemuir Angus
59 L1 Kirstead Green Norfk
97 P4 Kirtlebridge D & G
57 N9 Kirtling Cambs
57 N9 Kirtling Green Cambs
43 K8 Kirtlington Oxon
150 D4 Kirtomy Highld
68 F4 Kirton Lincs
78 H10 Kirton Notts
47 N4 Kirton Suffk
68 F4 Kirton End Lincs
113 M6 Kirtonhill W Duns
68 E4 Kirton Holme Lincs
79 M4 Kirton in Lindsey N Linc
95 M7 Kirwaugh D & G
135 Q8 Kishorn Highld
54 H9 Kislingbury Nhants
42 F5 Kitebrook Warwks
53 N7 Kite Green Warwks
54 D7 Kites Hardwick Warwks
7 J5 Kitleigh Cnwll
75 P3 Kitt Green Wigan
20 H9 Kittisford Somset
26 E4 Kittle Swans
53 M3 Kitt's Green Birm
133 M3 Kittybrewster C Aber
25 L7 Kitwood Hants
40 C5 Kivernoll Herefs
78 E7 Kiveton Park Rothm
79 L7 Knaith Lincs
79 L6 Knaith Park Lincs
22 H8 Knap Corner Dorset
32 D10 Knaphill Surrey
21 L8 Knapp Somset
24 G8 Knapp Hill Hants
79 J12 Knapthorpe Notts
85 R5 Knapton C York
92 H11 Knapton N York
71 L5 Knapton Norfk
51 M10 Knapton Green Herefs
56 F8 Knapwell Cambs
85 M4 Knaresborough N York
99 K7 Knarsdale Nthumb
141 L7 Knaven Abers
91 Q9 Knayton N York
45 J7 Knebworth Herts
86 D9 Knedlington E R Yk
78 H11 Kneesall Notts
55 K3 Kneesworth Cambs
66 H3 Kneeton Notts
26 C4 Knelston Swans
64 G5 Knenhall Staffs
58 E4 Knettishall Suffk
19 M5 Knightacott Devon
54 C9 Knightcote Warwks
64 E7 Knightley Staffs
64 F7 Knightley Dale Staffs
66 G12 Knighton C Leic
4 H7 Knighton Devon
10 F2 Knighton Dorset
11 P5 Knighton Poole
51 J6 Knighton Powys
21 K4 Knighton Somset
64 D4 Knighton Staffs
64 D7 Knighton Staffs
30 G8 Knighton Wilts
52 B6 Knighton on Teme Worcs
29 K6 Knightsbridge Gloucs
6 F8 Knightsmill Cnwll
52 D9 Knightwick Worcs
51 J8 Knill Herefs
67 K6 Knipton Leics
100 E8 Knitsley Dur
65 N2 Kniveton Derbys
89 R1 Knock Cumb
127 M2 Knock Highld
140 E5 Knock Moray
152 f3 Knock W Isls
144 F3 Knockally Highld
139 M7 Knockando Moray
137 P7 Knockbain Highld
138 B5 Knockbain Highld
113 J8 Knock Castle N Ayrs
151 L4 Knockdee Highld
112 G7 Knockdow Ag & B
29 N5 Knockdown Wilts
104 F10 Knockeen S Ayrs
103 Q4 Knockenkelly N Ayrs
104 G2 Knockentiber E Ayrs
33 Q7 Knockhall Kent
33 M10 Knockholt Kent
33 M10 Knockholt Pound Kent
63 K7 Knockin Shrops
104 H2 Knockinlaw E Ayrs
33 Q10 Knockmill Kent
94 D5 Knocknain D & G
111 M7 Knockrome Ag & B
102 c4 Knocksharry IoM
96 C2 Knocksheen D & G
96 F4 Knockvennie Smithy D & G
59 N8 Knodishall Suffk
59 N8 Knodishall Common Suffk
22 B8 Knole Somset
29 J6 Knole Park S Glos
76 E8 Knolls Green Ches E
63 L4 Knolton Wrexhm
23 L5 Knook Wilts
67 K10 Knossington Leics
83 J5 Knott End-on-Sea Lancs
55 P8 Knotting Bed
55 P8 Knotting Green Bed
85 Q10 Knottingley Wakefd
75 L5 Knotty Ash Lpool
32 D4 Knotty Green Bucks
51 P6 Knowbury Shrops
95 K4 Knowe D & G
105 L11 Knowehead D & G
104 E7 Knoweside S Ayrs
29 J8 Knowle Bristl
8 E4 Knowle Devon
9 J3 Knowle Devon
9 K8 Knowle Devon
19 J6 Knowle Devon
51 P6 Knowle Shrops
53 M5 Knowle Solhll
20 E5 Knowle Somset
9 K5 Knowle Cross Devon
98 E7 Knowlefield Cumb
83 P7 Knowle Green Lancs
32 E8 Knowle Hill Surrey
9 Q2 Knowle St Giles Somset
13 J3 Knowle Village Hants
84 D10 Knowle Wood Calder
46 D3 Knowl Green Essex
32 B6 Knowl Hill W & M
11 N3 Knowlton Dorset
35 M11 Knowlton Kent
75 M4 Knowsley Knows
75 M5 Knowsley Safari Park Knows
20 C3 Knowstone Devon
85 L4 Knox N York
16 D3 Knox Bridge Kent
51 J6 Knucklas Powys
55 M7 Knuston Nhants
76 D8 Knutsford Ches E
76 D8 Knutsford Services Ches E
64 F3 Knutton Staffs
84 G11 Krumlin Calder
2 H11 Kuggar Cnwll
135 M10 Kyleakin Highld
135 M10 Kyle of Lochalsh Highld
135 P11 Kylerhea Highld
148 F10 Kylesku Highld
127 P6 Kylesmorar Highld
152 e5 Kyles Scalpay W Isls
148 F9 Kylestrome Highld
41 K4 Kynaston Herefs
63 K8 Kynaston Shrops
64 C9 Kynnersley Wrekin
51 Q8 Kyre Green Worcs
52 B8 Kyre Park Worcs
51 Q7 Kyrewood Worcs
20 G9 Kyrle Somset

## L

12 c3 La Bellieuse Guern
152 e4 Lacasaigh W Isls
152 f3 Lacasdal W Isls
80 D2 Laceby NE Lin
32 B2 Lacey Green Bucks
76 D9 Lach Dennis Ches W
92 B3 Lackenby R & Cl
57 Q6 Lackford Suffk
57 Q6 Lackford Green Suffk
29 Q8 Lacock Wilts
54 C9 Ladbroke Warwks
64 H1 Ladderedge Staffs
16 C1 Laddingford Kent
68 H1 Lade Bank Lincs
3 L4 Ladock Cnwll
152 n2 Lady Ork
124 F11 Ladybank Fife
7 L7 Ladycross Cnwll
106 B4 Ladygill S Lans
88 G9 Lady Hall Cumb
117 K11 Ladykirk Border
41 J5 Ladyridge Herefs
57 P9 Lady's Green Suffk
53 K3 Ladywood Birm
52 F8 Ladywood Worcs
12 d1 La Fontenelle Guern
12 c3 La Fosse Guern
96 H1 Lag D & G
127 L12 Laga Highld
111 J12 Lagavulin Ag & B
103 P5 Lagg N Ayrs
129 K5 Laggan Highld
130 B5 Laggan Highld
130 F4 Lagganlia Highld
12 c1 La Greve Guern
13 a1 La Greve de Lecq Jersey
13 d2 La Hougue Bie Jersey
12 b2 La Houguette Guern
149 J5 Laid Highld
143 P7 Laide Highld
126 H7 Laig Highld
113 N11 Laigh Clunch E Ayrs
104 H1 Laigh Fenwick E Ayrs
105 L5 Laigh Glenmuir E Ayrs
114 C10 Laighstonehall S Lans
34 E4 Laindon Essex
145 N4 Lairg Highld
85 J3 Laisterdyke C Brad
98 F11 Laithes Cumb
7 P7 Lake Devon
19 L7 Lake Devon
13 K8 Lake IoW
11 N6 Lake Poole
23 P5 Lake Wilts
88 H5 Lake District National Park Cumb
57 N4 Lakenheath Suffk
14 F4 Laker's Green Surrey
57 K1 Lakesend Norfk
89 K9 Lakeside Cumb
32 F8 Laleham Surrey
27 L5 Laleston Brdgnd
3 J8 Lamanva Cnwll
46 F4 Lamarsh Essex
71 K7 Lamas Norfk
108 E1 Lambden Border
16 E4 Lamberhurst Kent
16 B4 Lamberhurst Down Kent
117 L9 Lamberton Border
33 K6 Lambeth Gt Lon
33 K8 Lambeth Crematorium Gt Lon
57 M10 Lambfair Green Suffk
66 C3 Lambley Notts
99 K6 Lambley Nthumb
30 C6 Lambourn W Berk
33 N3 Lambourne End Essex
30 C7 Lambourn Woodlands W Berk
83 Q7 Lamb Roe Lancs
15 J5 Lambs Green W Susx
36 H7 Lambston Pembks
4 C4 Lamellion Cnwll
7 N9 Lamerton Devon
100 G7 Lamesley Gatesd
106 C4 Lamington S Lans
103 Q4 Lamlash N Ayrs
98 E11 Lamonby Cumb
3 P2 Lamorick Cnwll
2 C9 Lamorna Cnwll
3 L6 Lamorran Cnwll
4 B3 Lampen Cnwll
49 K11 Lampeter Cerdgn
37 M7 Lampeter Velfrey Pembks
37 K10 Lamphey Pembks
88 E3 Lamplugh Cumb
55 J6 Lamport Nhants
22 F6 Lamyatt Somset
7 K3 Lana Devon
7 L5 Lana Devon
106 A1 Lanark S Lans
83 L3 Lancaster Lancs
83 L2 Lancaster & Morecambe Crematorium Lancs
83 L5 Lancaster Services (Forton) Lancs
28 H3 Lancaut Gloucs
100 F9 Lanchester Dur
14 H10 Lancing W Susx
12 C1 L'Ancresse Guern
57 J7 Landbeach Cambs
19 J8 Landcross Devon
133 J5 Landerberry Abers
24 D9 Landford Wilts
151 M10 Land-hallow Highld
75 J6 Landican Crematorium Wirral
26 C4 Landimore Swans
19 L7 Landkey Devon
26 G3 Landore Swans
4 E4 Landrake Cnwll
5 N3 Landscove Devon
2 B9 Land's End Cnwll
2 B9 Land's End Cnwll
2 B8 Land's End Airport Cnwll
37 K8 Landshipping Pembks
7 L9 Landue Cnwll
4 F4 Landulph Cnwll
57 M7 Landwade Suffk
3 K2 Lane Cnwll
7 J8 Laneast Cnwll
84 C8 Lane Bottom Lancs
32 A4 Lane End Bucks
6 F11 Lane End Cnwll
25 J8 Lane End Hants
33 Q8 Lane End Kent
84 C6 Lane End Lancs
76 C6 Lane End Warrtn
22 H4 Lane End Wilts
65 N5 Lane Ends Derbys
84 B9 Lane Ends Lancs
86 E5 Lane Ends N York
64 G11 Lane Green Staffs
79 K8 Laneham Notts
91 J4 Lane Head Dur
99 N10 Lanehead Dur
99 M1 Lanehead Nthumb
76 B4 Lane Head Wigan
64 H12 Lane Head Wsall
83 K7 Lane Heads Lancs
84 D7 Laneshaw Bridge Lancs
84 B10 Lane Side Lancs
7 M5 Langaford Devon
21 L8 Langaller Somset
67 J5 Langar Notts
113 M6 Langbank Rens
84 G5 Langbar N York
92 B4 Langbaurgh N York
84 B2 Langcliffe N York
93 J8 Langdale End N York
7 K7 Langdon Cnwll
99 N12 Langdon Beck Dur
12 G3 Langdown Hants
124 G11 Langdyke Fife
46 H8 Langenhoe Essex
44 H3 Langford C Beds
9 J4 Langford Devon
46 E10 Langford Essex
28 F10 Langford N Som
79 K12 Langford Notts
42 F11 Langford Oxon
20 H9 Langford Budville Somset
22 H8 Langham Dorset
46 H5 Langham Essex
70 E4 Langham Norfk
67 L10 Langham Rutlnd
58 E6 Langham Suffk
83 Q8 Langho Lancs
98 D1 Langholm D & G
26 F5 Langland Swans
107 M3 Langlee Border
76 H9 Langley Ches E
66 D3 Langley Derbys
42 B6 Langley Gloucs
12 G4 Langley Hants
45 J7 Langley Herts
34 E12 Langley Kent
99 M6 Langley Nthumb
42 G8 Langley Oxon
76 F2 Langley Rochdl
32 E6 Langley Slough
20 H7 Langley Somset
25 P7 Langley W Susx
53 M8 Langley Warwks
29 Q7 Langley Burrell Wilts
32 F2 Langleybury Herts
99 N6 Langley Castle Nthumb
65 P5 Langley Common Derbys
65 P4 Langley Green Derbys
46 F7 Langley Green Essex
53 M8 Langley Green Warwks
45 N5 Langley Lower Green Essex
20 G7 Langley Marsh Somset
66 D3 Langley Mill Derbys
100 G10 Langley Moor Dur
100 G9 Langley Park Dur
71 M11 Langley Street Norfk
45 N5 Langley Upper Green Essex
16 A10 Langney E Susx
78 F6 Langold Notts
7 K7 Langore Cnwll
21 P8 Langport Somset
68 E2 Langrick Lincs
29 L8 Langridge BaNES
19 L9 Langridgeford Devon
97 N9 Langrigg Cumb
25 M8 Langrish Hants
77 N4 Langsett Barns
123 K10 Langside P & K
13 N4 Langstone Hants
28 E4 Langstone Newpt
91 L8 Langthorne N York
85 M2 Langthorpe N York
90 G6 Langthwaite N York
87 J2 Langtoft E R Yk
68 C9 Langtoft Lincs
91 K3 Langton Dur
80 E10 Langton Lincs
80 G9 Langton Lincs
86 E2 Langton N York
80 C8 Langton by Wragby Lincs
15 Q3 Langton Green Kent
58 H6 Langton Green Suffk
10 F8 Langton Herring Dorset
11 L4 Langton Long Blandford Dorset
11 N9 Langton Matravers Dorset
19 J10 Langtree Devon
19 J10 Langtree Week Devon
98 H11 Langwathby Cumb
151 K12 Langwell House Highld
78 E9 Langwith Derbys
78 E10 Langwith Junction Derbys
79 Q8 Langworth Lincs
3 Q2 Lanhydrock House & Gardens Cnwll
3 P2 Lanivet Cnwll
3 N4 Lanjeth Cnwll
6 F9 Lank Cnwll
3 Q3 Lanlivery Cnwll
2 H6 Lanner Cnwll
7 K9 Lanoy Cnwll
4 B5 Lanreath Cnwll
4 B6 Lansallos Cnwll
6 F8 Lanteglos Cnwll
4 A6 Lanteglos Highway Cnwll
107 P5 Lanton Border
108 E3 Lanton Nthumb
12 c1 La Passee Guern
8 D3 Lapford Devon
111 J12 Laphroaig Ag & B
64 G9 Lapley Staffs
13 a2 La Pulente Jersey
53 M6 Lapworth Warwks
120 D3 Larachbeg Highld
114 F5 Larbert Falk
83 K7 Larbreck Lancs
140 F9 Largie Abers
112 D4 Largiemore Ag & B
125 J11 Largoward Fife
113 J9 Largs N Ayrs
103 Q5 Largybeg N Ayrs
103 R5 Largymore N Ayrs
9 K5 Larkbeare Devon
113 K6 Larkfield Inver
34 C10 Larkfield Kent
114 D11 Larkhall S Lans
23 P4 Larkhill Wilts
58 E3 Larling Norfk
13 d3 La Rocque Jersey
12 c2 La Rousaillerie Guern
90 G3 Lartington Dur
30 C2 Lasborough Gloucs
25 L5 Lasham Hants
7 M3 Lashbrook Devon
7 N4 Lashbrook Devon
16 E3 Lashenden Kent
76 G12 Lask Edge Staffs
115 P8 Lasswade Mdloth
92 E8 Lastingham N York
21 P4 Latcham Somset
45 N1 Latchford Herts
31 N2 Latchford Oxon
34 F2 Latchingdon Essex
7 M10 Latchley Cnwll
76 C4 Lately Common Warrtn
44 C3 Lathbury M Keyn
151 M10 Latheron Highld
151 M10 Latheronwheel Highld
125 J11 Lathones Fife
32 E3 Latimer Bucks
29 K5 Latteridge S Glos
22 F8 Lattiford Somset
30 C3 Latton Wilts
116 C11 Lauder Border
37 Q8 Laugharne Carmth
79 L8 Laughterton Lincs
15 P8 Laughton E Susx
54 H3 Laughton Leics
67 Q6 Laughton Lincs
79 L4 Laughton Lincs
78 E6 Laughton-en-le-Morthen Rothm
7 J4 Launcells Cnwll
7 K4 Launcells Cross Cnwll
7 L8 Launceston Cnwll
43 M7 Launton Oxon
132 H10 Laurencekirk Abers
96 D5 Laurieston D & G
114 G5 Laurieston Falk
55 M10 Lavendon M Keyn
58 D10 Lavenham Suffk
28 A8 Lavernock V Glam
98 F6 Laversdale Cumb
23 P7 Laverstock Wilts
24 H4 Laverstoke Hants
42 C4 Laverton Gloucs
91 L12 Laverton N York
22 H3 Laverton Somset
12 c3 La Villette Guern
75 L12 Lavister Wrexhm
114 E10 Law S Lans
122 H5 Lawers P & K
47 K5 Lawford Essex
21 J6 Lawford Somset
114 E11 Law Hill S Lans
7 L8 Lawhitton Cnwll
84 A2 Lawkland N York
84 B2 Lawkland Green N York
64 C10 Lawley Wrekin
64 F7 Lawnhead Staffs
85 K7 Lawns Wood Crematorium Leeds
37 K9 Lawrenny Pembks
58 C10 Lawshall Suffk
58 C10 Lawshall Green Suffk
51 M9 Lawton Herefs
152 e4 Laxay W Isls
152 f5 Laxdale W Isls
102 f5 Laxey IoM
59 L6 Laxfield Suffk
148 F7 Laxford Bridge Highld
152 t5 Laxo Shet
86 E10 Laxton E R Yk
55 N1 Laxton Nhants
79 J10 Laxton Notts
84 F7 Laycock C Brad
46 G8 Layer Breton Essex
46 G7 Layer-de-la-Haye Essex
46 G8 Layer Marney Essex
47 J4 Layham Suffk
30 H9 Layland's Green W Berk
10 B4 Laymore Dorset
32 E4 Layter's Green Bucks
86 D7 Laytham E R Yk
97 P7 Laythes Cumb
92 C3 Lazenby R & Cl
98 G10 Lazonby Cumb
77 Q12 Lea Derbys
41 K7 Lea Herefs
79 L6 Lea Lincs
51 K3 Lea Shrops
63 L10 Lea Shrops
29 Q5 Lea Wilts
138 B7 Leachkin Highld
115 N10 Leadburn Border
67 N2 Leadenham Lincs
45 Q9 Leaden Roding Essex
100 E8 Leadgate Dur
100 E7 Leadgate Nthumb
106 A7 Leadhills S Lans
34 F12 Leadingcross Green Kent
77 N7 Leadmill Derbys
42 G8 Leafield Oxon
44 F7 Leagrave Luton
76 C10 Leahead Ches W
65 J7 Lea Heath Staffs
91 Q8 Leake N York
68 H2 Leake Common Side Lincs
92 F5 Lealholm N York
92 F5 Lealholm Side N York
135 J4 Lealt Highld
77 N8 Leam Derbys
53 M2 Lea Marston Warwks
54 D7 Leamington Hastings Warwks
53 Q7 Leamington Spa Warwks
101 J9 Leamside Dur
15 Q9 Leap Cross E Susx
89 M10 Leasgill Cumb
67 Q2 Leasingham Lincs
100 H12 Leasingthorne Dur
32 H11 Leatherhead Surrey
85 K6 Leathley N York
63 M8 Leaton Shrops
63 Q10 Leaton Wrekin
83 L9 Lea Town Lancs
34 H11 Leaveland Kent
46 G4 Leavenheath Suffk
86 E3 Leavening N York
33 M10 Leaves Green Gt Lon
90 C9 Lea Yeat Cumb
93 M10 Lebberston N York
12 b3 Le Bigard Guern
12 c3 Le Bourg Guern
13 d3 Le Bourg Jersey
30 E2 Lechlade on Thames Gloucs
110 G7 Lecht Gruinart Ag & B
89 Q11 Leck Lancs
123 J5 Leckbuie P & K
24 F6 Leckford Hants
43 P4 Leckhampstead Bucks
31 J7 Leckhampstead W Berk
31 J7 Leckhampstead Thicket W Berk
41 Q8 Leckhampton Gloucs
144 F7 Leckmelm Highld
27 R7 Leckwith V Glam
87 J6 Leconfield E R Yk
120 G5 Ledaig Ag & B
44 C7 Ledburn Bucks
41 L4 Ledbury Herefs
41 L5 Leddington Gloucs
51 L10 Ledgemoor Herefs
51 L8 Ledicot Herefs
144 G3 Ledmore Junction Highld
75 K9 Ledsham Ches W
85 P9 Ledsham Leeds
85 N9 Ledston Leeds
5 M7 Ledstone Devon
85 N9 Ledston Luck Leeds
43 J6 Ledwell Oxon
19 J4 Lee Devon
33 M7 Lee Gt Lon
24 F9 Lee Hants
63 L6 Lee Shrops
51 N1 Leebotwood Shrops
63 P7 Lee Brockhurst Shrops
82 G1 Leece Cumb
34 C5 Lee Chapel Essex
44 C10 Lee Clump Bucks
44 C11 Lee Common Bucks
34 E11 Leeds Kent
85 L8 Leeds Leeds
85 K7 Leeds Bradford Airport Leeds
34 E11 Leeds Castle Kent
2 F7 Leedstown Cnwll
76 C11 Lee Green Ches E
77 J12 Leek Staffs
53 P7 Leek Wootton Warwks
5 J5 Lee Mill Devon
84 F8 Leeming C Brad
91 M9 Leeming N York
91 M8 Leeming Bar N York
5 J4 Lee Moor Devon
13 J5 Lee-on-the-Solent Hants
84 F7 Lees C Brad
65 N5 Lees Derbys
76 H3 Lees Oldham
65 N5 Lees Green Derbys
67 K9 Leesthorpe Leics
15 K2 Lee Street Surrey
75 J11 Leeswood Flints
124 E8 Leetown P & K
76 C9 Leftwich Ches W
40 B8 Legar Powys
80 G7 Legbourne Lincs
89 J3 Legburthwaite Cumb
107 P1 Legerwood Border
32 D7 Legoland W & M
12 b3 Le Gron Guern
80 C6 Legsby Lincs
13 c3 Le Haguais Jersey
13 d3 Le Hocq Jersey
66 F11 Leicester C Leic
66 E11 Leicester Forest East Leics
66 E11 Leicester Forest East Services Leics
19 P11 Leigh Devon
10 F3 Leigh Dorset
41 P6 Leigh Gloucs
15 Q2 Leigh Kent
63 K11 Leigh Shrops
15 J1 Leigh Surrey
76 C4 Leigh Wigan
30 C4 Leigh Wilts
52 E10 Leigh Worcs
34 E6 Leigh Beck Essex
29 P6 Leigh Delamere Wilts
29 P6 Leigh Delamere Services Wilts
16 F4 Leigh Green Kent
114 B11 Leigh Knoweglass S Lans
20 G6 Leighland Chapel Somset
34 E5 Leigh-on-Sea Sthend
11 P5 Leigh Park Dorset
52 E10 Leigh Sinton Worcs
65 K12 Leighswood Wsall
29 N4 Leighterton Gloucs
91 K11 Leighton N York
62 H11 Leighton Powys
63 Q11 Leighton Shrops
22 F4 Leighton Somset
56 C5 Leighton Bromswold Cambs
44 C6 Leighton Buzzard C Beds
22 F4 Leigh upon Mendip Somset
28 H8 Leigh Woods N Som
51 M7 Leinthall Earls Herefs
51 M7 Leinthall Starkes Herefs
51 L6 Leintwardine Herefs
54 E3 Leire Leics
59 N8 Leiston Suffk
115 N6 Leith C Edin
108 C1 Leitholm Border
2 E7 Lelant Cnwll
87 N8 Lelley E R Yk
51 Q5 Lem Hill Worcs
108 C3 Lempitlaw Border
152 f4 Lemreway W Isls
45 J9 Lemsford Herts
42 B2 Lenchwick Worcs
104 C11 Lendalfoot S Ayrs
122 F11 Lendrick Stirlg
141 Q7 Lendrum Terrace Abers
34 F12 Lenham Kent
34 G12 Lenham Heath Kent
137 N10 Lenie Highld
108 D2 Lennel Border
96 C8 Lennox Plunton D & G
114 B6 Lennoxtown E Duns
32 D6 Lent Bucks
66 F4 Lenton C Nott
67 P6 Lenton Lincs
70 G8 Lenwade Norfk
114 B7 Lenzie E Duns
132 E2 Leochel-Cushnie Abers
65 L10 Leomansley Staffs
51 N9 Leominster Herefs
41 N11 Leonard Stanley Gloucs
13 a1 Leoville Jersey
12 G5 Lepe Hants
134 C6 Lephin Highld
86 E3 Leppington N York
85 J12 Lepton Kirk
120 F7 Lerags Ag & B
12 b2 L'Eree Guern
4 A5 Lerryn Cnwll
152 t7 Lerwick Shet
109 L7 Lesbury Nthumb
12 b3 Les Arquets Guern
12 c3 Les Hubits Guern
140 F11 Leslie Abers
115 N1 Leslie Fife
12 b2 Les Lohiers Guern
105 Q2 Lesmahagow S Lans
12 b3 Les Murchez Guern
6 G6 Lesnewth Cnwll
12 c3 Les Nicolles Guern
12 c2 Les Quartiers Guern
13 a2 Les Quennevais Jersey
12 b3 Les Sages Guern
71 M6 Lessingham Norfk
97 P8 Lessonhall Cumb
3 K9 Lestowder Cnwll
12 b3 Les Villets Guern
94 E5 Leswalt D & G
13 a1 L'Etacq Jersey
32 G3 Letchmore Heath Herts
45 J5 Letchworth Garden City Herts
30 H5 Letcombe Bassett Oxon
30 H5 Letcombe Regis Oxon
125 K3 Letham Angus
107 Q8 Letham Border
114 G4 Letham Falk
124 F10 Letham Fife
125 M4 Letham Grange Angus
124 C4 Lethendy P & K
140 F11 Lethenty Abers
141 K8 Lethenty Abers
59 K9 Letheringham Suffk
70 F4 Letheringsett Norfk
8 D8 Lettaford Devon
143 P11 Letterewe Highld
136 B11 Letterfearn Highld
129 J6 Letterfinlay Lodge Hotel Highld
127 N6 Lettermorar Highld
144 E7 Letters Highld
106 B6 Lettershaw S Lans
36 H4 Letterston Pembks
139 J12 Lettoch Highld
139 K9 Lettoch Highld
40 D2 Letton Herefs
51 L6 Letton Herefs
33 N10 Lett's Green Kent
45 K9 Letty Green Herts
78 F6 Letwell Rothm
125 J8 Leuchars Fife
152 f4 Leumrabhagh W Isls
152 f3 Leurbost W Isls
3 N5 Levalsa Meor Cnwll
64 G9 Levedale Staffs
45 N7 Level's Green Essex
87 L6 Leven E R Yk
115 Q1 Leven Fife
89 M9 Levens Cumb
45 L7 Levens Green Herts
76 G5 Levenshulme Manch
152 s9 Levenwick Shet
152 c6 Leverburgh W Isls
68 H10 Leverington Cambs
44 F10 Leverstock Green Herts
68 H3 Leverton Lincs
12 c2 Le Villocq Guern
47 M4 Levington Suffk
92 G8 Levisham N York
42 G10 Lew Oxon
7 K8 Lewannick Cnwll
7 N7 Lewdown Devon
15 M9 Lewes E Susx
36 H6 Leweston Pembks
33 M7 Lewisham Gt Lon
33 M8 Lewisham Crematorium Gt Lon
137 N10 Lewiston Highld
27 M5 Lewistown Brdgnd
51 K9 Lewis Wych Herefs
31 P3 Lewknor Oxon
7 L4 Leworthy Devon
19 N6 Leworthy Devon
34 G10 Lewson Street Kent
83 L8 Lewth Lancs
7 N7 Lewtrenchard Devon
46 G6 Lexden Essex
21 L6 Lexworthy Somset
4 B3 Ley Cnwll
34 B10 Leybourne Kent
91 J8 Leyburn N York
64 E3 Leycett Staffs
44 H7 Leygreen Herts
44 E11 Ley Hill Bucks
83 M10 Leyland Lancs
75 P4 Leyland Green St Hel
133 J2 Leylodge Abers
141 N5 Leys Abers
124 E5 Leys P & K
35 J8 Leysdown-on-Sea Kent
125 M3 Leysmill Angus
124 H3 Leys of Cossans Angus
51 P8 Leysters Herefs
33 M5 Leyton Gt Lon
33 M5 Leytonstone Gt Lon
7 L9 Lezant Cnwll
2 H8 Lezerea Cnwll
139 P4 Lhanbryde Moray
39 N6 Libanus Powys
106 C1 Libberton S Lans
115 N7 Liberton C Edin
65 L10 Lichfield Staffs
53 J5 Lickey Worcs
52 H6 Lickey End Worcs
52 H6 Lickey Rock Worcs
14 C5 Lickfold W Susx
7 N8 Liddaton Green Devon
127 P12 Liddesdale Highld
30 E6 Liddington Swindn
78 D8 Lidgate Derbys
57 N9 Lidgate Suffk
78 G4 Lidget Donc
78 G10 Lidgett Notts
16 E7 Lidham Hill E Susx
44 E4 Lidlington C Beds
34 D10 Lidsing Kent
124 G6 Liff Angus
53 K5 Lifford Birm
7 M8 Lifton Devon
7 L7 Liftondown Devon
53 Q9 Lighthorne Warwks
54 B9 Lighthorne Heath Warwks
32 D10 Lightwater Surrey
64 G4 Lightwood C Stke
64 B4 Lightwood Green Ches E
63 L4 Lightwood Green Wrexhm
54 F5 Lilbourne Nhants
108 G5 Lilburn Tower Nthumb
64 D9 Lilleshall Wrekin
44 G6 Lilley Herts
31 J6 Lilley W Berk
107 N5 Lilliesleaf Border
43 P4 Lillingstone Dayrell Bucks
43 P4 Lillingstone Lovell Bucks
22 E11 Lillington Dorset
11 N7 Lilliput Poole
21 J4 Lilstock Somset
64 D9 Lilyhurst Shrops
83 N12 Limbrick Lancs
44 F7 Limbury Luton
51 L7 Limebrook Herefs
76 E1 Limefield Bury
114 C11 Limekilnburn S Lans
115 K5 Limekilns Fife
114 F7 Limerigg Falk
12 G8 Limerstone IoW
99 M8 Limestone Brae Nthumb
41 N5 Lime Street Worcs

22 C9 **Limington** Somset
105 L4 **Limmerhaugh** E Ayrs
71 M11 **Limpenhoe** Norfk
29 M10 **Limpley Stoke** Wilts
33 M11 **Limpsfield** Surrey
33 M12 **Limpsfield Chart** Surrey
66 E2 **Linby** Notts
14 B5 **Linchmere** W Susx
97 K3 **Lincluden** D & G
79 N9 **Lincoln** Lincs
79 N9 **Lincoln Crematorium** Lincs
52 F7 **Lincomb** Worcs
5 M8 **Lincombe** Devon
19 K4 **Lincombe** Devon
89 L10 **Lindale** Cumb
88 H11 **Lindal in Furness** Cumb
15 L6 **Lindfield** W Susx
25 P6 **Lindford** Hants
84 H11 **Lindley** Kirk
85 K5 **Lindley** N York
76 F8 **Lindow End** Ches E
52 C7 **Lindridge** Worcs
46 B6 **Lindsell** Essex
46 H3 **Lindsey** Suffk
46 H3 **Lindsey Tye** Suffk
21 N6 **Liney** Somset
12 C3 **Linford** Hants
34 B6 **Linford** Thurr
84 G8 **Lingbob** C Brad
92 D3 **Lingdale** R & Cl
51 L7 **Lingen** Herefs
15 M2 **Lingfield** Surrey
71 M10 **Lingwood** Norfk
134 G2 **Linicro** Highld
41 N5 **Linkend** Worcs
30 H10 **Linkenholt** Hants
16 E5 **Linkhill** Kent
7 L10 **Linkinhorne** Cnwll
115 N3 **Linktown** Fife
139 N4 **Linkwood** Moray
51 K2 **Linley** Shrops
52 C10 **Linley Green** Herefs
52 C1 **Linleygreen** Shrops
114 H6 **Linlithgow** W Loth
108 E8 **Linshiels** Nthumb
145 M5 **Linsidemore** Highld
44 C7 **Linslade** C Beds
59 L5 **Linstead Parva** Suffk
98 E6 **Linstock** Cumb
53 J6 **Linthurst** Worcs
84 G12 **Linthwaite** Kirk
117 J9 **Lintlaw** Border
140 D3 **Lintmill** Moray
108 C4 **Linton** Border
45 Q2 **Linton** Cambs
65 P9 **Linton** Derbys
41 K6 **Linton** Herefs
34 D12 **Linton** Kent
85 N6 **Linton** Leeds
84 E3 **Linton** N York
109 L11 **Linton** Nthumb
65 P9 **Linton Heath** Derbys
41 K7 **Linton Hill** Herefs
85 P3 **Linton-on-Ouse** N York
12 C3 **Linwood** Hants
80 B6 **Linwood** Lincs
113 N8 **Linwood** Rens
152 b8 **Lionacleit** W Isls
152 f1 **Lional** W Isls
15 Q7 **Lions Green** E Susx
25 P7 **Liphook** Hants
64 D6 **Lipley** Shrops
75 J5 **Liscard** Wirral
20 D7 **Liscombe** Somset
4 C4 **Liskeard** Cnwll
120 F4 **Lismore** Ag & B
25 N8 **Liss** Hants
87 L4 **Lissett** E R Yk
25 N7 **Liss Forest** Hants
80 B7 **Lissington** Lincs
46 E3 **Liston** Essex
28 B6 **Lisvane** Cardif
28 D5 **Liswerry** Newpt
70 C8 **Litcham** Norfk
27 L6 **Litchard** Brdgnd
54 G10 **Litchborough** Nhants
24 G3 **Litchfield** Hants
75 K4 **Litherland** Sefton
45 K3 **Litlington** Cambs
15 P10 **Litlington** E Susx
57 K10 **Little Abington** Cambs
55 N6 **Little Addington** Nhants
95 M8 **Little Airies** D & G
44 H6 **Little Almshoe** Herts
53 L8 **Little Alne** Warwks
75 J2 **Little Altcar** Sefton
45 L9 **Little Amwell** Herts
90 A5 **Little Asby** Cumb
65 K12 **Little Aston** Staffs
12 H9 **Little Atherfield** IoW
92 B5 **Little Ayton** N York
46 D10 **Little Baddow** Essex
29 N5 **Little Badminton** S Glos
98 B7 **Little Bampton** Cumb
46 B5 **Little Bardfield** Essex
56 D9 **Little Barford** Bed
70 H5 **Little Barningham** Norfk
42 E9 **Little Barrington** Gloucs
75 M9 **Little Barrow** Ches W
92 F10 **Little Barugh** N York
100 C3 **Little Bavington** Nthumb
59 J11 **Little Bealings** Suffk
92 H6 **Littlebeck** N York
30 G9 **Little Bedwyn** Wilts
47 K6 **Little Bentley** Essex
45 K10 **Little Berkhamsted** Herts
55 K8 **Little Billing** Nhants
44 D7 **Little Billington** C Beds
40 G5 **Little Birch** Herefs
82 H7 **Little Bispham** Bpool
58 G11 **Little Blakenham** Suffk
98 F11 **Little Blencow** Cumb
65 J11 **Little Bloxwich** Wsall
14 E7 **Little Bognor** W Susx
65 P1 **Little Bolehill** Derbys
76 D6 **Little Bollington** Ches E
32 G11 **Little Bookham** Surrey
8 F3 **Littleborough** Devon
79 K7 **Littleborough** Notts
84 D12 **Littleborough** Rochdl
35 M10 **Littlebourne** Kent
43 K3 **Little Bourton** Oxon
55 J3 **Little Bowden** Leics
57 N10 **Little Bradley** Suffk
51 J8 **Little Brampton** Herefs
51 L4 **Little Brampton** Shrops
46 E8 **Little Braxted** Essex
132 F11 **Little Brechin** Angus
10 F7 **Littlebredy** Dorset
44 C5 **Little Brickhill** M Keyn
64 G7 **Little Bridgeford** Staffs
54 H8 **Little Brington** Nhants
47 K6 **Little Bromley** Essex
97 M11 **Little Broughton** Cumb
75 Q10 **Little Budworth** Ches W
138 B5 **Littleburn** Highld
34 B4 **Little Burstead** Essex
45 P4 **Littlebury** Essex
45 P4 **Littlebury Green** Essex
67 P8 **Little Bytham** Lincs
45 Q7 **Little Canfield** Essex
80 H6 **Little Carlton** Lincs
79 K12 **Little Carlton** Notts
67 P10 **Little Casterton** Rutlnd
87 L6 **Little Catwick** E R Yk
56 B6 **Little Catworth** Cambs
80 G7 **Little Cawthorpe** Lincs
32 E3 **Little Chalfont** Bucks
16 G2 **Little Chart** Kent
45 P3 **Little Chesterford** Essex
16 C2 **Little Cheveney** Kent
23 L3 **Little Cheverell** Wilts
45 M4 **Little Chishill** Cambs
47 L8 **Little Clacton** Essex
30 F2 **Little Clanfield** Oxon
88 E1 **Little Clifton** Cumb
80 E2 **Little Coates** NE Lin
41 Q3 **Little Comberton** Worcs
16 C9 **Little Common** E Susx
34 B11 **Little Comp** Kent
42 F6 **Little Compton** Warwks
98 F7 **Little Corby** Cumb
46 F4 **Little Cornard** Suffk
23 P3 **Littlecott** Wilts
51 Q10 **Little Cowarne** Herefs
30 G4 **Little Coxwell** Oxon
91 L8 **Little Crakehall** N York
55 L5 **Little Cransley** Nhants
70 C12 **Little Cressingham** Norfk
75 K3 **Little Crosby** Sefton
88 H1 **Little Crosthwaite** Cumb
65 M5 **Little Cubley** Derbys
67 K9 **Little Dalby** Leics
41 K9 **Littledean** Gloucs
40 H5 **Little Dewchurch** Herefs
57 M9 **Little Ditton** Cambs
40 H8 **Little Doward** Herefs
30 H10 **Littledown** Hants
57 K4 **Little Downham** Cambs
87 J4 **Little Driffield** E R Yk
70 C9 **Little Dunham** Norfk
123 P4 **Little Dunkeld** P & K
46 B7 **Little Dunmow** Essex
23 P6 **Little Durnford** Wilts
45 R7 **Little Easton** Essex
66 B4 **Little Eaton** Derbys
70 E12 **Little Ellingham** Norfk
22 F4 **Little Elm** Somset
54 F9 **Little Everdon** Nhants
56 G10 **Little Eversden** Cambs
30 F2 **Little Faringdon** Oxon
91 M8 **Little Fencote** N York
85 Q8 **Little Fenton** N York
70 D9 **Little Fransham** Norfk
44 E9 **Little Gaddesden** Herts
40 F7 **Little Garway** Herefs
56 C4 **Little Gidding** Cambs
59 L9 **Little Glemham** Suffk
41 L7 **Little Gorsley** Herefs
56 E9 **Little Gransden** Cambs
67 J3 **Little Green** Notts
22 G4 **Little Green** Somset
80 F5 **Little Grimsby** Lincs
79 J7 **Little Gringley** Notts
92 F11 **Little Habton** N York
45 N7 **Little Hadham** Herts
68 C4 **Little Hale** Lincs
66 D4 **Little Hallam** Derbys
45 P8 **Little Hallingbury** Essex
9 K8 **Littleham** Devon
18 H8 **Littleham** Devon
44 B11 **Little Hampden** Bucks
14 E10 **Littlehampton** W Susx
11 K2 **Little Hanford** Dorset
55 L6 **Little Harrowden** Nhants
31 N2 **Little Haseley** Oxon
87 M6 **Little Hatfield** E R Yk
71 K8 **Little Hautbois** Norfk
36 G8 **Little Haven** Pembks
14 H4 **Littlehaven** W Susx
65 L11 **Little Hay** Staffs
77 J6 **Little Hayfield** Derbys
65 J8 **Little Haywood** Staffs
64 G8 **Little Heath** Staffs
31 N7 **Little Heath** W Berk
5 N4 **Littlehempston** Devon
51 P7 **Little Hereford** Herefs
46 G5 **Little Horkesley** Essex
45 M6 **Little Hormead** Herts
15 N7 **Little Horsted** E Susx
84 H9 **Little Horton** C Brad
30 B10 **Little Horton** Wilts
43 R5 **Little Horwood** Bucks
78 C2 **Little Houghton** Barns
55 K8 **Little Houghton** Nhants
109 L6 **Littlehoughton** Nthumb
77 M8 **Little Hucklow** Derbys
76 D3 **Little Hulton** Salfd
31 L7 **Little Hungerford** W Berk
91 Q11 **Little Hutton** N York
55 M7 **Little Irchester** Nhants
87 L3 **Little Kelk** E R Yk
22 H4 **Little Keyford** Somset
44 B10 **Little Kimble** Bucks
53 Q10 **Little Kineton** Warwks
32 C3 **Little Kingshill** Bucks
96 G6 **Little Knox** D & G
89 J6 **Little Langdale** Cumb
23 N6 **Little Langford** Wilts
45 Q9 **Little Laver** Essex
76 B8 **Little Leigh** Ches W
46 C8 **Little Leighs** Essex
76 D2 **Little Lever** Bolton
44 B3 **Little Linford** M Keyn
21 P8 **Little Load** Somset
43 N9 **Little London** Bucks
56 H1 **Little London** Cambs
15 Q7 **Little London** E Susx
45 N6 **Little London** Essex
46 B5 **Little London** Essex
41 L8 **Little London** Gloucs
24 F3 **Little London** Hants
31 N10 **Little London** Hants
85 J7 **Little London** Leeds
68 E8 **Little London** Lincs
68 H7 **Little London** Lincs
80 F8 **Little London** Lincs
69 L8 **Little London** Norfk
50 E3 **Little London** Powys
77 M9 **Little Longstone** Derbys
64 E3 **Little Madeley** Staffs
41 M4 **Little Malvern** Worcs
75 K10 **Little Mancot** Flints
46 E5 **Little Maplestead** Essex
41 K4 **Little Marcle** Herefs
19 K11 **Little Marland** Devon
32 C5 **Little Marlow** Bucks
69 Q7 **Little Massingham** Norfk
70 H10 **Little Melton** Norfk
131 P5 **Littlemill** Abers
138 G6 **Littlemill** Highld
40 D11 **Little Mill** Mons
31 N2 **Little Milton** Oxon
32 C3 **Little Missenden** Bucks
35 P12 **Little Mongeham** Kent
78 B11 **Littlemoor** Derbys
21 M7 **Little Moor** Somset
43 L11 **Littlemore** Oxon
90 C4 **Little Musgrave** Cumb
63 L8 **Little Ness** Shrops
75 J8 **Little Neston** Ches W
37 J5 **Little Newcastle** Pembks
91 J3 **Little Newsham** Dur
21 Q10 **Little Norton** Somset
47 M6 **Little Oakley** Essex
55 M3 **Little Oakley** Nhants
55 N9 **Little Odell** Bed
44 G6 **Little Offley** Herts
90 B3 **Little Ormside** Cumb
98 D7 **Little Orton** Cumb
57 M3 **Little Ouse** Cambs
85 P3 **Little Ouseburn** N York
65 Q5 **Littleover** C Derb
55 J4 **Little Oxendon** Nhants
53 N4 **Little Packington** Warwks
16 C2 **Little Pattenden** Kent
56 D8 **Little Paxton** Cambs
6 C10 **Little Petherick** Cnwll
83 J8 **Little Plumpton** Lancs
71 L9 **Little Plumstead** Norfk
67 M6 **Little Ponton** Lincs
57 L3 **Littleport** Cambs
57 L3 **Littleport Bridge** Cambs
13 J4 **Little Posbrook** Hants
19 K10 **Little Potheridge** Devon
85 M9 **Little Preston** Leeds
54 F10 **Little Preston** Nhants
76 B10 **Littler** Ches W
56 E5 **Little Raveley** Cambs
86 E10 **Little Reedness** E R Yk
85 M4 **Little Ribston** N York
42 E7 **Little Rissington** Gloucs
42 G6 **Little Rollright** Oxon
77 N10 **Little Rowsley** Derbys
70 E6 **Little Ryburgh** Norfk
108 G7 **Little Ryle** Nthumb
63 N11 **Little Ryton** Shrops
98 H11 **Little Salkeld** Cumb
46 B5 **Little Sampford** Essex
32 B10 **Little Sandhurst** Br For
64 H10 **Little Saredon** Staffs
75 L10 **Little Saughall** Ches W
57 Q8 **Little Saxham** Suffk
137 L4 **Little Scatwell** Highld
57 J10 **Little Shelford** Cambs
53 N7 **Little Shrewley** Warwks
8 G3 **Little Silver** Devon
83 J7 **Little Singleton** Lancs
86 C7 **Little Skipwith** N York
85 Q11 **Little Smeaton** N York
70 D6 **Little Snoring** Norfk
29 M6 **Little Sodbury** S Glos
29 M5 **Little Sodbury End** S Glos
24 F7 **Little Somborne** Hants
29 Q5 **Little Somerford** Wilts
64 D6 **Little Soudley** Shrops
84 B2 **Little Stainforth** N York
91 N3 **Little Stainton** Darltn
75 L9 **Little Stanney** Ches W
56 B8 **Little Staughton** Bed
80 H11 **Little Steeping** Lincs
64 G5 **Little Stoke** Staffs
17 K6 **Littlestone-on-Sea** Kent
58 G8 **Little Stonham** Suffk
66 H12 **Little Stretton** Leics
51 M2 **Little Stretton** Shrops
89 P3 **Little Strickland** Cumb
56 D5 **Little Stukeley** Cambs
64 E6 **Little Sugnall** Staffs
75 L8 **Little Sutton** Ches W
51 N4 **Little Sutton** Shrops
99 Q3 **Little Swinburne** Nthumb
96 E7 **Little Sypland** D & G
42 H6 **Little Tew** Oxon
46 F7 **Little Tey** Essex
57 K5 **Little Thetford** Cambs
91 Q11 **Little Thirkleby** N York
70 F4 **Little Thornage** Norfk
83 J7 **Little Thornton** Lancs
101 L9 **Little Thorpe** Dur
54 E1 **Littlethorpe** Leics
85 L1 **Littlethorpe** N York
57 N10 **Little Thurlow** Suffk
57 N10 **Little Thurlow Green** Suffk
34 A7 **Little Thurrock** Thurr
124 G3 **Littleton** Angus
28 H9 **Littleton** BaNES
75 M10 **Littleton** Ches W
96 D7 **Littleton** D & G
11 L4 **Littleton** Dorset
24 G7 **Littleton** Hants
22 C7 **Littleton** Somset
14 D1 **Littleton** Surrey
32 F8 **Littleton** Surrey
29 N6 **Littleton Drew** Wilts
29 J4 **Littleton-on-Severn** S Glos
23 M3 **Littleton Pannell** Wilts
19 J10 **Little Torrington** Devon
46 F9 **Little Totham** Essex
88 H3 **Little Town** Cumb
101 J9 **Littletown** Dur
83 P8 **Little Town** Lancs
76 B5 **Little Town** Warrtn
65 Q11 **Little Twycross** Leics
88 H12 **Little Urswick** Cumb
34 G5 **Little Wakering** Essex
45 Q3 **Little Walden** Essex
46 G3 **Little Waldingfield** Suffk
70 D5 **Little Walsingham** Norfk
46 C9 **Little Waltham** Essex
33 R4 **Little Warley** Essex
42 A5 **Little Washbourne** Gloucs
87 J8 **Little Weighton** E R Yk
55 M3 **Little Weldon** Nhants
58 C8 **Little Welnetham** Suffk
80 F6 **Little Welton** Lincs
47 K4 **Little Wenham** Suffk
64 C10 **Little Wenlock** Wrekin
22 E8 **Little Weston** Somset
13 K7 **Little Whitefield** IoW
59 K5 **Little Whittingham Green** Suffk
100 C4 **Little Whittington** Nthumb
32 B6 **Littlewick Green** W & M
57 K9 **Little Wilbraham** Cambs
10 C4 **Littlewindsor** Dorset
41 P8 **Little Witcombe** Gloucs
52 E8 **Little Witley** Worcs
31 M4 **Little Wittenham** Oxon
42 F5 **Little Wolford** Warwks
64 H10 **Littlewood** Staffs
33 K10 **Little Woodcote** Gt Lon
44 C7 **Littleworth** Bucks
30 G3 **Littleworth** Oxon
64 H7 **Littleworth** Staffs
65 J10 **Littleworth** Staffs
14 H7 **Littleworth** W Susx
52 G10 **Littleworth** Worcs
53 J8 **Littleworth** Worcs
32 D5 **Littleworth Common** Bucks
46 C2 **Little Wratting** Suffk
55 N7 **Little Wymington** Bed
45 J6 **Little Wymondley** Herts
65 J11 **Little Wyrley** Staffs
63 P8 **Little Wytheford** Shrops
46 D4 **Little Yeldham** Essex
46 C8 **Littley Green** Essex
77 M8 **Litton** Derbys
90 E12 **Litton** N York
22 D2 **Litton** Somset
10 E6 **Litton Cheney** Dorset
152 f3 **Liurbost** W Isls
75 K5 **Liverpool** Lpool
85 J10 **Liversedge** Kirk
8 E9 **Liverton** Devon
92 E4 **Liverton** R & Cl
92 E3 **Liverton Mines** R & Cl
34 F12 **Liverton Street** Kent
115 K7 **Livingston** W Loth
115 J8 **Livingston Village** W Loth
74 G9 **Lixwm** Flints
2 H12 **Lizard** Cnwll
72 C7 **Llaingoch** IoA
50 E5 **Llaithddu** Powys
61 Q12 **Llan** Powys
61 K8 **Llanaber** Gwynd
60 F3 **Llanaelhaearn** Gwynd
49 M6 **Llanafan** Cerdgn
50 C9 **Llanafan-Fawr** Powys
50 D10 **Llanafan-fechan** Powys
72 H6 **Llanallgo** IoA
60 G4 **Llanarmon** Gwynd
62 G6 **Llanarmon Dyffryn Ceiriog** Wrexhm
74 G12 **Llanarmon-yn-Ial** Denbgs
48 G9 **Llanarth** Cerdgn
40 E9 **Llanarth** Mons
38 D7 **Llanarthne** Carmth
74 F7 **Llanasa** Flints
72 F6 **Llanbabo** IoA
49 K4 **Llanbadarn Fawr** Cerdgn
50 F5 **Llanbadarn Fynydd** Powys
50 F11 **Llanbadarn-y-garreg** Powys
28 E2 **Llanbadoc** Mons
72 F5 **Llanbadrig** IoA
28 E4 **Llanbeder** Newpt
61 K7 **Llanbedr** Gwynd
39 Q2 **Llanbedr** Powys
40 B7 **Llanbedr** Powys
74 G11 **Llanbedr-Dyffryn-Clwyd** Denbgs
72 H7 **Llanbedrgoch** IoA
60 E6 **Llanbedrog** Gwynd
73 N10 **Llanbedr-y-Cennin** Conwy
73 K11 **Llanberis** Gwynd
27 N8 **Llanbethery** V Glam
50 F6 **Llanbister** Powys
27 N7 **Llanblethian** V Glam
37 N6 **Llanboidy** Carmth
27 Q4 **Llanbradach** Caerph
62 B11 **Llanbrynmair** Powys
27 N8 **Llancadle** V Glam
27 P8 **Llancarfan** V Glam
40 E11 **Llancayo** Mons
40 G7 **Llancloudy** Herefs
49 L2 **Llancynfelyn** Cerdgn
27 R7 **Llandaff** Cardif
61 J6 **Llandanwg** Gwynd
26 H3 **Llandarcy** Neath
37 Q8 **Llandawke** Carmth
72 H9 **Llanddaniel Fab** IoA
38 D8 **Llanddarog** Carmth
49 J6 **Llanddeiniol** Cerdgn
73 J10 **Llanddeiniolen** Gwynd
62 D5 **Llandderfel** Gwynd
39 J7 **Llanddeusant** Carmth
72 E6 **Llanddeusant** IoA
39 P5 **Llanddew** Powys
26 C4 **Llanddewi** Swans
49 L9 **Llanddewi Brefi** Cerdgn
50 E11 **Llanddewi'r Cwm** Powys
40 D9 **Llanddewi Rhydderch** Mons
37 M7 **Llanddewi Velfrey** Pembks
50 F7 **Llanddewi Ystradenni** Powys
73 P11 **Llanddoget** Conwy
73 J8 **Llanddona** IoA
37 P7 **Llanddowror** Carmth
74 B8 **Llanddulas** Conwy
61 K8 **Llanddwywe** Gwynd
72 H8 **Llanddyfnan** IoA
61 L5 **Llandecwyn** Gwynd
39 N5 **Llandefaelog** Powys
39 Q6 **Llandefaelog-Tre'r-Graig** Powys
39 Q4 **Llandefalle** Powys
73 J9 **Llandegfan** IoA
62 H2 **Llandegla** Denbgs
50 G8 **Llandegley** Powys
28 D3 **Llandegveth** Mons
60 D6 **Llandegwning** Gwynd
38 F7 **Llandeilo** Carmth
39 P3 **Llandeilo Graban** Powys
39 L5 **Llandeilo'r Fan** Powys
36 G5 **Llandeloy** Pembks
40 F11 **Llandenny** Mons
28 E4 **Llandevaud** Newpt
28 F5 **Llandevenny** Mons
40 G6 **Llandinabo** Herefs
50 E3 **Llandinam** Powys
37 M6 **Llandissilio** Pembks
40 H11 **Llandogo** Mons
27 N8 **Llandough** V Glam
27 R8 **Llandough** V Glam
39 J5 **Llandovery** Carmth
27 M7 **Llandow** V Glam
38 G3 **Llandre** Carmth
49 K3 **Llandre** Cerdgn
37 M5 **Llandre Isaf** Pembks
62 E5 **Llandrillo** Denbgs
73 P7 **Llandrillo-yn-Rhos** Conwy
50 E8 **Llandrindod Wells** Powys
63 J8 **Llandrinio** Powys
73 N7 **Llandudno** Conwy
73 N8 **Llandudno Junction** Conwy
39 L3 **Llandulas** Powys
60 G1 **Llandwrog** Gwynd
38 F8 **Llandybie** Carmth
38 B9 **Llandyfaelog** Carmth
38 F8 **Llandyfan** Carmth
37 Q2 **Llandyfriog** Cerdgn
72 G6 **Llandyfrydog** IoA
73 K9 **Llandygai** Gwynd
37 P2 **Llandygwydd** Cerdgn
62 G3 **Llandynan** Denbgs
74 F10 **Llandyrnog** Denbgs
50 H2 **Llandyssil** Powys
38 B3 **Llandysul** Cerdgn
28 B6 **Llanedeyrn** Cardif
38 E10 **Llanedi** Carmth
39 P4 **Llaneglwys** Powys
61 K11 **Llanegryn** Gwynd
38 D7 **Llanegwad** Carmth
72 H5 **Llaneilian** IoA
73 Q8 **Llanelian-yn-Rhôs** Conwy
62 F2 **Llanelidan** Denbgs
40 A5 **Llanelieu** Powys
40 D9 **Llanellen** Mons
26 D2 **Llanelli** Carmth
38 E11 **Llanelli Crematorium** Carmth
61 M8 **Llanelltyd** Gwynd
40 B8 **Llanelly** Mons
50 E10 **Llanelwedd** Powys
61 K7 **Llanenddwyn** Gwynd
60 E7 **Llanengan** Gwynd
62 B9 **Llanerch** Gwynd
51 J2 **Llanerch** Powys
72 G7 **Llanerchymedd** IoA
62 E10 **Llanerfyl** Powys
72 E7 **Llanfachraeth** IoA
61 N7 **Llanfachreth** Gwynd
72 E9 **Llanfaelog** IoA
60 C7 **Llanfaelrhys** Gwynd
40 F8 **Llanfaenor** Mons
73 K8 **Llanfaes** IoA
39 N6 **Llanfaes** Powys
72 E6 **Llanfaethlu** IoA
61 K6 **Llanfair** Gwynd
62 F11 **Llanfair Caereinion** Powys
49 K10 **Llanfair Clydogau** Cerdgn
62 F1 **Llanfair Dyffryn Clwyd** Denbgs
73 L9 **Llanfairfechan** Conwy
40 D10 **Llanfair Kilgeddin** Mons
37 M3 **Llanfair-Nant-Gwyn** Pembks
73 J9 **Llanfair P G** IoA
74 C9 **Llanfair Talhaiarn** Conwy
50 H5 **Llanfair Waterdine** Shrops
72 E5 **Llanfairynghornwy** IoA
72 E8 **Llanfair-yn-Neubwll** IoA
37 M6 **Llanfallteg** Carmth
37 M6 **Llanfallteg West** Carmth
49 K5 **Llanfarian** Cerdgn
62 G8 **Llanfechain** Powys
72 F5 **Llanfechell** IoA
74 G11 **Llanferres** Denbgs
72 F6 **Llanfflewyn** IoA
72 E7 **Llanfigael** IoA
38 C4 **Llanfihangel-ar-arth** Carmth
62 D2 **Llanfihangel Glyn Myfyr** Conwy
39 M5 **Llanfihangel Nant Bran** Powys
50 G9 **Llanfihangel-nant-Melan** Powys
50 G7 **Llanfihangel Rhydithon** Powys
28 F5 **Llanfihangel Rogiet** Mons
39 Q6 **Llanfihangel Tal-y-llyn** Powys
38 D7 **Llanfihangel-uwch-Gwili** Carmth
49 L5 **Llanfihangel-y-Creuddyn** Cerdgn
62 E9 **Llanfihangel-yng-Ngwynfa** Powys
72 E8 **Llanfihangel yn Nhowyn** IoA
61 J3 **Llanfihangel-y-pennant** Gwynd
61 L10 **Llanfihangel-y-pennant** Gwynd
61 K5 **Llanfihangel-y-traethau** Gwynd
39 Q5 **Llanfilo** Powys
40 C9 **Llanfoist** Mons
62 C5 **Llanfor** Gwynd
28 D4 **Llanfrechfa** Torfn
61 K4 **Llanfrothen** Gwynd
39 P6 **Llanfrynach** Powys
74 F12 **Llanfwrog** Denbgs
72 E7 **Llanfwrog** IoA
62 G8 **Llanfyllin** Powys
38 E6 **Llanfynydd** Carmth
75 J12 **Llanfynydd** Flints
37 P4 **Llanfyrnach** Pembks
62 D10 **Llangadfan** Powys
38 B10 **Llangadog** Carmth
38 H6 **Llangadog** Carmth
72 F10 **Llangadwaladr** IoA
62 G6 **Llangadwaladr** Powys
72 G10 **Llangaffo** IoA
38 B8 **Llangain** Carmth
39 M2 **Llangammarch Wells** Powys
27 M7 **Llangan** V Glam
40 H7 **Llangarron** Herefs
39 Q6 **Llangasty-Talyllyn** Powys
38 E7 **Llangathen** Carmth
40 B8 **Llangattock** Powys
40 E7 **Llangattock Lingoed** Mons
40 F8 **Llangattock-Vibon-Avel** Mons
62 G7 **Llangedwyn** Powys
72 G8 **Llangefni** IoA
27 L5 **Llangeinor** Brdgnd
49 K8 **Llangeitho** Cerdgn
38 B4 **Llangeler** Carmth
61 K10 **Llangelynin** Gwynd
38 C9 **Llangendeirne** Carmth
26 E2 **Llangennech** Carmth
26 C4 **Llangennith** Swans
40 C8 **Llangenny** Powys
73 Q10 **Llangernyw** Conwy
60 E6 **Llangian** Gwynd
38 H10 **Llangiwg** Neath
36 H4 **Llangloffan** Pembks
37 N5 **Llanglydwen** Carmth
73 K8 **Llangoed** IoA
48 C11 **Llangoedmor** Cerdgn
62 H4 **Llangollen** Denbgs
37 M5 **Llangolman** Pembks
39 Q6 **Llangors** Powys
40 F10 **Llangovan** Mons
62 B6 **Llangower** Gwynd
48 E10 **Llangranog** Cerdgn
72 G9 **Llangristiolus** IoA
40 H8 **Llangrove** Herefs
40 E6 **Llangua** Mons
50 H6 **Llangunllo** Powys
38 C7 **Llangunnor** Carmth
50 B5 **Llangurig** Powys
62 C3 **Llangwm** Conwy
28 F2 **Llangwm** Mons
37 J8 **Llangwm** Pembks
60 C5 **Llangwnnadl** Gwynd
74 F10 **Llangwyfan** Denbgs
72 G8 **Llangwyllog** IoA
49 K6 **Llangwyryfon** Cerdgn
49 K10 **Llangybi** Cerdgn
60 G4 **Llangybi** Gwynd
28 E3 **Llangybi** Mons
26 F3 **Llangyfelach** Swans
74 F11 **Llangynhafal** Denbgs
39 R8 **Llangynidr** Powys
37 P6 **Llangynin** Carmth
37 R2 **Llangynllo** Cerdgn
37 R7 **Llangynog** Carmth
62 E7 **Llangynog** Powys
27 K5 **Llangynwyd** Brdgnd
39 P6 **Llanhamlach** Powys
27 N6 **Llanharan** Rhondd
27 N6 **Llanharry** Rhondd
28 E4 **Llanhennock** Mons
28 B2 **Llanhilleth** Blae G
72 H10 **Llanidan** IoA
50 C4 **Llanidloes** Powys
60 D5 **Llaniestyn** Gwynd
40 B4 **Llanigon** Powys
49 K6 **Llanilar** Cerdgn
27 M6 **Llanilid** Rhondd
48 F8 **Llanina** Cerdgn
49 L9 **Llanio** Cerdgn
28 A6 **Llanishen** Cardif
40 G11 **Llanishen** Mons
73 K10 **Llanllechid** Gwynd
50 C10 **Llanlleonfel** Powys
28 E3 **Llanllowell** Mons
62 E11 **Llanllugan** Powys
38 B8 **Llanllwch** Carmth
50 F2 **Llanllwchaiarn** Powys
38 D4 **Llanllwni** Carmth
60 H2 **Llanllyfni** Gwynd
26 C4 **Llanmadoc** Swans
27 M8 **Llanmaes** V Glam
28 E4 **Llanmartin** Newpt
50 G2 **Llanmerewig** Powys
27 M8 **Llanmihangel** V Glam
37 P9 **Llanmiloe** Carmth
26 D3 **Llanmorlais** Swans
74 D9 **Llannefydd** Conwy
38 E10 **Llannon** Carmth
60 F5 **Llannor** Gwynd
48 H7 **Llanon** Cerdgn
40 D10 **Llanover** Mons
38 B6 **Llanpumsaint** Carmth
62 F7 **Llanrhaeadr-ym-Mochnant** Powys
36 F4 **Llanrhian** Pembks
26 D4 **Llanrhidian** Swans
73 N7 **Llanrhos** Conwy
73 N11 **Llanrhychwyn** Conwy
72 E6 **Llanrhyddlad** IoA
49 J7 **Llanrhystud** Cerdgn
40 G8 **Llanrothal** Herefs
73 J11 **Llanrug** Gwynd
28 B6 **Llanrumney** Cardif
73 P11 **Llanrwst** Conwy
37 Q8 **Llansadurnen** Carmth
38 G5 **Llansadwrn** Carmth
73 J8 **Llansadwrn** IoA
38 B10 **Llansaint** Carmth
26 G3 **Llansamlet** Swans
73 P8 **Llansanffraid Glan Conwy** Conwy
74 C10 **Llansannan** Conwy
27 N7 **Llansannor** V Glam
39 Q7 **Llansantffraed** Powys
50 C7 **Llansantffraed-Cwmdeuddwr** Powys
50 F9 **Llansantffraed-in-Elvel** Powys
49 J7 **Llansantffraid** Cerdgn
62 H8 **Llansantffraid-ym-Mechain** Powys
38 F4 **Llansawel** Carmth
62 H6 **Llansilin** Powys
40 F11 **Llansoy** Mons
39 N6 **Llanspyddid** Powys
37 J9 **Llanstadwell** Pembks
37 R8 **Llansteffan** Carmth
39 Q3 **Llanstephan** Powys
28 D4 **Llantarnam** Torfn
37 N8 **Llanteg** Pembks
40 D8 **Llanthewy Skirrid** Mons
40 C6 **Llanthony** Mons
40 E8 **Llantilio-Crossenny** Mons
40 D8 **Llantilio Pertholey** Mons
72 F7 **Llantrisant** IoA
28 E3 **Llantrisant** Mons
27 P6 **Llantrisant** Rhondd
27 P8 **Llantrithyd** V Glam
27 P5 **Llantwit Fardre** Rhondd
27 M8 **Llantwit Major** V Glam
62 H3 **Llantysilio** Denbgs
61 Q6 **Llanuwchllyn** Gwynd
28 F4 **Llanvaches** Newpt
28 F4 **Llanvair Discoed** Mons
40 E9 **Llanvapley** Mons
40 E8 **Llanvetherine** Mons
40 D5 **Llanveynoe** Herefs
40 D7 **Llanvihangel Crucorney** Mons
40 D9 **Llanvihangel Gobion** Mons
40 F9 **Llanvihangel-Ystern-Llewern** Mons
40 G6 **Llanwarne** Herefs
62 D8 **Llanwddyn** Powys
40 C8 **Llanwenarth** Mons
38 D3 **Llanwenog** Cerdgn
28 E5 **Llanwern** Newpt
37 P5 **Llanwinio** Carmth
72 H12 **Llanwnda** Gwynd
36 H3 **Llanwnda** Pembks
38 D2 **Llanwnnen** Cerdgn
50 D2 **Llanwnog** Powys
27 N3 **Llanwonno** Rhondd
38 H5 **Llanwrda** Carmth
61 N11 **Llanwrin** Powys
50 D8 **Llanwrthwl** Powys
49 Q11 **Llanwrtyd** Powys
39 L2 **Llanwrtyd Wells** Powys
62 E12 **Llanwyddelan** Powys
62 H7 **Llanyblodwel** Shrops
37 R8 **Llanybri** Carmth
38 D3 **Llanybydder** Carmth
37 L6 **Llanycefn** Pembks
37 J3 **Llanychaer Bridge** Pembks
38 F3 **Llanycrwys** Carmth
62 B8 **Llanymawddwy** Gwynd
63 J8 **Llanymynech** Powys
72 E7 **Llanynghenedl** IoA
74 F11 **Llanynys** Denbgs
63 L2 **Llan-y-pwll** Wrexhm
50 E8 **Llanyre** Powys
60 H4 **Llanystumdwy** Gwynd
39 Q6 **Llanywern** Powys
37 L7 **Llawhaden** Pembks
62 H6 **Llawnt** Shrops
50 C2 **Llawryglyn** Powys
63 K1 **Llay** Wrexhm
72 F7 **Llechcynfarwy** IoA
39 P6 **Llechfaen** Powys
39 Q10 **Llechrhyd** Caerph
37 N2 **Llechryd** Cerdgn
72 E8 **Llechylched** IoA
49 L6 **Lledrod** Cerdgn
60 E5 **Lleyn Peninsula** Gwynd
61 Q4 **Llidiardau** Gwynd
38 E4 **Llidiartnenog** Carmth
62 F3 **Llidiart-y-parc** Denbgs
60 F4 **Llithfaen** Gwynd
74 G8 **Lloc** Flints
40 B3 **Llowes** Powys
39 N10 **Llwydcoed** Rhondd
39 N10 **Llwydcoed Crematorium** Rhondd
62 E9 **Llwydiarth** Powys
74 E10 **Llwyn** Denbgs
48 G8 **Llwyncelyn** Cerdgn
48 F9 **Llwyndafydd** Cerdgn
62 H11 **Llwynderw** Powys
37 P4 **Llwyn-drain** Pembks
40 C8 **Llwyn-du** Mons
60 F4 **Llwyndyrys** Gwynd
61 K10 **Llwyngwril** Gwynd
26 E2 **Llwynhendy** Carmth
62 H5 **Llwynmawr** Wrexhm
39 N9 **Llwyn-on** Myr Td
37 N7 **Llwyn-y-brain** Carmth
49 K9 **Llwyn-y-groes** Cerdgn
27 N4 **Llwynypia** Rhondd
63 J7 **Llynclys** Shrops
72 G8 **Llynfaes** IoA
74 H10 **Llyn-y-pandy** Flints
74 B8 **Llysfaen** Conwy
48 G8 **Llyswen** Cerdgn
39 Q4 **Llyswen** Powys
27 M7 **Llysworney** V Glam
37 K6 **Llys-y-frân** Pembks
39 K6 **Llywel** Powys
77 P6 **Load Brook** Sheff
114 H6 **Loan** Falk
117 L11 **Loanend** Nthumb
115 P8 **Loanhead** Mdloth
97 J7 **Loaningfoot** D & G
104 F3 **Loans** S Ayrs
19 J6 **Lobb** Devon
7 N7 **Lobhillcross** Devon
127 P8 **Lochailort** Highld
120 C4 **Lochaline** Highld
94 F7 **Lochans** D & G
97 K2 **Locharbriggs** D & G
120 H9 **Lochavich** Ag & B
121 L7 **Lochawe** Ag & B
152 b10 **Loch Baghasdail** W Isls
152 b10 **Lochboisdale** W Isls
119 Q8 **Lochbuie** Ag & B
136 B8 **Lochcarron** Highld
120 D6 **Lochdon** Ag & B
120 D6 **Lochdonhead** Ag & B
111 R6 **Lochead** Ag & B
122 G8 **Lochearnhead** Stirlg
124 H6 **Lochee** C Dund
128 D8 **Locheilside Station** Highld
137 Q8 **Lochend** Highld
152 b7 **Locheport** W Isls
152 b7 **Loch Euphoirt** W Isls
96 H3 **Lochfoot** D & G
112 D3 **Lochgair** Ag & B
115 M3 **Lochgelly** Fife
112 C4 **Lochgilphead** Ag & B
113 J1 **Lochgoilhead** Ag & B
124 E10 **Lochieheads** Fife
139 P3 **Lochill** Moray
138 H9 **Lochindorb Lodge** Highld
148 C12 **Lochinver** Highld
122 D10 **Loch Lomond and The Trossachs National Park**
137 K3 **Lochluichart** Highld
97 M2 **Lochmaben** D & G
152 c7 **Lochmaddy** W Isls
143 N11 **Loch Maree Hotel** Highld
152 c7 **Loch nam Madadh** W Isls
137 P10 **Loch Ness** Highld
115 M2 **Lochore** Fife
112 D11 **Lochranza** N Ayrs
132 H11 **Lochside** Abers
97 J3 **Lochside** D & G
138 E5 **Lochside** Highld
146 F9 **Lochslin** Highld
95 J2 **Lochton** S Ayrs
132 E11 **Lochty** Angus
125 K11 **Lochty** Fife
120 E2 **Lochuisge** Highld
113 L9 **Lochwinnoch** Rens
106 E10 **Lochwood** D & G
3 P2 **Lockengate** Cnwll
97 N2 **Lockerbie** D & G
30 D9 **Lockeridge** Wilts
24 E8 **Lockerley** Hants
28 E10 **Locking** N Som
76 B5 **Locking Stumps** Warrtn
87 J6 **Lockington** E R Yk
66 D6 **Lockington** Leics
64 C6 **Lockleywood** Shrops
33 M9 **Locksbottom** Gt Lon
12 G6 **Locksgreen** IoW
12 H3 **Locks Heath** Hants
92 G9 **Lockton** N York
67 K11 **Loddington** Leics
55 K5 **Loddington** Nhants
5 M7 **Loddiswell** Devon
71 M12 **Loddon** Norfk
57 K8 **Lode** Cambs
53 M4 **Lode Heath** Solhll
10 D6 **Loders** Dorset
53 J4 **Lodge Hill Crematorium** Birm
14 D6 **Lodsworth** W Susx
85 L10 **Lofthouse** Leeds
91 J12 **Lofthouse** N York
85 L10 **Lofthouse Gate** Wakefd
92 E3 **Loftus** R & Cl
105 L6 **Logan** E Ayrs
88 G8 **Loganbeck** Cumb
114 H9 **Loganlea** W Loth
64 D5 **Loggerheads** Staffs
132 H11 **Logie** Angus
124 H8 **Logie** Fife
139 J6 **Logie** Moray
132 C3 **Logie Coldstone** Abers
140 G8 **Logie Newton** Abers
132 G11 **Logie Pert** Angus
123 N2 **Logierait** P & K
141 M10 **Logierieve** Abers
37 M6 **Login** Carmth
56 G8 **Lolworth** Cambs
135 M5 **Lonbain** Highld
86 F6 **Londesborough** E R Yk
33 K6 **London** Gt Lon
3 N4 **London Apprentice** Cnwll
16 F3 **London Beach** Kent
44 H11 **London Colney** Herts
91 M9 **Londonderry** N York
55 M7 **London End** Nhants
32 H3 **London Gateway Services** Gt Lon
67 N4 **Londonthorpe** Lincs
143 M9 **Londubh** Highld
143 L9 **Lonemore** Highld
28 H8 **Long Ashton** N Som
52 E6 **Long Bank** Worcs
67 L3 **Long Bennington** Lincs
100 H4 **Longbenton** N Tyne
42 E6 **Longborough** Gloucs
10 E7 **Long Bredy** Dorset
53 J5 **Longbridge** Birm
53 P8 **Longbridge** Warwks
23 J5 **Longbridge Deverill** Wilts
54 G7 **Long Buckby** Nhants
98 C6 **Longburgh** Cumb
22 E10 **Longburton** Dorset
5 N4 **Long Cause** Devon
67 J7 **Long Clawson** Leics
65 N1 **Longcliffe** Derbys
5 P5 **Longcombe** Devon
24 H10 **Long Common** Hants
64 F7 **Long Compton** Staffs
42 G5 **Long Compton** Warwks
30 F4 **Longcot** Oxon
43 P10 **Long Crendon** Bucks
11 N3 **Long Crichel** Dorset
97 P6 **Longcroft** Cumb
32 E9 **Longcross** Surrey
63 M11 **Longden** Shrops
63 M11 **Longden Common** Shrops
32 H9 **Long Ditton** Surrey
65 K9 **Longdon** Staffs
41 N4 **Longdon** Worcs
65 K9 **Longdon Green** Staffs
41 N4 **Longdon Heath** Worcs
63 Q9 **Longdon upon Tern** Wrekin
8 G6 **Longdown** Devon
3 J7 **Longdowns** Cnwll
86 C9 **Long Drax** N York
78 D9 **Long Duckmanton** Derbys
66 D5 **Long Eaton** Derbys
33 R8 **Longfield** Kent
54 B4 **Longford** Covtry
65 N5 **Longford** Derbys
41 N7 **Longford** Gloucs
32 F7 **Longford** Gt Lon
33 P11 **Longford** Kent
64 B5 **Longford** Shrops
64 D8 **Longford** Wrekin
124 F7 **Longforgan** P & K
116 F10 **Longformacus** Border
109 J9 **Longframlington** Nthumb
75 N9 **Long Green** Ches W
41 N5 **Long Green** Worcs
11 P5 **Longham** Dorset
70 D9 **Longham** Norfk
43 J9 **Long Hanborough** Oxon
141 Q8 **Longhaven** Abers
68 G3 **Long Hedges** Lincs
109 L12 **Longhirst** Nthumb
41 L8 **Longhope** Gloucs
152 j6 **Longhope** Ork
109 J11 **Longhorsley** Nthumb
109 L7 **Longhoughton** Nthumb
54 C7 **Long Itchington** Warwks
98 B11 **Longlands** Cumb
65 N4 **Longlane** Derbys

54 D5 Long Lawford Warwks
22 H4 Longleat Safari Park Wilts
41 N8 Longlevens Gloucs
84 G10 Longley Calder
77 L2 Longley Kirk
52 D10 Longley Green Worcs
124 F4 Longleys P & K
21 P8 Long Load Somset
140 H3 Longmanhill Abers
44 C8 Long Marston Herts
85 Q5 Long Marston N York
53 M11 Long Marston Warwks
89 Q2 Long Marton Cumb
51 L4 Long Meadowend Shrops
46 F3 Long Melford Suffk
25 N7 Longmoor Camp Hants
139 N4 Longmorn Moray
76 G9 Longmoss Ches E
29 P4 Long Newnton Gloucs
107 P4 Longnewton Border
116 C8 Long Newton E Loth
91 P3 Longnewton S on T
41 M9 Longney Gloucs
116 B6 Longniddry E Loth
63 N12 Longnor Shrops
77 K10 Longnor Staffs
24 G4 Longparish Hants
98 E6 Longpark Cumb
84 C4 Long Preston N York
83 N8 Longridge Lancs
64 G9 Longridge Staffs
114 H9 Longridge W Loth
114 E7 Longriggend N Lans
87 L7 Long Riston E R Yk
2 D8 Longrock Cnwll
64 H1 Longsdon Staffs
75 P3 Longshaw Wigan
141 P6 Longside Abers
76 G2 Long Sight Oldham
64 C5 Longslow Shrops
56 H7 Longstanton Cambs
24 F6 Longstock Hants
37 M8 Longstone Pembks
56 F9 Longstowe Cambs
59 J2 Long Stratton Norfk
55 K11 Long Street M Keyn
23 P3 Longstreet Wilts
25 M4 Long Sutton Hants
68 H7 Long Sutton Lincs
21 P8 Long Sutton Somset
56 C1 Longthorpe C Pete
58 E7 Long Thurlow Suffk
89 L2 Longthwaite Cumb
64 G3 Longton C Stke
83 L10 Longton Lancs
98 D4 Longtown Cumb
40 D6 Longtown Herefs
13 c3 Longueville Jersey
51 P2 Longville in the Dale Shrops
64 B9 Long Waste Wrekin
66 D7 Long Whatton Leics
43 R10 Longwick Bucks
31 L4 Long Wittenham Oxon
108 H12 Longwitton Nthumb
96 E6 Longwood D & G
63 Q10 Longwood Shrops
30 H2 Longworth Oxon
116 D8 Longyester E Loth
26 H3 Lon-las Swans
141 N4 Lonmay Abers
134 E6 Lonmore Highld
4 C6 Looe Cnwll
34 D12 Loose Kent
8 D4 Loosebeare Devon
68 F7 Loosegate Lincs
32 B2 Loosley Row Bucks
140 F5 Lootcherbrae Abers
24 D6 Lopcombe Corner Wilts
21 P10 Lopen Somset
63 M6 Loppington Shrops
108 G8 Lorbottle Nthumb
13 N3 Lordington W Susx
69 L9 Lordsbridge Norfk
34 D10 Lords Wood Medway
124 D4 Lornty P & K
66 C3 Loscoe Derbys
10 D5 Loscombe Dorset
147 N11 Lossiemouth Moray
64 B6 Lostford Shrops
3 N5 Lost Gardens of Heligan Cnwll
76 C8 Lostock Gralam Ches W
76 C9 Lostock Green Ches W
83 M10 Lostock Hall Lancs
76 C2 Lostock Hall Fold Bolton
76 C2 Lostock Junction Bolton
3 Q3 Lostwithiel Cnwll
146 G3 Lothbeg Highld
84 E6 Lothersdale N York
146 H3 Lothmore Highld
32 C4 Loudwater Bucks
66 E8 Loughborough Leics
66 E8 Loughborough Crematorium Leics
26 E3 Loughor Swans
33 M3 Loughton Essex
44 B4 Loughton M Keyn
52 B4 Loughton Shrops
67 Q8 Lound Lincs
78 H6 Lound Notts
71 P12 Lound Suffk
8 E9 Lounston Devon
66 C8 Lount Leics
80 F6 Louth Lincs
84 B9 Love Clough Lancs
25 L10 Lovedean Hants
24 C9 Lover Wilts
78 F4 Loversall Donc
46 B10 Loves Green Essex
91 N7 Lovesome Hill N York
37 L9 Loveston Pembks
22 D7 Lovington Somset
85 P11 Low Ackworth Wakefd
100 E1 Low Angerton Nthumb
41 M5 Lowbands Gloucs
94 E5 Low Barbeth D & G
80 B9 Low Barlings Lincs
92 E7 Low Bell End N York
83 P1 Low Bentham N York
89 P11 Low Biggins Cumb
89 P6 Low Borrowbridge Cumb
77 N5 Low Bradfield Sheff
84 F5 Low Bradley N York
98 E10 Low Braithwaite Cumb
79 K3 Low Burnham N Linc
109 L8 Low Buston Nthumb
88 C2 Lowca Cumb
86 D4 Low Catton E R Yk
91 L4 Low Coniscliffe Darltn
98 F6 Low Crosby Cumb
66 H3 Lowdham Notts
91 N4 Low Dinsdale Darltn
63 N6 Lowe Shrops
65 J1 Lowe Hill Staffs
91 L10 Low Ellington N York
21 K6 Lower Aisholt Somset
11 J4 Lower Ansty Dorset
41 P6 Lower Apperley Gloucs
43 M8 Lower Arncott Oxon
8 F8 Lower Ashton Devon
31 Q5 Lower Assendon Oxon
83 J9 Lower Ballam Lancs
83 L8 Lower Bartle Lancs
31 M6 Lower Basildon W Berk
51 L9 Lower Bearwood Herefs
15 J5 Lower Beeding W Susx
55 N3 Lower Eenefield Nhants
53 J7 Lower Eentley Worcs
52 E2 Lower Eeobridge Shrops
66 C1 Lower Eirchwood Deroys
54 D10 Lower Eoddington Nhants
2 B7 Lower Eoscaswell Cnwll
25 P4 Lower Eourne Surrey
42 G4 Lower Brailes Warwks
135 M11 Lower Breakish Highld
76 G5 Lower Bredbury Stockp
52 E9 Lower Broadheath Worcs
51 L9 Lower Broxwood Herefs
41 J5 Lower Buckenhill Herefs
40 G4 Lower Bullingham Herefs
23 P10 Lower Burgate Hants
9 J5 Lower Burrowton Devon
51 M9 Lower Burton Herefs
44 H2 Lower Caldecote C Beds
29 M2 Lower Cam Gloucs
28 E10 Lower Canada N Som
54 E9 Lower Catesby Nhants
39 N4 Lower Chapel Powys
23 L7 Lower Chicksgrove Wilts
24 E3 Lower Chute Wilts
33 L5 Lower Clapton Gt Lon
52 G5 Lower Clent Worcs
8 F4 Lower Creedy Devon
77 K7 Lower Crossings Derbys
77 N2 Lower Cumberworth Kirk
83 Q10 Lower Darwen Bl w D
55 Q7 Lower Dean Bed
77 N2 Lower Denby Kirk
135 P4 Lower Diabaig Highld
15 Q8 Lower Dicker E Susx
51 M4 Lower Dinchope Shrops
51 K4 Lower Down Shrops
85 N2 Lower Dunsforth N York
41 J3 Lower Egleton Herefs
77 K12 Lower Elkstone Staffs
65 L4 Lower Ellastone Staffs
43 P10 Lower End Bucks
44 D4 Lower End M Keyn
55 K9 Lower End Nhants
55 L8 Lower End Nhants
24 C2 Lower Everleigh Wilts
12 G5 Lower Exbury Hants
35 N12 Lower Eythorne Kent
28 G7 Lower Failand N Som
25 M6 Lower Farringdon Hants
32 F8 Lower Feltham Gt Lon
14 E7 Lower Fittleworth W Susx
102 c5 Lower Foxdale IoM
63 L6 Lower Frankton Shrops
37 J8 Lower Freystrop Pembks
25 N4 Lower Froyle Hants
5 Q3 Lower Gabwell Devon
145 N7 Lower Gledfield Highld
21 Q5 Lower Godney Somset
52 G2 Lower Gornal Dudley
44 G5 Lower Gravenhurst C Beds
44 H5 Lower Green Herts
45 M5 Lower Green Herts
15 Q3 Lower Green Kent
16 A2 Lower Green Kent
70 E5 Lower Green Norfk
64 G10 Lower Green Staffs
57 P7 Lower Green Suffk
59 L9 Lower Hacheston Suffk
32 F9 Lower Halliford Surrey
10 E3 Lower Halstock Leigh Dorset
34 F9 Lower Halstow Kent
11 N6 Lower Hamworthy Poole
35 L11 Lower Hardres Kent
51 J8 Lower Harpton Herefs
34 E9 Lower Hartlip Kent
66 C2 Lower Hartshay Derbys
43 R9 Lower Hartwell Bucks
64 F5 Lower Hatton Staffs
88 G9 Lower Hawthwaite Cumb
51 J9 Lower Hergest Herefs
43 K7 Lower Heyford Oxon
83 K3 Lower Heysham Lancs
34 C8 Lower Higham Kent
47 L5 Lower Holbrook Suffk
63 L6 Lower Hordley Shrops
14 E7 Lower Horncroft W Susx
84 B8 Lowerhouse Lancs
84 H12 Lower Houses Kirk
52 E11 Lower Howsell Worcs
76 D5 Lower Irlam Salfd
66 B3 Lower Kilburn Derbys
29 M4 Lower Kilcott Gloucs
102 B1 Lower Killeyan Ag & B
10 E5 Lower Kingcombe Dorset
33 J11 Lower Kingswood Surrey
75 K11 Lower Kinnerton Ches W
28 F10 Lower Langford N Som
124 H12 Lower Largo Fife
65 J5 Lower Leigh Staffs
42 E5 Lower Lemington Gloucs
50 C7 Lower Llanfadog Powys
19 K8 Lower Lovacott Devon
19 M6 Lower Loxhore Devon
41 J8 Lower Lydbrook Gloucs
51 L7 Lower Lye Herefs
28 B5 Lower Machen Newpt
40 D5 Lower Maes-coed Herefs
11 P4 Lower Mannington Dorset
22 G4 Lower Marston Somset
40 H10 Lower Meend Gloucs
21 K6 Lower Merridge Somset
43 L3 Lower Middleton Cheney Nhants
22 C4 Lower Milton Somset
41 R2 Lower Moor Worcs
29 K4 Lower Morton S Glos
45 M10 Lower Nazeing Essex
53 N8 Lower Norton Warwks
22 G9 Lower Nyland Dorset
28 A8 Lower Penarth V Glam
52 G1 Lower Penn Staffs
12 E6 Lower Pennington Hants
83 M10 Lower Penwortham Lancs
76 D9 Lower Peover Ches E
76 G1 Lower Place Rochdl
43 P9 Lower Pollicott Bucks
42 E2 Lower Quinton Warwks
34 E9 Lower Rainham Medway
47 J4 Lower Raydon Suffk
20 G5 Lower Roadwater Somset
83 N3 Lower Salter Lancs
29 Q6 Lower Seagry Wilts
45 P9 Lower Sheering Essex
44 E3 Lower Shelton C Beds
31 Q6 Lower Shiplake Oxon
54 D8 Lower Shuckburgh Warwks
42 D7 Lower Slaughter Gloucs
85 K10 Lower Soothill Kirk
41 K9 Lower Soudley Gloucs
17 M3 Lower Standen Kent
29 Q6 Lower Stanton St Quintin Wilts
34 E7 Lower Stoke Medway
29 K3 Lower Stone Gloucs
65 K11 Lower Stonnall Staffs
58 E2 Lower Stow Bedon Norfk
11 K5 Lower Street Dorset
16 C8 Lower Street E Susx
71 K5 Lower Street Norfk
57 Q10 Lower Street Suffk
58 G10 Lower Street Suffk
76 B7 Lower Stretton Warrtn
10 C5 Lower Stroud Dorset
44 F6 Lower Sundon C Beds
12 H3 Lower Swanwick Hants
42 E6 Lower Swell Gloucs
43 J4 Lower Tadmarton Oxon
9 K4 Lower Tale Devon
65 J4 Lower Tean Staffs
71 N12 Lower Thurlton Norfk
2 G8 Lower Town Cnwll
8 D10 Lower Town Devon
41 K3 Lower Town Herefs
37 J3 Lower Town Pembks
7 L9 Lower Trebullett Cnwll
3 J7 Lower Treluswell Cnwll
42 H3 Lower Tysoe Warwks
59 L10 Lower Ufford Suffk
8 G8 Lower Upcott Devon
25 J9 Lower Upham Hants
34 D8 Lower Upnor Medway
20 H6 Lower Vexford Somset
75 Q6 Lower Walton Warrtn
10 H6 Lower Waterston Dorset
21 N3 Lower Weare Somset
54 G9 Lower Weedon Nhants
51 J10 Lower Welson Herefs
41 Q4 Lower Westmancote Worcs
11 K4 Lower Whatcombe Dorset
22 G4 Lower Whatley Somset
75 Q8 Lower Whitley Ches W
29 L3 Lower Wick Gloucs
52 F10 Lower Wick Worcs
25 L5 Lower Wield Hants
15 Q10 Lower Willingdon E Susx
76 E9 Lower Withington Ches E
32 B5 Lower Woodend Bucks
23 P6 Lower Woodford Wilts
10 E4 Lower Wraxhall Dorset
41 M3 Lower Wyche Worcs
84 H10 Lower Wyke C Brad
67 J10 Lowesby Leics
59 Q2 Lowestoft Suffk
88 F3 Loweswater Cumb
100 H6 Low Fell Gatesd
15 K3 Lowfield Heath W Susx
113 P4 Low Gartachorrans Stirlg
99 P5 Low Gate Nthumb
98 G6 Low Gettbridge Cumb
89 Q7 Lowgill Cumb
83 P2 Lowgill Lancs
85 K1 Low Grantley N York
85 J3 Low Green N York
52 E5 Low Habberley Worcs
21 P7 Low Ham Somset
85 L4 Low Harrogate N York
93 J5 Low Hawsker N York
98 F9 Low Hesket Cumb
86 E2 Low Hutton N York
89 J9 Lowick Cumb
55 N4 Lowick Nhants
108 G2 Lowick Nthumb
89 J9 Lowick Bridge Cumb
89 J9 Lowick Green Cumb
89 N3 Low Knipe Cumb
85 J2 Low Laithe N York
91 J2 Lowlands Dur
28 C3 Lowlands Torfn
80 C8 Low Langton Lincs
77 J6 Low Leighton Derbys
88 F2 Low Lorton Cumb
92 G11 Low Marishes N York
79 K10 Low Marnham Notts
109 J3 Low Middleton Nthumb
92 D7 Low Mill N York
84 H9 Low Moor C Brad
101 J9 Low Moorsley Sundld
88 D3 Low Moresby Cumb
89 L10 Low Newton Cumb
97 P9 Low Row Cumb
98 D11 Low Row Cumb
98 H6 Low Row Cumb
90 G7 Low Row N York
94 E5 Low Salchrie D & G
79 N1 Low Santon N Linc
53 M7 Lowsonford Warwks
71 L7 Low Street Norfk
34 B7 Low Street Thurr
59 J2 Low Tharston Norfk
89 N2 Lowther Cumb
89 N2 Lowther Castle Cumb
87 K3 Lowthorpe E R Yk
8 C4 Lowton Devon
21 K9 Lowton Somset
75 Q4 Lowton Wigan
76 B4 Lowton Common Wigan
76 B4 Lowton St Mary's Wigan
115 J4 Low Torry Fife
80 E9 Low Toynton Lincs
78 C3 Low Valley Barns
89 K10 Low Wood Cumb
91 P5 Low Worsall N York
89 K6 Low Wray Cumb
20 E10 Loxbeare Devon
14 E3 Loxhill Surrey
19 M5 Loxhore Devon
19 M6 Loxhore Cott Devon
53 N10 Loxley Warwks
65 K6 Loxley Green Staffs
41 L3 Loxter Herefs
21 N2 Loxton N Som
14 E4 Loxwood W Susx
149 N7 Loyal Lodge Highld
54 H3 Lubenham Leics
68 H3 Lucasgate Lincs
32 D10 Lucas Green Surrey
20 E5 Luccombe Somset
13 K9 Luccombe Village IoW
109 J4 Lucker Nthumb
7 M10 Luckett Cnwll
46 E5 Lucking Street Essex
29 N5 Luckington Wilts
124 H8 Lucklawhill Fife
29 N8 Lucknam Wilts
20 D5 Luckwell Bridge Somset
51 M8 Lucton Herefs
91 L4 Lucy Cross N York
152 b10 Ludag W Isls
80 F4 Ludborough Lincs
5 L6 Ludbrook Devon
37 M8 Ludchurch Pembks
84 F10 Luddenden Calder
84 F10 Luddenden Foot Calder
34 H9 Luddenham Court Kent
34 B9 Luddesdown Kent
86 F12 Luddington N Linc
53 M10 Luddington Warwks
56 B4 Luddington in the Brook Nhants
80 D6 Ludford Lincs
51 N6 Ludford Shrops
43 N8 Ludgershall Bucks
24 D3 Ludgershall Wilts
2 D8 Ludgvan Cnwll
71 M8 Ludham Norfk
51 N5 Ludlow Shrops
21 N11 Ludney Somset
23 K9 Ludwell Wilts
101 J10 Ludworth Dur
45 K6 Luffenhall Herts
7 L6 Luffincott Devon
116 B5 Luffness E Loth
105 L5 Lugar E Ayrs
116 E6 Luggate Burn E Loth
51 M8 Lugg Green Herefs
114 D7 Luggiebank N Lans
113 N10 Lugton E Ayrs
40 H3 Lugwardine Herefs
135 K10 Luib Highld
120 D10 Luing Ag & B
40 F3 Lulham Herefs
65 N9 Lullington Derbys
15 P10 Lullington E Susx
22 H3 Lullington Somset
28 G9 Lulsgate Bottom N Som
52 D9 Lulsley Worcs
11 K8 Lulworth Camp Dorset
84 F11 Lumb Calder
84 C10 Lumb Lancs
84 E10 Lumbutts Calder
85 P9 Lumby N York
114 B7 Lumloch E Duns
132 F3 Lumphanan Abers
115 M3 Lumphinnans Fife
140 D11 Lumsden Abers
125 N2 Lunan Angus
125 J2 Lunanhead Angus
124 C7 Luncarty P & K
86 H5 Lund E R Yk
86 C8 Lund N York
124 F5 Lundie Angus
124 H12 Lundin Links Fife
124 H12 Lundin Mill Fife
18 C4 Lundy Devon
59 K2 Lundy Green Norfk
120 D11 Lunga Ag & B
152 t5 Lunna Shet
34 C10 Lunsford Kent
16 C8 Lunsford's Cross E Susx
75 K3 Lunt Sefton
51 L9 Luntley Herefs
9 M3 Luppitt Devon
5 M6 Lupridge Devon
85 L11 Lupset Wakefd
89 N10 Lupton Cumb
14 D5 Lurgashall W Susx
20 E10 Lurley Devon
80 G10 Lusby Lincs
5 N5 Luscombe Devon
5 J7 Luson Devon
113 M3 Luss Ag & B
111 N4 Lussagiven Ag & B
134 E4 Lusta Highld
8 E8 Lustleigh Devon
51 N8 Luston Herefs
132 G10 Luthermuir Abers
124 G9 Luthrie Fife
52 H4 Lutley Dudley
8 G9 Luton Devon
9 K4 Luton Devon
44 F7 Luton Luton
34 D9 Luton Medway
44 G7 Luton Airport Luton
54 E4 Lutterworth Leics
5 J5 Lutton Devon
5 L4 Lutton Devon
68 H7 Lutton Lincs
56 C3 Lutton Nhants
20 F6 Luxborough Somset
3 P3 Luxulyan Cnwll
76 H3 Luzley Tamesd
151 N9 Lybster Highld
51 K3 Lydbury North Shrops
19 N6 Lydcott Devon
17 J6 Lydd Kent
17 J6 Lydd Airport Kent
17 N2 Lydden Kent
35 P9 Lydden Kent
55 L1 Lyddington Rutlnd
20 H7 Lydeard St Lawrence Somset
31 P11 Lyde Green Hants
7 P8 Lydford Devon
22 D7 Lydford on Fosse Somset
84 D10 Lydgate Calder
84 E12 Lydgate Rochdl
51 K2 Lydham Shrops
30 C5 Lydiard Green Wilts
30 C5 Lydiard Millicent Wilts
30 C5 Lydiard Tregoze Swindn
75 L3 Lydiate Sefton
52 H5 Lydiate Ash Worcs
22 G10 Lydlinch Dorset
41 K11 Lydney Gloucs
37 L11 Lydstep Pembks
52 G4 Lye Dudley
28 G10 Lye Cross N Som
44 D11 Lye Green Bucks
15 P4 Lye Green E Susx
53 M7 Lye Green Warwks
52 D6 Lye Head Worcs
22 H4 Lye's Green Wilts
30 H3 Lyford Oxon
17 K2 Lymbridge Green Kent
9 Q6 Lyme Regis Dorset
17 L3 Lyminge Kent
12 E5 Lymington Hants
14 E10 Lyminster W Susx
76 C6 Lymm Warrtn
17 K4 Lympne Kent
21 M2 Lympsham Somset
9 J8 Lympstone Devon
19 N4 Lynbridge Devon
130 E4 Lynchat Highld
70 H11 Lynch Green Norfk
12 E3 Lyndhurst Hants
67 M11 Lyndon Rutlnd
53 L4 Lyndon Green Birm
106 G2 Lyne Border
32 E9 Lyne Surrey
63 M5 Lyneal Shrops
41 K5 Lyne Down Herefs
8 F9 Lyneham Devon
42 F7 Lyneham Oxon
30 B6 Lyneham Wilts
30 B6 Lyneham Airport Wilts
98 G4 Lyneholmford Cumb
109 M11 Lynemouth Nthumb
133 J2 Lyne of Skene Abers
90 H2 Lynesack Dur
152 j6 Lyness Ork
70 F8 Lyng Norfk
21 M7 Lyng Somset
19 P3 Lynmouth Devon
65 K11 Lynn Staffs
64 E9 Lynn Wrekin
34 G10 Lynsted Kent
7 J4 Lynstone Cnwll
19 N3 Lynton Devon
10 G4 Lyon's Gate Dorset
51 K9 Lyonshall Herefs
11 M6 Lytchett Matravers Dorset
11 M6 Lytchett Minster Dorset
151 N4 Lyth Highld
83 J9 Lytham Lancs
82 H9 Lytham St Anne's Lancs
63 M10 Lythbank Shrops
92 G4 Lythe N York
151 J3 Lythmore Highld

## M

3 J7 Mabe Burnthouse Cnwll
81 K7 Mablethorpe Lincs
76 G9 Macclesfield Ches E
76 G9 Macclesfield Crematorium Ches E
140 H3 Macduff Abers
103 K8 Macharioch Ag & B
28 B4 Machen Caerph
103 N3 Machrie N Ayrs
102 H5 Machrihanish Ag & B
111 J3 Machrins Ag & B
61 N12 Machynlleth Powys
26 D3 Machynys Carmth
65 P5 Mackworth Derbys
116 B7 Macmerry E Loth
7 Q6 Maddaford Devon
123 N8 Madderty P & K
23 N4 Maddington Wilts
114 G6 Maddiston Falk
14 E8 Madehurst W Susx
64 E3 Madeley Staffs
64 C11 Madeley Wrekin
64 E3 Madeley Heath Staffs
9 M3 Madford Devon
56 H8 Madingley Cambs
40 F4 Madley Herefs
52 E11 Madresfield Worcs
2 D8 Madron Cnwll
72 G7 Maenaddwyn IoA
73 N10 Maenan Conwy
37 L5 Maenclochog Pembks
27 N7 Maendy V Glam
3 K8 Maenporth Cnwll
61 L4 Maentwrog Gwynd
48 F9 Maen-y-groes Cerdgn
7 J3 Maer Cnwll
64 E4 Maer Staffs
38 G6 Maerdy Carmth
27 M3 Maerdy Rhondd
63 J8 Maesbrook Shrops
63 J7 Maesbury Shrops
63 K7 Maesbury Marsh Shrops
28 D5 Maes-glas Newpt
37 N6 Maesgwynne Carmth
74 H11 Maeshafn Denbgs
38 A3 Maesllyn Cerdgn
39 N2 Maesmynis Powys
50 E10 Maesmynis Powys
27 K4 Maesteg Brdgnd
38 E8 Maesybont Carmth
27 R3 Maesycwmmer Caerph
45 P10 Magdalen Laver Essex
139 P7 Maggieknockater Moray
45 N6 Maggots End Essex
15 R8 Magham Down E Susx
75 L3 Maghull Sefton
54 E4 Magna Park Leics
28 F5 Magor Mons
28 F5 Magor Services Mons
15 K4 Maidenbower W Susx
22 H5 Maiden Bradley Wilts
5 Q3 Maidencombe Torbay
9 P6 Maidenhayne Devon
28 H9 Maiden Head N Som
32 C6 Maidenhead W & M
100 F8 Maiden Law Dur
10 F5 Maiden Newton Dorset
104 D8 Maidens S Ayrs
32 C8 Maiden's Green Br For
80 F8 Maidenwell Lincs
37 J10 Maiden Wells Pembks
54 G10 Maidford Nhants
43 P4 Maids Moreton Bucks
34 D11 Maidstone Kent
34 E11 Maidstone Services Kent
55 J5 Maidwell Nhants
152 t7 Mail Shet
28 D5 Maindee Newpt
152 k4 Mainland Ork
152 s6 Mainland Shet
101 J12 Mainsforth Dur
132 D11 Mains of Balhall Angus
132 F9 Mains of Balnakettle Abers
139 L9 Mains of Dalvey Highld
132 H9 Mains of Haulkerton Abers
140 D10 Mains of Lesmoir Abers
125 L2 Mains of Melgunds Angus
97 J7 Mainsriddle D & G
51 J3 Mainstone Shrops
41 N7 Maisemore Gloucs
53 L5 Major's Green Worcs
66 B3 Makeney Derbys
5 L8 Malborough Devon
77 K7 Malcoff Derbys
32 H10 Malden Rushett Gt Lon
46 E10 Maldon Essex
84 D3 Malham N York
134 H3 Maligar Highld
127 M5 Mallaig Highld
127 M5 Mallaigvaig Highld
115 L8 Malleny Mills C Edin
45 N6 Mallows Green Essex
72 G10 Malltraeth IoA
61 Q9 Mallwyd Gwynd
29 Q5 Malmesbury Wilts
20 B4 Malmsmead Devon
63 N3 Malpas Ches W
3 K6 Malpas Cnwll
28 D4 Malpas Newpt
41 L7 Malswick Gloucs
80 F7 Maltby Lincs
78 E5 Maltby Rothm
91 Q4 Maltby S on T
81 J7 Maltby le Marsh Lincs
46 H7 Malting Green Essex
16 F2 Maltman's Hill Kent
92 F12 Malton N York
41 M3 Malvern Hills
52 E11 Malvern Link Worcs
41 M3 Malvern Wells Worcs
52 C6 Mamble Worcs
40 D11 Mamhilad Mons
3 J9 Manaccan Cnwll
62 F11 Manafon Powys
152 d6 Manais W Isls
8 E8 Manaton Devon
80 H6 Manby Lincs
53 Q1 Mancetter Warwks
76 F4 Manchester Manch
76 F7 Manchester Airport Manch
75 K10 Mancot Flints
129 K4 Mandally Highld
116 H10 Manderston House Border
57 J3 Manea Cambs
53 L2 Maney Birm
91 L4 Manfield N York
10 D5 Mangerton Dorset
29 K7 Mangotsfield S Glos
44 G7 Mangrove Green Herts
2 H8 Manhay Cnwll
152 d6 Manish W Isls
84 E10 Mankinholes Calder
75 N9 Manley Ches W
40 A11 Manmoel Caerph
118 D5 Mannel Ag & B
30 D10 Manningford Bohune Wilts
30 D10 Manningford Bruce Wilts
84 H8 Manningham C Brad
14 H5 Manning's Heath W Susx
11 P4 Mannington Dorset
47 K5 Manningtree Essex
133 M3 Mannofield C Aber
37 L11 Manorbier Pembks
37 K10 Manorbier Newton Pembks
38 G6 Manordeilo Carmth
107 Q3 Manorhill Border
36 H3 Manorowen Pembks
33 M5 Manor Park Gt Lon
33 M5 Manor Park Crematorium Gt Lon
40 E3 Mansell Gamage Herefs
40 F3 Mansell Lacy Herefs
89 P10 Mansergh Cumb
105 L7 Mansfield E Ayrs
78 E11 Mansfield Notts
78 E12 Mansfield & District Crematorium Notts
78 E11 Mansfield Woodhouse Notts
89 J10 Mansriggs Cumb
22 H10 Manston Dorset
35 P9 Manston Kent
85 M8 Manston Leeds
11 N3 Manswood Dorset
67 M5 Manthorpe Lincs
67 Q9 Manthorpe Lincs
79 M3 Manton N Linc
78 G8 Manton Notts
67 L11 Manton Rutlnd
30 E8 Manton Wilts
45 P6 Manuden Essex
45 Q9 Manwood Green Essex
22 F8 Maperton Somset
78 H11 Maplebeck Notts
32 E4 Maple Cross Herts
31 N7 Mapledurham Oxon
25 M3 Mapledurwell Hants
14 H6 Maplehurst W Susx
33 Q9 Maplescombe Kent
65 M3 Mapleton Derbys
15 N1 Mapleton Kent
66 C4 Mapperley Derbys
66 F4 Mapperley Park C Nott
10 D5 Mapperton Dorset
53 K7 Mappleborough Green Warwks
87 N6 Mappleton E R Yk
77 Q2 Mapplewell Barns
10 H3 Mappowder Dorset
3 K4 Marazanvose Cnwll
2 E8 Marazion Cnwll
63 P3 Marbury Ches E
56 H1 March Cambs
106 C7 March S Lans
31 K3 Marcham Oxon
63 Q6 Marchamley Shrops
63 Q6 Marchamley Wood Shrops
65 L6 Marchington Staffs
65 L6 Marchington Woodlands Staffs
60 E7 Marchros Gwynd
63 K3 Marchwiel Wrexhm
12 F3 Marchwood Hants
27 L8 Marcross V Glam
40 H2 Marden Herefs
16 D2 Marden Kent
30 C10 Marden Wilts
45 Q11 Marden Ash Essex
16 C2 Marden Beech Kent
15 P4 Mardens Hill E Susx
16 D2 Marden Thorn Kent
45 K8 Mardlebury Herts
40 D8 Mardy Mons
67 J10 Marefield Leics
80 E11 Mareham le Fen Lincs
80 F10 Mareham on the Hill Lincs
66 C3 Marehay Derbys
14 F7 Marehill W Susx
15 N6 Maresfield E Susx
87 L9 Marfleet C KuH
75 K12 Marford Wrexhm
27 J5 Margam Neath
27 J5 Margam Crematorium Neath
22 H9 Margaret Marsh Dorset
45 Q9 Margaret Roding Essex
34 B2 Margaretting Essex
34 B2 Margaretting Tye Essex
35 P8 Margate Kent
103 Q3 Margnaheglish N Ayrs
96 C8 Margrie D & G
92 D4 Margrove Park R & Cl
69 N10 Marham Norfk
7 J4 Marhamchurch Cnwll
68 C11 Marholm C Pete
72 H7 Marian-glas IoA
19 P9 Mariansleigh Devon
34 G7 Marine Town Kent
132 H3 Marionburgh Abers
135 J3 Marishader Highld
4 G4 Maristow Devon
97 M2 Marjoriebanks D & G
21 N4 Mark Somset
15 N2 Markbeech Kent
81 J8 Markby Lincs
21 N4 Mark Causeway Somset
15 Q4 Mark Cross E Susx
65 Q5 Markeaton C Derb
65 Q5 Markeaton Crematorium C Derb
66 C11 Market Bosworth Leics
68 C10 Market Deeping Lincs
64 C5 Market Drayton Shrops
55 J3 Market Harborough Leics
23 M3 Market Lavington Wilts
67 M9 Market Overton Rutlnd
80 B6 Market Rasen Lincs
80 E7 Market Stainton Lincs
78 F10 Market Warsop Notts
86 G7 Market Weighton E R Yk
58 E5 Market Weston Suffk
66 D10 Markfield Leics
27 R2 Markham Caerph
79 J9 Markham Moor Notts
115 P1 Markinch Fife
85 L2 Markington N York
116 D6 Markle E Loth
29 K10 Marksbury BaNES
12 H6 Mark's Corner IoW
46 F7 Marks Tey Essex
4 E5 Markwell Cnwll
44 F8 Markyate Herts
30 E8 Marlborough Wilts
51 N9 Marlbrook Herefs
52 H6 Marlbrook Worcs
53 L10 Marlcliff Warwks
5 P4 Marldon Devon
15 Q7 Marle Green E Susx
59 L9 Marlesford Suffk
35 L12 Marley Kent
35 P11 Marley Kent
63 P3 Marley Green Ches E
100 G6 Marley Hill Gatesd
70 H10 Marlingford Norfk
36 F9 Marloes Pembks
32 B5 Marlow Bucks
51 L5 Marlow Herefs
32 B5 Marlow Bottom Bucks
15 N1 Marlpit Hill Kent
15 N5 Marlpits E Susx
16 C8 Marlpits E Susx
66 D3 Marlpool Derbys
22 H9 Marnhull Dorset
76 H6 Marple Stockp
76 H6 Marple Bridge Stockp
78 E3 Marr Donc
90 H7 Marrick N York
37 N9 Marros Carmth
77 K1 Marsden Kirk
101 K5 Marsden S Tyne
84 C8 Marsden Height Lancs
90 E9 Marsett N York
44 A10 Marsh Bucks
84 F8 Marsh C Brad
9 P3 Marsh Devon
44 H8 Marshall's Heath Herts
44 H10 Marshalswick Herts
71 J7 Marsham Norfk
31 M3 Marsh Baldon Oxon
31 J9 Marsh Benham W Berk
35 P11 Marshborough Kent
51 M3 Marshbrook Shrops
80 G4 Marshchapel Lincs
44 F6 Marsh Farm Luton
28 C6 Marshfield Newpt
29 M7 Marshfield S Glos
6 H6 Marshgate Cnwll
43 N7 Marsh Gibbon Bucks
9 K6 Marsh Green Devon
15 N2 Marsh Green Kent
63 Q9 Marsh Green Wrekin
69 K10 Marshland St James Norfk
78 C8 Marsh Lane Derbys
41 J10 Marsh Lane Gloucs
83 J11 Marshside Sefton
20 F4 Marsh Street Somset
10 B5 Marshwood Dorset
91 J6 Marske N York
92 D2 Marske-by-the-Sea R & Cl
76 C4 Marsland Green Wigan
76 C8 Marston Ches W
51 L9 Marston Herefs
67 M3 Marston Lincs
43 L10 Marston Oxon
64 F9 Marston Staffs
64 G7 Marston Staffs
53 N2 Marston Warwks
29 Q11 Marston Wilts
53 M4 Marston Green Solhll
54 B3 Marston Jabbet Warwks
22 D9 Marston Magna Somset
30 D3 Marston Meysey Wilts
65 L5 Marston Montgomery Derbys
44 E3 Marston Moretaine C Beds
65 N6 Marston on Dove Derbys
43 L3 Marston St Lawrence Nhants
51 P9 Marston Stannett Herefs
54 H3 Marston Trussell Nhants
40 H8 Marstow Herefs
44 C8 Marsworth Bucks
30 G10 Marten Wilts
76 E8 Marthall Ches E
71 N8 Martham Norfk
23 N9 Martin Hants
17 P1 Martin Kent
80 C11 Martin Lincs
80 E10 Martin Lincs
89 L3 Martindale Cumb
80 D11 Martin Dales Lincs
23 N9 Martin Drove End Hants
19 N4 Martinhoe Devon
52 G8 Martin Hussingtree Worcs
76 C6 Martinscroft Warrtn
10 G7 Martinstown Dorset
47 N2 Martlesham Suffk
47 M3 Martlesham Heath Suffk
37 K8 Martletwy Pembks
52 D8 Martley Worcs
21 P9 Martock Somset
76 F10 Marton Ches E
76 B10 Marton Ches W
88 H11 Marton Cumb
87 M1 Marton E R Yk
87 M7 Marton E R Yk
79 L7 Marton Lincs
92 B3 Marton Middsb
85 N3 Marton N York
92 E10 Marton N York
63 J11 Marton Shrops
54 C7 Marton Warwks
85 M1 Marton-le-Moor N York
32 F11 Martyr's Green Surrey
24 H7 Martyr Worthy Hants
152 j3 Marwick Ork
19 K6 Marwood Devon
137 N5 Marybank Highld
137 P4 Maryburgh Highld
133 K4 Maryculter Abers
116 H9 Marygold Border
113 Q7 Maryhill C Glas
113 Q7 Maryhill Crematorium C Glas
132 G11 Marykirk Abers
40 G10 Maryland Mons
33 K6 Marylebone Gt Lon
75 P2 Marylebone Wigan
139 M8 Marypark Moray
97 L11 Maryport Cumb
94 G11 Maryport D & G
7 N8 Marystow Devon
7 P9 Mary Tavy Devon
125 N2 Maryton Angus
132 F5 Marywell Abers
133 M4 Marywell Abers
125 M4 Marywell Angus
91 L10 Masham N York
46 B9 Mashbury Essex
100 G3 Mason N u Ty
89 Q11 Masongill N York
104 G6 Masonhill Crematorium S Ayrs
78 D8 Mastin Moor Derbys
45 P9 Matching Essex
45 P9 Matching Green Essex
45 P9 Matching Tye Essex
100 D4 Matfen Nthumb
16 B2 Matfield Kent
28 H4 Mathern Mons
41 L2 Mathon Herefs
36 G4 Mathry Pembks
70 H5 Matlask Norfk
77 P11 Matlock Derbys
77 P11 Matlock Bank Derbys
77 P12 Matlock Bath Derbys
77 P12 Matlock Dale Derbys
41 N8 Matson Gloucs
89 L2 Matterdale End Cumb
78 H6 Mattersey Notts
78 H6 Mattersey Thorpe Notts
31 Q10 Mattingley Hants
70 F10 Mattishall Norfk
70 F9 Mattishall Burgh Norfk
105 J4 Mauchline E Ayrs

141 M6 **Maud** Abers
13 d2 **Maufant** Jersey
42 E7 **Maugersbury** Gloucs
102 g4 **Maughold** IoM
137 L8 **Mauld** Highld
44 F4 **Maulden** C Beds
89 Q3 **Maulds Meaburn** Cumb
91 N9 **Maunby** N York
51 P10 **Maund Bryan** Herefs
20 G7 **Maundown** Somset
71 P9 **Mautby** Norfk
65 K9 **Mavesyn Ridware** Staffs
80 G10 **Mavis Enderby** Lincs
97 M9 **Mawbray** Cumb
83 L12 **Mawdesley** Lancs
27 J6 **Mawdlam** Brdgnd
2 H9 **Mawgan** Cnwll
6 B11 **Mawgan Porth** Cnwll
76 D12 **Maw Green** Ches E
2 H5 **Mawla** Cnwll
3 K9 **Mawnan** Cnwll
3 J9 **Mawnan Smith** Cnwll
55 K5 **Mawsley** Nhants
81 J9 **Mawthorpe** Lincs
68 C10 **Maxey** C Pete
53 N3 **Maxstoke** Warwks
17 K2 **Maxted Street** Kent
107 P4 **Maxton** Border
17 N3 **Maxton** Kent
97 J3 **Maxwell Town** D & G
7 J6 **Maxworthy** Cnwll
26 F4 **Mayals** Swans
64 F3 **May Bank** Staffs
104 E8 **Maybole** S Ayrs
32 E10 **Maybury** Surrey
14 G3 **Mayes Green** Surrey
15 Q5 **Mayfield** E Susx
115 Q8 **Mayfield** Mdloth
65 M3 **Mayfield** Staffs
32 E11 **Mayford** Surrey
41 L7 **May Hill** Gloucs
46 G11 **Mayland** Essex
46 F11 **Maylandsea** Essex
15 Q7 **Maynard's Green** E Susx
53 K5 **Maypole** Birm
35 M9 **Maypole** Kent
40 G8 **Maypole** Mons
59 N2 **Maypole Green** Norfk
58 D9 **Maypole Green** Suffk
59 K7 **Maypole Green** Suffk
31 Q6 **May's Green** Oxon
32 F11 **May's Green** Surrey
18 E9 **Mead** Devon
29 K10 **Meadgate** BaNES
44 A10 **Meadle** Bucks
100 G10 **Meadowfield** Dur
63 K12 **Meadowtown** Shrops
7 M8 **Meadwell** Devon
64 G5 **Meaford** Staffs
89 N7 **Meal Bank** Cumb
97 N9 **Mealrigg** Cumb
97 P10 **Mealsgate** Cumb
85 L8 **Meanwood** Leeds
84 B3 **Mearbeck** N York
21 P5 **Meare** Somset
21 L9 **Meare Green** Somset
21 M8 **Meare Green** Somset
113 Q10 **Mearns** E Rens
55 L7 **Mears Ashby** Nhants
65 Q9 **Measham** Leics
89 L10 **Meathop** Cumb
87 L7 **Meaux** E R Yk
4 H3 **Meavy** Devon
55 K2 **Medbourne** Leics
18 F10 **Meddon** Devon
78 F9 **Meden Vale** Notts
68 F1 **Medlam** Lincs
83 K8 **Medlar** Lancs
32 A5 **Medmenham** Bucks
100 E7 **Medomsley** Dur
25 L6 **Medstead** Hants
34 D10 **Medway Crematorium** Kent
34 E9 **Medway Services** Medway
77 J11 **Meerbrook** Staffs
51 K10 **Meer Common** Herefs
45 M5 **Meesden** Herts
64 C8 **Meeson** Wrekin
7 Q3 **Meeth** Devon
57 P9 **Meeting Green** Suffk
71 L6 **Meeting House Hill** Norfk
37 Q6 **Meidrim** Carmth
62 G9 **Meifod** Powys
124 F4 **Meigle** P & K
105 P7 **Meikle Carco** D & G
114 C10 **Meikle Earnock** S Lans
112 F9 **Meikle Kilmory** Ag & B
123 Q5 **Meikle Obney** P & K
124 D5 **Meikleour** P & K
140 H9 **Meikle Wartle** Abers
38 C9 **Meinciau** Carmth
64 H4 **Meir** C Stke
64 H4 **Meir Heath** Staffs
45 M3 **Melbourn** Cambs
66 C7 **Melbourne** Derbys
86 D6 **Melbourne** E R Yk
3 M3 **Melbur** Cnwll
18 G9 **Melbury** Devon
23 K9 **Melbury Abbas** Dorset
10 F3 **Melbury Bubb** Dorset
10 E3 **Melbury Osmond** Dorset
10 E4 **Melbury Sampford** Dorset
55 P7 **Melchbourne** Bed
11 J4 **Melcombe Bingham** Dorset
7 Q6 **Meldon** Devon
100 E1 **Meldon** Nthumb
100 E1 **Meldon Park** Nthumb
45 M2 **Meldreth** Cambs
114 C1 **Meldrum** Stirlg
120 F10 **Melfort** Ag & B
74 E7 **Meliden** Denbgs
37 N8 **Melinau** Pembks
61 P12 **Melin-byrhedyn** Powys
39 K11 **Melincourt** Neath
73 P11 **Melin-y-coed** Conwy
62 F10 **Melin-y-ddol** Powys
62 E2 **Melin-y-wig** Denbgs
89 P2 **Melkinthorpe** Cumb
99 L5 **Melkridge** Nthumb
29 P9 **Melksham** Wilts
2 H9 **Mellangoose** Cnwll
31 K7 **Mell Green** W Berk
98 F9 **Mellguards** Cumb
83 N1 **Melling** Lancs
75 L4 **Melling** Sefton
75 L3 **Melling Mount** Sefton
58 G6 **Mellis** Suffk
143 M7 **Mellon Charles** Highld
143 N6 **Mellon Udrigle** Highld
83 P9 **Mellor** Lancs
77 J6 **Mellor** Stockp
83 P9 **Mellor Brook** Lancs
22 G4 **Mells** Somset
59 M5 **Mells** Suffk
99 J10 **Melmerby** Cumb
90 H9 **Melmerby** N York
91 N11 **Melmerby** N York
149 M4 **Melness** Highld
58 C9 **Melon Green** Suffk
10 D5 **Melplash** Dorset
107 N3 **Melrose** Border
152 j6 **Melsetter** Ork
91 K5 **Melsonby** N York
77 L2 **Meltham** Kirk
77 L2 **Meltham Mills** Kirk
86 H10 **Melton** E R Yk
59 K10 **Melton** Suffk
86 E5 **Meltonby** E R Yk
70 F5 **Melton Constable** Norfk
67 J8 **Melton Mowbray** Leics
79 Q2 **Melton Ross** N Linc
143 K8 **Melvaig** Highld
63 K9 **Melverley** Shrops
63 K8 **Melverley Green** Shrops
150 F4 **Melvich** Highld
9 P4 **Membury** Devon
30 G7 **Membury Services** W Berk
141 N3 **Memsie** Abers
124 H1 **Memus** Angus
3 Q4 **Menabilly** Cnwll
2 H5 **Menagissey** Cnwll
73 J9 **Menai Bridge** IoA
59 K4 **Mendham** Suffk
22 D5 **Mendip Crematorium** Somset
22 C3 **Mendip Hills**
58 G7 **Mendlesham** Suffk
58 G8 **Mendlesham Green** Suffk
4 D4 **Menheniot** Cnwll
52 D7 **Menithwood** Worcs
105 Q8 **Mennock** D & G
85 J6 **Menston** C Brad
114 F2 **Menstrie** Clacks
86 C8 **Menthorpe** N York
44 C8 **Mentmore** Bucks
127 P7 **Meoble** Highld
63 N10 **Meole Brace** Shrops
25 K9 **Meonstoke** Hants
34 B9 **Meopham** Kent
34 B9 **Meopham Green** Kent
34 B9 **Meopham Station** Kent
56 H4 **Mepal** Cambs
44 G4 **Meppershall** C Beds
40 D3 **Merbach** Herefs
76 D7 **Mere** Ches E
22 H7 **Mere** Wilts
83 K11 **Mere Brow** Lancs
84 C9 **Mereclough** Lancs
65 L12 **Mere Green** Birm
52 H8 **Mere Green** Worcs
76 C9 **Mere Heath** Ches W
34 E9 **Meresborough** Medway
34 B11 **Mereworth** Kent
53 N4 **Meriden** Solhll
134 G9 **Merkadale** Highld
11 N5 **Merley** Poole
37 J7 **Merlin's Bridge** Pembks
63 M8 **Merrington** Shrops
36 H11 **Merrion** Pembks
21 P11 **Merriott** Somset
7 Q9 **Merrivale** Devon
32 E12 **Merrow** Surrey
11 N4 **Merry Field Hill** Dorset
32 G3 **Merry Hill** Herts
52 G1 **Merryhill** Wolves
66 D11 **Merry Lees** Leics
4 D3 **Merrymeet** Cnwll
47 J8 **Mersea Island** Essex
17 J3 **Mersham** Kent
33 K11 **Merstham** Surrey
14 C10 **Merston** W Susx
13 J8 **Merstone** IoW
3 L5 **Merther** Cnwll
38 A7 **Merthyr** Carmth
39 N4 **Merthyr Cynog** Powys
27 Q8 **Merthyr Dyfan** V Glam
27 L7 **Merthyr Mawr** Brdgnd
39 P10 **Merthyr Tydfil** Myr Td
27 P2 **Merthyr Vale** Myr Td
19 K11 **Merton** Devon
33 J8 **Merton** Gt Lon
70 D12 **Merton** Norfk
43 M8 **Merton** Oxon
19 P9 **Meshaw** Devon
46 F8 **Messing** Essex
79 M3 **Messingham** N Linc
59 L4 **Metfield** Suffk
4 F3 **Metherell** Cnwll
79 Q11 **Metheringham** Lincs
115 Q1 **Methil** Fife
115 Q1 **Methilhill** Fife
85 N10 **Methley** Leeds
85 N10 **Methley Junction** Leeds
141 K8 **Methlick** Abers
123 P7 **Methven** P & K
57 P2 **Methwold** Norfk
57 N2 **Methwold Hythe** Norfk
59 M3 **Mettingham** Suffk
71 J5 **Metton** Norfk
3 P5 **Mevagissey** Cnwll
78 D4 **Mexborough** Donc
151 N2 **Mey** Highld
60 C6 **Meyllteyrn** Gwynd
30 D2 **Meysey Hampton** Gloucs
152 d3 **Miabhig** W Isls
152 d3 **Miavaig** W Isls
40 H6 **Michaelchurch** Herefs
40 D5 **Michaelchurch Escley** Herefs
50 H10 **Michaelchurch-on-Arrow** Powys
28 C5 **Michaelstone-y-Fedw** Newpt
27 Q8 **Michaelston-le-Pit** V Glam
6 F9 **Michaelstow** Cnwll
29 L3 **Michaelwood Services** Gloucs
5 L3 **Michelcombe** Devon
24 H5 **Micheldever** Hants
24 H5 **Micheldever Station** Hants
24 F8 **Michelmersh** Hants
58 H8 **Mickfield** Suffk
78 E5 **Micklebring** Donc
92 G4 **Mickleby** N York
85 N8 **Micklefield** Leeds
32 F3 **Micklefield Green** Herts
32 H11 **Mickleham** Surrey
65 P5 **Mickleover** C Derb
84 G7 **Micklethwaite** C Brad
98 C8 **Micklethwaite** Cumb
90 F2 **Mickleton** Dur
42 D3 **Mickleton** Gloucs
85 N9 **Mickletown** Leeds
75 M9 **Mickle Trafford** Ches W
77 Q8 **Mickley** Derbys
91 L11 **Mickley** N York
58 B9 **Mickley Green** Suffk
100 D6 **Mickley Square** Nthumb
141 M3 **Mid Ardlaw** Abers
152 k2 **Midbea** Ork
132 F4 **Mid Beltie** Abers
12 B5 **Mid Bockhampton** Dorset
115 K8 **Mid Calder** W Loth
151 P9 **Mid Clyth** Highld
140 G3 **Mid Culbeuchly** Abers
31 Q5 **Middle Assendon** Oxon
43 K6 **Middle Aston** Oxon
43 J6 **Middle Barton** Oxon
97 P3 **Middlebie** D & G
130 G11 **Middlebridge** P & K
21 Q10 **Middle Chinnock** Somset
43 P6 **Middle Claydon** Bucks
78 C3 **Middlecliffe** Barns
8 D7 **Middlecott** Devon
41 R10 **Middle Duntisbourne** Gloucs
91 J9 **Middleham** N York
78 C8 **Middle Handley** Derbys
58 E3 **Middle Harling** Norfk
4 D3 **Middlehill** Cnwll
29 N8 **Middlehill** Wilts
51 N3 **Middlehope** Shrops
112 D3 **Middle Kames** Ag & B
42 C2 **Middle Littleton** Worcs
64 E3 **Middle Madeley** Staffs
40 D5 **Middle Maes-coed** Herefs
10 G3 **Middlemarsh** Dorset
65 L3 **Middle Mayfield** Staffs
36 F5 **Middle Mill** Pembks
7 P10 **Middlemore** Devon
16 F3 **Middle Quarter** Kent
80 B6 **Middle Rasen** Lincs
5 Q3 **Middle Rocombe** Devon
83 N3 **Middle Salter** Lancs
91 R3 **Middlesbrough** Middsb
98 E10 **Middlesceugh** Cumb
89 N9 **Middleshaw** Cumb
91 J12 **Middlesmoor** N York
21 J9 **Middle Stoford** Somset
34 E7 **Middle Stoke** Medway
100 H12 **Middlestone** Dur
100 G11 **Middlestone Moor** Dur
21 P3 **Middle Stoughton** Somset
85 K11 **Middlestown** Wakefd
41 M10 **Middle Street** Gloucs
4 B4 **Middle Taphouse** Cnwll
107 R1 **Middlethird** Border
118 C4 **Middleton** Ag & B
89 Q9 **Middleton** Cumb
65 P1 **Middleton** Derbys
77 M11 **Middleton** Derbys
46 F4 **Middleton** Essex
24 G4 **Middleton** Hants
51 P7 **Middleton** Herefs
83 K3 **Middleton** Lancs
85 L9 **Middleton** Leeds
84 H5 **Middleton** N York
92 F9 **Middleton** N York
55 L3 **Middleton** Nhants
69 M9 **Middleton** Norfk
100 D1 **Middleton** Nthumb
108 H3 **Middleton** Nthumb
124 C11 **Middleton** P & K
76 F3 **Middleton** Rochdl
51 P5 **Middleton** Shrops
63 K6 **Middleton** Shrops
59 N7 **Middleton** Suffk
26 B5 **Middleton** Swans
65 M12 **Middleton** Warwks
43 K3 **Middleton Cheney** Nhants
76 G2 **Middleton Crematorium** Rochdl
65 J5 **Middleton Green** Staffs
108 F5 **Middleton Hall** Nthumb
90 F2 **Middleton-in-Teesdale** Dur
59 N7 **Middleton Moor** Suffk
91 N4 **Middleton One Row** Darltn
91 Q5 **Middleton-on-Leven** N York
14 D10 **Middleton-on-Sea** W Susx
51 P7 **Middleton on the Hill** Herefs
86 H5 **Middleton on the Wolds** E R Yk
133 M2 **Middleton Park** C Aber
52 B3 **Middleton Priors** Shrops
91 N11 **Middleton Quernhow** N York
91 N4 **Middleton St George** Darltn
52 C3 **Middleton Scriven** Shrops
43 L7 **Middleton Stoney** Oxon
91 L5 **Middleton Tyas** N York
88 C5 **Middletown** Cumb
2 b3 **Middle Town** IoS
28 F8 **Middletown** N Som
63 K9 **Middletown** Powys
42 H3 **Middle Tysoe** Warwks
24 E6 **Middle Wallop** Hants
76 C10 **Middlewich** Ches E
24 D7 **Middle Winterslow** Wilts
7 K9 **Middlewood** Cnwll
40 C3 **Middlewood** Herefs
23 P6 **Middle Woodford** Wilts
58 G8 **Middlewood Green** Suffk
105 J3 **Middleyard** E Ayrs
41 N11 **Middle Yard** Gloucs
21 N7 **Middlezoy** Somset
91 L2 **Middridge** Dur
29 M10 **Midford** BaNES
83 L10 **Midge Hall** Lancs
99 J6 **Midgeholme** Cumb
31 L9 **Midgham** W Berk
84 F10 **Midgley** Calder
85 K12 **Midgley** Wakefd
14 H2 **Mid Holmwood** Surrey
77 N4 **Midhopestones** Sheff
14 C6 **Midhurst** W Susx
13 Q3 **Mid Lavant** W Susx
107 N4 **Midlem** Border
137 M8 **Mid Mains** Highld
22 C8 **Midney** Somset
112 F9 **Midpark** Ag & B
22 F3 **Midsomer Norton** BaNES
149 M4 **Midtown** Highld
80 G12 **Midville** Lincs
53 P8 **Mid Warwickshire Crematorium** Warwks
76 G7 **Midway** Ches E
152 t3 **Mid Yell** Shet
132 C3 **Migvie** Abers
22 F9 **Milborne Port** Somset
11 K5 **Milborne St Andrew** Dorset
22 F9 **Milborne Wick** Somset
100 E3 **Milbourne** Nthumb
29 Q5 **Milbourne** Wilts
99 J12 **Milburn** Cumb
29 K4 **Milbury Heath** S Glos
85 N2 **Milby** N York
43 J5 **Milcombe** Oxon
46 G2 **Milden** Suffk
57 N6 **Mildenhall** Suffk
30 E8 **Mildenhall** Wilts
51 K6 **Milebrook** Powys
16 D2 **Milebush** Kent
30 A8 **Mile Elm** Wilts
46 H6 **Mile End** Essex
41 J9 **Mile End** Gloucs
59 L3 **Mile End** Suffk
70 D8 **Mileham** Norfk
15 J9 **Mile Oak** Br & H
16 B2 **Mile Oak** Kent
65 M11 **Mile Oak** Staffs
51 P7 **Miles Hope** Herefs
115 K4 **Milesmark** Fife
76 F4 **Miles Platting** Manch
34 G7 **Mile Town** Kent
108 E3 **Milfield** Nthumb
66 B3 **Milford** Derbys
18 E9 **Milford** Devon
50 F2 **Milford** Powys
64 H8 **Milford** Staffs
14 D2 **Milford** Surrey
36 H9 **Milford Haven** Pembks
12 D6 **Milford on Sea** Hants
41 J10 **Milkwall** Gloucs
13 a1 **Millais** Jersey
25 P8 **Milland** W Susx
25 P8 **Milland Marsh** W Susx
84 F11 **Mill Bank** Calder
88 H2 **Millbeck** Cumb
141 N7 **Millbreck** Abers
25 P5 **Millbridge** Surrey
44 E4 **Millbrook** C Beds
24 F10 **Millbrook** C Sotn
4 F6 **Millbrook** Cnwll
13 b2 **Millbrook** Jersey
76 H4 **Millbrook** Tamesd
76 H6 **Mill Brow** Stockp
133 J2 **Millbuie** Abers
137 P5 **Millbuie** Highld
5 N7 **Millcombe** Devon
71 L11 **Mill Common** Norfk
59 N4 **Mill Common** Suffk
16 E6 **Millcorner** E Susx
145 P11 **Millcraig** Highld
5 M4 **Mill Cross** Devon
65 L1 **Milldale** Staffs
31 R5 **Mill End** Bucks
56 F4 **Mill End** Cambs
29 M3 **Millend** Gloucs
45 L5 **Mill End** Herts
115 P7 **Millerhill** Mdloth
77 L9 **Miller's Dale** Derbys
65 P2 **Millers Green** Derbys
45 Q10 **Miller's Green** Essex
114 B8 **Millerston** C Glas
84 D11 **Millgate** Lancs
46 A3 **Mill Green** Cambs
34 B2 **Mill Green** Essex
45 J9 **Mill Green** Herts
68 E7 **Mill Green** Lincs
58 H4 **Mill Green** Norfk
64 C6 **Millgreen** Shrops
65 K12 **Mill Green** Staffs
65 K8 **Mill Green** Staffs
46 G3 **Mill Green** Suffk
58 E9 **Mill Green** Suffk
58 H8 **Mill Green** Suffk
59 L8 **Mill Green** Suffk
51 J11 **Millhalf** Herefs
9 N4 **Millhayes** Devon
83 L1 **Millhead** Lancs
114 D11 **Millheugh** S Lans
16 A9 **Mill Hill** E Susx
33 J4 **Mill Hill** Gt Lon
112 D7 **Millhouse** Ag & B
98 D10 **Millhouse** Cumb
97 M1 **Millhousebridge** D & G
77 N3 **Millhouse Green** Barns
78 C3 **Millhouses** Barns
77 Q7 **Millhouses** Sheff
113 N9 **Milliken Park** Rens
37 J7 **Millin Cross** Pembks
86 F5 **Millington** E R Yk
64 F5 **Millmeece** Staffs
89 N10 **Millness** Cumb
123 L9 **Mill of Drummond** P & K
113 M5 **Mill of Haldane** W Duns
88 G10 **Millom** Cumb
6 H5 **Millook** Cnwll
2 F8 **Millpool** Cnwll
6 G10 **Millpool** Cnwll
112 H10 **Millport** N Ayrs
89 M10 **Mill Side** Cumb
34 C11 **Mill Street** Kent
70 F8 **Mill Street** Norfk
58 F6 **Mill Street** Suffk
77 P8 **Millthorpe** Derbys
89 Q8 **Millthrop** Cumb
133 K4 **Milltimber** C Aber
131 N2 **Milltown** Abers
132 D1 **Milltown** Abers
3 Q3 **Milltown** Cnwll
98 D3 **Milltown** D & G
78 B11 **Milltown** Derbys
19 L5 **Milltown** Devon
132 G4 **Milltown of Campfield** Abers
139 N8 **Milltown of Edinvillie** Moray
132 F4 **Milltown of Learney** Abers
124 C11 **Milnathort** P & K
113 Q6 **Milngavie** E Duns
76 G1 **Milnrow** Rochdl
89 M10 **Milnthorpe** Cumb
85 M11 **Milnthorpe** Wakefd
134 C6 **Milovaig** Highld
52 B6 **Milson** Shrops
34 F10 **Milstead** Kent
23 Q4 **Milston** Wilts
68 C6 **Milthorpe** Lincs
43 M2 **Milthorpe** Nhants
64 G2 **Milton** C Stke
57 J8 **Milton** Cambs
98 H6 **Milton** Cumb
95 J7 **Milton** D & G
96 G4 **Milton** D & G
65 P7 **Milton** Derbys
135 N7 **Milton** Highld
137 N9 **Milton** Highld
137 Q6 **Milton** Highld
146 D10 **Milton** Highld
151 P6 **Milton** Highld
113 L7 **Milton** Inver
34 B7 **Milton** Kent
139 M12 **Milton** Moray
140 D3 **Milton** Moray
28 D10 **Milton** N Som
28 E5 **Milton** Newpt
78 H9 **Milton** Notts
31 K4 **Milton** Oxon
43 K5 **Milton** Oxon
131 K12 **Milton** P & K
37 K10 **Milton** Pembks
21 P9 **Milton** Somset
113 P1 **Milton** Stirlg
113 N6 **Milton** W Duns
11 K4 **Milton Abbas** Dorset
7 M9 **Milton Abbot** Devon
115 N8 **Milton Bridge** Mdloth
44 D6 **Milton Bryan** C Beds
22 F6 **Milton Clevedon** Somset
4 G3 **Milton Combe** Devon
43 N11 **Milton Common** Oxon
7 M3 **Milton Damerel** Devon
30 D2 **Milton End** Gloucs
41 L9 **Milton End** Gloucs
55 P9 **Milton Ernest** Bed
75 M12 **Milton Green** Ches W
31 K4 **Milton Hill** Oxon
44 B4 **Milton Keynes** M Keyn
30 E10 **Milton Lilbourne** Wilts
55 J9 **Milton Malsor** Nhants
122 G5 **Milton Morenish** P & K
132 E4 **Milton of Auchinhove** Abers
115 P1 **Milton of Balgonie** Fife
113 N3 **Milton of Buchanan** Stirlg
114 B6 **Milton of Campsie** E Duns
138 C7 **Milton of Leys** Highld
133 L4 **Milton of Murtle** C Aber
132 B5 **Milton of Tullich** Abers
22 H7 **Milton on Stour** Dorset
34 F9 **Milton Regis** Kent
15 P10 **Milton Street** E Susx
42 F8 **Milton-under-Wychwood** Oxon
20 H8 **Milverton** Somset
53 P7 **Milverton** Warwks
64 H6 **Milwich** Staffs
74 G8 **Milwr** Flints
112 E2 **Minard** Ag & B
23 L10 **Minchington** Dorset
29 P2 **Minchinhampton** Gloucs
108 D3 **Mindrum** Nthumb
20 F4 **Minehead** Somset
63 J2 **Minera** Wrexhm
30 B4 **Minety** Wilts
61 K4 **Minffordd** Gwynd
127 M10 **Mingarrypark** Highld
80 F11 **Miningsby** Lincs
7 K10 **Minions** Cnwll
104 F7 **Minishant** S Ayrs
61 Q9 **Minllyn** Gwynd
95 M5 **Minnigaff** D & G
35 N8 **Minnis Bay** Kent
141 J4 **Minnonie** Abers
76 C11 **Minshull Vernon** Ches E
85 M2 **Minskip** N York
12 D3 **Minstead** Hants
25 Q9 **Minsted** W Susx
34 G8 **Minster** Kent
35 P9 **Minster** Kent
63 L11 **Minsterley** Shrops
42 G9 **Minster Lovell** Oxon
41 M8 **Minsterworth** Gloucs
10 G4 **Minterne Magna** Dorset
10 G4 **Minterne Parva** Dorset
80 D9 **Minting** Lincs
141 N6 **Mintlaw** Abers
69 M8 **Mintlyn Crematorium** Norfk
107 N6 **Minto** Border
51 M2 **Minton** Shrops
37 K8 **Minwear** Pembks
53 M2 **Minworth** Birm
88 C4 **Mirehouse** Cumb
151 P4 **Mireland** Highld
85 J11 **Mirfield** Kirk
41 Q10 **Miserden** Gloucs
27 P3 **Miskin** Rhondd
27 P6 **Miskin** Rhondd
78 H5 **Misson** Notts
54 F4 **Misterton** Leics
79 J5 **Misterton** Notts
10 C3 **Misterton** Somset
47 K5 **Mistley** Essex
47 K5 **Mistley Heath** Essex
33 K8 **Mitcham** Gt Lon
41 K8 **Mitcheldean** Gloucs
3 L4 **Mitchell** Cnwll
106 C10 **Mitchellslacks** D & G
40 G9 **Mitchel Troy** Mons
100 F1 **Mitford** Nthumb
3 J4 **Mithian** Cnwll
64 G9 **Mitton** Staffs
43 M5 **Mixbury** Oxon
84 G9 **Mixenden** Calder
58 F9 **Moats Tye** Suffk
76 E8 **Mobberley** Ches E
65 J4 **Mobberley** Staffs
40 E3 **Moccas** Herefs
73 P8 **Mochdre** Conwy
50 E3 **Mochdre** Powys
95 L9 **Mochrum** D & G
12 B3 **Mockbeggar** Hants
16 C1 **Mockbeggar** Kent
88 E2 **Mockerkin** Cumb
5 L6 **Modbury** Devon
64 G5 **Moddershall** Staffs
72 H6 **Moelfre** IoA
62 G6 **Moelfre** Powys
60 H1 **Moel Tryfan** Gwynd
106 E8 **Moffat** D & G
56 C10 **Moggerhanger** C Beds
65 P9 **Moira** Leics
35 J12 **Molash** Kent
126 H2 **Mol-chlach** Highld
74 H11 **Mold** Flints
84 H12 **Moldgreen** Kirk
45 Q7 **Molehill Green** Essex
46 C7 **Molehill Green** Essex
87 J7 **Molescroft** E R Yk
100 F1 **Molesden** Nthumb
55 Q5 **Molesworth** Cambs
20 C7 **Molland** Devon
75 L9 **Mollington** Ches W
54 D11 **Mollington** Oxon
114 C7 **Mollinsburn** N Lans
48 H8 **Monachty** Cerdgn
133 J8 **Mondynes** Abers
59 K9 **Monewden** Suffk
123 Q7 **Moneydie** P & K
32 C7 **Moneyrow Green** W & M
105 P11 **Moniaive** D & G
125 K6 **Monifieth** Angus
125 K5 **Monikie** Angus
124 F10 **Monimail** Fife
37 M2 **Monington** Pembks
78 B2 **Monk Bretton** Barns
33 J3 **Monken Hadley** Gt Lon
85 Q9 **Monk Fryston** N York
41 J3 **Monkhide** Herefs
98 D6 **Monkhill** Cumb
52 B2 **Monkhopton** Shrops
51 M9 **Monkland** Herefs
19 J9 **Monkleigh** Devon
27 L8 **Monknash** V Glam
7 Q4 **Monkokehampton** Devon
101 J4 **Monkseaton** N Tyne
58 E11 **Monks Eleigh** Suffk
14 H5 **Monk's Gate** W Susx
76 F9 **Monks Heath** Ches E
31 M11 **Monk Sherborne** Hants
17 K3 **Monks Horton** Kent
20 G6 **Monksilver** Somset
54 D4 **Monks Kirby** Warwks
59 J7 **Monk Soham** Suffk
53 L5 **Monkspath** Solhll
44 A10 **Monks Risborough** Bucks
80 H10 **Monksthorpe** Lincs
45 R6 **Monk Street** Essex
40 D11 **Monkswood** Mons
9 M4 **Monkton** Devon
35 N9 **Monkton** Kent
104 F4 **Monkton** S Ayrs
101 J5 **Monkton** S Tyne
27 M8 **Monkton** V Glam
29 M10 **Monkton Combe** BaNES
23 J6 **Monkton Deverill** Wilts
29 N9 **Monkton Farleigh** Wilts
21 L8 **Monkton Heathfield** Somset
23 M10 **Monkton Up Wimborne** Dorset
9 Q5 **Monkton Wyld** Dorset
101 K6 **Monkwearmouth** Sundld
25 L7 **Monkwood** Hants
52 H1 **Monmore Green** Wolves
40 G9 **Monmouth** Mons
40 E3 **Monnington on Wye** Herefs
95 L10 **Monreith** D & G
22 C10 **Montacute** Somset
76 C1 **Montcliffe** Bolton
63 L9 **Montford** Shrops
63 M9 **Montford Bridge** Shrops
140 E12 **Montgarrie** Abers
50 H1 **Montgomery** Powys
76 E4 **Monton** Salfd
125 P1 **Montrose** Angus
12 b2 **Mont Saint** Guern
24 E4 **Monxton** Hants
77 L10 **Monyash** Derbys
132 G1 **Monymusk** Abers
123 M8 **Monzie** P & K
114 C7 **Moodiesburn** N Lans
124 G9 **Moonzie** Fife
85 L7 **Moor Allerton** Leeds
10 C6 **Moorbath** Dorset
80 F11 **Moorby** Lincs
51 K9 **Moorcot** Herefs
11 N3 **Moor Crichel** Dorset
11 Q6 **Moordown** Bmouth
75 P7 **Moore** Halton
44 D7 **Moor End** C Beds
84 F9 **Moor End** Calder
8 C3 **Moor End** Devon
41 L11 **Moorend** Gloucs
83 J6 **Moor End** Lancs
86 B7 **Moor End** N York
86 C12 **Moorends** Donc
24 H10 **Moorgreen** Hants
45 L6 **Moor Green** Herts
66 D3 **Moorgreen** Notts
77 P8 **Moorhall** Derbys
40 E2 **Moorhampton** Herefs
84 H8 **Moorhead** C Brad
85 K9 **Moor Head** Leeds
98 B8 **Moorhouse** Cumb
98 D7 **Moorhouse** Cumb
78 D2 **Moorhouse** Donc
79 J10 **Moorhouse** Notts
33 M11 **Moorhouse Bank** Surrey
21 M7 **Moorland** Somset
21 N6 **Moorlinch** Somset
85 Q4 **Moor Monkton** N York
88 D4 **Moor Row** Cumb
97 P8 **Moor Row** Cumb
92 E4 **Moorsholm** R & Cl
22 H9 **Moorside** Dorset
83 K8 **Moor Side** Lancs
83 L8 **Moor Side** Lancs
85 K8 **Moorside** Leeds
80 E12 **Moor Side** Lincs
76 H2 **Moorside** Oldham
17 K3 **Moorstock** Kent
53 J4 **Moor Street** Birm
34 E9 **Moor Street** Medway
4 C4 **Moorswater** Cnwll
78 D2 **Moorthorpe** Wakefd
7 P10 **Moortown** Devon
12 B4 **Moortown** Hants
12 G8 **Moortown** IoW
85 L7 **Moortown** Leeds
79 Q4 **Moortown** Lincs
63 Q8 **Moortown** Wrekin
146 D8 **Morangie** Highld
127 M6 **Morar** Highld
140 B3 **Moray Crematorium** Moray
56 C2 **Morborne** Cambs
8 E3 **Morchard Bishop** Devon
10 B6 **Morcombelake** Dorset
67 M12 **Morcott** Rutlnd
63 J6 **Morda** Shrops
11 M5 **Morden** Dorset
33 J8 **Morden** Gt Lon
40 H4 **Mordiford** Herefs
91 N1 **Mordon** Dur
51 K2 **More** Shrops
20 E8 **Morebath** Devon
108 C5 **Morebattle** Border
83 K2 **Morecambe** Lancs
30 D5 **Moredon** Swindn
144 E6 **Morefield** Highld
17 M3 **Morehall** Kent
5 M6 **Moreleigh** Devon
122 G6 **Morenish** P & K
88 D3 **Moresby Parks** Cumb
24 H8 **Morestead** Hants
11 K7 **Moreton** Dorset
45 P10 **Moreton** Essex
51 N8 **Moreton** Herefs
43 P10 **Moreton** Oxon
64 E8 **Moreton** Staffs
65 L6 **Moreton** Staffs
75 J6 **Moreton** Wirral
63 P7 **Moreton Corbet** Shrops
8 E7 **Moretonhampstead** Devon
42 E5 **Moreton-in-Marsh** Gloucs
51 Q11 **Moreton Jeffries** Herefs
63 P7 **Moretonmill** Shrops
53 P9 **Moreton Morrell** Warwks
40 G3 **Moreton on Lugg** Herefs
53 P9 **Moreton Paddox** Warwks
54 F11 **Moreton Pinkney** Nhants
64 B5 **Moreton Say** Shrops
41 M9 **Moreton Valence** Gloucs
48 E10 **Morfa** Cerdgn
61 J5 **Morfa Bychan** Gwynd
72 G12 **Morfa Dinlle** Gwynd
39 K10 **Morfa Glas** Neath
60 D4 **Morfa Nefyn** Gwynd
27 Q6 **Morganstown** Cardif
24 C9 **Morgan's Vale** Wilts
116 D7 **Morham** E Loth
49 K5 **Moriah** Cerdgn
89 P2 **Morland** Cumb
76 F7 **Morley** Ches E
66 C4 **Morley** Derbys
91 J1 **Morley** Dur
85 K9 **Morley** Leeds
76 F7 **Morley Green** Ches E
70 G12 **Morley St Botolph** Norfk
7 L10 **Mornick** Cnwll
115 N7 **Morningside** C Edin
114 E10 **Morningside** N Lans
59 J2 **Morningthorpe** Norfk
100 G1 **Morpeth** Nthumb
132 H11 **Morphie** Abers
65 L8 **Morrey** Staffs
65 J1 **Morridge Side** Staffs
26 G3 **Morriston** Swans
70 E3 **Morston** Norfk
19 J4 **Mortehoe** Devon
78 D6 **Morthen** Rothm
31 N9 **Mortimer** W Berk
31 N9 **Mortimer Common** W Berk
51 M8 **Mortimer's Cross** Herefs
31 N9 **Mortimer West End** Hants
32 H7 **Mortlake** Gt Lon
32 H7 **Mortlake Crematorium** Gt Lon
98 E7 **Morton** Cumb
98 F10 **Morton** Cumb
78 C11 **Morton** Derbys
13 K7 **Morton** IoW
68 B7 **Morton** Lincs
79 K5 **Morton** Lincs
67 J2 **Morton** Notts
63 J7 **Morton** Shrops
79 M11 **Morton Hall** Lincs
115 N7 **Mortonhall Crematorium** C Edin
91 N8 **Morton-on-Swale** N York
70 G9 **Morton on the Hill** Norfk
91 K2 **Morton Tinmouth** Dur
2 C7 **Morvah** Cnwll
4 C5 **Morval** Cnwll
136 D11 **Morvich** Highld
52 C2 **Morville** Shrops
52 C2 **Morville Heath** Shrops
4 G3 **Morwellham Quay** Devon
18 D10 **Morwenstow** Cnwll
78 C7 **Mosborough** Sheff
105 J2 **Moscow** E Ayrs
52 D3 **Mose** Shrops
98 D11 **Mosedale** Cumb
53 K4 **Moseley** Birm
52 H1 **Moseley** Wolves
52 E8 **Moseley** Worcs
76 D2 **Moses Gate** Bolton
118 C4 **Moss** Ag & B
86 B12 **Moss** Donc
63 J2 **Moss** Wrexhm
140 D12 **Mossat** Abers
152 t5 **Mossbank** Shet
75 N4 **Moss Bank** St Hel
88 C1 **Mossbay** Cumb
104 G5 **Mossblown** S Ayrs
76 D6 **Mossbrow** Traffd
107 Q6 **Mossburnford** Border
96 D4 **Mossdale** D & G
105 J9 **Mossdale** E Ayrs
83 K6 **Moss Edge** Lancs
76 C8 **Moss End** Ches E
114 D9 **Mossend** N Lans
88 F2 **Mosser Mains** Cumb
76 G11 **Mossley** Ches E
76 H3 **Mossley** Tamesd
107 L10 **Mosspaul Hotel** Border
97 P8 **Moss Side** Cumb
138 F5 **Moss-side** Highld
83 J9 **Moss Side** Lancs
75 L3 **Moss Side** Sefton
139 Q4 **Mosstodloch** Moray
95 Q8 **Mossyard** D & G
75 P1 **Mossy Lea** Lancs
10 C4 **Mosterton** Dorset
76 G3 **Moston** Manch
63 P7 **Moston** Shrops
76 D11 **Moston Green** Ches E
74 G7 **Mostyn** Flints
23 J8 **Motcombe** Dorset
5 K7 **Mothecombe** Devon
89 L1 **Motherby** Cumb
114 D10 **Motherwell** N Lans
33 J9 **Motspur Park** Gt Lon
33 M8 **Mottingham** Gt Lon
24 E8 **Mottisfont** Hants
12 G8 **Mottistone** IoW
77 J5 **Mottram in Longdendale** Tamesd
76 G8 **Mottram St Andrew** Ches E
12 c3 **Mouilpied** Guern
75 N9 **Mouldsworth** Ches W
123 N1 **Moulin** P & K
15 L9 **Moulsecoomb** Br & H
31 M5 **Moulsford** Oxon
44 C3 **Moulsoe** M Keyn
145 P11 **Moultavie** Highld
76 C9 **Moulton** Ches W
68 F7 **Moulton** Lincs
91 L6 **Moulton** N York
55 K7 **Moulton** Nhants
57 N8 **Moulton** Suffk
27 P8 **Moulton** V Glam
68 F8 **Moulton Chapel** Lincs
71 M10 **Moulton St Mary** Norfk
68 F6 **Moulton Seas End** Lincs
3 J3 **Mount** Cnwll
4 A3 **Mount** Cnwll
84 G11 **Mount** Kirk
84 G9 **Mountain** C Brad
27 P3 **Mountain Ash** Rhondd
115 L12 **Mountain Cross** Border
35 J11 **Mountain Street** Kent
2 H6 **Mount Ambrose** Cnwll
46 F5 **Mount Bures** Essex
16 C7 **Mountfield** E Susx
137 P3 **Mountgerald House** Highld
2 H5 **Mount Hawke** Cnwll
2 H11 **Mount Hermon** Cnwll
3 L2 **Mountjoy** Cnwll
115 N10 **Mount Lothian** Mdloth
34 A3 **Mountnessing** Essex
28 G4 **Mounton** Mons
76 F12 **Mount Pleasant** Ches E
65 P8 **Mount Pleasant** Derbys
65 Q2 **Mount Pleasant** Derbys
100 H11 **Mount Pleasant** Dur
87 N7 **Mount Pleasant** E R Yk
15 M7 **Mount Pleasant** E Susx
58 E2 **Mount Pleasant** Norfk
57 P11 **Mount Pleasant** Suffk
53 J7 **Mount Pleasant** Worcs
100 F7 **Mountsett Crematorium** Dur
66 F9 **Mountsorrel** Leics
23 M8 **Mount Sorrel** Wilts
84 G9 **Mount Tabor** Calder
14 D2 **Mousehill** Surrey
2 D9 **Mousehole** Cnwll
97 L4 **Mouswald** D & G
76 F12 **Mow Cop** Ches E
108 C5 **Mowhaugh** Border
66 F10 **Mowmacre Hill** C Leic
54 G3 **Mowsley** Leics
129 M8 **Moy** Highld
138 E9 **Moy** Highld
136 B12 **Moyle** Highld
48 A11 **Moylegrove** Pembks
103 J2 **Muasdale** Ag & B
133 L6 **Muchalls** Abers
40 G5 **Much Birch** Herefs
41 J2 **Much Cowarne** Herefs
40 G5 **Much Dewchurch** Herefs
21 P8 **Muchelney** Somset
21 P8 **Muchelney Ham** Somset
45 M8 **Much Hadham** Herts
83 L10 **Much Hoole** Lancs
83 L10 **Much Hoole Town** Lancs
4 C5 **Muchlarnick** Cnwll
41 K5 **Much Marcle** Herefs
64 B12 **Much Wenlock** Shrops
126 G8 **Muck** Highld
34 B6 **Mucking** Thurr
34 B6 **Muckingford** Thurr
70 G3 **Muckleburgh Collection** Norfk
10 G6 **Muckleford** Dorset
64 D5 **Mucklestone** Staffs
52 B2 **Muckley** Shrops
80 G7 **Muckton** Lincs
19 L6 **Muddiford** Devon
15 Q8 **Muddles Green** E Susx
12 C6 **Mudeford** Dorset
22 D9 **Mudford** Somset
22 D9 **Mudford Sock** Somset
21 P4 **Mudgley** Somset
34 H8 **Mud Row** Kent
113 Q6 **Mugdock** Stirlg
134 H8 **Mugeary** Highld
65 P4 **Mugginton** Derbys
65 P3 **Muggintonlane End** Derbys
100 D8 **Muggleswick** Dur
140 H5 **Muirden** Abers
125 L5 **Muirdrum** Angus
140 H6 **Muiresk** Abers
124 G6 **Muirhead** Angus
124 F11 **Muirhead** Fife
114 C7 **Muirhead** N Lans
105 N4 **Muirkirk** E Ayrs
114 D4 **Muirmill** Stirlg
132 E2 **Muir of Fowlis** Abers
139 M4 **Muir of Miltonduff** Moray
137 P6 **Muir of Ord** Highld
128 G8 **Muirshearlich** Highld
141 N8 **Muirtack** Abers
123 N10 **Muirton** P & K
137 M5 **Muirton Mains** Highld
124 D4 **Muirton of Ardblair** P & K
90 E7 **Muker** N York
71 J12 **Mulbarton** Norfk
139 Q6 **Mulben** Moray
2 D7 **Mulfra** Cnwll
119 Q6 **Mull** Ag & B
19 K4 **Mullacott Cross** Devon
2 H10 **Mullion** Cnwll
2 G11 **Mullion Cove** Cnwll
81 K9 **Mumby** Lincs
52 C10 **Munderfield Row** Herefs
52 C10 **Munderfield Stocks** Herefs
71 L5 **Mundesley** Norfk

57 Q2 **Mundford** Norfk
59 L1 **Mundham** Norfk
46 F11 **Mundon Hill** Essex
16 F2 **Mundy Bois** Kent
98 D12 **Mungrisdale** Cumb
138 B5 **Munlochy** Highld
113 K11 **Munnoch** N Ayrs
41 K3 **Munsley** Herefs
51 N3 **Munslow** Shrops
8 C7 **Murchington** Devon
42 C4 **Murcot** Worcs
43 M8 **Murcott** Oxon
29 Q4 **Murcott** Wilts
151 L3 **Murkle** Highld
128 D6 **Murlaggan** Highld
25 N2 **Murrell Green** Hants
125 J6 **Murroes** Angus
68 G10 **Murrow** Cambs
44 B6 **Mursley** Bucks
34 G9 **Murston** Kent
125 J1 **Murthill** Angus
124 C5 **Murthly** P & K
86 C5 **Murton** C York
90 B2 **Murton** Cumb
101 K9 **Murton** Dur
101 J4 **Murton** N Tyne
117 L11 **Murton** Nthumb
9 P6 **Musbury** Devon
92 E10 **Muscoates** N York
115 Q7 **Musselburgh** E Loth
67 K5 **Muston** Leics
93 M10 **Muston** N York
52 F6 **Mustow Green** Worcs
33 K4 **Muswell Hill** Gt Lon
96 E8 **Mutehill** D & G
59 P3 **Mutford** Suffk
123 M9 **Muthill** P & K
9 J4 **Mutterton** Devon
64 D9 **Muxton** Wrekin
151 L6 **Mybster** Highld
39 J5 **Myddfai** Carmth
63 M7 **Myddle** Shrops
48 G9 **Mydroilyn** Cerdgn
83 L7 **Myerscough** Lancs
3 K7 **Mylor** Cnwll
3 K7 **Mylor Bridge** Cnwll
37 M4 **Mynachlog ddu** Pembks
74 G9 **Myndd-llan** Flints
51 L3 **Myndtown** Shrops
28 G3 **Mynydd-bach** Mons
26 G3 **Mynydd-Bach** Swans
49 M5 **Mynydd Buch** Cerdgn
38 C10 **Mynyddgarreg** Carmth
75 J11 **Mynydd Isa** Flints
73 K10 **Mynydd Llandygai** Gwynd
60 E6 **Mynytho** Gwynd
132 H4 **Myrebird** Abers
107 P10 **Myredykes** Border
32 C11 **Mytchett** Surrey
84 E9 **Mytholm** Calder
84 F10 **Mytholmroyd** Calder
83 J8 **Mythop** Lancs
85 N2 **Myton-on-Swale** N York

## N

143 M8 **Naast** Highld
83 N9 **Nab's Head** Lancs
152 d5 **Na Buirgh** W Isls
86 B6 **Naburn** C York
84 H7 **Nab Wood Crematorium** C Brad
17 J2 **Naccolt** Kent
35 L11 **Nackington** Kent
47 M4 **Nacton** Suffk
87 K3 **Nafferton** E R Yk
29 P3 **Nag's Head** Gloucs
41 K8 **Nailbridge** Gloucs
21 K7 **Nailsbourne** Somset
28 G8 **Nailsea** N Som
66 C10 **Nailstone** Leics
29 N2 **Nailsworth** Gloucs
138 G5 **Nairn** Highld
15 J2 **Nalderswood** Surrey
2 G8 **Nancegollan** Cnwll
2 D7 **Nancledra** Cnwll
60 D6 **Nanhoron** Gwynd
74 G9 **Nannerch** Flints
66 E8 **Nanpantan** Leics
3 N3 **Nanpean** Cnwll
2 B8 **Nanquidno** Cnwll
6 F11 **Nanstallon** Cnwll
39 N8 **Nant-ddu** Powys
48 F9 **Nanternis** Cerdgn
38 D7 **Nantgaredig** Carmth
27 Q5 **Nantgarw** Rhondd
50 D7 **Nant-glas** Powys
74 D11 **Nantglyn** Denbgs
50 D5 **Nantgwyn** Powys
61 L2 **Nant Gwynant** Gwynd
60 H2 **Nantlle** Gwynd
63 J7 **Nantmawr** Shrops
50 E7 **Nantmel** Powys
61 K3 **Nantmor** Gwynd
73 K12 **Nant Peris** Gwynd
64 C2 **Nantwich** Ches E
39 Q9 **Nant-y-Bwch** Blae G
38 C8 **Nant-y-caws** Carmth
40 D10 **Nant-y-derry** Mons
27 K4 **Nantyffyllon** Brdgnd
40 B9 **Nantyglo** Blae G
62 H6 **Nant-y-gollen** Shrops
27 M4 **Nant-y-moel** Brdgnd
73 M9 **Nant-y-pandy** Conwy
32 B3 **Naphill** Bucks
52 F11 **Napleton** Worcs
84 C4 **Nappa** N York
54 D8 **Napton on the Hill** Warwks
37 L7 **Narberth** Pembks
54 E1 **Narborough** Leics
69 P9 **Narborough** Norfk
4 E5 **Narkurs** Cnwll
60 H2 **Nasareth** Gwynd
54 H5 **Naseby** Nhants
43 Q5 **Nash** Bucks
33 M9 **Nash** Gt Lon
51 K8 **Nash** Herefs
28 D5 **Nash** Newpt
51 Q6 **Nash** Shrops
52 E4 **Nash End** Worcs
44 B10 **Nash Lee** Bucks
25 L4 **Nash's Green** Hants
34 B8 **Nash Street** Kent
55 Q1 **Nassington** Nhants
41 M10 **Nastend** Gloucs
45 L7 **Nasty** Herts
90 C5 **Nateby** Cumb
83 L6 **Nateby** Lancs
65 M9 **National Memorial Arboretum** Staffs
66 F10 **National Space Science Centre** C Leic
89 N9 **Natland** Cumb
58 F10 **Naughton** Suffk
42 D7 **Naunton** Gloucs
41 P4 **Naunton** Worcs
52 H10 **Naunton Beauchamp** Worcs
79 N12 **Navenby** Lincs
33 P3 **Navestock** Essex
33 Q3 **Navestock Side** Essex
147 J2 **Navidale House Hotel** Highld
138 E3 **Navity** Highld
92 D9 **Nawton** N York
46 H5 **Nayland** Suffk
45 M10 **Nazeing** Essex
45 M10 **Nazeing Gate** Essex
12 C5 **Neacroft** Hants
53 Q4 **Neal's Green** Warwks
152 t6 **Neap** Shet
65 K3 **Near Cotton** Staffs
89 K7 **Near Sawrey** Cumb
33 J5 **Neasden** Gt Lon
91 N5 **Neasham** Darltn
26 H3 **Neath** Neath
25 M5 **Neatham** Hants
71 L8 **Neatishead** Norfk
49 J7 **Nebo** Cerdgn
61 P1 **Nebo** Conwy
60 H2 **Nebo** Gwynd
72 H5 **Nebo** IoA
70 C10 **Necton** Norfk
148 D10 **Nedd** Highld
100 G2 **Nedderton** Nthumb
58 E11 **Nedging** Suffk
58 F10 **Nedging Tye** Suffk
59 J4 **Needham** Norfk
58 G9 **Needham Market** Suffk
57 N7 **Needham Street** Suffk
56 G6 **Needingworth** Cambs
52 C5 **Neen Savage** Shrops
52 C6 **Neen Sollars** Shrops
52 B3 **Neenton** Shrops
60 E4 **Nefyn** Gwynd
113 P10 **Neilston** E Rens
27 Q3 **Nelson** Caerph
84 C7 **Nelson** Lancs
105 Q1 **Nemphlar** S Lans
28 H10 **Nempnett Thrubwell** BaNES
99 L9 **Nenthall** Cumb
99 M9 **Nenthead** Cumb
107 R2 **Nenthorn** Border
8 E5 **Neopardy** Devon
15 J8 **Nep Town** W Susx
74 H11 **Nercwys** Flints
110 F10 **Nereabolls** Ag & B
114 B10 **Nerston** S Lans
108 F3 **Nesbit** Nthumb
84 G5 **Nesfield** N York
75 J8 **Ness** Ches W
75 J8 **Ness Botanic Gardens** Ches W
63 L8 **Nesscliffe** Shrops
75 J8 **Neston** Ches W
29 P8 **Neston** Wilts
52 B2 **Netchwood** Shrops
76 F8 **Nether Alderley** Ches E
23 P4 **Netheravon** Wilts
107 N1 **Nether Blainslie** Border
141 J4 **Netherbrae** Abers
66 H7 **Nether Broughton** Leics
114 E11 **Netherburn** S Lans
10 D5 **Netherbury** Dorset
98 E4 **Netherby** Cumb
85 M6 **Netherby** N York
10 G5 **Nether Cerne** Dorset
97 M1 **Nethercleuch** D & G
22 D10 **Nether Compton** Dorset
54 E8 **Nethercote** Warwks
7 L5 **Nethercott** Devon
19 J5 **Nethercott** Devon
141 K11 **Nether Crimond** Abers
139 Q3 **Nether Dallachy** Moray
29 J2 **Netherend** Gloucs
8 H5 **Nether Exe** Devon
16 C7 **Netherfield** E Susx
66 F9 **Netherfield** Leics
66 G4 **Netherfield** Notts
106 B7 **Nether Fingland** S Lans
79 J4 **Nethergate** N Linc
70 F6 **Nethergate** Norfk
23 P7 **Netherhampton** Wilts
78 C8 **Nether Handley** Derbys
124 G4 **Nether Handwick** Angus
78 C4 **Nether Haugh** Rothm
10 C4 **Netherhay** Dorset
79 J8 **Nether Headon** Notts
66 B2 **Nether Heage** Derbys
54 H9 **Nether Heyford** Nhants
106 D7 **Nether Howcleugh** S Lans
83 L2 **Nether Kellet** Lancs
141 P7 **Nether Kinmundy** Abers
65 L6 **Netherland Green** Staffs
78 E9 **Nether Langwith** Notts
96 F9 **Netherlaw** D & G
133 K6 **Netherley** Abers
106 D12 **Nethermill** D & G
141 L7 **Nethermuir** Abers
33 K11 **Netherne-on-the-Hill** Surrey
84 H11 **Netheroyd Hill** Kirk
77 N8 **Nether Padley** Derbys
113 P10 **Netherplace** E Rens
85 R4 **Nether Poppleton** C York
98 C10 **Nether Row** Cumb
65 P9 **Netherseal** Derbys
91 Q8 **Nether Silton** N York
51 J6 **Nether Skyborry** Shrops
21 K5 **Nether Stowey** Somset
45 Q9 **Nether Street** Essex
29 R9 **Netherstreet** Wilts
77 L2 **Netherthong** Kirk
78 D9 **Netherthorpe** Derbys
125 L1 **Netherton** Angus
8 G10 **Netherton** Devon
52 H3 **Netherton** Dudley
30 H10 **Netherton** Hants
40 H6 **Netherton** Herefs
77 L1 **Netherton** Kirk
114 E10 **Netherton** N Lans
108 F8 **Netherton** Nthumb
31 J2 **Netherton** Oxon
124 C2 **Netherton** P & K
52 D4 **Netherton** Shrops
113 Q5 **Netherton** Stirlg
85 L11 **Netherton** Wakefd
42 A3 **Netherton** Worcs
88 C5 **Nethertown** Cumb
151 Q1 **Nethertown** Highld
83 Q8 **Nethertown** Lancs
65 L8 **Nethertown** Staffs
115 K12 **Netherurd** Border
24 E6 **Nether Wallop** Hants
88 F6 **Nether Wasdale** Cumb
98 D9 **Nether Welton** Cumb
42 E7 **Nether Westcote** Gloucs
53 N2 **Nether Whitacre** Warwks
105 Q6 **Nether Whitecleuch** S Lans
43 Q9 **Nether Winchendon** Bucks
108 H11 **Netherwitton** Nthumb
139 J11 **Nethy Bridge** Highld
12 G3 **Netley** Hants
24 E10 **Netley Marsh** Hants
31 P5 **Nettlebed** Oxon
22 E4 **Nettlebridge** Somset
10 D6 **Nettlecombe** Dorset
13 J9 **Nettlecombe** IoW
44 E9 **Nettleden** Herts
79 P8 **Nettleham** Lincs
34 B12 **Nettlestead** Kent
34 B12 **Nettlestead Green** Kent
13 K6 **Nettlestone** IoW
100 H8 **Nettlesworth** Dur
80 B4 **Nettleton** Lincs
29 N6 **Nettleton** Wilts
29 N7 **Nettleton Shrub** Wilts
5 J7 **Netton** Devon
23 P6 **Netton** Wilts
38 G7 **Neuadd** Carmth
50 C5 **Neuadd-ddu** Powys
34 D4 **Nevendon** Essex
37 L3 **Nevern** Pembks
55 K2 **Nevill Holt** Leics
97 K5 **New Abbey** D & G
141 L3 **New Aberdour** Abers
33 M9 **New Addington** Gt Lon
85 J6 **Newall** Leeds
25 K7 **New Alresford** Hants
124 E3 **New Alyth** P & K
68 D12 **Newark** C Pete
152 n2 **Newark** Ork
67 K1 **Newark-on-Trent** Notts
87 J6 **New Arram** E R Yk
114 E9 **Newarthill** N Lans
33 R9 **New Ash Green** Kent
67 K2 **New Balderton** Notts
17 L3 **Newbarn** Kent
34 A8 **New Barn** Kent
33 K3 **New Barnet** Gt Lon
55 L8 **New Barton** Nhants
115 P8 **Newbattle** Mdloth
108 H6 **New Bewick** Nthumb
97 N5 **Newbie** D & G
82 G1 **Newbiggin** Cumb
88 E8 **Newbiggin** Cumb
89 Q1 **Newbiggin** Cumb
98 F12 **Newbiggin** Cumb
98 H8 **Newbiggin** Cumb
90 E1 **Newbiggin** Dur
100 F8 **Newbiggin** Dur
90 F8 **Newbiggin** N York
90 G9 **Newbiggin** N York
109 M12 **Newbiggin-by-the-Sea** Nthumb
124 F4 **Newbigging** Angus
124 H5 **Newbigging** Angus
125 K5 **Newbigging** Angus
115 J12 **Newbigging** S Lans
90 B6 **Newbiggin-on-Lune** Cumb
54 D5 **New Bilton** Warwks
78 B9 **Newbold** Derbys
66 C8 **Newbold** Leics
54 D5 **Newbold on Avon** Warwks
42 F2 **Newbold on Stour** Warwks
53 P9 **Newbold Pacey** Warwks
54 D4 **Newbold Revel** Warwks
66 D11 **Newbold Verdon** Leics
80 F12 **New Bolingbroke** Lincs
68 D11 **Newborough** C Pete
72 G10 **Newborough** IoA
65 L7 **Newborough** Staffs
43 L4 **Newbottle** Nhants
101 J8 **Newbottle** Sundld
79 N9 **New Boultham** Lincs
47 N3 **Newbourne** Suffk
44 B3 **New Bradwell** M Keyn
78 B9 **New Brampton** Derbys
100 G10 **New Brancepeth** Dur
115 L7 **Newbridge** C Edin
28 B3 **Newbridge** Caerph
48 H9 **Newbridge** Cerdgn
2 C8 **Newbridge** Cnwll
3 K6 **Newbridge** Cnwll
97 J2 **Newbridge** D & G
24 E10 **Newbridge** Hants
12 G7 **Newbridge** IoW
92 G9 **New Bridge** N York
31 J2 **Newbridge** Oxon
63 J4 **Newbridge** Wrexhm
41 N4 **Newbridge Green** Worcs
28 E3 **Newbridge-on-Usk** Mons
50 D9 **Newbridge on Wye** Powys
75 J10 **New Brighton** Flints
75 K5 **New Brighton** Wirral
66 D2 **New Brinsley** Notts
92 E3 **New Brotton** R & Cl
99 N5 **Newbrough** Nthumb
63 K2 **New Broughton** Wrexhm
58 G3 **New Buckenham** Norfk
8 E4 **Newbuildings** Devon
141 M4 **Newburgh** Abers
141 N10 **Newburgh** Abers
124 E9 **Newburgh** Fife
75 N2 **Newburgh** Lancs
92 B11 **Newburgh Priory** N York
100 F5 **Newburn** N u Ty
76 D3 **New Bury** Bolton
22 F3 **Newbury** Somset
31 K9 **Newbury** W Berk
22 H5 **Newbury** Wilts
33 N5 **Newbury Park** Gt Lon
89 P2 **Newby** Cumb
84 B6 **Newby** Lancs
83 Q1 **Newby** N York
92 A4 **Newby** N York
93 K8 **Newby** N York
89 K9 **Newby Bridge** Cumb
98 D7 **Newby Cross** Cumb
98 F6 **Newby East** Cumb
89 P2 **Newby Head** Cumb
141 K5 **New Byth** Abers
98 D7 **Newby West** Cumb
91 N9 **Newby Wiske** N York
40 F8 **Newcastle** Mons
50 H4 **Newcastle** Shrops
100 F4 *Newcastle Airport* Nthumb
37 Q2 **Newcastle Emlyn** Carmth
107 M12 **Newcastleton** Border
64 F3 **Newcastle-under-Lyme** Staffs
100 G5 **Newcastle upon Tyne** N u Ty
37 P3 **Newchapel** Pembks
64 F1 **Newchapel** Staffs
15 L2 **Newchapel** Surrey
40 A9 **Newchurch** Blae G
51 K10 **Newchurch** Herefs
13 J7 **Newchurch** IoW
17 J4 **Newchurch** Kent
28 F3 **Newchurch** Mons
50 H10 **Newchurch** Powys
65 L7 **Newchurch** Staffs
84 B7 **Newchurch in Pendle** Lancs
71 J10 **New Costessey** Norfk
97 M9 **New Cowper** Cumb
115 P7 **Newcraighall** C Edin
85 M11 **New Crofton** Wakefd
49 L5 **New Cross** Cerdgn
33 L7 **New Cross** Gt Lon
21 P9 **New Cross** Somset
105 L7 **New Cumnock** E Ayrs
16 E7 **New Cut** E Susx
141 L6 **New Deer** Abers
100 H2 **New Delaval** Nthumb
77 J2 **New Delph** Oldham
32 F5 **New Denham** Bucks
14 H2 **Newdigate** Surrey
54 H8 **New Duston** Nhants
86 B4 **New Earswick** C York
66 D3 **New Eastwood** Notts
78 E4 **New Edlington** Donc
139 N3 **New Elgin** Moray
87 M7 **New Ellerby** E R Yk
32 C8 **Newell Green** Br For
33 N8 **New Eltham** Gt Lon
53 K8 **New End** Worcs
16 E5 **Newenden** Kent
68 D12 **New England** C Pete
46 C3 **New England** Essex
41 L6 **Newent** Gloucs
85 K9 **New Farnley** Leeds
75 K6 **New Ferry** Wirral
100 G11 **Newfield** Dur
100 G8 **Newfield** Dur
146 D9 **Newfield** Highld
56 D1 **New Fletton** C Pete
12 D3 **New Forest National Park**
25 K3 **Newfound** Hants
85 P10 **New Fryston** Wakefd
36 G6 **Newgale** Pembks
96 D3 **New Galloway** D & G
70 F4 **Newgate** Norfk
45 K10 **Newgate Street** Herts
125 J11 **New Gilston** Fife
2 b1 **New Grimsby** IoS
63 Q3 **Newhall** Ches E
65 P8 **Newhall** Derbys
109 K4 **Newham** Nthumb
100 H3 **New Hartley** Nthumb
115 N6 **Newhaven** C Edin
77 M11 **Newhaven** Derbys
15 N10 **Newhaven** E Susx
32 F9 **New Haw** Surrey
37 M10 **New Hedges** Pembks
101 J7 **New Herrington** Sundld
76 H1 **Newhey** Rochdl
70 C4 **New Holkham** Norfk
87 K10 **New Holland** N Linc
92 H5 **Newholm** N York
78 E10 **New Houghton** Derbys
69 Q6 **New Houghton** Norfk
114 E9 **Newhouse** N Lans
90 C12 **New Houses** N York
75 P3 **New Houses** Wigan
89 P8 **New Hutton** Cumb
34 C10 **New Hythe** Kent
15 M6 **Newick** E Susx
17 K4 **Newingreen** Kent
17 L3 **Newington** Kent
34 F9 **Newington** Kent
31 M3 **Newington** Oxon
51 M4 **Newington** Shrops
29 N3 **Newington Bagpath** Gloucs
38 C4 **New Inn** Carmth
28 D2 **New Inn** Torfn
51 J5 **New Invention** Shrops
71 J10 **New Lakenham** Norfk
106 A1 **New Lanark** S Lans
87 K9 **Newland** C KuH
89 J10 **Newland** Cumb
86 E9 **Newland** E R Yk
40 H9 **Newland** Gloucs
86 C10 **Newland** N York
42 H9 **Newland** Oxon
20 C6 **Newland** Somset
52 E11 **Newland** Worcs
115 Q9 **Newlandrig** Mdloth
107 M11 **Newlands** Border
98 D10 **Newlands** Cumb
100 E7 **Newlands** Nthumb
139 P6 **Newlands of Dundurcas** Moray
75 M1 **New Lane** Lancs
76 B5 **New Lane End** Warrtn
98 D1 **New Langholm** D & G
80 H12 **New Leake** Lincs
141 N5 **New Leeds** Abers
78 B2 **New Lodge** Barns
83 L10 **New Longton** Lancs
94 H5 **New Luce** D & G
2 D9 **Newlyn** Cnwll
3 K3 **Newlyn East** Cnwll
141 L12 **Newmachar** Abers
114 E10 **Newmains** N Lans
33 J8 **New Malden** Gt Lon
45 P9 **Newman's End** Essex
46 F3 **Newman's Green** Suffk
57 M8 **Newmarket** Suffk
152 f3 **Newmarket** W Isls
92 C2 **New Marske** R & Cl
43 L10 **New Marston** Oxon
63 K5 **New Marton** Shrops
133 J7 **New Mill** Abers
107 L7 **Newmill** Border
2 D7 **New Mill** Cnwll
44 C9 **New Mill** Herts
77 M2 **New Mill** Kirk
140 C5 **Newmill** Moray
85 L12 **Newmillerdam** Wakefd
132 C12 **Newmill of Inshewan** Angus
115 L8 **Newmills** C Edin
3 L4 **New Mills** Cnwll
77 J6 **New Mills** Derbys
115 J4 **Newmills** Fife
40 G10 **Newmills** Mons
62 F12 **New Mills** Powys
124 C7 **Newmiln** P & K
105 K2 **Newmilns** E Ayrs
12 D6 **New Milton** Hants
47 K5 **New Mistley** Essex
37 L5 **New Moat** Pembks
63 L5 **Newnes** Shrops
46 B10 **Newney Green** Essex
41 L9 **Newnham** Gloucs
25 M3 **Newnham** Hants
45 J4 **Newnham** Herts
34 G11 **Newnham** Kent
54 F9 **Newnham** Nhants
52 B7 **Newnham** Worcs
78 H10 **New Ollerton** Notts
53 L2 **New Oscott** Birm
141 L5 **New Pitsligo** Abers
6 D9 **New Polzeath** Cnwll
7 L7 **Newport** Cnwll
11 L6 **Newport** Dorset
86 F9 **Newport** E R Yk
45 P5 **Newport** Essex
29 L3 **Newport** Gloucs
151 L11 **Newport** Highld
12 H7 **Newport** IoW
28 D5 **Newport** Newpt
71 P8 **Newport** Norfk
37 L3 **Newport** Pembks
64 D8 **Newport** Wrekin
124 H7 **Newport-on-Tay** Fife
44 B3 **Newport Pagnell** M Keyn
44 B3 **Newport Pagnell Services** M Keyn
14 F5 **Newpound Common** W Susx
104 F5 **New Prestwick** S Ayrs
48 F8 **New Quay** Cerdgn
3 K2 **Newquay** Cnwll
46 H7 **New Quay** Essex
3 L2 *Newquay Airport* Cnwll
71 K9 **New Rackheath** Norfk
50 H8 **New Radnor** Powys
98 F11 **New Rent** Cumb
100 D6 **New Ridley** Nthumb
84 E6 **New Road Side** N York
17 J6 **New Romney** Kent
78 G4 **New Rossington** Donc
49 M6 **New Row** Cerdgn
83 P7 **New Row** Lancs
114 G2 **New Sauchie** Clacks
76 F10 **Newsbank** Ches E
140 H9 **Newseat** Abers
83 L8 **Newsham** Lancs
91 J5 **Newsham** N York
91 P10 **Newsham** N York
100 H2 **Newsham** Nthumb
85 M11 **New Sharlston** Wakefd
86 D9 **Newsholme** E R Yk
84 C5 **Newsholme** Lancs
109 K3 **New Shoreston** Nthumb
101 K7 **New Silksworth** Sundld
92 D3 **New Skelton** R & Cl
84 H12 **Newsome** Kirk
67 M5 **New Somerby** Lincs
33 K4 **New Southgate Crematorium** Gt Lon
75 Q2 **New Springs** Wigan
107 N3 **Newstead** Border
66 E2 **Newstead** Notts
109 J4 **Newstead** Nthumb
114 D9 **New Stevenston** N Lans
51 K9 **New Street** Herefs
66 C9 **New Swannington** Leics
85 P8 **Newthorpe** N York
66 D3 **Newthorpe** Notts
34 D4 **New Thundersley** Essex
15 K8 **Newtimber** W Susx
79 P6 **Newtoft** Lincs
112 F2 **Newton** Ag & B
107 P5 **Newton** Border
27 K7 **Newton** Brdgnd
45 J3 **Newton** C Beds
56 H10 **Newton** Cambs
68 H9 **Newton** Cambs
28 B6 **Newton** Cardif
75 L10 **Newton** Ches W
75 N11 **Newton** Ches W
75 N8 **Newton** Ches W
88 H12 **Newton** Cumb
78 D11 **Newton** Derbys
40 D5 **Newton** Herefs
51 L7 **Newton** Herefs
51 N10 **Newton** Herefs
137 Q6 **Newton** Highld
138 D6 **Newton** Highld
138 E3 **Newton** Highld
151 Q6 **Newton** Highld
82 H8 **Newton** Lancs
89 P11 **Newton** Lancs
67 P5 **Newton** Lincs
115 P7 **Newton** Mdloth
139 M3 **Newton** Moray
139 Q3 **Newton** Moray
92 H12 **Newton** N York
55 L4 **Newton** Nhants
70 B9 **Newton** Norfk
66 H4 **Newton** Notts
100 D5 **Newton** Nthumb
108 F8 **Newton** Nthumb
106 B3 **Newton** S Lans
114 C9 **Newton** S Lans
53 J2 **Newton** Sandw
63 M5 **Newton** Shrops
20 H6 **Newton** Somset
65 J7 **Newton** Staffs
46 G3 **Newton** Suffk
115 K6 **Newton** W Loth
54 E5 **Newton** Warwks
24 C9 **Newton** Wilts
8 F10 **Newton Abbot** Devon
97 P7 **Newton Arlosh** Cumb
91 M2 **Newton Aycliffe** Dur
91 Q1 **Newton Bewley** Hartpl
55 M10 **Newton Blossomville** M Keyn
55 P7 **Newton Bromswold** Nhants
66 B10 **Newton Burgoland** Leics
109 L5 **Newton-by-the-Sea** Nthumb
79 P6 **Newton by Toft** Lincs
4 E3 **Newton Ferrers** Cnwll
5 J7 **Newton Ferrers** Devon
152 c6 **Newton Ferry** W Isls
59 J1 **Newton Flotman** Norfk
115 P8 **Newtongrange** Mdloth
28 G4 **Newton Green** Mons
54 G1 **Newton Harcourt** Leics
76 G4 **Newton Heath** Manch
133 L5 **Newtonhill** Abers
85 L10 **Newton Hill** Wakefd
83 Q5 **Newton-in-Bowland** Lancs
85 P6 **Newton Kyme** N York
91 L9 **Newton-le-Willows** N York
75 Q4 **Newton-le-Willows** St Hel
115 P8 **Newtonloan** Mdloth
44 B5 **Newton Longville** Bucks
113 Q10 **Newton Mearns** E Rens
132 F11 **Newtonmill** Angus
130 C4 **Newtonmore** Highld
91 L5 **Newton Morrell** N York
37 J9 **Newton Mountain** Pembks
92 F4 **Newton Mulgrave** N York
124 D10 **Newton of Balcanquhal** P & K
125 K12 **Newton of Balcormo** Fife
85 Q3 **Newton on Ouse** N York
92 G8 **Newton-on-Rawcliffe** N York
63 N7 **Newton on the Hill** Shrops
109 K8 **Newton-on-the-Moor** Nthumb
79 L9 **Newton on Trent** Lincs
9 L7 **Newton Poppleford** Devon
43 N5 **Newton Purcell** Oxon
65 P10 **Newton Regis** Warwks
98 F12 **Newton Reigny** Cumb
8 G5 **Newton St Cyres** Devon
71 J8 **Newton St Faith** Norfk
29 L9 **Newton St Loe** BaNES
18 H11 **Newton St Petrock** Devon
65 P7 **Newton Solney** Derbys
24 G5 **Newton Stacey** Hants
95 M5 **Newton Stewart** D & G
24 C5 **Newton Tony** Wilts
19 K8 **Newton Tracey** Devon
92 B4 **Newton under Roseberry** R & Cl
100 F1 **Newton Underwood** Nthumb
86 D5 **Newton upon Derwent** E R Yk
25 M7 **Newton Valence** Hants
106 E10 **Newton Wamphray** D & G
83 K9 **Newton with Scales** Lancs
40 A9 **Newtown** Blae G
75 N8 **Newtown** Ches W
2 F8 **Newtown** Cnwll
7 K9 **Newtown** Cnwll
89 N2 **Newtown** Cumb
97 M8 **Newtown** Cumb
98 E6 **Newtown** Cumb
98 G6 **Newtown** Cumb
105 P8 **Newtown** D & G
77 J7 **Newtown** Derbys
9 K5 **Newtown** Devon
19 P8 **Newtown** Devon
10 D4 **Newtown** Dorset
11 N3 **New Town** Dorset
23 L10 **New Town** Dorset
23 L9 **New Town** Dorset
15 N7 **New Town** E Susx
41 K11 **Newtown** Gloucs
12 D3 **Newtown** Hants
25 K10 **Newtown** Hants
31 K9 **Newtown** Hants
40 H5 **Newtown** Herefs
41 J3 **Newtown** Herefs
41 L4 **Newtown** Herefs
51 N9 **Newtown** Herefs
129 L3 **Newtown** Highld
12 G6 **Newtown** IoW
83 L11 **Newtown** Lancs
55 N5 **New Town** Nhants
108 F3 **Newtown** Nthumb
108 G5 **Newtown** Nthumb
108 G9 **Newtown** Nthumb
11 P6 **Newtown** Poole
50 F2 **Newtown** Powys
27 P3 **Newtown** Rhondd
63 M8 **Newtown** Shrops
63 N6 **Newtown** Shrops
21 L10 **Newtown** Somset
65 J11 **Newtown** Staffs
76 G11 **Newtown** Staffs
75 P3 **Newtown** Wigan
23 K7 **Newtown** Wilts
30 G8 **New Town** Wilts
30 G9 **Newtown** Wilts
52 G9 **Newtown** Worcs
52 H5 **Newtown** Worcs
3 J10 **Newtown-in-St Martin** Cnwll
66 E10 **Newtown Linford** Leics
113 M9 **Newtown of Beltrees** Rens
107 P3 **Newtown St Boswells** Border
66 E11 **Newtown Unthank** Leics
39 Q11 **New Tredegar** Caerph
105 Q2 **New Trows** S Lans
78 C10 **New Tupton** Derbys
124 F5 **Newtyle** Angus
69 J10 **New Walsoken** Cambs
80 F3 **New Waltham** NE Lin
78 C8 **New Whittington** Derbys
116 B7 **New Winton** E Loth
42 H9 **New Yatt** Oxon
32 F5 **Newyears Green** Gt Lon
120 H10 **Newyork** Ag & B
68 E1 **New York** Lincs
101 J4 **New York** N Tyne
85 J3 **New York** N York
51 K9 **Nextend** Herefs
37 J9 **Neyland** Pembks
102 b6 **Niarbyl** IoM
41 K10 **Nibley** Gloucs
29 L6 **Nibley** S Glos
29 L3 **Nibley Green** Gloucs
20 H10 **Nicholashayne** Devon
26 D5 **Nicholaston** Swans
98 G5 **Nickies Hill** Cumb
85 L3 **Nidd** N York
133 M4 **Nigg** C Aber
146 E10 **Nigg** Highld
146 E11 **Nigg Ferry** Highld
29 M8 **Nimlet** BaNES
99 M7 **Ninebanks** Nthumb
30 C5 **Nine Elms** Swindn
36 F5 **Nine Wells** Pembks
16 C8 **Ninfield** E Susx
12 F7 **Ningwood** IoW
107 Q5 **Nisbet** Border
116 H11 **Nisbet Hill** Border
12 H9 **Niton** IoW
113 P9 **Nitshill** C Glas
33 Q10 **Noah's Ark** Kent
34 C4 **Noak Bridge** Essex
33 P3 **Noak Hill** Gt Lon
77 P3 **Noblethorpe** Barns
63 M10 **Nobold** Shrops
54 H8 **Nobottle** Nhants
79 Q11 **Nocton** Lincs
71 M12 **Nogdam End** Norfk
43 L9 **Noke** Oxon
36 G7 **Nolton** Pembks
36 G7 **Nolton Haven** Pembks
63 N3 **No Man's Heath** Ches W
65 P10 **No Man's Heath** Warwks
4 D5 **No Man's Land** Cnwll
20 C10 **Nomansland** Devon
24 D10 **Nomansland** Wilts
63 N6 **Noneley** Shrops
35 N11 **Nonington** Kent
89 N10 **Nook** Cumb
98 F2 **Nook** Cumb
32 H8 **Norbiton** Gt Lon
82 H7 **Norbreck** Bpool
41 L3 **Norbridge** Herefs
63 P3 **Norbury** Ches E
65 L4 **Norbury** Derbys
33 K8 **Norbury** Gt Lon
51 L2 **Norbury** Shrops
64 E7 **Norbury** Staffs
63 P2 **Norbury Common** Ches E
64 E7 **Norbury Junction** Staffs
52 F7 **Norchard** Worcs
75 Q7 **Norcott Brook** Ches W
82 H7 **Norcross** Lancs
69 K12 **Nordelph** Norfk
84 C12 **Norden** Rochdl
52 C1 **Nordley** Shrops
71 P10 **Norfolk Broads** Norfk
117 K11 **Norham** Nthumb
84 G10 **Norland Town** Calder
75 P9 **Norley** Ches W
12 F5 **Norleywood** Hants
15 N8 **Norlington** E Susx
79 P6 **Normanby** Lincs
86 G12 **Normanby** N Linc
92 E10 **Normanby** N York
92 B3 **Normanby** R & Cl
80 C5 **Normanby le Wold** Lincs
56 C2 **Norman Cross** Cambs
32 D12 **Normandy** Surrey
16 B9 **Norman's Bay** E Susx
9 K4 **Norman's Green** Devon
65 Q5 **Normanton** C Derb
67 K4 **Normanton** Leics
67 N3 **Normanton** Lincs
66 H1 **Normanton** Notts
67 M11 **Normanton** Rutlnd
85 M10 **Normanton** Wakefd
23 P5 **Normanton** Wilts
66 B9 **Normanton le Heath** Leics
66 E7 **Normanton on Soar** Notts
66 G5 **Normanton on the Wolds** Notts
79 K10 **Normanton on Trent** Notts
82 H7 **Normoss** Lancs
14 D2 **Norney** Surrey
29 P9 **Norrington Common** Wilts
4 F3 **Norris Green** Cnwll
75 L5 **Norris Green** Lpool
65 Q9 **Norris Hill** Leics
85 J10 **Norristhorpe** Kirk
58 E1 **Northacre** Norfk
44 D7 **Northall** Bucks
91 N8 **Northallerton** N York
70 E9 **Northall Green** Norfk
24 G11 **Northam** C Sotn
19 J7 **Northam** Devon
55 J8 **Northampton** Nhants
52 F7 **Northampton** Worcs
78 E7 **North Anston** Rothm
32 C8 **North Ascot** Br For
43 K6 **North Aston** Oxon
45 K11 **Northaw** Herts
9 P3 **Northay** Somset
24 F9 **North Baddesley** Hants
128 E12 **North Ballachulish** Highld
22 E7 **North Barrow** Somset
70 D5 **North Barsham** Norfk
34 D4 **North Benfleet** Essex
14 C10 **North Bersted** W Susx
116 D4 **North Berwick** E Loth
100 F11 **North Bitchburn** Dur
101 J2 **North Blyth** Nthumb
13 K3 **North Boarhunt** Hants
12 B5 **North Bockhampton** Dorset
68 C10 **Northborough** C Pete
35 P12 **Northbourne** Kent
8 D8 **North Bovey** Devon
23 J2 **North Bradley** Wilts
7 P8 **North Brentor** Devon
22 G6 **North Brewham** Somset
14 D3 **North Bridge** Surrey
16 C6 **Northbridge Street** E Susx
24 H5 **Northbrook** Hants
43 K7 **Northbrook** Oxon
45 K3 **North Brook End** Cambs
19 J5 **North Buckland** Devon
71 M10 **North Burlingham** Norfk
22 E8 **North Cadbury** Somset
79 N8 **North Carlton** Lincs
78 F7 **North Carlton** Notts
86 G8 **North Cave** E R Yk
42 B10 **North Cerney** Gloucs
15 M6 **North Chailey** E Susx
14 D5 **Northchapel** W Susx
24 C9 **North Charford** Hants
109 K5 **North Charlton** Nthumb
33 J9 **North Cheam** Gt Lon
22 F8 **North Cheriton** Somset
10 C6 **North Chideock** Dorset
44 D10 **Northchurch** Herts
86 G8 **North Cliffe** E R Yk
79 K9 **North Clifton** Notts
100 H11 **North Close** Dur
80 G5 **North Cockerington** Lincs
120 G6 **North Connel** Ag & B
27 K6 **North Cornelly** Brdgnd
3 J10 **North Corner** Cnwll
80 G4 **North Cotes** Lincs
7 L6 **Northcott** Devon
9 L3 **Northcott** Devon
20 H10 **Northcott** Devon
2 H6 **North Country** Cnwll
31 K3 **Northcourt** Oxon
59 P3 **North Cove** Suffk
91 M6 **North Cowton** N York
44 C3 **North Crawley** M Keyn
33 N8 **North Cray** Gt Lon
70 C4 **North Creake** Norfk
21 M8 **North Curry** Somset
86 H5 **North Dalton** E R Yk
85 N5 **North Deighton** N York
19 K7 **North Devon Crematorium** Devon
35 Q8 **Northdown** Kent
34 G11 **North Downs**
86 C8 **North Duffield** N York
142 D10 **North Duntulm** Highld
33 J9 **North East Surrey Crematorium** Gt Lon
78 B10 **Northedge** Derbys
17 L2 **North Elham** Kent
80 F5 **North Elkington** Lincs
70 E8 **North Elmham** Norfk
78 D1 **North Elmsall** Wakefd
31 Q4 **Northend** Bucks
13 L4 **North End** C Port
98 C6 **North End** Cumb
23 J8 **North End** Dorset
87 M7 **North End** E R Yk
87 P9 **North End** E R Yk
46 B8 **North End** Essex
23 N10 **North End** Hants
25 K7 **North End** Hants
66 F9 **North End** Leics
68 E4 **North End** Lincs
79 P4 **North End** Lincs
80 F3 **North End** Lincs
80 H6 **North End** Lincs
87 L10 **North End** N Linc
28 F9 **North End** N Som
55 N7 **North End** Nhants
58 E2 **North End** Norfk
109 J9 **North End** Nthumb
75 J3 **North End** Sefton
14 D10 **North End** W Susx
14 G9 **North End** W Susx
54 C10 **Northend** Warwks
76 F6 **Northenden** Manch
32 C4 **Northend Woods** Bucks
143 K9 **North Erradale** Highld
66 G11 **North Evington** C Leic
34 E3 **North Fambridge** Essex
87 J10 **North Ferriby** E R Yk
53 J5 **Northfield** Birm
133 L3 **Northfield** C Aber
87 J10 **Northfield** E R Yk
67 P10 **Northfields** Lincs
34 B7 **Northfleet** Kent
87 L5 **North Frodingham** E R Yk
12 B2 **North Gorley** Hants
59 J3 **North Green** Norfk
59 L8 **North Green** Suffk
59 M7 **North Green** Suffk
79 P9 **North Greetwell** Lincs
86 F2 **North Grimston** N York
34 C9 **North Halling** Medway
13 M4 **North Hayling** Hants
108 H3 **North Hazelrigg** Nthumb
19 P7 **North Heasley** Devon
14 F6 **North Heath** W Susx
20 G8 **North Hele** Devon
7 K9 **North Hill** Cnwll
32 F5 **North Hillingdon** Gt Lon
43 K10 **North Hinksey Village** Oxon
14 H1 **North Holmwood** Surrey
5 L5 **North Huish** Devon
79 N10 **North Hykeham** Lincs
16 E6 **Northiam** E Susx
44 G2 **Northill** C Beds
41 L10 **Northington** Gloucs
25 J6 **Northington** Hants
79 P3 **North Kelsey** Lincs
138 C6 **North Kessock** Highld
87 L11 **North Killingholme** N Linc
91 P9 **North Kilvington** N York
54 G4 **North Kilworth** Leics
12 B4 **North Kingston** Hants
68 C2 **North Kyme** Lincs
93 P12 **North Landing** E R Yk
68 G2 **Northlands** Lincs
42 D9 **Northleach** Gloucs
44 B10 **North Lee** Bucks
91 M12 **North Lees** N York
9 M5 **Northleigh** Devon
19 L6 **Northleigh** Devon
17 K1 **North Leigh** Kent
42 H9 **North Leigh** Oxon
79 K7 **North Leverton with Habblesthorpe** Notts
7 P5 **Northlew** Devon
53 K11 **North Littleton** Worcs
22 C5 **Northload Bridge** Somset
58 F4 **North Lopham** Norfk
67 M11 **North Luffenham** Rutlnd
25 P10 **North Marden** W Susx
43 Q7 **North Marston** Bucks
115 Q9 **North Middleton** Mdloth
108 G5 **North Middleton** Nthumb
141 K7 **North Millbrex** Abers

94 F7 North Milmain D & G
19 P7 North Molton Devon
43 J11 Northmoor Oxon
31 M4 North Moreton Oxon
124 H2 Northmuir Angus
14 C10 North Mundham W Susx
79 K12 North Muskham Notts
86 G8 North Newbald E R Yk
43 J4 North Newington Oxon
30 D11 North Newnton Wilts
21 L7 North Newton Somset
13 M4 Northney Hants
29 L3 North Nibley Gloucs
25 J2 North Oakley Hants
33 Q5 North Ockendon Gt Lon
32 G5 Northolt Gt Lon
74 H10 Northop Flints
75 J10 Northop Hall Flints
92 A3 North Ormesby Middsb
80 F5 North Ormsby Lincs
85 J11 Northorpe Kirk
68 B8 Northorpe Lincs
68 D5 Northorpe Lincs
79 M4 Northorpe Lincs
91 N9 North Otterington N York
22 B6 Northover Somset
22 C8 Northover Somset
79 Q5 North Owersby Lincs
84 H10 Northowram Calder
10 D3 North Perrott Somset
21 L7 North Petherton Somset
7 K7 North Petherwin Cnwll
70 C10 North Pickenham Norfk
52 H9 North Piddle Worcs
10 D5 North Poorton Dorset
11 M7 Northport Dorset
12 B3 North Poulner Hants
115 L5 North Queensferry Fife
19 P6 North Radworthy Devon
67 P3 North Rauceby Lincs
71 K4 Northrepps Norfk
80 G7 North Reston Lincs
85 L5 North Rigton N York
12 B5 North Ripley Hants
76 G10 North Rode Ches E
152 p1 North Ronaldsay Ork
152 p1 *North Ronaldsay Airport* Ork
97 P11 North Row Cumb
69 M9 North Runcton Norfk
82 F1 North Scale Cumb
79 L10 North Scarle Lincs
100 H1 North Seaton Nthumb
100 H1 North Seaton Colliery Nthumb
120 G4 North Shian Ag & B
101 J4 North Shields N Tyne
34 G5 North Shoebury Sthend
82 H8 North Shore Bpool
68 E12 North Side C Pete
97 K12 North Side Cumb
92 D3 North Skelton R & Cl
80 H4 North Somercotes Lincs
91 M11 North Stainley N York
90 D4 North Stainmore Cumb
33 R6 North Stifford Thurr
29 L8 North Stoke BaNES
31 M5 North Stoke Oxon
14 E8 North Stoke W Susx
57 L7 North Street Cambs
23 P9 North Street Hants
25 L7 North Street Hants
34 H10 North Street Kent
34 E7 North Street Medway
31 N8 North Street W Berk
109 K3 North Sunderland Nthumb
7 K5 North Tamerton Cnwll
8 C4 North Tawton Devon
114 D3 North Third Stirlg
80 F4 North Thoresby Lincs
109 L9 North Togston Nthumb
152 c6 Northton W Isls
7 P3 North Town Devon
22 D5 North Town Somset
32 C6 North Town W & M
70 F9 North Tuddenham Norfk
152 b7 North Uist W Isls
108 D9 Northumberland National Park Nthumb
100 F5 North Walbottle N u Ty
71 K6 North Walsham Norfk
25 J4 North Waltham Hants
25 M3 North Warnborough Hants
21 J7 Northway Somset
26 E4 Northway Swans
45 P11 North Weald Bassett Essex
79 J6 North Wheatley Notts
5 P3 North Whilborough Devon
76 C9 Northwich Ches W
29 J9 North Wick BaNES
28 H5 Northwick S Glos
21 M4 Northwick Somset
52 F9 Northwick Worcs
28 H10 North Widcombe BaNES
80 C6 North Willingham Lincs
78 C10 North Wingfield Derbys
67 M8 North Witham Lincs
57 P1 Northwold Norfk
64 G2 Northwood C Stke
77 P10 Northwood Derbys
32 G4 Northwood Gt Lon
12 H6 Northwood IoW
63 M5 Northwood Shrops
41 L8 Northwood Green Gloucs
22 E10 North Wootton Dorset
69 M7 North Wootton Norfk
22 D5 North Wootton Somset
29 N7 North Wraxall Wilts
30 D6 North Wroughton Swindn
92 F6 North York Moors National Park
85 Q12 Norton Donc
15 N10 Norton E Susx
41 P7 Norton Gloucs
75 P7 Norton Halton
45 J5 Norton Herts
12 E7 Norton IoW
40 F7 Norton Mons
28 D9 Norton N Som
86 E1 Norton N York
54 F8 Norton Nhants
78 F9 Norton Notts
51 J7 Norton Powys
91 Q2 Norton S on T
78 B7 Norton Sheff
51 M4 Norton Shrops
52 B4 Norton Shrops
63 P10 Norton Shrops
64 D12 Norton Shrops
58 D7 Norton Suffk
26 F5 Norton Swans
14 C9 Norton W Susx
29 P5 Norton Wilts
52 G10 Norton Worcs
53 K11 Norton Worcs
23 K5 Norton Bavant Wilts
64 F6 Norton Bridge Staffs
65 J10 Norton Canes Staffs
65 J10 Norton Canes Services Staffs
40 E2 Norton Canon Herefs
70 G6 Norton Corner Norfk
79 M11 Norton Disney Lincs
22 H6 Norton Ferris Wilts
21 K8 Norton Fitzwarren Somset
12 E7 Norton Green IoW
29 J9 Norton Hawkfield BaNES
45 R10 Norton Heath Essex
64 D4 Norton in Hales Shrops
64 G2 Norton in the Moors C Stke
65 Q10 Norton-Juxta-Twycross Leics
85 N1 Norton-le-Clay N York
53 N8 Norton Lindsey Warwks
58 E7 Norton Little Green Suffk
29 J9 Norton Malreward BaNES
45 Q10 Norton Mandeville Essex
22 H2 Norton St Philip Somset
59 N1 Norton Subcourse Norfk
21 P10 Norton sub Hamdon Somset
51 L11 Norton Wood Herefs
79 K11 Norwell Notts
79 J11 Norwell Woodhouse Notts
71 J10 Norwich Norfk
71 J9 *Norwich Airport* Norfk
71 J10 Norwich Cathedral Norfk
71 J9 Norwich (St Faith) Crematorium Norfk
152 u2 Norwick Shet
114 F3 Norwood Clacks
78 D7 Norwood Derbys
17 J5 Norwood Kent
45 Q10 Norwood End Essex
84 H10 Norwood Green Calder
32 G6 Norwood Green Gt Lon
15 J2 Norwood Hill Surrey
56 H1 Norwoodside Cambs
55 J1 Noseley Leics
5 J7 Noss Mayo Devon
91 M10 Nosterfield N York
46 B3 Nosterfield End Cambs
135 Q10 Nostie Highld
42 C7 Notgrove Gloucs
27 K7 Nottage Brdgnd
4 F4 Notter Cnwll
66 F4 Nottingham C Nott
10 G8 Nottington Dorset
77 Q1 Notton Wakefd
29 P8 Notton Wilts
46 D9 Nounsley Essex
52 E7 Noutard's Green Worcs
58 C8 Nowton Suffk
63 L10 Nox Shrops
31 N5 Nuffield Oxon
86 F6 Nunburnholme E R Yk
66 E1 Nuncargate Notts
98 F9 Nunclose Cumb
54 B2 Nuneaton Warwks
31 L2 Nuneham Courtenay Oxon
33 L7 Nunhead Gt Lon
87 L5 Nunkeeling E R Yk
85 Q4 Nun Monkton N York
22 G4 Nunney Somset
22 G4 Nunney Catch Somset
40 H3 Nunnington Herefs
92 D11 Nunnington N York
80 E2 Nunsthorpe NE Lin
86 B5 Nunthorpe C York
92 B4 Nunthorpe Middsb
92 B4 Nunthorpe Village Middsb
23 P8 Nunton Wilts
91 N11 Nunwick N York
99 N3 Nunwick Nthumb
29 J3 Nupdown S Glos
44 B8 Nup End Bucks
41 M10 Nupend Gloucs
32 C7 Nuptown Br For
24 F10 Nursling Hants
25 N9 Nursted Hants
30 B10 Nursteed Wilts
64 F12 Nurton Staffs
13 N4 Nutbourne W Susx
14 F7 Nutbourne W Susx
33 K12 Nutfield Surrey
66 E3 Nuthall Notts
45 M5 Nuthampstead Herts
14 H6 Nuthurst W Susx
15 N5 Nutley E Susx
25 K4 Nutley Hants
84 B12 Nuttall Bury
78 G3 Nutwell Donc
151 Q4 Nybster Highld
14 C11 Nyetimber W Susx
25 P9 Nyewood W Susx
8 D3 Nymet Rowland Devon
8 D5 Nymet Tracey Devon
29 N2 Nympsfield Gloucs
21 J9 Nynehead Somset
21 P6 Nythe Somset
14 D9 Nyton W Susx

## O

66 G12 Oadby Leics
34 F10 Oad Street Kent
52 E8 Oakall Green Worcs
65 K3 Oakamoor Staffs
115 K8 Oakbank W Loth
7 Q5 Oak Cross Devon
28 B3 Oakdale Caerph
21 J8 Oake Somset
64 F11 Oaken Staffs
83 M6 Oakenclough Lancs
64 C10 Oakengates Wrekin
75 J9 Oakenholt Flints
100 F10 Oakenshaw Dur
85 J9 Oakenshaw Kirk
66 C1 Oakerthorpe Derbys
48 G9 Oakford Cerdgn
20 E9 Oakford Devon
20 E9 Oakfordbridge Devon
76 G10 Oakgrove Ches E
67 L10 Oakham Rutlnd
64 E1 Oakhanger Ches E
25 N6 Oakhanger Hants
22 E4 Oakhill Somset
33 Q12 Oakhurst Kent
56 H8 Oakington Cambs
50 E10 Oaklands Powys
41 M8 Oakle Street Gloucs
55 P10 Oakley Bed
43 N9 Oakley Bucks
115 J3 Oakley Fife
25 J3 Oakley Hants
31 Q2 Oakley Oxon
11 N5 Oakley Poole
58 H5 Oakley Suffk
32 C7 Oakley Green W & M
50 D3 Oakley Park Powys
41 Q11 Oakridge Gloucs
83 P8 Oaks Lancs
63 M11 Oaks Shrops
30 A4 Oaksey Wilts
65 M5 Oaks Green Derbys
98 G3 Oakshaw Ford Cumb
25 N8 Oakshott Hants
65 Q9 Oakthorpe Leics
91 N4 Oak Tree Darltn
66 B4 Oakwood C Derb
99 P5 Oakwood Nthumb
84 F7 Oakworth C Brad
34 H9 Oare Kent
20 C4 Oare Somset
30 D9 Oare Wilts
67 P4 Oasby Lincs
21 N8 Oath Somset
125 J2 Oathlaw Angus
32 F9 Oatlands Park Surrey
120 F7 Oban Ag & B
120 G6 *Oban Airport* Ag & B
51 K5 Obley Shrops
123 P5 Obney P & K
22 E9 Oborne Dorset
68 B9 Obthorpe Lincs
58 H6 Occold Suffk
151 N9 Occumster Highld
105 J5 Ochiltree E Ayrs
66 C5 Ockbrook Derbys
52 H2 Ocker Hill Sandw
52 E8 Ockeridge Worcs
32 F11 Ockham Surrey
127 K10 Ockle Highld
14 G3 Ockley Surrey
41 J2 Ocle Pychard Herefs
87 J1 Octon E R Yk
22 C10 Odcombe Somset
29 M10 Odd Down BaNES
52 G9 Oddingley Worcs
42 E6 Oddington Gloucs
43 L8 Oddington Oxon
55 N9 Odell Bed
7 N4 Odham Devon
25 N3 Odiham Hants
84 H9 Odsal C Brad
45 K4 Odsey Cambs
23 P8 Odstock Wilts
66 C10 Odstone Leics
54 B7 Offchurch Warwks
42 B2 Offenham Worcs
76 G6 Offerton Stockp
101 J7 Offerton Sundld
15 M8 Offham E Susx
34 B11 Offham Kent
14 E9 Offham W Susx
64 E6 Offleymarsh Staffs
56 D7 Offord Cluny Cambs
56 D7 Offord D'Arcy Cambs
58 F10 Offton Suffk
9 M5 Offwell Devon
30 E8 Ogbourne Maizey Wilts
30 E8 Ogbourne St Andrew Wilts
30 E7 Ogbourne St George Wilts
84 G9 Ogden Calder
100 E2 Ogle Nthumb
75 M7 Oglet Lpool
27 L7 Ogmore V Glam
27 K7 Ogmore-by-Sea V Glam
27 M4 Ogmore Vale Brdgnd
73 K10 Ogwen Bank Gwynd
11 K3 Okeford Fitzpaine Dorset
8 B6 Okehampton Devon
77 P11 Oker Side Derbys
14 G3 Okewood Hill Surrey
8 G9 Olchard Devon
55 K6 Old Nhants
133 M3 Old Aberdeen C Aber
25 K6 Old Alresford Hants
148 D10 Oldany Highld
105 P10 Old Auchenbrack D & G
66 F3 Old Basford C Nott
25 L3 Old Basing Hants
70 E8 Old Beetley Norfk
53 L7 Oldberrow Warwks
108 H5 Old Bewick Nthumb
80 G10 Old Bolingbroke Lincs
85 K6 Old Bramhope Leeds
77 Q9 Old Brampton Derbys
96 F5 Old Bridge of Urr D & G
58 F2 Old Buckenham Norfk
31 K10 Old Burghclere Hants
33 Q11 Oldbury Kent
53 J3 Oldbury Sandw
52 D2 Oldbury Shrops
53 P2 Oldbury Warwks
29 J4 Oldbury Naite S Glos
29 J4 Oldbury-on-Severn S Glos
29 N5 Oldbury on the Hill Gloucs
92 B9 Old Byland N York
78 G3 Old Cantley Donc
101 J10 Old Cassop Dur
27 L6 Old Castle Brdgnd
40 D7 Oldcastle Mons
63 N3 Oldcastle Heath Ches W
71 J9 Old Catton Norfk
51 J2 Old Churchstoke Powys
80 F2 Old Clee NE Lin
20 G5 Old Cleeve Somset
78 G10 Old Clipstone Notts
73 Q8 Old Colwyn Conwy
78 F6 Oldcotes Notts
104 D10 Old Dailly S Ayrs
66 H7 Old Dalby Leics
77 L8 Old Dam Derbys
141 N6 Old Deer Abers
22 C3 Old Ditch Somset
78 E4 Old Edlington Donc
91 L1 Old Eldon Dur
87 M7 Old Ellerby E R Yk
47 P4 Old Felixstowe Suffk
84 F7 Oldfield C Brad
52 F7 Oldfield Worcs
56 D1 Old Fletton C Pete
22 H3 Oldford Somset
40 H8 Old Forge Herefs
40 G7 Old Furnace Herefs
77 K5 Old Glossop Derbys
86 D10 Old Goole E R Yk
2 b1 Old Grimsby IoS
45 L7 Old Hall Green Herts
58 C9 Oldhall Green Suffk
71 L5 Old Hall Street Norfk
76 G3 Oldham Oldham
116 G7 Oldhamstocks E Loth
45 N9 Old Harlow Essex
46 H7 Old Heath Essex
69 N4 Old Hunstanton Norfk
56 F5 Old Hurst Cambs
89 P9 Old Hutton Cumb
3 L6 Old Kea Cnwll
113 N7 Old Kilpatrick W Duns
45 J7 Old Knebworth Herts
71 J11 Old Lakenham Norfk
29 K8 Oldland S Glos
83 Q8 Old Langho Lancs
102 f5 Old Laxey IoM
68 H2 Old Leake Lincs
92 G12 Old Malton N York
141 K10 Oldmeldrum Abers
7 L10 Oldmill Cnwll
53 P7 Old Milverton Warwks
28 D10 Oldmixon N Som
58 F8 Old Newton Suffk
101 J10 Old Quarrington Dur
66 F4 Old Radford C Nott
50 H9 Old Radnor Powys
140 G10 Old Rayne Abers
17 J6 Old Romney Kent
15 J9 Old Shoreham W Susx
148 E5 Oldshoremore Highld
34 A11 Old Soar Kent
29 M6 Old Sodbury S Glos
67 N5 Old Somerby Lincs
92 B10 Oldstead N York
43 Q3 Old Stratford Nhants
130 E11 Old Struan P & K
109 K9 Old Swarland Nthumb
52 G4 Old Swinford Dudley
89 Q6 Old Tebay Cumb
91 Q10 Old Thirsk N York
84 F9 Old Town Calder
89 P10 Old Town Cumb
98 F9 Old Town Cumb
15 Q11 Old Town E Susx
2 b2 Old Town IoS
76 F4 Old Trafford Traffd
78 C10 Old Tupton Derbys
98 F6 Oldwall Cumb
26 D4 Oldwalls Swans
44 G3 Old Warden C Beds
20 D8 Oldways End Somset
56 B5 Old Weston Cambs
151 Q7 Old Wick Highld
32 D7 Old Windsor W & M
35 J11 Old Wives Lees Kent
32 E11 Old Woking Surrey
44 A3 Old Wolverton M Keyn
80 D10 Old Woodhall Lincs
63 M8 Old Woods Shrops
151 K6 Olgrinmore Highld
65 L8 Olive Green Staffs
24 G8 Oliver's Battery Hants
152 s4 Ollaberry Shet
135 J8 Ollach Highld
76 E8 Ollerton Ches E
78 G10 Ollerton Notts
64 C7 Ollerton Shrops
49 K9 Olmarch Cerdgn
46 A3 Olmstead Green Cambs
55 M10 Olney M Keyn
151 M3 Olrig House Highld
53 L4 Olton Solhll
29 J5 Olveston S Glos
52 F8 Ombersley Worcs
78 H10 Ompton Notts
99 L5 Once Brewed Nthumb
102 e5 Onchan IoM
65 K1 Onecote Staffs
58 F9 Onehouse Suffk
40 F9 Onen Mons
51 L7 Ongar Street Herefs
51 M5 Onibury Shrops
128 E12 Onich Highld
39 K9 Onllwyn Neath
64 D4 Onneley Staffs
46 B8 Onslow Green Essex
14 D1 Onslow Village Surrey
75 Q9 Onston Ches W
66 B3 Openwoodgate Derbys
143 K10 Opinan Highld
139 P4 Orbliston Moray
134 D7 Orbost Highld
81 J10 Orby Lincs
21 K9 Orchard Portman Somset
23 N4 Orcheston Wilts
40 G6 Orcop Herefs
40 G6 Orcop Hill Herefs
140 F4 Ord Abers
132 G2 Ordhead Abers
132 C4 Ordie Abers
139 Q4 Ordiequish Moray
99 Q6 Ordley Nthumb
78 H8 Ordsall Notts
16 E8 Ore E Susx
51 N7 Oreleton Common Herefs
52 C4 Oreton Shrops
59 N10 Orford Suffk
75 Q5 Orford Warrtn
11 M6 Organford Dorset
65 L9 Orgreave Staffs
16 H4 Orlestone Kent
51 N7 Orleton Herefs
52 C7 Orleton Worcs
55 L6 Orlingbury Nhants
88 H2 Ormathwaite Cumb
92 B3 Ormesby R & Cl
71 P9 Ormesby St Margaret Norfk
71 P9 Ormesby St Michael Norfk
143 M7 Ormiscaig Highld
116 A7 Ormiston E Loth
126 H11 Ormsaigmore Highld
111 Q7 Ormsary Ag & B
75 L2 Ormskirk Lancs
100 F8 Ornsby Hill Dur
110 H3 Oronsay Ag & B
152 j5 Orphir Ork
33 N9 Orpington Gt Lon
75 K4 Orrell Sefton
75 P3 Orrell Wigan
75 P3 Orrell Post Wigan
102 d3 Orrisdale IoM
96 F9 Orroland D & G
34 B6 Orsett Thurr
64 E9 Orslow Staffs
67 J4 Orston Notts
97 Q11 Orthwaite Cumb
83 M4 Ortner Lancs
89 Q5 Orton Cumb
55 K5 Orton Nhants
52 F2 Orton Staffs
56 D1 Orton Longueville C Pete
65 P11 Orton-on-the-Hill Leics
98 D8 Orton Rigg Cumb
56 C1 Orton Waterville C Pete
56 G10 Orwell Cambs
83 P9 Osbaldeston Lancs
83 P8 Osbaldeston Green Lancs
86 B5 Osbaldwick C York
66 C11 Osbaston Leics
63 K7 Osbaston Shrops
12 H6 Osborne IoW
13 J6 Osborne House IoW
67 Q4 Osbournby Lincs
75 N10 Oscroft Ches W
134 F7 Ose Highld
66 C8 Osgathorpe Leics
79 Q5 Osgodby Lincs
86 B8 Osgodby N York
93 L10 Osgodby N York
135 K8 Oskaig Highld
119 M5 Oskamull Ag & B
65 M3 Osmaston Derbys
10 H8 Osmington Dorset
10 H8 Osmington Mills Dorset
85 L8 Osmondthorpe Leeds
91 Q7 Osmotherley N York
43 K10 Osney Oxon
34 H10 Ospringe Kent
85 K11 Ossett Wakefd
79 J10 Ossington Notts
34 G3 Ostend Essex
32 H7 Osterley Gt Lon
92 C11 Oswaldkirk N York
83 Q9 Oswaldtwistle Lancs
63 J6 Oswestry Shrops
33 P10 Otford Kent
34 D11 Otham Kent
34 E11 Otham Hole Kent
21 N7 Othery Somset
85 J6 Otley Leeds
59 J9 Otley Suffk
59 J9 Otley Green Suffk
24 G9 Otterbourne Hants
84 C4 Otterburn N York
108 E11 Otterburn Nthumb
112 D4 Otter Ferry Ag & B
6 H6 Otterham Cnwll
21 L5 Otterhampton Somset
34 E9 Otterham Quay Kent
6 H7 Otterham Station Cnwll
152 c6 Otternish W Isls
32 E9 Ottershaw Surrey
152 t4 Otterswick Shet
9 K7 Otterton Devon
12 G4 Otterwood Hants
9 L5 Ottery St Mary Devon
17 L2 Ottinge Kent
87 P10 Ottringham E R Yk
98 C7 Oughterby Cumb
90 E10 Oughtershaw N York
97 M10 Oughterside Cumb
77 P5 Oughtibridge Sheff
76 C6 Oughtrington Warrtn
92 B12 Oulston N York
97 Q8 Oulton Cumb
85 M9 Oulton Leeds
70 H6 Oulton Norfk
64 E7 Oulton Staffs
64 G5 Oulton Staffs
59 Q2 Oulton Suffk
59 Q2 Oulton Broad Suffk
70 H7 Oulton Street Norfk
55 P3 Oundle Nhants
52 F2 Ounsdale Staffs
99 J11 Ousby Cumb
57 P8 Ousden Suffk
86 F10 Ousefleet E R Yk
100 H7 Ouston Dur
109 J3 Outchester Nthumb
35 M12 Out Elmstead Kent
89 K7 Outgate Cumb
90 C6 Outhgill Cumb
53 L7 Outhill Warwks
64 E6 Outlands Staffs
84 G11 Outlane Kirk
87 R11 Out Newton E R Yk
83 J7 Out Rawcliffe Lancs
69 K11 Outwell Norfk
23 P10 Outwick Hants
15 K2 Outwood Surrey
85 L10 Outwood Wakefd
76 E2 Outwood Gate Bury
66 C8 Outwoods Leics
64 E8 Outwoods Staffs
85 M10 Ouzlewell Green Leeds
84 G10 Ovenden Calder
56 G6 Over Cambs
76 B10 Over Ches W
41 N8 Over Gloucs
29 J6 Over S Glos
65 N4 Over Burrows Derbys
41 Q4 Overbury Worcs
10 H8 Overcombe Dorset
22 D10 Over Compton Dorset
76 C2 Overdale Crematorium Bolton
56 B2 Over End Cambs
77 Q9 Overgreen Derbys
53 M2 Over Green Warwks
77 M10 Over Haddon Derbys
83 M1 Over Kellet Lancs
43 J7 Over Kiddington Oxon
22 B6 Overleigh Somset
65 M9 Overley Staffs
40 G9 Over Monnow Mons
42 G6 Over Norton Oxon
76 E9 Over Peover Ches E
75 L8 Overpool Ches W
149 J12 Overscaig Hotel Highld
65 P9 Overseal Derbys
91 Q8 Over Silton N York
35 J11 Oversland Kent
53 L9 Oversley Green Warwks
55 K7 Overstone Nhants
21 J6 Over Stowey Somset
71 K4 Overstrand Norfk
21 P10 Over Stratton Somset
23 N6 Overstreet Wilts
76 D7 Over Tabley Ches E
43 K4 Overthorpe Nhants
133 L2 Overton C Aber
75 N8 Overton Ches W
24 H3 Overton Hants
83 K4 Overton Lancs
85 Q4 Overton N York
51 N6 Overton Shrops
26 C5 Overton Swans
85 K12 Overton Wakefd
63 L4 Overton Wrexhm
63 K4 Overton Bridge Wrexhm
76 E11 Overton Green Ches E
89 Q11 Overtown Lancs
114 E10 Overtown N Lans
30 D6 Overtown Swindn
85 M12 Overtown Wakefd
24 D6 Over Wallop Hants
53 N2 Over Whitacre Warwks
78 D9 Over Woodhouse Derbys
43 J6 Over Worton Oxon
31 M3 Overy Oxon
43 Q7 Oving Bucks
14 C10 Oving W Susx
15 L10 Ovingdean Br & H
100 E5 Ovingham Nthumb
91 J4 Ovington Dur
46 D3 Ovington Essex
25 J7 Ovington Hants
70 D11 Ovington Norfk
100 D5 Ovington Nthumb
12 H4 Ower Hants
24 E10 Ower Hants
11 J7 Owermoigne Dorset
51 K2 Owlbury Shrops
77 Q6 Owlerton Sheff
29 M3 Owlpen Gloucs
59 K7 Owl's Green Suffk
32 B10 Owlsmoor Br For
43 R10 Owlswick Bucks
79 P6 Owmby Lincs
79 Q3 Owmby Lincs
24 H8 Owslebury Hants
78 F1 Owston Donc
67 K10 Owston Leics
79 K4 Owston Ferry N Linc
87 P8 Owstwick E R Yk
87 Q9 Owthorne E R Yk
66 H5 Owthorpe Notts
101 M12 Owton Manor Hartpl
69 P11 Oxborough Norfk
10 D5 Oxbridge Dorset
80 F8 Oxcombe Lincs
78 D9 Oxcroft Derbys
46 B6 Oxen End Essex
89 N9 Oxenholme Cumb
84 F8 Oxenhope C Brad
89 J9 Oxen Park Cumb
21 P5 Oxenpill Somset
41 Q5 Oxenton Gloucs
30 G10 Oxenwood Wilts
43 L10 Oxford Oxon
43 K8 *Oxford Airport* Oxon
43 L10 Oxford Crematorium Oxon
43 N10 Oxford Services Oxon
32 G3 Oxhey Herts
100 F8 Oxhill Dur
42 G2 Oxhill Warwks
64 G11 Oxley Wolves
46 F9 Oxley Green Essex
16 C6 Oxley's Green E Susx
57 J3 Oxlode Cambs
108 A6 Oxnam Border
71 J7 Oxnead Norfk
32 G10 Oxshott Surrey
32 G10 Oxshott Heath Surrey
77 P3 Oxspring Barns
33 M12 Oxted Surrey
116 C10 Oxton Border
85 Q6 Oxton N York
66 G2 Oxton Notts
26 D5 Oxwich Swans
26 D5 Oxwich Green Swans
70 D7 Oxwick Norfk
145 J5 Oykel Bridge Hotel Highld
140 G10 Oyne Abers
26 F5 Oystermouth Swans
29 M4 Ozleworth Gloucs

## P

152 f3 Pabail W Isls
10 H3 Packers Hill Dorset
66 B9 Packington Leics
64 F1 Packmoor C Stke
53 P7 Packmores Warwks
124 H2 Padanaram Angus
43 P5 Padbury Bucks
33 K6 Paddington Gt Lon
76 B6 Paddington Warrtn
17 M3 Paddlesworth Kent
34 B10 Paddlesworth Kent
16 B2 Paddock Wood Kent
63 N6 Paddolgreen Shrops
77 J4 Padfield Derbys
76 B6 Padgate Warrtn
34 B3 Padhams Green Essex
84 B8 Padiham Lancs
84 H3 Padside N York
6 C9 Padstow Cnwll
31 M9 Padworth W Berk
100 G11 Page Bank Dur
14 C11 Pagham W Susx
34 G4 Paglesham Essex
5 Q4 Paignton Torbay
54 D4 Pailton Warwks
16 A6 Paine's Cross E Susx
65 J5 Painleyhill Staffs
40 A2 Painscastle Powys
100 D6 Painshawfield Nthumb
86 F4 Painsthorpe E R Yk
41 P9 Painswick Gloucs
34 H10 Painter's Forstal Kent
113 P8 Paisley Rens
113 P8 Paisley Woodside Crematorium Rens
59 Q3 Pakefield Suffk
58 D7 Pakenham Suffk
62 D5 Pale Gwynd
46 B3 Pale Green Essex
24 D5 Palestine Hants
32 B7 Paley Street W & M
53 J1 Palfrey Wsall
58 G5 Palgrave Suffk
11 J6 Pallington Dorset
6 H9 Palmersbridge Cnwll
33 K4 Palmers Green Gt Lon
105 J6 Palmerston E Ayrs
27 Q8 Palmerstown V Glam
96 G7 Palnackie D & G
95 N5 Palnure D & G
78 D10 Palterton Derbys
31 M10 Pamber End Hants
31 M10 Pamber Green Hants
31 M10 Pamber Heath Hants
41 Q5 Pamington Gloucs
11 N5 Pamphill Dorset
57 J11 Pampisford Cambs
21 Q4 Panborough Somset
125 L6 Panbride Angus
7 K4 Pancrasweek Devon
27 P8 Pancross V Glam
27 Q5 Pandy Caerph
61 K11 Pandy Gwynd
61 Q6 Pandy Gwynd
40 D7 Pandy Mons
62 B11 Pandy Powys
62 H5 Pandy Wrexhm
62 F2 Pandy'r Capel Denbgs
73 Q11 Pandy Tudur Conwy
46 C6 Panfield Essex
31 N7 Pangbourne W Berk
15 K8 Pangdean W Susx
52 B11 Panks Bridge Herefs
85 L5 Pannal N York
85 L4 Pannal Ash N York
132 B5 Pannanich Wells Hotel Abers
63 J8 Pant Shrops
74 G8 Pantasaph Flints
36 H4 Panteg Pembks
4 B3 Pantersbridge Cnwll
27 M5 Pant-ffrwyth Brdgnd
60 H3 Pant Glas Gwynd
49 N1 Pantglas Powys
38 E6 Pant-Gwyn Carmth
26 G2 Pant-lasau Swans
49 P4 Pant Mawr Powys
80 D8 Panton Lincs
74 E11 Pant-pastynog Denbgs
61 N11 Pantperthog Gwynd
50 D6 Pant-y-dwr Powys
62 G11 Pant-y-ffridd Powys
38 F9 Pantyffynnon Carmth
28 C2 Pantygaseg Torfn
27 L4 Pant-y-gog Brdgnd
37 M5 Pantymenyn Carmth
74 H10 Pant-y-mwyn Flints
71 M9 Panxworth Norfk
152 m1 *Papa Westray Airport* Ork
97 M12 Papcastle Cumb
151 Q6 Papigoe Highld
116 D7 Papple E Loth
66 F2 Papplewick Notts
56 F8 Papworth Everard Cambs
56 E8 Papworth St Agnes Cambs
3 Q4 Par Cnwll
35 N10 Paramour Street Kent
75 N2 Parbold Lancs
22 D6 Parbrook Somset
14 F6 Parbrook W Susx
61 Q5 Parc Gwynd
37 M7 Parc Gwyn Crematorium Pembks
48 D10 Parcllyn Cerdgn
28 F4 Parc Seymour Newpt
88 E2 Pardshaw Cumb
59 L8 Parham Suffk
106 B11 Park D & G
99 K6 Park Nthumb
2 G6 Park Bottom Cnwll
76 H3 Park Bridge Tamesd
15 P4 Park Corner E Susx
31 P5 Park Corner Oxon
32 B6 Park Corner W & M
83 J9 Park Crematorium Lancs
55 N10 Park End Bed
41 J10 Parkend Gloucs
99 N3 Park End Nthumb
16 A1 Parkers Green Kent
47 M5 Parkeston Essex
47 M5 Parkeston Quay Essex
16 H3 Park Farm Kent
75 J8 Parkgate Ches W
97 P9 Parkgate Cumb
106 D12 Parkgate D & G
16 C8 Parkgate E Susx
46 B6 Parkgate Essex
13 J3 Park Gate Hants
16 F4 Parkgate Kent
33 P9 Parkgate Kent
85 J7 Park Gate Leeds
14 H2 Parkgate Surrey
52 H6 Park Gate Worcs
45 N6 Park Green Essex
58 H8 Park Green Suffk
125 M3 Parkgrove Crematorium Angus
113 P7 Parkhall W Duns
18 H9 Parkham Devon
18 G9 Parkham Ash Devon
66 B1 Park Head Derbys
28 H2 Park Hill Gloucs
40 G11 Parkhouse Mons
26 E4 Parkmill Swans
32 H6 Park Royal Gt Lon
101 L8 Parkside Dur
114 E9 Parkside N Lans
63 L1 Parkside Wrexhm
11 P6 Parkstone Poole
44 G11 Park Street Herts
14 G4 Park Street W Susx
84 G10 Park Wood Crematorium Calder
11 Q5 Parley Green Dorset
31 R4 Parmoor Bucks
45 N10 Parndon Essex
45 N10 Parndon Wood Crematorium Essex
19 N4 Parracombe Devon
37 K3 Parrog Pembks
97 N10 Parsonby Cumb
77 Q5 Parson Cross Sheff
68 G10 Parson Drove Cambs
46 H6 Parson's Heath Essex
65 P7 Parson's Hill Derbys
113 Q8 Partick C Glas
76 D5 Partington Traffd
80 H10 Partney Lincs
88 C3 Parton Cumb
14 H7 Partridge Green W Susx
40 C7 Partrishow Powys
65 M1 Parwich Derbys
45 Q11 Paslow Wood Common Essex
43 Q4 Passenham Nhants
25 P6 Passfield Hants
33 P3 Passingford Bridge Essex
68 D11 Paston C Pete
71 L5 Paston Norfk
65 J7 Pasturefields Staffs
7 N5 Patchacott Devon
15 K9 Patcham Br & H
32 G3 Patchetts Green Herts
14 F9 Patching W Susx
19 M5 Patchole Devon
29 J6 Patchway S Glos
84 H2 Pateley Bridge N York
46 G8 Paternoster Heath Essex
21 N7 Pathe Somset
115 P3 Pathhead Fife
115 R8 Pathhead Mdloth
53 M9 Pathlow Warwks
124 B10 Path of Condie P & K
45 N6 Patmore Heath Herts
104 H7 Patna E Ayrs
30 C10 Patney Wilts
102 c5 Patrick IoM
91 L8 Patrick Brompton N York
76 D4 Patricroft Salfd
87 P10 Patrington E R Yk
87 P11 Patrington Haven E R Yk
35 L11 Patrixbourne Kent
89 L4 Patterdale Cumb
64 F12 Pattingham Staffs
54 H10 Pattishall Nhants
46 E7 Pattiswick Green Essex
51 P2 Patton Shrops
2 D9 Paul Cnwll
43 P3 Paulerspury Nhants
87 M10 Paull E R Yk
23 P7 Paul's Dene Wilts
29 K11 Paulton BaNES
52 C10 Paunton Herefs
108 H10 Pauperhaugh Nthumb
64 E9 Pave Lane Wrekin
55 N9 Pavenham Bed
21 L5 Pawlett Somset
108 D3 Pawston Nthumb
42 E4 Paxford Gloucs
117 L10 Paxton Border
34 G11 Payden Street Kent
9 L4 Payhembury Devon
2 G6 Paynter's Lane End Cnwll
84 B5 Paythorne Lancs
51 L6 Paytoe Herefs
15 M10 Peacehaven E Susx
77 K8 Peak Dale Derbys
77 M5 Peak District National Park
77 L8 Peak Forest Derbys
68 E9 Peak Hill Lincs
68 C11 Peakirk C Pete
16 C2 Pearson's Green Kent
41 J5 Peartree Green Herefs
29 L11 Peasedown St John BaNES
66 C2 Peasehill Derbys
70 F9 Peaseland Green Norfk
31 K7 Peasemore W Berk
59 M7 Peasenhall Suffk
15 J4 Pease Pottage W Susx
14 F2 Peaslake Surrey
75 N5 Peasley Cross St Hel
16 F6 Peasmarsh E Susx
21 M11 Peasmarsh Somset
14 E2 Peasmarsh Surrey
141 M3 Peathill Abers
125 J11 Peat Inn Fife
54 F2 Peatling Magna Leics
54 F3 Peatling Parva Leics
51 P4 Peaton Shrops
46 E5 Pebmarsh Essex
42 D2 Pebworth Worcs
84 E9 Pecket Well Calder
75 P12 Peckforton Ches E
33 L7 Peckham Gt Lon
66 D12 Peckleton Leics
62 F7 Pedairffordd Powys
17 L4 Pedlinge Kent
52 G4 Pedmore Dudley
21 P6 Pedwell Somset
106 H2 Peebles Border
102 c5 Peel IoM
83 J9 Peel Lancs
13 J4 Peel Common Hants
17 L3 Peene Kent
16 F5 Peening Quarter Kent
66 C8 Peggs Green Leics
44 G5 Pegsdon C Beds
109 L12 Pegswood Nthumb
35 Q9 Pegwell Kent
135 J9 Peinchorran Highld
134 G4 Peinlich Highld
36 H7 Pelcomb Pembks
36 H7 Pelcomb Bridge Pembks
36 H7 Pelcomb Cross Pembks
46 H8 Peldon Essex
16 B4 Pell Green E Susx
65 J11 Pelsall Wsall
65 J11 Pelsall Wood Wsall
100 G7 Pelton Dur
100 H8 Pelton Fell Dur
97 M8 Pelutho Cumb
4 B6 Pelynt Cnwll
26 D2 Pemberton Carmth
75 P3 Pemberton Wigan
16 F1 Pembles Cross Kent
26 C2 Pembrey Carmth
51 L9 Pembridge Herefs
37 J10 Pembroke Pembks
37 J10 Pembroke Dock Pembks
36 G6 Pembrokeshire Coast National Park Pembks
16 A3 Pembury Kent
40 H6 Pen-allt Herefs
40 H9 Penallt Mons
37 M10 Penally Pembks
3 N6 Penare Cnwll
28 B8 Penarth V Glam
37 M7 Penblewin Pembks
49 L4 Pen-bont Rhydybeddau Cerdgn
48 E10 Penbryn Cerdgn
38 C4 Pencader Carmth
60 G4 Pencaenewydd Gwynd
116 B7 Pencaitland E Loth
72 F9 Pencarnisiog IoA
38 E3 Pencarreg Carmth
6 G8 Pencarrow Cnwll

33 J8 **Putney Vale Crematorium** Gt Lon
19 J5 **Putsborough** Devon
44 C8 **Puttenham** Herts
14 D1 **Puttenham** Surrey
46 E4 **Puttock End** Essex
10 G8 **Putton** Dorset
43 Q3 **Puxley** Nhants
28 E9 **Puxton** N Som
26 D2 **Pwll** Carmth
36 H10 **Pwllcrochan** Pembks
40 C9 **Pwll-du** Mons
62 F1 **Pwll-glas** Denbgs
39 N5 **Pwllgloyw** Powys
60 F5 **Pwllheli** Gwynd
28 H4 **Pwllmeyric** Mons
37 P7 **Pwll Trap** Carmth
27 J4 **Pwll-y-glaw** Neath
73 P8 **Pydew** Conwy
66 D2 **Pye Bridge** Derbys
15 K8 **Pyecombe** W Susx
28 D5 **Pye Corner** Newpt
65 J9 **Pye Green** Staffs
27 K6 **Pyle** Brdgnd
20 H7 **Pyleigh** Somset
22 E6 **Pylle** Somset
57 J3 **Pymoor** Cambs
10 D6 **Pymore** Dorset
32 E10 **Pyrford** Surrey
31 P3 **Pyrton** Oxon
55 L6 **Pytchley** Nhants
7 K4 **Pyworthy** Devon

## Q

50 H4 **Quabbs** Shrops
68 E5 **Quadring** Lincs
68 E5 **Quadring Eaudike** Lincs
43 Q7 **Quainton** Bucks
27 P3 **Quaker's Yard** Myr Td
100 F8 **Quaking Houses** Dur
21 J6 **Quantock Hills** Somset
152 s8 **Quarff** Shet
24 D5 **Quarley** Hants
65 Q4 **Quarndon** Derbys
13 J6 **Quarr Hill** IoW
113 M8 **Quarrier's Village** Inver
67 Q3 **Quarrington** Lincs
101 J10 **Quarrington Hill** Dur
75 P10 **Quarrybank** Ches W
52 H3 **Quarry Bank** Dudley
139 M3 **Quarrywood** Moray
113 J9 **Quarter** N Ayrs
114 D11 **Quarter** S Lans
52 D2 **Quatford** Shrops
52 D3 **Quatt** Shrops
100 F9 **Quebec** Dur
41 N9 **Quedgeley** Gloucs
57 L4 **Queen Adelaide** Cambs
34 F8 **Queenborough** Kent
22 D8 **Queen Camel** Somset
29 K9 **Queen Charlton** BaNES
20 C10 **Queen Dart** Devon
122 E11 **Queen Elizabeth Forest Park** Stirlg
41 P4 **Queenhill** Worcs
22 H7 **Queen Oak** Dorset
13 J8 **Queen's Bower** IoW
84 G9 **Queensbury** C Brad
75 K10 **Queensferry** Flints
63 K7 **Queen's Head** Shrops
114 B8 **Queenslie** C Glas
55 P10 **Queen's Park** Bed
55 J8 **Queen's Park** Nhants
16 B2 **Queen Street** Kent
30 B5 **Queen Street** Wilts
114 C6 **Queenzieburn** N Lans
45 P6 **Quendon** Essex
66 G9 **Queniborough** Leics
42 D11 **Quenington** Gloucs
83 M3 **Quernmore** Lancs
53 K2 **Queslett** Birm
4 D4 **Quethiock** Cnwll
31 M7 **Quick's Green** W Berk
58 F3 **Quidenham** Norfk
25 J3 **Quidhampton** Hants
23 P7 **Quidhampton** Wilts
63 N5 **Quina Brook** Shrops
54 G10 **Quinbury End** Nhants
53 J4 **Quinton** Dudley
55 K10 **Quinton** Nhants
55 K10 **Quinton Green** Nhants
3 L2 **Quintrell Downs** Cnwll
65 L4 **Quixhall** Staffs
116 H8 **Quixwood** Border
7 M5 **Quoditch** Devon
123 L8 **Quoig** P & K
66 F9 **Quorn** Leics
106 C2 **Quothquan** S Lans
152 m5 **Quoyburray** Ork
152 j4 **Quoyloo** Ork

## R

135 K7 **Raasay** Highld
16 D1 **Rabbit's Cross** Kent
45 J8 **Rableyheath** Herts
97 P8 **Raby** Cumb
75 K8 **Raby** Wirral
106 E3 **Rachan Mill** Border
73 K10 **Rachub** Gwynd
20 C9 **Rackenford** Devon
14 F8 **Rackham** W Susx
71 K9 **Rackheath** Norfk
97 L3 **Racks** D & G
152 i5 **Rackwick** Ork
65 P5 **Radbourne** Derbys
76 E2 **Radcliffe** Bury
109 L9 **Radcliffe** Nthumb
66 G4 **Radcliffe on Trent** Notts
43 P5 **Radclive** Bucks
30 G2 **Radcot** Oxon
138 C4 **Raddery** Highld
20 F8 **Raddington** Somset
125 J11 **Radernie** Fife
53 Q4 **Radford** Covtry
53 Q8 **Radford Semele** Warwks
21 K6 **Radlet** Somset
32 H2 **Radlett** Herts
19 P8 **Radley** Devon
31 L3 **Radley** Oxon
46 A10 **Radley Green** Essex
63 Q1 **Radmore Green** Ches E
31 R3 **Radnage** Bucks
22 F2 **Radstock** BaNES
43 M4 **Radstone** Nhants
54 B11 **Radway** Warwks
55 P9 **Radwell** Bed
45 J4 **Radwell** Herts
45 R4 **Radwinter** Essex
45 R4 **Radwinter End** Essex
27 Q6 **Radyr** Cardif
67 P2 **RAF College (Cranwell)** Lincs
139 K4 **Rafford** Moray
66 H8 **Ragdale** Leics
51 M2 **Ragdon** Shrops
2 D9 **Raginnis** Cnwll
40 F10 **Raglan** Mons
79 K9 **Ragnall** Notts
138 E10 **Raigbeg** Highld
52 F9 **Rainbow Hill** Worcs
75 N3 **Rainford** St Hel
33 P6 **Rainham** Gt Lon
34 E9 **Rainham** Medway
75 N5 **Rainhill** St Hel
75 N6 **Rainhill Stoops** St Hel
76 H8 **Rainow** Ches E
76 E3 **Rainsough** Bury
91 N11 **Rainton** N York
78 F12 **Rainworth** Notts
89 Q5 **Raisbeck** Cumb
99 K9 **Raise** Cumb
86 F3 **Raisthorpe** N York
124 E7 **Rait** P & K
80 F7 **Raithby** Lincs
80 G10 **Raithby** Lincs
92 H4 **Raithwaite** N York
25 P8 **Rake** Hants
84 E12 **Rakewood** Rochdl
130 C5 **Ralia** Highld
38 E2 **Ram** Carmth
134 C7 **Ramasaig** Highld
2 H8 **Rame** Cnwll
4 F7 **Rame** Cnwll
29 K6 **Ram Hill** S Glos
16 H2 **Ram Lane** Kent
10 E4 **Rampisham** Dorset
82 G2 **Rampside** Cumb
56 H7 **Rampton** Cambs
79 K8 **Rampton** Notts
84 B11 **Ramsbottom** Bury
30 F8 **Ramsbury** Wilts
151 L11 **Ramscraigs** Highld
25 M9 **Ramsdean** Hants
31 M10 **Ramsdell** Hants
42 H8 **Ramsden** Oxon
41 Q2 **Ramsden** Worcs
34 C3 **Ramsden Bellhouse** Essex
34 C3 **Ramsden Heath** Essex
56 F4 **Ramsey** Cambs
47 M5 **Ramsey** Essex
102 f3 **Ramsey** IoM
56 F3 **Ramsey Forty Foot** Cambs
56 E4 **Ramsey Heights** Cambs
46 G10 **Ramsey Island** Essex
36 D6 **Ramsey Island** Pembks
56 F3 **Ramsey Mereside** Cambs
56 E3 **Ramsey St Mary's** Cambs
35 Q9 **Ramsgate** Kent
84 H1 **Ramsgill** N York
91 K2 **Ramshaw** Dur
99 Q9 **Ramshaw** Dur
47 P3 **Ramsholt** Suffk
108 B9 **Ramshope** Nthumb
65 K3 **Ramshorn** Staffs
8 C6 **Ramsley** Devon
14 D4 **Ramsnest Common** Surrey
80 E8 **Ranby** Lincs
78 G7 **Ranby** Notts
80 B8 **Rand** Lincs
32 H11 **Randalls Park Crematorium** Surrey
41 N10 **Randwick** Gloucs
113 M8 **Ranfurly** Rens
65 M7 **Rangemore** Staffs
29 L5 **Rangeworthy** S Glos
104 H7 **Rankinston** E Ayrs
67 L10 **Ranksborough** Rutlnd
46 D8 **Rank's Green** Essex
122 D1 **Rannoch Station** P & K
20 E5 **Ranscombe** Somset
78 G6 **Ranskill** Notts
64 F7 **Ranton** Staffs
64 F7 **Ranton Green** Staffs
71 M9 **Ranworth** Norfk
114 E2 **Raploch** Stirlg
152 m2 **Rapness** Ork
21 M10 **Rapps** Somset
96 G8 **Rascarrel** D & G
112 H5 **Rashfield** Ag & B
52 G7 **Rashwood** Worcs
85 P1 **Raskelf** N York
39 R9 **Rassau** Blae G
84 H10 **Rastrick** Calder
136 C11 **Ratagan** Highld
66 E11 **Ratby** Leics
65 Q12 **Ratcliffe Culey** Leics
66 E6 **Ratcliffe on Soar** Notts
66 G9 **Ratcliffe on the Wreake** Leics
23 P5 **Ratfyn** Wilts
141 N4 **Rathen** Abers
124 G8 **Rathillet** Fife
84 B3 **Rathmell** N York
115 L7 **Ratho** C Edin
115 L7 **Ratho Station** C Edin
140 C3 **Rathven** Moray
24 G8 **Ratlake** Hants
42 H2 **Ratley** Warwks
35 M11 **Ratling** Kent
51 L1 **Ratlinghope** Shrops
69 K9 **Rattan Row** Norfk
151 N2 **Rattar** Highld
98 C10 **Ratten Row** Cumb
98 E8 **Ratten Row** Cumb
83 K7 **Ratten Row** Lancs
5 M4 **Rattery** Devon
58 E9 **Rattlesden** Suffk
15 Q10 **Ratton Village** E Susx
124 D4 **Rattray** P & K
98 E8 **Raughton** Cumb
98 D9 **Raughton Head** Cumb
55 P6 **Raunds** Nhants
78 D5 **Ravenfield** Rothm
88 E7 **Ravenglass** Cumb
52 D9 **Ravenhills Green** Worcs
59 M1 **Raveningham** Norfk
93 K6 **Ravenscar** N York
114 D10 **Ravenscraig** N Lans
102 d4 **Ravensdale** IoM
55 Q10 **Ravensden** Bed
90 D6 **Ravenseat** N York
66 F1 **Ravenshead** Notts
64 B2 **Ravensmoor** Ches E
85 K11 **Ravensthorpe** Kirk
54 H6 **Ravensthorpe** Nhants
66 C9 **Ravenstone** Leics
55 L10 **Ravenstone** M Keyn
90 B6 **Ravenstonedale** Cumb
114 G12 **Ravenstruther** S Lans
91 J5 **Ravensworth** N York
93 J5 **Raw** N York
86 A4 **Rawcliffe** C York
86 C10 **Rawcliffe** E R Yk
86 C11 **Rawcliffe Bridge** E R Yk
85 J7 **Rawdon** Leeds
85 J7 **Rawdon Crematorium** Leeds
34 F10 **Rawling Street** Kent
78 D4 **Rawmarsh** Rothm
65 J9 **Rawnsley** Staffs
34 D4 **Rawreth** Essex
9 N3 **Rawridge** Devon
84 B10 **Rawtenstall** Lancs
47 J4 **Raydon** Suffk
108 E11 **Raylees** Nthumb
34 E4 **Rayleigh** Essex
9 Q5 **Raymond's Hill** Devon
46 C7 **Rayne** Essex
33 J8 **Raynes Park** Gt Lon
57 L7 **Reach** Cambs
84 A8 **Read** Lancs
31 P7 **Reading** Readg
31 P7 **Reading Crematorium** Readg
31 P8 **Reading Services** W Berk
16 G5 **Reading Street** Kent
35 Q8 **Reading Street** Kent
89 P3 **Reagill** Cumb
2 F7 **Realwa** Cnwll
146 D6 **Rearquhar** Highld
66 G9 **Rearsby** Leics
64 B1 **Rease Heath** Ches E
150 H4 **Reay** Highld
35 M8 **Reculver** Kent
20 H10 **Red Ball** Devon
37 L9 **Redberth** Pembks
44 G9 **Redbourn** Herts
79 N4 **Redbourne** N Linc
40 H9 **Redbrook** Gloucs
63 N4 **Redbrook** Wrexhm
16 G4 **Redbrook Street** Kent
138 H6 **Redburn** Highld
99 L5 **Redburn** Nthumb
92 C2 **Redcar** R & Cl
96 G5 **Redcastle** D & G
137 Q6 **Redcastle** Highld
97 Q9 **Red Dial** Cumb
114 G5 **Redding** Falk
114 G6 **Reddingmuirhead** Falk
76 G5 **Reddish** Stockp
53 K7 **Redditch** Worcs
53 K7 **Redditch Crematorium** Worcs
57 Q9 **Rede** Suffk
59 K4 **Redenhall** Norfk
24 E3 **Redenham** Hants
99 N2 **Redesmouth** Nthumb
133 J10 **Redford** Abers
125 L4 **Redford** Angus
25 Q8 **Redford** W Susx
107 K6 **Redfordgreen** Border
27 N5 **Redgate** Rhondd
124 B7 **Redgorton** P & K
58 F5 **Redgrave** Suffk
133 J3 **Redhill** Abers
11 Q5 **Red Hill** Bmouth
45 K5 **Redhill** Herts
28 G9 **Redhill** N Som
33 K12 **Redhill** Surrey
53 L9 **Red Hill** Warwks
59 N4 **Redisham** Suffk
29 J7 **Redland** Bristl
152 k3 **Redland** Ork
59 J6 **Redlingfield** Suffk
59 J6 **Redlingfield Green** Suffk
57 N6 **Red Lodge** Suffk
84 C12 **Red Lumb** Rochdl
22 F6 **Redlynch** Somset
24 C9 **Redlynch** Wilts
97 N11 **Redmain** Cumb
52 E7 **Redmarley** Worcs
41 M5 **Redmarley D'Abitot** Gloucs
91 P3 **Redmarshall** S on T
67 K5 **Redmile** Leics
90 H8 **Redmire** N York
133 J9 **Redmyre** Abers
53 J5 **Rednal** Birm
63 L6 **Rednal** Shrops
107 P3 **Redpath** Border
135 N2 **Redpoint** Highld
7 K4 **Red Post** Cnwll
75 P2 **Red Rock** Wigan
37 N8 **Red Roses** Carmth
109 L10 **Red Row** Nthumb
2 H6 **Redruth** Cnwll
29 Q9 **Redstocks** Wilts
124 D6 **Redstone** P & K
37 L7 **Redstone Cross** Pembks
64 F2 **Red Street** Staffs
76 E2 **Redvales** Bury
73 J7 **Red Wharf Bay** IoA
28 F5 **Redwick** Newpt
28 H5 **Redwick** S Glos
91 L2 **Redworth** Darltn
45 L4 **Reed** Herts
71 N11 **Reedham** Norfk
86 E10 **Reedness** E R Yk
80 D10 **Reeds Beck** Lincs
84 B10 **Reeds Holme** Lancs
79 P9 **Reepham** Lincs
70 G7 **Reepham** Norfk
90 H7 **Reeth** N York
53 N5 **Reeves Green** Solhll
102 f3 **Regaby** IoM
28 H9 **Regil** N Som
143 P2 **Reiff** Highld
33 J12 **Reigate** Surrey
93 N11 **Reighton** N York
141 L11 **Reisque** Abers
151 P6 **Reiss** Highld
3 K3 **Rejerrah** Cnwll
2 G8 **Releath** Cnwll
2 F8 **Relubbus** Cnwll
139 J6 **Relugas** Moray
31 Q5 **Remenham** Wokham
31 Q6 **Remenham Hill** Wokham
66 F7 **Rempstone** Notts
42 B9 **Rendcomb** Gloucs
59 L8 **Rendham** Suffk
59 L10 **Rendlesham** Suffk
113 P8 **Renfrew** Rens
56 B10 **Renhold** Bed
78 D8 **Renishaw** Derbys
109 K6 **Rennington** Nthumb
113 M6 **Renton** W Duns
98 H9 **Renwick** Cumb
71 N9 **Repps** Norfk
65 P7 **Repton** Derbys
138 C7 **Resaurie** Highld
3 N6 **Rescassa** Cnwll
3 N5 **Rescorla** Cnwll
127 N11 **Resipole** Highld
2 G6 **Reskadinnick** Cnwll
138 C3 **Resolis** Highld
39 K11 **Resolven** Neath
121 N11 **Rest and be thankful** Ag & B
117 K9 **Reston** Border
3 K7 **Restronguet** Cnwll
125 K3 **Reswallie** Angus
3 M2 **Reterth** Cnwll
78 H7 **Retford** Notts
3 N2 **Retire** Cnwll
34 D3 **Rettendon** Essex
3 L3 **Retyn** Cnwll
80 F11 **Revesby** Lincs
5 M9 **Rew** Devon
8 E10 **Rew** Devon
8 H5 **Rewe** Devon
12 H6 **Rew Street** IoW
7 M7 **Rexon** Devon
59 P5 **Reydon** Suffk
70 F11 **Reymerston** Norfk
37 L9 **Reynalton** Pembks
26 D4 **Reynoldston** Swans
7 L9 **Rezare** Cnwll
40 E11 **Rhadyr** Mons
39 J3 **Rhandirmwyn** Carmth
50 D7 **Rhayader** Powys
137 P6 **Rheindown** Highld
74 G9 **Rhes-y-cae** Flints
62 G3 **Rhewl** Denbgs
74 F11 **Rhewl** Denbgs
74 F7 **Rhewl-fawr** Flints
74 G7 **Rhewl Mostyn** Flints
148 C11 **Rhicarn** Highld
148 F6 **Rhiconich** Highld
146 C10 **Rhicullen** Highld
39 L10 **Rhigos** Rhondd
144 C6 **Rhireavach** Highld
146 E5 **Rhives** Highld
27 R6 **Rhiwbina** Cardif
61 M3 **Rhiwbryfdir** Gwynd
28 C5 **Rhiwderyn** Newpt
73 J11 **Rhiwen** Gwynd
27 N5 **Rhiwinder** Rhondd
62 C5 **Rhiwlas** Gwynd
73 K10 **Rhiwlas** Gwynd
62 H6 **Rhiwlas** Powys
27 P6 **Rhiwsaeson** Rhondd
21 L6 **Rhode** Somset
16 B2 **Rhoden Green** Kent
78 F7 **Rhodesia** Notts
17 L2 **Rhodes Minnis** Kent
36 E5 **Rhodiad-y-brenin** Pembks
96 F6 **Rhonehouse** D & G
27 P9 **Rhoose** V Glam
38 B5 **Rhos** Carmth
74 F11 **Rhos** Denbgs
38 H11 **Rhos** Neath
72 F5 **Rhosbeirio** IoA
73 J8 **Rhoscefnhir** IoA
72 D8 **Rhoscolyn** IoA
36 H10 **Rhoscrowther** Pembks
74 H10 **Rhosesmor** Flints
60 F4 **Rhos-fawr** Gwynd
72 H12 **Rhosgadfan** Gwynd
72 G6 **Rhosgoch** IoA
50 G11 **Rhosgoch** Powys
49 J8 **Rhos Haminiog** Cerdgn
37 N2 **Rhoshill** Pembks
60 C6 **Rhoshirwaun** Gwynd
60 H4 **Rhoslan** Gwynd
61 K11 **Rhoslefain** Gwynd
63 J3 **Rhosllanerchrugog** Wrexhm
72 H6 **Rhôs Lligwy** IoA
38 F7 **Rhosmaen** Carmth
72 H8 **Rhosmeirch** IoA
72 E9 **Rhosneigr** IoA
63 K2 **Rhosnesni** Wrexhm
73 P7 **Rhôs-on-Sea** Conwy
63 K2 **Rhosrobin** Wrexhm
26 B5 **Rhossili** Swans
72 H12 **Rhostryfan** Gwynd
63 K2 **Rhostyllen** Wrexhm
72 G6 **Rhosybol** IoA
62 F7 **Rhos y-brithdir** Powys
63 K5 **Rhosygadfa** Shrops
49 L6 **Rhos-y-garth** Cerdgn
62 C5 **Rhos-y-gwaliau** Gwynd
60 D5 **Rhos-y-llan** Gwynd
63 J4 **Rhosymedre** Wrexhm
51 J7 **Rhos-y-meirch** Powys
113 K4 **Rhu** Ag & B
74 E8 **Rhuallt** Denbgs
112 F6 **Rhubodach** Ag & B
75 P11 **Rhuddall Heath** Ches W
38 D3 **Rhuddlan** Cerdgn
74 D8 **Rhuddlan** Denbgs
50 F10 **Rhulen** Powys
111 Q11 **Rhunahaorine** Ag & B
61 L4 **Rhyd** Gwynd
38 C6 **Rhydargaeau** Carmth
38 E4 **Rhydcymerau** Carmth
41 N3 **Rhydd** Worcs
61 J2 **Rhyd-Ddu** Gwynd
26 H3 **Rhydding** Neath
74 D10 **Rhydgaled** Conwy
61 P2 **Rhydlanfair** Conwy
48 E11 **Rhydlewis** Cerdgn
60 C6 **Rhydlios** Gwynd
62 B2 **Rhyd-lydan** Conwy
38 C3 **Rhydowen** Cerdgn
49 J7 **Rhydrosser** Cerdgn
40 C2 **Rhydspence** Herefs
62 H1 **Rhydtalog** Flints
62 B5 **Rhyd-uchaf** Gwynd
60 E5 **Rhyd-y-clafdy** Gwynd
62 H6 **Rhydycroesau** Shrops
49 K5 **Rhydyfelin** Cerdgn
27 P5 **Rhydyfelin** Rhondd
74 B8 **Rhyd-y-foel** Conwy
38 H10 **Rhydyfro** Neath
73 K10 **Rhyd-y-groes** Gwynd
61 P8 **Rhydymain** Gwynd
40 D10 **Rhyd-y-meirch** Mons
74 H10 **Rhydymwyn** Flints
49 L3 **Rhyd-y pennau** Cerdgn
61 K11 **Rhyd-yr-onnen** Gwynd
61 M4 **Rhyd-y-sarn** Gwynd
74 D7 **Rhyl** Denbgs
39 Q10 **Rhymney** Caerph
124 D9 **Rhynd** P & K
140 D10 **Rhynie** Abers
146 F9 **Rhynie** Highld
52 E6 **Ribbesford** Worcs
83 M9 **Ribbleton** Lancs
83 J9 **Ribby** Lancs
83 P8 **Ribchester** Lancs
77 P11 **Riber** Derbys
80 D2 **Riby** Lincs
86 B7 **Riccall** N York
107 N10 **Riccarton** Border
104 H3 **Riccarton** E Ayrs
51 N7 **Richards Castle** Herefs
32 E6 **Richings Park** Bucks
32 H7 **Richmond** Gt Lon
91 K6 **Richmond** N York
78 C7 **Richmond** Sheff
12 b2 **Richmond Fort** Guern
21 J6 **Rich's Holford** Somset
64 G8 **Rickerscote** Staffs
28 G10 **Rickford** N Som
5 M9 **Rickham** Devon
58 F5 **Rickinghall** Suffk
45 P5 **Rickling** Essex
45 P6 **Rickling Green** Essex
32 F3 **Rickmansworth** Herts
107 N5 **Riddell** Border
66 C2 **Riddings** Derbys
19 M10 **Riddlecombe** Devon
84 G6 **Riddlesden** C Brad
28 H11 **Ridge** BaNES
11 M7 **Ridge** Dorset
33 J2 **Ridge** Herts
23 L7 **Ridge** Wilts
50 E8 **Ridgebourne** Powys
15 K1 **Ridge Green** Surrey
53 P2 **Ridge Lane** Warwks
17 M2 **Ridge Row** Kent
78 C7 **Ridgeway** Derbys
53 K8 **Ridgeway** Worcs
41 L2 **Ridgeway Cross** Herefs
46 C3 **Ridgewell** Essex
15 N7 **Ridgewood** E Susx
44 D4 **Ridgmont** C Beds
100 C6 **Riding Mill** Nthumb
34 A9 **Ridley** Kent
99 M5 **Ridley** Nthumb
63 P1 **Ridley Green** Ches E
71 L6 **Ridlington** Norfk
67 L11 **Ridlington** Rutlnd
71 L6 **Ridlington Street** Norfk
99 P1 **Ridsdale** Nthumb
92 C9 **Rievaulx** N York
92 C9 **Rievaulx Abbey** N York
98 C5 **Rigg** D & G
114 D7 **Riggend** N Lans
138 G5 **Righoul** Highld
89 P9 **Rigmadon Park** Cumb
80 H8 **Rigsby** Lincs
105 R3 **Rigside** S Lans
83 N10 **Riley Green** Lancs
65 L9 **Rileyhill** Staffs
7 K10 **Rilla Mill** Cnwll
7 K10 **Rillaton** Cnwll
92 H11 **Rillington** N York
84 B6 **Rimington** Lancs
22 E9 **Rimpton** Somset
87 P9 **Rimswell** E R Yk
37 J5 **Rinaston** Pembks
52 D2 **Rindleford** Shrops
96 E7 **Ringford** D & G
77 P7 **Ringinglow** Sheff
70 H9 **Ringland** Norfk
15 N6 **Ringles Cross** E Susx
34 F11 **Ringlestone** Kent
76 E3 **Ringley** Bolton
15 N8 **Ringmer** E Susx
5 K7 **Ringmore** Devon
8 H10 **Ringmore** Devon
75 M2 **Ring o'Bells** Lancs
139 N7 **Ringorm** Moray
68 H11 **Ring's End** Cambs
59 M3 **Ringsfield** Suffk
59 N3 **Ringsfield Corner** Suffk
44 E9 **Ringshall** Herts
58 F10 **Ringshall** Suffk
58 F10 **Ringshall Stocks** Suffk
55 N5 **Ringstead** Nhants
69 N4 **Ringstead** Norfk
12 B4 **Ringwood** Hants
17 P1 **Ringwould** Kent
2 F9 **Rinsey** Cnwll
2 F9 **Rinsey Croft** Cnwll
15 P9 **Ripe** E Susx
66 C2 **Ripley** Derbys
12 B5 **Ripley** Hants
85 L3 **Ripley** N York
32 F11 **Ripley** Surrey
86 H9 **Riplingham** E R Yk
25 L8 **Riplington** Hants
85 L1 **Ripon** N York
68 B6 **Rippingale** Lincs
35 P12 **Ripple** Kent
41 P4 **Ripple** Worcs
84 F11 **Ripponden** Calder
102 B1 **Risabus** Ag & B
51 P9 **Risbury** Herefs
86 G12 **Risby** N Linc
57 Q7 **Risby** Suffk
28 B4 **Risca** Caerph
87 M7 **Rise** E R Yk
16 A5 **Riseden** E Susx
16 C4 **Riseden** Kent
68 D6 **Risegate** Lincs
79 N8 **Riseholme** Lincs
97 L11 **Risehow** Cumb
55 P8 **Riseley** Bed
31 P9 **Riseley** Wokham
58 H7 **Rishangles** Suffk
83 Q9 **Rishton** Lancs
84 F11 **Rishworth** Calder
84 B10 **Rising Bridge** Lancs
66 D5 **Risley** Derbys
76 C5 **Risley** Warrtn
85 K1 **Risplith** N York
30 G10 **Rivar** Wilts
46 E8 **Rivenhall End** Essex
17 N2 **River** Kent
14 D6 **River** W Susx
57 K7 **River Bank** Cambs
137 P5 **Riverford** Highld
33 P11 **Riverhead** Kent
22 H10 **Rivers Corner** Dorset
83 N12 **Rivington** Lancs
20 C9 **Roachill** Devon
55 J10 **Roade** Nhants
59 K2 **Road Green** Norfk
98 G3 **Roadhead** Cumb
114 F11 **Roadmeetings** S Lans
105 K6 **Roadside** E Ayrs
151 L4 **Roadside** Highld
20 G6 **Roadwater** Somset
134 E7 **Roag** Highld
82 F2 **Roa Island** Cumb
104 E9 **Roan of Craigoch** S Ayrs
45 N5 **Roast Green** Essex
28 B7 **Roath** Cardif
107 L7 **Roberton** Border
106 B4 **Roberton** S Lans
16 C6 **Robertsbridge** E Susx
85 J10 **Roberttown** Kirk
37 L7 **Robeston Wathen** Pembks
97 Q4 **Robgill Tower** D & G
76 G12 **Robin Hill** Staffs
75 N1 **Robin Hood** Lancs
85 L9 **Robin Hood** Leeds
53 L4 **Robin Hood Crematorium** Solhll
78 H4 ***Robin Hood Doncaster Sheffield Airport*** Donc
46 C4 **Robinhood End** Essex
93 J6 **Robin Hood's Bay** N York
4 H4 **Roborough** Devon
19 L10 **Roborough** Devon
75 M5 **Roby** Knows
75 N2 **Roby Mill** Lancs
65 L4 **Rocester** Staffs
36 G6 **Roch** Pembks
76 G1 **Rochdale** Rochdl
76 G1 **Rochdale Crematorium** Rochdl
3 N2 **Roche** Cnwll
34 D8 **Rochester** Medway
108 D10 **Rochester** Nthumb
34 F4 **Rochford** Essex
52 B7 **Rochford** Worcs
36 G6 **Roch Gate** Pembks
6 D9 **Rock** Cnwll
27 J4 **Rock** Neath
109 K6 **Rock** Nthumb
14 G8 **Rock** W Susx
52 D6 **Rock** Worcs
9 J6 **Rockbeare** Devon
23 P9 **Rockbourne** Hants
98 D6 **Rockcliffe** Cumb
96 G7 **Rockcliffe** D & G
98 D6 **Rockcliffe Cross** Cumb
76 G12 **Rock End** Staffs
5 Q4 **Rockend** Torbay
75 K6 **Rock Ferry** Wirral
146 G8 **Rockfield** Highld
40 G8 **Rockfield** Mons
19 P4 **Rockford** Devon
12 B3 **Rockford** Hants
51 N5 **Rockgreen** Shrops
29 K4 **Rockhampton** S Glos
6 F8 **Rockhead** Cnwll
51 J5 **Rockhill** Shrops
52 H7 **Rock Hill** Worcs
55 L2 **Rockingham** Nhants
58 E1 **Rockland All Saints** Norfk
71 L11 **Rockland St Mary** Norfk
58 E1 **Rockland St Peter** Norfk
78 H8 **Rockley** Notts
30 D8 **Rockley** Wilts
84 C10 **Rockliffe** Lancs
113 J3 **Rockville** Ag & B
31 R5 **Rockwell End** Bucks
20 H9 **Rockwell Green** Somset
41 N10 **Rodborough** Gloucs
30 D5 **Rodbourne** Swindn
29 Q6 **Rodbourne** Wilts
51 K8 **Rodd** Herefs
108 G6 **Roddam** Nthumb
10 F8 **Rodden** Dorset
100 F11 **Roddymoor** Dur
22 H3 **Rode** Somset
76 E12 **Rode Heath** Ches E
76 G10 **Rode Heath** Ches E
152 d6 **Rodel** W Isls
63 P9 **Roden** Wrekin
20 F5 **Rodhuish** Somset
63 Q9 **Rodington** Wrekin
63 P9 **Rodington Heath** Wrekin
41 M9 **Rodley** Gloucs
85 K8 **Rodley** Leeds
29 Q3 **Rodmarton** Gloucs
15 M9 **Rodmell** E Susx
34 G10 **Rodmersham** Kent
34 G10 **Rodmersham Green** Kent
22 B3 **Rodney Stoke** Somset
65 M4 **Rodsley** Derbys
21 L5 **Rodway** Somset
85 M2 **Roecliffe** N York
77 J4 **Roe Cross** Tamesd
45 J10 **Roe Green** Herts
45 K5 **Roe Green** Herts
76 D3 **Roe Green** Salfd
33 J7 **Roehampton** Gt Lon
14 H4 **Roffey** W Susx
146 C5 **Rogart** Highld
25 P8 **Rogate** W Susx
89 K7 **Roger Ground** Cumb
28 C5 **Rogerstone** Newpt
152 d6 **Roghadal** W Isls
28 F5 **Rogiet** Mons
31 N4 **Roke** Oxon
101 K6 **Roker** Sundld
71 N9 **Rollesby** Norfk
67 J12 **Rolleston** Leics
67 J2 **Rolleston** Notts
65 N6 **Rolleston on Dove** Staffs
87 N6 **Rolston** E R Yk
28 E10 **Rolstone** N Som
16 E4 **Rolvenden** Kent
16 E5 **Rolvenden Layne** Kent
90 G2 **Romaldkirk** Dur
29 M9 **Roman Baths & Pump Room** BaNES
91 N8 **Romanby** N York
115 L11 **Romanno Bridge** Border
19 P9 **Romansleigh** Devon
16 F2 **Romden Castle** Kent
134 G5 **Romesdal** Highld
11 P3 **Romford** Dorset
33 P4 **Romford** Gt Lon
76 H5 **Romiley** Stockp
33 Q10 **Romney Street** Kent
24 F9 **Romsey** Hants
52 E4 **Romsley** Shrops
52 H5 **Romsley** Worcs
135 L4 **Rona** Highld
111 Q10 **Ronachan** Ag & B
29 P11 **Rood Ashton** Wilts
99 P9 **Rookhope** Dur
12 H8 **Rookley** IoW
12 H8 **Rookley Green** IoW
21 N3 **Rooks Bridge** Somset
20 H6 **Rooks Nest** Somset
91 L9 **Rookwith** N York
87 P9 **Roos** E R Yk
82 F1 **Roose** Cumb
82 G2 **Roosebeck** Cumb
56 B9 **Roothams Green** Bed
25 L7 **Ropley** Hants
25 L7 **Ropley Dean** Hants
25 L6 **Ropley Soke** Hants
67 N5 **Ropsley** Lincs
141 P6 **Rora** Abers
63 J12 **Rorrington** Shrops
140 B6 **Rosarie** Moray
3 J4 **Rose** Cnwll
83 K8 **Roseacre** Lancs
20 B9 **Rose Ash** Devon
114 E11 **Rosebank** S Lans
37 L5 **Rosebush** Pembks
6 H5 **Rosecare** Cnwll
3 K3 **Rosecliston** Cnwll
92 E7 **Rosedale Abbey** N York
46 F6 **Rose Green** Essex
46 G4 **Rose Green** Suffk
46 H3 **Rose Green** Suffk
14 C11 **Rose Green** W Susx
145 L5 **Rosehall** Highld
141 M2 **Rosehearty** Abers
15 N7 **Rose Hill** E Susx
84 B9 **Rose Hill** Lancs
63 M9 **Rosehill** Shrops
139 L2 **Roseisle** Moray
16 A10 **Roselands** E Susx
37 J9 **Rosemarket** Pembks
138 D4 **Rosemarkie** Highld
21 J10 **Rosemary Lane** Devon
124 D4 **Rosemount** P & K
6 D11 **Rosenannon** Cnwll
3 K10 **Rosenithon** Cnwll
15 Q7 **Roser's Cross** E Susx
3 P3 **Rosevean** Cnwll
3 L7 **Rosevine** Cnwll
2 F7 **Rosewarne** Cnwll
115 P9 **Rosewell** Mdloth
91 P2 **Roseworth** S on T
2 F6 **Roseworthy** Cnwll
89 N3 **Rosgill** Cumb
2 B10 **Roskestal** Cnwll
134 E7 **Roskhill** Highld
3 K9 **Roskorwell** Cnwll
98 C9 **Rosley** Cumb
115 N8 **Roslin** Mdloth
65 N9 **Rosliston** Derbys
113 K5 **Rosneath** Ag & B
96 D9 **Ross** D & G
109 J2 **Ross** Nthumb
75 L12 **Rossett** Wrexhm
85 L5 **Rossett Green** N York
78 G4 **Rossington** Donc
113 N7 **Rossland** Rens
41 J7 **Ross-on-Wye** Herefs
151 N8 **Roster** Highld
76 D7 **Rostherne** Ches E
88 H4 **Rosthwaite** Cumb
65 L4 **Roston** Derbys
2 E8 **Rosudgeon** Cnwll
115 L4 **Rosyth** Fife
108 H9 **Rothbury** Nthumb
66 H9 **Rotherby** Leics
15 Q5 **Rotherfield** E Susx
31 P6 **Rotherfield Greys** Oxon
31 P6 **Rotherfield Peppard** Oxon
78 C5 **Rotherham** Rothm
78 D5 **Rotherham Crematorium** Rothm
55 J9 **Rothersthorpe** Nhants
55 J9 **Rothersthorpe Services** Nhants
31 P11 **Rotherwick** Hants
139 P6 **Rothes** Moray
112 G8 **Rothesay** Ag & B
141 J8 **Rothiebrisbane** Abers
140 E6 **Rothiemay** Moray
130 H3 **Rothiemurchus Lodge** Highld
140 H8 **Rothienorman** Abers
66 F9 **Rothley** Leics
108 G12 **Rothley** Nthumb
140 G9 **Rothmaise** Abers
85 M9 **Rothwell** Leeds
80 C4 **Rothwell** Lincs
55 K4 **Rothwell** Nhants
87 K5 **Rotsea** E R Yk
132 B10 **Rottal Lodge** Angus
15 L10 **Rottingdean** Br & H
88 C4 **Rottington** Cumb
97 L3 **Roucan** D & G
97 L3 **Roucan Loch Crematorium** D & G
12 H8 **Roud** IoW
70 B8 **Rougham** Norfk
58 D8 **Rougham Green** Suffk
64 G4 **Rough Close** Staffs
35 K10 **Rough Common** Kent
84 C7 **Roughlee** Lancs
131 Q2 **Roughpark** Abers
80 E10 **Roughton** Lincs
71 J5 **Roughton** Norfk
52 D2 **Roughton** Shrops
34 A11 **Roughway** Kent
34 F2 **Roundbush** Essex
32 G3 **Round Bush** Herts
45 Q8 **Roundbush Green** Essex
44 G7 **Round Green** Luton
10 C3 **Roundham** Somset
85 M8 **Roundhay** Leeds
52 H3 **Rounds Green** Sandw
34 B8 **Round Street** Kent
14 F5 **Roundstreet Common** W Susx
30 B9 **Roundway** Wilts
124 H3 **Roundyhill** Angus
152 k3 **Rousay** Ork
9 P6 **Rousdon** Devon
43 K7 **Rousham** Oxon
53 J10 **Rous Lench** Worcs
113 J9 **Routenburn** N Ayrs
87 K7 **Routh** E R Yk
31 R3 **Rout's Green** Bucks
6 G9 **Row** Cnwll
89 M9 **Row** Cumb
99 J11 **Row** Cumb
98 E3 **Rowanburn** D & G
113 M2 **Rowardennan** Stirlg
77 J6 **Rowarth** Derbys
25 J10 **Row Ash** Hants
28 F10 **Rowberrow** Somset
12 H8 **Rowborough** IoW
29 R10 **Rowde** Wilts
8 C5 **Rowden** Devon
73 N9 **Rowen** Conwy
65 M2 **Rowfield** Derbys
99 K6 **Rowfoot** Nthumb
21 K8 **Rowford** Somset
46 D7 **Row Green** Essex
47 J7 **Rowhedge** Essex
14 G4 **Rowhook** W Susx
53 M7 **Rowington** Warwks
77 N9 **Rowland** Derbys
13 M3 **Rowland's Castle** Hants
100 F6 **Rowland's Gill** Gatesd
25 P5 **Rowledge** Surrey
100 E8 **Rowley** Dur
86 H8 **Rowley** E R Yk
63 J11 **Rowley** Shrops
85 J12 **Rowley Hill** Kirk
52 H3 **Rowley Regis** Sandw
52 H3 **Rowley Regis Crematorium** Sandw
40 E6 **Rowlstone** Herefs
14 F3 **Rowly** Surrey
13 K4 **Rowner** Hants
53 K6 **Rowney Green** Worcs
24 F10 **Rownhams** Hants
24 F9 **Rownhams Services** Hants
88 E3 **Rowrah** Cumb
44 B8 **Rowsham** Bucks
77 N10 **Rowsley** Derbys
76 F8 **Rows of Trees** Ches E
31 K4 **Rowstock** Oxon
80 B12 **Rowston** Lincs
78 D10 **Rowthorne** Derbys
75 M11 **Rowton** Ches W
51 L4 **Rowton** Shrops
63 L9 **Rowton** Shrops
63 Q8 **Rowton** Wrekin
32 E9 **Row Town** Surrey
108 A4 **Roxburgh** Border
86 G11 **Roxby** N Linc
92 F3 **Roxby** N York
56 C9 **Roxton** Bed
46 B10 **Roxwell** Essex
32 H7 **Royal Botanic Gardens** Gt Lon
91 L2 **Royal Oak** Darltn
75 L3 **Royal Oak** Lancs
64 B4 **Royal's Green** Ches E
129 J8 **Roy Bridge** Highld
77 N1 **Roydhouse** Kirk
45 M9 **Roydon** Essex
58 G4 **Roydon** Norfk
69 N7 **Roydon** Norfk
45 M10 **Roydon Hamlet** Essex
78 B1 **Royston** Barns
45 L4 **Royston** Herts
76 G2 **Royton** Oldham
13 d1 **Rozel** Jersey
63 J3 **Ruabon** Wrexhm
118 E3 **Ruaig** Ag & B
3 M6 **Ruan High Lanes** Cnwll
3 L6 **Ruan Lanihorne** Cnwll
2 H11 **Ruan Major** Cnwll
2 H11 **Ruan Minor** Cnwll
41 J8 **Ruardean** Gloucs
41 K8 **Ruardean Hill** Gloucs
41 J8 **Ruardean Woodside** Gloucs
53 J5 **Rubery** Birm
152 b10 **Rubha Ban** W Isls
98 G9 **Ruckcroft** Cumb
40 F4 **Ruckhall** Herefs
17 J4 **Ruckinge** Kent
80 F8 **Ruckland** Lincs
63 P12 **Ruckley** Shrops
91 Q5 **Rudby** N York
100 E5 **Rudchester** Nthumb
66 F5 **Ruddington** Notts
41 K9 **Ruddle** Gloucs
3 N3 **Ruddlemoor** Cnwll
41 M7 **Rudford** Gloucs
23 J3 **Rudge** Somset
29 J5 **Rudgeway** S Glos
14 F4 **Rudgwick** W Susx
41 J6 **Rudhall** Herefs
76 C9 **Rudheath** Ches W
76 D9 **Rudheath Woods** Ches E
46 E11 **Rudley Green** Essex
29 N8 **Rudloe** Wilts
28 B5 **Rudry** Caerph
87 L2 **Rudston** E R Yk
76 H12 **Rudyard** Staffs
107 P6 **Ruecastle** Border
83 K12 **Rufford** Lancs
85 Q5 **Rufforth** C York
62 E3 **Rug** Denbgs
54 E5 **Rugby** Warwks
65 K8 **Rugeley** Staffs
21 L8 **Ruishton** Somset
32 F5 **Ruislip** Gt Lon
126 G5 **Rùm** Highld
140 B5 **Rumbach** Moray
115 J1 **Rumbling Bridge** P & K
59 L4 **Rumburgh** Suffk
100 F11 **Rumby Hill** Dur
6 C10 **Rumford** Cnwll
114 G6 **Rumford** Falk
28 B6 **Rumney** Cardif
21 K8 **Rumwell** Somset
75 N7 **Runcorn** Halton
14 C10 **Runcton** W Susx
69 M10 **Runcton Holme** Norfk
14 B1 **Runfold** Surrey
70 F10 **Runhall** Norfk
71 P10 **Runham** Norfk
71 Q10 **Runham** Norfk
20 H9 **Runnington** Somset
46 D10 **Runsell Green** Essex
83 M11 **Runshaw Moor** Lancs
92 G3 **Runswick** N York
131 P10 **Runtaleave** Angus
34 D3 **Runwell** Essex
31 R7 **Ruscombe** Wokham
41 K5 **Rushall** Herefs
59 J4 **Rushall** Norfk
23 P2 **Rushall** Wilts
65 J12 **Rushall** Wsall
58 C8 **Rushbrooke** Suffk
51 N2 **Rushbury** Shrops
45 K5 **Rushden** Herts
55 N7 **Rushden** Nhants
34 F8 **Rushenden** Kent
15 R5 **Rusher's Cross** E Susx
7 N9 **Rushford** Devon
58 D4 **Rushford** Norfk
47 L8 **Rush Green** Essex
33 P5 **Rush Green** Gt Lon
45 J7 **Rush Green** Herts
76 C6 **Rush Green** Warrtn
16 A7 **Rushlake Green** E Susx
59 P3 **Rushmere** Suffk
47 M2 **Rushmere St Andrew** Suffk
14 B3 **Rushmoor** Surrey
51 K9 **Rushock** Herefs
52 G6 **Rushock** Worcs
76 F5 **Rusholme** Manch
75 P11 **Rushton** Ches W
55 L4 **Rushton** Nhants
63 Q10 **Rushton** Shrops
76 H11 **Rushton Spencer** Staffs
52 F10 **Rushwick** Worcs
91 M1 **Rushyford** Dur
114 B1 **Ruskie** Stirlg
68 B2 **Ruskington** Lincs
89 K9 **Rusland Cross** Cumb
14 H3 **Rusper** W Susx
41 K9 **Ruspidge** Gloucs
46 D9 **Russell Green** Essex
31 P4 **Russell's Water** Oxon
59 K6 **Russel's Green** Suffk
15 J3 **Russ Hill** Surrey
15 Q3 **Rusthall** Kent
14 F10 **Rustington** W Susx
93 J10 **Ruston** N York

87 K3 Ruston Parva E R Yk
92 H5 Ruswarp N York
51 Q3 Ruthall Shrops
107 Q4 Rutherford Border
114 B9 Rutherglen S Lans
6 E11 Ruthernbridge Cnwll
74 F12 Ruthin Denbgs
133 M3 Ruthrieston C Aber
140 D6 Ruthven Abers
124 F3 Ruthven Angus
130 D4 Ruthven Highld
3 M2 Ruthvoes Cnwll
97 P11 Ruthwaite Cumb
97 M5 Ruthwell D & G
33 N8 Ruxley Corner Gt Lon
40 H8 Ruxton Green Herefs
63 L8 Ruyton-XI-Towns Shrops
100 C3 Ryal Nthumb
10 B6 Ryall Dorset
41 P3 Ryall Worcs
34 B10 Ryarsh Kent
43 P10 Rycote Oxon
89 K5 Rydal Cumb
13 K6 Ryde IoW
16 G7 Rye E Susx
63 N6 Ryebank Shrops
41 K7 Ryeford Herefs
16 F6 Rye Foreign E Susx
16 G7 Rye Harbour E Susx
87 N10 Ryehill E R Yk
31 P9 Ryeish Green Wokham
41 M4 Rye Street Worcs
67 P10 Ryhall Rutlnd
91 M12 Ryhill Wakefd
101 K7 Ryhope Sundld
78 D10 Rylah Derbys
79 P8 Ryland Lincs
66 E5 Rylands Notts
84 E3 Rylstone N York
10 F3 Ryme Intrinseca Dorset
85 Q7 Ryther N York
100 F5 Ryton Gatesd
92 F11 Ryton N York
64 E11 Ryton Shrops
54 C3 Ryton Warwks
54 C6 Ryton-on-Dunsmore Warwks
100 F6 Ryton Woodside Gatesd

S

84 B7 Sabden Lancs
33 Q3 Sabine's Green Essex
45 L8 Sacombe Herts
45 L8 Sacombe Green Herts
100 G9 Sacriston Dur
91 N3 Sadberge Darltn
103 L3 Saddell Ag & B
54 H2 Saddington Leics
69 L9 Saddle Bow Norfk
15 K8 Saddlescombe W Susx
89 M6 Sadgill Cumb
45 P4 Saffron Walden Essex
37 L10 Sageston Pembks
70 D11 Saham Hills Norfk
70 C11 Saham Toney Norfk
75 M11 Saighton Ches W
117 K8 St Abbs Border
116 F8 St Agnes Border
2 H4 St Agnes Cnwll
2 b3 St Agnes IoS
44 G10 St Albans Herts
3 K4 St Allen Cnwll
12 c2 St Andrew Guern
125 K9 St Andrews Fife
125 K9 St Andrews Botanic Garden Fife
27 Q8 St Andrew's Major V Glam
10 D6 St Andrews Well Dorset
82 H9 St Anne's Lancs
106 E11 St Ann's D & G
7 M10 St Ann's Chapel Cnwll
5 L7 St Ann's Chapel Devon
3 J9 St Anthony Cnwll
16 A10 St Anthony's Hill E Susx
28 H3 St Arvans Mons
74 E9 St Asaph Denbgs
27 N9 St Athan V Glam
13 b2 St Aubin Jersey
3 P4 St Austell Cnwll
88 C4 St Bees Cumb
3 Q4 St Blazey Cnwll
3 P4 St Blazey Gate Cnwll
107 P4 St Boswells Border
13 a2 St Brelade Jersey
13 a3 St Brelade's Bay Jersey
6 E10 St Breock Cnwll
6 G9 St Breward Cnwll
40 H10 St Briavels Gloucs
36 F8 St Brides Pembks
27 L7 St Bride's Major V Glam
28 F4 St Brides Netherwent Mons
27 P7 St Brides super-Ely V Glam
28 C6 St Brides Wentlooge Newpt
4 G5 St Budeaux C Plym
42 D4 Saintbury Gloucs
2 C9 St Buryan Cnwll
29 M8 St Catherine BaNES
121 L11 St Catherines Ag & B
41 N11 St Chloe Gloucs
37 Q7 St Clears Carmth
4 C3 St Cleer Cnwll
3 L6 St Clement Cnwll
13 d3 St Clement Jersey
7 J8 St Clether Cnwll
112 F8 St Colmac Ag & B
3 M2 St Columb Major Cnwll
3 K2 St Columb Minor Cnwll
3 M3 St Columb Road Cnwll
141 P3 St Combs Abers
59 L4 St Cross South Elmham Suffk
133 J11 St Cyrus Abers
123 N9 St David's P & K
36 E5 St David's Pembks
2 H6 St Day Cnwll
20 G5 St Decumans Somset
3 M3 St Dennis Cnwll
40 F5 St Devereux Herefs
48 B11 St Dogmaels Pembks
37 J5 St Dogwells Pembks
4 F3 St Dominick Cnwll
27 M8 St Donats V Glam
29 R9 St Edith's Marsh Wilts
6 E9 St Endellion Cnwll
3 L3 St Enoder Cnwll
3 L4 St Erme Cnwll
4 E5 St Erney Cnwll
2 E7 St Erth Cnwll
2 F7 St Erth Praze Cnwll
6 C10 St Ervan Cnwll
6 C11 St Eval Cnwll
3 N5 St Ewe Cnwll
27 Q7 St Fagans Cardif
27 Q7 St Fagans Welsh Life Museum Cardif
141 Q5 St Fergus Abers
122 H8 St Fillans P & K
37 L10 St Florence Pembks
6 H5 St Gennys Cnwll
74 D8 St George Conwy
28 E10 St Georges N Som
27 Q7 St George's V Glam
32 F10 St George's Hill Surrey
4 E5 St Germans Cnwll
19 K9 St Giles in the Wood Devon
7 L7 St Giles-on-the-Heath Devon
3 K7 St Gluvia's Cnwll
50 D6 St Harmon Powys
91 K1 St Helen Auckland Dur
97 L11 St Helens Cumb
16 E8 St Helens E Susx
13 K7 St Helens IoW
75 N5 St Helens St Hel
75 N4 St Helens Crematorium St Hel
33 J9 St Helier Gt Lon
13 c2 St Helier Jersey
2 E8 St Hilary Cnwll
27 N8 St Hilary V Glam
9 L3 Saint Hill Devon
15 M4 Saint Hill W Susx
40 B11 St Illtyd Blae G
44 H6 St Ippollitts Herts
36 G9 St Ishmael's Pembks
6 D10 St Issey Cnwll
4 D3 St Ive Cnwll
4 D3 St Ive Cross Cnwll
56 F6 St Ives Cambs
2 E6 St Ives Cnwll
11 Q4 St Ives Dorset
71 K8 St James Norfk
55 J8 St James's End Nhants
59 L4 St James South Elmham Suffk
6 D10 St Jidgey Cnwll
4 F6 St John Cnwll
13 b1 St John Jersey
100 D11 St Johns Dur
102 c5 St John's IoM
33 P11 St Johns Kent
32 D10 St Johns Surrey
52 F10 St Johns Worcs
19 K7 St John's Chapel Devon
99 N10 St John's Chapel Dur
69 K9 St John's Fen End Norfk
69 K9 St John's Highway Norfk
106 C3 St John's Kirk S Lans
96 C2 St John's Town of Dalry D & G
33 K6 St John's Wood Gt Lon
102 e3 St Jude's IoM
2 B8 St Just Cnwll
3 L7 St Just-in-Roseland Cnwll
141 J9 St Katherines Abers
3 K10 St Keverne Cnwll
6 E9 St Kew Cnwll
6 F9 St Kew Highway Cnwll
4 C4 St Keyne Cnwll
6 F11 St Lawrence Cnwll
46 G11 St Lawrence Essex
13 J9 St Lawrence IoW
13 b2 St Lawrence Jersey
35 Q9 St Lawrence Kent
44 C10 St Leonards Bucks
11 Q4 St Leonards Dorset
16 E9 St Leonards E Susx
34 B11 St Leonard's Street Kent
2 B10 St Levan Cnwll
27 Q8 St Lythans V Glam
6 F10 St Mabyn Cnwll
124 D8 St Madoes P & K
40 E5 St Margarets Herefs
45 M9 St Margarets Herts
17 P2 St Margaret's at Cliffe Kent
152 k6 St Margaret's Hope Ork
59 L4 St Margaret South Elmham Suffk
102 d6 St Marks IoM
3 J9 St Martin Cnwll
4 C6 St Martin Cnwll
12 c3 St Martin Guern
13 d2 St Martin Jersey
2 c1 St Martin's IoS
124 D7 St Martin's P & K
63 K5 St Martins Shrops
63 K5 St Martin's Moor Shrops
13 b1 St Mary Jersey
24 G3 St Mary Bourne Hants
5 Q3 St Marychurch Torbay
27 N8 St Mary Church V Glam
33 N8 St Mary Cray Gt Lon
27 M7 St Mary Hill V Glam
17 J5 St Mary in the Marsh Kent
33 J4 St Marylebone Crematorium Gt Lon
2 b2 St Mary's IoS
152 k5 St Mary's Ork
17 K5 St Mary's Bay Kent
28 F8 St Mary's Grove N Som
34 E7 St Mary's Hoo Medway
40 F8 St Maughans Mons
40 G8 St Maughans Green Mons
3 L8 St Mawes Cnwll
6 C11 St Mawgan Cnwll
4 F4 St Mellion Cnwll
28 B6 St Mellons Cardif
6 C10 St Merryn Cnwll
3 N4 St Mewan Cnwll
3 N6 St Michael Caerhays Cnwll
21 M7 St Michael Church Somset
3 L6 St Michael Penkevil Cnwll
16 F4 St Michaels Kent
51 P7 St Michaels Worcs
83 K7 St Michael's on Wyre Lancs
59 L4 St Michael South Elmham Suffk
6 D9 St Minver Cnwll
116 C1 St Monans Fife
4 B3 St Neot Cnwll
56 D8 St Neots Cambs
36 H3 St Nicholas Pembks
27 P7 St Nicholas V Glam
35 N9 St Nicholas at Wade Kent
114 E3 St Ninians Stirlg
71 N12 St Olaves Norfk
47 K8 St Osyth Essex
13 c2 St Ouen Jersey
40 H7 St Owens Cross Herefs
33 N8 St Pauls Cray Gt Lon
44 H7 St Paul's Walden Herts
13 b2 St Peter Jersey
12 c2 St Peter Port Guern
12 b3 St Peter's Guern
35 Q8 St Peter's Kent
56 E6 St Peter's Hill Cambs
37 J11 St Petrox Pembks
4 B4 St Pinnock Cnwll
104 G5 St Quivox S Ayrs
2 H11 St Ruan Cnwll
12 d1 St Sampson Guern
12 b2 St Saviour Guern
13 c2 St Saviour Jersey
3 M4 St Stephen Cnwll
4 F5 St Stephens Cnwll
7 L7 St Stephens Cnwll
6 F8 St Teath Cnwll
6 F9 St Tudy Cnwll
37 J11 St Twynnells Pembks
4 A6 St Veep Cnwll
125 M4 St Vigeans Angus
6 D11 St Wenn Cnwll
40 G7 St Weonards Herefs
27 Q7 St y-Nyll V Glam
5 M9 Salcombe Devon
9 M7 Salcombe Regis Devon
46 G9 Salcott-cum-Virley Essex
76 E5 Sale Traffd
81 J8 Saleby Lincs
52 H9 Sale Green Worcs
16 D6 Salehurst E Susx
38 F6 Salem Carmth
49 L4 Salem Cerdgn
119 P4 Salen Ag & B
127 M11 Salen Highld
83 P8 Salesbury Lancs
44 D4 Salford C Beds
42 G6 Salford Oxon
76 E4 Salford Salfd
53 K10 Salford Priors Warwks
15 K2 Salfords Surrey
71 L9 Salhouse Norfk
115 J3 Saline Fife
23 P7 Salisbury Wilts
23 P7 Salisbury Cathedral Wilts
23 P7 Salisbury Crematorium Wilts
23 N4 Salisbury Plain Wilts
98 G10 Salkeld Dykes Cumb
70 G7 Salle Norfk
80 F9 Salmonby Lincs
42 C7 Salperton Gloucs
55 Q10 Salph End Bed
114 E8 Salsburgh N Lans
64 H6 Salt Staffs
97 M9 Salta Cumb
84 H7 Saltaire C Brad
4 F5 Saltash Cnwll
146 C11 Saltburn Highld
92 D3 Saltburn-by-the-Sea R & Cl
67 L7 Saltby Leics
97 P7 Salt Coates Cumb
88 E7 Saltcoats Cumb
104 D2 Saltcoats N Ayrs
83 J9 Saltcotes Lancs
15 M10 Saltdean Br & H
88 C11 Salterbeck Cumb
84 D6 Salterforth Lancs
76 B10 Salterswall Ches W
30 C11 Salterton Wilts
81 J5 Saltfleet Lincs
81 J5 Saltfleetby All Saints Lincs
81 J5 Saltfleetby St Clement Lincs
80 H6 Saltfleetby St Peter Lincs
29 K9 Saltford BaNES
70 G3 Salthouse Norfk
53 L5 Saltley Birm
28 D6 Saltmarsh Newpt
86 E10 Saltmarshe E R Yk
75 L10 Saltney Flints
92 E10 Salton N York
19 J9 Saltrens Devon
100 H6 Saltwell Crematorium Gatesd
100 F2 Saltwick Nthumb
17 L4 Saltwood Kent
14 G9 Salvington W Susx
52 G8 Salwarpe Worcs
10 C5 Salway Ash Dorset
53 K8 Sambourne Warwks
64 D7 Sambrook Wrekin
83 N9 Samlesbury Lancs
83 N9 Samlesbury Bottoms Lancs
20 H9 Sampford Arundel Somset
20 H5 Sampford Brett Somset
8 B4 Sampford Courtenay Devon
20 H9 Sampford Moor Somset
20 G10 Sampford Peverell Devon
7 P10 Sampford Spiney Devon
152 n3 Samsonlane Ork
47 K8 Samson's Corner Essex
116 B7 Samuelston E Loth
110 F7 Sanaigmore Ag & B
2 C8 Sancreed Cnwll
86 G7 Sancton E R Yk
21 P4 Sand Somset
127 N4 Sandaig Highld
97 Q10 Sandale Cumb
85 M11 Sandal Magna Wakefd
126 H7 Sandavore Highld
152 n7 Sanday Ork
152 n2 Sanday Airport Ork
76 D11 Sandbach Ches E
76 E11 Sandbach Services Ches E
112 H5 Sandbank Ag & B
11 P7 Sandbanks Poole
140 E3 Sandend Abers
33 L10 Sanderstead Gt Lon
90 B3 Sandford Cumb
8 F4 Sandford Devon
11 M7 Sandford Dorset
12 B4 Sandford Hants
13 J8 Sandford IoW
28 F10 Sandford N Som
105 N1 Sandford S Lans
63 K7 Sandford Shrops
63 P5 Sandford Shrops
43 L11 Sandford-on-Thames Oxon
22 E9 Sandford Orcas Dorset
43 J6 Sandford St Martin Oxon
17 M4 Sandgate Kent
141 M2 Sandhaven Abers
94 G8 Sandhead D & G
78 D4 Sandhill Rothm
10 F5 Sandhills Dorset
10 G3 Sandhills Dorset
85 M7 Sand Hills Leeds
43 L10 Sandhills Oxon
14 C4 Sandhills Surrey
100 B5 Sandhoe Nthumb
112 E5 Sandhole Ag & B
86 E8 Sand Hole E R Yk
86 F9 Sandholme E R Yk
68 G5 Sandholme Lincs
32 B10 Sandhurst Br For
41 N7 Sandhurst Gloucs
16 E5 Sandhurst Kent
16 D5 Sandhurst Cross Kent
86 C3 Sand Hutton N York
91 P10 Sandhutton N York
66 D5 Sandiacre Derbys
81 K7 Sandilands Lincs
75 Q9 Sandiway Ches W
23 P10 Sandleheath Hants
31 K2 Sandleigh Oxon
22 H8 Sandley Dorset
34 D10 Sandling Kent
76 E10 Sandlow Green Ches E
152 r6 Sandness Shet
46 C10 Sandon Essex
45 L5 Sandon Herts
64 H6 Sandon Staffs
64 H6 Sandon Bank Staffs
13 K8 Sandown IoW
4 C5 Sandplace Cnwll
44 H9 Sandridge Herts
29 Q9 Sandridge Wilts
69 N6 Sandringham Norfk
32 B4 Sands Bucks
92 H4 Sandsend N York
88 H10 Sand Side Cumb
89 M10 Sandside Cumb
79 J2 Sandtoft N Linc
34 F12 Sandway Kent
35 P10 Sandwich Kent
89 L3 Sandwick Cumb
152 s9 Sandwick Shet
152 f3 Sandwick W Isls
88 C4 Sandwith Cumb
88 C4 Sandwith Newtown Cumb
56 D10 Sandy C Beds
68 E1 Sandy Bank Lincs
75 K10 Sandycroft Flints
15 Q7 Sandy Cross E Susx
52 C9 Sandy Cross Herefs
106 G11 Sandyford D & G
8 G9 Sandygate Devon
102 e3 Sandygate IoM
36 G9 Sandy Haven Pembks
96 H9 Sandyhills D & G
83 K3 Sandylands Lancs
84 H8 Sandy Lane C Brad
64 D5 Sandylane Staffs
26 E9 Sandylane Swans
29 Q8 Sandy Lane Wilts
63 L4 Sandy Lane Wrexhm
8 D7 Sandy Park Devon
98 E5 Sandysike Cumb
40 G6 Sandyway Herefs
149 J3 Sangobeg Highld
149 J3 Sangomore Highld
75 P6 Sankey Bridges Warrtn
52 E7 Sankyn's Green Worcs
126 H10 Sanna Bay Highld
152 f9 Sanndabhaig W Isls
112 E12 Sannox N Ayrs
105 P8 Sanquhar D & G
88 E6 Santon Cumb
102 d6 Santon IoM
88 F6 Santon Bridge Cumb
58 B3 Santon Downham Suffk
54 D2 Sapcote Leics
52 C8 Sapey Common Herefs
58 D5 Sapiston Suffk
56 E6 Sapley Cambs
65 M5 Sapperton Derbys
41 Q11 Sapperton Gloucs
67 P5 Sapperton Lincs
68 G7 Saracen's Head Lincs
151 Q8 Sarclet Highld
12 H3 Sarisbury Hants
27 L6 Sarn Brdgnd
60 D6 Sarn Gwynd
62 H12 Sarn Powys
50 H2 Sarn Powys
37 Q7 Sarnau Carmth
48 E10 Sarnau Cerdgn
62 C4 Sarnau Gwynd
39 N5 Sarnau Powys
62 H9 Sarnau Powys
60 E7 Sarn Bach Gwynd
51 L10 Sarnesfield Herefs
27 L6 Sarn Park Services Brdgnd
38 J9 Sarn-wen Powys
38 B4 Saron Carmth
38 F9 Saron Carmth
72 H12 Saron Gwynd
73 J10 Saron Gwynd
32 F2 Sarratt Herts
35 N9 Sarre Kent
42 G7 Sarsden Oxon
24 E4 Sarson Hants
100 E9 Satley Dur
17 N3 Satmar Kent
57 P7 Satron N York
19 N9 Satterleigh Devon
89 K8 Satterthwaite Cumb
31 P6 Satwell Oxon
132 H2 Sauchen Abers
124 D6 Saucher P & K
132 G10 Sauchieburn Abers
41 M10 Saul Gloucs
79 K6 Saundby Notts
37 M9 Saundersfoot Pembks
44 A11 Saunderton Bucks
19 J6 Saunton Devon
80 G10 Sausthorpe Lincs
3 J5 Saveock Cnwll
64 H4 Saverley Green Staffs
85 K11 Savile Town Kirk
54 E7 Sawbridge Warwks
45 N8 Sawbridgeworth Herts
93 J9 Sawdon N York
66 D6 Sawley Derbys
84 B6 Sawley Lancs
85 K2 Sawley N York
57 J11 Sawston Cambs
56 C4 Sawtry Cambs
67 K8 Saxby Leics
79 P6 Saxby Lincs
87 J12 Saxby All Saints N Linc
66 H8 Saxelbye Leics
59 K8 Saxham Street Suffk
79 M8 Saxilby Lincs
70 F4 Saxlingham Norfk
59 K1 Saxlingham Green Norfk
59 J1 Saxlingham Nethergate Norfk
59 J1 Saxlingham Thorpe Norfk
59 M8 Saxmundham Suffk
66 H4 Saxondale Notts
57 N9 Saxon Street Cambs
59 K7 Saxtead Suffk
59 K8 Saxtead Green Suffk
59 K7 Saxtead Little Green Suffk
70 G6 Saxthorpe Norfk
85 P8 Saxton N York
15 K7 Sayers Common W Susx
92 D12 Scackleton N York
88 G5 Scafell Pike Cumb
78 H5 Scaftworth Notts
92 G12 Scagglethorpe N York
111 J2 Scalasaig Ag & B
86 F9 Scalby E R Yk
93 K8 Scalby N York
55 P9 Scald End Bed
55 J6 Scaldwell Nhants
98 F5 Scaleby Cumb
98 F5 Scalebyhill Cumb
98 H9 Scale Houses Cumb
88 H12 Scales Cumb
89 K1 Scales Cumb
98 F8 Scalesceugh Cumb
67 J7 Scalford Leics
92 F4 Scaling N York
92 F4 Scaling Dam R & Cl
152 s7 Scalloway Shet
135 L9 Scalpay Highld
80 E8 Scamblesby Lincs
84 F12 Scammonden Kirk
127 Q9 Scamodale Highld
92 H11 Scampston N York
79 N8 Scampton Lincs
138 B8 Scaniport Highld
84 G12 Scapegoat Hill Kirk
120 D12 Scarba Ag & B
93 L9 Scarborough N York
3 M4 Scarcewater Cnwll
78 E10 Scarcliffe Derbys
85 M7 Scarcroft Leeds
151 N2 Scarfskerry Highld
90 H4 Scargill Dur
118 E4 Scarinish Ag & B
75 L1 Scarisbrick Lancs
97 P12 Scarness Cumb
70 D9 Scarning Norfk
67 J4 Scarrington Notts
75 M2 Scarth Hill Lancs
85 P8 Scarthingwell N York
80 E2 Scartho NE Lin
152 s5 Scatsta Airport Shet
79 N3 Scawby N Linc
78 E3 Scawsby Donc
78 F2 Scawthorpe Donc
92 B10 Scawton N York
15 L6 Scayne's Hill W Susx
39 Q6 Scethrog Powys
76 F12 Scholar Green Ches E
84 H8 Scholemoor Crematorium C Brad
77 M2 Scholes Kirk
85 J10 Scholes Kirk
85 M8 Scholes Leeds
78 C5 Scholes Rothm
75 Q3 Scholes Wigan
91 L2 School Aycliffe Dur
84 H8 School Green C Brad
76 B11 School Green Ches W
31 Q9 Schoolgreen Wokham
10 B4 School House Dorset
77 N2 Scissett Kirk
36 H4 Scleddau Pembks
78 G7 Scofton Notts
58 H5 Scole Norfk
124 C7 Scone P & K
135 J9 Sconser Highld
115 Q1 Scoonie Fife
79 Q12 Scopwick Lincs
144 C6 Scoraig Highld
87 J6 Scorborough E R Yk
2 H6 Scorrier Cnwll
5 L3 Scorriton Devon
83 L5 Scorton Lancs
91 L7 Scorton N York
71 K8 Sco Ruston Norfk
98 F7 Scotby Cumb
91 L6 Scotch Corner N York
83 L3 Scotforth Lancs
64 E3 Scot Hay Staffs
79 P8 Scothern Lincs
67 P6 Scotland Lincs
100 H1 Scotland Gate Nthumb
115 M1 Scotlandwell P & K
76 B2 Scot Lane End Bolton
151 K5 Scotscalder Station Highld
98 E4 Scotsdike Cumb
100 D1 Scot's Gap Nthumb
140 E12 Scotsmill Abers
113 Q8 Scotstoun C Glas
100 G5 Scotswood N u Ty
79 L4 Scotter Lincs
79 L3 Scotterthorpe Lincs
67 Q8 Scottlethorpe Lincs
79 M4 Scotton Lincs
85 L3 Scotton N York
91 K7 Scotton N York
71 K7 Scottow Norfk
67 Q5 Scott Willoughby Lincs
70 E12 Scoulton Norfk
65 K6 Scounslow Green Staffs
148 E7 Scourie Highld
148 D8 Scourie More Highld
152 s9 Scousburgh Shet
76 H3 Scouthead Oldham
151 K3 Scrabster Highld
107 Q6 Scraesburgh Border
80 F10 Scrafield Lincs
108 F8 Scrainwood Nthumb
68 G4 Scrane End Lincs
66 G11 Scraptoft Leics
71 P9 Scratby Norfk
86 D3 Scrayingham N York
16 D7 Scrays E Susx
68 B4 Scredington Lincs
80 H10 Scremby Lincs
117 M11 Scremerston Nthumb
67 J3 Screveton Notts
80 E10 Scrivelsby Lincs
85 M3 Scriven N York
78 G5 Scrooby Notts
65 M6 Scropton Derbys
68 E1 Scrub Hill Lincs
91 M8 Scruton N York
98 F3 Scuggate Cumb
149 N4 Scullomie Highld
70 C6 Sculthorpe Norfk
79 M2 Scunthorpe N Linc
26 C5 Scurlage Swans
21 M10 Sea Somset
10 C3 Seaborough Dorset
64 F3 Seabridge Staffs
17 L4 Seabrook Kent
101 K6 Seaburn Sundld
75 K5 Seacombe Wirral
85 M8 Seacroft Leeds
81 L11 Seacroft Lincs
68 F5 Seadyke Lincs
134 H7 Seafield Highld
115 J8 Seafield W Loth
115 P6 Seafield Crematorium C Edin
15 N11 Seaford E Susx
75 K4 Seaforth Sefton
66 G8 Seagrave Leics
29 Q8 Seagry Heath Wilts
101 K8 Seaham Dur
109 L3 Seahouses Nthumb
33 Q11 Seal Kent
14 C1 Seale Surrey
91 R5 Seamer N York
93 K10 Seamer N York
113 J12 Seamill N Ayrs
71 N7 Sea Palling Norfk
79 Q3 Searby Lincs
35 K9 Seasalter Kent
88 D6 Seascale Cumb
88 H4 Seathwaite Cumb
88 H7 Seathwaite Cumb
89 K10 Seatle Cumb
88 H4 Seatoller Cumb
4 D6 Seaton Cnwll
97 K12 Seaton Cumb
9 N6 Seaton Devon
101 K8 Seaton Dur
87 M6 Seaton E R Yk
35 M10 Seaton Kent
101 J3 Seaton Nthumb
55 M1 Seaton Rutlnd
100 G3 Seaton Burn N Tyne
101 M12 Seaton Carew Hartpl
100 H3 Seaton Delaval Nthumb
86 E7 Seaton Ross E R Yk
101 J3 Seaton Sluice Nthumb
10 G6 Seatown Dorset
92 B7 Seave Green N York
13 K6 Seaview IoW
97 N7 Seaville Cumb
21 N10 Seavington St Mary Somset
21 N10 Seavington St Michael Somset
28 C3 Sebastopol Torfn
98 D10 Sebergham Cumb
65 N10 Seckington Warwks
89 Q8 Sedbergh Cumb
28 H4 Sedbury Gloucs
90 E8 Sedbusk N York
42 B4 Sedgeberrow Worcs
67 L4 Sedgebrook Lincs
57 M4 Sedge Fen Suffk
91 N1 Sedgefield Dur
69 N5 Sedgeford Norfk
23 J8 Sedgehill Wilts
21 N3 Sedgemoor Services Somset
52 G2 Sedgley Dudley
76 F3 Sedgley Park Bury
89 N9 Sedgwick Cumb
16 D7 Sedlescombe E Susx
44 A9 Sedrup Bucks
34 G11 Seed Kent
29 Q10 Seend Wilts
29 Q10 Seend Cleeve Wilts
32 D4 Seer Green Bucks
59 L1 Seething Norfk
75 K3 Sefton Sefton
75 K4 Sefton Town Sefton
100 H3 Seghill Nthumb
64 G7 Seighford Staffs
73 J10 Seion Gwynd
52 F2 Seisdon Staffs
63 J5 Selattyn Shrops
25 N6 Selborne Hants
86 B9 Selby N York
14 D7 Selham W Susx
33 L9 Selhurst Gt Lon
107 M4 Selkirk Border
40 H6 Sellack Herefs
152 t3 Sellafirth Shet
2 C8 Sellan Cnwll
21 K9 Sellick's Green Somset
17 K3 Sellindge Kent
35 J11 Selling Kent
29 Q10 Sells Green Wilts
53 K4 Selly Oak Birm
15 P9 Selmeston E Susx
33 L10 Selsdon Gt Lon
41 N11 Selsey Gloucs
13 Q6 Selsey W Susx
15 L4 Selsfield Common W Susx
89 N7 Selside Cumb
90 C11 Selside N York
17 M2 Selsted Kent
66 D2 Selston Notts
20 E4 Selworthy Somset
46 H2 Semer Suffk
29 P10 Semington Wilts
23 K8 Semley Wilts
68 C5 Sempringham Lincs
32 E11 Send Surrey
32 E11 Send Marsh Surrey
27 Q4 Senghenydd Caerph
2 B9 Sennen Cnwll
2 B9 Sennen Cove Cnwll
39 L6 Sennybridge Powys
78 G6 Serlby Notts
91 Q11 Sessay N York
69 M9 Setchey Norfk
12 E5 Setley Hants
116 B6 Seton Mains E Loth
84 B2 Settle N York
86 F1 Settrington N York
21 J7 Seven Ash Somset
42 B7 Sevenhampton Gloucs
30 E4 Sevenhampton Swindn
47 M3 Seven Hills Crematorium Suffk
33 N5 Seven Kings Gt Lon
33 P11 Sevenoaks Kent
33 P12 Sevenoaks Weald Kent
39 K10 Seven Sisters Neath
41 Q8 Seven Springs Gloucs
46 G6 Seven Star Green Essex
28 H5 Severn Beach S Glos
41 P3 Severn Stoke Worcs
28 H4 Severn View Services S Glos
56 B10 Sevick End Bed
17 J3 Sevington Kent
45 Q4 Sewards End Essex
33 M3 Sewardstonebury Essex
44 E7 Sewell C Beds
87 M2 Sewerby E R Yk
2 H8 Seworgan Cnwll
67 M8 Sewstern Leics
91 Q5 Sexhow N York
42 E5 Sezincote Gloucs
152 g1 Sgiogarstaigh W Isls
43 N10 Shabbington Bucks
64 F11 Shackerley Shrops
66 B10 Shackerstone Leics
66 C5 Shacklecross Derbys
14 D2 Shackleford Surrey
84 D10 Shade Calder
152 f2 Shader W Isls
101 J10 Shadforth Dur
59 N4 Shadingfield Suffk
16 H3 Shadoxhurst Kent
85 M7 Shadwell Leeds
58 D4 Shadwell Norfk
45 M4 Shaftenhoe End Herts
23 J9 Shaftesbury Dorset
78 F2 Shaftholme Donc
78 C2 Shafton Barns
78 C2 Shafton Two Gates Barns
76 C3 Shakerley Wigan
30 G9 Shalbourne Wilts
12 F7 Shalcombe IoW
25 M5 Shalden Hants
25 M5 Shalden Green Hants
8 H10 Shaldon Devon
12 G7 Shalfleet IoW
46 C6 Shalford Essex
14 E1 Shalford Surrey
46 C6 Shalford Green Essex
64 G6 Shallowford Staffs
35 K11 Shalmsford Street Kent
43 N4 Shalstone Bucks
14 E2 Shamley Green Surrey
132 D11 Shandford Angus
113 K4 Shandon Ag & B
146 F10 Shandwick Highld
55 J1 Shangton Leics
100 H3 Shankhouse Nthumb
13 K8 Shanklin IoW
89 P4 Shap Cumb
152 m4 Shapinsay Ork
11 M4 Shapwick Dorset
21 P6 Shapwick Somset
53 M3 Shard End Birm
66 C6 Shardlow Derbys
64 H11 Shareshill Staffs
85 N11 Sharlston Wakefd
85 N11 Sharlston Common Wakefd
53 L5 Sharman's Cross Solhll
34 D7 Sharnal Street Medway
55 N8 Sharnbrook Bed
84 C10 Sharneyford Lancs
54 D2 Sharnford Leics
83 K8 Sharoe Green Lancs
91 N12 Sharow N York
44 F5 Sharpenhoe C Beds
108 F9 Sharperton Nthumb
71 M8 Sharp Green Norfk
41 K11 Sharpness Gloucs
15 L4 Sharpthorne W Susx
7 K10 Sharptor Cnwll
52 H7 Sharpway Gate Worcs
70 F5 Sharrington Norfk
52 E4 Shatterford Worcs
35 N10 Shatterling Kent
77 M7 Shatton Derbys
4 H4 Shaugh Prior Devon
10 C5 Shave Cross Dorset
64 C2 Shavington Ches E
84 F8 Shaw C Brad
76 H2 Shaw Oldham
30 D5 Shaw Swindn
31 K8 Shaw W Berk
29 P9 Shaw Wilts
64 B9 Shawbirch Wrekin
152 e2 Shawbost W Isls
63 P8 Shawbury Shrops
84 D12 Shawclough Rochdl
41 L6 Shaw Common Gloucs
108 H7 Shawdon Hill Nthumb
54 E5 Shawell Leics
24 H8 Shawford Hants
84 D11 Shawforth Lancs
45 K5 Shaw Green Herts
83 M11 Shaw Green Lancs
85 K5 Shaw Green N York
96 H3 Shawhead D & G
85 K3 Shaw Mills N York
114 E11 Shawsburn S Lans
23 J5 Shear Cross Wilts
97 L5 Shearington D & G
54 G2 Shearsby Leics
21 L7 Shearston Somset
7 N3 Shebbear Devon
64 E7 Shebdon Staffs
151 J4 Shebster Highld
113 Q10 Sheddens E Rens
25 J10 Shedfield Hants
77 L11 Sheen Staffs
78 B9 Sheepbridge Derbys
100 F7 Sheep Hill Dur
84 H11 Sheepridge Kirk
85 L8 Sheepscar Leeds
41 P9 Sheepscombe Gloucs
5 J3 Sheepstor Devon
7 P3 Sheepwash Devon
100 H1 Sheepwash Nthumb
28 G7 Sheepway N Som
65 Q12 Sheepy Magna Leics
65 Q11 Sheepy Parva Leics
45 P9 Sheering Essex
34 G7 Sheerness Kent
32 F10 Sheerwater Surrey
25 N8 Sheet Hants
2 D9 Sheffield Cnwll
78 B6 Sheffield Sheff
31 N8 Sheffield Bottom W Berk
78 B6 Sheffield City Road Crematorium Sheff
15 M6 Sheffield Green E Susx
44 G4 Shefford C Beds
148 E4 Sheigra Highld
63 Q11 Sheinton Shrops
51 L5 Shelderton Shrops
53 L4 Sheldon Birm
77 M10 Sheldon Derbys
9 L3 Sheldon Devon
34 H11 Sheldwich Kent
34 H11 Sheldwich Lees Kent
84 H9 Shelf Calder
58 G4 Shelfanger Norfk
53 L8 Shelfield Warwks
65 J11 Shelfield Wsall
53 L8 Shelfield Green Warwks
66 H4 Shelford Notts
54 C3 Shelford Warwks
108 E11 Shellacres Nthumb
45 Q10 Shelley Essex
77 M2 Shelley Kirk
47 J4 Shelley Suffk
77 M2 Shelley Far Bank Kirk
30 G4 Shellingford Oxon
45 R10 Shellow Bowells Essex
52 D8 Shelsley Beauchamp Worcs
52 D8 Shelsley Walsh Worcs
55 P7 Shelton Bed
59 J2 Shelton Norfk
67 K3 Shelton Notts
63 M9 Shelton Shrops
59 J3 Shelton Green Norfk
66 B6 Shelton Lock C Derb
64 F4 Shelton Under Harley Staffs
63 K12 Shelve Shrops
40 H3 Shelwick Herefs
33 R3 Shenfield Essex
42 H3 Shenington Oxon
32 H2 Shenley Herts
44 B5 Shenley Brook End M Keyn
44 H11 Shenleybury Herts
44 B4 Shenley Church End M Keyn
40 E4 Shenmore Herefs
95 L5 Shennanton D & G
65 L11 Shenstone Staffs
52 F6 Shenstone Worcs
65 L12 Shenstone Woodend Staffs
66 C12 Shenton Leics
139 N10 Shenval Moray
68 F9 Shepeau Stow Lincs
45 J7 Shephall Herts
33 J6 Shepherd's Bush Gt Lon
31 P6 Shepherd's Green Oxon
41 L10 Shepherds Patch Gloucs
17 N1 Shepherdswell Kent
77 M2 Shepley Kirk
29 J3 Shepperdine S Glos
32 F9 Shepperton Surrey
32 F9 Shepperton Green Surrey
56 H11 Shepreth Cambs
66 D8 Shepshed Leics
21 N10 Shepton Beauchamp Somset
22 E5 Shepton Mallet Somset
22 F7 Shepton Montague Somset
34 D11 Shepway Kent
101 L11 Sheraton Dur
22 F9 Sherborne Dorset
42 E8 Sherborne Gloucs
22 D2 Sherborne Somset
25 K2 Sherborne St John Hants
53 N8 Sherbourne Warwks
101 J10 Sherburn Dur
93 J11 Sherburn N York
101 J10 Sherburn Hill Dur
85 P8 Sherburn in Elmet N York
14 F1 Shere Surrey
70 C6 Shereford Norfk
24 D9 Sherfield English Hants
31 P10 Sherfield on Loddon Hants
84 B10 Sherfin Lancs
5 N8 Sherford Devon
11 M6 Sherford Dorset
64 D9 Sheriffhales Shrops
86 C2 Sheriff Hutton N York
70 H3 Sheringham Norfk
44 C2 Sherington M Keyn
14 H7 Shermanbury W Susx
69 N6 Shernborne Norfk
23 L5 Sherrington Wilts
29 N5 Sherston Wilts
66 F3 Sherwood C Nott
66 F1 Sherwood Forest Notts
78 H10 Sherwood Forest Crematorium Notts
114 B8 Shettleston C Glas
75 P2 Shevington Wigan
75 P2 Shevington Moor Wigan
75 N2 Shevington Vale Wigan
4 E6 Sheviock Cnwll
84 G9 Shibden Head C Brad
12 H7 Shide IoW
108 C2 Shidlaw Nthumb
136 C12 Shiel Bridge Highld
135 P5 Shieldaig Highld
97 L1 Shieldhill D & G
114 G6 Shieldhill Falk
106 C2 Shieldhill House Hotel S Lans
114 D10 Shields N Lans
127 M10 Shielfoot Highld
124 H1 Shielhill Angus
113 K7 Shielhill Inver
42 H11 Shifford Oxon
64 D10 Shifnal Shrops
109 K8 Shilbottle Nthumb
91 L1 Shildon Dur
113 N10 Shillford E Rens
20 F8 Shillingford Devon
31 M4 Shillingford Oxon
8 G7 Shillingford Abbot Devon
8 G7 Shillingford St George Devon
11 K2 Shillingstone Dorset
44 G5 Shillington C Beds
108 E8 Shillmoor Nthumb
42 F10 Shilton Oxon
54 C4 Shilton Warwks
58 H4 Shimpling Norfk
58 C10 Shimpling Suffk
58 C10 Shimpling Street Suffk
100 H10 Shincliffe Dur
101 J8 Shiney Row Sundld

31 Q8 **Shinfield** Wokham
45 K2 **Shingay** Cambs
47 Q3 **Shingle Street** Suffk
5 N4 **Shinnersbridge** Devon
145 M2 **Shinness** Highld
33 Q12 **Shipbourne** Kent
70 E10 **Shipdham** Norfk
28 F11 **Shipham** Somset
5 Q7 **Shiphay** Torbay
31 Q7 **Shiplake** Oxon
31 Q6 **Shiplake Row** Oxon
21 E11 **Shiplate** N Som
84 H8 **Shipley** C Brad
66 D3 **Shipley** Derbys
52 E1 **Shipley** Shrops
14 G6 **Shipley** W Susx
15 K3 **Shipley Bridge** Surrey
16 H3 **Shipley Hatch** Kent
59 M3 **Shipmeadow** Suffk
57 M4 **Shippea Hill Station** Cambs
31 K3 **Shippon** Oxon
42 F4 **Shipston on Stour** Warwks
43 Q6 **Shipton** Bucks
42 B8 **Shipton** Gloucs
85 Q3 **Shipton** N York
51 P2 **Shipton** Shrops
24 C4 **Shipton Bellinger** Hants
10 D6 **Shipton Gorge** Dorset
13 P5 **Shipton Green** W Susx
29 P4 **Shipton Moyne** Gloucs
43 K8 **Shipton-on-Cherwell** Oxon
86 F6 **Shiptonthorpe** E R Yk
42 G8 **Shipton-under-Wychwood** Oxon
31 P3 **Shirburn** Oxon
75 K1 **Shirdley Hill** Lancs
99 J11 **Shire** Cumb
78 E10 **Shirebrook** Derbys
78 B5 **Shiregreen** Sheff
28 H7 **Shirehampton** Bristl
101 J4 **Shiremoor** N Tyne
28 G4 **Shirenewton** Mons
65 K11 **Shire Oak** Wsall
78 F7 **Shireoaks** Notts
16 G4 **Shirkoak** Kent
78 C12 **Shirland** Derbys
52 C1 **Shirlett** Shrops
24 F10 **Shirley** C Sotn
65 N4 **Shirley** Derbys
33 L9 **Shirley** Gt Lon
53 L5 **Shirley** Solhll
51 M8 **Shirl Heath** Herefs
25 J10 **Shirrell Heath** Hants
112 C4 **Shirvan** Ag & B
19 L6 **Shirwell** Devon
103 N4 **Shiskine** N Ayrs
100 C10 **Shittlehope** Dur
51 L8 **Shobdon** Herefs
12 C3 **Shobley** Hants
8 G4 **Shobrooke** Devon
66 H8 **Shoby** Leics
63 M2 **Shocklach** Ches W
63 M2 **Shocklach Green** Ches W
34 G5 **Shoeburyness** Sthend
35 P12 **Sholden** Kent
12 G2 **Sholing** C Sotn
63 L9 **Shoot Hill** Shrops
6 C10 **Shop** Cnwll
18 E10 **Shop** Cnwll
14 C9 **Shopwyke** W Susx
84 D11 **Shore** Rochdl
33 L6 **Shoreditch** Gt Lon
21 K9 **Shoreditch** Somset
33 P10 **Shoreham** Kent
14 H9 **Shoreham Airport** W Susx
15 J10 **Shoreham-by-Sea** W Susx
117 L12 **Shoreswood** Nthumb
25 K8 **Shorley** Hants
30 B3 **Shorncote** Gloucs
34 C8 **Shorne** Kent
4 D5 **Shorta Cross** Cnwll
15 N6 **Shortbridge** E Susx
25 P5 **Shortfield Common** Surrey
15 P8 **Shortgate** E Susx
53 L2 **Short Heath** Birm
25 N6 **Shortheath** Hants
64 H12 **Short Heath** Wsall
3 K5 **Shortlanesend** Cnwll
104 H5 **Shortlees** E Ayrs
44 F2 **Shortstown** Bed
12 G8 **Shorwell** IoW
29 L11 **Shoscombe** BaNES
71 K12 **Shotesham** Norfk
34 D4 **Shotgate** Essex
47 M4 **Shotley** Suffk
100 E7 **Shotley Bridge** Dur
70 D7 **Shotleyfield** Nthumb
47 M5 **Shotley Gate** Suffk
47 M5 **Shotley Street** Suffk
35 J11 **Shottenden** Kent
14 C4 **Shottermill** Surrey
53 M9 **Shottery** Warwks
43 J3 **Shotteswell** Warwks
47 P3 **Shottisham** Suffk
65 P2 **Shottle** Derbys
65 Q3 **Shottlegate** Derbys
91 N2 **Shotton** Dur
101 K10 **Shotton** Dur
75 K10 **Shotton** Flints
100 G3 **Shotton** Nthumb
108 D4 **Shotton** Nthumb
101 K10 **Shotton Colliery** Dur
114 F9 **Shotts** N Lans
75 K9 **Shotwick** Ches W
139 M5 **Shougle** Moray
69 N10 **Shouldham** Norfk
69 M10 **Shouldham Thorpe** Norfk
52 E9 **Shoulton** Worcs
15 P6 **Shover's Green** E Susx
64 E2 **Shraleybrook** Staffs
63 L9 **Shrawardine** Shrops
52 E7 **Shrawley** Worcs
32 E6 **Shreding Green** Bucks
53 N7 **Shrewley** Warwks
63 N9 **Shrewsbury** Shrops
23 N5 **Shrewton** Wilts
14 D10 **Shripney** W Susx
30 F4 **Shrivenham** Oxon
58 E2 **Shropham** Norfk
46 H7 **Shrub End** Essex
41 J3 **Shucknall** Herefs
46 A3 **Shudy Camps** Cambs
120 E11 **Shuna** Ag & B
41 Q8 **Shurdington** Gloucs
32 B7 **Shurlock Row** W & M
53 J8 **Shurnock** Worcs
151 J5 **Shurrery** Highld
151 J5 **Shurrery Lodge** Highld
21 K4 **Shurton** Somset
53 N3 **Shustoke** Warwks
8 G5 **Shute** Devon
9 N5 **Shute** Devon
42 H4 **Shutford** Oxon
64 F8 **Shut Heath** Staffs
41 P5 **Shuthonger** Gloucs
55 J10 **Shutlanger** Nhants
8 H9 **Shutterton** Devon
64 G10 **Shutt Green** Staffs
65 N11 **Shuttington** Warwks
78 D9 **Shuttlewood** Derbys
84 B11 **Shuttleworth** Bury
152 e2 **Siabost** W Isls
152 f2 **Siadar** W Isls
54 H4 **Sibbertoft** Nhants
51 L4 **Sibdon Carwood** Shrops
42 H4 **Sibford Ferris** Oxon
42 H4 **Sibford Gower** Oxon
46 D5 **Sible Hedingham** Essex
46 A6 **Sibley's Green** Essex
7 J10 **Siblyback** Cnwll
68 G2 **Sibsey** Lincs
68 G2 **Sibsey Fenside** Lincs
56 B1 **Sibson** Cambs
66 B12 **Sibson** Leics
151 P6 **Sibster** Highld
67 J3 **Sibthorpe** Notts
79 J9 **Sibthorpe** Notts
59 M7 **Sibton** Suffk
58 C8 **Sicklesmere** Suffk
85 M5 **Sicklinghall** N York
21 L8 **Sidbrook** Somset
9 L6 **Sidbury** Devon
52 C3 **Sidbury** Shrops
78 C2 **Sid Cop** Barns
28 F11 **Sidcot** N Som
33 N8 **Sidcup** Gt Lon
97 K12 **Siddick** Cumb
76 F9 **Siddington** Ches E
30 B2 **Siddington** Gloucs
52 F6 **Sidemoor** Worcs
71 K4 **Sidestrand** Norfk
9 L7 **Sidford** Devon
13 Q5 **Sidlesham** W Susx
13 P5 **Sidlesham Common** W Susx
16 C9 **Sidley** E Susx
9 L7 **Sidmouth** Devon
51 N4 **Siefton** Shrops
8 E10 **Sigford** Devon
87 M6 **Sigglesthorne** E R Yk
27 M8 **Sigingstone** V Glam
42 P4 **Signet** Oxon
31 N10 **Silchester** Hants
66 G9 **Sileby** Leics
88 F10 **Silecroft** Cumb
70 G12 **Silfield** Norfk
49 J10 **Silian** Cerdgn
24 G8 **Silkstead** Hants
77 P3 **Silkstone** Barns
77 P3 **Silkstone Common** Barns
67 Q4 **Silk Willoughby** Lincs
97 M7 **Silloth** Cumb
93 K8 **Silpho** N York
84 F6 **Silsden** C Brad
44 F4 **Silsoe** C Beds
22 H7 **Silton** Dorset
115 M9 **Silverburn** Mdloth
89 M11 **Silverdale** Lancs
64 E3 **Silverdale** Staffs
46 E8 **Silver End** Essex
141 J3 **Silverford** Abers
70 H6 **Silvergate** Norfk
59 L8 **Silverlace Green** Suffk
59 L5 **Silverley's Green** Suffk
43 N3 **Silverstone** Nhants
34 F10 **Silver Street** Kent
22 C7 **Silver Street** Somset
8 H4 **Silverton** Devon
3 J5 **Silverwell** Cnwll
52 B5 **Silvington** Shrops
76 F2 **Simister** Bury
77 J5 **Simmondley** Derbys
99 N3 **Simonburn** Nthumb
19 P5 **Simonsbath** Somset
21 J10 **Simonsburrow** Devon
84 B8 **Simonstone** Lancs
90 E8 **Simonstone** N York
117 J12 **Simprim** Border
44 C4 **Simpson** M Keyn
36 H6 **Simpson Cross** Pembks
116 H11 **Sinclair's Hill** Border
105 J6 **Sinclairston** E Ayrs
91 N10 **Sinderby** N York
99 N8 **Sinderhope** Nthumb
76 D6 **Sinderland Green** Traffd
31 Q8 **Sindlesham** Wokham
65 Q6 **Sinfin** C Derb
43 Q5 **Singleborough** Bucks
33 N10 **Single Street** Gt Lon
16 H3 **Singleton** Kent
83 J7 **Singleton** Lancs
14 C8 **Singleton** W Susx
34 B8 **Singlewell** Kent
16 E2 **Sinkhurst Green** Kent
132 D2 **Sinnarhard** Abers
92 F8 **Sinnington** N York
52 F8 **Sinton** Worcs
52 F9 **Sinton** Worcs
52 E8 **Sinton Green** Worcs
32 F7 **Sipson** Gt Lon
39 Q9 **Sirhowy** Blae G
16 D3 **Sissinghurst** Kent
29 J7 **Siston** S Glos
7 L6 **Sitcott** Devon
2 G8 **Sithney** Cnwll
2 G9 **Sithney Common** Cnwll
2 G8 **Sithney Green** Cnwll
34 F9 **Sittingbourne** Kent
52 E3 **Six Ashes** Shrops
40 B11 **Six Bells** Blae G
80 D6 **Sixhills** Lincs
57 L9 **Six Mile Bottom** Cambs
17 K2 **Sixmile Cottages** Kent
23 M10 **Sixpenny Handley** Dorset
13 b1 **Six Rues** Jersey
89 M9 **Sizergh Castle** Cumb
59 P8 **Sizewell** Suffk
152 m5 **Skaill** Ork
105 K6 **Skares** E Ayrs
133 L6 **Skateraw** Abers
116 G6 **Skateraw** E Loth
134 G6 **Skeabost** Highld
91 K6 **Skeeby** N York
67 J11 **Skeffington** Leics
87 Q11 **Skeffling** E R Yk
78 D11 **Skegby** Notts
79 K9 **Skegby** Notts
81 L11 **Skegness** Lincs
146 E6 **Skelbo** Highld
146 E6 **Skelbo Street** Highld
78 E1 **Skelbrooke** Donc
68 G5 **Skeldyke** Lincs
79 M9 **Skellingthorpe** Lincs
76 G7 **Skellorn Green** Ches E
78 E2 **Skellow** Donc
77 N2 **Skelmanthorpe** Kirk
75 M2 **Skelmersdale** Lancs
113 J8 **Skelmorlie** N Ayrs
150 C5 **Skelpick** Highld
96 G1 **Skelston** D & G
85 R4 **Skelton** C York
98 E11 **Skelton** Cumb
86 E10 **Skelton** E R Yk
85 M2 **Skelton** N York
91 J6 **Skelton** N York
92 D3 **Skelton** R & Cl
89 K6 **Skelwith Bridge** Cumb
80 H9 **Skendleby** Lincs
133 J2 **Skene House** Abers
40 F7 **Skenfrith** Mons
87 K4 **Skerne** E R Yk
149 P4 **Skerray** Highld
148 F6 **Skerricha** Highld
83 L3 **Skerton** Lancs
54 C2 **Sketchley** Leics
26 F4 **Sketty** Swans
26 H3 **Skewen** Neath
86 B1 **Skewsby** N York
71 K7 **Skeyton** Norfk
71 K7 **Skeyton Corner** Norfk
151 J3 **Skiall** Highld
80 H5 **Skidbrooke** Lincs
80 H5 **Skidbrooke North End** Lincs
87 J8 **Skidby** E R Yk
152 g1 **Skigersta** W Isls
20 F8 **Skilgate** Somset
67 M7 **Skillington** Lincs
97 M7 **Skinburness** Cumb
114 G5 **Skinflats** Falk
134 D6 **Skinidin** Highld
31 K9 **Skinners Green** W Berk
92 E3 **Skinningrove** R & Cl
112 C9 **Skipness** Ag & B
98 D2 **Skipper's Bridge** D & G
98 E9 **Skiprigg** Cumb
87 M4 **Skipsea** E R Yk
87 M4 **Skipsea Brough** E R Yk
84 E5 **Skipton** N York
91 N10 **Skipton-on-Swale** N York
86 C7 **Skipwith** N York
87 L7 **Skirlaugh** E R Yk
106 E2 **Skirling** Border
31 Q4 **Skirmett** Bucks
86 D4 **Skirpenbeck** E R Yk
99 J11 **Skirwith** Cumb
90 B12 **Skirwith** N York
151 Q3 **Skirza** Highld
98 F5 **Skitby** Cumb
43 Q11 **Skittle Green** Bucks
36 E9 **Skokholm Island** Pembks
36 E8 **Skomer Island** Pembks
135 M11 **Skulamus** Highld
51 J6 **Skyborry Green** Shrops
46 F7 **Skye Green** Essex
138 H11 **Skye of Curr** Highld
84 G3 **Skyreholme** N York
84 G9 **Slack** Calder
76 H2 **Slackcote** Oldham
89 M11 **Slack Head** Cumb
81 K9 **Slackholme End** Lincs
141 K7 **Slacks of Cairnbanno** Abers
41 P10 **Slad** Gloucs
9 L3 **Slade** Devon
19 K4 **Slade** Devon
20 C8 **Slade** Devon
31 M4 **Slade End** Oxon
33 P7 **Slade Green** Gt Lon
64 G11 **Slade Heath** Staffs
78 E6 **Slade Hooton** Rothm
6 E10 **Sladesbridge** Cnwll
41 N5 **Slades Green** Worcs
99 K8 **Slaggyford** Nthumb
83 Q5 **Slaidburn** Lancs
84 G12 **Slaithwaite** Kirk
114 F7 **Slamannan** Falk
77 P12 **Slaley** Derbys
100 B7 **Slaley** Nthumb
44 D7 **Slapton** Bucks
5 N7 **Slapton** Devon
43 N2 **Slapton** Nhants
76 G2 **Slattocks** Rochdl
15 J5 **Slaugham** W Susx
29 N7 **Slaughterford** Wilts
55 K2 **Slawston** Leics
25 P6 **Sleaford** Hants
67 Q3 **Sleaford** Lincs
89 P3 **Sleagill** Cumb
63 N7 **Sleap** Shrops
64 B9 **Sleapford** Wrekin
44 H10 **Sleapshyde** Herts
145 P6 **Sleasdairidh** Highld
37 K7 **Slebech** Pembks
41 N5 **Sledge Green** Worcs
86 H2 **Sledmere** E R Yk
98 G3 **Sleetbeck** Cumb
11 N5 **Sleight** Dorset
90 F5 **Sleightholme** Dur
92 H5 **Sleights** N York
11 M6 **Slepe** Dorset
151 P5 **Slickly** Highld
103 N5 **Sliddery** N Ayrs
135 J10 **Sligachan** Highld
112 H3 **Sligrachan** Ag & B
41 L11 **Slimbridge** Gloucs
64 F6 **Slindon** Staffs
14 D9 **Slindon** W Susx
14 G4 **Slinfold** W Susx
73 K10 **Sling** Gwynd
92 E11 **Slingsby** N York
44 F8 **Slip End** C Beds
45 K4 **Slip End** Herts
55 N5 **Slipton** Nhants
65 J8 **Slitting Mill** Staffs
112 B2 **Slockavullin** Ag & B
71 K7 **Sloley** Norfk
8 D7 **Sloncombe** Devon
81 J9 **Sloothby** Lincs
32 D6 **Slough** Slough
32 D6 **Slough Crematorium** Bucks
21 L9 **Slough Green** Somset
15 K5 **Slough Green** W Susx
136 B8 **Slumbay** Highld
32 E12 **Slyfield Green** Surrey
83 L2 **Slyne** Lancs
107 Q2 **Smailholm** Border
84 D12 **Smallbridge** Rochdl
8 G5 **Smallbrook** Devon
29 J2 **Smallbrook** Gloucs
71 L7 **Smallburgh** Norfk
77 L8 **Smalldale** Derbys
77 M7 **Smalldale** Derbys
15 J8 **Small Dole** W Susx
66 C3 **Smalley** Derbys
66 C4 **Smalley Common** Derbys
66 C3 **Smalley Green** Derbys
15 K2 **Smallfield** Surrey
53 L3 **Small Heath** Birm
16 F5 **Small Hythe** Kent
9 P4 **Smallridge** Devon
64 G2 **Smallthorne** C Stke
91 J4 **Smallways** N York
76 E11 **Smallwood** Ches E
83 J5 **Small Wood Hey** Lancs
58 E4 **Smallworth** Norfk
24 F4 **Smannell** Hants
90 B5 **Smardale** Cumb
16 F2 **Smarden** Kent
16 F2 **Smarden Bell** Kent
15 P2 **Smart's Hill** Kent
108 H2 **Smeafield** Nthumb
127 L9 **Smearisary** Highld
9 M3 **Smeatharpe** Devon
17 J3 **Smeeth** Kent
54 H2 **Smeeton Westerby** Leics
85 J2 **Smelthouses** N York
151 L10 **Smerral** Highld
52 F2 **Smestow** Staffs
53 J3 **Smethwick** Sandw
76 E11 **Smethwick Green** Ches E
65 Q8 **Smisby** Derbys
13 J6 **Smitheclose** IoW
52 E10 **Smith End Green** Worcs
98 F5 **Smithfield** Cumb
83 L4 **Smith Green** Lancs
78 B2 **Smithies** Barns
9 K2 **Smithincott** Devon
45 M4 **Smith's End** Herts
45 Q7 **Smith's Green** Essex
46 B4 **Smith's Green** Essex
143 L9 **Smithstown** Highld
138 D7 **Smithton** Highld
84 D12 **Smithy Bridge** Rochdl
76 D9 **Smithy Green** Ches E
76 G6 **Smithy Green** Stockp
66 C3 **Smithy Houses** Derbys
54 D3 **Smockington** Leics
149 J3 **Smoo** Highld
46 G8 **Smythe's Green** Essex
96 G1 **Snade** D & G
63 L11 **Snailbeach** Shrops
57 M7 **Snailwell** Cambs
93 J10 **Snainton** N York
86 B10 **Snaith** E R Yk
77 L5 **Snake Pass Inn** Derbys
91 M10 **Snape** N York
59 N9 **Snape** Suffk
83 J12 **Snape Green** Lancs
59 M9 **Snape Street** Suffk
33 M4 **Snaresbrook** Gt Lon
65 Q10 **Snarestone** Leics
79 P7 **Snarford** Lincs
16 H5 **Snargate** Kent
16 H5 **Snave** Kent
52 G10 **Sneachill** Worcs
51 K2 **Snead** Powys
58 H3 **Sneath Common** Norfk
92 H5 **Sneaton** N York
92 H5 **Sneatonthorpe** N York
79 Q7 **Snelland** Lincs
76 E8 **Snelson** Ches E
65 L3 **Snelston** Derbys
58 E2 **Snetterton** Norfk
69 N5 **Snettisham** Norfk
66 C9 **Snibston** Leics
41 M6 **Snig's End** Gloucs
108 G9 **Snitter** Nthumb
79 N5 **Snitterby** Lincs
53 N8 **Snitterfield** Warwks
77 P11 **Snitterton** Derbys
51 P5 **Snitton** Shrops
16 G2 **Snoadhill** Kent
40 D4 **Snodhill** Herefs
34 C10 **Snodland** Kent
16 B1 **Snoll Hatch** Kent
77 N4 **Snowden Hill** Barns
61 K1 **Snowdon** Gwynd
61 P6 **Snowdonia National Park**
45 M5 **Snow End** Herts
42 C5 **Snowshill** Gloucs
58 G4 **Snow Street** Norfk
13 L2 **Soake** Hants
27 P6 **Soar** Cardif
5 L9 **Soar** Devon
39 M5 **Soar** Powys
126 H2 **Soay** Highld
25 K10 **Soberton** Hants
25 K10 **Soberton Heath** Hants
89 M1 **Sockbridge** Cumb
91 N5 **Sockburn** Darltn
74 F9 **Sodom** Denbgs
63 K4 **Sodylt Bank** Shrops
57 L6 **Soham** Cambs
57 L6 **Soham Cotes** Cambs
152 b6 **Solas** W Isls
36 H8 **Solbury** Pembks
7 L3 **Soldon** Devon
7 L3 **Soldon Cross** Devon
25 L6 **Soldridge** Hants
17 K1 **Sole Street** Kent
34 B9 **Sole Street** Kent
53 M5 **Solihull** Solhll
51 M9 **Sollers Dilwyn** Herefs
41 J5 **Sollers Hope** Herefs
83 K11 **Sollom** Lancs
36 F6 **Solva** Pembks
98 C3 **Solwaybank** D & G
67 K10 **Somerby** Leics
79 Q2 **Somerby** Lincs
66 C1 **Somercotes** Derbys
12 B6 **Somerford** Dorset
30 B3 **Somerford Keynes** Gloucs
13 P5 **Somerley** W Susx
59 P1 **Somerleyton** Suffk
65 L5 **Somersal Herbert** Derbys
80 G9 **Somersby** Lincs
56 G5 **Somersham** Cambs
58 G11 **Somersham** Suffk
43 K6 **Somerton** Oxon
22 C7 **Somerton** Somset
57 Q10 **Somerton** Suffk
63 P9 **Somerwood** Shrops
14 H10 **Sompting** W Susx
31 Q7 **Sonning** Wokham
31 P6 **Sonning Common** Oxon
31 Q7 **Sonning Eye** Oxon
63 K3 **Sontley** Wrexhm
12 B5 **Sopley** Hants
29 N5 **Sopworth** Wilts
95 N9 **Sorbie** D & G
151 L4 **Sordale** Highld
126 E11 **Sorisdale** Ag & B
105 K4 **Sorn** E Ayrs
151 N4 **Sortat** Highld
80 D8 **Sotby** Lincs
80 C11 **Sots Hole** Lincs
59 N4 **Sotterley** Suffk
74 H10 **Soughton** Flints
44 C6 **Soulbury** Bucks
90 B4 **Soulby** Cumb
98 G12 **Soulby** Cumb
43 L5 **Souldern** Oxon
55 N8 **Souldrop** Bed
64 B3 **Sound** Ches E
140 B5 **Sound Muir** Moray
29 K7 **Soundwell** S Glos
7 P6 **Sourton** Devon
88 H10 **Soutergate** Cumb
69 Q9 **South Acre** Norfk
17 N2 **South Alkham** Kent
32 G6 **Southall** Gt Lon
5 N9 **South Allington** Devon
114 F3 **South Alloa** Falk
41 R6 **Southam** Gloucs
54 C8 **Southam** Warwks
14 C7 **South Ambersham** W Susx
24 G11 **Southampton** C Sotn
24 G10 **Southampton Airport** Hants
24 G10 **Southampton Crematorium** Hants
78 E7 **South Anston** Rothm
32 C8 **South Ascot** W & M
78 G7 **South Ashford** Kent
12 F5 **South Baddesley** Hants
121 K1 **South Ballachulish** Highld
86 B5 **South Bank** C York
92 B3 **South Bank** R & Cl
22 E8 **South Barrow** Somset
33 K9 **South Beddington** Gt Lon
7 K6 **South Beer** Cnwll
34 D5 **South Benfleet** Essex
14 D10 **South Bersted** W Susx
12 B5 **South Bockhampton** Dorset
33 M9 **Southborough** Gt Lon
15 Q2 **Southborough** Kent
12 B6 **Southbourne** Bmouth
13 N4 **Southbourne** W Susx
10 C5 **South Bowood** Dorset
78 F6 **South Bramwith** Donc
5 L5 **South Brent** Devon
22 G6 **South Brewham** Somset
28 H8 **South Bristol Crematorium** Bristl
109 L10 **South Broomhill** Nthumb
70 E11 **Southburgh** Norfk
71 M10 **South Burlingham** Norfk
87 J4 **Southburn** E R Yk
22 E8 **South Cadbury** Somset
79 N8 **South Carlton** Lincs
78 F7 **South Carlton** Notts
86 G9 **South Cave** E R Yk
30 B3 **South Cerney** Gloucs
15 M7 **South Chailey** E Susx
9 Q4 **South Chard** Somset
109 K6 **South Charlton** Nthumb
22 F8 **South Cheriton** Somset
91 L1 **South Church** Dur
34 F5 **Southchurch** Sthend
91 J3 **South Cleatlam** Dur
86 E8 **South Cliffe** E R Yk
79 K9 **South Clifton** Notts
80 G6 **South Cockerington** Lincs
27 K6 **South Cornelly** Brdgnd
6 H6 **Southcott** Cnwll
7 Q6 **Southcott** Devon
8 E8 **Southcott** Devon
19 J10 **Southcott** Devon
30 E10 **Southcott** Wilts
44 A9 **Southcourt** Bucks
59 P4 **South Cove** Suffk
70 C5 **South Creake** Norfk
77 L1 **South Crosland** Kirk
66 H10 **South Croxton** Leics
86 H6 **South Dalton** E R Yk
33 Q8 **South Darenth** Kent
15 L9 **South Downs National Park**
86 C8 **South Duffield** N York
15 M10 **Southease** E Susx
80 F6 **South Elkington** Lincs
78 D1 **South Elmsall** Wakefd
103 J8 **Southend** Ag & B
87 R11 **South End** E R Yk
23 N10 **South End** Hants
41 L3 **South End** N Linc
87 L11 **South End** N Linc
58 E3 **South End** Norfk
30 E7 **Southend** Wilts
34 F4 **Southend Airport** Essex
34 F5 **Southend Crematorium** Sthend
34 F5 **Southend-on-Sea** Sthend
98 D10 **Southerby** Cumb
17 L2 **Southernden** Kent
27 L7 **Southerndown** V Glam
97 K7 **Southerness** D & G
143 K11 **South Erradale** Highld
9 K6 **Southerton** Devon
57 M2 **Southery** Norfk
33 Q5 **South Essex Crematorium** Gt Lon
34 F3 **South Fambridge** Essex
30 H6 **South Fawley** W Berk
87 J11 **South Ferriby** N Linc
87 J10 **South Field** E R Yk
114 F7 **Southfield** Falk
33 R8 **Southfleet** Kent
13 J9 **Southford** IoW
33 K3 **Southgate** Gt Lon
69 N5 **Southgate** Norfk
70 C5 **Southgate** Norfk
70 H7 **Southgate** Norfk
26 E5 **Southgate** Swans
15 L1 **South Godstone** Surrey
12 B3 **South Gorley** Hants
100 G5 **South Gosforth** N u Ty
34 B4 **South Green** Essex
47 J8 **South Green** Essex
34 E10 **South Green** Kent
70 F10 **South Green** Norfk
58 H5 **South Green** Suffk
115 M7 **South Gyle** C Edin
34 C3 **South Hanningfield** Essex
25 N9 **South Harting** W Susx
13 M5 **South Hayling** Hants
108 H3 **South Hazelrigg** Nthumb
44 C11 **South Heath** Bucks
15 N10 **South Heighton** E Susx
101 K9 **South Hetton** Dur
78 C1 **South Hiendley** Wakefd
7 L10 **South Hill** Cnwll
21 Q8 **South Hill** Somset
43 L11 **South Hinksey** Oxon
18 E9 **South Hole** Devon
14 H2 **South Holmwood** Surrey
33 P5 **South Hornchurch** Gt Lon
22 D4 **South Horrington** Somset
5 L8 **South Huish** Devon
79 M10 **South Hykeham** Lincs
101 J7 **South Hylton** Sundld
44 H3 **Southill** C Beds
24 H3 **Southington** Hants
79 P4 **South Kelsey** Lincs
138 C6 **South Kessock** Highld
87 L12 **South Killingholme** N Linc
91 P10 **South Kilvington** N York
54 G4 **South Kilworth** Leics
78 D2 **South Kirkby** Wakefd
8 F10 **South Knighton** Devon
68 D2 **South Kyme** Lincs
114 C10 **South Lanarkshire Crematorium** S Lans
9 N6 **Southleigh** Devon
43 J10 **South Leigh** Oxon
79 K7 **South Leverton** Notts
42 C2 **South Littleton** Worcs
33 K8 **South London Crematorium** Gt Lon
58 F4 **South Lopham** Norfk
67 M11 **South Luffenham** Rutlnd
15 M8 **South Malling** E Susx
30 E5 **South Marston** Swindn
33 K12 **South Merstham** Surrey
108 G5 **South Middleton** Nthumb
85 P9 **South Milford** N York
5 L8 **South Milton** Devon
33 J2 **South Mimms** Herts
33 J2 **South Mimms Services** Herts
34 G2 **Southminster** Essex
19 N8 **South Molton** Devon
100 F8 **South Moor** Dur
31 J3 **Southmoor** Oxon
31 M5 **South Moreton** Oxon
124 H2 **Southmuir** Angus
14 C10 **South Mundham** W Susx
79 K12 **South Muskham** Notts
86 G8 **South Newbald** E R Yk
43 J5 **South Newington** Oxon
23 N6 **South Newton** Wilts
78 D12 **South Normanton** Derbys
33 L8 **South Norwood** Gt Lon
15 K1 **South Nutfield** Surrey
33 Q6 **South Ockendon** Thurr
56 D8 **Southoe** Cambs
59 J7 **Southolt** Suffk
80 G8 **South Ormsby** Lincs
67 Q11 **Southorpe** C Pete
91 M2 **South Otterington** N York
71 N9 ... 

## T

61 M5 **Trawsfynydd** Gwynd
27 N4 **Trealaw** Rhondd
83 K8 **Treales** Lancs
72 D8 **Trearddur Bay** IoA
134 G5 **Treaslane** Highld
6 C9 **Treator** Cnwll
27 N8 **Tre Aubrey** V Glam
27 N4 **Trebanog** Rhondd
38 H11 **Trebanos** Neath
7 K9 **Trebartha** Cnwll
6 F7 **Trebarwith** Cnwll
7 J7 **Trebeath** Cnwll
6 D9 **Trebetherick** Cnwll
20 F6 **Treborough** Somset
3 L2 **Trebudannon** Cnwll
7 L9 **Trebullett** Cnwll
6 F9 **Treburgett** Cnwll
7 L9 **Treburley** Cnwll
6 B10 **Treburrick** Cnwll
3 Q2 **Trebyan** Cnwll
39 L6 **Trecastle** Powys
7 K8 **Trecogo** Cnwll
8 C5 **Trecott** Devon
37 J4 **Trecwn** Pembks
39 N11 **Trecynon** Rhondd
7 J8 **Tredaule** Cnwll
2 D9 **Tredavoe** Cnwll
39 Q10 **Tredegar** Blae G
6 F10 **Tredethy** Cnwll
41 P6 **Tredington** Gloucs
42 F3 **Tredington** Warwks
3 P3 **Tredinnick** Cnwll
4 B3 **Tredinnick** Cnwll
4 C5 **Tredinnick** Cnwll
4 D5 **Tredinnick** Cnwll
6 D10 **Tredinnick** Cnwll
39 Q5 **Tredomen** Powys
37 L2 **Tredrissi** Pembks
6 D9 **Tredrizzick** Cnwll
28 E3 **Tredunnock** Mons
39 Q5 **Tredustan** Powys
2 B10 **Treen** Cnwll
2 C7 **Treen** Cnwll
3 Q3 **Treesmill** Cnwll
78 C6 **Treeton** Rothm
36 H3 **Trefasser** Pembks
72 G9 **Trefdraeth** IoA
39 Q5 **Trefecca** Powys
50 C3 **Trefeglwys** Powys
49 K7 **Trefenter** Cerdgn
37 J6 **Treffgarne** Pembks
36 G5 **Treffgarne Owen** Pembks
27 P4 **Trefforest** Rhondd
36 G5 **Treffynnon** Pembks
39 Q9 **Trefil** Blae G
49 J9 **Trefilan** Cerdgn
36 G4 **Trefin** Pembks
63 J7 **Treflach Wood** Shrops
62 H9 **Trefnannau** Powys
74 E9 **Trefnant** Denbgs
63 J7 **Trefonen** Shrops
60 F3 **Trefor** Gwynd
72 F7 **Trefor** IoA
6 G8 **Trefrew** Cnwll
73 N11 **Trefriw** Conwy
7 K8 **Tregadillett** Cnwll
40 H10 **Tre-gagle** Mons
72 G7 **Tregaian** IoA
40 F9 **Tregare** Mons
3 J10 **Tregarne** Cnwll
49 L8 **Tregaron** Cerdgn
73 K10 **Tregarth** Gwynd
3 L2 **Tregaswith** Cnwll
6 F7 **Tregatta** Cnwll
6 E11 **Tregawne** Cnwll
7 J7 **Tregeare** Cnwll
62 G5 **Tregeiriog** Wrexhm
72 F5 **Tregele** IoA
6 E9 **Tregellist** Cnwll
3 L6 **Tregenna** Cnwll
2 B8 **Tregeseal** Cnwll
3 K7 **Tregew** Cnwll
39 N10 **Tre-Gibbon** Rhondd
3 J10 **Tregidden** Cnwll
3 P5 **Tregiskey** Cnwll
36 F5 **Treglemais** Pembks
6 H5 **Tregole** Cnwll
3 J7 **Tregolls** Cnwll
6 D10 **Tregonce** Cnwll
3 N2 **Tregonetha** Cnwll
3 M5 **Tregony** Cnwll
6 G8 **Tregoodwell** Cnwll
3 P4 **Tregorrick** Cnwll
3 N2 **Tregoss** Cnwll
40 B4 **Tregoyd** Powys
3 P4 **Tregrehan Mills** Cnwll
38 B3 **Tre-groes** Cerdgn
3 P2 **Tregullon** Cnwll
6 D10 **Tregunna** Cnwll
7 J8 **Tregunnon** Cnwll
6 B11 **Tregurrian** Cnwll
50 F1 **Tregynon** Powys
38 B8 **Tre-gynwr** Carmth
27 P4 **Trehafod** Rhondd
4 F5 **Trehan** Cnwll
27 P3 **Treharris** Myr Td
6 E9 **Treharrock** Cnwll
6 C10 **Trehemborne** Cnwll
38 E2 **Treherbert** Carmth
27 M3 **Treherbert** Rhondd
4 D4 **Trehunist** Cnwll
7 L9 **Trekenner** Cnwll
6 F7 **Treknow** Cnwll
3 J10 **Trelan** Cnwll
6 H7 **Trelash** Cnwll
3 L4 **Trelassick** Cnwll
4 C6 **Trelawne** Cnwll
74 F8 **Trelawnyd** Flints
3 K10 **Treleague** Cnwll
3 J11 **Treleaver** Cnwll
37 Q4 **Trelech** Carmth
37 Q5 **Trelech a'r Betws** Carmth
36 E5 **Treleddyd-fawr** Pembks
3 K7 **Trelew** Cnwll
27 Q3 **Trelewis** Myr Td
6 F8 **Treligga** Cnwll
6 E9 **Trelights** Cnwll
6 F9 **Trelill** Cnwll
7 K8 **Trelinnoe** Cnwll
3 M4 **Trelion** Cnwll
3 K6 **Trelissick** Cnwll
3 K6 **Trelissick Garden** Cnwll
40 G10 **Trellech** Mons
28 G2 **Trelleck Grange** Mons
74 F7 **Trelogan** Flints
6 D10 **Trelow** Cnwll
2 H9 **Trelowarren** Cnwll
4 D5 **Trelowia** Cnwll
3 L7 **Treluggan** Cnwll
63 J11 **Trelystan** Powys
61 J4 **Tremadog** Gwynd
6 H7 **Tremail** Cnwll
48 C11 **Tremain** Cerdgn
7 J7 **Tremaine** Cnwll
4 C3 **Tremar** Cnwll
4 F5 **Trematon** Cnwll
4 C4 **Trembraze** Cnwll
74 F9 **Tremeirchion** Denbgs
2 C8 **Tremethick Cross** Cnwll
6 E11 **Tremore** Cnwll
74 G8 **Tre-Mostyn** Flints
3 K10 **Trenance** Cnwll
6 B11 **Trenance** Cnwll
6 D10 **Trenance** Cnwll
3 P5 **Trenarren** Cnwll
64 C9 **Trench** Wrekin
31 P7 **Trench Green** Oxon
3 L4 **Trendeal** Cnwll
2 D6 **Trendrine** Cnwll
6 E10 **Treneague** Cnwll
2 H8 **Trenear** Cnwll
7 J7 **Treneglos** Cnwll
2 F7 **Trenerth** Cnwll
4 B6 **Trenewan** Cnwll
6 F9 **Trenewth** Cnwll
6 H6 **Trengune** Cnwll
3 K2 **Treninnick** Cnwll
3 K3 **Trenowah** Cnwll
3 J8 **Trenoweth** Cnwll
22 D9 **Trent** Dorset
64 G4 **Trentham** C Stke
19 M4 **Trentishoe** Devon
66 D6 **Trentlock** Derbys
79 L7 **Trent Port** Lincs
64 F3 **Trent Vale** C Stke
2 G8 **Trenwheal** Cnwll
27 M7 **Treoes** V Glam
27 M3 **Treorchy** Rhondd
6 E9 **Trequite** Cnwll
49 L2 **Tre'r-ddol** Cerdgn
27 N7 **Trerhyngyll** V Glam
4 E5 **Trerulefoot** Cnwll
48 D10 **Tresaith** Cerdgn
3 L5 **Tresawle** Cnwll
2 b1 **Tresco** IoS
2 b1 ***Tresco Heliport*** IoS
52 F1 **Trescott** Staffs
2 F8 **Trescowe** Cnwll
3 J3 **Tresean** Cnwll
29 M4 **Tresham** Gloucs
118 H5 **Treshnish Isles** Ag & B
3 L5 **Tresillian** Cnwll
6 G8 **Tresinney** Cnwll
7 J5 **Treskinnick Cross** Cnwll
7 J7 **Tresmeer** Cnwll
6 G6 **Tresparrett** Cnwll
130 E12 **Tressait** P & K
152 s6 **Tresta** Shet
152 u3 **Tresta** Shet
79 K8 **Treswell** Notts
2 G6 **Treswithian** Cnwll
2 G6 **Treswithian Downs Crematorium** Cnwll
49 L2 **Tre Taliesin** Cerdgn
6 F7 **Trethevey** Cnwll
2 B9 **Trethewey** Cnwll
28 A4 **Trethomas** Caerph
3 M4 **Trethosa** Cnwll
3 P3 **Trethurgy** Cnwll
36 F5 **Tretio** Pembks
40 G7 **Tretire** Herefs
40 B7 **Tretower** Powys
75 J12 **Treuddyn** Flints
7 K9 **Trevadlock** Cnwll
6 F7 **Trevalga** Cnwll
75 L12 **Trevalyn** Wrexhm
6 D9 **Trevanger** Cnwll
6 E10 **Trevanson** Cnwll
2 D8 **Trevarrack** Cnwll
3 M2 **Trevarren** Cnwll
6 B11 **Trevarrian** Cnwll
3 N6 **Trevarrick** Cnwll
2 H6 **Trevarth** Cnwll
37 N7 **Trevaughan** Carmth
38 B7 **Tre-Vaughan** Carmth
2 D6 **Treveal** Cnwll
3 J3 **Treveal** Cnwll
6 F9 **Treveighan** Cnwll
3 J4 **Trevellas Downs** Cnwll
4 B4 **Trevelmond** Cnwll
3 K3 **Trevemper** Cnwll
3 N6 **Treveor** Cnwll
3 L5 **Treverbyn** Cnwll
3 P3 **Treverbyn** Cnwll
3 J8 **Treverva** Cnwll
2 B9 **Trevescan** Cnwll
40 C11 **Trevethin** Torfn
6 G8 **Trevia** Cnwll
4 E3 **Trevigro** Cnwll
3 K7 **Trevilla** Cnwll
3 L3 **Trevilson** Cnwll
3 M3 **Treviscoe** Cnwll
3 M6 **Treviskey** Cnwll
3 L2 **Trevithick** Cnwll
3 N5 **Trevithick** Cnwll
3 K3 **Trevoll** Cnwll
6 C9 **Trevone** Cnwll
63 J4 **Trevor** Wrexhm
2 C9 **Trevorgans** Cnwll
6 D10 **Trevorrick** Cnwll
6 B9 **Trevose** Cnwll
2 F8 **Trew** Cnwll
6 F8 **Trewalder** Cnwll
39 R5 **Trewalkin** Powys
6 F7 **Trewarmett** Cnwll
6 H7 **Trewassa** Cnwll
2 F9 **Trewavas** Cnwll
7 J8 **Treween** Cnwll
2 B8 **Trewellard** Cnwll
7 J8 **Trewen** Cnwll
2 H9 **Trewennack** Cnwll
37 K11 **Trewent** Pembks
63 J10 **Trewern** Powys
6 E8 **Trewetha** Cnwll
6 E9 **Trewethern** Cnwll
4 C5 **Trewidland** Cnwll
3 J11 **Trewillis** Cnwll
4 D4 **Trewint** Cnwll
7 J8 **Trewint** Cnwll
3 L7 **Trewithian** Cnwll
7 L10 **Trewoodloe** Cnwll
2 H10 **Trewoon** Cnwll
3 N4 **Trewoon** Cnwll
3 L6 **Treworga** Cnwll
3 K4 **Treworgan** Cnwll
3 L7 **Treworlas** Cnwll
6 G6 **Treworld** Cnwll
3 L7 **Treworthal** Cnwll
40 D7 **Tre-wyn** Mons
6 B10 **Treyarnon** Cnwll
25 P9 **Treyford** W Susx
11 Q4 **Trickett's Cross** Dorset
98 H5 **Triermain** Cumb
37 J6 **Triffleton** Pembks
7 K7 **Trillacott** Cnwll
101 K11 **Trimdon** Dur
101 K11 **Trimdon Colliery** Dur
101 K11 **Trimdon Grange** Dur
71 K4 **Trimingham** Norfk
47 N4 **Trimley Lower Street** Suffk
47 N4 **Trimley St Martin** Suffk
47 N4 **Trimley St Mary** Suffk
52 E5 **Trimpley** Worcs
38 C10 **Trimsaran** Carmth
45 N8 **Trims Green** Herts
19 K5 **Trimstone** Devon
130 D11 **Trinafour** P & K
28 B2 **Trinant** Caerph
44 C9 **Tring** Herts
44 C9 **Tringford** Herts
44 C9 **Tring Wharf** Herts
132 F12 **Trinity** Angus
13 c1 **Trinity** Jersey
123 N9 **Trinity Gask** P & K
21 J6 **Triscombe** Somset
128 F9 **Trislaig** Highld
3 K4 **Trispen** Cnwll
109 K11 **Tritlington** Nthumb
3 L3 **Troan** Cnwll
123 P5 **Trochry** P & K
39 Q10 **Troedrhiwfuwch** Caerph
48 E11 **Troedyraur** Cerdgn
39 P11 **Troedyrhiw** Myr Td
73 Q9 **Trofarth** Conwy
13 b2 **Trois Bois** Jersey
2 G7 **Troon** Cnwll
104 F4 **Troon** S Ayrs
85 L7 **Tropical World Roundhay Park** Leeds
122 E11 **Trossachs** Stirlg
122 E11 **Trossachs Pier** Stirlg
58 C6 **Troston** Suffk
7 J6 **Troswell** Cnwll
52 G9 **Trotshill** Worcs
34 B10 **Trottiscliffe** Kent
25 P9 **Trotton** W Susx
108 D11 **Troughend** Nthumb
84 D11 **Trough Gate** Lancs
89 L1 **Troutbeck** Cumb
89 L6 **Troutbeck** Cumb
89 L7 **Troutbeck Bridge** Cumb
78 C8 **Troway** Derbys
29 P10 **Trowbridge** Wilts
66 D4 **Trowell** Notts
66 E4 **Trowell Services** Notts
29 N10 **Trowle Common** Wilts
44 F9 **Trowley Bottom** Herts
71 K10 **Trowse Newton** Norfk
85 K7 **Troy** Leeds
22 G5 **Trudoxhill** Somset
21 K9 **Trull** Somset
78 F1 **Trumfleet** Donc
134 D4 **Trumpan** Highld
41 K4 **Trumpet** Herefs
56 H9 **Trumpington** Cambs
32 E9 **Trumpsgreen** Surrey
71 K5 **Trunch** Norfk
82 H6 **Trunnah** Lancs
3 K5 **Truro** Cnwll
3 K5 **Truro Cathedral** Cnwll
7 K7 **Truscott** Cnwll
8 F8 **Trusham** Devon
65 N5 **Trusley** Derbys
81 K7 **Trusthorpe** Lincs
52 F2 **Trysull** Staffs
31 J3 **Tubney** Oxon
5 N5 **Tuckenhay** Devon
52 E3 **Tuckhill** Shrops
2 G6 **Tuckingmill** Cnwll
23 L7 **Tuckingmill** Wilts
12 B6 **Tuckton** Bmouth
3 N5 **Tucoyse** Cnwll
57 P6 **Tuddenham** Suffk
59 J11 **Tuddenham** Suffk
16 A2 **Tudeley** Kent
100 H11 **Tudhoe** Dur
41 J7 **Tudorville** Herefs
60 D5 **Tudweiliog** Gwynd
14 D2 **Tuesley** Surrey
41 N8 **Tuffley** Gloucs
24 G4 **Tufton** Hants
37 K5 **Tufton** Pembks
67 J12 **Tugby** Leics
51 P3 **Tugford** Shrops
109 K4 **Tughall** Nthumb
114 F2 **Tullibody** Clacks
138 B10 **Tullich** Highld
146 F10 **Tullich** Highld
123 P2 **Tulliemet** P & K
141 J9 **Tulloch** Abers
112 E2 **Tullochgorm** Ag & B
129 L8 **Tulloch Station** Highld
124 D2 **Tullymurdoch** P & K
140 E12 **Tullynessle** Abers
33 K8 **Tulse Hill** Gt Lon
38 E9 **Tumble** Carmth
46 E6 **Tumbler's Green** Essex
80 E11 **Tumby** Lincs
80 E12 **Tumby Woodside** Lincs
123 K1 **Tummel Bridge** P & K
15 Q3 **Tunbridge Wells** Kent
97 N2 **Tundergarth** D & G
71 K6 **Tungate** Norfk
29 L10 **Tunley** BaNES
64 F2 **Tunstall** C Stke
87 P9 **Tunstall** E R Yk
34 F10 **Tunstall** Kent
89 P12 **Tunstall** Lancs
91 L7 **Tunstall** N York
71 N10 **Tunstall** Norfk
64 E6 **Tunstall** Staffs
59 M9 **Tunstall** Suffk
101 K7 **Tunstall** Sundld
77 L8 **Tunstead** Derbys
71 L8 **Tunstead** Norfk
77 J7 **Tunstead Milton** Derbys
25 L4 **Tunworth** Hants
40 H4 **Tupsley** Herefs
31 P10 **Turgis Green** Hants
42 C8 **Turkdean** Gloucs
54 H2 **Tur Langton** Leics
29 N10 **Turleigh** Wilts
52 E4 **Turleygreen** Shrops
84 B11 **Turn** Lancs
40 E4 **Turnastone** Herefs
104 D8 **Turnberry** S Ayrs
4 H6 **Turnchapel** C Plym
65 P3 **Turnditch** Derbys
83 N9 **Turner Green** Lancs
16 B7 **Turner's Green** E Susx
53 M7 **Turner's Green** Warwks
15 L4 **Turner's Hill** W Susx
11 K6 **Turners Puddle** Dorset
45 L10 **Turnford** Herts
115 L6 **Turnhouse** C Edin
11 K3 **Turnworth** Dorset
140 H6 **Turriff** Abers
83 Q12 **Turton Bottoms** Bl w D
56 G1 **Turves** Cambs
55 N10 **Turvey** Bed
31 Q4 **Turville** Bucks
31 Q4 **Turville Heath** Bucks
43 M4 **Turweston** Bucks
107 J6 **Tushielaw Inn** Border
65 N6 **Tutbury** Staffs
53 J6 **Tutnall** Worcs
28 H3 **Tutshill** Gloucs
71 J7 **Tuttington** Norfk
7 M9 **Tutwell** Cnwll
79 J9 **Tuxford** Notts
152 j3 **Twatt** Ork
152 s6 **Twatt** Shet
114 C6 **Twechar** E Duns
107 N3 **Tweedbank** Border
117 M10 **Tweedmouth** Nthumb
106 E5 **Tweedsmuir** Border
3 J6 **Twelveheads** Cnwll
16 C7 **Twelve Oaks** E Susx
76 E10 **Twemlow Green** Ches E
68 C8 **Twenty** Lincs
29 L9 **Twerton** BaNES
32 H7 **Twickenham** Gt Lon
41 N7 **Twigworth** Gloucs
15 J7 **Twineham** W Susx
15 J7 **Twineham Green** W Susx
29 M10 **Twinhoe** BaNES
46 F4 **Twinstead** Essex
20 B7 **Twitchen** Devon
51 L5 **Twitchen** Shrops
35 N11 **Twitham** Kent
8 B9 **Two Bridges** Devon
77 P11 **Two Dales** Derbys
65 N12 **Two Gates** Staffs
5 P3 **Two Mile Oak Cross** Devon
19 K4 **Two Pots** Devon
44 F10 **Two Waters** Herts
65 Q11 **Twycross** Leics
65 P11 **Twycross Zoo** Leics
43 N6 **Twyford** Bucks
24 H8 **Twyford** Hants
67 J10 **Twyford** Leics
67 M7 **Twyford** Lincs
70 F7 **Twyford** Norfk
31 R7 **Twyford** Wokham
40 G5 **Twyford Common** Herefs
39 Q10 **Twyn-carno** Caerph
96 D7 **Twynholm** D & G
41 P4 **Twyning Green** Gloucs
38 H7 **Twynllanan** Carmth
27 Q7 **Twyn-yr-Odyn** V Glam
40 F10 **Twyn-y-Sheriff** Mons
55 N5 **Twywell** Nhants
40 E4 **Tyberton** Herefs
53 L2 **Tyburn** Birm
38 F9 **Tycroes** Carmth
72 E9 **Ty Croes** IoA
62 F8 **Tycrwyn** Powys
69 J8 **Tydd Gote** Lincs
68 H9 **Tydd St Giles** Cambs
68 H8 **Tydd St Mary** Lincs
13 M4 **Tye** Hants
45 P7 **Tye Green** Essex
45 Q4 **Tye Green** Essex
46 D7 **Tye Green** Essex
85 J8 **Tyersal** C Brad
76 C3 **Tyldesley** Wigan
35 L10 **Tyler Hill** Kent
32 C4 **Tylers Green** Bucks
45 P10 **Tyler's Green** Essex
33 L12 **Tylers Green** Surrey
27 N3 **Tylorstown** Rhondd
50 D5 **Tylwch** Powys
62 D3 **Ty-nant** Conwy
62 B7 **Ty-nant** Gwynd
121 Q6 **Tyndrum** Stirlg
62 H4 **Ty'n-dwr** Denbgs
101 K4 **Tynemouth** N Tyne
101 J4 **Tynemouth Crematorium** N Tyne
27 M3 **Tynewydd** Rhondd
116 E5 **Tyninghame** E Loth
105 P11 **Tynron** D & G
28 G8 **Tyntesfield** N Som
27 N5 **Ty'n-y-bryn** Rhondd
28 B5 **Ty'n-y-coedcae** Caerph
72 H7 **Tynygongl** IoA
49 M7 **Tynygraig** Cerdgn
73 N9 **Ty'n-y-Groes** Conwy
27 P5 **Tyn-y-nant** Rhondd
44 B2 **Tyringham** M Keyn
53 L4 **Tyseley** Birm
27 K6 **Tythegston** Brdgnd
76 G8 **Tytherington** Ches E
29 K5 **Tytherington** S Glos
22 H4 **Tytherington** Somset
23 K5 **Tytherington** Wilts
9 Q4 **Tytherleigh** Devon
29 Q7 **Tytherton Lucas** Wilts
44 H10 **Tyttenhanger** Herts
3 Q4 **Tywardreath** Cnwll
3 Q3 **Tywardreath Highway** Cnwll
73 N8 **Tywyn** Conwy
61 K12 **Tywyn** Gwynd

## U

59 L6 **Ubbeston Green** Suffk
28 H10 **Ubley** BaNES
91 L6 **Uckerby** N York
15 N6 **Uckfield** E Susx
41 P4 **Uckinghall** Worcs
41 Q7 **Uckington** Gloucs
63 P10 **Uckington** Shrops
114 C9 **Uddingston** S Lans
105 Q3 **Uddington** S Lans
16 F7 **Udimore** E Susx
141 L10 **Udny Green** Abers
141 L11 **Udny Station** Abers
30 D7 **Uffcott** Wilts
20 G10 **Uffculme** Devon
67 Q10 **Uffington** Lincs
30 G4 **Uffington** Oxon
63 N9 **Uffington** Shrops
68 B11 **Ufford** C Pete
59 L10 **Ufford** Suffk
54 C8 **Ufton** Warwks
31 N9 **Ufton Nervet** W Berk
103 L4 **Ugadale** Ag & B
5 L5 **Ugborough** Devon
59 N5 **Uggeshall** Suffk
92 H5 **Ugglebarnby** N York
77 N5 **Ughill** Sheff
45 P6 **Ugley** Essex
45 P6 **Ugley Green** Essex
92 G4 **Ugthorpe** N York
152 b9 **Uibhist A Deas** W Isls
152 b7 **Uibhist A Tuath** W Isls
118 G2 **Uig** Ag & B
134 C5 **Uig** Highld
134 G3 **Uig** Highld
152 d3 **Uig** W Isls
134 H6 **Uigshader** Highld
119 L9 **Uisken** Ag & B
151 P8 **Ulbster** Highld
89 L2 **Ulcat Row** Cumb
80 H9 **Ulceby** Lincs
87 L12 **Ulceby** N Linc
87 L12 **Ulceby Skitter** N Linc
16 E1 **Ulcombe** Kent
97 Q10 **Uldale** Cumb
29 M3 **Uley** Gloucs
109 L11 **Ulgham** Nthumb
144 E6 **Ullapool** Highld
53 L7 **Ullenhall** Warwks
41 Q8 **Ullenwood** Gloucs
85 Q7 **Ulleskelf** N York
54 E3 **Ullesthorpe** Leics
78 D6 **Ulley** Rothm
51 Q10 **Ullingswick** Herefs
134 F8 **Ullinish Lodge Hotel** Highld
88 E2 **Ullock** Cumb
89 L3 **Ullswater** Cumb
88 G8 **Ulpha** Cumb
89 M10 **Ulpha** Cumb
87 M4 **Ulrome** E R Yk
152 t4 **Ulsta** Shet
46 E10 **Ulting Wick** Essex
119 L5 **Ulva** Ag & B
53 L4 **Ulverley Green** Solhll
89 J11 **Ulverston** Cumb
11 N8 **Ulwell** Dorset
105 P8 **Ulzieside** D & G
19 L8 **Umberleigh** Devon
148 F10 **Unapool** Highld
89 M8 **Underbarrow** Cumb
98 F2 **Under Burnmouth** Border
85 J8 **Undercliffe** C Brad
63 N9 **Underdale** Shrops
16 D2 **Underling Green** Kent
33 Q12 **Under River** Kent
66 D2 **Underwood** Notts
57 N4 **Undley** Suffk
28 F5 **Undy** Mons
102 d6 **Union Mills** IoM
16 C4 **Union Street** E Susx
152 u2 **Unst** Shet
78 B8 **Unstone** Derbys
78 B8 **Unstone Green** Derbys
98 E8 **Unthank** Cumb
98 F11 **Unthank** Cumb
98 H10 **Unthank** Cumb
77 P8 **Unthank** Derbys
117 M11 **Unthank** Nthumb
23 P2 **Upavon** Wilts
10 G4 **Up Cerne** Dorset
34 E9 **Upchurch** Kent
19 P7 **Upcott** Devon
51 K10 **Upcott** Herefs
57 N9 **Upend** Cambs
8 H4 **Up Exe** Devon
70 H8 **Upgate** Norfk
58 G2 **Upgate Street** Norfk
59 K2 **Upgate Street** Norfk
10 E4 **Uphall** Dorset
115 K7 **Uphall** W Loth
8 G3 **Upham** Devon
25 J9 **Upham** Hants
51 L8 **Uphampton** Herefs
52 F7 **Uphampton** Worcs
28 D10 **Uphill** N Som
75 N3 **Up Holland** Lancs
113 N10 **Uplawmoor** E Rens
41 M6 **Upleadon** Gloucs
92 D3 **Upleatham** R & Cl
34 H9 **Uplees** Kent
10 D6 **Uploders** Dorset
20 F10 **Uplowman** Devon
9 Q6 **Uplyme** Devon
25 N10 **Up Marden** W Susx
33 Q5 **Upminster** Gt Lon
22 D9 **Up Mudford** Somset
25 M3 **Up Nately** Hants
9 N3 **Upottery** Devon
51 M3 **Upper Affcot** Shrops
145 N7 **Upper Ardchronie** Highld
52 E4 **Upper Arley** Worcs
43 M8 **Upper Arncott** Oxon
43 L4 **Upper Astrop** Nhants
31 M7 **Upper Basildon** W Berk
85 K10 **Upper Batley** Kirk
14 H8 **Upper Beeding** W Susx
55 N3 **Upper Benefield** Nhants
53 J7 **Upper Bentley** Worcs
150 F5 **Upper Bighouse** Highld
66 D1 **Upper Birchwood** Derbys
27 Q5 **Upper Boat** Rhondd
54 D10 **Upper Boddington** Nhants
49 K3 **Upper Borth** Cerdgn
42 G4 **Upper Brailes** Warwks
135 M11 **Upper Breakish** Highld
40 G4 **Upper Breinton** Herefs
52 E9 **Upper Broadheath** Worcs
66 H7 **Upper Broughton** Notts
31 L8 **Upper Bucklebury** W Berk
23 P10 **Upper Burgate** Hants
34 C9 **Upper Bush** Medway
98 E7 **Upperby** Cumb
44 H2 **Upper Caldecote** C Beds
28 E10 **Upper Canada** N Som
24 D10 **Upper Canterton** Hants
54 E9 **Upper Catesby** Nhants
52 H6 **Upper Catshill** Worcs
39 N4 **Upper Chapel** Powys
21 K7 **Upper Cheddon** Somset
23 L7 **Upper Chicksgrove** Wilts
24 E3 **Upper Chute** Wilts
33 L5 **Upper Clapton** Gt Lon
24 F5 **Upper Clatford** Hants
41 R8 **Upper Coberley** Gloucs
14 H10 **Upper Cokeham** W Susx
65 K3 **Upper Cotton** Staffs
63 P11 **Upper Cound** Shrops
78 C2 **Upper Cudworth** Barns
77 N2 **Upper Cumberworth** Kirk
139 Q3 **Upper Dallachy** Moray
35 Q12 **Upper Deal** Kent
55 P7 **Upper Dean** Bed
77 N2 **Upper Denby** Kirk
99 J5 **Upper Denton** Cumb
15 Q9 **Upper Dicker** E Susx
51 M4 **Upper Dinchope** Shrops
150 H3 **Upper Dounreay** Highld
47 M5 **Upper Dovercourt** Essex
122 H11 **Upper Drumbane** Stirlg
85 N3 **Upper Dunsforth** N York
14 D2 **Upper Eashing** Surrey
138 E3 **Upper Eathie** Highld
41 K3 **Upper Egleton** Herefs
77 K12 **Upper Elkstone** Staffs
65 L3 **Upper Ellastone** Staffs
77 K8 **Upper End** Derbys
24 F3 **Upper Enham** Hants
52 E2 **Upper Farmcote** Shrops
25 M6 **Upper Farringdon** Hants
41 M9 **Upper Framilode** Gloucs
25 N5 **Upper Froyle** Hants
134 F5 **Upperglen** Highld
22 B5 **Upper Godney** Somset
44 G4 **Upper Gravenhurst** C Beds
40 E8 **Upper Green** Mons
57 P7 **Upper Green** Suffk
30 H9 **Upper Green** W Berk
40 H6 **Upper Grove Common** Herefs
77 P11 **Upper Hackney** Derbys
25 P3 **Upper Hale** Surrey
32 F8 **Upper Halliford** Surrey
34 C9 **Upper Halling** Medway
67 M10 **Upper Hambleton** Rutlnd
35 K10 **Upper Harbledown** Kent
35 L12 **Upper Hardres Court** Kent
51 L9 **Upper Hardwick** Herefs
15 N4 **Upper Hartfield** E Susx
66 C2 **Upper Hartshay** Derbys
41 Q7 **Upper Hatherley** Gloucs
64 F5 **Upper Hatton** Staffs
78 C4 **Upper Haugh** Rothm
51 N4 **Upper Hayton** Shrops
85 J11 **Upper Heaton** Kirk
86 C4 **Upper Helmsley** N York
51 J9 **Upper Hergest** Herefs
54 H8 **Upper Heyford** Nhants
43 K6 **Upper Heyford** Oxon
51 M10 **Upper Hill** Herefs
33 P8 **Upper Hockenden** Kent
85 J11 **Upper Hopton** Kirk
52 E11 **Upper Howsell** Worcs
77 J11 **Upper Hulme** Staffs
14 E4 **Upper Ifold** Surrey
30 E3 **Upper Inglesham** Swindn
29 M5 **Upper Kilcott** Gloucs
26 E4 **Upper Killay** Swans
121 M7 **Upper Kinchrackine** Ag & B
30 G6 **Upper Lambourn** W Berk
64 H11 **Upper Landywood** Staffs
28 F10 **Upper Langford** N Som
78 E9 **Upper Langwith** Derbys
124 H12 **Upper Largo** Fife
65 J5 **Upper Leigh** Staffs
28 H9 **Upper Littleton** N Som
132 H5 **Upper Lochton** Abers
65 K9 **Upper Longdon** Staffs
44 H5 **Upper & Lower Stondon** C Beds
52 E2 **Upper Ludstone** Shrops
151 N9 **Upper Lybster** Highld
41 J8 **Upper Lydbrook** Gloucs
40 G3 **Upper Lyde** Herefs
51 L7 **Upper Lye** Herefs
40 D5 **Upper Maes-coed** Herefs
77 N4 **Upper Midhope** Sheff
77 J3 **Uppermill** Oldham
52 E6 **Upper Milton** Worcs
30 B4 **Upper Minety** Wilts
52 H11 **Upper Moor** Worcs
85 K9 **Upper Moor Side** Leeds
139 Q5 **Upper Mulben** Moray
51 Q2 **Upper Netchwood** Shrops
65 K5 **Upper Nobut** Staffs
14 D7 **Upper Norwood** W Susx
77 N8 **Upper Padley** Derbys
12 E5 **Upper Pennington** Hants
43 P9 **Upper Pollicott** Bucks
85 Q4 **Upper Poppleton** C York
42 E2 **Upper Quinton** Warwks
24 E8 **Upper Ratley** Hants
42 E7 **Upper Rissington** Gloucs
52 B7 **Upper Rochford** Worcs
96 B6 **Upper Ruscoe** D & G
52 C8 **Upper Sapey** Herefs
29 Q6 **Upper Seagry** Wilts
44 E3 **Upper Shelton** C Beds
70 H4 **Upper Sheringham** Norfk
113 J8 **Upper Skelmorlie** N Ayrs
42 D7 **Upper Slaughter** Gloucs
41 K9 **Upper Soudley** Gloucs
51 K10 **Upper Spond** Herefs
17 M3 **Upper Standen** Kent
56 C8 **Upper Staploe** Bed
71 K11 **Upper Stoke** Norfk
54 G9 **Upper Stowe** Nhants
23 P9 **Upper Street** Hants
58 H5 **Upper Street** Norfk
71 L8 **Upper Street** Norfk
71 M9 **Upper Street** Norfk
47 L5 **Upper Street** Suffk
57 P10 **Upper Street** Suffk
58 G10 **Upper Street** Suffk
41 P4 **Upper Strensham** Worcs
44 F6 **Upper Sundon** C Beds
42 E6 **Upper Swell** Gloucs
77 Q4 **Upper Tankersley** Barns
59 J2 **Upper Tasburgh** Norfk
65 J4 **Upper Tean** Staffs
77 L2 **Upperthong** Kirk
78 D7 **Upperthorpe** Derbys
79 J4 **Upperthorpe** N Linc
63 M3 **Upper Threapwood** Ches W
14 D6 **Upperton** W Susx
65 N2 **Upper Town** Derbys
77 Q10 **Uppertown** Derbys
100 D10 **Upper Town** Dur
51 P11 **Upper Town** Herefs
151 Q1 **Uppertown** Highld
28 H9 **Upper Town** N Som
58 D7 **Upper Town** Suffk
38 E9 **Upper Tumble** Carmth
42 H3 **Upper Tysoe** Warwks
59 K10 **Upper Ufford** Suffk
30 B3 **Upperup** Gloucs
30 F7 **Upper Upham** Wilts
34 D8 **Upper Upnor** Medway
125 K5 **Upper Victoria** Angus
22 F3 **Upper Vobster** Somset
43 K3 **Upper Wardington** Oxon
44 A4 **Upper Weald** M Keyn
54 G9 **Upper Weedon** Nhants
41 M3 **Upper Welland** Worcs
15 N8 **Upper Wellingham** E Susx
29 L9 **Upper Weston** BaNES
59 J5 **Upper Weybread** Suffk
52 F10 **Upper Wick** Worcs
25 K5 **Upper Wield** Hants
43 Q9 **Upper Winchendon** Bucks
77 P12 **Upperwood** Derbys
23 P6 **Upper Woodford** Wilts
25 K2 **Upper Wootton** Hants
29 N7 **Upper Wraxall** Wilts
41 M3 **Upper Wyche** Worcs
8 G3 **Uppincott** Devon
67 L12 **Uppingham** Rutlnd
11 N3 **Uppington** Dorset
63 Q10 **Uppington** Shrops
91 Q9 **Upsall** N York
117 K12 **Upsettlington** Border
33 M2 **Upshire** Essex
24 F7 **Up Somborne** Hants
35 M9 **Upstreet** Kent
10 F4 **Up Sydling** Dorset
58 E6 **Upthorpe** Suffk
43 Q9 **Upton** Bucks
68 B12 **Upton** C Pete
56 D5 **Upton** Cambs
75 L10 **Upton** Ches W
7 J4 **Upton** Cnwll
7 K10 **Upton** Cnwll
98 C10 **Upton** Cumb
5 L8 **Upton** Devon
9 L4 **Upton** Devon
10 H8 **Upton** Dorset
11 N6 **Upton** Dorset
87 L4 **Upton** E R Yk
75 N6 **Upton** Halton
24 F10 **Upton** Hants
24 F2 **Upton** Hants
66 B12 **Upton** Leics
79 L6 **Upton** Lincs
55 J8 **Upton** Nhants
71 M9 **Upton** Norfk
67 J1 **Upton** Notts
79 J8 **Upton** Notts
31 L5 **Upton** Oxon
42 F9 **Upton** Oxon
37 K9 **Upton** Pembks
92 F3 **Upton** R & Cl
32 D6 **Upton** Slough
20 F7 **Upton** Somset
21 P8 **Upton** Somset
78 D1 **Upton** Wakefd
53 L9 **Upton** Warwks
23 J7 **Upton** Wilts
75 J6 **Upton** Wirral
41 K6 **Upton Bishop** Herefs
29 L8 **Upton Cheyney** S Glos
52 C2 **Upton Cressett** Shrops
41 K6 **Upton Crews** Herefs
7 K10 **Upton Cross** Cnwll
44 G5 **Upton End** C Beds
25 M4 **Upton Grey** Hants
75 L9 **Upton Heath** Ches W
8 F4 **Upton Hellions** Devon
23 L5 **Upton Lovell** Wilts
63 P9 **Upton Magna** Shrops
22 G5 **Upton Noble** Somset
8 G5 **Upton Pyne** Devon
41 P8 **Upton St Leonards** Gloucs
23 J4 **Upton Scudamore** Wilts
52 H9 **Upton Snodsbury** Worcs
2 F6 **Upton Towans** Cnwll
41 N4 **Upton upon Severn** Worcs
52 H7 **Upton Warren** Worcs
14 D8 **Upwaltham** W Susx
57 K6 **Upware** Cambs
69 J11 **Upwell** Norfk
10 G7 **Upwey** Dorset
45 N7 **Upwick Green** Herts
56 E4 **Upwood** Cambs
30 B11 **Urchfont** Wilts
51 N11 **Urdimarsh** Herefs
91 N12 **Ure Bank** N York
91 P4 **Urlay Nook** S on T
76 E5 **Urmston** Traffd
139 P3 **Urquhart** Moray
92 B6 **Urra** N York
137 N5 **Urray** Highld
125 P2 **Usan** Angus
100 G9 **Ushaw Moor** Dur
28 E2 **Usk** Mons
80 B5 **Usselby** Lincs
100 H7 **Usworth** Sundld
75 P10 **Utkinton** Ches W
84 F6 **Utley** C Brad
8 F5 **Uton** Devon
80 F5 **Utterby** Lincs
65 K5 **Uttoxeter** Staffs
60 B7 **Uwchmynydd** Gwynd
32 F5 **Uxbridge** Gt Lon
152 u3 **Uyeasound** Shet
37 J7 **Uzmaston** Pembks

## V

12 c1 **Vale** Guern
27 Q8 **Vale of Glamorgan Crematorium** V Glam
49 M5 **Vale of Rheidol Railway** Cerdgn
72 D8 **Valley** IoA
32 D9 **Valley End** Surrey
6 G8 **Valley Truckle** Cnwll
135 J3 **Valtos** Highld
152 d3 **Valtos** W Isls
34 C5 **Vange** Essex
40 C10 **Varteg** Torfn
152 t3 **Vatsetter** Shet
134 E7 **Vatten** Highld
39 P9 **Vaynor** Myr Td
12 b2 **Vazon Bay** Guern
152 s7 **Veensgarth** Shet
40 B4 **Velindre** Powys
20 H5 **Vellow** Somset
18 F8 **Velly** Devon
7 M2 **Venngreen** Devon
63 K10 **Vennington** Shrops
9 K6 **Venn Ottery** Devon
8 F5 **Venny Tedburn** Devon
7 L10 **Venterdon** Cnwll
13 J9 **Ventnor** IoW
5 J5 **Venton** Devon
30 H11 **Vernham Dean** Hants
30 H11 **Vernham Street** Hants
51 N4 **Vernolds Common** Shrops
11 Q3 **Verwood** Dorset
3 M6 **Veryan** Cnwll
3 M6 **Veryan Green** Cnwll
9 N7 **Vicarage** Devon
82 F1 **Vickerstown** Cumb
77 M3 **Victoria** Barns
40 A10 **Victoria** Blae G
3 N2 **Victoria** Cnwll
152 t5 **Vidlin** Shet
139 P3 **Viewfield** Moray
114 C9 **Viewpark** N Lans
34 B10 **Vigo** Kent
12 c3 **Village de Putron** Guern
13 a1 **Ville la Bas** Jersey
12 b3 **Villiaze** Guern
16 D7 **Vinehall Street** E Susx
15 Q7 **Vines Cross** E Susx
34 D11 **Vinters Park Crematorium** Kent
32 E9 **Virginia Water** Surrey
7 M6 **Virginstow** Devon
22 F4 **Vobster** Somset
152 s6 **Voe** Shet
40 E4 **Vowchurch** Herefs
75 P5 **Vulcan Village** St Hel

## W

88 E8 **Waberthwaite** Cumb
91 K2 **Wackerfield** Dur
58 H2 **Wacton** Norfk
52 G11 **Wadborough** Worcs
43 Q8 **Waddesdon** Bucks
5 P5 **Waddeton** Devon
75 L4 **Waddicar** Sefton
79 N4 **Waddingham** Lincs
83 Q6 **Waddington** Lancs
79 N11 **Waddington** Lincs
8 G9 **Waddon** Devon
10 F7 **Waddon** Dorset
6 E10 **Wadebridge** Cnwll
9 Q3 **Wadeford** Somset
55 P4 **Wadenhoe** Nhants
45 L8 **Wadesmill** Herts
16 B4 **Wadhurst** E Susx
77 P9 **Wadshelf** Derbys
29 N9 **Wadswick** Wilts
78 F4 **Wadworth** Donc
74 D11 **Waen** Denbgs
74 F10 **Waen** Denbgs
62 H8 **Waen** Powys
62 H8 **Waen Fach** Powys
73 K10 **Waen-pentir** Gwynd
73 K10 **Waen-wen** Gwynd
63 L11 **Wagbeach** Shrops
28 C2 **Wainfelin** Torfn
81 J12 **Wainfleet All Saints** Lincs
81 J11 **Wainfleet Bank** Lincs
81 J12 **Wainfleet St Mary** Lincs
59 L3 **Wainford** Norfk
6 H6 **Wainhouse Corner** Cnwll
34 D8 **Wainscott** Medway
28 E8 **Wain's Hill** N Som
84 F9 **Wainstalls** Calder
90 B5 **Waitby** Cumb
80 F4 **Waithe** Lincs
85 M11 **Wakefield** Wakefd
85 L12 **Wakefield Crematorium** Wakefd
53 K4 **Wake Green** Birm
67 N12 **Wakerley** Nhants
46 F6 **Wakes Colne** Essex
59 P6 **Walberswick** Suffk
14 D9 **Walberton** W Susx
100 F5 **Walbottle** N u Ty
96 F4 **Walbutt** D & G
98 F6 **Walby** Cumb
22 D4 **Walcombe** Somset
67 Q5 **Walcot** Lincs
86 G11 **Walcot** N Linc
51 K4 **Walcot** Shrops
63 Q9 **Walcot** Shrops
30 D5 **Walcot** Swindn
53 L9 **Walcot** Warwks
54 F4 **Walcote** Leics
58 H4 **Walcot Green** Norfk
80 C12 **Walcott** Lincs
71 M6 **Walcott** Norfk
90 G10 **Walden** N York
90 F10 **Walden Head** N York
85 Q11 **Walden Stubbs** N York
34 D9 **Walderslade** Medway
13 N3 **Walderton** W Susx
10 D6 **Walditch** Dorset
65 L5 **Waldley** Derbys
100 G8 **Waldridge** Dur
47 N3 **Waldringfield** Suffk
15 Q7 **Waldron** E Susx
78 D7 **Wales** Rothm
22 D8 **Wales** Somset
80 C5 **Walesby** Lincs
78 H9 **Walesby** Notts
41 J7 **Walford** Herefs
51 L6 **Walford** Herefs
63 M8 **Walford** Shrops
64 F5 **Walford** Staffs
63 M8 **Walford Heath** Shrops
64 C2 **Walgherton** Ches E
55 K6 **Walgrave** Nhants
12 E5 **Walhampton** Hants
76 D3 **Walkden** Salfd
100 H5 **Walker** N u Ty
107 K2 **Walkerburn** Border
83 P7 **Walker Fold** Lancs
79 J5 **Walkeringham** Notts
79 K5 **Walkerith** Lincs
45 K6 **Walkern** Herts
51 N11 **Walker's Green** Herefs
53 K5 **Walker's Heath** Birm
115 N1 **Walkerton** Fife
12 C6 **Walkford** Dorset
4 H3 **Walkhampton** Devon
87 J8 **Walkington** E R Yk
77 Q6 **Walkley** Sheff

89 N2 Whale Cumb
78 E9 Whaley Derbys
77 J7 Whaley Bridge Derbys
78 E9 Whaley Thorns Derbys
151 P8 Whaligoe Highld
83 Q8 Whalley Lancs
83 Q8 Whalley Banks Lancs
152 u5 Whalsay Shet
100 E2 Whalton Nthumb
68 F7 Whaplode Lincs
68 F9 Whaplode Drove Lincs
54 C10 Wharf Warwks
84 B1 Wharfe N York
83 K8 Wharles Lancs
44 D3 Wharley End C Beds
77 P5 Wharncliffe Side Sheff
86 F2 Wharram-le-Street N York
76 C10 Wharton Ches W
51 N9 Wharton Herefs
91 K5 Whashton N York
89 N10 Whasset Cumb
42 G3 Whatcote Warwks
65 N12 Whateley Warwks
47 J2 Whatfield Suffk
10 B3 Whatley Somset
22 G4 Whatley Somset
29 K6 Whatley's End S Glos
16 D7 Whatlington E Susx
17 K2 Whatsole Street Kent
65 Q1 Whatstandwell Derbys
67 J4 Whatton Notts
95 M8 Whauphill D & G
90 G6 Whaw N York
2 H5 Wheal Rose Cnwll
59 P2 Wheatacre Norfk
31 P2 Wheatfield Oxon
44 H9 Wheathampstead Herts
52 B4 Wheathill Shrops
22 D7 Wheathill Somset
84 G10 Wheatley Calder
25 N5 Wheatley Hants
43 M10 Wheatley Oxon
101 K10 Wheatley Hill Dur
78 F3 Wheatley Hills Donc
84 C7 Wheatley Lane Lancs
64 F9 Wheaton Aston Staffs
63 K2 Wheatsheaf Wrexhm
20 E5 Wheddon Cross Somset
17 L2 Wheelbarrow Town Kent
32 A4 Wheeler End Bucks
31 Q8 Wheeler's Green Wokham
16 E2 Wheeler's Street Kent
14 D3 Wheelerstreet Surrey
76 D12 Wheelock Ches E
76 D12 Wheelock Heath Ches E
83 N11 Wheelton Lancs
85 P10 Wheldale Wakefd
86 C6 Wheldrake C York
30 D3 Whelford Gloucs
44 E10 Whelpley Hill Bucks
98 C10 Whelpo Cumb
74 H8 Whelston Flints
45 K7 Whempstead Herts
86 B1 Whenby N York
58 B9 Whepstead Suffk
47 L3 Wherstead Suffk
24 F5 Wherwell Hants
77 L8 Wheston Derbys
16 B2 Whetsted Kent
33 J4 Whetstone Gt Lon
54 F1 Whetstone Leics
97 P8 Wheyrigg Cumb
88 F10 Whicham Cumb
42 G5 Whichford Warwks
100 G6 Whickham Gatesd
7 N5 Whiddon Devon
8 C6 Whiddon Down Devon
47 K3 Whight's Corner Suffk
125 J4 Whigstreet Angus
54 G7 Whilton Nhants
7 L4 Whimble Devon
9 K5 Whimple Devon
71 M6 Whimpwell Green Norfk
70 E10 Whinburgh Norfk
83 J7 Whin Lane End Lancs
96 E8 Whinnie Liggate D & G
98 C8 Whinnow Cumb
141 P9 Whinnyfold Abers
91 P3 Whinny Hill S on T
12 H6 Whippingham IoW
44 E8 Whipsnade C Beds
8 H6 Whipton Devon
77 P7 Whirlow Sheff
79 M10 Whisby Lincs
67 K9 Whissendine Rutlnd
70 D7 Whissonsett Norfk
113 J3 Whistlefield Ag & B
112 H3 Whistlefield Inn Ag & B
31 R7 Whistley Green Wokham
75 N5 Whiston Knows
55 L8 Whiston Nhants
78 D6 Whiston Rothm
64 G9 Whiston Staffs
65 J3 Whiston Staffs
64 E11 Whiston Cross Shrops
65 K3 Whiston Eaves Staffs
53 N2 Whitacre Fields Warwks
88 F10 Whitbeck Cumb
52 D9 Whitbourne Herefs
101 K6 Whitburn S Tyne
114 H8 Whitburn W Loth
75 L8 Whitby Ches W
92 H4 Whitby N York
75 L9 Whitbyheath Ches W
116 G9 Whitchester Border
29 J9 Whitchurch BaNES
44 A7 Whitchurch Bucks
27 R6 Whitchurch Cardif
7 P10 Whitchurch Devon
24 H4 Whitchurch Hants
40 H8 Whitchurch Herefs
31 N7 Whitchurch Oxon
36 F5 Whitchurch Pembks
63 P4 Whitchurch Shrops
10 B6 Whitchurch Canonicorum Dorset
31 N6 Whitchurch Hill Oxon
10 H7 Whitcombe Dorset
51 L2 Whitcot Shrops
51 J4 Whitcott Keysett Shrops
17 K1 Whiteacre Kent
53 N2 Whiteacre Heath Warwks
46 D5 Whiteash Green Essex
20 H9 White Ball Somset
129 N1 Whitebridge Highld
40 H10 Whitebrook Mons
141 M12 Whitecairns Abers
33 L6 Whitechapel Gt Lon
83 M7 White Chapel Lancs
37 M3 Whitechurch Pembks
40 H9 Whitecliffe Gloucs
46 F6 White Colne Essex
83 N11 White Coppice Lancs
115 Q7 Whitecraig E Loth
41 J10 Whitecroft Gloucs
94 H7 Whitecrook D & G
2 E7 Whitecross Cnwll
2 H10 White Cross Cnwll
6 D10 Whitecross Cnwll
114 H6 Whitecross Falk
41 M5 White End Worcs
146 C7 Whiteface Highld
103 M1 Whitefarland N Ayrs
104 E8 Whitefaulds S Ayrs
76 E2 Whitefield Bury
19 N6 Whitefield Devon
20 G7 Whitefield Somset
75 M6 Whitefield Lane End Knows
140 H10 Whiteford Abers
76 B10 Whitegate Ches W
25 N3 Whitehall Hants
152 n3 Whitehall Ork
14 G6 Whitehall W Susx
88 C3 Whitehaven Cumb
34 H10 Whitehill Kent
66 C10 Whitehill Leics
25 N6 Whitehill and Bordon Hants
140 G3 Whitehills Abers
132 F1 Whitehouse Abers
112 B9 Whitehouse Ag & B
53 L1 Whitehouse Common Birm
116 E5 Whitekirk E Loth
100 C11 White Kirkley Dur
10 H5 White Lackington Dorset
21 N10 Whitelackington Somset
52 G10 White Ladies Aston Worcs
44 B10 Whiteleaf Bucks
100 F7 White-le-Head Dur
13 J3 Whiteley Hants
13 J8 Whiteley Bank IoW
76 G8 Whiteley Green Ches E
32 F10 Whiteley Village Surrey
15 K6 Whitemans Green W Susx
38 C7 White Mill Carmth
138 H5 Whitemire Moray
66 E4 Whitemoor C Nott
3 N3 Whitemoor Cnwll
66 B3 Whitemoor Derbys
76 G11 Whitemoor Staffs
152 s7 Whiteness Shet
46 D8 White Notley Essex
42 H9 Whiteoak Green Oxon
29 L10 White Ox Mead BaNES
24 D8 Whiteparish Wilts
80 G8 White Pit Lincs
141 K11 Whiterashes Abers
45 Q9 White Roding Essex
151 Q7 Whiterow Highld
139 J4 Whiterow Moray
41 N10 Whiteshill Gloucs
15 P8 Whitesmith E Susx
83 M10 White Stake Lancs
9 P3 Whitestaunton Somset
8 G6 Whitestone Devon
40 H3 White Stone Herefs
8 G6 Whitestone Cross Devon
46 H4 Whitestreet Green Suffk
86 E1 Whitewall Corner N York
32 B7 White Waltham W & M
29 L9 Whiteway BaNES
41 Q9 Whiteway Gloucs
83 P6 Whitewell Lancs
8 B10 Whiteworks Devon
125 J6 Whitfield C Dund
17 N2 Whitfield Kent
43 M4 Whitfield Nhants
99 M7 Whitfield Nthumb
29 K4 Whitfield S Glos
99 M7 Whitfield Hall Nthumb
9 P5 Whitford Devon
74 G8 Whitford Flints
86 E10 Whitgift E R Yk
64 G6 Whitgreave Staffs
95 N10 Whithorn D & G
103 Q4 Whiting Bay N Ayrs
85 M8 Whitkirk Leeds
37 N7 Whitland Carmth
107 M7 Whitlaw Border
104 G5 Whitletts S Ayrs
85 R11 Whitley N York
31 P8 Whitley Readg
77 Q5 Whitley Sheff
29 P9 Whitley Wilts
101 J4 Whitley Bay N Tyne
101 J3 Whitley Bay Crematorium N Tyne
99 P7 Whitley Chapel Nthumb
64 F7 Whitley Heath Staffs
85 J11 Whitley Lower Kirk
33 P11 Whitley Row Kent
53 L5 Whitlock's End Solhll
41 M10 Whitminster Gloucs
11 P3 Whitmore Dorset
64 E4 Whitmore Staffs
20 G10 Whitnage Devon
53 Q8 Whitnash Warwks
40 C2 Whitney-on-Wye Herefs
97 P10 Whitrigg Cumb
97 P6 Whitrigg Cumb
97 P7 Whitrigglees Cumb
23 P9 Whitsbury Hants
117 J11 Whitsome Border
28 E6 Whitson Newpt
35 K9 Whitstable Kent
7 K5 Whitstone Cnwll
108 H7 Whittingham Nthumb
51 M3 Whittingslow Shrops
78 C8 Whittington Derbys
42 B7 Whittington Gloucs
89 P11 Whittington Lancs
69 N12 Whittington Norfk
63 K6 Whittington Shrops
52 F4 Whittington Staffs
65 M10 Whittington Staffs
65 P12 Whittington Warwks
52 G10 Whittington Worcs
78 B9 Whittington Moor Derbys
43 P3 Whittlebury Nhants
83 N11 Whittle-le-Woods Lancs
56 E1 Whittlesey Cambs
57 J11 Whittlesford Cambs
83 Q11 Whittlestone Head Bl w D
86 G10 Whitton N Linc
108 H9 Whitton Nthumb
51 J7 Whitton Powys
91 P2 Whitton S on T
51 P6 Whitton Shrops
58 H11 Whitton Suffk
30 G8 Whittonditch Wilts
100 D7 Whittonstall Nthumb
31 K10 Whitway Hants
78 E8 Whitwell Derbys
44 H7 Whitwell Herts
13 J9 Whitwell IoW
91 M7 Whitwell N York
67 M10 Whitwell Rutlnd
86 D2 Whitwell-on-the-Hill N York
70 G8 Whitwell Street Norfk
66 D9 Whitwick Leics
85 N10 Whitwood Wakefd
84 D11 Whitworth Lancs
63 N5 Whixall Shrops
85 N4 Whixley N York
91 J4 Whorlton Dur
91 Q6 Whorlton N York
51 P8 Whyle Herefs
33 L10 Whyteleafe Surrey
28 H3 Wibdon Gloucs
84 H9 Wibsey C Brad
54 D3 Wibtoft Warwks
52 E8 Wichenford Worcs
34 G11 Wichling Kent
12 B6 Wick Bmouth
9 M4 Wick Devon
151 Q6 Wick Highld
29 L8 Wick S Glos
21 K4 Wick Somset
21 N8 Wick Somset
27 L8 Wick V Glam
14 E10 Wick W Susx
23 Q9 Wick Wilts
41 Q3 Wick Worcs
151 Q6 *Wick Airport* Highld
57 L6 Wicken Cambs
43 Q4 Wicken Nhants
45 P5 Wicken Bonhunt Essex
80 B7 Wickenby Lincs
55 N10 Wick End Bed
70 B6 Wicken Green Village Norfk
78 D5 Wickersley Rothm
46 H3 Wicker Street Green Suffk
34 D4 Wickford Essex
13 K2 Wickham Hants
31 J8 Wickham W Berk
46 E9 Wickham Bishops Essex
35 M10 Wickhambreaux Kent
57 P9 Wickhambrook Suffk
42 C3 Wickhamford Worcs
58 G7 Wickham Green Suffk
31 J8 Wickham Green W Berk
31 J8 Wickham Heath W Berk
59 L9 Wickham Market Suffk
71 N11 Wickhampton Norfk
46 E4 Wickham St Paul Essex
58 G7 Wickham Skeith Suffk
57 P10 Wickham Street Suffk
58 G7 Wickham Street Suffk
70 G11 Wicklewood Norfk
70 H5 Wickmere Norfk
28 E9 Wick St Lawrence N Som
15 P9 Wickstreet E Susx
29 L5 Wickwar S Glos
45 P5 Widdington Essex
84 D8 Widdop Calder
109 L10 Widdrington Nthumb
109 L11 Widdrington Station Nthumb
8 D9 Widecombe in the Moor Devon
4 D5 Widegates Cnwll
7 J4 Widemouth Bay Cnwll
100 G4 Wide Open N Tyne
46 C10 Widford Essex
45 M8 Widford Herts
30 C5 Widham Wilts
13 L3 Widley Hants
32 C3 Widmer End Bucks
66 G6 Widmerpool Notts
33 M8 Widmore Gt Lon
75 N7 Widnes Halton
75 N6 Widnes Crematorium Halton
9 N5 Widworthy Devon
75 P3 Wigan Wigan
75 Q3 Wigan Crematorium Wigan
21 P10 Wigborough Somset
9 L6 Wiggaton Devon
69 L9 Wiggenhall St Germans Norfk
69 L10 Wiggenhall St Mary Magdalen Norfk
69 L9 Wiggenhall St Mary the Virgin Norfk
46 B3 Wiggens Green Essex
77 K11 Wiggenstall Staffs
63 K5 Wiggington Shrops
86 B3 Wigginton C York
44 D9 Wigginton Herts
42 H5 Wigginton Oxon
65 N11 Wigginton Staffs
44 D10 Wigginton Bottom Herts
84 B4 Wigglesworth N York
98 C7 Wiggonby Cumb
14 F7 Wiggonholt W Susx
85 P6 Wighill N York
70 D4 Wighton Norfk
52 F1 Wightwick Wolves
77 P9 Wigley Derbys
24 E10 Wigley Hants
51 L7 Wigmore Herefs
34 D9 Wigmore Medway
79 L9 Wigsley Notts
55 P4 Wigsthorpe Nhants
54 G1 Wigston Leics
66 F12 Wigston Fields Leics
54 D3 Wigston Parva Leics
78 F7 Wigthorpe Notts
68 E5 Wigtoft Lincs
97 Q8 Wigton Cumb
95 N7 Wigtown D & G
77 N4 Wigtwizzle Sheff
85 M7 Wike Leeds
55 K3 Wilbarston Nhants
86 D5 Wilberfoss E R Yk
57 J6 Wilburton Cambs
55 L7 Wilby Nhants
58 F3 Wilby Norfk
59 K6 Wilby Suffk
30 D10 Wilcot Wilts
63 L8 Wilcott Shrops
28 F5 Wilcrick Newpt
77 Q9 Wilday Green Derbys
76 H10 Wildboarclough Ches E
56 B9 Wilden Bed
52 F6 Wilden Worcs
57 N5 Wilde Street Suffk
24 F3 Wildhern Hants
45 J10 Wildhill Herts
114 E10 Wildmanbridge S Lans
52 H5 Wildmoor Worcs
79 K4 Wildsworth Lincs
66 F5 Wilford C Nott
66 F5 Wilford Hill Crematorium Notts
64 B4 Wilkesley Ches E
146 G8 Wilkhaven Highld
115 L7 Wilkieston W Loth
44 H10 Wilkin's Green Herts
80 F11 Wilksby Lincs
9 K3 Willand Devon
16 C6 Willards Hill E Susx
64 C2 Willaston Ches E
75 K8 Willaston Ches W
44 C3 Willen M Keyn
54 B5 Willenhall Covtry
52 H1 Willenhall Wsall
87 J9 Willerby E R Yk
93 K11 Willerby N York
42 C4 Willersey Gloucs
40 D2 Willersley Herefs
17 J2 Willesborough Kent
17 J2 Willesborough Lees Kent
33 J5 Willesden Gt Lon
19 L6 Willesleigh Devon
29 N5 Willesley Wilts
20 H6 Willett Somset
64 C12 Willey Shrops
54 E4 Willey Warwks
32 D12 Willey Green Surrey
43 K3 Williamscot Oxon
27 N4 Williamstown Rhondd
45 J5 Willian Herts
53 M10 Willicote Warwks
45 Q10 Willingale Essex
15 Q10 Willingdon E Susx
56 H6 Willingham Cambs
79 L7 Willingham by Stow Lincs
57 M10 Willingham Green Cambs
56 C10 Willington Bed
65 P6 Willington Derbys
100 G11 Willington Dur
34 D11 Willington Kent
42 F4 Willington Warwks
75 N10 Willington Corner Ches W
101 J5 Willington Quay N Tyne
86 D8 Willitoft E R Yk
20 H5 Williton Somset
81 J9 Willoughby Lincs
54 E7 Willoughby Warwks
68 G3 Willoughby Hills Lincs
66 G7 Willoughby-on-the-Wolds Notts
54 F2 Willoughby Waterleys Leics
79 M5 Willoughton Lincs
75 Q8 Willow Green Ches W
46 C8 Willows Green Essex
29 K8 Willsbridge S Glos
7 P8 Willsworthy Devon
21 N8 Willtown Somset
53 M9 Wilmcote Warwks
29 L10 Wilmington BaNES
9 N5 Wilmington Devon
15 Q10 Wilmington E Susx
33 P8 Wilmington Kent
76 F7 Wilmslow Ches E
65 N12 Wilnecote Staffs
83 Q8 Wilpshire Lancs
84 G8 Wilsden C Brad
67 P4 Wilsford Lincs
23 P5 Wilsford Wilts
30 C11 Wilsford Wilts
19 P4 Wilsham Devon
77 L2 Wilshaw Kirk
85 J2 Wilsill N York
16 D3 Wilsley Green Kent
16 D3 Wilsley Pound Kent
40 H7 Wilson Herefs
66 C7 Wilson Leics
114 H10 Wilsontown S Lans
44 F3 Wilstead Bed
68 B9 Wilsthorpe Lincs
44 C9 Wilstone Herts
44 C9 Wilstone Green Herts
88 D4 Wilton Cumb
41 J7 Wilton Herefs
92 H10 Wilton N York
92 C3 Wilton R & Cl
23 N7 Wilton Wilts
30 F10 Wilton Wilts
107 M7 Wilton Dean Border
45 Q4 Wimbish Essex
45 R5 Wimbish Green Essex
33 J8 Wimbledon Gt Lon
56 H2 Wimblington Cambs
76 C11 Wimboldsley Ches W
11 N5 Wimborne Minster Dorset
11 P2 Wimborne St Giles Dorset
69 M11 Wimbotsham Norfk
56 G10 Wimpole Cambs
53 N11 Wimpstone Warwks
22 G7 Wincanton Somset
80 F10 Winceby Lincs
76 C8 Wincham Ches W
115 K6 Winchburgh W Loth
42 B6 Winchcombe Gloucs
16 F7 Winchelsea E Susx
16 G7 Winchelsea Beach E Susx
24 H7 Winchester Hants
25 J6 Winchester Services Hants
16 C3 Winchet Hill Kent
25 N2 Winchfield Hants
32 D3 Winchmore Hill Bucks
33 K3 Winchmore Hill Gt Lon
76 H10 Wincle Ches E
78 C5 Wincobank Sheff
88 D3 Winder Cumb
89 L7 Windermere Cumb
42 G3 Winderton Warwks
137 P6 Windhill Highld
76 H6 Windlehurst Stockp
32 D9 Windlesham Surrey
6 C9 Windmill Cnwll
77 M8 Windmill Derbys
16 B8 Windmill Hill E Susx
21 M10 Windmill Hill Somset
42 E9 Windrush Gloucs
140 E4 Windsole Abers
32 D7 Windsor W & M
32 D7 Windsor Castle W & M
29 N2 Windsoredge Gloucs
58 C9 Windsor Green Suffk
53 P6 Windy Arbour Warwks
115 Q1 Windygates Fife
76 F9 Windyharbour Ches E
63 J1 Windy Hill Wrexhm
15 J7 Wineham W Susx
87 P10 Winestead E R Yk
84 D7 Winewall Lancs
58 G4 Winfarthing Norfk
13 J8 Winford IoW
28 H9 Winford N Som
40 C2 Winforton Herefs
11 K8 Winfrith Newburgh Dorset
44 C7 Wing Bucks
67 M11 Wing Rutlnd
101 K11 Wingate Dur
76 C2 Wingates Bolton
108 H10 Wingates Nthumb
78 C10 Wingerworth Derbys
44 E6 Wingfield C Beds
59 J5 Wingfield Suffk
29 N11 Wingfield Wilts
59 J5 Wingfield Green Suffk
35 M11 Wingham Kent
17 L2 Wingmore Kent
44 B8 Wingrave Bucks
78 H12 Winkburn Notts
32 C8 Winkfield Br For
32 C8 Winkfield Row Br For
65 K2 Winkhill Staffs
15 P1 Winkhurst Green Kent
8 B3 Winkleigh Devon
85 K1 Winksley N York
12 B5 Winkton Dorset
100 F6 Winlaton Gatesd
100 F6 Winlaton Mill Gatesd
151 P6 Winless Highld
62 H8 Winllan Powys
83 L6 Winmarleigh Lancs
24 H7 Winnall Hants
31 Q8 Winnersh Wokham
76 B9 Winnington Ches W
88 D2 Winscales Cumb
28 F11 Winscombe N Som
76 C10 Winsford Ches W
20 D6 Winsford Somset
19 K5 Winsham Devon
10 B3 Winsham Somset
65 P7 Winshill Staffs
26 G3 Winshwen Swans
98 H11 Winskill Cumb
25 L4 Winslade Hants
29 M10 Winsley Wilts
43 Q6 Winslow Bucks
42 C10 Winson Gloucs
24 E10 Winsor Hants
89 L8 Winster Cumb
77 N11 Winster Derbys
91 J3 Winston Dur
58 H8 Winston Suffk
41 Q9 Winstone Gloucs
19 J10 Winswell Devon
10 H7 Winterborne Came Dorset
11 K4 Winterborne Clenston Dorset
10 H7 Winterborne Herringston Dorset
11 K4 Winterborne Houghton Dorset
11 L5 Winterborne Kingston Dorset
10 G7 Winterborne Monkton Dorset
11 K4 Winterborne Stickland Dorset
11 L5 Winterborne Tomson Dorset
11 K5 Winterborne Whitechurch Dorset
11 L5 Winterborne Zelston Dorset
29 K6 Winterbourne S Glos
31 K8 Winterbourne W Berk
10 F6 Winterbourne Abbas Dorset
30 C7 Winterbourne Bassett Wilts
24 B6 Winterbourne Dauntsey Wilts
24 B6 Winterbourne Earls Wilts
24 B6 Winterbourne Gunner Wilts
30 C8 Winterbourne Monkton Wilts
10 F7 Winterbourne Steepleton Dorset
23 N5 Winterbourne Stoke Wilts
31 M5 Winterbrook Oxon
84 D3 Winterburn N York
86 H10 Winteringham N Linc
76 D12 Winterley Ches E
85 M12 Wintersett Wakefd
24 C7 Winterslow Wilts
86 H11 Winterton N Linc
71 P8 Winterton-on-Sea Norfk
81 L10 Winthorpe Lincs
79 K12 Winthorpe Notts
11 Q6 Winton Bmouth
90 C5 Winton Cumb
15 P10 Winton E Susx
91 P7 Winton N York
92 H12 Wintringham N York
56 B4 Winwick Cambs
54 G6 Winwick Nhants
75 Q5 Winwick Warrtn
65 P1 Wirksworth Derbys
75 J6 Wirral
63 P3 Wirswall Ches E
69 J10 Wisbech Cambs
68 H10 Wisbech St Mary Cambs
14 F5 Wisborough Green W Susx
37 M9 Wiseman's Bridge Pembks
79 J6 Wiseton Notts
41 Q9 Wishanger Gloucs
114 E10 Wishaw N Lans
53 M2 Wishaw Warwks
32 F10 Wisley Surrey
32 F10 Wisley Gardens Surrey
80 D9 Wispington Lincs
16 F3 Wissenden Kent
59 M5 Wissett Suffk
57 M1 Wissington Norfk
46 G5 Wissington Suffk
51 M4 Wistanstow Shrops
64 C6 Wistanswick Shrops
64 C1 Wistaston Ches E
64 C1 Wistaston Green Ches E
76 F9 Wisterfield Ches E
37 K7 Wiston Pembks
106 C3 Wiston S Lans
14 G8 Wiston W Susx
56 E4 Wistow Cambs
54 G2 Wistow Leics
86 B8 Wistow N York
83 R7 Wiswell Lancs
57 J5 Witcham Cambs
11 N3 Witchampton Dorset
57 J5 Witchford Cambs
21 Q9 Witcombe Somset
46 E9 Witham Essex
22 G5 Witham Friary Somset
67 P9 Witham on the Hill Lincs
79 M11 Witham St Hughs Lincs
80 F7 Withcall Lincs
15 K9 Withdean Br & H
16 B5 Witherenden Hill E Susx
20 C10 Witheridge Devon
53 Q1 Witherley Leics
80 H7 Withern Lincs
87 Q9 Withernsea E R Yk
87 M7 Withernwick E R Yk
59 K4 Withersdale Street Suffk
57 M11 Withersfield Suffk
89 L10 Witherslack Cumb
6 E11 Withiel Cnwll
20 F7 Withiel Florey Somset
6 E11 Withielgoose Cnwll
42 B8 Withington Gloucs
40 H3 Withington Herefs
76 F5 Withington Manch
63 P9 Withington Shrops
65 J5 Withington Staffs
76 E9 Withington Green Ches E
40 H3 Withington Marsh Herefs
20 D10 Withleigh Devon
83 P10 Withnell Lancs
53 J6 Withybed Green Worcs
54 D4 Withybrook Warwks
20 F5 Withycombe Somset
15 P4 Withyham E Susx
29 K11 Withy Mills BaNES
20 C6 Withypool Somset
28 H9 Withywood Bristl
14 D3 Witley Surrey
58 H10 Witnesham Suffk
42 H9 Witney Oxon
67 Q11 Wittering C Pete
16 F5 Wittersham Kent
53 K2 Witton Birm
71 L10 Witton Norfk
71 L6 Witton Norfk
100 G9 Witton Gilbert Dur
71 N11 Witton Green Norfk
100 F12 Witton le Wear Dur
100 F12 Witton Park Dur
20 H8 Wiveliscombe Somset
25 L6 Wivelrod Hants
15 L7 Wivelsfield E Susx
15 L7 Wivelsfield Green E Susx
15 L7 Wivelsfield Station W Susx
47 J7 Wivenhoe Essex
47 J7 Wivenhoe Cross Essex
70 F4 Wiveton Norfk
47 L6 Wix Essex
53 K9 Wixford Warwks
47 L6 Wix Green Essex
63 P6 Wixhill Shrops
46 C3 Wixoe Suffk
44 D5 Woburn C Beds
44 D5 Woburn Abbey C Beds
44 C4 Woburn Sands M Keyn
31 N9 Wokefield Park W Berk
32 E10 Woking Surrey
32 D10 Woking Crematorium Surrey
32 A8 Wokingham Wokham
8 F10 Wolborough Devon
33 L11 Woldingham Surrey
93 L12 Wold Newton E R Yk
80 E4 Wold Newton NE Lin
106 D3 Wolfclyde S Lans
52 C8 Wolferlow Herefs
69 M6 Wolferton Norfk
54 E7 Wolfhampcote Warwks
124 D6 Wolfhill P & K
99 L6 Wolf Hills Nthumb
37 J5 Wolf's Castle Pembks
36 H6 Wolfsdale Pembks
52 G4 Wollaston Dudley
55 M8 Wollaston Nhants
63 K9 Wollaston Shrops
66 E4 Wollaton C Nott
8 F8 Wolleigh Devon
64 B6 Wollerton Shrops
52 H4 Wollescote Dudley
65 J8 Wolseley Bridge Staffs
100 D10 Wolsingham Dur
64 F3 Wolstanton Staffs
84 C12 Wolstenholme Rochdl
54 C5 Wolston Warwks
97 M8 Wolsty Cumb
43 K9 Wolvercote Oxon
64 G12 Wolverhampton Wolves
52 F2 *Wolverhampton Business Airport* Staffs
63 M6 Wolverley Shrops
52 F5 Wolverley Worcs
31 L10 Wolverton Hants
17 N2 Wolverton Kent
44 B3 Wolverton M Keyn
53 N8 Wolverton Warwks
22 H7 Wolverton Wilts
31 M10 Wolverton Common Hants
28 F2 Wolvesnewton Mons
54 C3 Wolvey Warwks
54 D3 Wolvey Heath Warwks
91 Q2 Wolviston S on T
92 D10 Wombleton N York
52 G2 Wombourne Staffs
78 C3 Wombwell Barns
35 M12 Womenswold Kent
85 Q11 Womersley N York
40 G9 Wonastow Mons
14 E2 Wonersh Surrey
8 H6 Wonford Devon
8 C7 Wonson Devon
10 H3 Wonston Dorset
24 H5 Wonston Hants
32 C5 Wooburn Bucks
32 C5 Wooburn Green Bucks
32 C4 Wooburn Moor Bucks
7 M3 Woodacott Devon
90 G11 Woodale N York
78 D7 Woodall Rothm
78 D7 Woodall Services Rothm
71 L9 Woodbastwick Norfk
79 K8 Woodbeck Notts
53 K9 Wood Bevington Warwks
66 G3 Woodborough Notts
30 C10 Woodborough Wilts
9 M6 Woodbridge Devon
23 J9 Woodbridge Dorset
59 K10 Woodbridge Suffk
43 P2 Wood Burcote Nhants
9 J7 Woodbury Devon
9 J7 Woodbury Salterton Devon
41 N11 Woodchester Gloucs
16 G4 Woodchurch Kent
75 J6 Woodchurch Wirral
20 E4 Woodcombe Somset
33 K10 Woodcote Gt Lon
31 N6 Woodcote Oxon
64 E9 Woodcote Wrekin
52 G6 Woodcote Green Worcs
24 G2 Woodcott Hants
28 H3 Woodcroft Gloucs
23 L10 Woodcutts Dorset
70 G7 Wood Dalling Norfk
57 M9 Woodditton Cambs
43 L9 Woodeaton Oxon
64 F8 Wood Eaton Staffs
37 M9 Wooden Pembks
44 E2 Wood End Bed
56 B7 Wood End Bed
56 G5 Wood End Cambs
32 G6 Wood End Gt Lon
45 L6 Wood End Herts
127 P12 Woodend Highld
54 G11 Woodend Nhants
65 M7 Woodend Staffs
114 G7 Woodend W Loth
13 P3 Woodend W Susx
53 L6 Wood End Warwks
53 N1 Wood End Warwks
53 P3 Wood End Warwks
64 H12 Wood End Wolves
80 E11 Wood Enderby Lincs
45 Q6 Woodend Green Essex
24 C9 Woodfalls Wilts
18 E10 Woodford Cnwll
5 N6 Woodford Devon
29 L3 Woodford Gloucs
33 M4 Woodford Gt Lon
55 N5 Woodford Nhants
76 G7 Woodford Stockp
33 M4 Woodford Bridge Gt Lon
54 E10 Woodford Halse Nhants
33 M4 Woodford Wells Gt Lon
53 J4 Woodgate Birm
20 H10 Woodgate Devon
70 C9 Woodgate Norfk
70 F9 Woodgate Norfk
14 D10 Woodgate W Susx
52 H7 Woodgate Worcs
33 K4 Wood Green Gt Lon
24 B10 Woodgreen Hants
42 H9 Woodgreen Oxon
90 F8 Woodhall N York
85 J8 Woodhall Hill Leeds
80 D11 Woodhall Spa Lincs
43 P8 Woodham Bucks
91 M1 Woodham Dur
32 F10 Woodham Surrey
34 D2 Woodham Ferrers Essex
46 E10 Woodham Mortimer Essex
46 E10 Woodham Walter Essex
64 H11 Wood Hayes Wolves
141 J8 Woodhead Abers
52 D4 Woodhill Shrops
21 M8 Woodhill Somset
109 M12 Woodhorn Nthumb
109 M12 Woodhorn Demesne Nthumb
85 L8 Woodhouse Leeds
66 E9 Woodhouse Leics
78 C7 Woodhouse Sheff
85 M11 Woodhouse Wakefd
66 E9 Woodhouse Eaves Leics
76 G11 Woodhouse Green Staffs
115 N8 Woodhouselee Mdloth
98 E3 Woodhouselees D & G
78 C6 Woodhouse Mill Sheff
98 C8 Woodhouses Cumb
76 G4 Woodhouses Oldham
65 K10 Woodhouses Staffs
65 M8 Woodhouses Staffs
5 Q6 Woodhuish Devon
56 F5 Woodhurst Cambs
15 L9 Woodingdean Br & H
85 K10 Woodkirk Leeds
141 L11 Woodland Abers
5 K5 Woodland Devon
5 N3 Woodland Devon
90 H1 Woodland Dur
17 L3 Woodland Kent
104 C10 Woodland S Ayrs
8 E5 Woodland Head Devon
133 J5 Woodlands Abers
78 E2 Woodlands Donc
11 P3 Woodlands Dorset
12 E2 Woodlands Hants
33 Q10 Woodlands Kent
85 L4 Woodlands N York
21 J5 Woodlands Somset
53 M3 Woodlands (Coleshill) Crematorium Warwks
32 B6 Woodlands Park W & M
30 G7 Woodlands St Mary W Berk
93 K9 Woodlands (Scarborough) Crematorium N York
79 L2 Woodlands (Scunthorpe) Crematorium N Linc
22 C6 Woodland Street Somset
77 P6 Woodland View Sheff
63 L5 Wood Lane Shrops
64 E2 Wood Lane Staffs
5 M7 Woodleigh Devon
85 M9 Woodlesford Leeds
76 H5 Woodley Stockp
31 Q7 Woodley Wokham
29 M3 Woodmancote Gloucs
41 R6 Woodmancote Gloucs
42 B10 Woodmancote Gloucs
13 N3 Woodmancote W Susx
15 J8 Woodmancote W Susx
41 P3 Woodmancote Worcs
25 J5 Woodmancott Hants
87 K7 Woodmansey E R Yk
25 Q8 Woodmansgreen W Susx
33 K10 Woodmansterne Surrey
9 J7 Woodmanton Devon
23 J2 Woodmarsh Wilts
65 L8 Woodmill Staffs
23 M9 Woodminton Wilts
35 P11 Woodnesborough Kent
55 P2 Woodnewton Nhants
66 D2 Woodnook Notts
70 E6 Wood Norton Norfk
83 L8 Woodplumpton Lancs
70 E11 Woodrising Norfk
85 M9 Wood Row Leeds
52 G5 Woodrow Worcs
16 B7 Wood's Corner E Susx
51 J11 Woods Eaves Herefs
64 C6 Woodseaves Shrops
64 E7 Woodseaves Staffs
30 E7 Woodsend Wilts
78 F7 Woodsetts Rothm
11 J6 Woodsford Dorset
16 B4 Wood's Green E Susx
32 D8 Woodside Br For
97 L11 Woodside Cumb
45 N11 Woodside Essex
124 H11 Woodside Fife
33 L9 Woodside Gt Lon
12 E6 Woodside Hants
45 J10 Woodside Herts
124 D5 Woodside P & K
34 F11 Woodside Green Kent
43 K8 Woodstock Oxon
37 K5 Woodstock Pembks
56 D1 Woodston C Pete
71 M8 Wood Street Norfk
32 D12 Wood Street Village Surrey
78 D9 Woodthorpe Derbys
66 E9 Woodthorpe Leics
80 H7 Woodthorpe Lincs
59 K2 Woodton Norfk
18 H8 Woodtown Devon
75 K2 Woodvale Sefton
15 L9 Woodvale Crematorium Br & H
65 P8 Woodville Derbys
64 E6 Woodwall Green Staffs
56 D4 Wood Walton Cambs
23 M9 Woodyates Dorset
19 N4 Woody Bay Devon
51 N7 Woofferton Shrops
22 C4 Wookey Somset
22 C4 Wookey Hole Somset
11 K7 Wool Dorset
19 J5 Woolacombe Devon
17 M1 Woolage Green Kent
35 M12 Woolage Village Kent
29 J2 Woolaston Gloucs
29 J2 Woolaston Common Gloucs
21 M5 Woolavington Somset
14 C6 Woolbeding W Susx
9 L7 Woolbrook Devon
20 F7 Woolcotts Somset
77 M2 Wooldale Kirk
108 G4 Wooler Nthumb
8 F3 Woolfardisworthy Devon
18 G9 Woolfardisworthy Devon
76 E1 Woolfold Bury
115 J10 Woolfords S Lans
31 M9 Woolhampton W Berk
41 J4 Woolhope Herefs
11 J3 Woolland Dorset
29 K9 Woollard BaNES
45 L9 Woollensbrook Herts
29 M8 Woolley BaNES
56 C6 Woolley Cambs
18 E10 Woolley Cnwll
78 B11 Woolley Derbys
77 Q1 Woolley Wakefd
77 J5 Woolley Bridge Derbys
85 L12 Woolley Edge Services Wakefd
32 B6 Woolley Green W & M
52 H8 Woolmere Green Worcs
45 J8 Woolmer Green Herts
21 L6 Woolmerston Somset
10 C3 Woolminstone Somset
16 E3 Woolpack Kent
58 E8 Woolpit Suffk
58 E8 Woolpit Green Suffk
54 E7 Woolscott Warwks
8 E4 Woolsgrove Devon
100 F4 Woolsington N u Ty
51 M1 Woolstaston Shrops
67 L5 Woolsthorpe Lincs
67 M7 Woolsthorpe-by-Colsterworth Lincs
12 G3 Woolston C Sotn
5 M6 Woolston Devon
5 M8 Woolston Devon
51 M3 Woolston Shrops
63 K7 Woolston Shrops
20 H5 Woolston Somset
22 E8 Woolston Somset
76 C6 Woolston Warrtn
41 Q5 Woolstone Gloucs
44 C4 Woolstone M Keyn
30 G5 Woolstone Oxon
5 N3 Woolston Green Devon
75 M6 Woolton Lpool
31 J10 Woolton Hill Hants
47 L4 Woolverstone Suffk
22 H3 Woolverton Somset
33 N6 Woolwich Gt Lon
51 K10 Woonton Herefs
51 P8 Woonton Herefs
108 G6 Wooperton Nthumb
64 D4 Woore Shrops
59 J6 Wootten Green Suffk
44 E3 Wootton Bed
12 D5 Wootton Hants
51 K10 Wootton Herefs
13 J6 Wootton IoW
17 M2 Wootton Kent
87 K12 Wootton N Linc
55 J9 Wootton Nhants
43 J7 Wootton Oxon
43 K11 Wootton Oxon
63 K6 Wootton Shrops

64 F7 Wootton Staffs
65 L3 Wootton Staffs
30 C6 Wootton Bassett Wilts
13 J6 Wootton Bridge IoW
44 E3 Wootton Broadmead Bed
13 J6 Wootton Common IoW
20 E5 Wootton Courtenay Somset
10 B5 Wootton Fitzpaine Dorset
30 E9 Wootton Rivers Wilts
25 K3 Wootton St Lawrence Hants
53 M8 Wootton Wawen Warwks
52 F9 Worcester Worcs
33 J9 Worcester Park Gt Lon
52 G3 Wordsley Dudley
52 D1 Worfield Shrops
11 L7 Worgret Dorset
56 B10 Workhouse End Bed
88 D1 Workington Cumb
78 F8 Worksop Notts
80 G8 Worlaby Lincs
79 P1 Worlaby N Linc
44 B10 Worlds End Bucks
25 L11 Worlds End Hants
31 K7 World's End W Berk
15 L7 Worlds End W Susx
28 E9 Worle N Som
76 C12 Worleston Ches E
59 N3 Worlingham Suffk
19 P10 Worlington Devon
57 N6 Worlington Suffk
59 J7 Worlingworth Suffk
85 L2 Wormald Green N York
40 F5 Wormbridge Herefs
69 M10 Wormegay Norfk
40 G6 Wormelow Tump Herefs
77 L9 Wormhill Derbys
40 F4 Wormhill Herefs
46 G5 Wormingford Essex
43 N10 Worminghall Bucks
42 B4 Wormington Gloucs
22 D5 Worminster Somset
124 H7 Wormit Fife
54 D10 Wormleighton Warwks
45 L10 Wormley Herts
14 D3 Wormley Surrey
45 L10 Wormleybury Herts
86 C12 Wormley Hill Donc
34 F11 Wormshill Kent
51 M11 Wormsley Herefs
32 D11 Worplesdon Surrey
77 P5 Worrall Sheff
41 J8 Worrall Hill Gloucs
78 B3 Worsbrough Barns
78 B3 Worsbrough Bridge Barns
78 B3 Worsbrough Dale Barns
76 D4 Worsley Salfd
71 L7 Worstead Norfk
84 C8 Worsthorne Lancs
5 J6 Worston Devon
84 A6 Worston Lancs
35 P11 Worth Kent
22 C4 Worth Somset
15 K4 Worth W Susx
58 G5 Wortham Suffk
63 K11 Worthen Shrops
63 M3 Worthenbury Wrexhm
70 E8 Worthing Norfk
14 G10 Worthing W Susx
14 G9 Worthing Crematorium W Susx
66 C8 Worthington Leics
11 N9 Worth Matravers Dorset
40 G9 Worthybrook Mons
25 K3 Worting Hants
77 P4 Wortley Barns
85 K8 Wortley Leeds
90 F8 Worton N York
29 R11 Worton Wilts
59 K4 Wortwell Norfk
63 J12 Wotherton Shrops
67 P11 Wothorpe C Pete
5 J4 Wotter Devon
14 G1 Wotton Surrey
29 M4 Wotton-under-Edge Gloucs
43 P8 Wotton Underwood Bucks
44 C4 Woughton on the Green M Keyn
34 C9 Wouldham Kent
52 E2 Woundale Shrops
47 L5 Wrabness Essex
19 J6 Wrafton Devon
80 C8 Wragby Lincs
85 N11 Wragby Wakefd
70 G11 Wramplingham Norfk
5 L5 Wrangaton Devon
78 E1 Wrangbrook Wakefd
68 H2 Wrangle Lincs
68 H1 Wrangle Common Lincs
68 H2 Wrangle Lowgate Lincs
20 H9 Wrangway Somset
21 M9 Wrantage Somset
79 P2 Wrawby N Linc
28 G8 Wraxall N Som
22 E6 Wraxall Somset
83 N2 Wray Lancs
89 K6 Wray Castle Cumb
32 E7 Wraysbury W & M
89 P12 Wrayton Lancs
83 J9 Wrea Green Lancs
88 H9 Wreaks End Cumb
89 M2 Wreay Cumb
98 E8 Wreay Cumb
25 P4 Wrecclesham Surrey
100 H6 Wrekenton Gatesd
92 F9 Wrelton N York
63 Q3 Wrenbury Ches E
93 K9 Wrench Green N York
70 H12 Wreningham Norfk
59 P4 Wrentham Suffk
85 L10 Wrenthorpe Wakefd
63 M11 Wrentnall Shrops
86 D9 Wressle E R Yk
79 N2 Wressle N Linc
56 E11 Wrestlingworth C Beds
69 N12 Wretton Norfk
63 K2 Wrexham Wrexhm
52 E5 Wribbenhall Worcs
52 B3 Wrickton Shrops
75 P1 Wrightington Bar Lancs
45 P8 Wright's Green Essex
64 D3 Wrinehill Staffs
28 G9 Wrington N Som
22 F2 Writhlington BaNES
46 B10 Writtle Essex
64 B9 Wrockwardine Wrekin
78 H3 Wroot N Linc
85 J8 Wrose C Brad
33 R10 Wrotham Kent
34 B10 Wrotham Heath Kent
64 F12 Wrottesley Staffs
30 D6 Wroughton Swindn
13 J9 Wroxall IoW
53 N6 Wroxall Warwks
63 P10 Wroxeter Shrops
71 L8 Wroxham Norfk
43 J3 Wroxton Oxon
65 M4 Wyaston Derbys
33 Q2 Wyatt's Green Essex
68 F4 Wyberton East Lincs
68 F4 Wyberton West Lincs
56 C9 Wyboston Bed
64 C2 Wybunbury Ches E
52 G7 Wychbold Worcs
15 M4 Wych Cross E Susx
65 M9 Wychnor Staffs
25 N5 Wyck Hants
42 E7 Wyck Rissington Gloucs
91 J4 Wycliffe Dur
84 D7 Wycoller Lancs
67 K7 Wycomb Leics
32 C4 Wycombe Marsh Bucks
45 L5 Wyddial Herts
17 J1 Wye Kent
40 G9 Wyesham Mons
67 K8 Wyfordby Leics
84 H10 Wyke C Brad
8 G5 Wyke Devon
9 P5 Wyke Devon
22 H8 Wyke Dorset
64 C11 Wyke Shrops
32 C12 Wyke Surrey
22 F6 Wyke Champflower Somset
93 K10 Wykeham N York
54 B4 Wyken Covtry
52 E2 Wyken Shrops
10 G9 Wyke Regis Dorset
63 L7 Wykey Shrops
54 C2 Wykin Leics
100 E5 Wylam Nthumb
53 L2 Wylde Green Birm
23 M6 Wylye Wilts
66 G7 Wymeswold Leics
55 N8 Wymington Bed
67 L8 Wymondham Leics
70 G12 Wymondham Norfk
27 M4 Wyndham Brdgnd
10 F5 Wynford Eagle Dorset
91 Q2 Wynyard Park S on T
91 P1 Wynyard Village S on T
52 F6 Wyre Forest Crematorium Worcs
52 H11 Wyre Piddle Worcs
66 G7 Wysall Notts
51 N7 Wyson Herefs
53 K5 Wythall Worcs
43 K10 Wytham Oxon
89 J4 Wythburn Cumb
76 F6 Wythenshawe Manch
97 N12 Wythop Mill Cumb
56 E6 Wyton Cambs
87 M8 Wyton E R Yk
58 F7 Wyverstone Suffk
58 F7 Wyverstone Street Suffk
67 L6 Wyville Lincs

## Y

79 M2 Yaddlethorpe N Linc
12 G8 Yafford IoW
91 N8 Yafforth N York
5 P5 Yalberton Torbay
34 C12 Yalding Kent
89 N1 Yanwath Cumb
42 C9 Yanworth Gloucs
86 E5 Yapham E R Yk
14 D10 Yapton W Susx
28 E10 Yarborough N Som
13 K7 Yarbridge IoW
80 G5 Yarburgh Lincs
9 N3 Yarcombe Devon
19 P9 Yard Devon
53 L3 Yardley Birm
53 L4 Yardley Crematorium Birm
43 Q3 Yardley Gobion Nhants
55 L9 Yardley Hastings Nhants
53 L5 Yardley Wood Birm
50 H9 Yardro Powys
21 K7 Yarford Somset
41 J3 Yarkhill Herefs
22 C4 Yarley Somset
22 E7 Yarlington Somset
91 P4 Yarm S on T
12 F7 Yarmouth IoW
19 M7 Yarnacott Devon
23 J2 Yarnbrook Wilts
8 E9 Yarner Devon
64 F6 Yarnfield Staffs
19 L8 Yarnscombe Devon
43 K9 Yarnton Oxon
51 M7 Yarpole Herefs
107 K4 Yarrow Border
21 N4 Yarrow Somset
107 J5 Yarrow Feus Border
107 L4 Yarrowford Border
40 F2 Yarsop Herefs
55 Q1 Yarwell Nhants
29 L6 Yate S Glos
32 B10 Yateley Hants
30 C8 Yatesbury Wilts
31 L7 Yattendon W Berk
51 M7 Yatton Herefs
28 F9 Yatton N Som
29 P7 Yatton Keynell Wilts
13 K7 Yaverland IoW
9 Q6 Yawl Devon
79 M5 Yawthorpe Lincs
70 E10 Yaxham Norfk
56 D2 Yaxley Cambs
58 G6 Yaxley Suffk
40 E2 Yazor Herefs
32 G6 Yeading Gt Lon
85 J7 Yeadon Leeds
89 N11 Yealand Conyers Lancs
89 N11 Yealand Redmayne Lancs
89 M11 Yealand Storrs Lancs
5 J6 Yealmbridge Devon
5 J6 Yealmpton Devon
92 C2 Yearby R & Cl
97 N9 Yearngill Cumb
92 C11 Yearsley N York
63 M8 Yeaton Shrops
65 M4 Yeaveley Derbys
108 E4 Yeavering Nthumb
92 H11 Yedingham N York
42 H10 Yelford Oxon
152 t4 Yell Shet
19 J7 Yelland Devon
56 E8 Yelling Cambs
54 F5 Yelvertoft Nhants
4 H3 Yelverton Devon
71 K11 Yelverton Norfk
22 G9 Yenston Somset
8 E5 Yeoford Devon
7 L7 Yeolmbridge Cnwll
20 C8 Yeo Mill Devon
18 H8 Yeo Vale Devon
22 D10 Yeovil Somset
22 C10 Yeovil Crematorium Somset
22 C9 Yeovil Marsh Somset
22 D9 Yeovilton Somset
22 D8 Yeovilton Fleet Air Arm Museum Somset
37 L8 Yerbeston Pembks
152 j4 Yesnaby Ork
108 G8 Yetlington Nthumb
10 F3 Yetminster Dorset
5 N5 Yetson Devon
9 K7 Yettington Devon
115 J1 Yetts o'Muckhart Clacks
84 G9 Yews Green C Brad
53 J2 Yew Tree Sandw
73 J10 Y Felinheli Gwynd
48 C10 Y Ferwig Cerdgn
60 F4 Y Ffor Gwynd
74 E12 Y Gyffylliog Denbgs
55 P7 Yielden Bed
52 G5 Yieldingtree Worcs
114 F11 Yieldshields S Lans
32 F6 Yiewsley Gt Lon
62 D3 Y Maerdy Conwy
63 J2 Y Nant Wrexhm
27 P3 Ynysboeth Rhondd
28 A4 Ynysddu Caerph
26 G2 Ynysforgan Swans
27 N4 Ynyshir Rhondd
49 K2 Ynyslas Cerdgn
27 N5 Ynysmaerdy Rhondd
38 H10 Ynysmeudwy Neath
26 G2 Ynystawe Swans
39 K9 Ynyswen Powys
27 M3 Ynyswen Rhondd
27 P3 Ynysybwl Rhondd
61 K11 Ynysymaengwyn Gwynd
90 E11 Yockenthwaite N York
63 L10 Yockleton Shrops
86 F10 Yokefleet E R Yk
113 P7 Yoker C Glas
86 B5 York C York
83 Q8 York Lancs
86 B5 York City Crematorium C York
35 K9 Yorkletts Kent
41 K10 Yorkley Gloucs
86 B5 York Minster C York
90 E11 Yorkshire Dales National Park
32 B10 York Town Surrey
63 N7 Yorton Heath Shrops
77 N11 Youlgreave Derbys
86 E4 Youlthorpe E R Yk
85 P3 Youlton N York
45 L8 Youngsbury Herts
46 C8 Young's End Essex
65 L8 Yoxall Staffs
59 M7 Yoxford Suffk
60 C6 Y Rhiw Gwynd
49 N5 Ysbyty Cynfyn Cerdgn
61 P2 Ysbyty Ifan Conwy
49 M6 Ysbyty Ystwyth Cerdgn
74 G9 Ysceifiog Flints
49 L2 Ysgubor-y-Coed Cerdgn
39 J10 Ystalyfera Neath
27 N3 Ystrad Rhondd
49 J9 Ystrad Aeron Cerdgn
39 M9 Ystradfellte Powys
39 J2 Ystrad Ffin Carmth
39 J9 Ystradgynlais Powys
49 M7 Ystrad Meurig Cerdgn
27 Q3 Ystrad Mynach Caerph
27 N7 Ystradowen V Glam
49 M5 Ystumtuen Cerdgn
141 L9 Ythanbank Abers
140 G8 Ythanwells Abers
141 L9 Ythsie Abers

## Z

8 D4 Zeal Monachorum Devon
22 H7 Zeals Wilts
3 K4 Zelah Cnwll
2 D7 Zennor Cnwll
3 J10 Zoar Cnwll
66 E7 Zouch Notts
44 E8 ZSL Whipsnade Zoo C Beds